THE ENCYCLOPEDIA OF

CELTIC MYTHOLOGY
AND FOLKLORE

PATRICIA MONAGHAN

Checkmark Books
An imprint of Infobase Publishing

The Encyclopedia of Celtic Mythology and Folklore

Checkmark Books
An imprint of Infobase Publishing
132 West 31st Street
New York NY 10001

ISBN-13: 978-0-8160-4524-2 (hc)
ISBN-13: 978-0-8160-7556-0 (pbk)

Library of Congress Cataloging-in-Publication Data

Monaghan, Patricia.
The encyclopedia of Celtic mythology and folklore / Patricia Monaghan.
p. cm.
Includes bibliographical references and index.
ISBN 0-8160-4524-0 (hc: alk. paper)—0-8160-7556-5 (pbk: alk. paper)
1. Mythology, Celtic—Encyclopedias. 2. Celts—Folklore—Encyclopedias.
3. Legends—Europe—Encyclopedias. I. Title.

BL900.M66 2003
299'.16—dc21   2003044944

Checkmark Books are available at special discounts when purchased in bulk quantities
for businesses, associations, institutions, or sales promotions. Please call our Special
Sales Department in New York at (212) 967-8800 or (800) 322-8755.

You can find Facts On File on the World Wide Web at http://www.factsonfile.com

Text design by Erika K. Arroyo
Cover design by Jooyoung An

Printed in the United States of America

VB Hermitage 10   9   8   7   6   5   4   3   2   1

This book is printed on acid-free paper.

CONTENTS

INTRODUCTION

Who Were the Celts?

The terms *Celt* and *Celtic* seem familiar today—familiar enough that many people assume that they are ethnic descriptions, words that define a people related by blood and culture. Such people are imagined as fair-skinned, possibly red-haired, often freckled. More important, it is presumed they share an inborn mystical inclination. They see in ways that others do not or cannot. They acknowledge a world beyond the world of the senses. Some even have the second sight, the ability to see fairies and other spirits dancing through the soft evening. For evening always gathers around the Celts, a misty twilight where things are never quite solid and defined.

The image is a charming one; it has drawn many to the study of Celtic culture. But it is also incorrect. The word *Celt* is not as exact as many people presume. It does not define a race or a tribe; the alleged Celtic mysticism is not an invariably inherited trait. Nor does "Celtic" describe a culture that was so centralized that all Celts everywhere felt the same way toward nature, worshiped the same gods, and performed rituals in the same fashion.

No ancient people called themselves "the Celts." They called themselves Belgae, Cantii, Icini, Brigantes, Voconces, Arverni, or by any one of scores of other tribal names. Where contemporary imagination sees a single culture, these ancient people themselves knew dozens of linguistically related groups, each bearing a name derived from an ancestor, a god or a goddess, a totem animal, a sacred location. The word *Celt* may originally have been one of these tribal names, used by other Europeans as a generic term for the whole people.

If the name itself is not exact, neither is what it names. There is no one agreed-upon definition of what constituted Celtic society and the Celtic worldview. Indeed, some claim that Celtic peoples adapted themselves to and absorbed influences from pre-Celtic cultures wherever they lived and that, therefore, the idea of a Celtic culture is itself hopelessly flawed. Narrowly, a Celt can be defined as someone who spoke or speaks a Celtic language. Beyond that, scholars and other experts disagree as much as they agree.

The Celts in Classical Literature

Literacy is not a value shared by all cultures. The Celts did not write down their myths and histories, honoring instead the spoken word and the human memory. As a result, we have no written documents from early Celtic times, when they were settling central Europe. Instead, the earliest writings we have about the Celts are in the languages of their enemies: the Greeks and, later, the Romans.

The Celts were already a mature culture when they began to appear in the writings of their southern neighbors. Until then, they lived too far away to be of interest, and besides, they were no threat to the wealth and power of Greece and Rome. In the last several centuries before the common era, however, the Celts began to seek new territories. Whether this was because they were being pushed out of traditional homelands by other invaders, or because a population explosion put pressure on resources, we do not know. But within a few hundred years of their first appearance in historical documents the Celts posed a real threat to the safety and stability of the Mediterranean world. Simply put, the Greeks and Romans had land and resources that the Celts needed. Conflict was inevitable.

The earliest written reference to the Celtic tribes is found in the late sixth century B.C.E. in the works of Hecataeus of Miletus, who described Narbonne, in today's France, as a city of the Celts. A hundred years later, the Greek geographer Herodotus described a people, the *Keltoí*, as the most westerly of the European people but also holding territories at the source of the Danube River. The fourth-century B.C.E. Greek writer Ephoros described the Celts as one of the four great barbarian races, the equal of the powerful Libyans, Persians, and Scythians to the south, east, and north of the Greeks respectively. These writers were reporting what they had learned from travelers; they had no firsthand experience of Celtic ways.

For two centuries, central and western Europe was essentially under Celtic control. Then the Celts began to expand, moving south and west. At the height of their expansion, Celtic tribes occupied territory that stretched from Galatia in Asia Minor—today's Turkey—west to Ireland, and from northern Germany to Italy. They were the first truly European civilization.

They were also aggressive in expanding their territories. Around 387 B.C.E. the Celts reached the steps of the Roman capital, where the city leaders were hiding in terror. A siege ensued, broken when the sacred geese in the temple of Juno called an alarm that roused the captives against the last rush of the invasion. Had the geese not squawked when they did, Europe may well have been a Celtic continent. But the tides of fortune turned against the Celts, and by the first century C.E. a Roman empire stretched across much of the ancient Celtic territory.

It is from this period that we learn the most about Celtic traditions, religion, and ritual. But the source is suspect: The writer was their fiercest enemy, the Roman general who would become emperor, Julius Caesar, who fought the Celtic people and recorded what he knew of them in his *Commentaries on the Gallic Wars*. In the Celts, whom he called Gauls, Caesar faced the most significant impediment to his imperial plans. As aggressive as the Celts had been in their period of expansion, the Romans under Caesar were just as aggressive.

This time, the Celts were fighting to maintain their home territories, not to move into new ones. Classical sources tell us of the fierceness of Gaulish and British warriors, but if the Celts were a people to be feared, they also occupied lands the Romans wished to conquer. And because the Celtic warriors fought individually, for personal glory, while the trained Roman legions were pawns in a larger economic game, the Celts were ultimately beaten back. Classical literature tells of the carnage of battle and the horror of massacre that, even from the point of view of the victors, was unendurable. Roman historian Tacitus tells us of the rebellion of the British queen Boudicca against the invading Romans who had raped her daughters; Polybius tells of the powerful Celtic warriors who wore little clothing apart from their great gold neckpieces and who sliced off the heads of their vanquished enemies, only to die as miserable captives after being paraded naked through the streets of Rome.

Because the Celtic people themselves left no written records, we only hear the voices of their literate enemies. Although Caesar, Ammianus Marcellinus, Tacitus, Diodorus Siculus, and others recorded many interesting details about Celtic culture, we cannot rely solely upon them. They were writing, after all, for an audience that cheered the extermination of this fierce foe. The temptation was strong to portray the Celts as more savage and brutal than they were in reality. Such Roman material must be read with suspicion. When Marcellinus speaks of the "great pride and insolence" of the Celtic warrior, for instance, it is easy to dismiss the comment as intended to drive fear into the hearts of the Roman citizenry. But what of his claim that

Celtic women helped their men in battle? Was this an observed fact, or a way of showing the Celts to be more barbaric than the Romans, who left their wives at home when they invaded Celtic lands? When Strabo says that the Celts are "war-mad and uncouth," we can recognize his propagandizing tone, but what of his report that the Celts placed a premium on education and eloquence?

Despite their defeat, the Celtic peoples were not exterminated. Many remained in their old territories, intermarrying with Roman soldiers to become the ancestors of many of today's Europeans and, by further migration, European-Americans. Others migrated into territories traditionally occupied by the Germans, whom they fought or married or both. Celtic languages and Celtic customs continued to migrate and adapt.

Both on the Continent and in Britain, the Celts had constant contact with the German or Teutonic tribes, who spoke a different language and had different customs, but who shared enough of their characteristics philosophically and socially that at times the two groups are difficult to distinguish. The Anglo-Saxons, a Germanic group that invaded England in early historic times, encountered Celtic people there; the resulting British culture combined features of the two parent cultures. There, and in other Celtic lands as well, contact with Scandinavians occurred when Vikings raided, and sometimes settled in, the coastal areas; these visitors brought their own languages and religions, so that in the ancient Celtic lands we often find words, myths, and folklore of Scandinavian origin.

Thus what we know today as "Celtic culture" is based in part upon biased literature written by enemies of the Celts, and in part upon oral traditions written down in medieval or later times in lands where the Celts mingled with other tribal people; both sources raise questions even as they answer them. But scholars have other ways of finding information about the Celts that are not reliant upon these potentially tainted sources. They are archaeological excavations of Celtic sites (material culture) and analysis of Celtic languages (nonmaterial culture).

Archaeological Traces

Where language cannot reach, the archaeologist reads instead the artifacts of ancient cultures. Unlike warrior generals who slander their opponents, potsherds and earthen walls do not deliberately lie nor distort the facts. But because time destroys anything not made of stone, metal, or bone, even the richest site leaves many unanswered questions about cultures of the past. Leather, cloth, and even ceramics can decay after several hundred, much less several thousand, years. Thus archaeologists are forced to piece together a picture of Celtic life that relies solely on non-decaying materials, sometimes comparing their finds with the written texts in a search for common themes. It is impossible to know with certainty how close the re-created Celtic culture is to the original.

The search for the origins of the Celts begins more than three thousand years ago, in Bronze-Age central Europe. There, faint traces of an energetic people have been found and categorized by scholars, who seek to determine which of the related and contiguous cultures were proto-Celtic and which were not. The analysis of archaeological remains points to religious and social changes that led, with unusual rapidity, to the creation of a dynamic culture. At what point this culture can be called Celtic is a subject of debate.

Approximately 1,400 years before the common era, people buried their dead in a distinctive way, by building mounds or "barrows" over the graves. A few hundred years later, burial practices changed: after cremation, ashes of the dead were placed in urns and buried in designated cemeteries. This, the Urnfield stage, was the first of many steps in the development of a distinctive Celtic culture; the culture of this time is usually considered proto-Celtic, for while it is not yet fully Celtic, it appears related.

The Celts remained in prehistory longer than other Europeans did, for they did not develop writing, except for a rudimentary script called ogham that was used for short inscriptions. But illiterate does not mean unintelligent or lacking in genius. The Celts were both inventive and artistic, as the beautifully wrought objects from the second stage of Celtic culture—named for its primary archaeological site, Hallstatt in Austria—reveal. By this time, the Celts had become metalworkers of some renown in the ancient world. The mirrors, jewelry, weapons, and other splendid metal objects from the Hallstatt culture were created during the Iron Age, from 800 to 450 B.C.E.; most were found in barrow graves, for unlike the preceding Urnfield people, those of Hallstatt had resumed erecting great mounds over their gravesites. Examples of their workmanship have been found in non-Celtic areas of Europe, showing that there was significant trade in their metalwork.

The manufacture of ornate but useful objects continued in the late Iron Age culture called La Tène, from "the shallows" of Lake Neuchâtel in Switzerland, where a hoard of metal objects was discovered and dated to approximately 450 B.C.E. From then until the 1st century B.C.E., the fluid style developed at La Tène was the dominant one among the European Celts; its influence affected neighboring people as well, while the skillful artists and artisans of La Tène expanded their repertoire by using designs inspired by the Etruscans, the Scythians, and other distant cultures. Some scholars date the beginning of Celtic culture to this period.

From these early sites in central Europe, the Celtic tribes moved out to settle throughout western Europe. Celtic migrations began early, with people colonizing today's Spain and France in the Hallstatt period. Later, Celtic people moved from their continental homelands to the islands off the west coast of Europe. First Britain and then Ireland were invaded by groups of Celts who found earlier, non-Celtic people in residence. Joining with or fighting these groups, the Celts created what is called insular Celtic culture, in which elements of earlier culture survived in vestigial form. Scholars disagree about when the Celts arrived, but agree that the migra-tion took place in several, or many, waves—a belief that is found as well in ancient literature and medieval scholarship.

After the arrival of the Roman legions, Celtic art and artifacts changed. Whereas in earlier times, the Celtic people did not portray their divinities in human form, later artists adopted Roman styles, probably to please their patrons and clients. From this period (ca. 100–400 C.E.) we find statues and reliefs of gods and goddesses, many clad in Roman togas but wearing Celtic jewelry or carrying Celtic cult objects. Some such sculptures are inscribed with names of the divinity depicted. Because the Roman legions practiced what was called the "interpretatio Romana," giving the names of their gods to those of the people they colonized, many Celtic gods were labeled with Latin names. In some cases, the original name was included, but often not even that survived. Thus Celtic and Roman cultures were also melded and can be difficult to distinguish.

Celtic Languages

At base, the term *Celtic* refers not to a culture but to a language group. In addition to the similarities of archaeological finds like the Urnfield burials and the swirling metal patterns of the La Tène artists, similar words are found across the old Celtic lands—today's nations of Germany, Austria, France, England, Scotland, Wales, and Ireland. While the names of gods and goddesses may differ, some words found in place-names suggest the spiritual values of the people who used Celtic languages, like *nemeton* for "sacred grove" and *find* for both "white" and "radiant." What the word *Celtic* itself means is unknown; if it was not, as many assume, the name of a small group within the larger Celtic world, it may derive from the Old Norse word for "war," for the Celts were known as a warrior people.

Celtic is a branch of the great Indo-European language family that includes Germanic languages such as English and Dutch; Romance languages such as Italian, Spanish, and French; Slavic languages such as Russian; the Baltic languages, Lithuanian and Latvian; Sanskrit, the language of ancient India; and the odd outpost of Tocharian along the Silk Road near China. The Indo-European-speaking people are not, as was assumed in the 19th century, all racially related. But they share a linguistic family tree that reaches back to central Europe in approximately 2,500 B.C.E. The Celtic tongues were among the first to branch off from the trunk of that tree; thus some ancient verbal forms are maintained in the Celtic tongues that were lost in later branches of the language tree.

Today, six Celtic tongues are known. They fall into two groups, divided by pronunciation and, to a lesser extent, by grammar. Irish and Scottish, both called Gaelic, and Manx, the dying language of the tiny Isle of Man, are called Goidelic Celtic or P-Celtic, while Welsh, Breton, and Cornish are called Brythonic or Q-Celtic. The Goidelic languages are more grammatically complicated, while the Brythonic tongues are slightly more streamlined; in addition, the letter pronounced as Q (or C) in the Brythonic languages became P in the Goidelic, hence their alternate names. For instance, the number "four" in Irish is *ceathar;* the same word in Cornish becomes *peswar.* Similarly, "head" and "son" in Irish are *cenn* and *mac,* while in Cornish they are *pen* and *map.*

Although these languages have lasted more than three thousand years, they are in danger today. Some 16.5 million people live in the ancient Celtic lands, but only approximately 2 million people speak Celtic tongues, and fewer still speak them as first languages. Political and cultural pressure has meant that other languages—notably French and English—are the official tongues of Celtic countries. Only in Ireland is the indigenous language the language of the state, and even there English is used for most communication. Scots Gaelic is spoken on both sides of the Atlantic, in the Cape Breton Island and in the aptly named Nova Scotia as well as in Scotland itself, but it is a minority language, as is the case in Wales, where the Celtic tongue, Welsh, was not officially recognized until 1969.

Breton boasts 1 million speakers, but because the peninsula of Brittany has been part of France for the last six hundred years, schoolchildren there are taught French, not Breton. The last native speaker of Manx, Ned Maddrell, died in 1974; in Cornwall the language lost its native status more than a hundred years ago. Both languages are now the domain of scholars and cultural enthusiasts.

The economic value of speaking English, the world's major language for commerce, has been a primary reason for the decline in the use of Celtic languages over the last several centuries. Because Celts are not racially distinct people but people who speak Celtic languages, if those languages die, so do the Celts.

The Oral Tradition

Literate people often presume that something transcribed into writing is permanent and unalterable, while the spoken word disappears quickly and can be readily changed. But written works are more fragile, and memorized works more enduring, than is commonly believed. The Greek poet Sappho was only known from a few lines quoted by other writers and from her reputation as one of the great poets of antiquity, until a mummy was discovered whose embalmer had used strips from an old manuscript of Sappho's poems in his work. The burning of libraries, as at Alexandria in Egypt in the third century C.E., has meant incalculable loss to human learning. If the written word is not necessarily permanent, neither is it unalterable. Changes in dialect or in spelling can create misunderstandings at a distance in time or place. Writing something down does not in itself insure that it will survive as the author intended.

Conversely, skilled storytellers have been found by researchers to be astonishingly accurate in their recall of details and compositional frameworks. It is now believed that the epics of Homer, despite their great length, began as orally transmitted works and were written down only later; the *Iliad* and the *Odyssey* were composed aloud and shared through public recitation rather than private reading. In addition, oral societies have social structures that support frequent recitation of stories, dispersing those stories through the community in a way that the solitary experience of reading cannot match.

So although they were not literate, the Celts did not lack learning or poetry or historical knowledge. They believed that words gained power by being spoken rather than written. To the Irish Celts, the craft of poetry was a form of magic, related to incantation and enchantment. Especially powerful was the satire, a stinging verbal rebuke so strong and effective that it could change the physical world. A satire could raise boils on the skin of a stingy king or twist the arm of a thief. While we do not know whether the continental Celts held the same beliefs, evidence from classical writers emphasizes the importance they placed on eloquence.

Even after literacy was introduced, it was not widespread, and extemporaneous composition of stories and poems continued. At the same time, works held in the oral tradition were written down, so that early Celtic literature was preserved and passed along by a newly literate class: the monks, who in Christian times took the place of the bards of antiquity. Ireland, which was spared the ravages of Roman invasion and therefore never developed artistic styles that imitated those of the conquerors, is the source of the greatest number and variety of written sources, with Wales and Britain trailing behind, while little remains to tell us the myths of the continental Celts.

Celtic Textual Sources

For the earliest periods of Celtic culture and for the continental Celts into historical times, archaeologists must listen to the mute testimony of artifacts. Few texts exist from ancient Gaul. After Roman occupation, some Celts became literate, no doubt for economic and social advancement. From several of these literate Celts, we have inscriptions connected to religious practices. Written on rugged lead tablets, the inscriptions were found in graves and at cult sites;

although short, they reveal some information (names of gods, social rank, family names) about the people who inscribed and deposited them.

Among the insular Celts, the situation was dramatically different. Celtic languages continued to be spoken after the arrival of literacy, which in most cases was contemporaneous with Christianization. In Ireland many early poems and epics—previously recited and memorized by the bardic classes—were written down by monks who belonged to the culture whose works they were transcribing. In Wales the same thing occurred, although somewhat later. While the transcribers may not have felt any temptation to propagandize against their Celtic ancestors, they may also have been uncomfortable with some of the values expressed in the stories they were writing down. Especially when it comes to women, the insular Celtic written sources must be read with care. But compared to the works of their Roman enemies, the words of the Celtic storytellers offer complex and nuanced information about the society from which they sprang.

In some cases, the works were transcribed in the original languages; in a few cases, the language used was classical Latin, the language of the Church. Sources in Celtic languages carry with them some of the values embedded and encoded in the words and structure, while Latin and other tongues may occasionally convey different meanings than the original may have intended. The greatest number of Celtic-language texts are in Irish, which boasts the distinction of being Europe's third-oldest literary language, after Greek and Latin.

In addition to works of direct transcription of myths, we have some early writings by Celtic people themselves that reveal religious beliefs and practices, such as the geographical and historical works of the historian Nennius and the author Giraldus Cambrensis (Gerald of Wales). These are not necessarily free from bias, whether deliberate or not, for authors can only write from their own perspective, which is necessarily limited.

Texts were typically written on fragile material like vellum made from sheepskin or on parchment made from plant fibers. Unless such materials are carefully preserved, they can quickly deteriorate. In addition, the vagaries of history—including several centuries of Viking raids—meant that some great works were lost to fire, water, and other destruction. What we have today often survived by an accident of history. It is impossible to know if other surviving texts may someday be unearthed and might change our view of the Celtic past.

Nonetheless a number of significant manuscripts have survived for more than a thousand years. The most famous, the *Book of Kells*, records no mythic material but is completely devoted to Christian scripture. More useful for the scholar of mythology are the *Book of the Dun Cow*, written down in the 11th century (allegedly on the hide of a cow whose milk-giving powers recall a mythological image of abundance); the *Book of Leinster*, written in the late 12th century; the *Book of Úi Maine*, written in 1394 by Faelán mac Gabhann; the *Book of Ballymote*, transcribed ca. 1400 C.E.; and the *Yellow Book of Lecan*, composed by three scribes in 1417. Each of these compilations includes a number of stories and poems, some of which are called "books" (as in the *Book of Invasions*); because this can be confusing to the nonspecialist, we will use the term *book* to refer to any compilation and the term *text* to refer to a single story.

One of the oldest of the texts is the *Book of Invasions* (also called the *Book of the Taking of Ireland*), which was written down in the 12th century in several versions. This text describes the history of Ireland from the beginning of time. While there are obvious biblical interpolations (Noah, for instance, appears as an ancestral figure), there are also many mythical figures prominent in the works; thus the *Book of Invasions* is a major source for information about Irish, and through it Celtic, mythology.

Another text written down at about the same time, but based on much older material, is the *Dindshenchas* or place-poetry. Each poem tells the history of a place-name, and as many such names derive from their connection to myth, the poems of the *Dindshenchas* provide valuable mythic information. In addition, a series of Irish texts variously categorized as adventures, visions, wooings, cattle raids, elopements, and voyages provide vivid images of Celtic life. Some of the most important are the Irish epic called the *Táin bó Cuailnge;* the legal texts called the *Senchas Mór;* the short poems called the *Triads;* the collection of Welsh myths, the *Mabinogion;* and the poems of the great and presumedly historical Welsh bard Taliesin.

Unfortunately, less than one-quarter of the known texts have been translated into English. Many of those are difficult for the average reader to obtain. In addition, even when translated, the texts often present problems in interpretation. The valuable medieval texts that make up the *Dindshenchas*, for instance, are filled with allusions to stories and figures who are now unknown.

Because all of these texts were created after Christianization, it is impossible to tell whether the stories were altered to fit the new worldview or whether they truly reflect the viewpoint of the Celts. In general, where a story conveys a meaning different from the later (in this case Christian) worldview, it can be assumed to be correctly transcribed, while anything that agrees is suspect. If, for instance, a monk describes a world-destroying event as a flood, it would be impossible to tell whether that was originally a Celtic idea or whether it was imported from biblical sources. Conversely, if the same monk described a god who wheeled a huge mallet around on a cart—a figure not found in the Bible—we can assume that the image was originally Celtic.

In addition to the 500 or so tales and poems that survive from ancient Ireland, some texts are known from other insular Celtic societies. After Ireland, the greatest wealth of mythological material was transcribed in Wales: the *White Book of Rhydderech*, composed in the early 14th century, and the *Red Book of Hergst*, composed some fifty years later. Together, the tales compiled in the two books comprise the *Mabinogion*, a great cycle of myths as complex and rich as any known to the literate world.

Although in early times the literary language of Scotland was "common Gaelic" or Irish, by the late Middle Ages some works were being transcribed in the local language, Scots Gaelic. An important source from that time is the *Book of the Dean of Lismore*, written in 1516, which includes stories known from Irish sources as well as some original to the document. On the Isle of Man a ballad written down in 1770 reveals the extent of the island's oral tradition, while in Cornwall only fragments of mythic material remain, leaving us to guess at the great tales that have been lost. In Brittany written texts are mostly late, from the 15th century and beyond, but 12th-century French poets Marie de France and Chrétien de Troyes appear to have based their romances on oral Celtic sources.

The Folklore Movement

Literacy and the oral tradition came together in the late 19th century, when across Europe literate people began to be aware of the depth and richness of their indigenous cultures. Rural life, which had gone on relatively unchanged for many generations, was suddenly threatened by increasing industrialization. In places where for generations the same festivals had been held, the same stories told, railroads now cut through quaint villages, luring young people to factory work in the increasingly crowded cities. The old tales, based as they were in ancient religious and cultural visions, were in danger of being lost, as storytellers died with no one to carry on after them.

The great era of folklore collection began then. In Germany the Grimm brothers, Jacob and Wilhelm, gathered scores of stories from country residents. Some of these, like "Cinderella" and "Snow White," are now part of the collective heritage of the world's children, for although originally myths describing the actions of gods and goddesses, the subjugation of these ancient religious ways meant the diminishment of deities into mere human heroes and heroines, their grand adventures becoming merely amusing tales.

In Finland Elias Lönnrot trekked through the winter weather to collect stories that are clearly mythical. He wrote them in a curious chanting rhythm into a collection called the *Kalevala*, still one of the primary texts for those who desire to learn about ancient Finnish religion. In Lithuania collectors transcribed thousands of *daina* or folk songs, most of them addressing the land's ancient goddesses; the songs permit scholars to tentatively reconstruct the ancient mythology of the Baltic region.

In the Celtic lands, too, the folklore movement made its mark. But rather than being merely a cultural effort, in Scotland and Wales and, especially, in Ireland, folklore and literature joined forces. It began with the curious case of James Macpherson, a Scottish poet who created a sensation with the release of his collections of "ancient" poetry from the Highlands. A jaded public was inspired by the Celtic passion of Macpherson's work, then scandalized to learn that it was not word-by-word translation but an imaginative reconstruction—what today would be called ethnopoetic transcription.

But if Macpherson himself fell from favor, a renaissance of Celtic learning had begun. Suddenly collectors in Wales, Brittany, and Ireland were transcribing the stories and songs that had, only a decade previously, been scorned as the inconsequential yarn-spinning of illiterates. William Carleton and T. Crofton Croker set down Irish legends, the great J. F. Campbell published huge collections of Scottish tales, and Lady Charlotte Guest published the first English translations of the *Mabinogion*. The movement continued and deepened in Ireland with the "Celtic Revival" movement spearheaded by the great poet William Butler Yeats, and it continues to some extent today as rock bands name themselves after ancient Celtic goddesses and movie directors mine the tales of the past for new entertainments.

Celtic Life and Society

That Celts did not develop writing did not mean that they had no way to record their history and beliefs. As we have seen, Celtic peoples placed great emphasis on the spoken word as a means of conveying both historical and religious information, leaving us ancient documents describing Celtic life and beliefs. Examination of contemporaneous texts by Roman and other Mediterranean writers offers information naturally biased by their enmity toward the Celts. Archaeology supplements the written word with artifacts found in Celtic sites, both on the Continent and on the islands. Finally, vestiges of Celtic beliefs can be traced through oral recitation and storytelling.

Scholars and writers rely on these three major points of access for information about the Celts, but every statement made is necessarily conjectural. There is much we do not know about the Celts. Over the last two hundred years, theories about how they lived and what they believed have been espoused and then discarded. Many aspects of Celtic life remain subject to intense, often acrimonious, debate. With no definitive text to illuminate questions, such debate is likely to continue. Nonetheless, some features of Celtic life are accepted by most scholars.

Celtic society was based upon a balance of powers among the leaders, who included both kings and druid-poets. Kings could not continue ruling if the land ceased to be productive for the farmers and herders, in which case the druid-poets had to use their magic to end the king's reign. This balance of powers was symbolized by the "marriage" of the king, at his inauguration, to the goddess of the land. As her consort and spouse, the king's job was to keep her happy; the goddess revealed her contentedness by permitting the land to produce food in abundance. Should the king, however, lose the favor of the goddess, pestilence and famine would follow. Thus the king did not expect his people to serve him; rather, he served them as the goddess's husband.

The role of the druid-poet was complex. In both Continental and insular Celtic society, great importance was placed upon eloquence. Since Celtic culture was nonliterate, recitation played a very important role in conveying historical, genealogical, and mythological information from generation to generation. As a result, members of the druidic orders were highly trained in memorization and extemporaneous composition. In addition, they practiced what we might call psychic skills: casting oracles, interpreting dreams, reading omens.

The druids were the priests of the Celts; they were also the poets, historians, judges, troubadours, and professors. Not all druids practiced all of these arts. Some specialized in one or the other, but all fell within the social role of the druid. Nor did the druids form a separate class in the way priests today typically do. They were, rather, spread through society, where they satisfied their various roles.

These social roles remained, to some extent, in Celtic lands even after Roman conquest, Christianization, and occupation by Germanic and Norse overlords. The Romans, who had already cut down the sacred groves on the Continent, destroyed the last druid sanctuary, on Anglesey island off Britain, in ca. 64 C.E. Roman historian Tacitus described the massacre, as robed priestesses and monks fought desperately to preserve their sacred land. As they were cut down, one by one, the knowledge they carried was killed, just as surely as if a great library had been burned to rubble and ash.

The position of Celtic women is hotly contested among scholars. Evidence can be found that Celtic women fought alongside male warriors when their lands were threatened, that queens ruled and led armies into battle, that women were poets and druids. But some scholars dismiss such evidence as indicating only occasional extraordinary women, arguing that the average Celtic woman had few legal rights and served her husband in all matters. This area is one of the most contentious in contemporary scholarship, with some scholars arguing that evidence of matrilineal succession (passage of property and social standing through the mother's family) suggests a non-patriarchal social organization, while others assert that the Celts were a fervently patriarchal warrior culture and any counterevidences were vestiges of pre-Celtic cultures.

Celtic Religion

Most religious systems begin with a creation myth that explains how the world we know came into being. There is, however, no extant Celtic creation myth. One may have existed that has been lost, but we find no references or allusions that suggest as much. This has led some scholars to describe the Celts as positing a world that is continually creating itself, or one that has been always in existence as it is today.

That world, however, does not only include what is tangible to our senses, for according to Celtic belief an Otherworld exists beyond our immediate reality. This Otherworld resembles the Dreamtime of the Australian peoples, for it is a place contiguous with our world, where deities and other powerful beings dwell and from which they can affect our world. These beings cannot enter and leave at will, but only at points in time and space where access is possible.

The Celts also believed that human beings could enter the Otherworld. Some did so accidentally, by mistaking it for this world. Others were kidnapped into it—for example, by a fairy lover who desired the human as a companion, or by a fairy hostess looking for a fine musician for a dance. The Otherworld looked like this world, only more beautiful and changeless. Trees bore blossom and fruit at the same time there; no one ever aged or grew infirm; death had no dominion in the Otherworld.

This world was not mundane as opposed to sacred; the Celts appear to have had no such dualistic conceptions. Although different from the magical Otherworld, this world had its sacred points as well. The four directions were oriented around a sacred center, not necessarily physical nor located in the center. The sacred center was a concept rather than a specific place; it could move, it could multiply, it could even leave this world entirely and become part of the Otherworld.

In the Otherworld lived the great gods. There is no specific pantheon of gods found among all Celtic peoples. Rather, there were many gods, most of which were specific to a region or environment. So polytheistic were the Celts that the standard oath was, "I swear by the gods my people swear by." But however decentralized was the pantheon, some divinities appear in many places, usually under various names. These include the triple mothers, a horned god, and divinities of rivers and other landscape features.

The Celts typically did not depict their divinities in human form. Because divinities had the power of shape-shifting—assuming multiple forms, including those of humans and animals—there was no native tradition of sculpting or painting them in physical form. It was only after the Roman conquest that we find examples of the Mediterranean tradition of showing gods and goddesses in the forms of Roman men and women.

Similarly, the Celts did not bandy about the names of their deities. If all words had power, how powerful were the names of the gods, which were not to be casually invoked. We are not even certain if the words recorded, often by non-Celtic authors, represented divine names or titles. Christians refer to the same deity as Jesus, Christ, Our Lord, the Savior, and the Son of God; a non-Christian reader, finding those names in various texts, might make the understandable mistake of imagining five different gods. It is impossible now to be completely certain whether the names recorded in Roman times and later refer to one or many gods.

Nonetheless, scholars generally agree that the Celts did not have an organized, hierarchical pantheon. Rather than a court arranged in descending order under a king of gods, they saw divinities as arranged in families, as for example the descendants of Danu or Dôn, both mother goddesses. These gods did not live in the sky but in mountains and the sea, in trees and in running streams. This form of religious vision, seeing the divine within the physical world, is known as pantheism and is distinct from those religions that see divinity as separate from or transcendent over nature.

Although all Celts did not share the same gods and goddesses, each group having its own divinities associated with features of their land, there are some commonalities among the tribes.

The Celts all believed in a goddess whose generosity and fecundity made life possible. Often this mother goddess was the ancestor of the entire people, while at other times she was viewed as the ancestor of the gods themselves. Her name in myth is Danu or Anu or Dôn, which has been connected with a hypothesized central European goddess Dan, whose name survives in such rivers as the Danube and the Don. Although she was a goddess of the land, the mother goddess also ruled the rivers that watered the soil; thus most rivers in Celtic lands are, even today, named for goddesses.

The goddesses are often depicted as triple. During Roman times, they were the Deae Matres, the "mother goddesses," shown as three women with similar features, two apparently younger than the third. As contemporary genetics has shown that a woman with at least two daughters is most likely to pass her inheritance through the ages, the ancient portraits of three goddesses may represent a mother-ancestor and her descendants rather than, as was commonly assumed, the same woman passing through different phases of life.

The powers of the god matched and complemented those of the goddess. Although not invariably matched into pairs and rarely into monogamous units, Celtic gods and goddesses are often associated. The male force was imagined as representing skill, as compared to the goddess's powers of fecundity. Many gods were called "many-skilled" or "many-gifted" because they offered their gifts of magic, craft, and poetry to humanity. Gods appeared both as mature men and as young, even vulnerable, sons. The latter could be stolen or lost, and then regained, as several myth-cycles attest.

Celtic Rituals

Archaeology tells us that the Celts did not build many temples. Rather, they celebrated their religion in the open air, a setting appropriate to a people who envisioned divinity as resident in the natural world. Their ritual sites were on hilltops, where great blazes marked the turning seasons; at wells of fresh water, which were honored for their connection to the goddess of sovereignty who empowered kings; and in groves of trees, especially oaks, where ceremonies were held.

Because of the lack of written documents, we have little idea what these rituals entailed. Classical writers liked to claim they had witnessed butchery: animals and even humans killed as sacrifices to the gods. Such commentary, long believed to be merely propaganda by enemies of the Celts, has more recently been examined in light of bodies found in bogs. Because the sterile waters and tannic acid of boggy lands preserve organic material for centuries, even millennia, it is possible to autopsy such corpses to determine the manner of death. Several bog-bodies found in Celtic lands show that the victims were people of leisure, well-fed and well-groomed, who were killed by being strangled, stabbed, and then drowned. This "threefold death" corresponds to some textual evidence, suggesting that in times of crisis human sacrifice may indeed have been practiced.

It is not, however, believed to have been a standard component of Celtic ritual. Most Celtic ceremonies were, rather, centered on the turning of the seasons. Although some scholars argue that the four recognized Celtic holidays were in fact only Irish, most agree that the Celts marked two seasons, each of which had a beginning and an ending half, thus making four seasonal festivals. The two most important were at the turning points of the year: from summer to winter at Samhain on November 1, and from winter back to summer on Beltane on May 1. The secondary festivals marked the midpoints between those great events: Imbolc, on February 1, when winter moved towards spring; and Lughnasa, on August 1, when summer died into fall.

These festivals are distinctively Celtic, for other people marked their year off by noting the solar shifts of solstices (June 21 and December 21) and equinoxes (March 21 and September 21). That the Celts marked the season's midpoint rather than the point of change may relate to the insistence upon the sacredness of the center, which is both a geographical and a spiritual concept.

Tales of Arthur

Some of the most famous tales of western Europe are those of the Matter of Britain, also known as the Arthurian Cycle. From the historian Nennius, who rarely let himself be inhibited by fact, we learn of a Celtic king of the island named Arthur, who rallied his fellows and fought against the Germanic Saxon invaders sometime in the early Christian era, approximately the sixth century C.E. References to the same or a similar figure appear in the Welsh annals, so it appears that there is some historical reality to the regal figure of Arthur, who finally was killed in an internecine battle with his fellow Celts.

Whatever the facts, the story that grew around the figure of Arthur is more mythical than historical. A single Celtic theme repeats itself in the tales, which were developed by writers and artists over many centuries, so that the originating pattern became embedded in complication and elaboration. That theme is the power of the goddess of sovereignty, without whose approving presence the king's right to rule is in danger. The love triangle between the queen and her two lovers (which appears in the Tristan-Iseult-Mark story as well as that of Lancelot-Guinevere-Arthur) is a human reflection of the myth of a goddess who marries one king after another. Similarly, when the Fisher King is wounded in his generative organ and therefore unmanned, the land becomes barren, for in the Celtic framework, a blemished king finds no favor with the land's goddess. Thus although not part of Celtic religion, the tales of Camelot and the knights of the Round Table form an important cultural expression of Celtic ideas and ideals.

The Fairy Faith

Much of oral tradition in Celtic lands involves tales of fairies, beings of the Otherworld who interact with humanity. In Ireland such figures are diminished gods, the race of the Tuatha Dé Danann (tribe of the goddess Danu) who went into hiding within the hills and bogs of Ireland after being defeated by the human invaders, the Milesians. Similarly, in Brittany the old gods became *korrigans*, while in other areas of the ancient Celtic world, we find magical beings whose behavior suggests that they were originally divine.

The early scholar W. Y. Evans-Wentz named these tales and traditions the "fairy faith," claiming that it was a functional religion. In other words, there was both myth (or in this case, legend) and ritual to be found among believers in the fairy people. Stories about the likelihood of being kidnapped by fairies on certain days were connected to rituals of protection, such as wearing clothing backward or carrying iron implements. Although the claim that the fairy faith is a true religion is controversial, there appear to be religious elements to the belief system.

Whether that belief system is connected to earlier Celtic beliefs is similarly controversial. Legend claims that the fairies were originally gods, and some, like the familiar leprechaun, bear the names of divinities known from mythological texts (in this case, Lugh). While some scholars dismiss or question the connection between folkloric figures and the great gods and goddesses of mythology, most see resonances between what has been recorded from oral folkloric sources and the written evidence found in manuscripts that record early myths. The heroic figure of Fionn mac Cumhaill, for instance, appears in folklore as the somewhat less-than-heroic giant Finn McCool, and many similar tales are told of them.

Pronunciation and Spelling

Celtic mythology did not begin in text; it began in story. When transcribers (whether monks or folklorists) wrote down these stories, they spelled in various ways, caring less about the orthography and more about plot and character. For years, indeed for centuries, there was little standardization among Celtic names. As a result, various texts will offer various spellings—sometimes several spellings in a single text.

To popularize their work, 19th- and early 20th-century writers often anglicized Celtic words, creating a hybrid language that was easy on the eyes of the English-speaking reader but that had no scholarly support. Because Celtic languages and the people who speak them have so often been politically disadvantaged in comparison to their English conquerors, the anglicization of Celtic words can be offensive to some. Yet the variations of ancient, early modern, and late modern spellings, with and without diacritical marks, can be confusing and off-putting, especially when accompanied by a pedantic insistence on one formulation over another. Because this book is aimed not at the specialist but at the general reader, the entries include as many alternative spellings as were available. For words in Celtic languages, the spelling that most scholars accept is used as the primary entry name. When that represents a challenge to English-speaking readers, the anglicized spelling appears as the first alternative as a guide to acceptable pronunciation. In the rare case where an anglicized spelling is so common as to render the Celtic spelling not readily recognizable—as with the magician Merlin, correctly spelled Myrddin—the procedure is reversed, with the most acceptable Celtic spelling appearing in brackets immediately after the entry. Latinized names of continental Celtic divinities, which are readily pronounced by English speakers, are not given anglicized forms.

A

Abarta (Ábartach, Ábhartach)   Irish god. This minor figure in Irish mythology—one of the FOMORIANS, an ancient and monstrous race—appears in texts devoted to the band of heroes called the FIANNA. Ambitious to join the warrior elite, Abarta came to them pretending to be a lazy man in search of a job. FIONN MAC CUMHAILL, leader of the Fianna, inexplicably agreed to take him into service, calling him Gialla Deacair, or "lazy servant." Abarta tricked Fianna into mounting his apparently frail old horse and carried them away to the OTHERWORLD. There he held them hostage until Fionn, after many magical adventures and battles, located and freed them. After this crime, Fionn did not offer Abarta membership in his band.

Source: Joyce, P. W. *Ancient Celtic Romances.* London: Parkgate Books, 1997, pp. 223 ff.

Abbey Lubber   British folkloric figure. The Abbey Lubber haunted the wine cellar of any British abbey where lazy monks were overfond of drink. The best known was a spectral horse who dressed in a monkish robe and lived in a monastery under the name of Friar Rush. The wealthy and dissolute prior attempted to chastise the alleged friar for behavior more alcoholic than was welcome in that liberal establishment, but the Abbey Lubber assumed his real form and

vanished, leaving the monks both frightened and chastened. Tales about this creature may derive not from actual mythology but from satirists of the Middle Ages, when corruption in monasteries caused public dismay.

Abbots Bromley   British folkloric site. A vestige of the worship of the horned god CERNUNNOS may survive in the small English town of Abbots Bromley, which is located in the area where the Celtic tribe called the Curnovii or "horned ones" once lived. There, early each September, men wearing ANTLERS are "hunted" through the town streets, after which the Horn Dance is performed, a luck-bringing performance said to lose efficacy if performed outside the town limits. As Celtic beliefs often continue under folkloric disguises, the community festival may have ancient antecedents.

Abcán   Irish god. The TUATHA DÉ DANANN, the early Celtic divinities of Ireland, had a dwarf poet by this name who figures in the story of RUAD, a maiden goddess after whom the famous waterfall of ASSAROE may have been named. It was in Abcán's boat, with its bronze hull and tin sail, that Ruad traveled to this world from the OTHERWORLD. But she did not live long in Ireland, for she died at the waterfall, lured by the singing of MERMAIDS from Abcán's boat into the swirling waters. In another text, Abcán was captured by the great hero of ULSTER, CÚCHULAINN, but freed himself by playing lullabies so irresistible that the warrior fell sound asleep. The figure of Abcán had much in common with, and may be related to, the dwarf musician FER Í.

Abnoba Celtic goddess. Known in both Britain and on the Continent, Abnoba gave her name to the many rivers named Avon, including the famous one in England that flows through the town where playwright William Shakespeare was born; she also ruled the source of the Danube River in central Europe and was associated with the Black Forest, perhaps because of its numerous rivers. Sometimes this goddess was called Dea Abnoba, which means simply "the goddess Abnoba." Inscriptions to Abnoba from the Black Forest suggest that the Romans identified her with their woodland goddess DIANA. She is sometimes depicted as a huntress accompanied by a hunting DOG and a STAG.

Accalon Arthurian hero. The lover of MORGAN, Accalon was said to hail from Gaul and to have been one of king ARTHUR's last opponents in battle. After Morgan stole the scabbard from EXCALIBUR, thus removing Arthur's magical protection against any fatal wound, Accalon hoped to be victorious over the king. But the magician MERLIN strengthened Arthur's hand, and Accalon fell beneath his blows.

Achall Irish heroine. A hill just east of TARA, Ireland's ancient center of royal power, bears the name of this ULSTER princess who died of sorrow when CONALL CERNACH killed her brother, ERC. She was considered one of the six noblest women in Ireland because of her sisterly love.

Achtan (Étain) Irish heroine. Mother of the Irish hero CORMAC MAC AIRT, she conceived and bore him under unusual circumstances. The king of TARA, ART MAC CUINN, was traveling to a battle in which he expected to die, for a vision had warned him of his fate. He stopped overnight in Achtan's home, where her father, the SMITH Olc Acha, revealed to Art a prophecy that sleeping with Achtan would ensure everlasting fame to her lover. Art went eagerly to Achtan's bed. In order to assure fosterage for any offspring resulting from the tryst, Art told Achtan that his friend Lugna would be responsible should she conceive. And conceive she did, though Achtan never saw her child's father again, for Art died in battle soon after.

Near her term, Achtan started for Lugna's home in CONNACHT, making it to the border of the province before going into labor under a thundering sky. A mother WOLF protected and suckled the child when Achtan stumbled away looking for aid, and the new mother was unable to find her child when she returned. Some years later a hunter found the robust young man who had been raised by that wolf-mother. Reunited, human mother and son went to Tara to claim the throne, and there he reigned as Cormac mac Airt. Achtan married the hunter and lived thereafter near her son.

Ádammair Irish god. The husband of the Irish woodland goddess FLIDAIS is obscure in comparison to his consort and has few known myths.

adder See SERPENT.

adder stone See SERPENT STONE.

Ade Arthurian heroine. This obscure figure is named in some texts as the second wife of the knight of the ROUND TABLE, LANCELOT, after an unnamed first wife. In such texts, Lancelot does not become the lover of queen GUINEVERE.

ad-hene Manx spirits. As in other Celtic lands, the residents of the Isle of Man called their neighbors in the ghostly OTHERWORLD by euphemisms such as this one, which means simply "Themselves." See NAMES FOR THE FAIRIES.

Adhnúall (Adnual) Irish mythological animal. One of the hunting DOGS of the Irish hero FIONN MAC CUMHAILL, Adhnúall accompanied his master less frequently than Fionn's primary companion hounds, BRAN and SCEOLAN.

Adra Irish hero. In the *BOOK OF INVASIONS*, the mythic history of Ireland, Adra "the ancient" was the husband of CESAIR, the land's first settler. Theirs was an incestuous marriage, for BITH was the father of both. The multiple and sometimes contradictory texts make it difficult to determine if Adra is the same character as LADRA, otherwise said to be Cesair's mate.

Adsagsona Continental Celtic goddess. Adsagsona was invoked as "weaver of spells," for she was a divinity of magic and the OTHERWORLD, and as "she who seeks out," for she could find the object of any curse or blessing.

adventure Irish literary form. One class of ancient Irish texts that often includes mythological material is the Adventure *(echtra)*; often, an Adventure includes a journey to the OTHERWORLD, although the class of stories called VOYAGES *(imram)* also describe Otherworldly visitations. The most famous texts of this genre are: the *Adventure of ART* Son of Conn, which tells of the desire of the fairy woman BÉ CHUMA for the king of TARA's son Art; the *Adventure of the Sons of EOCHAID* (Mugmedón), which relates the birth of NIALL, another king of Tara; the *Adventure of NERA*, in which a warrior enters the Otherworld through the cave of CRUACHAN; the *Adventure of CONNLA*, in which a FAIRY woman lures Connla to the Otherworld; the *Adventure of CORMAC*, in which that king is lured by FAIRY MUSIC to seek an Otherworld lover; and the *Adventure of LAOGHAIRE* (Mac Crimthann), in which the titular king helps

an Otherworldly peer gain the release of his wife from captivity in the surface world.

Áeb (Aebh, Aobh) Irish heroine. In the famous Irish story of the CHILDREN OF LIR, this unfortunate woman was the birth mother of the fated children of the title. The daughter of BODB DERG, a great magician, Áeb died giving birth to her second set of twins; Áeb's only daughter, the loyal FIONNUALA, is the heroine of the tale, for she replaced her mother after the children were bereaved. Áeb's death brought her evil foster-sister, childless AÍFE, into Lir's household and led to the curse that turned Áeb's children into singing swans.

Áed (Aedh, Aodh) Irish hero and divinity. Anglicized as Hugh, this common ancient Irish name gives rise to contemporary surnames including Hay, Hayes, Hughes, McHugh, and MacKay. Among the many legendary figures bearing this name are:

- **Áed Abrat,** a FAIRY king and father of the renowned fairy queens FAND and LÍ BAN; little legend remains to define him.
- **Áed, son of Eochaid Lethderg** of Leinster, who was held captive by two fairy women for three years; unlike most such captives (see FAIRY KIDNAPPING), he sought to escape the beautiful if sterile land in which he was held. After successfully doing so, Áed traveled to see ST. PATRICK, who freed him from the vestigial bonds of FAIRYLAND. While the former part of the tale is consistent with Irish mythology (see FAIRY LOVER), the latter seems to have been added after Christianization of the land.
- **Áed, son of LIR,** one of the enchanted princes of the tale of the CHILDREN OF LIR, turned into a swan for 900 years by his jealous stepmother.
- **Áed, king of TARA.** A sixth-century king who owned a magical COW that he thought would keep him safe in battle; this assumption may have been correct, but Áed left the cow at home when he went to war and was killed.

- **Áed Minbhrec,** son of the DAGDA, seduced the wife of the hero COINCHEANN who killed Áed Minbhrec in retaliation. The Dagda condemned Coincheann to carry Áed's corpse until he found a boulder big enough to cover it. This story is connected with GRIANÁN AILEACH, where Coincheann died of exhaustion from bearing boulder and body. But some variations have Áed alive still and ruling from his FAIRY MOUND at Mullaghnasee, near Ballyshannon in Co. Donegal.
- **Áed, husband of Aíbell,** a queen of CONNACHT; the powerful and lusty king MONGÁN shape-shifted into Áed's form to sleep with Aíbell, putting a transfigured crone into Áed's bed to cover the deception.
- **Áed Alain,** husband of the birth goddess BÉBINN, sister of BÓAND.
- **Áed Ruad** (Rua, Ruadh), father of the goddess and queen MACHA Mong Rua, who ruled jointly with two other ULSTER kings, CIMBÁETH and DÍTHORBA, in periods of seven years each. When Áed Ruad drowned in the famous waterfall ASSAROE in Co. Donegal, Macha went to war for the right to succeed him. This Áed has been considered an Otherworldly figure, sometimes identified with GOLL MAC MORNA, rather than a mere human king.
- **Áed, son of Miodhchaoin,** killer of (and killed by) the SONS OF TUIREANN, the most tragic of Irish heroes.
- **Áed Eangach,** long-awaited king of Ireland who was to be born miraculously from the side of a pillar on TARA. This "red-handed" king was never born, but the expectation of his imminent arrival was a staple of Irish poetic lore for centuries.
- **Áed Slaine,** see SLANE.
- **Áed Srónmár.** Human lover of the goddess or FAIRY RUAD, he plays little part in myth except to inspire his beloved's fatal trip from the OTHERWORLD to join him on earth; Ruad died before reaching him.

Sources: Gwynn, Edward. *The Metrical Dindshenchas.* Part IV. Royal Irish Academy, Todd Lecture Series. Dublin: Hodges, Figgis, and Co., Ltd., 1906–1924, pp. 3–9, 95, 103, 298, 375–376; MacCulloch, J. A. *The Religion of the Ancient Celts.* London: Constable, 1911, p. 65; MacNeill, Máire. *The Festival of Lughnasa, Parts I and II.* Dublin: Comhairle Bhéaloideas Éireann, 1982, p. 84; O'Rahilly, Thomas. *Early Irish History and Mythology.* Dublin: The Dublin Institute for Advanced Studies, 1946, p. 319; Squire, Charles. *Mythology of the Celtic People.* London: Bracken Books, 1996, pp. 143, 105.

Aeí (Plain of Aeí) Irish mythological site. In the greatest Irish epic, the TÁIN BÓ CUAILNGE, which tells the story of the CATTLE RAID of CONNACHT against ULSTER, the two great bulls of the opposing peoples fight a final battle on the plain of Aeí. Actually reborn human enemies destined to fight in every lifetime, the bulls fought for three days and three nights, tearing each other apart so that at the end of the battle, both lay dead. The plain of Aeí has been variously located in the actual Irish landscape.

Aeracura (Aericura, Heracura) Celtic goddess. Known in Switzerland and Germany as partner to DIS PATER, Aeracura is believed to have been similar to Greek Hecate, whose name resembles hers, for she was depicted holding a CORNUCOPIA or basket of fruit, common emblems of goddesses of fecundity and the OTHERWORLD. See also DEAE MATRES.

áes dána (*aos dana, aes dana*) Irish hero, heroine. This phrase, which today in Ireland designates a group of nationally acclaimed artists, derives from the Old Irish term for poets; the term was also sometimes applied to DRUIDS, BREHONS, or lawyers. To gain the gift of inspiration, one had to drink from the WELL of wisdom, eat the HAZEL nuts floating there, or taste the flesh of the SALMON who swam in it.

áes sídhe (*aos shee, aos sidhe*) See FAIRIES.

Aeval (Eevell, Aoibheall, Aibell, Aebill, Aoibhell, Aoibhil, Aibhinn)   Irish spirit. Ireland has many ancient goddesses who come into literature and folklore as FAIRY QUEENS. Among the most famous is Aeval, connected with the southwestern region of MUNSTER and specifically with a FAIRY MOUND at Killaloe in east Co. Clare, near which a well called Tobereevul ("well of Aeval") gushes from beneath the crag Craganeevul ("rock of Aeval"); she is also associated with the mountain Slieve Bernaugh, where she was said to have lived.

Her name means "beautiful" or "the lovely one," but her behavior was more threatening than loving. Queen of the two-dozen BANSHEES of the region whose appearance predicted death, she appeared as a WASHER AT THE FORD before disasters like the defeat of the historical hero Brian Boru; she was especially connected with the O'Brien family. Aeval judged the famous Midnight Court of the poet Brian Merriman, in which prudish Irishmen were found guilty of not being satisfactory lovers. Her rival was the sea fairy CLÍDNA, who turned Aeval into a white CAT.

Sources: Dames, Michael. *Mythic Ireland.* London: Thames and Hudson, 1992, p. 236; Gregory, Lady Augusta. *Gods and Fighting Men: The Story of the Tuatha De Danaan and of the Fianna of Ireland.* New York: Oxford University Press, 1970, p. 87; Merriman, Brian. *The Midnight Court.* Trans. Frank O'Connor. Dublin: The O'Brien Press, 1989.

Afagddu (Avagddu, Morfran)   Welsh god. Afagddu ("utter darkness") was a boy so ugly that his mother, the HAG-goddess CERIDWEN, feared he would never attract a mate. Thinking that poetry might draw maidens even to an uncomely man, Ceridwen mixed herbs of inspiration for her son in her magical CAULDRON—but the young servant boy GWION sipped the brew prematurely, thus draining its magic and becoming the great poet TALIESIN as a result. (In Irish myth, inspiration is gained from drinking from a sacred water-source, apparently a corollary of Ceridwen's cauldron.) After this theft, we hear nothing more in myth of Afagddu. It is unclear whether MORFRAN was an equally ugly brother or another name for Afagddu.

Sources: MacCulloch, J. A. *The Religion of the Ancient Celts.* London: Constable, 1911, p. 116; Straffon, Cheryl. *The Earth Goddess: Celtic and Pagan Legacy of the Landscape.* London: Blandford, 1997, p. 43.

afanc (avanc)   Welsh monster. The *afanc* haunted a whirlpool in the River Conwy in north Wales in the form of a massive beaver—or sometimes a crocodile, though that tropical reptile is otherwise rare in the vicinity. The monstrous size of the *afanc* clashes with its name, which means "dwarf" or "water-dwarf." The *afanc* could be tamed, but only if lured (like a unicorn) to the lap of a maiden, where it could be harnessed by chains. One maiden, however, who tried to do so lost her life as the monster fled back to the safety of its lake home.

Source: Rhys, John. *Celtic Folklore: Welsh and Manx.* Oxford: Clarendon Press, 1941, pp. 130 ff.

Agallamh na Seanóarch   See COLLOQUY OF THE ELDERS.

Aglovale   Arthurian hero. This minor figure in Arthurian legend was killed by LANCELOT as that great knight was rescuing his beloved GUINEVERE from death at the stake.

Agnoman   Irish hero. He never reached Ireland, but this mythological figure nonetheless figures in the Irish mythic history, the *BOOK OF INVASIONS.* Agnoman's son was NEMED, founder of the vaguely described race called the Nemedians who followed him from the family home in SCYTHIA to migrate to Ireland. Some scholars believe that such myths are vestiges of otherwise lost history; Elizabethan English poet and political apologist Edmund Spenser took the story literally and argued vehemently that the Irish were originally Scythian savages.

Agravaine Arthurian hero. This minor figure in the legends of king ARTHUR and his knights of the ROUND TABLE was a member of that renowned assembly, as were his brothers GAWAIN, GAHERIS, and GARETH. He was killed by LANCELOT for plotting with the evil MORDRED.

agricultural rituals Although the Celts enter history as migratory herding tribes, they soon developed agriculture, perhaps as a result of contact with settled people; new religious rites developed to reflect and support the new lifestyle. Whether the rites were Celtic inventions or adaptations from rituals of pre-Celtic cultures is a matter of debate. In Ireland, we find rituals connected both with herding (as in the driving of animals between the BELTANE fires) and with agriculture (as in the offering of fruits to the god CROM DUBH on SAMHAIN), suggesting a mixed economy and the need to sustain both herds and fields through ritual. More clearly agricultural are the Irish myths and rituals that reflect the belief that the king was married to the goddess of the region, its FERTILITY being reliant upon the rectitude of his actions (see SOVEREIGNTY, INAUGURATION). In Wales the god AMAETHON, who appears in the epic poem *KULHWCH AND OLWEN*, was a human farmer able to make even the most unlikely wastelands bloom; although he was a god of agricultural fertility, the rituals offered to him were not recorded.

Source: MacCulloch, J. A. *The Religion of the Ancient Celts.* London: Constable, 1911, pp. 57, 80.

Agretes Arthurian hero. Long before king ARTHUR took the throne of CAMELOT, Agretes reigned there. Because he refused to assist a pilgrim from the Holy Land who bore a great chalice called the GRAIL, he was stricken mad and died.

Agrona British goddess. An obscure goddess of war found in Britain and perhaps in Wales, she has been described as cognate with the MÓRRÍGAN, the Irish death queen.

Aguigrenons Arthurian hero. A minor figure in legends of the great ROUND TABLE knights, he was their enemy who was finally vanquished by the pure PERCIVAL.

Aí (Aoi, Aoi mac Ollamain) Irish god. This minor Irish divinity was a poet of the magical race of Ireland, the TUATHA DÉ DANANN; at his birth a prophet predicted that he would wield great power. This prompted a king to try to murder the babe, but his father saved Aí so that his destiny could be fulfilled; however, the specifics of that destined greatness are lost.

aiats See DIRECTIONS.

Aíbgréne (Abgrenia) Irish heroine. In some texts, this otherwise-unknown heroine is the daughter of the doomed lovers, DEIRDRE and NOÍSIU.

Aibheaeg Irish divinity or fairy. This FAIRY QUEEN or goddess of Donegal was worshiped at a "well of fire" whose waters were held to be an effective treatment for toothache; the petitioner was to leave a white stone as a substitute for the afflicted tooth. Connection of WELLS with toothache was less common than with HEALING of eye diseases; see BRIGIT.

Sources: Logan, Patrick. *The Holy Wells of Ireland.* Gerrards Cross: Colin Smyth, 1980, p. 67; Monaghan, Patricia. *O Mother Sun: A New View of the Cosmic Feminine.* Freedom, Calif.: The Crossing Press, 1994, p. 70.

Aidín (Aideen) Irish heroine. A minor figure in Irish lore, Aidín was the wife of OSCAR, a warrior of the elite FIANNA, and she died of grief at her husband's death. The BARD, OISÍN, buried her with high honors under a CAIRN on the hill called BENN ÉTAIR.

Aífe (Eefa, Eva, Aoife, Aife, Aeife) Irish heroine. Several legendary Irish figures bear this name, which means "radiant" or "beautiful." These include:

- **Aífe of Scotland,** a great warrior who trained Irish heroes. She was the daughter, sister, and/or double of the fearsome, SCÁTHACH, one of the great WARRIOR WOMEN. After the ULSTER hero CÚCHULAINN showed his virile strength by besting her in battle, Aífe bore his child, CONNLA. The hero later unwittingly killed the young man, finding—too late—the ring he had given Aífe as a memento for their child. This tragedy has been the inspiration for several literary works, notably W. B. Yeats's play *On Baile's Strand.* In some myths, Aífe was Scáthach's rival rather than her sister.
- **Aífe, stepmother of the CHILDREN OF LIR,** a jealous woman who took the place of her unfortunate foster sister ÁEB as wife of Lir after Áeb died giving birth to her second set of twins. But the children did not fare well in Aífe's care: she turned FIONNUALA and her brothers into swans for 900 years.
- **Aífe of the crane bag,** a woman magically transformed into a CRANE (sometimes, HERON) by a jealous rival, Iuchra; after spending a lifetime on the sea, she was again transformed by the sea god MANANNÁN MAC LIR, who created the mythological CRANE BAG from her skin to carry all his mythic treasures, including the letters of the alphabet. Sometimes described as a muse figure, she is occasionally conflated with the stepmother of Fionnuala.

Sources: Condren, Mary. *The Serpent and the Goddess: Women, Religion and Power in Ancient Ireland.* San Francisco: Harper & Row, 1989, pp. 122–123; Gwynn, Edward. *The Metrical Dindshenchas.* Royal Irish Academy, Todd Lecture Series. Dublin: Hodges, Figgis, and Co., Ltd., 1906–1924, p. 133; Hull, Eleanor. *The Cuchullin Saga in Irish Literature.* London: David Nutt, 1898, p. xxxi; Joyce, P. W. *Ancient Celtic Romances.* London: Parkgate Books, 1997, pp. 1–32.

Aifi Irish heroine. This obscure figure is named in the *BOOK OF INVASIONS* as one of the FIVE wives of the hero PARTHOLÓN, along with Elgnad or DEALGNAID, Cerbnat, Cichban, and Nerbgen. She is otherwise unknown.

Aige Irish heroine. A malicious FAIRY, urged on by neighbors envious of Aige's grace and charm, turned this woman into a wild doe. In that form she wandered the island, fleeing from hunters, until the warrior Meilge killed her while he was hunting. Aige's brother FAIFNE, a satirist, tried to avenge her death but lost his own life instead.

Source: Gwynn, Edward. *The Metrical Dindshenchas.* Part II. Vol. IX. Royal Irish Academy, Todd Lecture Series. Dublin: Hodges, Figgis, and Co., Ltd., 1906–1924, p. 67.

Aigle Irish hero. This CONNACHT prince was slain by his uncle, Cromderg, in retaliation for Aigle's own murder of a woman named Cliara who was under Cromderg's care. For a time Aigle's name was given to one of Connacht's most important mountains. First called Cruachan Garbrois, the pyramidal peak then became Cruachan Aigle; now the mountain, called CROAGH PATRICK for the last 1,600 years, is honored as the site of the final conflict between the Christian missionary and Ireland's ancient pagan powers.

Source: Gwynn, Edward. *The Metrical Dindshenchas.* Royal Irish Academy, Todd Lecture Series. Dublin: Hodges, Figgis, and Co., Ltd., 1906–1924, p. 281.

Ailbe (Ailba) Irish mythological beast. A famous hunting DOG owned by the warrior MAC DATHÓ, Ailbe was desired by two powerful provincial kings, each of whom his owner wished to satisfy. Promising the dog to both CONCOBAR MAC NESSA and AILILL MAC MATA, kings of ULSTER and CONNACHT respectively, Mac Dathó set in motion an argument in which the dog was killed.

Aileach   See GRIANÁN AILEACH.

Ailill (Aleel, Aileel, Allil)   Irish hero. Ancient Irish literature boasts many heroes and kings by this name, which means "elf" or "sprite" and is similar to the goddess name ÉLE; it is often anglicized into Oliver. Mythic figures of this name include:

• **Ailill mac Máta** (mac Matach), the most famous bearer of the name, was consort of queen MEDB of CONNACHT. In the Irish epic, *TÁIN BÓ CUAILNGE*, an argument between Ailill and Medb (the famous "pillow-talk") set off a murderous CATTLE RAID on ULSTER. Medb announced that she had married Ailill for his generosity, bravery, and lack of jealousy; Ailill showed the latter by ignoring Medb's flagrant affair with the well-endowed FERGUS. Ailill claimed the right to rule Connacht because his mother Máta—after whom he is called mac ("son of") Máta—was the province's queen, although in some stories he was a mere man-at-arms raised to consort status by Medb's desire; in either case, his claim to power comes through relationship to a woman. In addition to the *Táin bó Cuailnge*, Ailill also appears in the *Táin bó Fraéch*, the *Cattle Raid of Fraéch*, in which he set obstacles in the way of the hero FRAÉCH who wished to wed FINNABAIR, Ailill and Medb's daughter.

Ailill also makes a significant appearance in *Echtra Nerai*, the *Adventure of NERA*, for it was at Ailill's instigation that the hero NERA descended into the OTHERWORLD on SAMHAIN, the day when the veils between worlds were

thinnest. Despite his forbearance about her many lovers, Medb did not return the favor; Ailill met his death when she found him unfaithful and convinced the hero CONALL CERNACH to kill him. That Ailill was not without fault is emphasized by the derogatory reference in the *SENCHAS MÓR*, a compilation of ancient legal texts, which censures him for "sudden judgements," apparently meaning hasty and ill-conceived opinions.

• **Ailill, a MILESIAN** king of LEINSTER and father of the romantic heroine ÉTAIN. When the god of beauty, AONGHUS Óg, asked for Étain's hand for his foster-father, the FAIRY king MIDIR, Ailill exploited the situation by demanding the clearing of 12 vast agricultural plains—a task that the sturdy DAGDA, Aonghus's father, performed. Not yet satisfied, Ailill demanded that 12 rivers be created to irrigate the new fields; again the Dagda complied. Then Ailill asked for his daughter's weight in silver and again in gold, and once again the Dagda did as asked. And so finally Ailill agreed to grant Midir permission to court his daughter, setting in motion events that affected Étain for several lifetimes. The name Ailill also appears later in Étain's story, the result either of poetic doubling or of the derivation of both figures from a lost original.

• **Ailill Anglonnach** (Anguba), who seduced Étain, queen of TARA, wife of his brother EOCHAID Airem. Ailill feigned illness to attract Étain. Not wishing to betray her marriage bed but convinced that only making love to him would save Ailill's life, Étain agreed to meet him on a nearby hill. A man looking exactly like Ailill approached, and she made love with him—but the man was, in fact, her FAIRY husband from a former lifetime, MIDIR, who thus spared her honor.

• **Ailill Olom** (Ailill Aulomm, Ailill Ólom), mythological king of ancient MUNSTER and ancestor of that province's historical Eóganacht dynasty. He was said to have lived for nearly a century as the mate of the land goddess ÁINE, but alternative stories say that he raped her on the feast of SAMHAIN and that, in defending herself, she ripped off his ear—hence his nickname, "bare-eared Ailill." Ailill was foster father of the hero LUGAIDH mac Conn, who despite that relationship turned against Ailill and his ally ART MAC CUINN. After defeating them at the battle of MAG MUCRAMHAN, Lugaidh gave Tara's kingship to Art's son, COR-MAC MAC AIRT, and traveled south to make amends to Ailill. But the Munster king, unwilling to accept Lugaidh's apology, poisoned his son with his breath.

• **Ailill of Aran,** father of two wives of king LIR: ÁEB, who gave birth to his children, including the heroic FIONNAULA; and the envious AÍFE, who bewitched the children into swans, according to the story of the CHILDREN OF LIR, one of the THREE SORROWS OF IRELAND.

• **Ailill Áine,** mythological ancestral father of the historical Lagin people of ancient LEINSTER.

Sources: Evans-Wentz, W. Y. *The Fairy-Faith in Celtic Countries.* Gerrards Cross: Colin Smythe Humanities Press, 1911, pp. 288–289; Gantz, Jeffrey, ed. and trans. *Early Irish Myths and Sagas.* New York: Penguin Books, 1984, pp. 37 ff, 113 ff; Green, Miranda. *Celtic Goddesses: Warriors, Virgins and Mothers.* London: British Museum Press, 1995, p. 122; Green, Miranda. *The Gods of the Celts.* Gloucester: Alan Sutton, 1986, p. 15; Hull, Eleanor. *The Cuchullin Saga in Irish Literature.* London: David Nutt, 1898, pp. 111 ff; Joyce, P. W. *Ancient Celtic Romances.* London: Parkgate Books, 1997, p. 3; Kiernan, Thomas J. *The White Hound on the Mountain and Other Irish Folk Tales.* New York: Devin-Adair, 1962, pp. 129–152; Markale, Jean. *Women of the Celts.* Rochester, Vt.: Inner Traditions, 1986; Squire, Charles. *Mythology of the Celtic People.* London: Bracken Books, 1996, pp. 147 ff; Kinsella, Thomas, trans. *The Táin.* Dublin: The Dolmen Press, 1969, pp. 52 ff.

Ailinn (Aillinn, Aillin) Irish heroine. One of Ireland's greatest romances revolves around this princess of the southeastern PROVINCE of LEIN-STER and her lover Baile Binnbhéarlach ("sweet-spoken Baile"), prince of ULSTER in the northeast. As each traveled separately to a trysting place midway between their realms, a maleficent FAIRY told the prince—falsely—that his lover was dead, whereupon he died of grief at Baile's Strand, a seashore near today's Dundalk; the spiteful sprite then carried the same story (sadly true this time) to Ailinn, who also fell down dead of grief. From their adjacent graves grew two entwined trees: a yew from his, an apple from hers. Seven years later, poets cut down the trees and carved them into magical tablets, engraving all of Ulster's tragic love songs on the yew, while those of Leinster were recorded on the apple-wood; thus their provinces were joined as closely as the lovers had once been. When the king of TARA, CORMAC MAC AIRT, held the two tablets near each other, they clapped together and could never again be separated. A variant holds that Ailinn was abducted and raped, dying of shame over her treatment; an apple tree grew from her grave, while nearby a yew ascended from the grave of her beloved pet DOG Baile.

Sources: Condren, Mary. *The Serpent and the Goddess: Women, Religion and Power in Ancient Ireland.* San Francisco: Harper & Row, 1989, p. 66; Hull, Eleanor. *The Cuchullin Saga in Irish Literature.* London: David Nutt, 1898, p. xxx.

Aillén (Ellen, Aillene) Irish hero, heroine, or spirit. A number of legendary Irish figures bear this name, which is related to words for "sprite" and "monster." Several are sufficiently similar that they may be the same or derivatives of the same original.

• **Aillén mac Midgna** (Midna, Midhna) The most famous Aillén, he was called "the burner." This destructive musician of the magical tribe called the TUATHA DÉ DANANN burned down the great halls of TARA for 23 consecutive years, each time lulling its defenders to sleep with FAIRY MUSIC so rapturously soporific that no one could resist. After each year's success, Aillén crept back to his FAIRY MOUND at Finnachaid (the tragic king LIR was sometimes said to live there as well); each year after his departure, Tara was rebuilt. Finally the hero FIONN MAC CUMHAILL killed Aillén, using a poisoned spear whose fumes were so noxious that no one could sleep after breathing them, not even those lulled by Aillén's magical music.

- **Aillén Trechenn** (Trechend) "Triple-headed Aillen" regularly attacked Ireland's great capital TARA, as well as the regional capital of EMAIN MACHA in ULSTER; described as sometimes male, sometimes female, this fiend lived in the cave called OWEYNAGAT at the CONNACHT capital of CRUACHAN. The poet AMAIRGIN finally dispatched the monster and freed Tara from its stranglehold. As Oweynagat's usual resident is the MÓRRÍGAN, this figure may be associated with her. The distinction between this murderous monster and Aillén mac Midgna is difficult to discern.
- **Aillén, brother of** ÁINE, goddess of FAIRY QUEEN of MUNSTER, he fell in love with the wife of the sea god MANANNÁN MAC LIR.

Source: Briggs, Katherine M. *An Encyclopedia of Fairies: Hobgoblins, Brownies, Bogies, and Other Supernatural Creatures.* New York: Pantheon Books, 1976, p. 3.

Aill na Mireann   See STONE OF DIVISIONS.

Ailna   Irish heroine. When the bold warriors of the FIANNA killed her husband Mergah, this woman set out to gain vengeance. Transforming herself into a deer (see SHAPE-SHIFTING), she led the Fianna leader FIONN MAC CUMHAILL and his musician pal DÁIRE on a desperate chase until they were exhausted. Then she surrounded them with a DRUID'S FOG so that they could not find their way home. When the Fianna heard Dáire's music and attempted a rescue, they too got lost

in the thick fog. Wandering, Fionn and Dáire met another lost traveler, Glanlua, who asked them for aid. Then FAIRY MUSIC arose from within the fog, and all fell asleep.

When the fog cleared, Fionn found himself on the shores of a lake, from which there arose a GIANT and a beautiful woman: Ailna and her brother, DRYANTORE, demanding recompense for the murder of Mergah in battle and for the deaths of his nephews, Dryantore's sons, as well. The pair imprisoned the heroes in a dungeon, but Glanlua became Ailna's companion and from her learned of a magical drinking horn that would restore health and strength. When the Fianna were finally able to locate Fionn, the wily Conan slipped the vessel to Fionn so that, strengthened, he was able to break his bonds and escape.

Source: Joyce, P. W. *Ancient Celtic Romances.* London: Parkgate Books, 1997, pp. 362 ff.

Aimend   Irish goddess. This obscure goddess appears to have been an early solar divinity.

Áine (Enya)   Irish goddess, heroine or spirit. Irish legend offers several figures of this name, which means "brightness" or "splendor." Historical figures of this name tend to be male and are connected with the Limerick/north Kerry area of the southwestern province of MUNSTER; mythological figures are female and are typically connected to the same area, although the name is found as far away as ULSTER. The most prominent Áines of myth may be ultimately the same or may derive from the same original.

- **Áine of** KNOCKAINY [Cnoc Áine], usually described as a FAIRY QUEEN although she is probably a diminished goddess, who inhabits a hill near storied LOUGH GUR in east Co. Limerick. Several scholars connect her with ANU (DANU), the great goddess of MUNSTER who gave her name to the TUATHA DÉ DANANN, the tribe of the goddess Danu.

There are indications that she was a SUN goddess, for she was connected with solar wells like Tobar Áine near Lissan in Ulster as well as being linked with the sun goddess GRIAN, her sister; but at other times she is described as related to FINNEN, "white," an obscure goddess of the Lough Gur region. As sun goddess, Áine could assume the form of an unbeatable HORSE, Lair Derg ("red mare").

Áine's special feast was held on either MID-SUMMER night, the summer solstice on June 21, or on LUGHNASA, the Celtic feast on August 1. At that time, straw torches were waved over animals that were then driven up the slopes of Knockainy to solicit Áine's protection. She is sometimes called Áine Chlair, either from the connection with the "cliars" or torches used in such ceremonies, or from Cliu/Cliach, the ancient name for the territory. "The best-hearted woman that ever lived," as she was locally called, was reported to have been seen on the slopes of her mountain even into recent times, offering help to those in need.

The long list of Áine's lovers includes both gods and mortals. Among the former was the sea god MANANNÁN MAC LIR. Áine's brother AILLÉN fell in love with Manannán's wife, and Manannán with Áine, so Manannán gave his wife to Aillén in exchange for the charms of Áine. (A variant has Áine as daughter rather than lover to Manannán.) Although a lustful goddess, she also has a matronly aspect, for her "birth chair" (see SUIDEACHAN) can be seen on the mountain Knockadoon.

Áine was the lover of Maurice (Muiris), the human Earl of Desmond, who stole her cloak in order to capture her (see SWAN MAIDEN); once captured, she bore him a son, GERÓID IARLA or Gerald the waterbird. Warned against showing any surprise at their magical son's behavior, Maurice remained composed at all times—until Geróid was fully grown and showed himself able to shrink almost into invisibility at will. When his father called out in astonishment, Geróid disappeared; he is said to live still in Lough Gur and to ride around it every seven years on a white horse. The descendants of Áine's son—the Geraldines or Fitzgeralds—long claimed sovereignty in western Munster through this descent from the goddess of the land.

Áine did not always go willingly to prospective lovers; she was responsible for the death of the hero ÉTAR, who expired of a broken heart when she rejected him. She was also said to have resisted AILILL Olom, who took her against her will and whose ear she ripped off in her unsuccessful fight against him; the child of the rape was Eógan, a story that some scholars describe as an invention of his descendants, the Eóganacht rulers, to affirm control of the lands under Áine's SOVEREIGNTY.

Some legends connect Áine with madness, for those who sat on her stone chair went mad, and if they sat there three times, they would never recover their wits. Those who were already mad, however, could regain their sanity through the same process.

- **Áine of Donegal,** from the parish of Teelin in the townland of Cruachlann, near another mountain called Cnoc Áine; there Áine was said to have been a human woman who disappeared into the mountain to escape a savage father. She now spends her time spinning sunbeams, this story says, suggesting that the folkloric figure disguises an ancient SUN goddess. A folk verse from the area has Áine telling discontented wives how to weaken their husbands with "corn warm from the kiln and sheep's milk on the boil."

- **Áine of the FENIAN CYCLE,** daughter of either the fairy king CUILENN or a Scottish king, was the lover of FIONN MAC CUMHAIL, by whom she had two sons. Áine and her sister MILUCRA fought for Fionn's affections; Milucra turned him into a graybearded ancient who would be uncompelled by lust, but Áine restored him to youth with a magical drink. Fionn, however, married neither of the sisters.

Sources: Dames, Michael. *Mythic Ireland.* London: Thames and Hudson, 1992, pp. 62–67; Gregory,

Lady Augusta. *Gods and Fighting Men: The Story of the Tuatha De Danaan and of the Fianna of Ireland.* New York: Oxford University Press, 1970, p. 86; Joyce, P. W. *Ancient Celtic Romances.* London: Parkgate Books, 1997, pp. 351 ff; O hEochaidh, Séan. *Fairy Legends of Donegal.* Translated by Máire MacNeill. Dublin: Comhairle Bhéaloideas Éireann, 1977, p. 39; O'Rahilly, Thomas. *Early Irish History and Mythology.* Dublin: The Dublin Institute for Advanced Studies, 1946, pp. 286 ff; Straffon, Cheryl. *The Earth Goddess: Celtic and Pagan Legacy of the Landscape.* London: Blandford, 1997, p. 36.

Ainge Irish goddess. This daughter of the DAGDA magically defended against the theft of the logs she was gathering by transforming them into living trees. She owned a tub or CAULDRON in which water would ebb and flow as though it were the tide.

Airech Irish hero. The foster son of the great BARD of the MILESIANS, AMAIRGIN, Airech plays little part in Irish mythology except as the man who steered the ship of the mysterious DONN. As Donn is sometimes interpreted as ruler of death, Airech may be the steersman of the death barge.

Airmid (Airmed, Airmedh) Irish goddess. A member of the TUATHA DÉ DANANN, the tribe of the goddess DANU, Airmid was an herbalist, daughter of the divine physician DIAN CÉCHT. With her beloved brother MIACH, Airmid healed the wounded hand of king NUADA so that he could continue to reign, for a BLEMISHED KING could not lead the people. Her father had already tried, but Dian Cécht was only able to craft a hand of silver, while his children made a far superior replacement: They made flesh grow around their father's prosthesis, creating a lifelike limb. Furious with envy, Dian Cécht killed Miach. As Airmid tended the flowers on her brother's grave, she observed hundreds of healing plants among them, and she sat down to classify the herbs, fail-ing to notice her father creeping up on her. He allowed Airmid to finish her task, then scattered all the herbs. Airmid's order has never been restored, and the ancient Irish said that the loss of her medical knowledge greatly increased the pain that humans must endure.

aisling (ashling, aislinge) Irish literary form. A traditional form of Irish poetry, this word means "vision" or "dream." The most famous such poem is the *Aislinge Óenguso*, or *The Vision of AONGHUS*, which tells of the love of that god for a SWAN MAIDEN named CÁER; another renowned poem in the genre is the *Aislinge Meic Con Glinne* or *The Vision of MAC CONGLINNE*, a satirical poem about a wise scholar who travels around an Ireland burdened by the corruption of its clergy and poets. Many later (17th–19th century) aislings were patriotic poems that described the poet encountering the goddess of SOVEREIGNTY, now betrayed and alone, walking the roads of Ireland searching for a hero.

See DREAMS, *SPÉIR-BHEAN.*

Aithirne (Aitherne, Athairne) Irish hero. A poet who appears in a number of medieval texts, Airthirne "the Importunate" represents a degraded form of the magical BARD of ancient times. He lived by taking advantage of the Irish custom that it was wrong to refuse the request of a poet. He was so greedy that even before birth his *in utero* noises caused ale barrels to burst; later he used his poetic gift to satirize anyone—or anything, for he even satirized a river—that did not give him food. It was because of Aithirne that a bridge of bundled saplings was built over the River Liffey where the city of Dublin now lies (in Irish, the city is Baile Átha Cliath, the town on the wicker ford); when he wanted to drive some stolen sheep across the river, the men of the region, frightened of his merciless reputation, built the bridge for him. He then repaid them—by stealing their wives.

Aithirne traveled to the FAIRY MOUND of BRÍ LÉITH to steal the HERONS of inhospitality, which he intended to install in his own house, in direct defiance of the requirement that householders be generous and hospitable. His greed extended to the sexual realm; he demanded to sleep with one queen immediately after she gave birth. Finally he went too far, demanding access to the bed of Luaine, the bride of ULSTER's king CONCOBAR MAC NESSA. When she refused, Aithirne composed a satire that caused her to break out in blisters so virulent that they killed her. In retaliation, the Ulster warriors set fire to Aithirne's house, and the greedy poet was devoured by greedy flames.

Sources: Dames, Michael. *Mythic Ireland.* London: Thames and Hudson, 1992, p. 138; Hull, Eleanor. *The Cuchullin Saga in Irish Literature.* London: David Nutt, 1898, pp. 87 ff; Kennedy, Patrick. *Legendary Fictions of the Irish Celts.* New York: Benjamin Blom, 1969, p. 311.

Alain   See FISHER KING.

Alator   British warrior or healing god. His name, which appears to mean "he who rears and nourishes his people," is found in several British sites, and versions of it appear in Ireland as well. Alator was associated by the Romans with MARS, which suggests that he ruled war or healing.

Alauna   Continental Celtic goddess. Alauna was a river divinity found in Brittany (in the river Alaunus) and in Wales (in the river Alun in Pembrokeshire), and possibly in England's Alun, a tributary of the Dee, from which fish reputedly came ashore to stare at human men and to wink suggestively at women.

Albinal (Albu, Alba)   British goddess. According to the Roman author Pliny, this was the name of the chief goddess of the island of Britain, sometimes called Albion after her; some authors refer to her as Alba, although that name is also used to refer to Scotland. The

early medieval British historian Holinshed mentioned a figure of this name, a princess who landed on the British shore in ships with 50 fugitive women who had killed their husbands; a parallel figure in Irish mythology, CESAIR, similarly landed with boatloads of women, although in that case several men were permitted aboard. Albina's name may mean "white," suggesting a connection to the chalky soil of southeast Britain, although others have derived the word from an ancient term for "height" (as in "Alps").

Albion   British hero. According to the medieval writer Geoffrey of Monmouth, there was once a giant of this name whose father was a sea god. The name has been seen as cognate with that of the continental Celtic god ALBIORIX.

Albiorix   Continental Celtic god. This name may mean "king of the world" and is found in several inscriptions from Gaul; the Romans identified this deity with their own god of war, MARS.

alder   Celtic sacred tree. On slender, graceful branches, the alder (genus *Alnus*) carries tiny cones and dangling catkins at the same time; perhaps it was this evidence of the simultaneity of seasons past with those to come that led the Celts to connect alder with DIVINATION and prognostication, a connection that lasted into the early modern period in Scotland. When cut, the wood turns from white to red as though bleeding, which may have suggested that the trees sustain a humanlike spirit; in ancient times, the felling of alder trees was forbidden as a kind of murder. The sacredness of alders is emphasized in tales that the FAIRY folk used it to cover their theft of cattle from humans, leaving enchanted boughs of alder in place of the cattle they spirited away. In Wales the alder was associated with the hero BRÂN, THE BLESSED for the poet GWYDION was able to ascertain Brân's identity because of the alder branch he carried.

ale (*dergfhlaith*) Ritual object. This hearty drink of hops and malt—a favorite of the ancient Irish, who also fermented honey into mead—had a ritual significance as the symbol of the goddess of SOVEREIGNTY, who offered a cup of *dergfhlaith* ("red ale") to the new king at his inauguration. The legendary but little-known PARTHOLONIANS were said to have brought the beverage to Ireland, but it was a later mythological race, the TUATHA DÉ DANANN, who refined the art of brewing until the ale of their SMITH and brewer GOIBNIU was strong enough to endow the drinker with immortality. Irish epics such as *The Drunkenness of the Ulstermen* and the *Adventure of Nera* connect ale with the festival of SAMHAIN, when the boundaries between this world and the OTHERWORLD were blurred. Archaeology has revealed ancient brewing cauldrons but no indication of storage vessels; thus drinking may have been a seasonal event in ancient Ireland.

Aleine Arthurian heroine. A minor figure in legends of king ARTHUR, Aleine was the niece of GAWAIN and lover of PERCIVAL.

Alend Irish goddess. The great ancient capital of the eastern Irish province of LEINSTER, Almu, was named for this otherwise obscure goddess or heroine, who was described as royal and heroic, but with little narrative to reveal why. The hill where the capital once stood is now known as the Hill of Allen, in Co. Kildare; this goddess also gave her name to the BOG OF ALLEN.

Source: Gwynn, Edward. *The Metrical Dindshenchas.* Part II. Vol. IX. Royal Irish Academy, Todd Lecture Series. Dublin: Hodges, Figgis, and Co., Ltd., 1906–1924, pp. 81 ff.

Alfasem Arthurian hero. One of the BLEM-ISHED KINGS of Arthurian legend, he attempted to gaze at the GRAIL before his soul was pure enough for him to do so. As a result he was stricken in his reproductive organs and remained wounded until the Grail quest was completed.

Alice la Beale Pilgrim Arthurian heroine. A minor character of Arthurian legend, Alice kept her face always veiled; she was a cousin of the fair knight LANCELOT and the lover of ALISANDER LE ORPHELIN.

Alisander le Orphelin (Alixandre l'Orphelin) Arthurian hero. This minor figure in Arthurian legend was held prisoner by MORGAN, who appears in this story as a FAIRY QUEEN who unsuccessfully attempted to seduce the pure knight. The same story is told of LANCELOT, leading some to believe they are the same or parallel figures.

Alisanos (Alisanus) Continental Celtic god. An obscure Gaulish god whose name may have been given to the important settlement of Alesia, variously believed to mean stone, alder, or rowan.

All Saints' Day See SAMHAIN.

Almu Irish goddess. Almu was honored in the eastern PROVINCE of Ireland, LEINSTER, on the Hill of Allen—once the sacred capital of the province from which the regional kings reigned. Surrounded by the immense BOG OF ALLEN, the hill was personified as Almu, "all-white," a term also used to describe the royal citadel on the hill's crest. An invisible entrance to the OTHERWORLD was reputed to exist on the hill, and the Otherworldly king NUADA was described as its original possessor, until the hero FIONN MAC CUMHAILL won it from him by strength of arms. The hill was often named as the birthplace of Fionn, whose "chair"—a small mound—was atop its summit. Almu has been frequently confused with Dún Ailinne or KNOCKAULIN, near Kilcullen, the former residence of the kings of Leinster.

Sources: Gwynn, Edward. *The Metrical Dindshenchas.* Part II. Vol. IX. Royal Irish Academy, Todd

Lecture Series. Dublin: Hodges, Figgis, and Co., Ltd., 1906–1924, pp. 78 ff; O'Rahilly, Thomas. *Early Irish History and Mythology.* Dublin: The Dublin Institute for Advanced Studies, 1946, p. 280.

alp-luachra   Irish folkloric figure. A water sprite who could be accidentally swallowed, the *alp-luachra* was no end of trouble, causing stomach ailments until it was lured back out of the mouth. Some contended that the problems arose when a person accidentally swallowed a newt, a small amphibian that turned into an *alp-luachra* within the body. To get rid of one, the sufferer had to eat salty food without washing it down with liquids, then sleep next to a stream; dying of thirst, the *alp-luachra* leapt from the afflicted one's mouth and into the water.

Source: Hyde, Douglas. *Beside the Fire: A Collection of Irish Gaelic Folk Stories.* London: David Nutt, 1890, p. 47.

altar   Celtic ritual object. Although a number of stone altars engraved with dedications to Celtic divinities have been found in Britain and on the Continent, such altars represented Roman rather than Celtic custom. Several authors, including the Roman Cicero and the Irish Cormac, speak of Celtic altars used for sacrifice, but these seem to have been rather different than the stone imitations of dining tables that arrived in Celtic lands with the Roman legions. In keeping with Celtic custom of worshiping out of doors rather than inside a building, the original altars of the Celts were probably unshaped boulders or piles of large rock. See SACRIFICE.

Source: MacCulloch, J. A. *The Religion of the Ancient Celts.* London: Constable, 1911, p. 283.

Amadán (Amadáin, Amadáin Mhóir)   Irish hero or spirit. Just as every FAIRY MOUND had its queen, so also did it have a fool, the Amadán, who served the queen loyally, even blindly, unaware of the difficulties he caused. It was the Amadán who could cause a stroke by the mere touch of his hand over human flesh (see FAIRY STROKE). While some describe the Amadán as malicious—and certainly his behavior caused difficulties for his victims—he is more often depicted as too dim-witted to understand the (sometimes dire) consequences he wrought.

The fool also appears in oral folklore and in written texts as a hapless human simpleton, as in the story of "Shawn an Omadawn," recorded by several early collectors, wherein a somewhat stupid boy winds up outwitting his more intelligent siblings or companions. In a tale from the FENIAN CYCLE called the *Adventure of the Great Amadán* (*Eachtra an Amadáin Mhóir*), the fool was really the son of a king, dispossessed of his lands by invasion. Hiding in the wildwood, he grew into a hairy giant who, despite his unattractive features, married into the usurping family, only to kill his in-laws in retribution for their crimes. After many adventures and battles, the Amadán was restored to his own family and went forth to battle other giants.

Sources: Curtin, Jeremiah. *Hero-Tales of Ireland.* New York: Benjamin Blom, 1894, p. 140; Hyde, Douglas. *Beside the Fire: A Collection of Irish Gaelic Folk Stories.* London: David Nutt, 1890, p. xi.

Amaethon (Amatheon)   Welsh god. Amaethon's name means "ploughman," suggesting that he was a spirit of earthly FERTILITY. Despite his name, he was associated with wild animals such as the DEER, and thus seems connected not strictly with agriculture but with fruitfulness of all kinds. In the Welsh TRIADS, Amaethon owned a DOG, a deer, and a lapwing that he stole from the king of ANNWN, the OTHERWORLD, suggesting that the source of this world's abundance rests in the mysterious realm beyond. This relatively obscure god was one of the children of the mother goddess DÔN.

Amairgin (Amargen, Amhairghin, Amairgin, Amairgein, Amorgin)   Irish hero. This name, which means "wondrously born" or "song-conception" is borne by two legendary poets:

- **Amairgin, son of Míl** and the first great poet of Ireland, was reputed to have lived in the sixth century C.E. When the TUATHA DÉ DANANN, who then had control of Ireland, blew up a magical storm to keep the invading MILESIANS from landing, Amairgin's magical words calmed the storm and allowed his people to land, with Amairgin himself becoming the first of his race to set foot on Irish soil. As he did so, he recited his most famous poem, the "Song of Amairgin," in which he describes himself SHAPE-SHIFTING into a SALMON, a sunbeam, a flower, a spear; similar poems ascribed to the Irish poet TUAN MAC CAIRILL and to the Welsh bard TALIESIN show the connection in the Celtic mind between magical transformation and poetry. As the Milesians traveled through Ireland, they encountered three goddesses of the land, each of whom demanded that they name the island after her (see FÓDLA and BANBA); it was Amairgin's decision to call it after ÉRIU. As chief poet of the Milesians, Amairgin was simultaneously judge and seer, so his decision was unchangeable.
- **Amairgin of Ulster,** whose wife Findchóem was the sister of king CONCOBAR MAC NESSA; this Amairgin saved TARA by killing the monster AILLÉN TRECHENN who raided the capital at destructive intervals. He fostered the hero CÚCHULAINN, who thus became foster-brother to Amairgin's own son, CONALL CERNACH. Amairgin was once visited by the bitter poet AITHIRNE, but Amairgin's words were too slippery to provide Aithirne a foothold for satirizing him. Amairgin was a warrior as well as a poet; in the epic TÁIN BÓ CUAILNGE, Amairgin was so powerful that the dead piled up around him.

Sources: Hull, Eleanor. *The Cuchullin Saga in Irish Literature.* London: David Nutt, 1898, pp. 111 ff;

Ó hÓgain, Dáithí. *Myth, Legend and Romance: An Encyclopedia of the Irish Folk Tradition.* New York: Prentice-Hall Press, 1991, pp. 25–26.

Amangons   Arthurian hero. This evil king set the quest for the GRAIL in motion when he and his warriors raped the maidens who protected the sacred WELLS deep in Britain's forests.

Amr (Anir)   Arthurian hero. This obscure figure was said to have been the son of king ARTHUR and slain accidentally by him. His grave in Wales cannot be measured (see COUNTLESS STONES), since it continually gives a new measurement to those who try.

amulet   Ritual object. Some people distinguish a TALISMAN, an object worn or carried to bring good luck, from an amulet, typically an object of warding power, used for protection against some force or entity. The distinction is not always observed, however, so that we read of amulets dedicated to certain gods but intended to attract rather than to keep their powers at bay. Celtic peoples wore amulets of various sorts. Some were made of precious metal such as gold and embossed with the symbol of a divinity: A wheel for the solar deity, for instance, was common. Other amulets included coral, which was worn as both a decorative jewel and, as Pliny attests, an amulet of protection. Amber and quartz were graven into balls, and tiny animal figures (boars, horses, bulls) were shaped from stone or bone, both to be worn on thongs around the neck. In Scotland nuts were hung around the necks of children as amulets against the evil EYE. For the most famous Celtic amulet, see SERPENT STONE.

Ana Life (Ana Liffey)   Irish heroine. James Joyce called her "Anna Livia Plurabelle" in his great modernist novel *Finnegans Wake;* she is invoked in the invented word that begins the book, "riverrun," and is implied in its ending, which circles back to the beginning like water from the River Liffey running to the sea and then returning to the source through rain. Although Anna Livia Plurabelle is Joyce's invention, there is precedent for personifying the river in this way, for Ana Life is the name given to the only female visage among the sculpted river divinities on Dublin's bridges, apparently joining the early Irish land-goddess name ANU with the Irish name of the river, Life. Despite being a sculptural invention, Ana Life is the most mythically accurate of the bridge sculptures, for Irish rivers are almost invariably goddesses rather than gods; the correct name of the goddess of the Liffey is LÍFE. In his flowing and abundant archetypal feminine figure, Joyce similarly reflected ancient Celtic beliefs. The Liffey is an especially archetypal river, rising from the BOG OF ALLEN (not in the Devil's Glen in Wicklow, as Joyce says) and flowing south, west, north, and finally east, forming a great "c" shape before disgorging itself in the sea.

Ancamna Continental Celtic goddess. Consort of MARS (a Roman name given to Celtic war gods; not her mate's original name), Ancamna appears to have been a maternal goddess of prosperity and HEALING.

ancestors To the Celts, ancestral spirits always remained close to their families, often still cohabiting their dwelling places by remaining around the hearth. Generally these spirits were seen to be neutral or even protective, though in need of regular attention to keep their energies positive. Ancestor-honoring may have been ancestor-worship in early Celtic society, where goddesses and gods were addressed as "mother" and "father" of the tribe; in Christian times, veneration for a family's special saint may be a vestigial form of such devotion.

In Brittany and other parts of France, it was common to water graves with milk, as though the dead needed its nourishment. In Ireland the dead were said to come back and visit—have a drink, smoke a pipe, sit by the fire in their usual chair—on SAMHAIN, the day when the veils between this world and the OTHERWORLD grew thinnest. Food and tobacco were often left out for them. Implicit in such rituals is the idea that, if unattended to, the dead may grow angry and cause disruptions in the earthly world.

Sources: MacCulloch, J. A. *The Religion of the Ancient Celts.* London: Constable, 1911, p. 170; Ross, Anne, and Michael Cyprien. *A Traveller's Guide to Celtic Britain.* Harrisburg, Pa.: Historical Times, 1985, p. 67.

Andarta Continental Celtic goddess. Goddess of a continental Celtic tribe, the Voconces, Andarta's name is similar to that of the war goddess ANDRASTE, which has given rise to an identification of the two; she has also been interpreted as a goddess of wildlife because the second syllable of her name, *art*, is found in the names of many Celtic BEAR divinities.

Andraste British goddess. Andraste, whose name means "invincibility," was invoked in a sacred grove by the warrior queen BOUDICCA of the British tribe, the Iceni, before she led her troops into battle against the Roman invaders. In her ritual to Andraste, Boudicca released a HARE, found in Ireland as an occasional symbol of the warrior queen MEDB; although at first the hare seems a timid beast for a war divinity, it can grow fierce when threatened and is thus an appropriate image of defense. Boudicca came near to succeeding in her quest to drive the Romans from her land, but when the tides of war turned against her, she committed suicide rather than submit to the ignominies the Romans heaped upon their conquered enemies.

Andred Arthurian hero. This cousin of the romantic hero TRISTAN served as a spy for king MARK, husband of Tristan's lover ISEULT. Some texts claim that he murdered Tristan to curry favor with the king.

Anfortas   See FISHER KING.

Angharad (Angharad Law Eurawc, Angharad of the Golden Hand)   Arthurian heroine. The knight PEREDUR courted this otherwise obscure maiden, who may have originated as a goddess of the land's SOVEREIGNTY.

Anglesey (Mona)   British and Welsh sacred site. Location of Druidic college. According to the Roman historian Tacitus, this island off Wales was the site of a DRUID sanctuary destroyed in a fierce attack by Roman soldiers in ca. 59–64 C.E. Celtic women or priestesses, robed in black, screamed like the RAVEN-goddess MÓRRÍGAN as their fellow priests fought fiercely against the invaders. As the Romans had ruthlessly cut down the NEMETONS or sacred groves of other Celtic peoples and massacred the clergy, the druids of Anglesey knew what fate held in store for them and their honored trees. And indeed, the druids were killed in battle or executed, and the great forests burned. But evidence of the wealth and glory of Anglesey survived. The BOGS and lakes of Anglesey have yielded up great troves of goods in Celtic design, suggesting that the Druids hid them during or before the invasion.

The island may have been sacred to pre-Celtic people, as attested by an ancient CAIRN atop the hill of Bryn-Celli-Dhu. Celts typically absorbed the holy sites of their predecessors, so Anglesey would be typical. The destruction of Anglesey has been depicted in several works of contemporary fantasy, most notably Diana Paxon's Arthurian trilogy.

Source: Straffon, Cheryl. *The Earth Goddess: Celtic and Pagan Legacy of the Landscape.* London: Blandford, 1997, pp. 16, 169.

Angwish (Anwisance)   Arthurian hero. A king of Ireland and father of the fair ISEULT around whom one of the greatest Arthurian romances centers, Angwish was the enemy of king ARTHUR but later became his ally. His brother, the fierce MORHOLT, caused the battle that brought the fated lover TRISTAN to Angwish's court, where he first laid infatuated eyes on Iseult.

animal divination   See BULL-SLEEP.

animals   In both Continental and insular Celtic mythology, divinities are pictured or described as accompanied by animals and birds: NEHALENNIA and CÚCHULAINN with the DOG, SEQUANA with the DUCK, CERNUNNOS with the STAG, MOCCUS with the PIG, and EPONA with the HORSE. Such animals are often interpreted as the servants of the divinity, but it is more appropriate to describe them as the god or goddess in shape-shifted form. In some cases, as with the CAILLEACH, who is said to appear in the form of a HARE, or OISÍN, whose mother gave birth to him while in the shape of a deer, such SHAPE-SHIFTING is part of the figure's mythology; more often, as in Gaul, where Romanization left names and figures but no myths, we lack narrative descriptions of the relationship between animal and divinity.

It was not only gods who could shape-shift into animals; poets were thought to have the ability, as were WITCHES. Several legendary poets, including AMAIRGIN and TUAN MAC CAIR-ILL, describe themselves as having lived many times in different forms, including those of animals; this can be viewed as evidence either of shape-shifting or of transmigration of souls. This connection of magical transformation with the art of poetry is typical of insular Celtic society and may have extended as well to the Continent.

The folkloric belief in witches' ability to take on animal form, however, is not clearly Celtic and may as well derive from pre- or post-Celtic beliefs. Like the haggish Cailleach, human witches were thought to disguise themselves as hares in order to be about their nefarious deeds; if a suspected witch were found with a bad wound in her thigh the morning after a night-roving hare was shot in its back leg, it was clear to all that the hare had been the shape-shifted witch.

According to classical writers, animals were offered as SACRIFICE in early Celtic rituals. The most famous description of such sacrifice comes from Julius Caesar, who claimed that annually the Celts of Gaul burned animals caged with human captives alive; there is, however, substantial doubt that Caesar—who was in the business of conquering the Celts abroad and may have yielded to the temptation to paint them as savages at home— was correct in this description. However, there is evidence of the sacrifice of the BULL, a sacred animal; such sacrificed animals were doubtless eaten, so the distinction between a sacrifice and a feast is sometimes difficult to discern.

The eating of some animals was generally forbidden. Caesar said that the Britons would not kill nor eat hare, hen, or GOOSE. Yet such taboo beasts could, upon certain occasions, be sacrificed; there is evidence that the Briton queen BOUDICCA sacrificed a hare to divine her people's future. Often taboos were linked to imagined descent from divine beasts, as is made clear in the story of the Irish king CONAIRE who, because his mother was a BIRD, was forbidden to hunt or eat them. Irish folk belief that such families as the O'Flahertys and the Coneelys were descended from SEALS points to such an ancient tradition, as was the idea that such families would be drowned or otherwise killed should they attempt to hunt their erstwhile kin. Ancient Celtic tribal names often incorporate an animal reference, as the Bribroci (beavers) of Britain, who may have pictured themselves as descended from an ancestral beaver goddess. Scots clan names, too, incorporate references to animals, as in the Cinel Gabran, "clan of the little GOAT," or Cinel Loarn, "clan of the FOX." Some Irish names are similarly suggestive of ancestral connection to animals, the McMurrows from OTTERS and the McMahons from BEARS, for instance. Such divine ancestors tended to be wild rather than domesticated animals.

See also BADGER, BOAR, CAT, CATTLE, COCK, COW, CRANE, CROW, DEER, DOVE, EAGLE, EGRET, EEL, FISH, FROG, HERON, OX, RAT, RAVEN, SALMON, SERPENT, SWALLOW, SWAN, WOLF, WREN.

animism   Religious concept. The Celts, like many other ancient peoples, seem to have imbued the world in which they lived with animating spirit. This did not take, as in some cultures, the form of a single abstracted divinity of nature but rather was radically place-based and polytheistic. A startling outcropping of rocks, for instance, might be animated by a goddess, or a huge ancient tree by a god. Often these divinities were known only in the immediate locality; the spirits of various WELLS, for instance, did not move freely about the landscape making the acquaintance of distant tribes but remained within their own sacred waters. Many writers have argued that this animism, which may have originated with pre-Celtic peoples, in turn became part of the Celtic Christian tradition.

See also *GENIUS LOCI.*

Anind   Irish hero. One of the sons of the early invader NEMED, Anind is connected with an important feature of the Irish landscape, Lough Ennell in Co. Westmeath. That part of Ireland had no surface water until Anind's grave was dug, whereupon the lake suddenly flooded forth. Such tales of landscape formation often indicate the presence of an ancient divinity with creative powers.

Anna   Arthurian heroine. This obscure figure is named as the sister of king ARTHUR in some texts.

Annals of Ireland *(Annals of the Four Masters)* Irish text. One of the textual sources for the mythological history of Ireland, this book (in Irish, *Annála Ríoghachta Éireann*) was compiled between 1632 and 1636 C.E. by Micheál Ó Cléirigh of Donegal and three other unnamed "masters," probably Franciscan friars or lay brothers. While the later entries in the *Annals* are roughly historical, early entries date to "forty days after the Flood" and include much myth and legend. Irish monks are credited with the preservation of most of Ireland's most important Celtic legends, for despite their differing theology, the monks recognized the narrative treasures of the ancient tales. Such texts must be read with suspicion, however, and with alertness for the insertion of Christian beliefs and motifs.

Annaugh (Anna) Irish goddess. This obscure Irish goddess was known in only one place, Collins Wood in Connemara, where she was the GENIUS LOCI.

Annowre Arthurian heroine. This WITCH or sorceress (possibly the double of MORGAN) conceived a lust for the great king ARTHUR and lured him to her forest, but she was not to have her way with him. When he rejected her, she held him captive and sent knights to challenge him in single combat, hoping he would be killed. Arthur was able to hold them off, so she sent the challengers after him in pairs, and they overpowered him. But with the assistance of NIMUE, the knight TRISTAN was able to free the king, after which Arthur killed Annowre.

Annwn (Annwyn, Annwfn) Welsh mythological site. Like the Irish who proposed multiple sites for the OTHERWORLD, the Welsh saw Annwn ("abyss") in various ways: as a seagirt castle (Caer Siddi); as a court of intoxication (Caer Feddwid); as a palace of glass (Caer Wydyr). Like TIR NA NÓG, the Irish island of the blessed, Annwn was a place of sweetness and charm, whose residents did not age nor suffer, eating their fill from a magic CAULDRON and quenching their thirst at an ever-flowing WELL. Two kings ruled in Annwn, ARAWN and HAFGAN, who were perpetually at war; Arawn figures more prominently in legend.

Antenociticus British god. A temple dedicated to Antenociticus was excavated at Benwell

in Condercum; like many other Celtic gods, he is known only in a single site and may have been the GENIUS LOCI or spirit of the place.

antlers Symbolic image. Celtic divinities often appeared in animal form, suggesting a connection to shamanic transformation (see CELTIC SHAMANISM). At other times, deities would be seen in human form but with animal characteristics; most commonly, this meant either HORNS or antlers, the latter representing prosperity and worn by both gods and goddesses. See CERNUNNOS.

Anu (Ana, Danu) Irish goddess. In southwestern Ireland, two identical rounded hills are capped with prehistoric CAIRNS, stone nipples on the great breasts of the mother goddess. The hills are called Dá Chich Danann, conventionally and rather prudishly translated PAPS OF DANU. Alternatively, the hills are called after the presumed goddess Anu, of which little is known.

No narratives describe this supposed goddess of abundance, who is listed by the early glossarist Cormac as "mother of the gods of Ireland." She is considered by many identical to DANU, purported ancestor of the TUATHA DÉ DANANN. Others argue that she is a separate goddess of Ireland's abundance; still others connect her with ÁINE of Limerick or with BLACK ANNIS of Britain. In Christian times, she became conflated with St. Anne, grandmother of Jesus, to whom many holy WELLS are dedicated, most impressively that of Llanmihangel in Glamorgan, South Wales, where St. Anne is depicted in a fountain, with water gushing from her nipples. Welsh mythology has a shadow figure named Ána or Anu, connected by Rhys and others with the Irish mother goddess Anu.

Sources: Briggs, Katherine M. *An Encyclopedia of Fairies: Hobgoblins, Brownies, Bogies, and Other Supernatural Creatures.* New York: Pantheon Books, 1976, p. 9; MacCulloch, J. A. *The Religion of the Ancient Celts.* London: Constable, 1911, pp. 67 ff; Rhys, John. *The Welsh People.*

London: T. Fisher Unwin, 1906, p. 42; Straffon, Cheryl. *The Earth Goddess: Celtic and Pagan Legacy of the Landscape.* London: Blandford, 1997, pp. 36, 71.

Aonbárr Irish mythological beast. The enchanted steed of the Irish sea god MANANNÁN MAC LIR, whose name ("froth") suggests the seafoam.

Aoncos Irish mythological site. One of the many magical islands of the Irish OTHERWORLD, Aoncos was distinguished by the silver pillar that held it aloft above the ocean waves.

Aonghus (Angus, Aengus, Oengus) Irish and Scottish hero or god. Several mythological and heroic figures of Ireland and Scotland bear this name, which means "strength" or "vigor."

- **Aonghus Óg,** who also goes by the name Aonghus mac Óg or "Angus son of youth": he was god of beauty and poetry among the TUATHA DÉ DANANN and corresponds to the Welsh god MABON. His conception was miraculous, even for a god: His father the DAGDA "borrowed" his mother Eithne from her husband ELCMAR, then caused the sun to remain overhead for nine months so that the goddess could gestate the child without Elcmar's realizing that more than a day had passed; upon his birth Aonghus Óg was immediately given to the god MIDIR to foster. In another version, the cuckolded husband was NECHTAN, the mother was BÓAND, and the foster father Elcmar. In either case, the young son took after his father, gaining by trickery the great carved-stone palace called the BRÚ NA BÓINNE, where trees held out tempting fruit and two pigs took turns being cooked and eaten, only to spring to life again. Several commentators connect these legends with other traditions in which a son defeats or replaces his father, as in the Greek myth of

Saturn and Uranus, or Zeus and Saturn. The place-poems called the DINDSHENCHAS call him "Aonghus of the many exploits" and "mighty Mac in Oc."

Four white SWANS flew about Aonghus Óg's head when he traveled. When he fell in love, it was with a woman he had seen only in a dream, as recorded in the *Aislinge Óenguso*, the *Dream of Aonghus.* His lover visited him in dreams for a year, until he sickened with desire to be with her in the flesh. With the help of the magician BODB DERG, Aonghus found his beloved, CÁER, and flew away with her in the shape of white swans whose song was so lovely that it enchanted people to sleep for three days and three nights. It was this legend that inspired William Butler Yeats's poem, "The Song of Wandering Aengus," while an earlier version of the god appears in James Stephens's comic novel, *The Crock of Gold.*

- **Aonghus, brother of FAND** and LÍ BAN, a fairy who lured the hero CÚCHULAINN to the OTHERWORLD to meet his lustful sisters.
- **Aonghus of the FIR BOLG,** after whom the great stone fort on the Aran Islands, DÚN Aonghusa, was named.

Sources: Gwynn, Edward. *The Metrical Dindshenchas.* Royal Irish Academy, Todd Lecture Series. Dublin: Hodges, Figgis, and Co., Ltd., 1906–1924, pp. 65–67; Ó hÓgain, Dáithí. *Myth, Legend and Romance: An Encyclopedia of the Irish Folk Tradition.* New York: Prentice-Hall Press, 1991, pp. 39–40.

Apollo Romano-Celtic god. The Roman legions were under orders to bring conquered lands into the Roman empire. One way to do that was through the INTERPRETATIO ROMANA, in which local divinities were given Latin names. But when the Romans began to conquer the territories of their longtime rivals, the Celts, their hierarchical pantheon met a polytheism so extreme that the generic Celtic oath was "I swear by the gods my people swear by." Nonetheless they set about renaming divinities, in some cases keeping the original Celtic name as an appendage, while in other cases tossing it into the dustbin of history.

Oversimplifying Celtic religion grandly, the legions affixed to dozens of gods the name Apollo—ironically enough, not originally a Roman god's name but one adopted from conquered Greeks, for whom Apollo was a sun deity; these Celtic Apollos may have had little or nothing to do with the Roman, much less the Greek, original. In turn, the Celts adopted Apollo into their ever-flexible pantheon, providing him with a consort that the classical Apollo lacked but who was necessary in the Celtic worldview. As the Roman Apollo was both a god of HEALING and of light, divinities of hot SPRINGS, used by the Celts (as they are today) as healing spas, were often retitled with his name. Some Celtic Apollos are:

- **Apollo Amarcolitanus,** "of the distant gaze," found on the Continent.
- **Apollo Anextiomarus** (Anextlomarus), Continental god of healing or protection.
- **Apollo Atepomarus,** god of horses and the SUN, often linked to CERNUNNOS, but also to BELENUS.
- **Apollo Canumagus** (Cunomaglus), a British god connected with DOGS.
- **Apollo Grannus** (Grannos), god of healing springs across Europe and Scotland, consort of SIRONA; his name seems to derive from the same source as the Irish sun goddess GRIAN; around Auvergne, in France, he was honored in a ritual in which sheaves of grain were set on fire and people sang, "Granno, my friend; Granno, my father; Granno, my mother," which suggests that the god may have been seen as of dual or ambiguous gender.
- **Apollo Moritasgus,** healing god of France, consort of DAMONA.
- **Apollo Vindonnus,** healer of EYE diseases.

Sources: Green, Miranda. *Symbol and Image in Celtic Religious Art.* London: Routledge, 1989, pp. 89, 61; MacCulloch, J. A. *The Religion of the Ancient Celts.* London: Constable, 1911, pp. 42 ff, 135.

apple   Symbolic fruit. The most magical of fruits to the Celts, the apple appears in many myths and legends. It hides in the word for the Arthurian OTHERWORLD, AVALON; it is the fruit on which the hero CONNLA of the Golden Hair was fed by his FAIRY LOVER; the soul of king CÚ ROÍ rested in an apple within the stomach of a SALMON; it was one of the goals of the fated SONS OF TUIREANN. Its significance continues into folkloric uses such as that in the British Cotswolds, where an apple tree blooming out of season meant coming death. Symbolizing harmony and immortality, abundance and love, the apple was considered a talisman of good fortune and prosperity. Some have connected the word to APOLLO, whose name may have originally been Apellon, a word derived from the same source as our word "apple."

Aquae Sulis   British goddess. Roman name for the shrine and hot SPRINGS at BATH in England, dedicated to the SUN goddess SUL.

Arawn   Welsh god. The lord of ANNWN, the Welsh OTHERWORLD, Arawn owned a magical CAULDRON, which suggests a parallel with the Irish father god, the DAGDA. Arawn had magical PIGS (another motif associated with the Dagda) that he presented as a gift to the mortal king PRYDERI; when the bard GWYDION stole them, he was apprehended and imprisoned in Annwn. Three magical animals belonging to Arawn were stolen by the obscure divinity AMAETHON; the motif seems to point to a belief that domesticated animals originally belonged to the gods and had to be brought by force or trickery to this world. In one tale, Arawn was said to have exchanged identities for a year with the mortal king PWYLL, who during his stay in the Otherworld killed Arawn's enemy and rival for power in Annwn, HAFGAN. Arawn's world is a typical Celtic Otherworld, beautiful and unchanging, not entirely unlike our world but without any pain, death, disfigurement, or disease; its residents spend their time in merrymaking and games.

Sources: Gantz, Jeffrey, trans. *The Mabinogion.* New York: Barnes & Noble Books, 1976, pp. 47–51, 100; MacCulloch, J. A. *The Religion of the Ancient Celts.* London: Constable, 1911, pp. 368–387.

Arberth   Welsh mythological site. This name is given in Welsh mythological texts to a magical FAIRY MOUND in the kingdom of PWYLL, where people see visions. It is sometimes associated with the town of Narberth in the region of southwestern Wales called Dyfed.

Ard Éireann   Irish mythological site. The mountains in central Ireland called Slieve Bloom include a peak called by this name, which means "height of Ireland," although it is not the highest geographical point in the land; the summit was mythically the birthplace of the island of Ireland.

Ard-Greimne   Irish hero. This otherwise obscure figure was the father of the great WARRIOR WOMEN of the Isle of SKYE, SCÁTHACH and her sister/rival AÍFE.

Ard Macha   See EMAIN MACHA.

ard rí *(ard ri, ard righe)*   See HIGH KING.

Arduinna (Ardwinna, Arduenna, Arduanna) Continental Celtic goddess. Sometimes conflated with the Roman DIANA or the Greek ARTEMIS, Arduinna rode, mounted on a wild BOAR, through the Gaulish forest that bore her name, the Ardennes. Hunters were welcome in her forests only if they left money as payment for the animals they killed. Her name may incorporate *ard*, the syllable for "height" or "highland."

Argante   British heroine or goddess. Queen of the OTHERWORLD island of AVALON, she has been variously described as a form of ARIANRHOD and of MORGAN Le Fay. It was to Argante that king ARTHUR was taken to be cured of his mortal wounds; from her realm he has not yet returned.

Arianrhod (Arianrod, Aranrhod)   Welsh heroine or goddess. In the fourth branch of the Welsh MABINOGION we find the tale of this heroine, who may be a diminished form of an earlier goddess. The story begins with the rape of GOEWIN, who served a strange office for king MATH: As his life depended upon his feet resting in the lap of a virgin, Goewin sat endlessly on the floor beneath his throne serving as footholder. GWYDION and GILFAETHWY, Math's nephews, were responsible for the violation, in recompense for which Math married Goewin and cast a spell on the rapists.

To preserve the king's life, Gwydion nominated his sister Arianrhod, daughter of the mother goddess DÔN, to serve as footholder. Asked if she were a virgin, the beautiful Arianrhod said that, as far as she knew, she was. Math asked her to step over his wand to prove her purity, but when she did so, she gave birth to two children she had conceived unawares: DYLAN and LLEU LLAW GYFFES. The first, child of the sea, immediately escaped into that watery realm; the second was rejected by Arianrhod but claimed by Gwydion, whose son he may have been, and raised in a magical chest. But when Lleu was grown, Arianrhod refused to give him either a name or weapons—two prerogatives of a Welsh mother—and once again Gwydion tricked her so that Lleu could attain his manhood.

The story is a confusing one, especially in its lack of clarity about whether Arianrhod's children were conceived parthenogenetically (as would befit a goddess) or without her knowledge (as befits deceitful Gwydion); she seems as surprised as anyone at the children issuing from her womb, so it does not seem likely that she was lying. Her name means "silver wheel," and many have seen in Arianrhod the remnants or reflection of an ancient moon goddess; conversely, she may be a mother goddess of the land, since such goddesses were often described as virgin mothers; yet again, she has been called a dawn goddess because she is mother of both light (Lleu) and darkness (Dylan). She was said to live surrounded by her maidens in her castle on the coastal island of CAER ARIANRHOD, which is also an idiomatic Welsh name for the constellation called Corona Borealis. In that seagirt (or starry) realm, she lived wantonly, which suggests a parallel to the Breton figure of DAHUT. She has also been compared to the ancestral goddess BRANWEN, for the Welsh TRIADS name her as one of the "three fair maidens" or "white ladies" of the isle of Britain.

Sources: Gantz, Jeffrey, trans. *The Mabinogion.* New York: Barnes & Noble Books, 1976, pp. 97 ff; MacCulloch, J. A. *The Religion of the Ancient Celts.* London: Constable, 1911, pp. 104–109; Spence, Lewis. *The Minor Traditions of British Mythology.* New York: Benjamin Blom, Inc., 1972, p. 27; Straffon, Cheryl. *The Earth Goddess: Celtic and Pagan Legacy of the Landscape.* London: Blandford, 1997, p. 41.

Armorica   See BRITTANY.

Arnemetia   British goddess. This name of this British goddess is related to the word NEMETON and means "in front of the sacred grove." The Romans called her shrine—today's Buxton Spa in Derbyshire—Aquae Arnementiae, "waters of Arnemetia," for two mineral SPRINGS that rose in close proximity. After Christianization, Arnemetia became St. Anne.

Art mac Cuinn   (Art Son of Conn)   Irish hero. He was the best known of the Irish heroes and champions given the name Art, which means BEAR. His father, CONN of the Hundred Battles, ruled at TARA with a woman named BÉ CHUMA,

who both lusted after Art and sent him into exile. When he returned, she sent him on a quest to gain the affections of a woman of the OTHERWORLD, DELBCHÁEM. After many feats of arms, he won Delbchém and brought her back to Tara, where she forced the sly Bé Chuma to depart. In other texts, Art is the consort of MEDB Lethderg, a form of the goddess of SOVEREIGNTY. Art was was mythically important as father to the great hero CORMAC MAC AIRT, who was conceived by the magical heroine ACHTAN immediately before Art's death at the battle of Mag Mucrama.

Sources: Cross, Tom Peete, and Clark Harris Slover, eds. *Ancient Irish Tales.* New York: Henry Holt and Co., 1936, p. 491; Curtin, Jeremiah. *Hero-Tales of Ireland.* New York: Benjamin Blom, 1894, p. 312.

Artaios   See MERCURY.

Artemis   Greek goddess. The paradoxical Greek goddess of FERTILITY and chastity found several parallels in Celtic lands; the name is linked with figures as diverse as the HAG named the CAILLEACH of Scotland and Ireland and the unnamed DOG goddess of Galatia to whom coins were offered annually as payment for every animal killed in the hunt. This tendency to associate Celtic divinities with those of the classical Mediterranean began early, with the assimilation of Celtic deities to Roman ones in areas subdued by the legions, who called Artemis-like goddesses by the Roman name of DIANA. These goddesses were associated with wild lands, which they were imagined as occupying with a company of untamed maidens.

Arthur   British hero. The tale of the great king of CAMELOT was first recorded in sixth-century Wales and was popularized by the 12th-century British writer Geoffrey of Monmouth, whose *History of the Kings of Britain* (ca. 1136) mingled romance, history, and mythology and inspired poets and storytellers in both England and France. The verse romances of the 12th-century French poet Chrétien de Troyes were another important contribution to the Arthurian cycle, introducing the GRAIL theme into Arthurian legend. From Sir Thomas Malory's *Le Morte d'Arthur* (1485) and through Alfred Tennyson's *Idylls of the King* (1859–85) and T. H. White's *The Once and Future King* (1958), the Arthurian cycle has inspired both literary and popular treatments in English and French; related tales of PERCIVAL and TRISTAN, including the related FISHER KING and Grail cycles, expand the corpus of Arthurian renderings into thousands of works. The story of king Arthur continues to inspire poets and authors today; the popular musical *Camelot*, the movie *Excalibur*, and the bestselling novel *The Mists of Avalon* are among the most recent of hundreds of works of art inspired by the theme of the noble but flawed (and betrayed) king.

The cycle of Arthurian tales, often called the MATTER OF BRITAIN, has roots in Celtic myth but has been altered and amplified through literary transmission. While it is possible to glimpse Celtic and even pre-Celtic mythological motifs behind the characters and plot twists of the story as we know it, especially given the parallel Celtic love-triangles of MARK-Tristan-ISEULT from Brittany and FIONN-DIARMAIT-GRÁINNE from Ireland, such interpretation is necessarily speculative. For much of the past thousand years, Arthur has been viewed in the popular imagination as an historical king of sixth-century C.E. Britain, his court at Camelot offering a true picture of the possibility of nobleness as well as a tragic depiction of betrayal. The reality of an early Celtic king named Arthur now seems assured, but the power of his story is mythical rather than merely historical.

Although there are many variants of Arthur's legend—which began to be recorded even as Celtic influence in Britain and France, the lands most connected with the legends, began to wane—the story usually follows roughly similar outlines. Arthur was born of royal blood after his father, UTHER PENDRAGON, slept with his mother IGRAINE through deceit, using the great MERLIN's magic to appear in the form of her husband, the duke of Cornwall, GORLOIS. Arthur was snatched away at birth by the omnipresent Merlin and fostered away from the royal seat. Despite his royal blood, Arthur was only accepted as ruler when he performed a feat no one else had managed: to extract a magical sword (often confused with, but actually distinct from, EXCALIBUR, the magical sword later given to Arthur by the LADY OF THE LAKE) from a stone that it pierced. Assuming his rightful place as king, Arthur established an idealistic and idealized court of noble knights (among whom were PERCIVAL, LANCELOT, KAY, and others) who met around a great ROUND TABLE at Camelot. He married the rapturously beautiful GUINEVERE, and all of Britain was at peace under their reign.

Arthur in these legends appears as the epitome of manhood and KINGSHIP. He is strong, an excellent warrior and strategist who drives opposing forces from his land; he is also an inspiring leader who draws to himself the noblest knights and wins their affection and loyalty. He is a trickster figure in some legends, as when he steals the CAULDRON of plenty from the OTHERWORLD. He is even a BARD, fluent in poetry and song.

Despite the king's gifts and good nature, all was not to be well in Camelot. The beautiful Lancelot and queen Guinevere fell in love, and Lancelot exiled himself rather than betray his king. Finally their love grew too strong to resist. Although they kept it secret, the land knew the truth; the crops failed for seven years while Arthur attempted to discover the cause. At the same time, his estranged son MORDRED—born of a secret liaison with his own sister MORGAUSE—began to war against Arthur. In the chaos of battle, Arthur was mortally wounded. He did not die, however; casting Excalibur into a lake, he was borne across its waters to AVALON by mysterious women, thus becoming the "once and future king."

Among the mythological motifs that point to a Celtic origin for the tale is the emphasis on the rectitude of the king, upon which the land itself depends. Yet Camelot falls not through the king's ungenerosity—the usual downfall of Celtic kings—but because of his unwillingness to doubt his wife and apparently loyal knight. This divergence from the Celtic norm has suggested to some a pre-Celtic basis for the tales, with Guinevere standing in for an early goddess who chose and discarded kings, a motif employed by Marion Zimmer Bradley in her popular novel, *The Mists of Avalon.* Whether Arthur was originally a British or Welsh god, as suggested by his name's connection to the divine BEAR (in Welsh, *arth*), is arguable; some scholars find in the figure evidence of a Celtic (probably Brythonic) divinity, while others consider him a culture hero, perhaps based on an historical king.

Sources: Evans-Wentz, W. Y. *The Fairy-Faith in Celtic Countries.* Gerrards Cross: Colin Smythe Humanities Press, 1911, pp. 308 ff; Geoffrey of Monmouth. *Histories of the Kings of Britain.* London: J. M. Dent and Sons, 1912, pp. 164 ff.; Herm, Gerhard. *The Celts: The People Who Came out of the Darkness.* New York: St. Martin's Press, 1975, pp. 274–286; MacCulloch, J. A. *The Religion of the Ancient Celts.* London: Constable, 1911, pp. 119 ff.

Artio (Dea Artio, Andarta)   British and continental Celtic goddess. In Britain and Gaul, the goddess of wilderness and wildlife was worshiped in the form of a BEAR (the meaning of Artio's name), while the name ANDARTA is found in inscriptions in Switzerland (especially in Berne, "bear city") and France for a similar goddess, the second syllable of her name suggesting a bear connection. Not only in name but in function, Artio is similar to the Greek goddess ARTEMIS, also envisioned as a bear. A bear god, Artaios or Artaius, is also found in some regions.

Arvalus   Continental Celtic god. This obscure Celtic god of HEALING was equated with APOLLO by the invading Romans. As that name was often applied to divinities of thermal SPRINGS, Arvalus may have once ruled such a shrine.

Arvernorix (Arvernus)   Continental Celtic god. This obscure god, known from only a few inscriptions, may have been the tribal divinity of the Arverni. It is also unclear whether the two spellings represent different gods or the same one.

Asenora (Senara, Senora)   Cornish heroine. A legend in Cornwall tells of a princess of Brittany, Asenora, who was thrown into the sea in a barrel while pregnant. Despite its origin in a historically Celtic land, the motif may derive from non-Celtic sources, for it is found in the Greek story of Danae, mother of the hero Perseus. Asenora's barrel drifted to Ireland, where she was rescued. She tried to return to Brittany but only made it as far as Zenor, where she founded a church and where she is honored as St. Senara. In that church is found a famous 600-year-old carving of a MERMAID, believed to be originally a sea goddess of the region. Interestingly, unlike the Greek version, Asenora herself is the focus of the Cornish tale; legend tells nothing of the offspring with whom she was pregnant when cast adrift.

Source: Straffon, Cheryl. *The Earth Goddess: Celtic and Pagan Legacy of the Landscape.* London: Blandford, 1997, p. 85.

ash   Symbolic tree. Despite being a common TREE in many climates, the ash (genus *Fraxinus*) plays a significant role in Scandinavian and Germanic as well as Celtic mythologies. It is a large but graceful tree whose sweeping, upturned branches make a dramatic pattern against the winter sky and whose feathery compound leaves create a dappled shade in summer. Together with the OAK and the THORN, the ash is one of the magical trees of Celtic tradition. Because it is connected with the FAIRIES, it was also believed to ward them off; for this reason

Scots Highland mothers burned a green ash branch until it oozed sap, which was fed to a newborn as its first food. In the Cotswolds the ash was believed to be protective against WITCHCRAFT if crafted into a whip handle. It cured earthly as well as Otherworldly diseases: as a protection against rickets, children were passed through young ash branches slashed in two, after which the branches were sutured up and left to heal; should such healing not occur, which in the hardy ash was uncommon, the child was thought doomed to be as twisted as the tree. Ashwood was believed to be a general charm against evil.

The ash tree is especially associated with BELTANE, the spring festival celebrated on May 1. In Ireland the most important site for that festival was the hill of UISNEACH, so ash trees on that site were considered especially potent. One great ash on Uisneach's summit was said to have fallen in prehistory, its tip reaching across the country to near the town of Longford; such an impossibly tall tree (over 30 miles high) suggests a world-axis that may originally have been envisioned to ascend from Uisneach. Another famous Irish ash was the holy tree of Clenore, where the spirit or saint Creeva was thought to live. So important was the ash in Ireland that three of the five most significant mythological trees were ash.

The ash family has many branches, including the square-twigged blue ash and the common green ash; it is distinct from the ROWAN or mountain ash, which is a different genus. Ash trees love water, which is why many are found at holy WELLS; such a combination of ash and water source was held to be especially powerful. Miracles were said to be possible when ash trees "bled" or leaked sap into the well, and people would gather the liquid to use as an elixir.

See TREE ALPHABET.

Sources: Briggs, Katharine M. *The Folklore of the Cotswolds.* London: B. T. Batsford Ltd., 1974, p. 123; Dorson, Richard M., ed. *Peasant Customs and Savage Myths: Selections from the British Folklorists.* Vol II. Chicago: University of Chicago Press, 1968, pp. 58, 329; Spence, Lewis. *The Minor Traditions of British Mythology.* New York: Benjamin Blom, Inc., 1972, p. 108.

ashes Symbolic material. Remnant ash from peat fires was part of many Irish folk traditions. Some derived from Christian tradition regarding Ash Wednesday, the beginning of the penitential season of Lent; ashes were thrown at unmarried people then, which gave rise to the saying "You'll have the ash-bag thrown at you," meaning that a person was unmarriageable. Older, probably pre-Christian traditions use ashes as a MIDSUMMER fertility symbol (from which the Lenten rite may have evolved); ashes from the LUGHNASA bonfires were used to bless cattle, fields, and people.

Source: Danaher, Kevin. *The Year in Ireland.* Cork: Mercier Press, 1922, pp. 50, 135.

Assa See NESSA.

Assaroe Irish mythological site. The waterfall Assaroe on the River ERNE in Co. Sligo, famous in legend, was flooded when a hydroelectric dam was erected nearby in the mid-20th century. It was there, according to some stories, that FIONN MAC CUMHAILL accidentally ate the SALMON of wisdom (named GOLL Essa Ruaid), which the druid FINNÉCES had been awaiting for seven years. It was there that the father of the warrior woman MACHA Mong Rua, ÁED RUAD (Áed the red), died, giving his name to the falls, which in Irish are Eas Ruadh, "the red waterfall." A variant holds that the falls are named for a goddess, RUAD, who drowned there after being lured to her death by the singing of MERMAIDS. Sailing in the ship of the poet ABCÁN, she traveled from the OTHERWORLD in order to pursue a human lover (see FAIRY LOVER) but drowned before reaching him. The drowning of a goddess in a river is common in Irish mythology and typically represents the dissolving of her divine power into the water, which then gives life to the land.

Source: Gwynn, Edward. *The Metrical Dindshenchas.* Part IV. Royal Irish Academy, Todd Lecture Series. Dublin: Hodges, Figgis, and Co., Ltd., 1906–1924, pp. 3–9.

Assembly   See ÓENACH.

Assembly of the Wondrous Head   See BRÂN THE BLESSED.

Assipattle   Scottish hero. This Scottish Cinderfella is found in many folktales and resembles the Irish AMADÁN. Unlike Cinderella, typically a girl of good birth cast down to servitude, Assipattle was born poor and looked to stay that way, being lazy and unambitious. Finally stirred to action by some crisis (a threatening dragon does nicely), Assipattle performs heroically.

astrology   The Celts, like other tribal peoples whose way of life required them to be outdoors much of the time, knew the stars well. They may have elaborated this knowledge into an arcane science in which the changing patterns of the planets had impact on earthly life; Julius Caesar claimed that the DRUIDS were master astrologers. There is evidence that in Ireland the starting date of the Christian St. Columba's education was determined by starry aspects, and legend holds that the druid CATHBAD cast a horoscope to see the future of the child who would grow up to become DEIRDRE of the Sorrows.

A Celtic astrology would not be surprising, as the druids were skilled at divination of various sorts, but only the faintest hints remain of this supposed system, including the Irish word *néladóir,* used of someone who divines from the sky (although it has also been translated "cloud-diviner"). The Celts conveyed such sensitive and powerful material orally, and thus it is unlikely that any Celtic astrological text will ever be found.

Atesmerta, Atesmerius   Continental Celtic goddess and god. Divinities of these names are attested from several inscriptions from Gaul, but nothing more than their names is known of them.

athach   Scottish monster. A monstrous creature that haunted the Scottish Highlands, killing passersby and throwing them into gorges or down rocky hills. *Athachs* included the female *luideag* of Skye and the male *díreach* of Glen Etive, who had one hand growing out of his chest and one eye in his forehead.

See also *FACHAN.*

autumn equinox   Astronomical feast. The EQUINOXES and SOLSTICES were not celebrated by the Celts, who instead celebrated the solar year's fixed points (IMBOLC, BELTANE, LUGHNASA, SAMHAIN). But in Ireland, after the coming of the Normans and of Christianity, an equinoctial feast was celebrated on or about September 29. This feast of St. Michael the Archangel or Michaelmas was, in many regions, defined as the date on which rents and loans were repaid and contracts settled. Elected officials took and left office on Michaelmas, which was often celebrated with harvest fairs. Michaelmas marked the Fomhar na nGéan, the goose harvest, when butchering began; farmers were expected to be generous at that season and to give meat to the poor. In England the fall equinox period was devoted to harvest fairs marked by mummers' parades in which mythological characters like ROBIN HOOD and Maid Marion danced with animal archetypes like the HOBBYHORSE.

Avalon   (Afallon)   British mythological site. When ARTHUR, ruler of CAMELOT, was ready to pass from this world, mysterious women carried him in a boat to Avalon, the Island of Apples, a typical Celtic OTHERWORLD. Avalon was a beautiful place of mild weather and eternal spring, where flowers and fruit were found simultaneously on the trees and where no storms ever raged. A queen ruled there, sometimes named as ARGANTE; she and her maiden attendants were great healers. There may have also been a king of Avalon, for a shadowy figure named Avalloc appears in some legends. Although today Glastonbury in southwest England is often linked with Avalon, this seems to be a post-Celtic association, perhaps deriving from the town's ancient name Ynys-witrin, "glass island." To the Celts, Avalon was clearly one of those western isles of the Otherworld where the dead and the divine mingle.

Sources: MacCulloch, J. A. *The Religion of the Ancient Celts.* London: Constable, 1911, pp. 120, 369; Evans-Wentz, W. Y. *The Fairy-Faith in Celtic Countries.* Gerrards Cross: Colin Smythe Humanities Press, 1911, pp. 314–315.

Avebury British mythological site. The great STONE CIRCLES at Avebury have been associated with the DRUIDS for centuries, although they in fact date from thousands of years before the Celts arrived in Britain. When the Celts arrived in what is now north Wiltshire, they found a huge ditch-encircled site with four openings, one at each of the cardinal directions, with great stones standing upright within that circle, as well as a double parade of stones standing like sentinels along a pathway toward a nearby hill. Although there is some evidence that the Celts may have adapted the site to their own ritual purposes, as appears to have been the case with the similar monument of STONEHENGE, Avebury was not built by the Celts but by the mysterious pre-Celtic people of the MEGALITHIC CIVILIZATION. The site is so large that an entire village has sprung up within its boundaries.

Source: Malone, Caroline. *English Heritage Book of Avebury.* London: B. T. Batsford, Ltd./English Heritage, 1989.

Avenable Arthurian heroine. This ambitious and vital young British woman, dissatisfied with her options at home, dressed herself up as a young man, renamed herself Grisandole, and headed for adventure. She soon found a job in Rome, as seneschal or steward to the emperor himself. As one of his nearest confidants, Avenable heard him complain about a haunting dream in which a PIG was crowned with jewels. The dream told him that only a wild man could interpret it. Avenable found the wild man—none other than the great magician MERLIN, living in the woods during his period of madness—who indeed interpreted the dream. Rome's empress was in fact a pig who had engaged in SHAPE-SHIFTING, and her offspring were not really knights but piglets. In horror, the emperor had her killed and, once she had revealed her true gender, married Avenable.

Aveta Continental Celtic goddess. The goddess of the healing SPRING of Trier in Germany was depicted as a nursing mother, suggesting that she may have been a tribal ancestor; she is also shown with baskets of fruit, suggestive of a control over FERTILITY, as well as with DOGS, linked by the Celts to OTHERWORLD or after-life powers.

away FAIRIES were said to lust or yearn for humans—babies, lovely maidens, hearty young men, fiddlers, and midwives were at particular risk—whom they stole away from ordinary life into the beauteous but sterile FAIRYLAND. Such people were said to be "away" or to have been "taken." When stolen people returned, they were usually unaware of how much time had passed, for a night in fairyland might be hundreds of years in our world. Sometimes a stolen person was replaced by a replica; sometimes they just disappeared. Children were especially at risk of being "taken," for fairy children were often weak or wizened while human babies are plump and happy; putting a piece of iron in the cradle was said to protect the child from being replaced by a CHANGELING. In Ireland the stolen person was thought to be able to escape by removing the vision of fairyland by wiping the EYES with an ointment made of four-leafed clovers or SHAMROCKS. The belief in changelings occasioned several murders, most notably the death by burning of the seamstress Bridget Cleary in 1895. On the Isle of Man, belief in FAIRY KIDNAPPING survived into recent times as well.

See also FAIRY LOVER.

Sources: Bourke, Angela. *The Burning of Bridget Cleary.* London: Pimlico, 1999; Killip, Margaret. *The Folklore of the Isle of Man.* London: B. T. Batsford, Ltd., 1975, p. 28; O hEochaidh, Séan. *Fairy Legends of Donegal.* Trans. Máire MacNeill, Dublin: Comhairle Bhéaloideas Éireann, 1977, p. 231.

Ba'al (Baal) Non-Celtic divinity. This title, meaning "the lord," was given to various gods of the Phoenicians, the sea-trading ancient people of the eastern Mediterranean; Ba'al was parallel to, and perhaps consort of, the goddess named Ba'alat, "the lady." Ba'al is sometimes mistakenly described as the Celtic corollary to a hypothesized seasonal god named Bel, after whom the spring feast of BELTANE, celebrated on May 1, was presumably named. There is no evidence of such a divinity; no inscriptions to or sculptures of Bel have been found, although we do find a god named BELENUS whose name may have been incorporated into the springtime festival. Unlike Ba'al, who was typically a god of the atmosphere (and especially of stormy weather), Belenus was associated with healing spring and, at times, with the sun.

Bacorbladhra Irish hero. A member of the obscure mythological race, the PARTHOLONIANS, Bacorbladhra is distinguished as the first teacher to have lived in Ireland.

Badb (Bave, Badhbh, Baobh, Badb Catha) Irish goddess. One of ancient Ireland's war furies, Badb joins with the MÓRRÍGAN and MACHA under the title "the three Mórrígna"; she and the Mórrígan also appear with MEDB, FEA ("the hate-ful"), and NEMAIN ("the venomous") to form another fearful group of war goddesses. Sometimes Badb's name is used for the entire group, while at other times she seems a separate entity. As a result, it is difficult to tease out Badb's distinct identity from those of other Irish war furies.

Her name means "hoodie CROW" or "scald crow," and she was often envisioned as a carrion bird screaming over the battlefield, inciting warriors to provide more meat for her hungry beak. At other times she was conflated with the mournful BANSHEE, weeping over battlefields and sometimes predicting death by wailing before a battle or washing the clothes of those about to die (see WASHER AT THE FORD). Badb's function as a prophet—usually of doom—is pointed up by her appearance after the final mythical battle for control of Ireland, on the plain of MAG TUIRED; at that significant moment she described not a peaceful future but evils yet to come. Until recently in Ireland, because its call betokened doom, farmers would abandon projects if they heard a crow scream.

Badb may be related to the Gaulish war goddess named CATHUBODUA, sometimes depicted as a RAVEN riding a HORSE. Inscriptions to Cathubodua are found in the Haute-Savoie, as well as in tribal names like Boduogenos, "people of Bodua," in Gaul. It may have been Badb who was imitated in battle by black-robed women

DRUIDS who stood by the sidelines and screamed to incite the warriors to greater deeds, as was witnessed in the massacre and destruction of the druidic college at ANGLESEY.

Whether Badb and the other war goddesses were originally Celtic or pre-Celtic is debated. Scholars have argued that her bird form connects her to the unnamed Neolithic or New Stone Age goddess who was frequently depicted in that form.

Sources: Dexter, Miriam Robbins. *Whence the Goddesses: A Sourcebook.* New York: Pergamon Press, 1990, pp. 89–90; Green, Miranda. *Symbol and Image in Celtic Religious Art.* London: Routledge, 1989, p. 26.

Bademagu (Maelwas)   Arthurian hero. In one of the many lesser-known tales of the cycle of ARTHUR, he was the father of MELEAGANT, the king or god of the OTHERWORLD who carried away queen GUINEVERE, intending to force her to become his consort. The knight KAY followed after the kidnapped queen but, unable to win her escape, was himself held hostage. Thus LANCELOT, the queen's beloved, had to find and free the pair; the pure knight GAWAIN accompanied him. The site of their captivity, in the city of Gorre, was difficult to find; once there, the heroes were faced with a terrifyingly turbulent river, which they could cross either over a sword-sharp bridge or through a safer underwater route; Gawain chose the latter, but Lancelot, eager for Guinevere, raced across the upper bridge and thus was deeply wounded. In that state, Lancelot had to fight Meleagant—whose father, the kindly king Bademagu, forced his son to return the kidnapped queen.

badger   Symbolic animal. Like the SEAL, the badger was sometimes seen as a SHAPE-SHIFTING person; the Irish hero TADG found their meat revolting, unconsciously aware that they were really his cousins.

Baile   See AILINN.

Bairrind   Irish heroine. This otherwise obscure figure appears as the wife of the early invader BITH; her activities parallel the more important CESAIR.

Balan   See BALIN.

Balin (Balin le Sauvage)   Arthurian hero. A minor role in Arthurian legend is played by this knight, brother of Pelles, the FISHER KING; he struck the DOLOROUS BLOW and thus was responsible for the Fisher King's crippling wound.

ball seirc   Irish mythological motif. This "love spot" miraculously drew the heroine GRÁINNE to the handsome hero DIARMAIT. The *ball seirc* was a kind of dimple or other mark on his forehead (sometimes, on his shoulder) that made Diarmait irresistible to women, for which reason he usually wore bangs or a cap. But Diarmait's fate was sealed when, struggling with some active dogs, he accidentally revealed the *ball seirc*; Gráinne fell in love at that moment, and she tricked Diarmait into escaping with her.

Balor (Balar, Bolar, Balor of the Evil Eye)   Irish god. Before the Celts came to Ireland, other peoples whose names are lost to history lived there. The mythological history of Ireland, the *BOOK OF INVASIONS*, describes various waves of arrivals on Ireland's shores, each of whom had to do battle with the monstrous FOMORIANS who owned the island before the first invaders arrived.

Balor was king of the Fomorians; his daughter was the fair EITHNE, who a prophecy warned would give birth to a son destined to kill his grandfather. Balor attempted to outwit the prophecy by imprisoning his daughter in a tower, on the understandable assumption that if Eithne never laid eyes on a man, she could never become pregnant, thus sparing Balor's life.

But Balor's own greed led to his downfall, for he stole a magical COW, the GLAS GHAIBH-LEANN, who belonged to a SMITH and was tended by a man named CIAN. Threatened with death by the Glas's owner unless he reclaimed the cow, Cian found his way to Balor's domain and, discovering the tower in which Eithne was imprisoned, disguised himself as a woman to gain access to her. Eithne bore Cian three sons, all of whom were thrown into the sea by their furious, frightened grandfather when he discovered their existence. Cian was able to save one, who became the god and hero LUGH. (Because myth is rarely consistent, Eithne's husband is sometimes named MacInelly.)

It was Lugh who fulfilled the feared prophecy at the second battle of MAG TUIRED, when the Fomorians were finally defeated and the island wrested from their control. Lugh, despite being half-Fomorian, fought on the side of the TUATHA DÉ DANANN, the tribe of the goddess DANU, and it was his sharp aim that brought victory when he blinded Balor with a slingshot or a magical spear crafted by the smith god GOIBNIU. Lugh then used the spear to cut off Balor's head, after which his one remaining baleful EYE continued to have such power that it could split boulders.

Balor's evil eye was sometimes described as a third eye in the middle of his forehead, spitting flames and destruction. Alternatively, it may have been a conventionally placed eye that leaked poison from fumes cooked up by his father's DRUIDS. That maleficent eye never opened unless four men lifted its heavy lid, and then it caused anyone looking into it to fall to the ground helpless as a babe. Because of his ocular peculiarity, the god is called Balor of the Evil Eye (Birug-derc) or the Strong-Smiting one (Bailcbhémneach). His consort CETHLION also had poisonous powers that killed the good god DAGDA.

Balor was associated with Mizen Head (Carn Uí Néit, "the Burial-Place of Neit's Grandson") in Co. Cork and Land's End in Wales. For this reason he is sometimes interpreted as a sun god, imaged as the single eye of the setting sun off such southwesterly promontories. Other interpretations connect him with the winter season, which smites growing plants with frost and chill, and as such he is sometimes said to be the Irish version of the continental OTHERWORLD god the Romans called DIS PATER. Balor lasted long in Irish folklore, where he appears as a pirate living on Tory Island, off the northwest coast, and struggling against those who would steal his magical cow.

Sources: Curtin, Jeremiah. *Hero-Tales of Ireland.* New York: Benjamin Blom, 1894, pp. 296, 304; MacCulloch, J. A. *The Religion of the Ancient Celts.* London: Constable, 1911, pp. 31–35, 89–90; Ó hÓgain, Dáithí. *Myth, Legend and Romance: An Encyclopedia of the Irish Folk Tradition.* New York: Prentice-Hall Press, 1991, p. 43.

banais ríghe See INAUGURATION, HORSE SACRIFICE.

Banba (Banbha) Irish goddess. When the MILESIANS—the mythological invaders often interpreted as the first Irish Celts—arrived, they were met by three goddesses or queens of the TUATHA DÉ DANANN, each of whom announced herself as ruler of the land. First was Banba, who according to the *BOOK OF INVASIONS* met the Milesians at Slieve Mis in Co. Kerry, although some sources say that she was found on the plain from which the royal hill of TARA rises; she promised the Milesians happiness and wealth so long as the land bore her name. Next was FÓDLA, on her mountain Slieve Felim in Co. Limerick, who made the same promise in exchange for the same honor. Finally, the Milesians met the most impressive goddess, ÉRIU, on the central hill of UISNEACH; she promised them they would forever live happily in her land if it bore her name, and to her they gave precedence.

The three earth goddesses have been connected with that continental Celtic triple goddess of FERTILITY called by the Latin name of DEAE MATRES, "the mother goddesses." Or they may have been not a trinity but three unrelated goddesses, rulers of their specific regions, who were brought together in a shared narrative by the newcomers. Banba may once have had her own mythological cycle; if so, it has been lost, her specific powers being discernable only through hints and vestiges. That she was an ancient divinity is shown by her statement to the Milesians that she had been in Ireland before the biblical Noah, whose descendant CESAIR was the first human to reach the land. Similarly, some versions of the *Book of Invasions* say that the Milesians banished her by singing SPELLS against her, suggesting the removal of an early divinity by invaders. What Banba's original meaning was, however, is conjectural.

Three gods or heroes are named as the husbands of Ireland's three goddesses, with Banba's being MAC CUILL, "son of HAZEL," suggesting a connection with poetic inspiration, for hazel nuts were said to feed the SALMON of wisdom. The PIG is sometimes cited as an emblem of Banba, whose name resembles the word for piglet, *banb;* pigs were images of the goddess of the underworld in many European cultures as far back as 6000 B.C.E. and were in Ireland especially connected with prosperity.

The name Banba remains today as a poetic term for Ireland. Despite that connection with the entire island, and despite her associations in myth with the southwestern province of MUNSTER and the eastern province of LEINSTER, Banba is most especially connected with the most northerly point in ULSTER, Malin Head, locally called Banba's Crown. Occasionally, Banba is given as an alternative name for Cesair, the earliest human arrival in Ireland.

Source: MacAlister, R. A. Stewart. *Lebor Gabála Érenn: The Book of the Taking of Ireland, Part 5.* Dublin: Irish Texts Society, 1956, pp. 35 ff.

bandrui   Woman druid; see DRUID.

bangaisgedaig   See WARRIOR WOMEN.

Ban Naemha (Ban Naema)   Irish mythological being. Throughout Ireland we find the story of a magical FISH that swims in a holy WELL. In Cork, the sun-well called Kil-na-Greina was the residence of Ban Naemha, the fish of wisdom that only those gifted with SECOND SIGHT could see. The well's ritual involved taking three sips of the well's water, crawling around the well three times between each drink, and offering a stone the size of a dove's egg with each circuit. Whether this series of actions was intended to lure the fish or simply to honor the place is unclear.

banshee (bean sídhe, ben síd, bean sí, ben síde in Scotland, ban-sìth, bean-shìth, bean sìth; on the Isle of Man, ben shee)   Celtic mythological being. The Irish word *bean-sídhe*—woman of the SÍDHE or FAIRY people—originally referred to any woman of the OTHERWORLD. Such beings were often early goddesses of the land or of SOVEREIGNTY, diminished into regional FAIRY QUEENS when their worshipers were conquered by those who honored other divinities. Over time, however, the banshee's domain narrowed, until she became a spirit who announced forthcoming death, a transformation that has been linked to the seizure of Irish lands by the English in the 16th and 17th centuries.

The banshee is similar to the WASHER AT THE FORD, who washes the clothes of those about to die in battle, save that she specializes in deaths from causes other than war. She is a folkloric rather than a literary character, not appearing in written documents until the 17th century, after which her presence is commonplace. She appears either as a HAG or as a lovely woman; the transformation of one into the other is frequent in folklore (see CAILLEACH), so there may be no difference between these forms. The banshee often has RED hair (a common signifier of fairy blood), or wears white or green clothing, or sports bright red shoes. Sometimes she combs her hair with a golden COMB as she wails in anticipatory grief, usually at noon.

Some Irish families have banshees who signal the deaths of their members; most of these families have names beginning with Ó or Mac and thus represent the ancient families of a region. This association perhaps reflects a lingering loyalty to ancient Celtic beliefs, for the banshee has been linked to Celtic goddesses such as ÁINE. These families' banshees are occasionally found in the New World, having followed their emigrating charges, as was the case with the banshee of the O'Gradys, who traveled to Canada to provide her lamentation services.

Sources: Croker, T. Crofton. *Fairy Legends and Traditions of the South of Ireland.* London: William Tegg, 1862, p. 110; Delaney, Mary Murray. *Of Irish Ways.* New York: Harper & Row, 1973, p. 170; MacDougall, James. *Folk Tales and Fairy Lore in Gaelic and English.* Edinburgh: John Grant, 1910, pp. 175–179; Westropp, T. J. *Folklore of Clare: A Folklore Survey of County Clare and County Clare Folk-Tales and Myths.* Ennis, Co. Clare: Clasp Press, 2000, pp. 6–10; Wilde, Lady. *Ancient Legends, Mystic Charms and Superstitions of Ireland.* London: Chatto and Windus, 1902, p. 136.

baptism   Celtic ritual. There is some textual indication that the Celts had a ritual of name-giving that required children to be splashed with water from a sacred water-source, for the hero AILILL Mac Máta was said to have been "baptized in druidic streams" while the Welsh GWRI was "baptized with the baptism which was usual." In Ireland the power of the local goddess was imagined as resident in holy WELLS; baptism with her waters might have symbolized acceptance into her people. Until recently, children in the Hebrides were protected at birth from FAIRY KIDNAPPING by the placing of three drops of water on their brows; this rite may descend from an ancient baptismal ritual.

bard   Celtic social role. Throughout the Celtic world, the poet was held in high esteem because of an assumed power to curse and to bless. Thus POETRY was connected to MAGIC, perhaps because both employed the power of transformation: in poetry, metaphor; in magic, SHAPE-SHIFTING. In addition, because of the emphasis that the Celts put upon honor (see ÉRIC) and reputation, the words of a satirist were greatly feared.

Although the term *bard* is often used today to describe Celtic poets, the usage is inexact; according to Roman writers, the bard was the lowest among the various types of poets found in Gaul. According to this system, a bard was a singer and reciter—no inconsequential thing in a world that relied upon recitation rather than writing. These bards were historians, under strict demand not to change any of the basic facts of a story or genealogy.

As memory was important to the bard, vision was significant to the higher orders; the VATES, who interpreted omens, and the DRUIDS or priests. In Ireland the bard was a low-ranked poet, a student still working to learn the nearly four hundred required myths and legends; as one ascended the scale, one became a *FILI*, a member of a more distinguished caste of poets, of which the OLLAM was the highest rank. Both Gaul and Ireland thus seem to reflect the same hierarchy: bards or reciters; diviners or prophets (vates and *fili*); and druids or magician-priests.

Open to both men and women, these social roles were not generally hereditary but were contingent upon the gifts of the potential bard. Intensive training, including the memorization of hundreds of narratives, was required before progressing to extemporaneous composition in highly structured forms; such composition demanded familiarity with altered states and was connected to PROPHECY and spell-casting. In Ireland such poet-seers could be called upon to discern the next king in the bloody rite called the BULL-SLEEP or *tarbhfleis*. Finally, the most elevated poet was the satirist whose stinging words could punish any king who proved ungenerous or unfit to rule. Thus the dividing lines between poet, judge, historian, and prophet were not crisply drawn among the ancient Irish.

Several bards appear in myth and legend, some holding heroic or semidivine status. One is the Irish TUAN MAC CAIRILL, who described himself as having lived in various bodies since the beginning of time; another is AMAIRGIN, the MILESIAN poet who spoke the first words upon the arrival of his people in Ireland. In Wales the greatest poet was TALIESIN, who had gained all knowledge by accidentally drinking the brew of the goddess CERIDWEN; pursued and persecuted by her, he took on the shapes of animals and birds but was unable to escape her. She finally ate him as a grain of wheat, when she was a hen; but she then bore him as a child that she threw into the sea. This shape-shifting motif shows that the poet was believed able to assume the bodies of animals and birds while maintaining human consciousness.

In Ireland poets originally moved freely about the countryside, accompanied by their students and retainers, demanding hospitality from every king. But later poets attached themselves to specific noble families. Even later, when their traditional patrons were driven out by English settlement, the bardic orders degraded into wandering poets like Anthony Raftery, an historical figure of Co. Galway in the 1700s; like Raftery many of these poetic practitioners were blind. In Wales a continuous line of poets can be traced to the sixth century C.E.; the Bardic Order (Bardd Teulu) served the Welsh kings for more than a millennium, with assemblies of bards called EISTEDDFOD known as early as 1176.

Sources: Henderson, George. *Survivals in Belief Among the Celts.* Glasgow: James MacLeose and Sons, 1911, pp. 11–14; Hull, Eleanor. *The Cuchullin Saga in Irish Literature.* London: David Nutt, 1898, p. xviii; Kelly, Fergus. *A Guide to Early Irish Law.* Dublin: School of Celtic Studies, Dublin Institute for Advanced Studies. Early Irish Law Series, Vol. III, 1988, pp. 43–51; MacCulloch, J. A. *The Religion of the Ancient Celts.* London: Constable, 1911, p. 117.

Barenton (Belenton)   Breton mythological site. The magical Fountain That Makes Rain was hidden in the center of Brittany's legendary forest, BROCÉLIANDE. Visitors who drew water from the fountain and sprinkled it around unleashed fierce storms. The fountain may be the same as that ruled over by Laudine, the LADY OF THE FOUNTAIN, lover of the Arthurian hero OWEIN. This legendary site may also reflect a folk memory of a NEMETON or Celtic sacred wood.

barguest   British and Scottish mythological being. Hard to distinguish from BOGIES and boggarts (see BROWNIE), the barguest found in Scotland and England could appear as a headless man, a ghostly rabbit, or a white CAT. The barguest could also take the form of a BLACK DOG, especially when locally prominent people died; at such times the fire-eyed barguest would set all the dogs in the region to howling infernally. The barguest was dangerous to encounter, for its bite refused to heal. The name has been interpreted to mean both "bear-ghost," and "BARROW-ghost," the latter referring to ancient stone graves it was reputed to haunt.

Barinthus (Saint Barrind)   Arthurian hero. The ferryman of the OTHERWORLD, Barinthus carried the wounded king ARTHUR away from the surface world to the Otherworld after his final battle.

barnacle goose   Symbolic animal. In Ireland until recently, this waterbird was considered a fish, so it could be eaten during the Lenten fast. Although this curious belief may not have mythological roots but may derive from later folklore, it has a basis in the ancient Celtic belief that BIRDS are beings of several elements and therefore magical. It is even possible that the folkloric prominence given to the bird reflects pre-Celtic belief, for a barnacle goose was excavated from a Neolithic house, where it appears to have been part of a foundation sacrifice, suggesting that it was viewed as a protective being.

The barnacle goose is a migratory wildfowl, which annually arrived in Ireland from parts unknown, and it may have had special significance because of that cyclic disappearance and reappearance.

See also GOOSE.

Barrax (Barrecis, Barrex)   British god. Known from one dedication only, this obscure British god was likened by the occupying Roman armies to their warrior god MARS; the Celtic name seems to mean "supreme" or "lordly."

barrow   Sacred site. A pre-Celtic grave made from stones set in a line ending in a grave, in which more than one burial is sometimes found. The Wiltshire Downs, whereon rises STONE-HENGE, has the greatest collection of barrow graves in England; such graves are also found throughout Ireland. Barrows were revered by those who dwelt around them, who told stories of hauntings by fairy creatures (BLACK DOGS, for instance) or ghosts at the site.

See FAIRY MOUND.

Bath   British mythological site. The great hot SPRINGS that bubble forth from the earth at Bath, a town in the southwest of England, have been renowned for HEALING for at least two thousand years. While some suggest that the springs were used in pre-Celtic times, what we know of AQUAE SULIS (the Roman name for Bath) dates to Celtic times. SUL, the Celtic goddess of the site, was conflated with the healing MINERVA by the Romans who built the colonnaded temples and interior bathing rooms still visible today. The Celtic custom of throwing coins into water-sources was practiced at Bath, as was the custom of writing curses on lead; 16,000 coins have been excavated from Bath and more than 50 cursing tables.

Source: Ross, Anne, and Michael Cyprien. *A Traveller's Guide to Celtic Britain.* Harrisburg, Pa.: Historical Times, 1985, p. 19.

Battle of Mag Tuired (Moyturra)   See MAG TUIRED.

Baudwin (Baudwin of Brittany)   Arthurian hero. One of the few knights to survive the brutal battle of CAMLAN at the end of the reign of king ARTHUR, he became a hermit thereafter.

bean nighe   See WASHER AT THE FORD.

bean tighe   See FAIRY HOUSEKEEPER.

bear   Symbolic animal. A dim-sighted but sharp-eared creature of impressive speed and climbing ability, the bear was feared and respected for its strength by all early people who encountered it. Perhaps because a skinned bear looks very much like the carcass of a person, and because the live animal can walk upright like a man, the bear was often imagined as nearly human.

The region where the Celts emerged, in mountainous central Europe, was supreme bear terrain. Prior to the Celts' appearance in the archaeological record, we find evidence of a bear cult centered in Alpine caves; this ancient religious vision may have influenced the Celtic sense of the bear's divinity. Swiss sites especially attest to the bear's early importance, as at the city of Berne (whose name means "bear"), where the sculpture of the Celtic bear goddess ARTIO was found; there is some evidence of a parallel bear god named Artaios, whom the Romans called by the name of MERCURY. The name of ANDARTA, an obscure Gaulish goddess, may mean "great bear." Other mythological figures with ursine names include ARTHUR and CORMAC MAC AIRT.

Beare (Bera, Béirre, Moméa)   Irish goddess. In the far southwest of Ireland, in the province of MUNSTER, a thin peninsula stretches out to sea: the Beare (Bheara) peninsula, rich in both antiquities and legend. The area gets its name from this woman, said to have been a Spanish princess; little legend remains of her. More mythically significant was the CAILLEACH Bhéirre, the Hag of Beare, an ancient land goddess of the pre-Celtic people; she is associated with the area even today, and she can be seen, in the shape of a boulder, looking out to sea on the north side of the peninsula. Occasionally the consonants mutate, making her name Moméa.

beating the bounds   British ritual. In some areas of rural England, the tradition of walking the boundaries of parishes on certain holidays was maintained until recent times. Although a priest or minister led the procession, the ritual itself probably harkens back to pre-Christian days. When the procession passed ancient STANDING STONES, children were pushed against the boulders; similarly, children were ducked in sacred springs or ponds along the route.

Beaumains   See GARETH.

Bébinn (Bebind, Bé Find, Be Bind, Be Find, Bebhionn, Befind, Befionn)   Irish goddess or heroine. This name is common in early Irish literature and legend. One Bébinn, the goddess of birth, was sister of BÓAND and mother of Ireland's most handsome hero, FRÁECH; another Bébinn, beautiful GIANT from Maiden's Land off the west coast, was always surrounded by magical BIRDS and may have originally been a goddess of pleasure. Of the latter, legend has it that she left the OTHERWORLD to live with the king of the Isle of Man but ran away from him after he began to beat her. In a sad but realistic ending, the king pursued his escaping wife and killed her.

Bebo   Irish heroine. The small wife of an equally tiny FAIRY king, IUBDAN, Bebo traveled with her husband to the land of ULSTER, which seemed to them to be populated by GIANTS. The lovely diminutive queen caught the eye of Ulster's king, FERGUS. Despite physical chal-

lenges (his phallus was bigger than her entire body), Bebo became Fergus's mistress for a year, until Iubdan offered a pair of magical shoes to Fergus in order to gain her back.

Bec   Irish hero. This name, which means "small," is borne by several characters in Irish legend. One, Bec mac Buain, was the father of the maiden guardians of a magical WELL, where the hero FIONN MAC CUMHAILL gained wisdom when one of the girls accidentally spilled some of the well water into his mouth. Another, Bec mac Dé, was a diviner who could answer nine questions simultaneously with one answer.

Becfhola (Becfola, Beagfhola)   Irish goddess or heroine. A mortal queen of TARA, she is protagonist of the *Tochmarc Becfhola (The Wooing of Becfhola)*, which tells of her affair with a FAIRY LOVER, FLANN ua Fedach. As Tara's queen represented SOVEREIGNTY, her unhappiness with king DIARMAIT and her preference for the hero CRIMTHANN might have caused Diarmait to lose his right to rule. But when Becfhola attempted an assignation with Crimthann, she met Flann instead and spent an enchanted night with him on an island in Lough ERNE. When she returned to Tara, it was as though no time had passed, for she had lived in fairy time with Flann, who soon came to take her away.

Source: Cross, Tom Peete, and Clark Harris Slover, eds. *Ancient Irish Tales*. New York: Henry Holt and Co., 1936, p. 533.

Bé Chuille (Becuille)   Irish goddess. Magical daughter of the woodland goddess FLIDAIS, she was the only member of the TUATHA DÉ DANANN able to combat the wicked sorceress CARMAN.

Bé Chuma (Bechuma, Bé Cuma, Bé cuma)   Irish goddess or heroine. A woman of Irish legend, one of the magical people called the TUATHA DÉ DANANN, Bé Chuma was known for her car-nal appetites. She originally came from the OTH-ERWORLD, where she left her powerful husband for another man, after which she was banished to this world. There she continued her fickle ways, lusting after her stepson ART MAC CUINN while married to the king of TARA, CONN of the Hundred Battles. Since Tara's queen represented SOVEREIGNTY over the land, Bé Chuma could have replaced one king with another. Instead, she was forced to leave Tara when Art returned with a wife who demanded Bé Chuma's ostracism.

Bedwyr (Bedivere, Bedwyr fab Bedrawg) Welsh hero. In the Welsh mythological text of *KULHWCH AND OLWEN*, this warrior was highly regarded; he was so brave that he never shied away from a fight. He was also beautiful (though not as handsome as ARTHUR, much less LANCELOT). In later Arthurian literature Bedwyr's importance diminished until he was only called Arthur's butler, though a remnant of his earlier significance remained in the story in that he was instructed to throw the great sword EXCALIBUR into the water so that it could be reclaimed by the magical LADY OF THE LAKE, after which Bedwyr placed the dying king in the boat headed to AVALON.

bee Symbolic insect. Bees do not often appear in Celtic legend; when they do, it is typically as a symbol of WISDOM. bees were believed to drop down to earth from heaven; on the Isle of Man, they were caught early in the spring by fishermen, who used them as AMULETS of safety when at sea. In Ireland bees have no pre-Christian symbolic importance, although some saints (the Welsh Domnóc and the MUNSTER nun GOBNAT) were associated with beekeeping.

Source: Killip, Margaret. *The Folklore of the Isle of Man.* London: B. T. Batsford, Ltd., 1975, p. 76.

beech Symbolic tree. One of the Celtic sacred trees, this large relative (genus *Fagus*) of the OAK, with its muscular gray trunk and low full branches, was especially honored by Celts in the Pyrenees mountains.

See TREE ALPHABET.

Belatucadros Continental Celtic god. This obscure Gaulish god, whose name means "beautiful in slaughter" or "fair slayer," was equated by the Romans with their war god MARS. Evidence of his worship found in numerous (though not elaborate) dedications in northwestern England suggests that his cult was strongest among lowly soldiers. He never appears with a consort.

Belenus (Bel, Belinus) Continental Celtic god. The spring festival of BELTANE was named for him, some have suggested. Not much is known of this continental Celtic god, whom the Romans compared to APOLLO and who was worshiped at HEALING waters including Aquae Borvonis (Bourbon-les-Bains) in France; the healing plant Belinuntia was reputedly named for him, strengthening the likelihood that his domain was health.

Belenus's worship appears to have been widespread, for many inscriptions to him are found throughout Gaul, and several classical writers refer to his cult. His name appears to mean "bright" or "shining one," so he may have been a solar divinity; such deities were often associated with healing SPRINGS on the theory that the SUN, leaving our sight at night, traveled under the world, heating the waters of thermal springs as it went. The ancient author Apollonius relates a Celtic story of a stream formed by the tears of Apollo Belenus when he was forced from heaven by his father; as Apollo was the Greek sun divinity, this textual evidence strengthens the argument that Belenus had solar connections.

In Britain a hero Belinus was mentioned by the early historian Geoffrey of Monmouth as twin to Brennius; the two went to war over the throne but ultimately agreed to share power. The continental Belinus is not described as warlike, so despite the similarity in names, it is not clear that the same figure is intended.

Source: Geoffrey of Monmouth. *Histories of the Kings of Britain.* London: J. M. Dent and Sons, 1912, pp. 38 ff.

Beli (Beli Mawr, Beli Mawr fab Mynogan) Celtic ancestral figure, possibly a god. This Welsh ancestral father may have been derived from the Celtic god BELENUS, although given how little is known about the latter, that is conjectural. In the MABINOGION, Beli appears as consort of the mother goddess DÔN and as father of the goddess ARIANRHOD and the warrior CASWALLAWN; in the story of MAXEN, Beli was said to have ruled Britain until the titular hero arrived with his legions, driving Beli into the sea. He has been described as a god of death as well as of the sea, the latter giving rise to the poetic description of the ocean as "Beli's liquor"; the London site of Billingsgate (Beli's gate) appears to contain his name. Some have connected him with the obscure Irish god Bile (see *BILE*).

Sources: Gantz, Jeffrey, trans. *The Mabinogion.* New York: Barnes & Noble Books, 1976, pp. 67, 85, 124, 129; Rhys, John. *The Welsh People.* London: T. Fisher Unwin, 1906, p. 43.

Belisama (Belesama, Belisma) Continental Celtic and British goddess. This powerful goddess, found in several places in the ancient Celtic world, was an unusual circumstance in that most divinities are found in only one site. She was both a cosmic goddess and one associated with the RIVERS that, to the Celts, sheltered the preeminent divinities of good fortune and abundance. As her name may be derived from words for "brightness" or "shining," it has been proposed that she is a continental Celtic corollary to BRIGIT, the Irish flame goddess of healing. That the Romans connected her to MINERVA, as they did the hot-spring goddess SUL of Bath, is also suggestive of Belisama's possible original rulership of healing, water, and the solar flame.

In Lancashire the River Ribble once bore Belisama's name, according to the ancient Egyptian geographer Ptolemy, and it is thought that the headless statue still to be found near the river represents her. More recently the spirit of the Ribble was said to be named PEG O'NELL, a tyrannized servant girl who drowned while fetching water and who vindictively returns to claim a victim every seventh year. The only way to avoid such a human tragedy on Peg's Night was to sacrifice small birds or animals to the waters, a tradition in which some have discerned a memory of human sacrifice to the water divinity.

Sources: Spence, Lewis. *The Minor Traditions of British Mythology.* New York: Benjamin Blom, Inc., 1972, p. 11; Straffon, Cheryl. *The Earth Goddess: Celtic and Pagan Legacy of the Landscape.* London: Blandford, 1997, p. 141.

Bellieus Arthurian hero. A minor character in the tales of king ARTHUR, Bellieus became a knight of the ROUND TABLE by a curious means: He found the pure knight LANCELOT in bed with his lady, which Lancelot claimed was entirely a mistake. Bellieus was honor-bound to challenge the invader, who proved much the better swordsman. Despite his wounds, Bellieus survived and joined Lancelot at Arthur's court, CAMELOT.

Beltane (Bealtaine, Beltain, Beltine, Beltaine, Bealtane, Là Beltain, May Eve, May Day, Cétshamain) Celtic festival. Celebrated on May 1, Beltane was one of the four great festivals of what is conventionally called the ancient Celtic year—although it has been argued that the CALENDAR, not found on the Continent, represents only the Irish seasonal cycle. Beltane is essentially an agricultural festival, its roots in the cycle of grazing and planting. Traditionally, Beltane marked the beginning of the summer and the movement of cattle from sheltered winter pastures to the mountain *buaile* or "booleys" of summer, where the grass would be fresh and green. As might be expected of a festival that begins an agricultural cycle, weather divination was important, with frost being deemed ominous of bad times ahead, while rain was a sign of good fortune and a strong harvest.

As with other such festivals, Beltane began at sundown on the eve of the festival day. Like SAMHAIN in the fall, Beltane was a day when the door to the OTHERWORLD opened sufficiently for FAIRIES and the dead to communicate with the living. Whereas Samhain was essentially a festival of the dead, Beltane was one for the living, when vibrant spirits were said to come forth seeking incarnation in human bodies or intercourse with the human realm.

The name is related to words referring to fire. The spurious connection with the Semitic god BA'AL has been long since disproven, but divinities such as BELENUS and BELISAMA have been connected with the bonfires of spring, which were the most significant part of the Beltane celebrations in several Celtic lands. On Beltane Eve, hearth fires were extinguished, then relit from a bonfire made on the nearest signal hill. In Ireland these fires were thought to have been lit around the land in response to the sacred fire of ÉRIU on the hill of UISNEACH, in the Island's center, or at its royal center at the Hill of TARA.

The famous story of the "Easter fire" or "Paschal fire" lit by ST. PATRICK as he attempted to Christianize Ireland is anachronistic, for there would have been no Easter fires in the pre-Christian period; the fires in question were for Beltane, and Patrick was being both sacrilegious and politically challenging by lighting his own fire on SLANE hill before the royal fire blazed.

Beltane fires, which may have originated simply in the need to burn off brush before the fields and pastures were put into use, were lit in Wales until 1840 and in Ireland regularly through the middle of the 20th century, with CATTLE being driven near or between fires in order to assure their safety in the coming year. It was considered especially significant if a white heifer was seen in the herds, presumably an incarnation of BÓAND, the white cow goddess of abundance. At the same time, Beltane was a night when evil could strike cattle, drying up

their milk and causing them to sicken and die. Thus many Beltane rituals, including hunting HARES (shape-shifted WITCHES), and speaking CHARMS over BUTTER churns, have a basis in the belief that agricultural produce is particularly vulnerable at this time of year.

There are strong indications that Beltane had its origins in a festival for the protection of cattle. In ULSTER, as in other parts of Ireland, cattle were driven around raths and other areas believed to be residences of the fairy race. There they were bled, and after their owners had tasted the blood, it was poured into the earth with prayers for the herds' safety. In Devon in Britain a ram was tied to a STANDING STONE and butchered, its blood pouring over the stone; the animal was then cooked, hide and all, and its burnt flesh devoured to bring good luck.

It was not only a time of prayers for animal well-being but of rituals for human health as well, Beltane being one of the days on which Irish holy WELLS were most frequently visited, together with IMBOLC on February 1 and LUGHNASA on August 1. Well visitors performed a PATTERN or ritual walk, usually sunwise around the well, then left offerings (coins or CLOOTIES, bits of cloth tied to the sacred trees that shade the well) while praying for health and healing. Usually no words were to be spoken except in prayer, and the visitor departed without turning back to look at the well. These rituals, still practiced in many parts of Ireland, may have once included the carrying of sacred water to Beltane ritual sites, where trees and fields were sprinkled with prayers for an abundant harvest.

Decoration of a "May bush" was popular until the late 19th century in rural Ireland and in urban areas as well, with groups vying for the most resplendent tree covered with flowers and ribbons and bits of bright fabric. The THORN tree, traditionally the abode of the fairy folk, was a favorite for May bushes, but others could substitute, especially the ASH, considered the premiere Beltane tree in Ireland. In Dublin and Belfast, bushes were cut outside town and then decorated in various neighborhoods, with attempts to steal another district's May bush causing much jollity. The disreputable behavior of some Beltane revelers caused the May bush to be outlawed in Victorian times. In Cornwall the sycamore was the favored "May tree"; celebrants stripped its new branches of leaves and crafted little flutes. In Liverpool the festival long survived in rudimentary form, with houses and horses being decked with flowers for the day.

Beltane dew was believed to have the power to increase sexual attractiveness. Maidens would roll in the grass or dip their fingers in the dew and salve their faces, hoping thus to become fairer. In Britain one of their number was chosen as the May Queen, who was ceremoniously married to the May King, an act that symbolized the joining of the land's fertile powers. But in some cases there was a queen only, without a consort, which some scholars view as evidence that the goddess was invoked rather than the god at this time; in Britain the May King was called the "Beltane carline" or "old woman," which has led to the same interpretation.

Sexual license, with the magical intention of increasing the land's yield, is believed to have been part of the annual event. English Beltane festivals focused on that transparently phallic symbol, the MAYPOLE, around which dancers cavorted (see MORRIS DANCING). The full ritual entailed bringing in a cut tree from the woodlands and erecting it in the town square or a similar public gathering place. In the Cotswolds the maypole was associated with "summer bowers" built of new-budding trees and decorated with flowers and a large china doll called the "lady." Plays about ROBIN HOOD and maze-games, both originally part of the Beltane festivals, slowly diminished into children's games rather than sacred calendrical rituals.

Remnants of the maypole festival are still found in some English towns, most notably in Chipping Campden, but maypole dancing today is usually a folkloric revival, for the dances were outlawed in Puritan England in 1644. It is probable that it was not so much the dances themselves that caused concern but the usual aftermath, the "greenwood weddings" of young people who spent Beltane night together under the pretext of gathering flowers to deck the town next morning, for the Puritans complained that girls who went a-maying "did not one of them return a virgin."

Virginity was not the only thing sacrificed to the new season. Animal sacrifices continued into historical times; in Dublin the skull and bones of a horse were burned. Some have suggested that human sacrifice occurred at this time, although perhaps only in times of plague and need. In Britain until the 18th century, part of the Beltane festival was the preparation of a round cake that was broken up and distributed; whoever got a blackened piece was designated the "devoted" and the other celebrants mimed pushing the selected into the fire, suggesting an ancient sacrificial ritual. Such round cakes, called Beltane bannocks, were typically made from the last sheaf of the previous year's harvest. In Britain parts of the cake were offered to the land, with the words, "I give you this, preserve my horses; I give you this, preserve my sheep; I give the FOXES this, preserve my lambs; I give this to the hoodie CROW and to the EAGLE."

On the Isle of Man, Beltane fires and the strewing of flowers were said to scare away witches, who were most active on this day but who could be most effectively countered then as well. DIVINATION on Beltane or Beltane Eve was common among the Manx islanders: Light blazing from a house meant a wedding was in the offing, while dim light meant a funeral. Girls placed snails on pewter dishes that night, watching until midnight after washing face and hands in dew from a wheatfield, in the hopes that the creatures would write their husband-to-be's name on the dish. Protection of cattle and home were also part of the Beltane ritual, for the doorway was strewn with rushes and primroses while ROWAN crosses were fastened to the cattle's necks. Leaves of ELDER trees were affixed to windows and doors as protection against fairy powers. But fairy beauty would leave its mark on the dew, which could be gathered and used as a beautifying potion. Until some 50 years ago, the Manx islanders celebrated Beltane with a contest between the Queen of Winter and the Queen of the May, represented by girls whose attendants staged mock battles that ended in a festival.

In Scotland cattle were preserved from the influence of witchcraft by placing garlands of rowan and honeysuckle around their necks; red threads tied in their hair or woven into the wreaths likewise protected dairy cattle from milk-stealing witches, who were especially active on Beltane. Records from the 18th century show that a pot of eggs, butter, oatmeal, and milk was placed on the Beltane fire, after a bit of the mixture had been thrown onto the ground to honor the spirits; once cooked, the oatcake was divided into nine parts and offered to the animals who might steal the harvest: one part to the crow, one to the eagle, one to the fox, and so forth. Even as late as the 19th century, Beltane fires were still being built in rural districts of Scotland and cattle driven between them for purification.

The Beltane festival is alluded to in several recent popular works, including the science-fiction cult classic, *The Illuminatus! Trilogy* by Robert Shea and Robert Anton Wilson, in which conspiratorial forces of the Bavarian Illuminati and their henchmen meet (and are defeated by) the orgiastic forces of alternative culture; in the film *The Wicker Man*, in which a remnant Celtic society sacrifices a puritanical policeman to increase the land's fertility; and in the "Lusty Month of May" sequence in the musical *Camelot*. See also GLEN LYON.

Sources: Bord, Janet, and Colin Bord. *The Secret Country: An interpretation of the folklore of ancient sites in the British Isles.* New York: Walker and Co. 1976, p. 40; Briggs, Katharine M. *The Folklore of the Cotswolds.* London: B. T. Batsford Ltd., 1974, p. 24; Burne, Charlotte Sophia. *Shropshire Folk-Lore: A Sheaf of Gleanings, Part II.* Yorkshire: EP Publishing, 1974, p. 354–363; Carmichael, Alexander. *Carmina Gadelica: Hymns and Incantations.* Hudson, N.Y.: Lindisfarne Press, 1992, pp. 83–85, 586 ff; Danaher, Kevin. "Irish Folk Tradition and the Celtic Calendar." In Robert O'Driscoll, ed. *The Celtic Consciousness.* New York: George Braziller, 1981, pp. 217–42; Danaher, Kevin. *The Year in Ireland.* Cork: Mercier Press, 1922, pp. 90 ff; Harland, John, and T. T. Wilkinson. *Lancashire Legends.* London: George Routledge and Sons, 1873, pp. 96–97; Hull, Eleanor. *Folklore of the British Isles.* London: Methuen & Co., Ltd., 1928, p. 248–260; Killip, Margaret. *The Folklore of the Isle of Man.* London: B. T. Batsford, Ltd., 1975, p. 64; MacNeill, Máire. *The Festival of Lughnasa, Parts I and II.* Dulbin: Comhairle Bhéaloideas Éireann, 1982, pp. 12, 63; Rhys, John. *Celtic Folklore: Welsh and Manx.* Oxford: Clarendon Press, 1941, pp. 308 ff; Ross, Anne. *Folklore of the Scottish Highlands.* London: B. T. Batsford, Ltd., 1976, pp. 67, 132; Whitlock, Ralph. *The Folklore of Wiltshire.* London: B. T. Batsford, Ltd., 1976, p. 42; Wilde, Lady. *Ancient Legends, Mystic Charms and Superstitions of Ireland.* London: Chatto and Windus, 1902, p. 101.

Beltany Irish mythological site. In the far northwestern county of Donegal, a huge circle of some 60 stones once caught the beams of the rising sun on the morning of BELTANE, May 1; an alignment between a pillar stone and a stone engraved with small indentations called cup marks indicates the sunrise on that day. While STONE CIRCLES indicating astronomical alignments are far from unusual in Ireland, most were engineered as much as 4,000 years before the Celts arrived with their four festivals marking the midpoints between solstices and equinoxes; the pre-Celtic builders of stone circles more typically marked the equinoxes themselves. Thus Beltany presents an archaeological puzzle: Is it a Celtic site, inspired by the stone circles that they found in Ireland? A pre-Celtic site whose orientation has been misread by enthusiasts? Or an astronomical accident?

Bendonner Irish folkloric figure. This Scottish GIANT terrorized the coast of ULSTER until the residents requested the aid of FINN MCCOOL, a folkloric version of the great Irish hero FIONN MAC CUMHAILL. Finn challenged the giant to battle, then dressed himself in swaddling clothes. When the monster came to call, he found an enormous baby in an immense cradle, and he became so terrified of its strength that he ran away without Finn's having to lift his weapons. He never bothered the people of Ulster again.

Ben Bulben Irish mythological site. Near a mound of stone atop this famous, dramatically sweeping peak on the coast above the town of Sligo in the western Irish province of CONNACHT, the romantic hero DIARMAIT Ua Duibne died as a result of a wound from a magical BOAR who had kidnapped him and to whose back the hero clung. Diarmait managed to kill the beast, but then accidentally brushed against the body, puncturing himself with a poisonous bristle. As Diarmait lay dying, FIONN MAC CUMHAILL—whose intended wife GRÁINNE's love for the much-younger Diarmait had consumed years of Fionn's waning energy as he pursued the lovers across Ireland— arrived on the scene. A healer, Fionn could have saved the young man, but instead he taunted Diarmait, who had been so beloved for his beauty, with his gory ugliness. The mountain is famous in contemporary letters as shadowing the site of the grave of William Butler Yeats.

Benn Étair (Ben Edair, Ben Edar) Irish mythological location. Now the well-known Hill of Howth near Dublin, Benn Étair appears in many legends. In the tale of the SONS OF TUIRE-ANN, the exhausted heroes believe if they were able to see Benn Étair their strength would return; the hill may have been thought to have healing power. The grieving widow of the hero OSCAR, AIDÍN, was buried there by the BARD, OISÍN. Benn Étair was also the dwelling place of a fairy woman, ÉTAIN of the Fair Hair, who died of grief after her mortal husband was killed; the hill is said to have been named for Étain's father, ÉTAR.

Ben-Varrey See MERMAID.

Berba Irish goddess. Tutelary goddess of the River Barrow.
　　See also CESAIR.

Bercilak See GAWAIN.

Berecynthia Continental Celtic goddess. This obscure goddess was described by the early Christian author Gregory of Tours as being conveyed, in the form of a white-veiled image, through the fields in spring and whenever crops threatened to fail. She may be related to the otherwise little-known BRIGINDO; both appear to have been regional Celtic FERTILITY goddesses. Since one of Gregory's coreligionists, Martin of Tours, destroyed most of the "pagan idols" of the region, it is unlikely that images of Berecynthia survive.

Berguisa Continental Celtic goddess. Goddess of crafts among the Celts of what is now eastern Burgundy, she was the consort of the god UCUETIS.

Berrey Dhone (Brown Berry) Manx goddess. On the Isle of Man, this HAG or WITCH lived either on top of North Barrule Mountain or inside it. Like other forms of the CAILLEACH, she was an Amazonian GIANT, and her rocky heelprint can still be seen on the mountainside.

Biddy Irish goddess. This nickname for BRIGIT was commonly used in Ireland on the spring feast of IMBOLC, when children went begging from house to house. In Kerry, white-garbed young men—the "Biddy Boys"—sang at each doorstep, "Something for poor Biddy! Her clothes are torn. Her shoes are worn. Something for poor Biddy!" Although the tradition faded during the latter part of the 20th century, it has been lately revived, with Biddy boys and girls in outrageous straw hats dancing in Kerry towns, begging donations for the poor.

Biddy Early Historical Irish heroine. The "White Witch of Clare" was a renowned healer in the eastern part of Co. Clare area of Ireland in the 19th century, and her name is still current almost a century and a half after her death. Legends about her, although exaggerated and often including mythological motifs, are clearly based on a real woman of Feakle, a parish in the rolling hills known as Slieve Aughty (see ECHTHGE). Biddy was reputed to have been given a magical blue bottle by the FAIRY folk, into which she peered to ascertain the cause of illness or unhappiness. She was frequently at odds with the local clergy, who deemed her powers devilish; one of the most famous tales tells how Biddy cursed a clergyman for making defamatory remarks about her, causing his horse to be pinned in place until she spoke words to free him. She had several husbands, each increasingly younger; when she died, she tossed her blue bottle in a stream (or lake, or river, depending on the speaker) where it reportedly still rests today.

Source: Lenihan, Edmund. *In Search of Biddy Early.* Cork: Mercier Press, 1987.

Biddy Mannion See FAIRY MIDWIFE.

bilberry Symbolic plant. This berry (*Vaccinium myrtillus*), also called the whortleberry or mulberry, was a significant calendar marker in Ireland up to the present. Festivals celebrating the Celtic summer feast of LUGHNASA included climbing hills to gather bilberries, which were eaten on the spot or saved to make pies and wine; after Lughnasa, the berries were said to lose their flavor. The start of bilberry season was also the start of harvest, and many omens were sought from the berry bushes at this time, for crops were expected to be good when berries were plentiful, but hunger threatened when the berries were scarce.

Source: MacNeil, Máire. *The Festival of Lughnasa, Parts 1 and II.* Dublin: Comhairle Bhéaloideas Éireann, 1982, pp. 182, 422.

bile (*bele*; pl., *bili*) Symbolic plant. A sacred TREE, often found near a holy WELL or other honored site, is even today in Ireland decorated with offerings, especially strips of cloth called *CLOOTIES*. In ancient times such a tree would have marked an INAUGURATION site, and its branches would have provided the wood used for the king's scepter. There is also a god of this name, ancestral father to the MILESIANS who were the last invaders of Ireland, but it is unclear if tree and god are connected; indications that Bile was an underworld divinity could be linked to the tree's function as a symbol of the unification of the underworld (roots) and upper world (branches).

The term *bile* was used to designate a sacred tree or any genus, although certain kinds of trees, including OAK, YEW, and ASH, were thought to have special powers. The Irish place-poems, the *DINDSHENCHAS*, describe five great trees of ancient Ireland, including an oak that bore nuts and apples at the same time as acorns, replicating the trees said to grow in the OTHERWORLD. The second sacred tree was the YEW OF ROSS, described as a "firm strong god," while the remaining three were ash trees, most notably the mythic Ash of UISNEACH, which, when felled, stretched 50 miles across the countryside.

In addition to having totem animals, the ancient Celts may have believed in ancestral tree-spirits; we find one ancient Irish group going by the name of Fir Bile, "tribe of the sacred tree," while the Continental Eburones were the "yew-tree tribe."

The cutting of sacred trees was utterly forbidden among the Celts, a tradition that sometimes continued into Christian times. Weapons were not permitted around the oak of BRIGIT in KILDARE, a tree that was probably sacred before the foundation of the convent at that site, for the town's name includes the words for church (*kil-*) and for oak (*-dare*). The tradition of protecting such trees survived in folklore until recently; in the Irish village of Borrisokane in east Co. Galway, it was said that if anyone so much as burned a broken-off branch of the town's sacred tree in his fireplace, his house would burn to the ground.

This reverence for trees is one of the most deep-rooted of Celtic beliefs. DRUIDS held their sacrifices in sacred groves called NEMETONS, the destruction of which by the Romans was a brutal blow to the heart of the people, as was the Christian demand that trees no longer be honored with offerings and prayers. Despite the heavy fines levied on those who broke these regulations, Celtic tree-worship continued, as is evidenced by the frequent fulminations against it, generation after generation, by churchmen. Martin of Tours, renowned for smashing idols, was unable to gain destructive access to a sacred pine tree in central France. Faced with such fervent devotion, the Church converted the trees along with their worshipers, declaring them sacred to the Virgin Mary or to lesser saints, decking them with saints' images, and using them as sites for Christian ritual.

Sources: Brenneman, Walter, and Mary Brenneman. *Crossing the Circle at the Holy Wells of Ireland*. Charlottesville: University of Virginia Press, 1995; MacCulloch, J. A. *The Religion of the Ancient Celts*. London: Constable, 1911, pp. 54, 60, 103, 162, 201.

Billy Blind   British folkloric figure. In northern England, this name was sometimes given to a male form of the BANSHEE, the FAIRY who predicts death; he also sometimes helped around the house like a BROWNIE.

birch   Symbolic plant. One of the Celtic sacred trees, the birch (species *betula*) stands for the second letter of the TREE ALPHABET. A short-lived but graceful white-barked tree, the birch provided wood for the MAYPOLES used in BELTANE dances.

bird   Symbolic animal. Birds are found as emblems or escorts of Celtic goddesses, especially the carrion-eaters, such as CROWS or RAVENS, that accompanied goddesses of war and death. Birds sometimes represented souls leaving the body, as their connection with warrior goddesses would suggest, but they also were seen as oracular. The designs formed by birds in flight were the basis of a now-lost system of DIVINATION.

Not all Celtic bird imagery was gloomy or foreboding. Sweetly singing birds surround goddesses such as RHIANNON, whose presence was always indicated by their joy-giving song, or CLÍDNA, whose bright-feathered companions eased the pain of the sick with their songs. Individual bird species had specific associated traditions.

See COCK, CRANE, DOVE, DUCK, EAGLE, EGRET, GOOSE, HERON, OWL, SWALLOW, SWAN, WREN.

Biróg   Irish heroine. In the Irish story of the conception of the hero LUGH, this woman DRUID helped Lugh's father, a human named CIAN, disguise himself in women's attire to gain entry to the prison of the fair EITHNE, daughter of BALOR of the Evil Eye.

birth   Mythic theme. FERTILITY, whether of the fields, of the herds, or of humans, was not taken for granted by the Celts. The number of recorded invocations and rituals that were offered to increase fertility suggest that it was a matter of serious concern. Birth itself was not without its dangers, and so protective rituals for a safe childbirth included drinking waters of holy WELLS or wearing clothing dipped in them. As many wells had oracular functions, it is likely that parents-to-be also consulted them about the expected child.

Bith   Irish hero or god. Son of the biblical Noah and father of CESAIR, the original settler of Ireland who fled the flood in her own ark. According to the *BOOK OF INVASIONS*, Bith came along, landing with Cesair in MUNSTER in the southwestern part of the island, then moved with 17 of Cesair's 50 handmaidens to ULSTER. There he died on Slieve Beagh, where he is said to have been buried under the now-destroyed Great Cairn (Carn Mór). As the Irish word *bith* means cosmos, this shadowy god may have originally had greater significance than his fragmentary myth implies.

Black Annis

Black Annis British mythological figure. Outside Leicester rise the Dane Hills, named after the ancestral goddess DANU and said to be haunted by the fearsome blue-faced Black Annis, a degraded goddess figure who may derive from Danu. In a cave known as Black Annis's Bower, she was said to ambush children and eat them. She was sometimes pictured as a HARE (spring ritual hare-hunting is known in the area) or a CAT (dragging a dead cat in front of hounds was another spring ritual of the area). In other stories, she is said to have been a nun who turned cannibal. She may be a form of the weather-controlling ancient goddess, the CAILLEACH.

Sources: Spence, Lewis. *The Minor Traditions of British Mythology.* New York: Benjamin Blom, Inc., 1972, p. 92; Straffon, Cheryl. *The Earth Goddess: Celtic and Pagan Legacy of the Landscape.* London: Blandford, 1997, p. 124.

Black Chanter

Black Chanter Scottish mythological instrument. An enchanted musical instrument, part of a bagpipe, of which many tales are told in Scotland. Given to the leader of the Chisholms of Strath Glas by a foreign magician, it permitted one to travel through the air if played by a Cameron, the traditional pipers of the area. The Black Chanter served as a kind of BANSHEE, predicting death by cracking the evening before a death in the family. Each time this occurred, a ring of silver was placed around the chanter to repair it, until the whole instrument was covered with silver rings.

Source: McKay, John G. *More West Highland Tales.* Vol. 2. Scottish Anthropological and Folklore Society. Edinburgh: Oliver and Boyd, 1969, pp. 57 ff.

Black Dog

Black Dog Irish, Scottish, and British mythological figure. This spectral creature, usually shaggy and as big as a calf, was familiar throughout the insular Celtic world as an indication of great change and probable death. Occasionally Black Dogs could be helpful, but it was necessary to be wary of them, for one glance of their eyes could kill.

In northern England this beast was sometimes called a BARGUEST and thought to be a portent of death; the barguest led all the dogs of a district on a rampage through an area where death was about to occur, all howling and creating a memorable disturbance. In East Anglia the dog is called Black Shuck, while in Cumbria it was Shriker. In Westmoreland the dog was called the Capelthwaite and performed doggy services, like rounding up herds, for the locals, while the same creature on the Isle of Man was called the Mauthe Doog. The Black Dog is also familiar to Irish folklore and has been sighted at Irish sacred sites as recently as the 1990s. It is likely that lore about this ghostly creature inspired Sir Arthur Conan Doyle's "The Hound of the Baskervilles."

Sources: Clarke, David, with Andy Roberts. *Twilight of the Celtic Gods: An Exploration of Britain's Hidden Pagan Traditions.* London: Blandford, 1996, p. 145; Coxhead, J. R. W. *Devon Traditions and Fairy-Tales.* Exmouth: The Raleigh Press, 1959, pp. 94–95; Lamb, Cynthia. "Following the Black Dog." In Patricia Monaghan, ed. *Irish Spirit: Pagan, Celtic, Christian, Global.* Dublin: Wolfhound Press, 2001, pp. 43 ff; Spence, Lewis. *The Minor Traditions of British Mythology.* New York: Benjamin Blom, Inc., 1972, p. 90.

Black Vaughan

Black Vaughan British folkloric figure. In Lancastershire this savage GHOST was said to have been so vile in life that he remained on earth to torment his neighbors after his death, even resorting to SHAPE-SHIFTING into a fly to drive their horses wild. The ghost was finally exorcised by a woman with a newborn baby, whose purity and innocence Black Vaughan could not tolerate.

Bladud   British hero or god. This king was said by Geoffrey of Monmouth to have founded the great spa at BATH, shrine to the Celtic goddess SUL, lighting the unquenchable fire of the goddess there; some argue that Bladud was not a human king at all but the spirit of the place, or *GENIUS LOCI*.

Blaí   Irish heroine. Mother of OISÍN, the poet of the band of heroes called the FIANNA, she was turned into a deer by a magical enemy and conceived her son while in that form. FIONN MAC CUMHAILL was the father. Oisín was born in human form, and Blaí was warned not to touch him. But she could not resist and stroked him gently with her tongue, leaving a small furry patch forever on Oisín's forehead. Often this heroine is given the name of SADB.

Source: Almqvist, Bo, Séamus Ó Catháin, and Páidaig ó Héalái. *The Heroic Process: Form, Function and Fantasy in Folk Epic.* Dublin: The Glendale Press, 1987, p. 4.

Blaise   Arthurian hero. Blaise, an otherwise obscure figure, taught magic to the great MERLIN.

Blanchefleur (Blancheflor)   Arthurian heroine. When the ROUND TABLE knight PERCIVAL entered the domain of the wounded FISHER KING, he met and wooed the beautiful Blanchefleur ("white flower"); in some texts, the name is given as belonging to Percival's sister, otherwise known as DINDRAINE.

Blarney Stone   Irish folkloric site. In Co. Cork, in the 15th-century Blarney Castle, is a stone that is said to convey eloquence (without the requirement of honesty) upon those who kiss it. The stone was blessed by CLÍDNA, the region's FAIRY QUEEN, after the local ruler Cormac MacCarthy had asked for help in winning a lawsuit. Kissing the stone at dawn as Clídna instructed, MacCarthy was instantly gifted with glibness and talked his way out of trouble. To prevent others from having the same advantage, MacCarthy had the stone installed in an inaccessible part of the castle wall, where it remains to this day, attracting tourists who hang upside down to plant a kiss on the stone and win Clídna's gift.

Bláthnat (Blanaid, Blathait, Bláithíne)   Irish goddess. This goddess, whose name means "little flower," was daughter either of MIDIR, king of the Irish FAIRIES, or of the human king of ULSTER, CONCOBAR MAC NESSA. In Irish legend, she was brought from the OTHERWORLD by the hero CÚCHULAINN, who also brought forth her magical CATTLE and CAULDRON. But his companion in that raid, CÚ ROÍ, then stole them all. To make matters worse, Cú Roí buried Cúchulainn in sand and shaved off his hair, subjecting him to humiliation by all passersby.

Bláthnat did not live happily with Cú Roí, as is evidenced by the fact that she plotted his assassination only a year later with Cúchulainn, who became her lover. She is thus the Irish version of the Welsh BLODEUWEDD, for she revealed to Cúchulainn the secret way to kill her husband. The story does not end with that bloodshed, for Cú Roí's poet FERCHERTNE pushed Bláthnat over a cliff, killing himself in the process. Despite her enslavement by Cú Roí, Bláthnat is often characterized as deceitful and traitorous for plotting his death. In Christian legend she is described as converting and entering the convent rather than being killed.

Sources: Condren, Mary. *The Serpent and the Goddess: Women, Religion and Power in Ancient Ireland.* San Francisco: Harper & Row, 1989, p. 71; MacCulloch, J. A. *The Religion of the Ancient Celts.* London: Constable, 1911, pp. 84, 381.

blemished king   Mythic theme. Among the Celts, a king could only claim the goddess of the land as his wife—and through her, the SOVEREIGNTY of the country—if he were whole and without blemish. If injured, he was forced to abdicate the throne, as was NUADA, who lost his arm at the first Battle of MAG TUIRED and who had to give up leadership of the TUATHA DÉ DANANN until he was provided with a magical prosthesis. The motif also forms the basis of the legends of the FISHER KING that are so important in the Arthurian cycle.

Blodeuwedd (Bloduwith, Blodeuedd)   Welsh goddess. When the presumably virginal ARIANRHOD was tricked into giving birth to a son of questionable parentage, she laid a curse on him that he would never have a name, weapons, or a wife. But her brother GWYDION tricked her again, so that she provided the first two items for the newly named LLEU LLAW GYFFES. Then with the help of his magician uncle MATH, Gwydion created a wife for the young man, who may have been his son.

In the fourth branch of the Welsh collection of myths, the *MABINOGION*, we hear how the two magicians constructed the aptly named Blodeuwedd ("flower-face") from nine kinds of wildflowers, including meadowsweet, oak, broom, primrose, and cockle. But this creature of no earthy race was unhappy with her lot. She grew restless as Lleu's wife and conceived a lust for a handsome hunter, GRONW PEBYR, whom she convinced to kill Lleu. Knowing that her husband could only be killed when bathing by the side of a river, under a thatched roof over a cauldron, while standing with one foot on a deer, she dared Lleu to assume that unlikely posture, whereupon her lover dispatched him with ease. For her part in the murder, she was turned into an OWL by her creators. It has been argued that this apparently treacherous woman is the shadow of an ancient goddess of death; Robert Graves finds in her an ancient queen whose ritual marriage to the king lasted but a year before his sacrifice.

Sources: Gantz, Jeffrey, trans. *The Mabinogion.* New York: Barnes & Noble Books, 1976, pp. 111–116; Graves, Robert. *The White Goddess: A Historical Grammar of Poetic Myth.* New York: Farrar, Strauss and Giroux, 1948, pp. 308–316.

Blondine (Velandinenn, Princess Velandinnen) Breton heroine. A folktale of Brittany tells of a lovely princess whose story is replete with mythological motifs, suggesting that she may be a degraded goddess. When the young man CADO insulted a mysterious FAIRY, she put a curse on him that could only be lifted by the unknown princess Blondine. No human could tell Cado the way to Blondine's land, but he overheard some CROWS talking about her and, hitching a ride on the back of one, found Blondine beneath a tree (see *BILE*) beside a mirror-bright WELL. Convincing her to marry him, Cado stole Blondine away from her magician father, who cast unsuccessful spells at the couple as they fled. Once on earth, however, Cado proved false to Blondine by losing the ring she had given him, whereupon his mind was wiped clean of any memory of her. He was betrothed to another woman, but when Blondine arrived at his wedding, wearing her matching ring, he regained his memory and his senses; his brother married the other bride, while Cado and Blondine were finally wed.

Source: Luzel, F. M. *Celtic Folk-Tales from Armorica.* Trans. by Derek Bryce. Dyfed, Wales: Llanerch Enterprises, 1985, pp. 35–44.

blood   Mythic theme. Roman writers contended that blood was sacred to the Celts and was used in grisly rituals such as drinking the blood of slain enemies. But whether such writers can be credited is difficult to say, for their audience consisted of people afraid of the Celts, whose warriors had almost conquered Rome itself; thus Roman authors must always be read with some suspicion when they paint the Celts as barbarians—in this case, bloodthirsty ones. Yet other indications support the picture of blood rituals among the Celts. Blood brotherhood, for instance, remained a tradition in the Scottish isles until historical times. And there seems little question that the blood of animal SACRIFICES was smeared on trees in the sacred groves or NEME-TONS. Blood may have been interpreted as bearing the essence or life force; thus drinking blood would restore the warrior.

Blue Men of the Minch (Fir Gorm, Fir Ghorma)   Scottish folkloric figures. Scotland's coastal waters between the inner and outer Hebrides, known as the Minch, are haunted by blue-skinned beings who may descend from SEALS or who may be fallen angels. The Blue Men control the weather in that region and, therefore, ship traffic as well. Even on calm days, it is said, the Minch can be turbulent because the Blue Men are swimming about, stirring the waters. The Minch is sometimes called the Blue Men's Stream or the Current of Destruction because its waters are so unpredictable and dangerous. Skippers who are not fast-witted are not encouraged to traverse the passage, for the Blue Men call out rhymes to them, and if another good couplet is not sung back to them, they capsize the boat.

Bóand (Boann, Bónn, Boinn, Bóinn, Boadan; possibly Bouvinda)   Irish goddess. Bóand's name means "woman of white cows" or "shining cow," although the COW does not appear in her legend, unless this goddess is the same as the similarly named BÓ FIND, the ancestor of all Ireland's cows. She may also be identical to the goddess referred to by the great Egyptian geographer Ptolemy as Bouvinda, a name that connects Bóand with other Indo-European cow goddesses.

Bóand gave her name to the River Boyne, along which Ireland's greatest ancient monuments stand. Of her, the story common to Ireland's RIVER goddesses is told: that she visited a forbidden WELL, where she lifted the stone that protected it. The waters of the well rose and drowned her,

forming the river as it did so. The well is called the well of SEGÁIS, which was Bóand's name in the OTHERWORLD. An alternative name for the Boyne is Sruth Segsa, "river of Segáis," further showing the identity of the two names.

Bóand is also a goddess of wisdom, for one root of her name meant both "white" and "wisdom"; in some stories, she was blinded by the rising river, reflecting a common connection of inner vision and outer blindness, as well as connecting her through the motif of the single EYE with the famous resident of the river source, the one-eyed SALMON sometimes called FINTAN. Irish folklore claimed that if you drank from Bóand's river in June, you would become a seer and poet. Finally, Bóand has associations of abundance and prosperity, for Celtic rivers were seen as sources of the FERTILITY of their watersheds.

Bóand is connected to the solar year, as goddess of the great tumulus of Newgrange—BRÚ NA BÓINNE or "palace of Bóand" in Irish—which is Ireland's most famous winter SOLSTICE site. There she was seduced by the good god DAGDA away from her husband NECHTAN (a name for NUADA; in some stories, ELCMAR). To hide their affair, Dagda caused the sun to stand still for nine months, so that Bóand could bear their child, AONGHUS Óg, without Nechtan's knowing that more than a day had passed. In some versions of the story, Bóand is given the name EITHNE.

Source: Gwynn, Edward. *The Metrical Dindshenchas.* Vol. III. Royal Irish Academy, Todd Lecture Series. Dulbin: Hodges, Figgis, and Co. Ltd., 1906–1924, pp. 27–39.

boar   Symbolic animal. The male PIG or wild boar, pictured in art and on coins from both insular and continental sources, was the most savage animal that the ancient Celts were likely to encounter. As a consequence, the boar came to represent strength and tenacity and sexual potency; its meat was often part of the CHAMPION'S PORTION lauded in song and story, while its skin was used for warriors' cloaks. (The word *boar* in several Gaelic languages is TORC, also the word for the warrior's neckpiece). Because its meat was so favored, the boar represented prosperity as well; on the Isle of Man, the Arkan Sonney or "lucky piggy" was a beautiful white FAIRY pig that brought good luck. The boar appears in several important cycles of Irish legend, most importantly the death of the romantic hero DIARMAIT Ua Duibine, who killed a boar that was terrorizing a region, only to die when he stepped on one of its poisonous bristles as he tried to measure its great size; there are also frequent mentions of an OTHERWORLD pig that could be carved up and devoured but that would endlessly replenish its own flesh. In the Welsh *MABINOGION*, boars originate in the Otherworld, which is perhaps the source of their fierce strength in the surface world.

Sources: Campbell, J. F. *Popular Tales of the West Highlands.* Vol. III. Edinburgh: Edmonston and Douglas, 1862, p. 81; Green, Miranda. *Symbol and Image in Celtic Religious Art.* London: Routledge, 1989, pp. 27, 139.

boat Symbolic object. An important image connected with the Celtic goddess of waters, found in sculptures from the Roman period; the unnamed goddess from Nuits-Saint-Georges in France holds a CORNUCOPIA while standing on the prow and rudder of a boat. As all these symbols are also associated with the Roman goddess Fortuna, the boat may link the ideas of FERTILITY (seen by the Celts as connected with the waters that fed the land) and abundance (seen by the Romans as the goddess of fortune).

See NEHALENNIA.

Bochtóg Irish heroine. In Ireland this FAIRY woman saved people from drowning by awakening them if they fell asleep on the shore as the tide rose. When visible, usually in rough weather, Bochtóg was a beautiful woman with waist-length blonde hair.

bodach *(carle)* Scottish folkloric figure. In the Highlands the bodach could appear either as a relatively harmless trickster or, as the Bodach Glas or Dark Gray Man, as a male BANSHEE who was seen just before a death. Its name refers to its appearance as an old man, who made beckoning motions or stared into windows after dark. He was, however, more frightening than truly dangerous. The Bodach á Chipein, or "Old Man with the Peg," was a friendly and approachable Highland FAIRY who watched humans at their ordinary tasks and wept whenever funerals went by. The word is sometimes found in Ireland, referring to the same figure.

Source: McKay, John G. *More West Highland Tales.* Vol. 2. Scottish Anthropological and Folklore Society. Edinburgh: Oliver and Boyd, 1969, p. 489.

Bodb Derg (Bove Derg, Bodhb, Bodhbh) Irish god or hero. The most powerful magician of the TUATHA DÉ DANANN, the wise Bodb Derg was the son of the good god DAGDA and brother of AONGHUS Óg, god of poetry. He reigned from a great palace on the shores of LOUGH DERG. Bodb Derg was elected king of the Tuatha Dé, much to the annoyance of LIR, who stormed from the meeting in protest. But upon his return home, he found his wife (whose name is not recorded) taken ill; she died after three days and Bodb Derg, in a gesture of sympathy and solidarity, sent his three handsome foster daughters to minister to Lir at SHEE FINNAHA, his palace.

Eldest of the three was ÁEB, with whom Lir quickly fell in love. But, after giving birth to FIONNUALA and her brothers, Áeb died. Lir married yet again, this time his wife's foster sister, AÍFE, who grew insanely envious of her stepchildren and enchanted them into SWANS. Although he could not undo her powerful spell, Bodb Derg punished Aífe by turning her into a demon or a CRANE.

Source: Joyce, P. W. *Ancient Celtic Romances.* London: Parkgate Books, 1997, pp. 1–36.

Bodhmall (Boghmin) Irish heroine. A DRUID, she was the foster mother of the great hero FIONN MAC CUMHAILL and instructed him in the occult arts.

Bó Find Irish goddess. When Ireland was a barren, empty island, this magical white COW appeared with her sisters, the red cow Bó Ruadh and the black cow Bó Dhu, and rose from the western sea. The red cow headed north, the black south, and Bó Find went to the island's center, all three creating life behind them as they traveled. When she reached the island's center, Bó Find gave birth to twin calves, one male and one female; from them descended all Ireland's CAT-TLE. Sites along her route often still bear names that incorporate the word "Bó," the most famous being her sacred island, Inis Bó Find, now known as Inisbofin, off the Galway coast. See BÓAND.

Source: Wilde, Lady. *Ancient Legends, Mystic Charms and Superstitions of Ireland.* London: Chatto and Windus, 1902, p. 22.

bog Symbolic site. Formed of centuries of sphagnum moss and other plants compacted in water, bogs were a prominent feature of the Irish and Scottish landscape until recent times. Peat, harvested from the bogs, is still dried into turf and burned as fuel in both countries. Until the middle of the 20th century, turf-harvesting was a labor-intensive process, but mechanical harvest-ing has meant the destruction of vast ancient bogs in both countries. With that destruction, folkloric sites have also been lost, for bogs are typically liminal zones (see LIMINALITY), neither dry nor wet, inhospitable for building roads or homes—and thus, perfect entrances to the OTH-ERWORLD. Bogs are also important archaeologi-cally, for the lack of oxygen and the excess of tannic acid in bog water mean that objects lost or sacrificed in bogs (see BOG PEOPLE) are astonish-ingly well preserved. Many of the archaeological riches viewable today in the National Museum of Ireland consist of bog discoveries.

Bog of Allen Irish mythological site. One of Ireland's most extensive BOGS, it covers much of the southeastern midlands and surrounds ALMU, ancient capital of LEINSTER; the bog and hill are both named for an obscure goddess or heroine named ALEND.

bog people (bog men) Archaeological arti-fact. Throughout Europe, those harvesting burnable peat from BOGS occasionally encounter bodies of people who were lost and drowned in bog lakes—or sacrificed in ancient times. Because of the preservative power of bog water, the bodies of these people are well preserved, although the tannic acid dyes their skin brown. Archaeologists have examined these bog bodies to determine if they died accidentally or, as is sometimes clear, were killed as part of a sacrifi-cial rite. Most sacrificed bodies come from European bogs, especially from Denmark, but there are also finds in Celtic lands. Found in 1984 at Lindow near Liverpool, the LINDOW MAN was garroted or strangled after being fed pollen of the sacred plant MISTLETOE; his body has been analyzed as evidence of HUMAN SACRI-FICE and of the THREEFOLD DEATH.

Source: Ross, Anne. "Lindow Man and the Celtic Tradition." In Stead, I. M., J. B. Bourke, and Don Brothwell. *The Lindow Man: The Body in the Bog.* Ithaca, N.Y.: Cornell University Press, 1986, pp. 162–169.

bogan (*buckawn, bòcan, bauchan*) Scottish (occasionally Irish) folkloric figure. This SHAPE-SHIFTING night sprite was a trickster, occasion-ally helpful but usually malicious. Found fre-quently in the Highlands and less often in Ireland, the bogan also appeared in America, having immigrated to the New World with those he served—or haunted. The MacDonald family of Morar lived with a bogan named Coluinn gun Cheann who was cheerful to the family but tended to murder visitors and leave their muti-lated bodies near the river. Finally he killed a man whose friend, a strong man named John Macleod, took revenge on the bogan, wrestling it to the ground and threatening to drag it into the dangerous daylight. But the bogan promised that, if freed, he would leave the land—and kept his promise.

Sources: Briggs, Katherine M. *An Encyclopedia of Fairies: Hobgoblins, Brownies, Bogies, and Other Supernatural Creatures.* New York: Pantheon Books, 1976, pp. 19, 79; Douglas, George *Scottish Fairy and Folk Tales.* West Yorkshire: EP Publishing, 1977, pp. 143 ff.

bogie (bogle, bug, bug-a-boo) Scottish mythological figure. A class of trickster figures found in the Scottish Highlands, where March 29 was Bogle Day, as well as in England, where bogies could go about in troops (see TROOPING FAIRIES) or alone (see SOLITARY FAIRIES). Bogies tended to settle in trees, attics, lofts, and other high places. There are many categories of bogie, depending upon attire and attitude; these included the helpful BROWNIE, the tormenting boggart, and the destructive *NUCKELAVEE*, as well as various goblins who appeared in devilish skeletal form.

boggart See BROWNIE.

Bolg See FIR BOLG.

Bolvinnus Continental Celtic god. Little is known of this god from Gaul whom the Romans identified with their warrior god MARS.

boobrie (tarbh boibhre) Scottish folkloric figure. The SHAPE-SHIFTING specter of Highland tradition sometimes appeared as a COW or as a WATER HORSE. Occasionally it was seen in the form of a huge insect with long tentacles, which sucked horses' blood. It haunted LAKES, crying like a strange bird; indeed, it commonly assumed the form of a waterbird, but one vastly larger than any duck or swan ever seen. Its footprint on land was said to be the size of a large deer's antlers. The *boobrie* preyed upon calves and lambs and thus was a danger to subsistence farmers; when cattle were not handy, he ate OTTERS.

Book of Invasions (Lebor Gabála Érenn) Literary text. Its Irish title, *Lebor Gabála Érenn,* literally means "the book of the takings of Ireland" or "the book of Irish conquests," but it is usually translated as the *Book of Invasions* or the *Book of Conquests.* It was compiled in a dozen separate manuscripts in approximately the 12th century, but portions date to much earlier; the poetic text describes the six invasions of Ireland from the time of the biblical flood to the arrival of the final settlers. Although the text is interrupted at times by recitations of biblical material, it is nonetheless an invaluable source for students of Celtic mythology.

First came CESAIR, granddaughter of Noah, escaping the flood in her own ark but not leaving many descendants; then the Partholonians (see PARTHOLÓN), also from the east and descendants of the GIANT MAGOG, who were destroyed by plague; and then the Nemedians, people from the Caspian Sea who followed their leader NEMED and who fought the monstrous FOMORIANS.

The Fomorians apparently never invaded Ireland, although they appear over and over as the story progresses, to be beaten back time and again by new arrivals; they seem to be always resident on the island rather than coming from elsewhere. The Fomorians drove out the Nemedians, who were forced to return to their earlier lands, where they were enslaved for many centuries. But finally, under the new name of FIR BOLG, the Nemedians returned to Ireland; nothing is mentioned of the Fomorians at this point, suggesting that either they left the Fir Bolg alone or the two groups made an alliance. When the final immortal race arrived, the TUATHA DÉ DANANN or people of the goddess DANU, they defeated both the Fir Bolg and the remnant Fomorians to become the rulers of Ireland for many centuries.

But even immortals have limits to their terms, and so the Tuatha Dé Danann too were forced to yield Ireland, this time to a mortal race, the Sons of Míl or the MILESIANS. The descendants and followers of a Scythian man who married a noble Irishwoman, they won Ireland from the Tuatha Dé—who did not depart but disappeared under the ground, where they became the FAIRY people.

Having been composed after Christianization, the *Book of Invasions* attempts to bring Ireland's history into Judeo-Christian tradition, with such obvious interpolations as Noah. But from this mélange of fact and myth, scholars construct connections with archaeologically proven migrations to Ireland. Thus the text is a useful tool for discovering Ireland's past, as well as a significant resource for study of Irish mythology.

Sources: Cross, Tom Peete, and Clark Harris Slover, eds. *Ancient Irish Tales*. New York: Henry Holt and Co., 1936; MacAlister, R. A. Stewart. *Lebor Gabála Érenn: The Book of the Taking of Ireland, Parts 1–4*. Dublin: Irish Texts Society, 1941; MacAlister, R. A. Stewart. *Lebor Gabála Érenn: The Book of the Taking of Ireland, Part 5*. Dublin: Irish Texts Society, 1956.

borrowed days   Mythic theme. The stormy days of late spring, when winter seems to have suddenly come back to life, were until recently called the Borrowed (or Borrowing) Days or the Skinning Days in the west of Ireland. Legend had it that the GLAS GHAIBHLEANN, the cow of abundance—also called the Old Brindled Cow or the Gray Cow—defied winter by claiming it could not kill her, but winter stole several days from spring and skinned the cow in retaliation.

Source: Danaher, Kevin. *The Year in Ireland*. Cork: Mercier Press, 1922, p. 85.

borrowing fire   Scottish and Irish ritual. It was vital, in ancient times, to keep the hearth fire alight, for the making of a new fire was an ardu-

ous procedure. Only once each year, on BELTANE Eve, was the fire allowed to die; the next day it was relit from one of the festival blazes. Should the fire die out at any other time, the householder would likely have to relight it using a fire-drill, a tool in which the whirling of a wooden stick in a small hole in a wooden plank creates sufficient friction for sparks to be born. Borrowing fire from the neighbors was unlikely, as it was believed that this gave the borrower power over the CATTLE—and thus, the wealth—of the lender.

Bors de Ganis   Arthurian hero. Only three knights of the ROUND TABLE were pure enough of heart to gain the magical chalice called the GRAIL: PERCIVAL, GALAHAD, and the least-known of the three, LANCELOT's cousin Bors de Ganis.

Borvo (Bormanus, Bormo)   Continental Celtic god. Among the Gauls, Borvo was the god of healing SPRINGS, a male version of the goddess known in the singular as SUL, in the plural as the SULEVIAE. Depicted as a warrior seated beneath a horned SERPENT, he was son of SIRONA and consort of DAMONA, also called Bormana. To the Romans, Borvo was identical with the healing APOLLO. His name may mean "boiling," an appropriate name for a god of hot springs.

Boudicca (Boudica, Boadicea)   British heroine. This historical Celtic queen achieved almost mythic status with her war against the invading Romans, which she launched shortly after the horrific destruction of the important DRUID sanctuary on the island of ANGLESEY. Her people, the Iceni of the southeastern part of Britain, had borne the earliest brunt of the Roman invasion. When her daughters were raped and her husband killed, Boudicca rallied her people and their allies to wage a strong, if ultimately unsuccessful, campaign. Having seen the treatment meted out to captive queens, Boudicca took her own life when defeated, calling out to the war goddess ANDRASTE as she died.

Braciaea Continental Celtic god. This obscure Gaulish god was equated by the Romans with their warrior god MARS. His name may derive from a Gaulish or Welsh word for "malt," suggesting a connection between drunkenness and aggression and recalling traditions that Celtic leaders gave their warriors alcoholic beverages before battle.

Bran Irish mythological beast. One of the primary hunting hounds of FIONN MAC CUMHAILL, whose name means "crow," Bran was born a DOG because Fionn's sister, UIRNE, was cursed by a jealous rival and turned into a bitch. After whelping Bran and SCEOLAN, Uirne was restored to human form, but her TWIN children (variously described as daughters or sons), remained trapped in canine bodies. Yellow-footed and red-eared, Bran became Fionn's favorite dog, so fast she could overtake flying birds. Bran had one offspring, a black female pup who was fed on milk. The woman who tended her was instructed to feed her all the cow's daily output, but she secretly held back some for herself. The hungry pup attacked a flock of wild SWANS and was killed when she could not be stopped.

Bran met her own death because of such exuberant hunting. She had almost caught a fawn—the enchanted poet OISÍN—and was about to close her jaws around him when Fionn opened his legs wide. The fawn ran between, followed closely by Bran, but Fionn snapped his legs shut on her, breaking her neck. Sadly, for he loved his hunting companion, Fionn buried her at Carnawaddy near Omeath in Co. Louth.

Source: Hyde, Douglas. *Beside the Fire: A Collection of Irish Gaelic Folk Stories.* London: David Nutt, 1890, pp. 15 ff.

Bran Meaning "crow" or "carrion eater," this name is common in heroic literature in several Celtic lands, applied to figures including:

• **Bran, the Breton hero** who was reincarnated as a CROW after dying in prison for his war against the Vikings.

• **Bran Galed,** a Welsh hero who owned an endlessly full drinking horn.

• **Bran mac Febail,** an Irish hero who in the *Imram Brain* or *Voyage of Bran*, fell asleep after hearing FAIRY MUSIC and, upon awakening, set out to find its source and the FAIRY LOVER who came to him in dreams. He found her in the OTHERWORLD, an island in the western sea, where they lived happily for years that seemed but moments in fairy time. When Bran returned to this world, his years caught up with him, but he was able to speak the story of his adventures before he turned to dust.

Sources: Cross, Tom Peete, and Clark Harris Slover, eds. *Ancient Irish Tales.* New York: Henry Holt and Co., 1936, p. 588; Gregory, Lady Augusta. *Gods and Fighting Men: The Story of the Tuatha De Danaan and of the Fianna of Ireland.* New York: Oxford University Press, 1970, pp. 30 ff; Hyde, Douglas. *Beside the Fire: A Collection of Irish Gaelic Folk Stories.* London: David Nutt, 1890, pp. 15 ff; Ó hÓgain, Dáithí. *Myth, Legend and Romance: An Encyclopedia of the Irish Folk Tradition.* New York: Prentice-Hall Press, 1991, p. 50.

Brangien (Braignwen, Brangaine, Golwg) Arthurian heroine. In the great romance of TRISTAN and ISEULT, the maidservant Brangien accidentally gave a love-potion—designed to be shared by Iseult with her husband king MARK on their wedding night—to the heroine and her escort Tristan as they were traveling by sea to Mark's court. The two fell into fated love, and, to ease her mistress's pain, Brangien took Iseult's place in the bed of Mark on their wedding night.

Brân the Blessed (Bendigeidfran, Brân Fendigeid, Bendigeid Fran, Bendigeit Vran, Brân Llyr) Welsh hero or god. One of the great heroes of the Welsh epic cycle, the *MABINOGION*, Brân was the son of LLYR and brother of the fair BRANWEN. He was so huge that not a single building could house him, so he lived happily in the open air. When Branwen was lured away to Ireland, where she was virtually imprisoned, Brân led an expedition to retrieve her, during which he suffered a fatal wound from a poisoned spear. Dying, he instructed his warriors to cut off his HEAD and carry it back to Wales. They did so, discovering along the way that Brân's head (called Urdawl Ben, "the noble head") was quite entertaining, singing and telling stories for 87 years before its burial, in an ongoing party called the Assembly of the Wondrous Head.

Brân is one of those hard-to-categorize figures over which scholarly debate rages, some contending that he is a literary figure while others find him an ancient god. Among those who contend the latter, Brân is variously a Celtic sea deity or a pre-Celtic divinity merged with a later god, a form of the British god BELATUCADROS, or an early version of the FISHER KING.

Sources: Gantz, Jeffrey, trans. *The Mabinogion.* New York: Barnes & Noble Books, 1976, pp. 67–84; Ross, Anne. *Pagan Celtic Britain: Studies in Iconography and Tradition.* London: Routledge & Kegan Paul, 1967, p. 119.

Branwen (Branwen ferch Llŷr)   Welsh heroine or goddess. In the second branch of the *MABINOGION*, Branwen ("white raven") was the daughter of LLYR and sister of the great hero BRÂN THE BLESSED. She was given in marriage to king MATHOLWCH of Ireland, but when her half-brother EFNISIEN insulted the Irish people by mutilating their horses, Branwen was put to work as a scullery maid in punishment. From her kitchen prison she trained a starling to carry messages back to Wales, describing her plight. Her brother Brân led an expedition to rescue her, but he was killed in the attempt, and Branwen died of her sorrow and was buried, according to tradition, in the barrow called Bedd Branwen. Branwen has many similarities to the Welsh goddess RHIANNON; both were exiled by marriage and enslaved by their husbands' people. The interpretation of this heroine as an

ancient goddess is strengthened by her connection with a nipple-cairned mountain peak in the Berwyn range of Wales called Branwen's Seat.

Source: Gantz, Jeffrey, trans. *The Mabinogion.* New York: Barnes & Noble Books, 1976, pp. 68–82.

Brastias   Arthurian hero. Although he served GORLOIS, duke of Cornwall, this knight helped the bewitched UTHER PENDRAGON enter the bedroom of IGRAINE, the duke's wife. No one else realized the treachery, for the great magician MERLIN had altered Uther's appearance so that he seemed to be Gorlois, home from battle to spend a night with his wife. Brastias, in league with Merlin, welcomed the disguised Uther, who conceived the future king ARTHUR with Igraine that night. When Arthur ascended the throne, Brastias became one of his strongest supporters.

Brâzil (Brazil)   See HY-BRÂZIL.

Brega (Bregia)   Irish mythological site. This great central plain, described in several ancient texts, is believed to be the rich agricultural region that is now Co. Meath and parts of Co. Westmeath.

Bregon   Irish hero. In the Irish mythological history, the *BOOK OF INVASIONS*, this man was an ancestor of the MILESIANS, who were the final conquerors of the island.

brehon   Irish judge. A member of the class of DRUIDS, the ancient Irish brehon (from the Irish *brithemain*, "judge") did not evaluate cases or enforce the law as today's lawyers and judges do, for both were prerogatives of the king. Rather, the brehons used precognitive skill and drew on the history and poetry they had memorized in their many years of training to guide their people. They were also bound by spiritual powers to be just in their actions; the great judge Sencha was said to have broken out in blotches when he pronounced a biased judgment regarding women. Some brehons wore special garments or jewelry that kept them just: MORANN wore a chain around his neck that, if he attempted to speak a false judgment, tightened and choked him, while it grew loose and comfortable when he spoke truly.

There are many historically renowned women brehons, and women were not barred from druidic training, yet many scholars contend that women were not permitted to function in this capacity. Many sources refer to the great Brig (or BRIGIT), an honored woman brehon; she healed Sencha's blotched face by correcting his biased judgment against women. Thus there is some evidence for women, perhaps the daughters of jurists, serving in this capacity, which some scholars have taken to indicate equity of opportunity between the sexes, while others argue that it was the exception rather than the norm. There is perhaps no other area of Celtic studies that draws such controversy, for where the evidence is slight, even scholars project their own desires and fears upon the past. The question of women brehons is far from settled.

The brehon laws, developed in ancient times and passed on through the oral tradition, were first codified in the fifth or sixth century. The brehons continued to practice until the 17th century; the Case of Tanistry in 1608 brought Ireland under British common law, on the grounds that the brehon laws caused "barbarism and desolation."

Bréifne (Breffni)   Irish goddess or heroine. One of the most famous territories of Ireland is named for this obscure figure, who may have been the goddess of the region's SOVEREIGNTY. According to the *DINDSHENCHAS*, the place-poetry of Ireland, Bréifne was a WARRIOR WOMAN who died defending her land and its people from evil invaders.

Brenhines-y-Nef   Welsh goddess. Ancient and obscure Welsh sky goddess and maternal force, ancestral mother of humanity.

Brennius (Brennus)   See BELENUS.

Bres (Breaseal)   Irish god. There are several figures of this name in Irish mythology.

- **Bres mac Elatha,** the most important figure of this name. Originally named Eochu, he was nicknamed Bres ("the beautiful one") because of the fairness of his appearance, but the actions of this crossbreed son of the TUATHA DÉ DANANN princess ÉRIU (or EITHNE) and the FOMORIAN king ELATHA did not match the splendor of his countenance. As king of TARA, he was so stingy that he would not light a fire in the great hall nor feed visitors anything but unbuttered crackers.

  Bres even refused beer to a BARD. That poet, CAIRBRE mac Éadoine, paid him back in kind, leveling a (literally) blistering SATIRE at the king: "Without food upon a dish, without a cow's milk on which calves grow, without a house in the gloomy night, without storytellers to entertain him, let this be Bres's future." Stung by the satire, Bres felt his face break out in boils. As a BLEMISHED KING could not rule, Bres was driven from the throne, whereupon he turned traitor and joined the forces of his father, fighting against his former people but losing in the second battle of MAG TUIRED.

  In some accounts Bres's consort was the goddess BRIGIT; their son, RUADÁN, was killed at Mag Tuired.

- **Bres,** a member of the Tuatha Dé Danann who was killed in the first battle of Mag Tuired.

- **Bres** (Breseal), lord of HY-BRÀZIL, an ISLAND of the OTHERWORLD that floats in the western ocean; whether he is the same as the half-Fomorian Bres is difficult to determine.

Breuse (Breuse sans Pitie)   Arthurian hero. An evil knight whose nickname means "without pity," Breuse was one of the great enemies of king ARTHUR of CAMELOT.

Brí Irish heroine. The mythologically important FAIRY MOUND of BRÍ LÉITH was named in part for this obscure heroine, who was loved by a warrior named LIATH. Daughter of MIDIR and resident in his SÍDHE or palace, Brí went to visit Liath in TARA, where both were killed, although the source is unclear as to how or why. Midir's great palace was named after the lovers, who were never united in the flesh but whose names were thereafter wedded.

Brian Irish god. This still-popular Irish name derives from an ancient god of the TUATHA DÉ DANANN, one of the tragic SONS OF TUIREANN. Son of the great goddess DANU and the otherwise obscure human hero TUIREANN, Brian was one of three brothers who ambushed CIAN, father of the great hero LUGH and an enemy of their father. To avoid a confrontation, Cian metamorphosed into a PIG, but not soon enough: Brian turned his brothers into DOGS who set out after their prey and showed mercy only by allowing Cian to turn back into a man as he died. Lugh then demanded, as recompense for the murder, that Brian and his brothers perform eight impossible feats; they completed seven but failed at the last one and were killed by Lugh and his companions.

The name was also borne by one of the most famous of Ireland's high kings, Brian Boru (Bóroma), whose historical reality has become enshrouded with legend. Hailing from Clare, near the mouth of the Shannon, Brian was originally ruler of a tiny kingdom, but taking on both foreign and Irish foes, he rose to be high king. He ruled for many years and finally died while mustering the Irish forces against the Vikings at Clontarf.

Briccriu (Bricriu, Bricriu Nemhthenga, Bricriu of the Poisonous Tongue) Irish hero. The bitter-tongued poet of the ULSTER CYCLE appears most notably in the epic *Briccriu's Feast*, in which he set great champions against each other for the CHAMPION'S PORTION, causing much bloodshed.

He acted similarly in the story of MAC DATHÓ's PIG. The texts commemorate the power of Irish poets, whose words were believed to have magical powers over men. Briccriu is said to have been killed near the Ulster lake that bears his name, Loughbrickland, where he made a slighting remark about the sexual appetite of queen MEDB and was brained by her lover FERGUS mac Róich.

Sources: Cross, Tom Peete, and Clark Harris Slover, eds. *Ancient Irish Tales.* New York: Henry Holt and Co., 1936, p. 254, Gantz, Jeffrey. *Early Irish Myths & Sagas.* New York: Penguin, 1981, p. 219. Gregory, Lady Augusta. *Gods and Fighting Men: The Story of the Tuatha De Danaan and of the Fianna of Ireland.* New York: Oxford University Press, 1970, p. 67.

brídeóg Symbolic object. A puppet said to represent St. Bridget, the Christian figure who assumed many of the traits of the earlier Celtic goddess BRIGIT, the *brídeóg* was constructed of two long clusters of green rushes plaited together to form a small square; the unplaited rushes were then drawn together and bound to form the body of the doll, while a second cluster of rushes, bound near each end to suggest hands, was attached crosswise to the body, the whole thing then being dressed in rags. Sometimes the figure was formed of a broom or churn-dash, again dressed in rags and with a turnip for a head. In Ireland until recent times, this effigy was carried on the eve of Brigit's day—the ancient Celtic feast of IMBOLC—from house to house by children demanding pennies "for poor BIDDY." In many villages, only unmarried girls could carry the *brídeóg* (which means "little Brigit"), although in other places both boys and girls participated in the procession.

Source: Danaher, Kevin. *The Year in Ireland.* Cork: Mercier Press, 1922, p. 24.

Brigantia Continental Celtic and British goddess. The northern half of the island of Britain—

the northern six counties of today's nation—was occupied in the early historical period by the Brigantes, a Brythonic Celtic people who worshiped this ancestral goddess, memorialized in the names of the rivers Braint in Anglesey and Brent in Middlesex. Sculptures of and inscriptions to her from Roman times conflate her with Victoria, Roman goddess of victory, and Caelestis, a Syrian sky goddess. Her name ("high one") may connect her to the Irish goddess BRIGIT; she has also been connected with the Gaulish goddess BRIGINDO. In Ireland, Brigit is not generally known as a RIVER goddess, but her connection there to holy WELLS may indicate that the Celts saw her as a divinity of water and the fertility it brings.

Brigindo   Celtic goddess. Obscure Continental Celtic protector goddess invoked to assure abundance of crops.

Brigit (Bride, Brigid, Brighid, Brid, Bridget, Briid)   Irish goddess. There are two important figures of this name: Brigit the goddess, and Brigit of Kildare, an early Christian saint who died ca. 525 C.E. Whether the latter is a Christianized version of the former is the subject of some contention, although even the most devout admit the accretion of implausible legends around a woman of dubious historicity. While there is all likelihood that a brilliant abbess who bore the name of a Celtic goddess lived in Kildare, it is not likely that she time-traveled back to Bethlehem to serve as midwife at the birth of Jesus, nor that she pulled out her eyes to avoid marriage and then replaced them with no damage to her sight, nor that she used sunbeams to hang up her wet mantle. Accidentally made a bishop by a god-intoxicated cleric, Brigit the saint has much of the power and magic of the earlier goddess.

As goddess, Brigit is a rarity among the Celts: a divinity who appears in many sites. Her name has numerous variants (Brig, Bride, Brixia, Brigindo). As Celtic divinities tended to be intensely place-bound, the apparently pan-Celtic nature of this figure is remarkable—sufficiently so that some argue that the variants of the name refer to the same figure. The Irish Brigit ruled transformation of all sorts: through POETRY, through smithcraft, through HEALING. Associated with FIRE and CATTLE, she was the daughter of the god of fertility, the DAGDA; as mother of RUADÁN, she invented KEENING when he was killed. Some texts call Brigit a triple goddess or say that there were THREE goddesses with the same name, who ruled smithcraft, healing, and poetry, respectively. This triplication, a frequent occurrence among the Celts, typically emphasized or intensified a figure's divine power.

It is not clear whether the Brigit mentioned in the great compilation of ancient Irish law called the SENCHAS MÓR as Brigh Ambui was the goddess; parallel male figures in that section of the text such as CAI and NIALL are mythological or quasi-historical. From Brigh Ambui, "female author of the men of Ireland," the renowned BREHON or judge Briathra Brighi got her name; the text implies that it was common for women judges to be called Brigit. The question of women's rights in the law and as lawyers is unsettled; however, Brigh Ambui is mentioned third in the *Senchas Mór*'s list of important figures in the lineage of Irish law.

Many scholars hypothesize an all-female priesthood of Brigit, even suggesting that men were excluded from her sanctuary. She may have been seen as a bringer of civilization, rather like other Indo-European hearth goddesses (Vesta, Hestia) who ruled the social contract from their position in the heart and hearth of each home. In Ireland the mythological Brigit was not imagined to be virginal; indeed, she was the consort of one of the prominent early kings of Ireland, the unfortunate BRES mac Elatha, and bore him a son, Ruadán.

Brigit's feast day was IMBOLC, February 1, still celebrated in Ireland today. Her special region was the southeast corner of Ireland, LEINSTER, also the historical home of the saint who bears her name. St. Brigit is still honored in KILDARE, ancient seat of her abbey. Little can be verified about her life, but legend has filled in the blanks. Brigit is said to have been born of a Christian slave mother and a pagan Celtic king, at dawn as her mother stood on the threshold of their home; miracles attended upon her birth, with light pouring from the child, who was named by the DRUIDS of the court after the pan-Celtic goddess described above. When grown, she refused marriage, pulling her eyes from their sockets to make herself so ugly no one would have her; but then she healed herself and set out in search of a place for her convent. Tricking a local king out of land, she established one of ancient Ireland's great religious centers at Kildare, whose name includes both *kil-* (church) and *dar-*(OAK, sacred to the druids), signifiers of two spiritual traditions of Ireland. There she was both abbess and bishop, for she was made a priest when St. Mel, overcome with the excitement of blessing the abbess, accidentally conferred holy orders on her.

The historian Giraldus Cambrensis reported in 1184 that nuns had for five hundred years kept an undying flame burning to St. Brigit, a tradition that recalls the fire rituals of SUL and BATH and may have had a basis in Celtic religion. The miraculous flame, which never produced any ash, was doused not long after Giraldus wrote, and the nuns dispersed; but in 1994, the Brigidine sisters returned to Kildare and relit Brigit's flame. An annual gathering on Imbolc brings pilgrims from around the world to see the fire returned to the ancient fire-temple, discovered on the grounds of the Protestant cathedral during restoration in the 1980s. Vigils at the WELL dedicated to Brigit and other ceremonial, artistic, and social-justice events make up the remainder of the celebration of Lá Féile Bhride, the feast of Bridget, in Kildare today.

The Irish conflation of goddess and saint seems even stronger outside Kildare, where various traditions of greeting the rising spring at Imbolc were sustained through the late years of the 20th century. February 1, ancient festival of Brigit the goddess, continues even today to be celebrated as the feast of Brigit the saint. Old folkways, some with clear pre-Christian roots, have died away in most lands, although only within recent memory. However, some traditions, like the BIDDY Boy processions in Co. Kerry and the *crios bridghe* ("Brigit girdle") in Co. Galway, have been recently revived. Workshops are now offered in many places in constructing the four-armed rush Brigit cross and the rush poppet called the *BRÍDEÓG* (little Brigit). Meanwhile, around the world, neopagans and Christians alike bring honor to Brigit in various ways, including on-line societies of Brigit.

Sources: Berger, Pamela. *The Goddess Obscured: Transformation of the Grain Protectress from Goddess to Saint.* Boston: Beacon Press, 1985, p. 70; Carmichael, Alexander. *Carmina Gadelica: Hymns and Incantations.* Hudson, N.Y.: Lindisfarne Press, 1992, pp. 81, 581; Condren, Mary. *The Serpent and the Goddess: Women, Religion and Power in Ancient Ireland.* San Francisco: Harper & Row, 1989, pp. 47 ff; Danaher, Kevin. *The Year in Ireland.* Cork: Mercier Press, 1922, pp. 13 ff; NightMare, M. Macha. "Bridey in Cyberspace" and Callan, Barbara. "In Search of the Crios Bhride." In Patricia Monaghan, ed. *Irish Spirit: Pagan, Celtic, Christian, Global.* Dublin: Wolfhound Press, 2001; Ó hÓgain, Dáithí. *The Hero in Irish Folk History.* Dublin: Gill & Macmillan, 1985, pp. 16 ff.

Brí Léith Irish mythological site. A famous FAIRY MOUND in the center of Ireland, Brí Léith was the palace of the greatest of fairy kings, MIDIR. Several mythic tales are set at Brí Léith, most notably that of ÉTAIN, the reborn heroine who was Midir's lover through several lifetimes. It is said to have been named for an obscure heroine named BRÍ, which may be another name for Étain.

Source: Gwynn, Edward. *The Metrical Dindshenchas.* Part II. Vol IX. Royal Irish Academy, Todd Lecture Series. Dublin: Hodges, Figgis, and Co. Ltd., 1906, pp. 3, 299–301.

Brisen Arthurian heroine. The friend of ELAINE—not the Lady of Shalott, but Elaine of Corbenic—Brisen was a magician who found a way to help her friend, who was infatuated with the splendid knight LANCELOT. Knowing that Lancelot was in love with queen GUINEVERE, Brisen got him drunk and whispered that the queen was waiting in a secret chamber. When he arrived there, Lancelot found a beautiful woman with whom he spent a blissful night, awaking to Brisen's trickery.

Britannia British goddess. There is some evidence that the ancient Celtic residents of the island of Britain saw their land as a goddess of SOVEREIGNTY, like ÉRIU of Ireland. This controversial view has detractors as well as supporters. A very early Roman coin (161 C.E.) from Britain shows a female figure mounted on a globe and bearing a shield and spear; she has been interpreted as Britannia, a name also used of England during its imperial period in the 18th and 19th centuries. The name may derive from the tribal name Pritani.

Source: Ross, Anne, and Michael Cyprien. *A Traveller's Guide to Celtic Britain.* Harrisburg, Pa.: Historical Times, 1985, p. 101.

Britovius Continental Celtic god. Little is known about this god of the region near Nîmes in France, whom the Romans saw as similar to their own warrior god MARS.

Brittany See GAUL.

Brixia (Bricta) Continental Celtic goddess. Known from only one site, the thermal SPRING of Luxeuil in southern France, this goddess has been linked to BRIGIT in her HEALING aspect.

Brocéliande (Broceliande) Arthurian site. This legendary forest in eastern Brittany is said to have been the site where the great magician MERLIN was imprisoned by his mistress, the fair but ambitious VIVIANE, in an attempt to trick his magical knowledge from him; legend claims that he lives forever within a great tree there. Also within the forest is a piercingly cold fountain that brews storms at the behest of its lady guardian (see OWEIN and BARENTON). As the Celts were known to believe in the sacredness of TREES, this still-standing primeval forest near Rennes (now called the Forest of Paimpont) may be Europe's last remaining *NEMETON.*

brollachan See *VOUGH.*

Bron See FISHER KING.

Bronach Irish heroine or goddess. In the west of Ireland, a famous line of cliffs mark the edge of the Co. Clare coast. The highest of them is Ceann na Cailighe, "hag's head," named for this mythological HAG, also called the "hag of Black Head" for another nearby rocky place. Some researchers claim the CAILLEACH of the area is not Bronach but MAL.

Bronwen Welsh goddess. Several writers have connected this obscure ancestral goddess of Wales with the later epic heroine BRANWEN, but others warn against such conflation. Her name, which may mean "white-bosomed one," is found as the name of a mountain in north Wales.

brounger British mythological figure. This British spirit, said to haunt the island's east coast and to levy a tax of fish upon fisherfolk, may have descended from a Celtic thunder god.

brownie Scottish and British folkloric figure. In naming the youngest branch of her Girl Scouts, feminist Juliette Gordon Low recalled the cheery, helpful household spirits of Scotland and the English midlands. Usually seen as a housebound and friendly member of the FAIRY race, there is some evidence that the brownie may in fact be a late mythological development with no roots in the Celtic or pre-Celtic world-view, arising from a kind of disguised ancestor worship in which the forebears are imagined as hanging about to help the living. But because of the brownie's close connection to the fairies, the little household sprite may have such an exalted past as well. The specialized brownie called the GRUAGACH in the Hebrides indeed seems to have been divine at some point, for until recently milk offerings were poured over its sacred stones to convince the *gruagach* to guard the herds.

Just as controversial as its origin is the matter of the brownie's appearance. Most observers claimed the brownie was a stout hairy man, while others said that although short, the brownie was not necessarily rotund, and his hair was fair and flowing. In either case, he usually wore ragged brown clothes. Despite Low's application of the term of little girls, the brownie was typically male.

The brownie specialized in doing barn work at night: threshing, tidying, currying horses, and the like. Outdoor work was not beyond his domain, for he would also help with sheepherding, mowing, and running errands. Obviously, a household with a brownie was a happy one; the brownie was not always invisible but could serve as a confidante and adviser if necessary. Sometimes the brownie was offered a libation of milk, left in a special pitcher or bowl, but as with other resident aliens, it was important not to make a fuss over his needs. It was especially crucial never to notice his raggedy clothing, for to offer him a suit of human clothes would result in the offended brownie leaving to seek employment elsewhere.

Often found in Cornwall, the boggart was a trickster version of the brownie, who caused destruction, tossing things about the house at whim; any brownie could become a boggart if mistreated by his family. Equivalent creatures in other Celtic areas include the BUCCA of Wales, the Highland BODACH, and the Manx fenodyree (see GLASTIG).

Sources: Briggs, Katherine. *The Fairies in Tradition and Literature.* London: Routledge & Kegan Paul, 1967, pp. 28 ff; Keightley, Thomas. *The Fairy Mythology.* London: H. G. Bohn, 1870, pp. 307, 357 ff; MacGregor, Alasdair Alpin. *The Peat-Fire Flame: Folk-Tales and Traditions of the Highlands & Islands.* Edinburgh: The Moray Press, 1937, pp. 44 ff.

Brú na Bóinne (Brug na Bóinne) Irish mythological site. Three great mounds of rock rise on the banks of the River Boyne, between the towns of Slane and Drogheda in east central Ireland: KNOWTH, Dowth, and Newgrange. The huge tumuli are each built around an interior passageway of STANDING STONES, many carved with exuberant SPIRALS, sunbursts, and stars. Additional massive boulders hold in place the base of the mounds, and standing stones circle the central mound, Newgrange.

These sites were not built by the Celts, who came into the land almost three millennia after their construction by unknown people approximately 5,000 years ago. The so-called MEGA-LITHIC CIVILIZATION also gave us the AVEBURY and STONEHENGE sites much later than the Irish structures. The engineering and astronomical genius of these people remains unsurpassed; the central mound, Newgrange, is carefully oriented to the winter SOLSTICE sunrise, incorporating awareness of the change in the obliquity of the ecliptic (the earth's wobble), which was only rediscovered in the last century. In addition, the great buildings are constructed so that 6,000 years of rain has fallen on them without penetrating their interiors, for a system of gutters draws the water away from the inner chambers.

Although the Celts did not build the mounds, they soon wove stories around the sites, which they may also have used for ritual or burials. Newgrange was the palace (*Brú*) of BÓAND, goddess of the river beneath the mound. It was Bóand (sometimes called EITHNE) who first lived there with ELCMAR (sometimes NECHTAN). When she decided to take the DAGDA as her lover, she asked him to hold the sun steady in the sky for nine months, so that her pregnancy could pass in what seemed to be a single day. This subterfuge worked, and AONGHUS óg was safely born. He later tricked his father into leaving the Brú so that he could make it his home.

The other two mounds on the site, Knowth and Dowth, do not figure so largely in Celtic myth, nor is much known about their astronomical orientation, although there are suggestions that they are oriented toward significant moments in the solar and lunar years. Dowth, whose name means "darkness" or "darkening," is slightly smaller than the other mounds; it contains two highly ornate inner chambers. Knowth, whose rock art is unsurpassed anywhere in Europe, has recently been opened to the public.

Sources: Cooney, Gabriel. *Landscapes of Neolithic Ireland.* London: Routledge, 2000; Gwynn, Edward. *The Metrical Dindshenchas.* Part II. Vol. IX. Royal Irish Academy, Todd Lecture Series. Dublin: Hodges, Figgis, and Co., Ltd., 1906, pp. 11–25; Moane, Geraldine. "A Womb Not a Tomb: Goddess Symbols and Ancient Ireland." Canadian Women's Studies: Les cahiers de la femme. Vol. 17, 1997, pp. 7–10; O'Sullivan, Muiris. *Megalithic Art in Ireland.* Dublin: Country House, 1993; Thomas, N. L. *Irish Symbols of 3500 BC.* Cork: Mercier Press, 1988.

Brunissen Continental Celtic heroine or goddess. In Provence, France, we find tales of a FAIRY QUEEN of this name, which means "the brown one" or "the brown queen"—tales whose motifs recall such Celtic BIRD goddesses as RHIANNON. Bereft of her family and left an orphan in the magical forest of BROCÉLIANDE, Brunissen wept constantly for seven years. Only the song of magical birds could ease her until a knight of the ROUND TABLE, Giflet (or Jaufré), who had passed through several tests as he traveled through the forest and who had then fallen into an enchanted sleep, drew Brunissen's attention away from her grief. Some

have called Brunissen a legendary form of the dark side of an ancient SUN goddess, the "black sun" of the OTHERWORLD.

Source: Markale, Jean. *Women of the Celts.* Rochester, Vt.: Inner Traditions, 1986, pp. 74–75, 111.

Bruno (Bruno le Noir, La Cote Male-Taile) Arthurian hero. The only rags-to-riches tale in the Arthurian canon is that of Bruno, who worked cleaning pots when he first came to CAMELOT but finally, after he married MALEDISANT, rose to become a landowner and knight.

buada (buadha) Irish ritual. The king, in ancient Ireland, was subjected after INAUGURATION to a series of mystic regulations. He was forbidden to do some things (see GEIS), while required to do others, called *buada*: eating certain foods, behaving in certain ways. The king at TARA, for instance, had to eat the meat of the HARES of Naas, a food apparently taboo to others. Breaking these rules would result in the land's ceasing to bear food, which in turn would lead to the king's removal from office.

See also KINGSHIP.

Buan Irish heroine. When the hero MAC DATHÓ was killed, his severed HEAD was brought home to his wife Buan. She asked questions of it, and, like the famous head of BRÂN THE BLESSED, it spoke back to her, revealing the treachery that had led to his death. Buan wept herself into her grave, from which the magical HAZEL Coll Buana grew; rods of such hazel bushes were used as DIVINATION tools. Buan may descend from the early goddess BÚANANN.

Búanann Irish heroine or goddess. Mentioned by the early Irish scholar Cormac as the mother of heroes, a common epithet for a goddess, Búanann is an obscure figure whom some have connected with deities of the land's abundance.

Her name is sometimes translated as "good mother," a phrase that may be impersonal rather than specific. Some texts contrast her with ANU, mother of the gods. Some stories from the FENIAN CYCLE name her as a WARRIOR WOMAN who trained the great hero, FIONN MAC CUMHAILL.

bucca (*bwca, bucca-boo, pwca, bwci, coblyn, bwbach, bwciod*) Welsh mythological being. This household sprite of Wales was very like a BROWNIE; he would work for food, but if a householder failed to leave out a bowl of milk or other treat, mischief was likely to result. Similarly, it was important not to ask the bucca its name, for the question would cause it to leave the farm in disgust. Some folklorists and storytellers distinguish between the helpful bucca gwidden and the evil bucca dhu. The name is sometimes used as a generic term for FAIRY.

bug Celtic folkloric figure. Variations of this syllable are found in the names of many sprites, especially meddlesome ones, in Celtic countries: bug-a-boo, bugbear, bullbeggar, bogle, BOGIE, BOGAN, boggart, boogyman. As *boge* is a word found in other Indo-European languages meaning "god," the frequency of this syllable's appearance in the names of spirits in Celtic countries has been used to support the argument that such creatures are diminished deities, although other scholars utterly reject this connection. Yet others have connected this word to BOG, often seen as a liminal location or opening to the OTHERWORLD.

On the Isle of Man, a bug or buggane haunted a church reputed to have been built in the 12th century by St. Ninian, which was called by a variant of his name, St. Trinian's. The church was never roofed, because every time roofers ascended to do so, a coarse-haired apparition destroyed their work. A tailor attempted to undo the buggane's magic by sewing the roof to the rafters, but even he was chased away by the buggane, who threw his own head at the tailor. The buggane was never seen after that, but the roofing project was also abandoned.

Sources: Killip, Margaret. *The Folklore of the Isle of Man.* London: B. T. Batsford, Ltd., 1975, p. 106; Ross, Anne. "Lindow Man and the Celtic Tradition." In Stead, I. M., J. B. Bourke, and Don Brothwell. *The Lindow Man: The Body in the Bog.* Ithaca, N.Y.: Cornell University Press, 1986, pp. 162–169; Spence, Lewis. *The Minor Traditions of British Mythology.* New York: Benjamin Blom, Inc. 1972, p. 87.

building to the west Mythic theme. In traditional Celtic countries, it was ill-advised to build an addition to your house on the west side, for you might be inadvertently building on FAIRY property. Places built on "gentle land" where fairies lived would find themselves the site of endless trouble. A youth building a cowhouse on one such place—to spite the old folks who warned him against it—found his cattle mysteriously dying, and darts (see FAIRY DARTS) thrown at him while he slept in his bed. He took the roof off the cowhouse to expose it to the elements, and all was well again.

Buitch (Fir as Mraane Obbee, or "man of enchantment"; Fir as Fysseree, or "man of knowledge") Manx witch. The generic Manx word for WITCH probably derives from that English word, just as *buitcheragh* probably comes from "witchcraft." The craft was considered generally harmful among residents of the Isle of Man, although some practitioners could use their skills for good.

bull Symbolic animal. Found iconographically in Europe before the rise of the Celts, the bull may derive from the pre-Celtic past. Both in image and story, the bull was embraced by the Celts, who associated it with ferocity on the one hand and agricultural abundance on the other. Some Continental sanctuaries show evidence of bull sacrifices; entrances to shrines were sometimes guarded by bull skulls. An important Continental god connected to the bull was ESUS, who also appeared as a woodsman cutting down trees in the presence of bulls; some scholars have seen the tree and bull as parallel images of sacrifice.

The bull as emblem of strength and ferocity appears in significant Irish texts, most importantly in the *TÁIN BÓ CUAILNGE*, where the great cattle raid on ULSTER is launched because of the residence in that province of a bull, DONN CUAILNGE (actually a transformed swineherd), the only equal on the island of the great white-horned bull of AILILL mac Máta, FINNBENNACH (also a transformed swineherd). The bull as emblem of abundance connects to the general importance of CATTLE among the herd-owning Celtic people, as does the reiteration of the image of the food-beasts in the reincarnated swineherds.

See also BULL-SLEEP, WATER BULL.

Sources: Green, Miranda. *The Gods of Roman Britain.* Aylesbury: Shire Publications Ltd., 1983, p. 8; Green, Miranda. *Symbol and Image in Celtic Religious Art.* London: Routledge, 1989, pp. 89, 149; Hull, Eleanor. *The Cuchullin Saga in Irish Literature.* London: David Nutt, 1898, pp. 111 ff; MacCulloch, J. A. *The Religion of the Ancient Celts.* London: Constable, 1911, p. 243.

bullaun Symbolic object. Round stones with holes in them, found at holy WELLS and other sacred sites in Ireland, *bullauns* have been described as feminine symbols like the yoni stones of India. They were held to have healing power, especially helping women to conceive or to survive difficult pregnancies. Some *bullauns* were large flat boulders with basins, either natural or artificial, from which women would drink water ritually. *Bullauns* were also used as receptacles for libations or fluid offerings.

bull-sleep (bull feast, tarbhfleis) Irish and Scottish ritual. One of the great DIVINATION rituals of ancient Ireland was the *tarbhfleis* or

bull-sleep, used to determine who was the rightful king of TARA. A poet, who had been trained as a seer, gorged on the flesh of a just-killed BULL, then slept wrapped in its bloody hide in an attempt to divine through dreams the identity of the next king. Should the poet fail, the punishment was death. Sometimes the poet's vision was cryptic, as when the king CONAIRE appeared as a naked man surrounded by BIRDS, approaching Tara. At that moment Conaire, whose mother was a bird, dreamed that he should approach Tara naked, thus fulfilling the prophecy.

A similar ritual was known among the Scottish Highlanders, who bound up a diviner in bulls' hides and left him to dream of the future. The ritual was apparently long-lasting; a literary tourist in 1769 described a ritual of "horrible solemnity" practiced in the Trotternish district in which a man was sewn up in an oxhide and slept under a high waterfall to gain precognitive knowledge.

Sources: MacCulloch, J. A. *The Religion of the Ancient Celts.* London: Constable, 1911, p. 249; Ross, Anne. *Folklore of the Scottish Highlands.* London: B. T. Batsford, Ltd., 1976, p. 58.

burial rites See FUNERAL RITES.

butter Mythic object. Butter was connected in folklore to FAIRIES and WITCHCRAFT. Irish and Scottish rural life revolved around CATTLE, which provided food in the form of milk, butter, and cheese, as well as meat. Churning butter from cows' milk was an important part of women's work in these lands: Milk was beaten until the butterfat congealed into a yellow mass. The leftover liquid, buttermilk, was consumed as a nourishing drink, while the butter itself was shaped and stored until use. At any point in the proceedings, the process could fail and the butter be spoiled, leaving only a half-congealed, half-liquid mess. The most common complaint was that, no matter how hard the woman churned, the butter did not "come" or thicken from the liquid milk. At such a time, it was alleged that someone was "stealing" the butter, which was indeed forming within the churn but was being spirited away. As fairies were thought to have a great hunger for butter, they were a common culprit, but WITCHES were also blamed.

See BUTTERY SPIRITS.

buttery spirits   British and Scottish mythological beings. Fairies loved rich food, so this was a generic name given to fairies who stole away butter.

See FAIRY FOOD.

Buxenus   Continental Celtic god. This Gaulish divinity, known only from a single inscription, was described by the occupying Romans as similar to their warrior god MARS.

bwca   See *BUCCA.*

Cabyll-Ushtey   Manx mythological creature. On the Isle of Man, this variety of the WATER HORSE was a monster that stole cattle (and sometimes people) from the safety of land and drowned them in lakes or in the sea.

Cado   Breton mythological figure. A sea god or sea monster of Brittany, he came to force the beautiful pagan princess DAHUT to live with him forever beneath the ocean waves. In the ensuing tumult, Dahut's magnificent city of YS was destroyed. Some versions of the tale call Dahut's companion the DEVIL. Cado also appears in the story of the princess BLONDINE as a forgetful suitor who betrays his intended bride after freeing her from her magician father's captivity.

Cáel (Caol)   Irish hero. One of the great romances of Ireland is that of Cáel, a slender hero of the FIANNA who won the heart of the maiden CRÉD by reciting praise-poetry to her. She had challenged the BARDS of Ireland to create a poem about her palace, into which no man had ever stepped, with the prize being her own hand. Using the telepathic abilities that resulted from his poetic training, Cáel crafted the winning verse. But he was soon killed in battle, and Créd, overcome with grief, climbed into the grave to lie beside him one last time, then died there of grief.

caepion   See LAKE.

Cáer (Cáer Ibormeith)   Irish heroine or goddess. A moving Irish romance tells of this woman, beloved of the sweet god of poetry, AONGHUS Óg. After dreaming repeatedly of a woman he had never met, Aonghus grew so lovesick that he set out wandering through the world, searching for his mysterious beloved. Finally, on the Lake of Dragon's Mouths, Aonghus found Cáer, swimming in the form of a SWAN decked in 130 golden chains. Immediately he, too, became a swan, and the two flew away, singing so sweetly that any who heard the melody slept soundly for three days and three nights. One of W. B. Yeats's most famous poems, "The Song of Wandering Aengus," is based upon this tale.

Caer Arianrhod (Caer Aranrhod)   Welsh mythological site. The great mythic castle of ARIANRHOD, goddess or heroine of the *MABINO-GION*, was said to have been destroyed, like the Breton city of YS, by an inundation brought on by the sinfulness of its inhabitants; this is probably a post-pagan belief reflecting a Christian judgment on the wanton, free-spirited behavior of the goddess, who was said to have had affairs with MERMEN. A rock off the coast of North

Wales, nearly a mile out to sea, is said to be the wreckage of Arianrhod's great castle, while other sources say it was moved to the heavens.

Caer Idris Welsh mythological site. At the top of a mountain in Merionethshire, there is a formation of rock reputed to have magical powers. Anyone who spent the night sitting in the stone chair would greet the dawn either insane or inspired with poetry.

Caer Nefenhir Welsh mythological site. The mysterious "castle of high heaven" was an OTHERWORLD location that appears in several ancient texts, including the story of KULHWCH AND OLWEN.

Caer Wydyr Welsh mythological site. The "glass fortress" was another Welsh term for ANNWYN, the mythic and magical OTHERWORLD.

Cai Irish hero. The first BREHON or judge in Ireland was the otherwise obscure Cai, a member of the race of MILESIANS. He had studied in Egypt, where he learned the law of Moses and arranged the marriage of Míl to SCOTA, daughter of the Pharaoh. When the great biblical flood occurred, Cai fled with Moses, with whom he endured the desert sojourn, but finally he joined his own people in central Europe. From there he sailed for Ireland, serving as brehon to the invaders. The Arthurian hero KAY is also called by this name.

Cailitin (Calatin, Calatán) Irish hero. There were 28 parts to this DRUID warrior: one man and his 27 identical sons, each of whom was missing his left hand and right foot. After serving an apprenticeship in sorcery in Scotland, the multiple Cailitin enlisted in the service of the great queen MEDB, who set him/them against the great hero CÚCHULAINN, who killed the entire Cailitin contingent. But the druid's wife promptly gave birth

to two posthumous sets of horrific triplets, one each of daughters and sons; the former included the battle-crow BADB, whom Medb trained in wizardry that ultimately was used to bring about Cúchulainn's death. The one-eyed daughters, in league with Cúchulainn's enemy LUGAIDH mac Con Ró, brought about the hero's death.

Cailleach (Callech, Caillech, Cailliach, Cailleach Bhéirre, Birrn, Béarra, Bhear, Beare, Birra in Ireland; Sentainne Bérri on the Isle of Man, Caillagh ny Groamagh in Ulster, Cally Berry; in Scotland, Cailleach Bheur, Cailliche, and Carlin). Scottish and Irish folkloric figure or goddess. This important figure probably descends from a pre-Celtic divinity; she is not found among the continental Celts but is widespread in place-name and legend in Ireland and Scotland. Her name, meaning "veiled one" or "hooded one," is not of Celtic origin but is still used in modern Irish and Scots Gaelic as a name for an old woman or HAG. Her antiquity is suggested by the names born by the largest mountains in those lands (Slieve na Cailleach, Knockycallanan) and by legends that she created the landscape by dropping rocks from her apron or throwing them angrily at an enemy; creation legends often are attached to the oldest divinities of a land, and settlement in Ireland preceded the Celts by some 7,000 years. The Cailleach was said to have formed the islands off MUNSTER, in Ireland's southwest, by towing land around with a straw rope, that broke, leaving the islands of Scariff and Deenish stranded in the sea. Another tale tells how she struck an escaping BULL with a rod as he swam away from her, turning him into an island of rock.

The Cailleach was described as an ancient woman with a blue-gray face and uncannily sharp eyesight, so sharp that she could see 20 miles as clearly as her hand before her—this despite having but a single eye. In spite of her advanced age, the Cailleach was said to have inordinate strength, so much so that she could best the fastest reaper in the land in a one-on-one contest. Although she was described as unappealing and even fearsome, legend does not show her acting in a threatening fashion toward humans. To the contrary, one of her primary activities was the bestowal of SOVEREIGNTY on the chosen king, who typically had to kiss or have intercourse with the Cailleach in her hag form before she revealed herself as a splendid young woman—a motif often interpreted as a poetic image of the land blossoming under the rule of a just king. Such tales may derive from a pre-Celtic cosmic tale in which the winter sun's daughter is born as an old woman and grows younger through the winter, ending as a lovely maid, which was adopted by the arriving Celts and melded to their own myth of kingly INAUGURATION.

In Ireland the Cailleach was especially associated with Munster, where she was called the Hag of Beare after a prominent peninsula there; sometimes she has the name of Beara, while at other times she is called Boí. Her divinity was emphasized by triplication, with identical sisters said to live on the nearby Dingle and Iveraugh peninsulas. These areas were associated with the OTHERWORLD, in this case especially as a location of the CAULDRON of plenty, for the Cailleach in that region was considered a goddess of abundance, as her personal name Boí (COW, symbol of plenty) suggests.

The Cailleach was preeminently the goddess of harvest, whose name was given to the last sheaf cut in each field; dressed in women's clothes and honored during the harvest festivities, the Cailleach sheaf was kept safe until the next year's harvest. The hag goddess was sometimes said to appear as a HARE or other small creature; a shout went up from harvesters as they approached the end of a field to "drive the Cailleach" into the next field. Some argue that this harvest Cailleach was a separate goddess from the Hag of Beare, although others see both as aspects of a creative and protective goddess of the land.

In Scotland Carlin was the name given to the spirit of SAMHAIN, the end of the harvest; the sheaf representing her was exhibited in the home to discourage Otherworldly visitors. The Scottish Cailleach was, however, less connected with agriculture than with the wildwood, for she was seen as a herder of DEER, whose milk she drank. Probably because fine weather was so important during harvest time, the Cailleach was seen as a weather spirit, sometimes called "the old gloomy woman" or envisioned as a crane with sticks in her beak which forecast storms. Winter storms were sometimes greeted by the descriptive phrase, "The Cailleach is trampling the blankets tonight." She was the "sharp old wife," the Cailleach Bhuer, the latter word ("cutting") probably referring to wintry winds; she was also called the "daughter of the little sun," presumably that of winter. Mumming dances drove her away in spring, when she was replaced by the figure of Bride, a maiden figure possibly related to BRIGIT, who married a hero once the winter-witch was frozen into stone; the day of her defeat was March 29.

On the Isle of Man, the Caillagh ny Groamagh ("gloomy old woman") was a WITCH who, around IMBOLC, the beginning of spring, went out to gather twigs for her fire; if it was fine and bright, she gathered enough wood to extend the winter, but if weather kept her indoors, she ran through her previously gathered woodpile, and spring came earlier.

A hag-like figure appears in many legends from the insular Celtic lands; she was guardian of the wildwood and its animal life, an ARTEMIS-like figure who may ultimately derive from a separate aged goddess conflated with the weather-witch Cailleach. This figure, called the Hag of the Hair or the Hag of the Long Teeth, was said to punish hunters who killed pregnant animals, choking them to death with her hair; she was often accompanied by a monstrous CAT. In a story told in Scotland, the Cailleach befriended a hunter, permitting him to see which deer she struck in her herd and thus marking it as prey.

The Cailleach appeared in Arthurian legend as the LOATHY LADY who begged a kiss of a kingly contender. She appeared as a hag to PERCIVAL, mocking him because he failed to answer the questions of the mysterious FISHER KING and thus lost the sacred GRAIL that would have healed the land. She also appeared under the name of RAGNELL in a famous Arthurian story, in which she assumed the alternative forms of hag and maiden.

One of the most famous Irish medieval poems, written ca. 900 C.E., depicts the Cailleach as a woman mourning her beauty and forced to take the veil in her old age; apparently the Christian author understood the veiled woman as a nun rather than as the earlier crone goddess. However much the author of the "Lament of the Hag of Beare" attempted to bring the Cailleach to heel, he could not entirely subdue her earlier nature, for she slipped in a boast about renewing her virginity like the self-renewing Cailleach of old. In addition to her appearances in Gaelic-language literatures, the Cailleach appeared as Milton's "blew, meager hag" and as the foul "olde wyf" in Chaucer's "The wife of Bath's Tale." The 20th-century Irish poet Austin Clarke updated the Cailleach's image in his poem. "The Young Woman of Beare."

See also GLEN LYON.

Sources: Hyde, Douglas. *Beside the Fire: A Collection of Irish Gaelic Folk Stories.* London: David Nutt, 1890, pp. 161 ff; MacNeill, Máire. *The Festival of Lughnasa, Parts I and II.* Dublin: Comhairle Bhéaloideas Éireann, 1982, pp. 160–161, 412–413, 207–208; MacKenzie, Donald A. *Scottish Folk-Lore and Folk Life: Studies in Race, Culture and Tradition.* Glasgow: Blackie & Sons, Ltd., 1935, pp. 136–155; McKay, John G. *More West Highland Tales.* Vol. 2. Scottish Anthropological and Folklore Society. Edinburgh: Oliver and Boyd, 1969, pp. 166, 379 ff; Paton, C. I. *Manx Calendar Customs.* Publications of the Folk-lore Society, reprinted. Nendeln/Liechtenstein: Kraus Reprint Limited, 1968, p. 37; Spence, Lewis. *The Minor Traditions of British Mythology.* New York: Benjamin Blom, Inc., 1972, p. 78; Straffon, Cheryl. *The Earth Goddess: Celtic and Pagan Legacy of the Landscape.* London: Blandford, 1997, pp. 45–52, 179–180.

Caílte (Cailte, Caoilte)   Irish hero. A nephew of FIONN MAC CUMHAILL and hunter for the fair GRÁINNE, this FIANNA hero was a poet who entertained after the evening meal with recitations and song. He was also an athlete renowned for his fleetness of foot. How fast was Caílte? So fast that he could herd rabbits by racing around them. So fast that he was able to pick up a fistful of sand from every beach in Ireland every morning, so that if any enemy had stepped upon the land, he could smell the intruder.

In several texts Caílte was described as running the entire length and breadth of Ireland in a single day. In others, he raced with the HAG goddess CAILLEACH at CRUACHAN, cutting off her head as he ran; in other stories about the Cailleach, this motif of decapitation resulted in a rebirth missing from this version, unless it can be found in what appears to be a separate story of Caílte racing with a young and beautiful woman; because hag and maiden together comprise the goddess of SOVEREIGNTY, it is possible that the two tales are mirror images or part of the same original.

Caílte was not fast enough to outrun change. In a famous passage in the COLLOQUY OF THE ELDERS, Caílte argued pagan values against ST. PATRICK, who preached for Christianity, the worldview that eventually won out against that of the Fianna.

Caíntigern   Irish goddess or heroine. This minor figure in Irish mythology was the mother of the magical king MONGÁN, whose father was the Irish sea god, MANANNÁN MAC LIR.

Cairbre (Carbry, Carpre, Cairpre, Corpre) This common male name was borne by several Irish legendary heroes:

- **Cairbre mac Éadaoine** (Corpre mac Étaine), a poet who bore the matronymic or personal name of his mother the poet ÉTAN; his father was OGMA, god of eloquence. Cairbre expected to be treated with the hospitality due a BARD, but when he visited the royal residence at TARA, he was shut into a stinking hut and fed nothing but stale bread. His SATIRE on the stingy ruler BRES mac Elatha raised sores on the king's face; as a BLEMISHED KING could not reign, Bres was forced to step down. Cairbre employed his magical poetic power next in the second battle of MAG TUIRED, assisting the TUATHA DÉ DANANN toward victory. When he died, his mother's heart broke and she died with him.

- **Cairbre Cinn-Chait** (Catcheann), a usurper who ruled over the MILESIANS. His name, "CAT-head," was given to him because he had the head of a feline. He seized the throne of TARA by ambushing and killing the heirs. But as the Irish land would not bear fruit under an unjust king, this Cairbre's short reign was followed by the resumption of the kingship by its rightful kings.

- **Cairbre Lifechair (of the Coffey)** This high king's outrage at being taxed for his daughter's wedding led to his waging war upon the wandering heroes of the FIANNA, which in turn led to the destruction of that legendary fighting force—but at the cost of Cairbre's life, at the renowned battle of GABHAIR.

- **Cairbre Nia Fer,** a king of TARA who opposed CÚCHULAINN and was killed by him; he was renowned for his 12 handsome daughters.

Sources: O hÓgain, Dáithí. *Myth, Legend and Romance: An Encyclopedia of the Irish Folk Tradition.* New York: Prentice-Hall Press, 1991, p. 70; Ross, Anne. *Pagan Celtic Britain: Studies in Iconography and Tradition.* London: Routledge & Kegan Paul, 1967, p. 100.

Cairenn Irish heroine. The consort of EOCHAID Mugmedón and mother of NIALL of the Nine Hostages, Cairenn was said to have been a British princess who was captured and enslaved in Ireland despite her regal status; thus the great king of TARA, ancestor of the O'Neill family, would have been half-British. Eochaid's first wife, MONGFHINN, was jealous of her husband, and thus Cairenn stole away from Tara's court to give birth near a sacred WELL. As with many early Irish kings, Niall's birth and later life are described in mythological terms.

cairn Mythological site. On the tops of mountains and at other significant places throughout the Celtic lands, mounds of rock are found, left by the unknown pre-Celtic people of the MEGALITHIC CIVILIZATION. Some of these have interior chambers, while others apparently do not. Many cairns were adapted by the Celts to their own mythological uses and became sites of legend and, possibly, ritual as well (see COURT TOMBS).

cait sith Scottish mythological animal. In the Scottish Highlands, this black spectral creature of ambiguous species (probably feline) was so large that it was sometimes mistaken for a BLACK DOG. Although its name ("fairy CAT") suggests that it was of the FAIRY race, it was also reported to be a shape-shifting WITCH or her familiar.

cake *(struan, strone)* Symbolic object. At certain feasts, cake (sometimes called bannock) was served, not only as a festive food but as part of a ritual. In some sites, the cake was displayed to all in attendance, then won by the best dancer or athlete, who was then charged with breaking and distributing the cake. One piece of the cake was sometimes blackened, and the person who drew that piece was said to be "devoted," a custom that may suggest an ancient rite of HUMAN SACRIFICE.

Sources: Carmichael, Alexander. *Carmina Gadelica: Hymns and Incantations.* Hudson, N.Y.: Lindisfarne Press, 1992, pp. 88, 624; Ross, Anne. "Lindow Man and the Celtic Tradition." In Stead, I. M., J. B. Bourke, and Don Brothwell. *The Lindow Man: The Body in the Bog.* Ithaca, N.Y.: Cornell University Press, 1986, pp. 162–169.

Caladbolg Irish mythological object. The sword of the great warrior FERGUS mac Róich may have been associated with king ARTHUR's magical EXCALIBUR, for its name reflects the Welsh name for the latter. Caladbolg caused rainbows whenever Fergus used it, as when he lopped off the tops of the midlands mountains, creating the flattened hills we see today.

calamity meat Irish folkloric motif. This term was used of animals that died accidentally, falling over a cliff or crushed by a boulder or in another unusual fashion. The bodies of such animals were supposed to be buried whole, with not a bite taken of them nor a steak cut off their flanks, for they were thought bewitched by the FAIRIES—or, even worse, to be the disguised body of an aged dead fairy, left behind when the living animal was stolen AWAY. It was best as well to puncture the animal's hide with an IRON nail before burying it, to protect the land in which it was buried from further fairy influence. Until recent times, rural people in Scotland and Ireland refused to eat calamity meat for fear of devouring a fairy cadaver.

Sources: MacGregor, Alasdair Alpin. *The Peat-Fire Flame: Folk-Tales and Traditions of the Highlands & Islands.* Edinburgh: The Moray Press, 1937, p. 3; O hEochaidh, Séan. *Fairy Legends of Donegal.* Trans. by Máire MacNeill. Dublin: Comhairle Bhéaloideas Éireann, 1977, p. 79.

Caledonia Celtic land. Now used poetically to mean Scotland, Caledonia was originally a tribal territory in northern Britain. When the Romans occupied the island, they encountered a people called the Cadedonii, who later united with other Celtic tribes including the Lugi, Taezali, Decantae, and Smeretae to form the Caledonian confederacy, which fiercely opposed Roman occupation. The Caledonian language, still not completely understood, has been claimed as an ancestor to or relative of Welsh. The ancient tribal name still hides in the name Dunkeld, the "fort of the Caledonians," in Scotland.

calendar Cosmological concept. Unlike most ancient people, the Celts did not divide the seasons at SOLSTICES (the year's longest and shortest days) and EQUINOXES (when day and night are equal). Rather, they began and ended seasons at the central points between the solar pivots. Thus winter began on SAMHAIN, November 1, midway between the autumnal equinox on September 21 and the winter solstice on December 21. Similarly, spring began on IMBOLC, February 1; summer on BELTANE, May 1; and fall on LUGHNASA, August 1. Some scholars have argued that this annual division was not Celtic but Irish, since such a calendar is not found among the continental Celts and since it more clearly reflects the seasonal cycle in Ireland than in France. Such great stone monuments as STONEHENGE and Newgrange (see BRÚ NA BÓINNE) are pre-Celtic, designed to mark points of the solar year rather than the midpoints celebrated by the Celts; nonetheless the Celts adapted them to their own use and wove myth and legend around them.

The Celts saw darkness as preceding light, both in the diurnal and the annual cycle. Thus a day began at sundown; Samhain began on the evening of October 31, which we now call Hallowe'en or the "hallowed evening." Similarly Samhain marked the beginning of the new year and the end of the old. This precedence of night over day has given rise alternatively to theories of a dualistic struggle between light and dark on the one hand, and a matrifocal society that honored women's cycles on the other; neither interpretation has been proved or disproved.

A break in this pattern came in the organization of the lunar months, which began with the full moon, perhaps because it was more readily visible than the dark new moon. The COLIGNY Calendar of the continental Celtic people shows the months as follows: Samonious (October/November), Dumannios (November/December), Ruaros (December/January), Anagantios (January/February), Ogronios (February/March), Cutios (March/April), Giamonios (April/May), Simivisonios (May/June), Equos (June/July), Elembiuos (July/August), Edrinios (August/

September), and Cantlos (September/October). A 13th month, Mid Samonious, was added every 30 months to adapt the lunar year to the longer solar year.

Source: Danaher, Kevin. "Irish Folk Tradition and the Celtic Calendar." In Robert O'Driscoll, ed. *The Celtic Consciousness.* New York: George Braziller, 1981, pp. 217–242.

Caliburn (Carliburnus, Caladfwlch, Caedvwlch) British mythological object. Alternative name for EXCALIBUR, the magical sword of ARTHUR.

Callanish (Callernish) Scottish mythological site. This STONE CIRCLE on the isle of Lewis and Harris, part of the Outer Hebrides off Scotland, is widely renowned. Every 18 years, the full moon, as seen from Callanish, rises from the feet of a woman-shaped hill and travels across her body until it sets behind her head. Celtic peoples probably converted such monuments, built by the MEGALITHIC CIVILIZATION some 4,000 years prior to their arrival in the land, to their own ritual purposes. Local tradition has it that the stones of Callanish, like many other stone circles, were originally GIANTS who were turned to stone, in this case for refusing the opportunity to convert to Christianity.

Sources: Grinsell, Leslie V. *Folklore of Prehistoric Sites in Britain.* London: David & Charles, 1976, p. 28; Straffon, Cheryl. *The Earth Goddess: Celtic and Pagan Legacy of the Landscape.* London: Blandford, 1997, p. 18.

Callirius British god. Equated by the Romans with the woodland god SILVANUS, Callirius was honored at a temple near Colchester; he may have been the *GENIUS LOCI* of the region.

Camelot Welsh and British mythological site. Several places in England and Wales lay claim to having been the site of the legendary court of King ARTHUR, where noble knights gathered around the ROUND TABLE to determine their next adventurous quest; a favorite contender is Cadbury Camp in Somerset. The great palace was said to have been erected overnight by the magician MERLIN. The name Camelot has come to mean an ideal kingdom, despite the downfall of its heroic king Arthur. Camelot should be distinguished from AVALON, the OTHERWORLD realm of the LADY OF THE LAKE and other powerful beings; Camelot was entirely of this world, though affected by influences from beyond.

Camlan (Camlaun, Camlann) Welsh mythological site. This unknown spot was said by early writers to be the site of the final battle of king ARTHUR's reign, at which he was defeated by his son/nephew MORDRED and from which he was taken to the OTHERWORLD by the mysterious LADY OF THE LAKE.

Camulos (Camulus) British god. Little is left to identify the significance of this god whose name was incorporated in the important town of Camulodunum, "fort of Camulos," now Colchester. The invading Romans identified him with their war god MARS. It has been theorized that he may be a parallel to the Irish ancestral father CUMHALL, father of the hero FIONN MAC CUMHAILL.

canach (catkin, *clòimh-chat*) Scottish folkloric motif. The fluffy white wool of the cattail, a reed that grows in marshes, was once thought to be shape-shifted WITCHES, riding to their secret gatherings on the winds. The same was said to be true of snowflakes, in which witches could hide as they traveled. The fibers of catkins or cat-wool, which carry the seeds of such trees as the birch and the poplar, could be twisted into little white cords that were reputed to keep away WITCHCRAFT and other evil.

Source: McKay, John G. *More West Highland Tales.* Vol. 2. Scottish Anthropological and Folklore Society. Edinburgh: Oliver and Boyd, 1969, pp. 369, 370.

Candlemas   See IMBOLC.

Canola   Irish heroine. The HARP, one of today's emblems of Ireland, was invented by this legendary woman. After arguing with a lover, Canola left his side to wander the night. At the seashore, she heard sweet music and, under its influence, fell asleep under the stars. Upon awakening, she discovered that the music had been made by sinews, still attached to the rib-bones of a whale, through which the wind was singing. This discovery inspired her to build the first harp.

Cano mac Gartnáin   Irish hero. This character is closely parallel to CÁEL, for both were warrior BARDS beloved of CRÉD, the princess of CONNACHT, daughter of the legendary king GUAIRE. Cano fled to Ireland after his father's murder, and although Créd was already married to a king, she and Cano fell hopelessly and instantly in love. Although he refused to consummate their affair until he had regained his kingdom, Cano gave his EXTERNAL SOUL to Créd in the form of a stone. Their attempt to meet for a tryst was thwarted by Créd's stepson, child of her rejected husband, and in despair the queen killed herself—crushing Cano's soul-stone in the process and thus killing him as well.

Caoimhe   (Keeva, Keeva of the White Skin) Irish heroine. The daughter of the great hero FIONN MAC CUMHAILL, she does not figure significantly in legend, except as the wife of Fionn's great enemy, GOLL MAC MORNA.

Caointeach   (Caoineag) Scottish mythological being. Highland names ("wailer" and "weeper" respectively) for the BANSHEE, who called out when death was imminent. She sat by a waterfall and wailed before any death, but made a particular commotion when disaster loomed; the Caointeach of the Macdonalds mourned for days in advance of the horrific massacre at Glencoe.

The Caointeach was sometimes seen to wash the clothing of the doomed at night, like the WASHER AT THE FORD. She was not an unfriendly spirit, despite the woe her presence predicted, and she found human grief to be desperately affecting, causing her to weep even more copiously. Like other FAIRIES, these beings were carefully ignored; it was especially important not to reward them for doing their jobs, which caused them to disappear leaving the family without a designated death-warner.

The Welsh version of this creature was called the Cyhyreath; her cries were said to imitate the sighs and groans of the dying.

Caolainn   Irish heroine or goddess. This name is given to a female figure associated with a healing WELL in Co. Roscommon, where Caolainn was said to have healed herself of a self-inflicted wound. When a man spoke admiringly of her beautiful eyes, Caolainn gouged them out and flung them at him, then groped her way to the well, tore rushes from its perimeter, and wiped her bloody sockets, whereupon her eyes grew back. The same story was told of BRIGIT, the Christian saint, who was also associated with wells that offer HEALING for eye complaints.

Caoranach   (Keeronagh, Caorthannach) Irish mythological being. This monstrous serpent lived in the waters of LOUGH DERG in Donegal, in Ireland's northern province of ULSTER. Near the Christian pilgrimage site of Station Island, a stone is still pointed out as the skeleton of this creature. Now called the Altar of Confession, the indented stone resembles a *BULLAUN*, an ancient pitted stone whose use and significance is unclear. The serpent Caoranach—like the sky demon CORRA (the DEVIL'S MOTHER), who may have been the same mythic creature—was killed by ST. PATRICK, who fought Caoranach for two nights and two days while both were submerged in the waters of her LAKE. Many legends say that Patrick did not succeed in killing Caoranach, who is allegedly still alive in the lake and appears during stormy weather. Like a WATER HORSE, she could suck men and cattle into her voracious mouth; she was also a portent of doom, for anyone who saw a light inside her cave would die within the year.

Earlier legends link Caoranach to mythological heroes like FIONN MAC CUMHAILL and his son, CONAN. When the shinbones of Fionn's mother were thrown into Lough Derg, they immediately came alive as Caoranach. The serpent swam instantly to shore and swallowed Conan, but the hero fought his way out from her belly, killing the serpent in the process. When Conan emerged, he was both skinless and hairless, thus earning the name Conan Muil, "bald Conan." The blood of the dying serpent stained the lake red, hence its name ("Dark Lake"). In a Christian version of this story, Patrick himself was swallowed by Caoranach, cutting his way out with his crosier.

See also GARRAVOGUE.

Source: MacNeill, Máire. *The Festival of Lughnasa, Parts I and II.* Dublin: Comhairle Bhéaloideas Éireann, 1982, p. 503.

captive fairies   Irish mythological theme. Although not easy to do, it was possible to ensnare some kinds of FAIRIES under certain circumstances. LEPRECHAUNS could be captured by grabbing the little fellows by their teeny shoulders; they employed all kinds of trickery to escape, and so rarely did their stash of hoarded GOLD pass into human hands. Fairy women who swam about earthly LAKES disguised as SWANS could be captured if one stole the swanskin robe that lay in the reeds by the side of the lake (see SWAN-MAIDEN). The robe, however, had to be kept from the maiden's sight thereafter, for no matter how many children an apparently contented fairy wife might bear to her human husband, should she reclaim her swanskin she would disappear into the nearest lake. The same was true of SEAL-wives or SILKIES, whose skin robes had to be similarly concealed; several famous

families of Ireland, including the Coneellys and the Flahertys, are said to have descended from such captured seal-wives.

captive in fairyland   See FAIRY KIDNAPPING.

Caradawg   (Carradoc, Caradog)   Welsh hero. In the Welsh mythological texts called the *MABINOGION*, Caradawg appeared as the son of the heroic king BRÂN THE BLESSED. Although still a youth, Caradawg was left behind as ruler of Wales when his father traveled to Ireland to wage war against the king who was holding Caradawg's aunt BRANWEN in an abusive marriage. But Caradawg was unable to hold his father's throne against a usurper, CASWALLAWN, who killed all the royal retainers but Caradawg; his failure to protect the throne caused Caradawg to die of heartbreak. Another Caradawg, who bears the name of Freichfras ("of the strong arm") or Briefbras ("short-armed"), is named in literature as an adviser to king ARTHUR.

Carlin   Scottish heroine or goddess. In Scotland, this was a name for the CAILLEACH as a harvest divinity.

Carman   Irish goddess or heroine. This powerful figure in Irish legend was said to have been one of the earliest rulers of Ireland, a mighty but destructive sorceress whose three sons were equally distressing: darkness (Dub), wickedness (Dothur), and violence (Dian). Together they maliciously blighted Ireland's corn until the people of the goddess DANU, the TUATHA DÉ DANANN, mustered sufficient magic to drive Carman's sons from the land.

Carman herself was a greater challenge. First the Tuatha Dé sent a BARD against her, but he failed to stop her destructive energy; then a satirist came, but he too failed; finally the sorceress BÉ CHUILLE cast a spell sufficient to undo Carman's. Upon hearing that her sons had been killed, Carman died of grief. Despite the enmity between the Tuatha Dé and Carman, a great festival was staged in her honor, called the ÓENACH CARMAN, whose site has been variously located on the Curragh in Co. Kildare and on the plains of the River Barrow in the same county, suggesting that she was a force to be propitiated. Similar festivals were also staged in honor of the goddesses TAILTIU and TLACHTGA, suggesting an ancient connection of such goddesses to the harvest season.

Sources: Gwynn, Edward. *The Metrical Dindshenchas.* Vol. III. Royal Irish Academy, Todd Lecture Series. Dublin: Hodges, Figgis, and Co., Ltd., 1906–1924, pp. 3–27; MacCulloch, J. A. *The Religion of the Ancient Celts.* London: Constable, 1911, p. 167; Raftery, Brian. *Pagan Celtic Ireland: The Enigma of the Irish Iron Age.* London: Thames and Hudson, 1994, p. 82.

Carravogue   See GARRAVOGUE.

Carrigogunnel   See GRANA.

cart   Continental Celtic symbol. In many parts of the continental Celtic world, archaeologists have found models of a feminine figure—assumed to be a GODDESS—being borne on a cart or wagon, some of them from the earliest Celtic era (ca. 800 B.C.E.). The bronze Strettweg cart shows this figure; the arguably Celtic or Celtic-inspired GUNDESTRUP CAULDRON shows small men riding alongside a cart on which a larger female figure is carried.

There is little textual evidence of a ritual involving a cart, except the description by the Roman historian Tacitus of a Germanic rite in which a goddess was carried in an ox-drawn wagon around the land in the spring. A similar rite was known in Celtic Gaul, where the goddess was called BERECYNTHIA, a name not otherwise known. In some areas, the annual conveyance of the goddess through the greening spring survived Christianization, for we have early medieval records of the goddess riding her cart through the fields to protect the crops.

Source: Berger, Pamela. *The Goddess Obscured: Transformation of the Grain Protectress from Goddess to Saint.* Boston: Beacon Press, 1985, p. 31.

Casan Buidhe   (Yellow Legs, Weaver of the Yellow Legs) Scottish folkloric figure. This famous wizard preyed upon travelers as they attempted to cross rivers. He shape-shifted into a large STAG and terrified those in the middle of the ford so that they dropped their treasures to run for safety, or drowned in fright, whereupon he helped himself to their wealth. Finally, a SMITH (always a magical being) confronted the wizard and destroyed him.

Source: McKay, John G. *More West Highland Tales.* Vol. 2. Scottish Anthropological and Folklore Society. Edinburgh: Oliver and Boyd, 1969, p. 461.

casting a glamour   See GLAMOUR.

Caswallawn   (Casswallon, Caswallan, Caswallan fab Beli Mawr) Welsh hero. In the Welsh stories compiled as the MABINOGION, this warrior wore a cloak of invisibility that gave him great advantage in battle. He used it to wage war against his own cousins, taking the throne of BRÂN THE BLESSED from his son CARADAWG while Brân was in Ireland fighting to free his hostage sister, BRANWEN. Caswallawn contended with the Roman emperor Julius Caesar for the love of the fair FFLUR, possibly a form of the goddess of SOVEREIGNTY whose approval permitted a man to rule.

cat   Folkloric animal. In ancient Ireland, wild cats resembling the cougar or mountain lion ranged the land; the pre-Celtic people of the MEGALITHIC CIVILIZATION may have honored them, if the burial of a cat at the great chamber of FOURKNOCKS is evidence of a religious rite. Although the big cats have long become extinct in all the ancient Celtic lands, they live on in myth and legend, and the smaller Scottish wild cat is still found in the woods and moors of northern Scotland.

Prowling the night with glowing eyes, showing extraordinary physical flexibility and agility, cats were believed to seek the companionship of old women who practiced magic as WITCHES. On the Isle of Man, all cats were believed unlucky, while in Ireland only black ones were to be avoided—unless their blood was needed for healing rituals. In Scotland black cats were believed to be SHAPE-SHIFTING witches, a belief that may explain some common American Hallowe'en decorations. The contemporary fear of black cats, like their association with witches and Hallowe'en, may be Celtic in origin, although some have traced the connection to the Greek goddess of witchcraft, Hecate, who was also associated with cats.

The connection of cats and witchcraft includes fortune-telling rituals; DIVINATION by killing cats was used in Scotland. Both witches and cats were believed to have the power to control or predict the weather. When a cat washed its face, rain was supposed to follow; if it walked away from the fire, a storm was brewing. Caution and even discomfort was the typical reaction to cats, hence the common Irish greeting, "God bless all here except the cat."

Several important mythological sites are named for cats, although there is little mythology left to explain the names. A cave in Ireland's Co. Roscommon, believed to open into the OTHERWORLD, is called OWEYNAGAT, the Cave of the Cats. It is not known whether Oweynagat is the cave recorded as the site of a divination rite involving a spectral cat. In Scotland's Black Wood of Chesthill in magical GLEN LYON, a tall megalith called Clach Taghairm nan Cat, "the stone of the devil cat," was said to be where cats gathered to celebrate Hallowe'en.

Cats are found in myth as well as folklore. Black cats, like BLACK DOGS, were often found at Otherworldly sites and events. Cats appear in a number of Celtic tales, usually in circumstances that suggest a connection to the Otherworld. In the *Voyage of MAELDUIN*, the hero came upon a magical island on which a majestic palace stood, all hung with gorgeous draperies. There a single cat lived in splendor. When one of the hero's companions attempted to steal some of the island's treasures, the cat shape-shifted into an arrow and brought the thief down.

The most famous extant legend regarding supernatural cats came from Ireland, where it was said that the land's chief BARD, Seanchán Toirpéist, was disgusted once when mice walked upon the banquet table and stuck their whiskers in the egg he was about to eat. This inspired him to compose a SATIRE in which he derided the Irish cats—including their high king—for failing to keep the island free of mice. Across the land, in his palace at the BRÚ NA BÓINNE, the king of cats Irusan magically overheard the satire and swelled up to twice his normal size in fury at the insult. He leapt across the land and grabbed the poet, fully intending to eat him, but when the grappling pair reached the abbey of Clonmacnoise, where the saints Kieran and Dunstan were doing some metalwork (see SMITH), the plot was foiled. The saints threw metal rods like javelins at the cat, which dropped the terrified poet and disappeared.

Sources: Campbell, John Grigorson. *Witchcraft and Second Sight in the Highlands and Islands of Scotland.* Detroit: Singing Tree Press, 1970, pp. 6, 31 ff; Kennedy, Patrick. *Legendary Fictions of the Irish Celts.* New York: Benjamin Blom, 1969, pp. 14–15.

Cathaír Mór (Cathaoir Mór) Irish hero. Before the great CONN of the Hundred Battles became king of TARA, this king—whose name means "great battle-lord"—reigned over the land. Although little was recorded of the king himself except his replacement by and death at the hands of Conn, Cáthaír was the father of several significant women: EITHNE Tháebfhota, wife of the hero and king CORMAC MAC AIRT and mother of his son CAIRBRE Lifechair; and COCHRANN, mother of the romantic hero DIARMAIT Ua Duibne. One text describes a dream of Cathaír's, in which a woman was pregnant an unduly long time, finally giving birth to a son near a fragrant, singing fruit tree. His DRUID explained to Cathaír that the lady was the River Slaney that ran near Tara, her child the harbor at its mouth, and the singing tree the king himself.

Cathbad (Cathbhadh)   Irish hero. A powerful DRUID of the court of king CONCOBAR MAC NESSA, Cathbad was an important figure in the ULSTER CYCLE. Lusting after the studious maiden Assa ("gentle"), Cathbad had her tutors killed to gain access to her; this violent destruction of her peaceful life turned the girl into a warrior who went by the name of NESSA ("ungentle"). Cathbad was undeterred, however, by his intended victim's fierce strength. Surprising Nessa at her bath—the only time she was without her weapons—he raped her and thereafter kept her hostage as his concubine.

But Nessa outwitted Cathbad. Skilled in reading omens, she realized that a WORM that she found floating in a glass of wine would impregnate her with a hero, whereupon she swallowed it, conceiving the king CONCOBAR MAC NESSA. Cathbad later became the teacher of Concobar's hero, CÚCHULAINN, and father of the heroine FINDCHÓEM, who employed the same method of insemination as had Nessa. Cathbad made an appearance in the romantic tale of DEIRDRE, before whose birth he predicted she would bring sorrow to Ulster.

Cathleen ni Houlihan (Caitlín Ní hUallacháin) Irish goddess. This name for the SOVEREIGNTY goddess was made popular by W. B. Yeats in his play of the same title, in which the resplendent actress and activist Maud Gonne appeared as Cathleen, a poor old woman who turned into a queen, echoing the tales of the CAILLEACH.

Cath Paluc   Welsh mythological figure. "Paluc's Cat" was a Welsh monster in feline form who ate 180 men at every meal. The presence of such figures in Celtic mythology has led some to argue for an ancient cult of the CAT, of which Cath Paluc is believed to be a vestige.

Cathubodua (Cauth Bova, Badb Catha)   Continental Celtic goddess. Gaulish goddess whose name means "Battle Raven." See BADB.

Cat Sith   Scottish folkloric figure. In the Highlands, this huge dark creature was believed to be either a FAIRY or a WITCH in disguise.

cattle   Symbolic animal. Cattle were an important economic resource to the Celts, who were predominantly a herding people. Thus cattle not only represented wealth symbolically but defined it in fact. In consequence, many Celtic divinities, rituals, and myths were connected with cattle. The white COW goddess BÓ FIND represented the abundance of stable, healthy herds, while the MÓRRÍGAN was the OTHERWORLD aspect of cattle, driving her herds through the narrow opening of the cave at OWEYNAGAT and away from the surface world. DIVINATION was performed by sleeping in the hide of a recently slaughtered BULL (see BULL-SLEEP); cattle were driven between signal fires on BELTANE, the beginning of the summer grazing season, to magically assure their health and well-being.

See also BUTTER.

cattle raid   Irish ritual and mythological text. Stealing CATTLE from neighboring kingdoms represented an ongoing and dangerous sport for young men, who gained acclaim and power through their prowess in the cattle raid. Because cattle represented wealth and power, there may have been a ritual aspect to these cattle raids; certainly they appear in numerous myths.

The cattle raid (Táin) was also an Irish literary form, the most famous of which described the epic raid by CONNACHT's queen MEDB against the PROVINCE of ULSTER, in order to steal a great BULL who could match her husband's legendary white bull FINNBENNACH; the story is told in the epic *TÁIN BÓ CUAILNGE*. Another famous cattle raid involved FRÁECH, husband of Medb's daughter FINNABAIR.

Caturix Continental Celtic god. Inscriptions to this obscure god, whose name seems to mean "king of battle," have been found in central European regions; the occupying Romans identified Caturix with their warrior god MARS.

caul Folkloric motif. Infants are sometimes born with a veil of skin, called a caul, over their faces. In most cultures, this was believed to set the child apart from others in some way; such was the case in Celtic lands, where the caul typically signified access to OTHERWORLD knowledge. On the seagirt Isle of Man, children born with a caul were believed to be blessed, as they could never drown; they grew up to become sought-after fishing mates. The caul was usually preserved and worn or carried as a charm against the sea's fury. In Ireland the caul was called the "cap of happiness" and was preserved as a good-luck charm.

Cauld Lad British folkloric figure. This form of the BROWNIE was occasionally found in Britain, where he shivered nakedly but helped around the house until the householder, worried about his condition, gave him a cloak, thus LAYING THE FAIRY and causing his disappearance.

cauldron Celtic symbolic object. The cauldron was both a domestic object, used in the home for brewing and stewing, and a sacred one, the secret place where new life was brewed and stewed. As such, it was a symbol of great power to the Celts. The Roman author Strabo described a sacramental cauldron sent by the Cimbri to Caesar Augustus; Strabo claimed that the Celts ritually cut the throats of prisoners over such cauldrons. A ritual of that sort may have been the reason for the creation of the GUNDESTRUP CAULDRON. This great silver vessel was found in Denmark, not commonly considered Celtic territory, but the mythic figures on the cauldron (including CERNUNNOS and an unidentified gigantic goddess), as well as interlacing abstract decorations, mark it as a likely Celtic product. Other, smaller cauldrons have been found deposited in BOGS and LAKES, apparently as offerings to the OTHERWORLD powers.

The cauldron's basic meaning was fullness and abundance; Ireland's "good god," called the DAGDA, had a cauldron forever filled with good things, while the Welsh goddess CERIDWEN used hers for cooking up a broth that endowed drinkers with unfathomable wisdom (see TALIESIN). Yet even abundance and plenty could be mismanaged. In the Welsh *MABINOGION*, we find a cauldron of rebirth—Irish in origin—wherein soldiers' bodies were thrown so that they might come back, alive yet soulless, to fight again.

cave Symbolic site. Openings to the OTHERWORLD held a special place in the Celtic imagination. These were to be found in such liminal zones as BOGS and swamps; in land surrounded by water, such as seagirt ISLANDS; and in places that join different levels of the world, such as caves and MOUNTAINS. The parallelism of cave and mountain was reinforced when raths or HILLFORTS were built near natural caves. In Ireland the most mythologically significant cave was OWEYNAGAT, the Cave of the Cats, a natural underground gallery beneath MEDB's rath at CRUACHAN in Co. Roscommon. Down its tiny entry, the great queen MÓRRÍGAN drove her Otherworldly cattle; within it, the great CAULDRON of abundance, once kept at Tara but later returned to the Otherworld, was stored. The cave, like other passages to the Otherworld, was considered especially powerful on SAMHAIN, when spirits rushed around it. Many of the epics set at Cruachan begin on Samhain, including the *Adventure of NERA* and the famous TÁIN BÓ CUAILNGE.

Ceasg Scottish mythological being. Sea captains were often born from the mating of this Highland MERMAID—half woman, half SALMON—who was also known as the *maighdean na tuinne* or "maiden of the wave." Like other captured FAIRIES, she was said to grant wishes to her captor. But like any other seagoing siren, she was also capable of capturing humans, who usually lost their lives upon entering her watery domain.

Ceibhfhionn (Cabfin) Irish goddess. This Irish goddess of inspiration stood beside the WELL of wisdom, filling a vessel with its water, which she then spilled on the ground rather than letting humans drink it. She may be a human form of the magical FISH that lived within the pool, an elusive being that kept wisdom for itself by eating the nuts that fell from enchanted HAZEL trees into the well's water.

Ceisnoidhe Uladh See DEBILITY OF THE ULSTERMEN.

Celidon (Cellydon) Arthurian site. Like the legendary forest BROCÉLIANDE in Brittany, the dense woods of Celidon in Britain appear in several legends, although their actual location is not known. An important battle that led to a victory for king ARTHUR's knights took place at Celidon; the magician MERLIN wandered there during his period of madness.

Cellach Irish hero. Rapist son of the good king CORMAC MAC AIRT, he played little role in myth except to cause the end of his father's reign; when Cormac fought the vengeful father of Cellach's victim, his eye was put out, thus forcing him to step down from the throne of TARA because a BLEMISHED KING could not reign.

Celtchair Irish hero. The laws of HOSPITALITY were taken very seriously by the Celts, and when the warrior Celtchair offended against this tradi-

tion by spilling blood on the FIDCHELL board on which his king, CONCOBAR MAC NESSA, was contending with the hero CÚCHULAINN, Celtchair was forced to take on three impossible tasks to repair the damage to his reputation. He managed two of them, but then was killed when a spectral DOG, scourge of the land, splattered its blood upon him as he killed it. The poisonous blood ended Celtchair's life, but he died with his honor intact.

Celtic pantheon Celtic religion was fundamentally pantheistic, based on a belief in many rather than one god. Fiercely tribal and extraordinarily local, the Celtic religious world was also radically different from the structured, hierarchical mythologies of Greece and Rome. Few Celtic GODS or GODDESSES are known from more than one carved inscription or a single mention in a text; the majority appear to have been divinities of a small region, a tiny unit of population, or both (see TUATH). This extreme polytheism gave rise to the oath used by Celts in Roman times, "I swear by the gods my people swear by." Any vision of an organized Celtic pantheon, with one divinity at the top and descending ranks beneath, cannot be supported by literature or archaeology.

The invading Romans dealt with the overwhelming number of Celtic divinities by interpreting them all as versions of Roman gods; thus we have dozens of titles for MERCURY or MINERVA. But how closely Celtic deities actually corresponded to Roman ones is impossible to know. The APOLLO of one place may have been a healing god, while the Apollo of another place downriver was a divinity of song and magic. Thus Roman renaming of regional divinities both preserved them in vestigial form and cloaked their true identities.

Source: Brunaux, Jean Louis. *The Celtic Gauls: Gods, Rites and Sanctuaries.* London: Seaby, 1988, pp. 68–70.

Celtic religion The differences between religion, mysticism, superstition, ritual, and myth have been carefully articulated by scholars, but there is often unacknowledged bias in the use of one or the other word to describe the practices and beliefs of people in Celtic lands. Religion is technically the practice of ritual based in a socially supported sequence of narratives; mysticism is a personal engagement with nature that results in a feeling of timeless unity; superstition is a baseless belief or ritualized behavior that often represents a degraded form of an earlier religion. Mythology and ritual are connected, the first being a narrative or narrative sequence, the second being actions or behaviors that evoke or reflect that myth.

Certain problems arise in defining and describing Celtic religion. The Celtic peoples did not employ writing, believing that religious secrets were better shared orally. Thus there is little textual evidence for what the Celts believed; what we have was written down after literacy arrived, along with Christianity, in Celtic lands. We also have some texts written by those who were at war with the Celts, including the Roman general (later emperor) Caesar and the army geographer Tacitus; whether they accurately recorded what their enemies believed is unclear, even doubtful. Thus the mythic basis of Celtic ritual may not be accurately known.

The same is true of Celtic ritual. The DRUIDS left no prayer books or other evidence of how they enlivened mythological narrative through ritual. We have only descriptions of Celtic rituals written by foreigners and enemies. Even when accuracy was their goal—and propaganda-conscious leaders writing to convince an audience to continue a war may have not made accuracy a prime intention—a writer might misapprehend the meaning of ritual, making a false analogy to a known ritual or failing to see references that the typical member of Celtic society would immediately recognize.

Besides written texts, Celtic religion can be studied through analysis of objects found by archaeologists. Here too, however, we face difficulties of interpretation. Whether an object was intended for ritual, was merely decorative, or was made for nonreligious use is not necessarily clear from examining it. Similarly, its connection to mythological narrative may not be known, either because the myth has been altered in transmission or because it has been completely lost. In addition, Celtic artists began to follow classical models after the Romanization of Celtic lands, so it becomes extremely difficult to tease out the solely Celtic part of Romano-Celtic finds.

Despite these difficulties, some aspects of Celtic religion are generally accepted. It was polytheistic, meaning that there were many gods (see POLYTHEISM). There were, in fact, so many gods and goddesses that some seem only to have been known in a very small area or among a small group. In addition, the Celts left no grand TEMPLES, leading scholars to picture a ritual life celebrated in NATURE. Together, these two facts lead to a description of Celtic religion as based in the natural aspects of the land, which varied greatly from place to place and therefore may have been quite differently celebrated.

Celtic revival Contemporary movement. In the last quarter-century, many people have been drawn to Celtic spirituality and mythology, seeking a spiritual vision rooted in heritage that meets contemporary needs. Ecological concerns draw those who find in the Celts a pre-capitalistic view of land that supports a post-capitalist utopian vision; to such seekers, the Celtic view of NATURE as permeated with spiritual meaning is significant and satisfying. Others cast a womanist or feminist eye on Celtic literature in which strong, active women play a major role. Still others are drawn by personal heritage and the search for deep roots in an imagined pagan past. Many of these people simply read books about Celtic matters and listen to spiritually inspired Celtic music; others take self-described pilgrimages to Celtic lands, while yet others form groups that practice rites allegedly derived from Celtic sources. Such seekers may call themselves DRUIDS, pagans (see PAGANISM), NEO-PAGANS, wiccans (see WICCA), or WITCHES.

Such attempts are not new; the British order of Druids, established almost a hundred years ago, grew from an earlier revival of interest in personal applications of real or imagined Celtic lore, while the great burst of Irish creativity called the CELTIC TWILIGHT was both ritual and artistic. Celtic revivalism has grown impressively in recent years, leading some scholars to object to—even to deride—its varied movements. From a scholarly point of view, many participants are indeed deficient; they do not read the original languages or even, in some cases, seek out competent translations of significant texts. Some of the material they believe traditional is of relatively recent origin; some of their rituals derive from Masonic rather than Celtic sources; some of their hopeful social attitudes are not yet supported by archaeology. Yet Celtic revivalism seems unlikely to wane in the near future. Should scholars become less resistant to the spiritual quest, they could find a ready audience for their work among practitioners, who in turn could root their reinvented religious practices more firmly in history.

Source: Carr-Gomm, Philip. *The Druid Renaissance*. London: Thorsons, 1996.

Celtic shamanism   Although found throughout the world, shamanism is often described as an arctic religion; the word *shaman* derives from the Tungus language of southern Siberia. Some scholars argue that aspects of Celtic religion suggest a connection with shamanic traditions, which may or may not mean a historical connection with the peoples of the arctic. Primary links between Celtic religion and shamanism are the role of the poet as SHAPE-SHIFTING seer (see BARD) and the vision of another world separate but linked to ours (see OTHERWORLD). According to this interpretation, the poet's ability to become "a wave of the sea, a tear of the sun"—as the famous "Song of AMAIRGIN" has it—is similar to the transformation of a shaman into a BEAR or other animal while in a trance induced by drumming and dancing;

similarly, the role of the poet in maintaining social balance through SATIRE can be seen as similar to the healing function of the traditional arctic shaman. Further, the Celtic Otherworld has been compared to the Dreamtime of the Australian aboriginals, a culture defined as shamanic.

Other aspects of traditional shamanism are arguably absent from Celtic life; it is not known, for instance, whether ingestion of psychotropic plants was known among the Celts, although there is strong evidence of alcohol use for that purpose (see ALE). Similarly, there is no indication of a Celtic version of the so-called arctic hysteria, a mental disorder that usually precedes shamanic initiation. Yet such acknowledged shamanic practitioners as the Okinawan *nuru* and the south Korean *mudang* are trained for many years and rarely suffer mental collapse, so the lack of "arctic hysteria" among the Celts does not in itself mean their religious culture cannot be called shamanic. The lack of scholarly agreement on this topic has not inhibited groups and individuals from promoting themselves or their organization as representatives of Celtic shamanism.

Some scholars object to the construction of Celtic religion as shamanic, arguing that the word is properly used to describe Asian religions and that there is little evidence of religious influence from that area on the Celts. Some academics evince discomfort with any reconstruction of historical religion, and, indeed, the more egregiously commercial versions of Celtic shamanism have little theoretical or spiritual basis. Serious scholars disagree, in some cases profoundly, on whether to consider Celtic religion as shamanic.

Sources: Cowan, Tom. *Fire in the Head: Shamanism and the Celtic Spirit*. San Francisco: HarperSanFrancisco, 1993; Lonigan, Paul, "Shamanism in the Old Irish Tradition." *Eire-Ireland*, Fall 1985, pp. 109–129; Matthews, John, and Caitlín Matthews. *Encyclopedia of Celtic Wisdom: A Celtic Shaman Sourcebook*. Rockport, Mass.: Element, 1994.

Celtic Twilight artistic movement This term describes an early 20th-century Irish movement, predominantly literary but also involving artists, politicians, and other visionaries who saw themselves living in a long dim evening after a glorious ancient "day" of Celtic heroism and romance. Such poets as William Butler Yeats, inspired by such ideas, wrote poems using the personae of ancient divinities or telling their myths; dramatists like Lady Augusta Gregory set their works in a (sometimes too imaginatively) reconstructed Celtic Ireland.

Some of the artworks of the period seem self-conscious, even contrived, especially when compared to early modernist art produced at the same time. Yet the ideals of the Celtic Twilight resulted in the recording of a significant amount of folklore and oral literature that might otherwise have been lost. In addition, part of the movement was the attention to the then-dying Irish language; Celtic Twilight ideals were in part responsible for the promotion of Irish as the national language of the new Republic and the insistence on teaching Irish in the new nation's schools, which led to the maintenance of the language during a critical time.

Center   See MÍDE.

ceó druídecta   See DRUID'S FOG.

Cera   Irish god. A name given to the DAGDA, perhaps signifying "creator," occasionally used in texts or place-names.

Cerbnat   Irish heroine. This obscure figure is named in the *BOOK OF INVASIONS* as one of the FIVE wives of the hero PARTHOLÓN, the others being Aifi, Elgnad or DEALGNAID, Cichban, and Nerbgen. She is otherwise unknown.

ceremony   Celtic ritual. Consistent with the decentralization of Celtic religion, there seem to have been no ceremonies shared by all Celts. Even the major holidays (see CALENDAR) conventionally associated with the Celtic year may have been only Irish; thus the presumption that BELTANE fires were lit throughout the Celtic world, for instance, or rush crosses were plaited everywhere at IMBOLC, cannot be upheld. In the same way, we find no evidence of rites of passage shared across Celtic Europe, no formulae for marriage or initiation; even death customs vary, with cremation and exhumation both being found, sometimes even within one tribe. There is significant evidence that the kingly INAUGURATION ritual—in which a woman representing the earth goddess offered a drink (and possibly, other refreshments as well) to the new king—was practiced throughout Ireland. Yet the ritual is not found in other European Celtic lands, leading some to argue that it originated among pre-Celtic people, while others claim similar rituals in India suggest an Indo-European origin.

What defines Celtic religion, therefore, is not shared ritual but shared COSMOLOGY or worldview. The Celts saw NATURE as sacred, therefore honoring the elements in outdoor festivals rather than by building temples or shrines. They were not dualistic in their worldview; paired divinities were complementary rather than in opposition. Many scholars perceive a threefold division of society (king, nobles, commoners) reflected in aspects of their religion. No evidence, however, has been found of a pan-Celtic ritual or ceremony.

Ceridwen (Caridwen, Cerridwen, Cariadwen, Keridwen)   Welsh goddess. On an island in the middle of Lake Bala (Llyn Tegid) in north Wales this fearsome goddess (sometimes called a WITCH or sorceress) lived with her mate, TEGID VOEL ("the bald"), and their two children, the beautiful Creirwy ("light") and the ugliest little boy in the world, AFAGDDU ("dark"). To compensate for his unfortunate appearance, Ceridwen planned to make her son a great seer, and to this end she brewed a powerful secret mixture of herbs. Into her CAULDRON she piled the herbs to simmer for a year and a day—a magical length of time appropriate to such a concoction.

The brew had to be stirred regularly, and Ceridwen was not always on hand to keep the brew mixed. So she set a little boy named GWION to stir the cauldron, warning him that he must on no account taste it. Three tiny drops splattered from the cooking pot onto Gwion's thumb, which he popped in his mouth to ease the burn. Immediately, all the wisdom and inspiration Ceridwen had intended for Afagddu was Gwion's.

When she discovered the boy's unwitting theft, Ceridwen was furious. But with his new insight, Gwion had foreseen her reaction and fled. Ceridwen started after him. Gwion transformed himself into a HARE; Ceridwen matched him, turning into a greyhound. He became a FISH, she an OTTER; he became a BIRD, she a hawk; finally he turned into a grain of wheat, she became a hen, and she ate him up.

In Celtic legends, eating is often a form of intercourse that leads to pregnancy; many heroines and goddesses become pregnant after drinking an insect in a glass of water. And so it was with Ceridwen, who was impregnated by the transformed Gwion; nine months later, she bore a boy child. Still angry at the thieving little boy but touched by his reborn beauty, Ceridwen set him adrift on the sea, from which he was rescued by a nobleman; he grew up to be the great poet TALIESIN.

Ceridwen, although clearly a mother in this tale, is described in terms more common to the CAILLEACH or HAG goddess. She was a magician or WITCH who possessed enviable occult knowledge, including that of SHAPE-SHIFTING. That she may have originally been a cosmic goddess of time and the seasons is suggested by the names of her two children. Some have interpreted the story of Ceridwen and Gwion's many transformations as a tale of initiation and rebirth.

The cauldron that is one of the primary emblems of Ceridwen appears in other Celtic myths as a symbol of abundance; in Ireland it is the OTHERWORLD vessel from which the fertility god DAGDA distributes wealth and plenty. Thus Ceridwen, despite her fierce appearance, may have originally been a goddess of the land whose fertility provided abundant food.

Source: Straffon, Cheryl. *The Earth Goddess: Celtic and Pagan Legacy of the Landscape.* London: Blandford, 1997, p. 43.

Cerne Abbas Giant   British mythological site and folkloric figure. On a hill near the village of Cerne Abbas in Dorset, England, the green turf has been removed down to the chalky white soil, outlining the shape of a man more than 200 feet tall. The figure bears no name, nor is it known who carved it in the turf. Another turf-cut figure, the WHITE HORSE OF UFFINGTON, has been recently dated to the Iron Age, when Celtic people lived in Britain, but it is not known whether the Cerne Abbas GIANT derives from the same period. Most scholars theorize that the Giant was already graven into the hillside by the time the Celtic tribe called the Durotriges arrived in the area.

Others argue, however, that aspects of the Giant connect him to other Celtic mythologies. Most noticeable about the figure is his enormous erection (30 feet long), which has led to an assumed connection with FERTILITY; a local belief of long standing was that the Giant helped women become pregnant, for which reason outdoor assignations on or near the figure were common. The Giant also carries a huge club, like the Irish DAGDA, held aloft to emphasize its phallic symbolism; a similar mallet-endowed god was known among the continental Celts as SUCELLUS.

Source: Newman, Paul. *Gods and Graven Images: The Chalk Hill-Figures of Britain.* London: Robert Hale, 1987, pp. 72–101.

Cernunnos   Celtic god. Cernunnos was one of the greatest and most ancient Celtic gods, his name and image found among both continental and insular peoples as far back as the fourth century B.C.E. His name, which appears in only one inscription from France, has been translated as "the horned one," although that is controversial and derives from iconographic rather than linguistic sources. For the image, if not the name, of a horned god is found elsewhere, including on the important GUNDESTRUP CAULDRON.

The horns Cernunnos wears are never those of domesticated animals, but rather those of a STAG, suggesting a connection with the powers of the wildwood. A link has also been suggested to the seasonal cycle, since DEER sprout antlers in the spring and shed them in the fall. Animals, both wild and domesticated, accompany him in virtually all known images; he is thus sometimes called the Master of Animals.

Often Cernunnos wears or bears a TORC, symbol of high status and holiness. He may have represented a force of abundance and prosperity, for he is often portrayed accompanied by symbols of plenty like the CORNUCOPIA and the moneybag. No myths are known of him, but he remains a common image today, for the horned DEVIL image apparently was derived from him.

Cesair (Cessair, Cesara, Kesair, Heriu, Berba) Irish goddess or heroine. According to the BOOK OF INVASIONS, this was the name of Ireland's first settler. The text was not written until after Ireland became Christian, and the scribes were monks with an interest in depicting Ireland as a holy land. So its authors combined Ireland's mythological history with biblical stories.

Thus Cesair was described as the granddaughter of the biblical Noah who escaped the great Flood by sailing away from the Holy Land. Whereas Noah had a boat full of animals, Cesair specialized in people, loading her ship with 50 women and three men. Four days before the waters raged, before Noah even boarded the ark, Cesair and her followers arrived in the safety of Ireland—which was never affected by the otherwise worldwide flood. Her route was far from direct, for after leaving from Meroe on a Tuesday, she sailed down the Nile and traveled to the Caspian and Cimmerian seas, then sailed over the drowned Alps, from which it took her nine days to sail to Spain and another nine to reach Ireland.

Arriving on the southwest coast, at Bantry Bay in Co. Cork, Cesair and her crew disembarked and divided the land among the crew. There being only three men, Cesair constituted three groups, each with more than a dozen women but only one man. But the demands of the women soon proved too much for Cesair's father, BITH, and brother, LADRA, who died from excessive sexual exertion, while the last man, FINTAN mac Bóchra, fled the eager women.

The names of the women who accompanied Cesair appear by their names to represent the world's ancestral mothers, for they included German (Germans), Espa (Spanish), Alba (British), Traige (Thracian), and Gothiam (Goth). Thus their arrival can be read as creating a microcosm of the entire world's population in Ireland. Several other companions, including BANBA and BÚANANN, echo the names of ancient Irish goddesses.

It has been theorized that Cesair was a goddess of the land, for she is sometimes thought to be the daughter of the earth goddess Banba, While at other times she is herself called Berba (the goddess of the River Barrow), or Heriu, a name similar to that of the primary land-goddess, ÉRIU. Thus Cesair may have been a form of, or assimilated to, those important divinities. The fact that THREE men divided the women among them, each taking a primary bride (Fintan with Cesair, Bith with Bairrind, and Ladra with Banba), makes Cesair and her companions a parallel grouping to the better-known trio Banba, FÓDLA, and Ériu.

Source: MacAlister, R. A. Stewart. *Lebor Gabála Érenn: The Book of the Taking of Ireland, Part 1.* Dublin: Irish Texts Society, 1941, pp. 166–248.

Cet (Cet mac Mágach) Irish hero. A great ULSTER warrior, Cet was said to have been eloquent as well as brave, especially in boasting about his prowess in battle. In some legends Cet named the boy who grew to be the greatest warrior of his people, CÚCHULAINN.

Cethern mac Fintain   Irish hero. This warrior is described as the tutor to the great hero FIONN MAC CUMHAILL, who gained all the world's wisdom by eating part of a SALMON named FINTAN. As Cethern's name shows that he is the son of Fintan, his presence in the stories may serve to intensify the connection between Fionn and Fintan.

Cethlion   (Cethlenn, Ceithlenn, Céthlionn, Caitlín, Kethlenda of the Crooked Teeth). Irish heroine or goddess. Buck-toothed queen of the ancient Irish race called the FOMORIANS and wife of their leader BALOR, Cethlion was a prophet who foresaw her people's defeat at the hands of the invading TUATHA DÉ DANANN at the second battle of MAG TUIRED. This foreknowledge did not stop her from waging a fierce battle in which she wounded or killed one of the chiefs of her enemies, the DAGDA.

cétnad   Irish ritual. This form of DIVINATION was practiced by BARDS, who chanted through their hands in order to locate stolen property, especially CATTLE. A special chant, addressed to the otherwise unknown seven Daughters of the Sea, was used to discover how long someone would live.

champion's portion   Irish mythological theme. Several Irish epics center on this traditional Celtic practice, whereby the most prominent warrior at a feast was given the *curad-mír*, or choicest portion, of the meat served, often interpreted as the thigh. Should two or more warriors claim the prize, a fight was immediately waged, sometimes with deadly results. This tradition, recorded as far back as the first century B.C.E., gave the sharp-tongued BRICCRIU an opportunity for troublemaking when he set several champions against each other.

changeling   Irish, Scottish, occasionally Breton folkloric figure. FAIRY babies were withered little raisinettes, ugly to look at, more like wizened old people than darling newborns. As a result, fairy parents were tempted to steal away chubby, cheery human babies, leaving enchanted fairy offspring in their place. Thus a strong tradition exists of protective rituals, including having nicknames for children so that the fairies cannot know their true names and thus gain power over the souls of the children.

A speedy baptism was important, because that Christian ritual made a child unattractive to fairies; burning old leather shoes in the birthing chamber was a good substitute. Should parents find a child changed—a bad-tempered, angry, and squalling brat where once there had been a sweet, placid babe—there was little recourse except a trip to FAIRYLAND to reclaim the stolen child. Sometimes the fairy enchantment (see GLAMOUR) was so strong that even the parents believed the changeling child to be human. But fairy behavior finally revealed itself, and if not, a test could be administered to the suspected fairy offspring. The suspicious parent must do something out of the ordinary, like beating an egg in its own shell rather than in a bowl or announcing an intent to brew beer from eggs. This caused no end of puzzlement to the changeling, which finally dropped its cover and demanded to know the purpose of the action. Having thus revealed itself, the fairy would nonetheless remain until the stolen child was located in the OTHERWORLD.

Sometimes human parents attempted to force the return of their children by exposing the changeling to the elements. There is tragic evidence that such beliefs were occasionally used to excuse the abuse and even murder of children who may have been unwanted or handicapped. In Wales, alleged changelings were driven away by being exposed to the elements, starved, or drowned, in the belief that the fairies would come rescue their lost kin.

Fairy changelings did not need to be infants; sometimes older humans were stolen away because the fairies needed their special gifts. MID-WIVES and musicians were especially at risk, as were beautiful people of either sex. Sometimes these stolen ones were replaced by an enchanted stock of wood. As with child changelings, there is evidence that people suffered torture and death at the hands of relatives who believed them to have been taken AWAY. In the 19th century, a young woman named Bridget Cleary was apparently burned to death by her family after taking unaccountably ill, showing that the belief was still strong at that point—or that it was used to do away with an ambitious and therefore troublesome woman of the community.

See also FAIRY KIDNAPPING.

Sources: Bourke, Angela. *The Burning of Bridget Cleary*. London: Pimlico, 1999; Briggs, Katherine. *The Fairies in Tradition and Literature*. London: Routledge & Kegan Paul, 1967, pp. 115 ff; Carmichael, Alexander. *Carmina Gadelica: Hymns and Incantations*. Hudson, N.Y.: Lindisfarne Press, 1992, p. 517; Croker, T. Crofton. *Fairy Legends and Traditions of the South of Ireland*. London: William Tegg, 1862, p. 36; Curtin, Jeremiah. *Tales of the Fairies and of the Ghost World Collected from Oral Tradition in South-West Munster*. New York: Lemma Publishing Corp., 1970, p. 23; Douglas, George. *Scottish Fairy and Folk Tales*. West Yorkshire: EP Publishing, 1977, pp. 125 ff; Kennedy, Patrick. *Legendary Fictions of the Irish Celts*. New York: Benjamin Blom, 1969, pp. 84, 89; Parry-Jones, D. *Welsh Legends and Fairy Lore*. London: B. T. Batsford, Ltd., 1953, p. 42.

chariot   Celtic symbolic object. The Celts were among the first European peoples to domesticate the HORSE. They did not ride upon the animals' backs but instead hitched them to speedy chariots, used for travel and, especially, for battle. Both gods and goddesses, heroes and heroines, are described or depicted as charioteers; in addition, parts of chariots—bridle, wheel—appear in the iconography of divinities, such as EPONA.

charm   The opposite of a CURSE—a formula designed to bring bad luck—is a charm (in Irish, *eólas*), a spell or incantation to attract good fortune; sometimes the word is used to mean both attracting good and repelling bad, as in, for instance, a "charm against the evil eye" used in Scotland, where a few words were spoken while gathering WATER from beneath a bridge that was later sprinkled protectively on the household. The Celtic lands provide many examples of charms, which entailed certain ritual gestures, specified offerings, the gathering of specific herbs, and/or incantatory words. Charms were sung to hasten the BUTTER, when the monotonous action of churning milk began to tire the milkmaid. Similarly there were waulking charms, to ease the labor of making linen. A milking charm collected in Scotland is typical: With each flow of milk a new verse was sung, calling on a different saint, for many ancient charms were Christianized and continued in use even until recent years. In Ireland, charms included stealing a DEAD HAND from a corpse and the liver of a black CAT, the first being effective in churning butter, the second dried into a foolproof love potion. In Cornwall charms were written out on bits of paper and kept in pockets and purses; one was simply the untranslatable word *nalgah* above a picture of a four-winged bird.

Sources: Carmichael, Alexander. *Carmina Gadelica: Hymns and Incantations*. Hudson, N.Y.: Lindisfarne Press, 1992, pp. 350, 377 ff, 643; Courtney, M. A. *Cornish Feasts and Folklore*. Penzance: Beare and Son, 1890, pp. 143 ff; Kavanagh, Peter. *Irish Mythology: A Dictionary*. Newbridge, Co. Kildare: The Goldsmith Press, Ltd., 1988, pp. 30–33.

Children of Lir   Irish heroine and heroes. Their story is called one of the THREE SORROWS OF IRELAND. Happily married to king LIR, the magician's daughter ÁEB gave birth first to a twin son and daughter, Áed and FIONNUALA. Her next pregnancy was less fortunate however, and she died giving birth to a pair of twin sons, FIACHRA and CONN. Orphaned when their beloved mother died, the four children of king LIR fell into the care of their aunt AÍFE who, filled with spite and envy, bewitched the children into SWANS and cursed them to live nine hundred years in that form. The children kept their human emotions and senses and were given hauntingly sweet singing voices. When their enchantment ended, they aged and died and turned to dust, all within moments.

Children of Llyr   Welsh heroes and heroines. The second branch of the Welsh *MABINOGION* tells the story of a war between Wales and Ireland. See BRANWEN.

Chimes Child   British folkloric figure. In rural Somerset, a child born after Friday midnight but before dawn on Saturday was believed to have the SECOND SIGHT and to be a healer.

Chlaus Haistig   Irish heroine. In the legends of the heroic FIANNA, we find a queen much harassed by the powers of the OTHERWORLD. Time after time a long hairy arm would reach into her home and steal one of her children, and the queen could do nothing to stop it. She required the hero FIONN MAC CUMHAILL to make a *GEIS*, a sacred vow, to help her. He stayed up all night to catch the WITCH Chlaus Haistig upon the roof, reaching down to steal the queen's children; holding the witch hostage, Fionn gained the release of the other boys and girls.

Source: Kennedy, Patrick. *Legendary Fictions of the Irish Celts*. New York: Benjamin Blom, 1969, p. 228.

Christianity   As Celtic religion was polytheistic in the extreme, the arrival of monotheistic Christianity might have meant the extirpation of Celtic practices. And indeed, the loss of much continental Celtic material can be traced to Christian campaigns such as that of idol-smashing Martin of Tours in what is now France. Yet reli-

gious practices proved harder to break than sculptures, although a series of edicts emphasized the need to eliminate traditions such as that of honoring STONES and TREES. The Edict of Arles (452 C.E.) proclaimed that "if any infidel either lighted torches, or worshiped trees, fountains or stones, or neglected to destroy them, he should be found guilty of sacrilege." A century later the Council of Tours recommended excommunication for those found guilty of the same practices. After another century, ancient traditions still held, so that the Decree of Nantes (658 C.E.) encouraged "bishops and their servants" to "dig up and remove and hide to places where they cannot be found, those stones that in remote and woody places are still worshiped."

Clearly people were continuing to find their way to the old sites of worship, some of which had been taken over by the Celts from pre-Celtic people and therefore had been in use for millennia. Finally the church took a clue from earlier Roman invaders and proposed a version of the INTERPRETATIO ROMANA. In the words of the seventh-century Pope Gregory, "Take advantage of well-built temples by purifying them from devil-worship and dedicating them to the service of the true God. In this way, I hope the people will leave their idolatry and yet continue to frequent the places as formerly, so coming to know and revere the true God."

This new attitude meant that ancient practices continued under the rubric of church ceremonies. Even with this expanded definition of Christian worship, pagan ceremonies seem to have continued in some areas, for the Church of Scotland appointed a commission in 1649 to eliminate "druidical customs" (see DRUID) still practiced in certain areas. More often, Celtic traditions were absorbed into Christianity, so that ancient Celtic festival days became Christian feasts, churches were built on old holy sites, and pagan divinities were "canonized" as saints.

In Ireland the same general pattern was followed, with ancient sites being consecrated to Christian uses. A difference between Ireland and the other Celtic countries rests in the role of monks and other literate Christians in sustaining the ancient traditions. The earliest written works of Irish literature we have, including the *TÁIN BÓ CUAILNGE*, were transcribed by Christian religious men. While it is likely that some motifs and beliefs in most flagrant discord with Christian values were altered or suppressed, without the monks' work even more of Celtic religion may well have been lost. Christianity therefore exists in a complex relationship to Celtic religion, as both preserver and destroyer.

Sources: Bord, Janet, and Colin Bord. *The Secret Country: An interpretation of the folklore of ancient sites in the British Isles.* New York: Walker and Co., 1976, p. 115; Bradley, Ian. *Celtic Christianity: Making Myths and Chasing Dreams.* New York: St. Martin's Press, 1999.

Christmas   See NOLLAIG.

Ciabhán (Keevan of the Curling Locks, Ciabhan)   Irish hero. Briefly a member of the FIANNA, the band of heroes led by FIONN MAC CUMHAILL, Ciabhán was asked to leave the heroic band because of his womanizing. So he set sail to the west, toward the FAIRYLAND of TÍR TAIRNGIRI, the Land of Promise, where he astonished observers with his juggling abilities. The fairy queen CLÍDNA took him as her lover but lost her life because of their affair: She drowned while awaiting his return from a hunting expedition.

Cian (Kian, Cian mac Cainte)   Irish hero. When BALOR, king of the FOMORIANS, was told that he would be killed by his grandson, he thought he could outwit the prophecy because his only daughter EITHNE was still a virgin. So he locked her in a high tower, where she would never meet a man and therefore never bear a child.

Balor proved his own undoing, for he coveted the magically abundant COW, the GLAS GHAIBHLEANN, which was in the keeping of Cian, a man from the mainland. Some tales say that Cian was the cow's owner, while others say

that he was merely the cowherd, the owner being a magical SMITH. Sailing over from his home on Tory Island, off the northwest coast of Ireland, Balor stole the cow and brought her back to his distant home. Unwilling to lose such a splendid beast, Cian went secretly across the waters, where he found a greater prize: the fair Eithne. Helped by a DRUID woman, BIRÓG, he decked himself in women's clothes and took up residence in the tower, where he seduced Eithne. She gave birth to three sons, two of whom were drowned by their grandfather; the surviving child was the hero LUGH. In variants of the story, Cian is called Kian or MacInelly; he is also said to have impregnated Eithne's other 12 handmaids, all of whom gave birth to SEALS.

In some stories, Cian is described as a son of the physician god, DIAN CÉCHT, which would make him one of the TUATHA DÉ DANANN, the people of the goddess DANU. He died when three brothers, the SONS OF TUIREANN, ambushed him because of enmity between Cian and their father. To his humiliation, he attempted to avoid the encounter with the armed warriors, turning himself into a PIG and pretending to scour the forest floor for acorns, but the brothers saw through the SHAPE-SHIFTING and turned themselves into DOGS to bring Cian down, only permitting him to return to human form just before death. The great earthwork called the Black Pig's Dyke is said to be his petrified body or to have been dug by him while in pig form.

Cichban   Irish heroine. This obscure figure is named in the *BOOK OF INVASIONS* as one of the FIVE wives of the hero PARTHOLÓN, the others being Aife, Elgnad or DEALGNAID, Nerbgen, and Cerbnat. She is otherwise unknown.

Cicollus   Continental Celtic god. An obscure god whose name seems to mean "great protector," he was worshiped in central Europe where inscriptions to him from Roman times—calling him a form of the warrior god MARS—were found. He may be the same as the protector god

APOLLO Anextiomarus. His consort was the goddess LITAVIS.

Cigfa (Kigva)   Welsh heroine or goddess. In the third branch of the Welsh MABINOGION, this woman became the wife of PRYDERI, son of the goddess RHIANNON and her consort PWYLL. After her husband became strangely entrapped with his mother in a magical FAIRY MOUND, Cigfa lived chastely with Rhiannon's second husband, MANAWYDAN, until the latter was able to find a way to break the enchantment on their spouses.

Source: Gantz, Jeffrey, trans. *The Mabinogion.* New York: Barnes & Noble Books, 1976, pp. 90–95.

Cill Dara   See KILDARE.

Cilydd   Welsh hero. The father of the hero KULHWCH, he encouraged his son to ask for assistance in finding his true love, OLWEN, by traveling to the court of his cousin, king ARTHUR of CAMELOT.

Cimbáeth (Cimbaoth)   Irish hero. With two other ULSTER kings, ÁED Ruad and DÍTHORBA, this legendary ruler agreed that each in turn would rule for seven years. The agreement, overseen by a committee of poets, nobles, and DRUIDS, worked until Áed Ruad was killed. When his daughter MACHA Mong Rua (Red-Haired Macha) took his place, both Cimbáeth and Díthorba opposed her claim in battle. However, she was the stronger and won, afterward wedding Cimbáeth and killing Díthorba.

City of Ys   See YS.

Clan Baíscne   Irish heroes. The followers of the great hero FIONN MAC CUMHAILL were called by this name, especially when they fought against the followers of the one-eyed GOLL MAC MORNA, who were called after him the CLAN MORNA. The two rival clans eventually joined to form the FIANNA.

Clan Morna   Irish heroes. This name is used to describe the followers or tribe of the great warrior GOLL MAC MORNA, traditional enemies of the CLAN BAÍSCNE who served the hero FIONN MAC CUMHAILL. After numerous skirmishes the rival clans joined to form the FIANNA.

Clarine   Arthurian heroine. In some texts, this is the name given to king ARTHUR's sister, although it is unclear whether she is the same individual as the one otherwise known as MORGAUSE.

Clarisant (Clarisse)   Arthurian heroine. Sister of a knight of the ROUND TABLE, GAWAIN, Clarisant was the daughter of king ARTHUR's half-sister MORGAUSE and the king of the remote northern island of Orkney. She lived in an enchanted castle with her lover, Guireomelant.

Clas Myrddin (Merlin's palace, Merlin's enclosure)   Arthurian site. The entire island of Britain was said to be the palace of the great magician MERLIN, who served as its guardian.

Clídna (Cleena, Clíodna, Cliodna, Clíona, Clidna Centfind)   Irish heroine or goddess. In every series of nine waves, Irish legend maintains, the ninth one is the largest; it is still called Clídna's wave, Tonn Clíodhna, for a goddess of the TUATHA DÉ DANANN who was the world's most beautiful woman, called Clídna of the Fair Hair. Especially associated with the southwestern province of MUNSTER, she is sometimes called its FAIRY QUEEN, although that title is also claimed by ÁINE and AEVAL. Clídna lived in the fairy hill in Cork called Carrig Cliodna; she is also associated with offshore rocks called Carrigcleena; thus like other fairy queens she may have originally been a goddess of the land.

   Many romantic tales are associated with Clídna. In one, she was courted by CIABHÁN, the womanizing outcast of the heroic band called the FIANNA, who won her hand in her homeland of TÍR TAIRNGIRI, the Land of Promise. Unlike most mortal lovers of fairy women, Ciabhán traveled back and forth between this world and the OTHERWORLD safely. While he went hunting on the Irish mainland, he took Clídna along to Glandore ("golden harbor"). Clídna's lover went ashore as she stole a nap in their boat. But a huge wave crashed over the boat, drowning the beautiful Clídna.

Despite this report of her watery demise, Clídna managed to live on to have more romantic adventures. She fell in love with a man named John Fitzjames, who already had a human lover named Caitileen Óg; this girl followed Clídna into the Otherworld, angrily demanding the return of her man. Although she came close to persuading Clídna to let her sweetheart go, even the witty tongue of Caitileen Óg was ultimately ineffective against Clídna's desires.

Clídna is connected with several important Irish families; she had affairs with Earl Gerald Fitzgerald of the Desmond Geraldines (son of the fairy queen ÁINE) and with Caomh, ancestor of the O'Keeffes. Cládna served as BANSHEE to the MacCarthys, to whom she told the secret of the BLARNEY STONE, that touching it with the lips would make anyone eloquent—a superstition that lasts to this day. Her connection with nobility suggests that Clídna was goddess of the SOVEREIGNTY of sea-lapped Munster.

Sources: Gregory, Lady Augusta. *Gods and Fighting Men: The Story of the Tuatha De Danaan and of the Fianna of Ireland.* New York: Oxford University Press, 1970, pp. 111 ff.; Gwynn, Edward. *The Metrical Dindshenchas.* Vol. III. Royal Irish Academy, Todd Lecture Series. Dublin: Hodges, Figgis, and Co., Ltd., 1906–1924, pp. 207–213.

clipping the church British ritual. In England some village churches were sites of a ritual wherein children performed a circle dance around the churchyard, touching ("clipping") the church's walls as they cavorted. As churches were often erected on ancient holy sites (see

CHRISTIANITY), this rite has been seen as reflecting a ritual once conducted beside or inside a stone circle, where the stones were touched by passing celebrants. In the Cotswolds the rite was celebrated when the YEWS in the churchyard were clipped around the AUTUMN EQUINOX.

clootie Ritual object. A *clootie* is a rag, ribbon, or strip of cloth tied to a sacred tree or BILE growing near a holy WELL or other honored site in Ireland and Scotland. Typically the rag was touched to a part of the body in need of HEALING before being tied to the tree; this practice continues to the present. In the case of one tree beside a well in Scotland, tens of thousands of ribbons deck the surrounding trees and shrubs.

Sources: Clarke, David, with Andy Roberts. *Twilight of the Celtic Gods: An Exploration of Britain's Hidden Pagan Traditions.* London: Blandford, 1996, p. 96 ff; MacCulloch, J. A. *The Religion of the Ancient Celts.* London: Constable, 1911, p. 201.

Clota (Clud, Clutoida) Scottish goddess. The eponymous goddess of Scotland's River Clyde and of the FERTILITY of its watershed, Clota also appeared on the Continent as the SPRING nymphs called the Clutoida.

Clothra (Clothru) Irish heroine or goddess. The legendary Irish king EOCHAID Fedlech had four impressive daughters: MEDB, EITHNE, MUGAIN, and Clothra, as well as three sons, all named Finn and collectively named the FINN Emna. Clothra bore a single son to her three brothers, LUGAIDH Riab nDerg, whose body was divided into three parts by red stripes, each section having been fathered by a different brother. Clothra then lay with her son Lugaidh, by whom she conceived the hero CRIMTHANN Nia Náir, who was born posthumously, for Clothra was killed by her jealous sister Medb. This sequence of incestuous matings suggests an ancestral goddess, as does Clothra's appearance in many Irish genealogies.

clover Symbolic object. The four-leafed clover was said to be magical or lucky because it alone could break through the GLAMOUR that FAIRIES used to disguise the reality of their surroundings. Holding up such a clover would permit one to see things as they really were: a CAVE where a cottage appeared, a toothless old man where a handsome one had stood seconds before. The oil of the four-leafed clover may have been the main ingredient in FAIRY OINTMENT.

cluricaune (*cluricane, cluracan*) Scottish and Irish mythological being. Whereas his kin, the LEPRECHAUN, was an industrious little fellow, this SOLITARY FAIRY was quite the opposite, preferring to lounge about and primp his handsome clothing: his silver-buckled shoes, cap with golden lace, and suit of RED—the typical color of the Solitary Fairy; TROOPING FAIRIES, by contrast, wore GREEN. Fond of tippling, the *cluricaune* would steal into wine cellars, especially those belonging to alcoholics, to steal a few bottles. He was hard to exterminate, for if an owner tried to move, the *cluricaune* would simply travel along inside a cask.

The name *cluricaune* was most often used of this fairy being in Co. Cork; in nearby Co. Kerry, he was the Luricaune; in Tipperary, the Lugirgadaune; in Ulster, the Loghery Man. One *cluricaune* named Little Wildbeam, who haunted a Quaker family in Cork, was most helpful if a servant left a bit of beer dripping from the cask; he shrank and wedged himself into the spigot so that not a drop was lost. If the maids did not feed him well, the fairy came out at night and beat them senseless. This all became too much for the family, and when the *cluricaune* would not vacate the premises, they packed up and moved, only to unpack and find their annoying helper had made his way to their new home.

Source: Croker, T. Crofton. *Fairy Legends and Traditions of the South of Ireland.* London: William Tegg, 1862, p. 73.

Cnabetius Continental Celtic god. His name has been translated as "the crippled one," but little is known of this god to whom inscriptions have been found in Celtic regions of Germany and Austria. The Romans connected him with their protective warrior god MARS; he has been linked by scholars with such wounded kingly figures as the Irish NUADA.

Cnoc Ailinee See KNOCKAULIN.

Cnoc Áine See KNOCKAINY.

Cnucha Irish heroine. This obscure Irish heroine or goddess was said to have been the nurse of CONN of the Hundred Battles. She died of a fever and was buried by her father, Connad, in the area near Dublin called Castleknock in her honor.

Cnú Deiréil Irish hero. Harpist of FIONN MAC CUMHAILL; see DWARF.

Cobhthach (Covac) Irish hero. This cruel king forced his young brother, LABHRAIGH Lore, to eat mice, whereupon the child was frightened into muteness. He is sometimes described as Labhraigh's uncle. He killed Labhraigh in his lust for the throne of the PROVINCE of LEINSTER.

Cochrann Irish heroine. She was the daughter of the king of TARA, CATHAÍR MÓR, and mother of the romantic hero DIARMAIT Ua Duibne. She also gave birth to Diarmait's nemesis, the great wild BOAR named DONN UA DUIBNE. She had betrayed Diarmait's father with a shepherd who had magical powers, and when she gave birth to a boy, Diarmait's father killed it. The shepherd waved a HAZEL wand over the child's body, restoring him to life. It was not a human life that Cochrann's child lived, however, for he awakened from death as a boar. From then on, he lived to confront his half-brother and exact his revenge for his unfortunate state.

Cocidius British god. The Romans associated this northern British god with their war god MARS, but despite being favored by soldiers, Cocidius's horns suggest that he was probably originally a hunters' god, as the alternative identification with SILVANUS also suggests. One inscription from Britain connects Cocidius with an otherwise obscure Celtic god named Vernostonus, although the significance of that linkage is not clear.

cock Symbolic animal. Although domestic chickens were more utilitarian than religious, the cock or rooster drew some superstitions to itself. Possibly because of its harsh call, the cock was believed to protect against danger that might approach from an unanticipated direction; this power was especially strong in March. Black cocks were viewed as lucky, while white cocks were just the opposite.

Coel (Coel Hen) British god. "Old King Cole was a merry old soul," the nursery rhyme says, but Coel was not actually a king at all—he was an ancient Celtic god, "old Coel," euhemerized or diminished into a mere human. His name remains in the town of Colchester.

cohuleen druith Irish folkloric object. Irish MERMAIDS wore this little cap, which allowed them to swim beneath the waters of lakes and sea without danger. Should her cap be lost or stolen, however, the mermaid henceforth was forced to remain landbound.

Cóiced Mythic theme. This term, which means "a fifth," was used to describe the ancient PROVINCES of Ireland. The four geographical provinces were LEINSTER in the east, MUNSTER in the southwest, CONNACHT in the west, and ULSTER in the north. The fifth province, MIDE, or Meath, was not so much a geographical as a cosmological concept, representing the true center, sometimes defined as the hill of UIS-NEACH or, more specifically, the rock called the STONE OF DIVISIONS on that hill. In historical times, the province of Meath was established near the center of Ireland's landmass, but the mystical connotations of the island's provincial divisions were never lost.

Coinchenn (Coinchend) Irish heroine. This WARRIOR WOMAN was put under a CURSE of death if her daughter DELBCHÁEM should ever wed, so she challenged every suitor who came seeking the maiden's fair hand. Coinchenn usually won her battles with the suitors, placing their heads on poles around her house to form a macabre fence and hiding her daughter in a high tower. One man was stronger than she, and then only with FAIRY help: the king of TARA, ART MAC CUINN, who eventually gained Delbcháem's hand.

coins Symbolic object. The Celts had no coinage before the Roman invasions; the means of their economic exchange is not entirely clear but seems to have been based on barter. Metal coins were a revolutionary invention; prior to the widespread acceptance of money, goods themselves had to be transported to market and goods gotten in exchange carried back. Early Roman-era coins show some Celtic designs, indicating that local craftspeople were finding ways to create appropriate coins. Ultimately, coins substituted for images of afflicted parts of the body in rituals at holy WELLS; throwing coins in fountains is still superstitiously practiced today, the result of such offerings being a vaguely described "good luck."

Colgrevance Arthurian hero. This knight of the ROUND TABLE played a minor role in the story of OWEIN and the LADY OF THE FOUNTAIN, for he was the first knight to encounter the fountain's guardian, the mysterious Black Knight who was the lady's husband. Defeated by him, Colgrevance returned to CAMELOT with the tale, which spurred Owein to attempt to win over the Black Knight.

Coligny Continental Celtic site. At this archaeological site in southeastern France, an artifact was found that has been very important in Celtic studies. The bronze fragments of the Coligny Calendar document five years, dividing time into a 12-month lunar or moon year with 355 days and inserting a 30-day month after every 30 months to bring the CALENDAR back into sequence with the solar or sun year. The calendar was found in a shrine to the Romano-Celtic MARS and is believed to have had a ritual function. It is the only Celtic calendar known to archaeology.

Colloquy of the Elders (Colloquy of the Sages or Ancients, Acallam na Senórach, Agallamh na Seanórach) Irish mythological text. An important Irish narrative text, source for many of the legends of the FIANNA, the *Colloquy of the Elders* was composed in the 12th century, presumably by Christian monks. It tells of two members of the Fianna, OISÍN and CAÍLTE, who after a long stay in FAIRYLAND met with ST. PATRICK and engaged him in a discussion of religion and values. They traveled with the Christian monk, pointing out the holy sites and telling stories connected with them (see *DINDSHENCHAS*). Despite being composed during Christian times, the text is satirical toward Patrick and reverent toward the two aging survivors of pagan Ireland.

Sources: Cross, Tom Peete, and Clark Harris Slover, eds. *Ancient Irish Tales*. New York; Henry Holt and Co., 1936, pp. 457 ff; Dillon, Myles, ed. *Irish Sagas*. Cork: The Mercier Press, 1968, p. 119; Evans-Wentz, W. Y. *The Fairy-Faith in Celtic Countries*. Gerrards Cross: Colin Smythe Humanities Press, 1911, pp. 283 ff.

comb Symbolic object. The comb is associated with the MERMAID, who was thought to sit on a rock combing her lovely HAIR, the better to lure sailors to their deaths. Invoking the principle of SYMPATHETIC MAGIC—like attracting like— Scottish girls were warned not to comb their hair in the evening when their brothers were at sea, because it might draw the energy of a dangerous mermaid to their ship. Combing one's hair on a Wednesday would result in sterility, although the reason for this belief is unclear.

In Ireland, the comb was especially associated with the goddess-queen MEDB, whose sexual potency was legendary. The comb appears to represent the feminine force, especially in its malevolent form, a motif that appears in Scottish lore that described bad girls as combing fleas and frogs from their hair, while good girls would release GOLD and jewels.

Conaire (Conare, Conaire Mór, Conaire Mess Buachalla) Irish hero. Born from the union of his mother, MESS BUACHALLA, with the bird god NEMGLAN, Conaire was the grandson of the great goddess or fairy queen ÉTAIN. His story points up how vital it was that every sacred vow or *GEIS* required of the ruler be followed. Conaire attained the throne of TARA after DIVINATION (see BULL-SLEEP) revealed that he was its rightful king. With INAUGURATION came a series of demands, including the stipulation that he must never stand between two competing vassals. He did so, however, inserting himself into an argument between his brothers.

As he returned to Tara from that expedition, he was forced to break other vows, letting red riders pass him on his horse, riding with Tara on his right hand, and entering a hostel after nightfall. A fearsome HAG appeared at the door and demanded entry, but Conaire clung to the last of his geasa, that no woman should be alone with him at night in Da Derga's hostel (see DA DERGA). At that, she cursed him while standing in a magical position, and he was stricken with an unquenchable thirst even as the hostel burst into flame. His inauguration had made him the spouse of the lady of the land's SOVEREIGNTY, and the fearsome hag who threatened him as his life ended may have been her in vengeful form.

Sources: Dillon, Myles, ed. *Irish Sagas*. Cork: The Mercier Press, 1968, p. 79; O'Rahilly, Thomas.

Early Irish History and Mythology. Dublin: The Dublin Institute for Advanced Studies, 1946, p. 124.

Conall This ancient name, often anglicized as Connell and meaning "wolf," is born by a number of heroic figures.

- **Conall, son of Eochaid**, whose sons were turned into BADGERS by the goddess GRIAN after they attacked her fort on the mountain of KNOCKGRANEY. In retaliation, he fought Grian. Neither was able to gain an advantage until Grian sprinkled him with FAIRY dust, whereupon Conall stumbled away and died.
- **Conall Cernach**, "victorious Conall," hero of the ULSTER CYCLE, son of the poet AMAIRGIN and queen FINDCHÓEM, foster brother to the hero CÚCHULAINN. He appears in several texts, in which he performs amazing feats like swallowing a boar whole. He killed many men, often brutally. He was the only warrior to survive the holocaust at the hostel of DA DERGA, where his king CONAIRE was killed.
- **Conall Gulban**, son of NIALL of the Nine Hostages and founder of the ancient kingdom of Tír Chonaill in Co. Donegal. His name, corrupted into Bulben, was given to a famous mountain in Co. Sligo (see BEN BULBEN), where he was said to have been killed while attempting to release the fair EITHNE from the hands of a kidnapping GIANT. Many folktales revolve around this figure, who appears as a hero second only in popularity to FIONN MAC CUMHAILL.

Source: Gardner, Alexander. *Popular Tales of the West Highlands.* Vol III. London: J. F. Campbell, 1892, p. 98.

Conán Irish hero. Common in Irish mythology, this name means "wolf" and was born by many minor figures in the heroic cycles, most importantly Conán mac Morna (Conan Maeol), a comic blusterer sometimes called "Conán of the Bitter Tongue," who has been compared to the Scandinavian trickster Loki. Bald and usually attired with a black fleece wig, he was a tubby buffoon who nonetheless was great friends with the heroic FIONN MAC CUMHAILL. Another hero of this name was Conan Muil or Conan the Bald, Fionn's son, who lost his scalp when swallowed by the great monster CAORANACH.

Conaran Irish goddess. This obscure goddess was mother of three magician daughters who, lusting after the great warriors of the FIANNA, set out to ensnare them—literally, for they spun a magical web that trapped the heroes. All three were killed by the warriors; see IRNAN. Sometimes Conaran is described as a male figure, a prince of the TUATHA DÉ DANANN.

Concobar mac Nessa (Conchubar, Conchobhar, Conachar) Irish hero. A great king of ULSTER, he figures in many of the tales called, the ULSTER CYCLE. Concobar bears a matronymic, for he is named for his mother NESSA, a studious gentle girl who became fierce and warlike after being raped by the DRUID CATHBAD, who may be Concobar's father, although his father is also given as Fachtna Fathach, king of Ulster. It may have been neither: Nessa drank a drink containing a magical worm that may have impregnated her by supernatural means.

After being widowed, Nessa was courted by the great king FERGUS MAC RÓICH, who gave up his throne at EMAIN MACHA for a year upon her request, so that Concobar's children might claim royal descent. When Fergus wanted his throne back, he found that Nessa prevented his reassuming power; angrily, he left Ulster to take up with CONNACHT's queen MEDB, a former wife of Concobar who later launched a cattle raid on Concobar's territory (see *TÁIN BÓ CUAILNGE*).

Like the other men of Ulster, Concobar suffered from debilitating pains whenever an invasion threatened, because of a curse put upon the region's warriors by the dying goddess MACHA. Concobar may himself have been responsible for that curse, for he demanded that the pregnant goddess race against his fastest horses (in some tellings, the blame is placed upon Macha's boastful husband CRUNNIUC). Fergus came close to killing Concobar at the end of Medb's cattle raid, but the Ulster king lived until hit with a ball made of calcified brains that ultimately felled him.

In addition to Medb, Concobar was married to all her three sisters: EITHNE Aittencháithrech, CLOTHRA, and MUGAIN; his sons and daughters figure in many Irish legends. He also lusted after other women, most notably DEIRDRE, whom he attempted to raise to become his concubine but who escaped with her true love; the sad conclusion to the tale shows Concobar as a scheming vindictive person, far from the ideal king of Celtic legend (see KINGSHIP).

Sources: Cross, Tom Peete, and Clark Harris Slover, eds. *Ancient Irish Tales*. New York: Henry Holt and Co., 1936, pp. 131 ff; Hull, Eleanor. *The Cuchullin Saga in Irish Literature*. London: David Nutt, 1898, pp. 267 ff.

Condatis British god. The shrines of the minor water deity Condatis were situated at the confluence of RIVERS.

Condwiramur Welsh heroine. In some legends, she was the wife of the heroic king PEREDUR and mother of their son Lohenergrain.

Conn (Con) Irish hero. Several important Irish figures go by this name, including:

• **Conn of the Hundred Battles** (Con Cétchathach, Conn Céadchathach), one of the great legendary kings of Ireland. He was the first to be recognized by the magical stone LIA FÁIL, which screamed when he approached it. So designated as the true king, he walked the ramparts of TARA each day to assure that his people's enemies, the monstrous FOMORIANS, would not catch him unawares.

Before becoming king at Tara, Conn controlled the northern part of Ireland, with a strong rival named EÓGAN Mór ruling over the southern part; the division between them was a row of glacial hills called the EISCIR RIADA. Conn was not happy to remain in his sector, invading Eógan's region and defeating him. Eógan fled and then returned with additional aid, but to no avail, for Conn once again won over him at the battle of Mag Léna, where Eógan Mór was killed. These and other wars won Conn the epithet "of the hundred battles" or "fighter of hundreds."

Many of the stories regarding Conn emphasize the need for the king to remain in right relationship to the land so that it might be fruitful. Offered the cup of SOVEREIGNTY by a beautiful unknown woman, he took as his queen the virtuous EITHNE Táebfhorta. The land, well pleased under such good kingship, bore three harvests every year. But when he married BÉ CHUMA, who had been evicted from the OTHERWORLD for her disreputable ways, Conn found the land did not agree with his actions, for not a COW gave milk until the FAIRY woman was sent away.

Conn is a major figure in stories from the FENIAN CYCLE, for it was during his reign that the great hero FIONN MAC CUMHAILL was born. Some stories tell of Conn's execution of Fionn's father, CUMHALL, for kidnapping and raping his mother, MURNA; despite this, Fionn was a friend to Conn. Conn's children include ART MAC CUINN and CONNLA.

• **Conn mac Lir** (son of Lir), one of the CHILDREN OF LIR who were turned into SWANS by their jealous stepmother AÍFE.

Connacht (Connaught, Connachta) Irish mythological site. Ancient Ireland was divided variously into four or five PROVINCES, called in Irish CÓICED. The most westerly was Connacht, named in some legends for king CONN of the Hundred Battles; the others were ULSTER, LEINSTER, MUNSTER, and, sometimes, MIDE. The first syllable in Connacht means "wisdom," and so the province is traditionally connected with that attribute, while its site in the WEST connects it with the FAIRY people who were thought to prefer that direction. Ancient associations with Connacht were education, stories and histories, science, eloquence, and all forms of learning. The capital of ancient Connacht was CRUACHAN.

The counties of Galway, Mayo, Sligo, Leitrim, and Roscommon make up modern Connacht, smallest of Ireland's provinces and one of its poorest. It has long been considered a bastion of traditional culture, for invaders tended to push the Irish "to hell or Connacht," in Oliver Cromwell's memorable phrase. Many Americans derive their heritage from this region, for its poverty led to massive emigration during the 19th-century famine years.

Connla (Conla, Conlaí, Conle) More than a dozen Irish mythological figures bear this name, some of them minor and several major.

- **Connla, son of CÚCHULAINN** (Finmole). In one of the most tragic of Irish myths, the boy Connla was conceived by the WARRIOR WOMAN AÍFE from her encounter with the hero-in-training Cúchulainn, who had come to study with Aífe's mother SCÁTHACH. Cúchulainn left a ring with Aífe as a token, should she conceive, of her child's parentage. When the boy had grown and wished to seek his father, Aífe gave him that ring and sent him to Ireland. Challenged to give his right to enter the court of ULSTER by Cúchulainn, Connla refused to give his name. The two fought, and Connla was killed by his own father.
- **Connla Cóel,** a FAIRY king.
- **Connla of the Golden Hair,** son of CONN of the Hundred Battles. Earthly power held no appeal for this son of the king of TARA once he had met a woman of the FAIRY race upon the mystical hill of UISNEACH. He traveled with her, according to the *Adventures of Connla*, to her land, where he was offered

eternal life and pleasure. He was never seen again on this earth.

See FAIRY LOVER.

Sources: Cross, Tom Peete, and Clark Harris Slover, eds. *Ancient Irish Tales.* New York: Henry Holt and Co., 1936, p. 488; Hull, Eleanor. *The Cuchullin Saga in Irish Literature.* London: David Nutt, 1898, p. 79; Joyce, P. W. *Ancient Celtic Romances.* London: Parkgate Books, 1997, pp. 106 ff.

Connla's Well (Cóelrind's well) Irish mythological site. It is not known for whom this WELL is named, whether FAIRY or mortal. Nor is it known where the well is located, whether under the sea, in the OTHERWORLD, or somewhere in Tipperary. The well could be recognized by the nine HAZEL trees that hung over it, dropping nuts into the water, and by the fat SALMON (or trout) that fed off the nuts, each nut staining the fishes' skin with mottled spots. If you found the well, you could eat the nuts yourself, or drink the water, or even catch the salmon and eat them; any of those actions would bring you WISDOM and inspiration. The river goddess SÍNANN was one of those who found the well, but she paid with her life for succeeding at her quest.

Continental Celts See GAUL.

Cooley See CUAILNGE.

Corann Irish heroine or goddess. This obscure figure gives her name to a wooded region of Co. Sligo in Ireland's northwest. When some of her favorite hunting dogs were killed by a wild BOAR, she buried them and raised a ceremonial mound over their bodies.

Corbenic Arthurian site. The name of the castle of the FISHER KING may derive from the Latin words for "blessed body."

Corc mac Luigthic (Conall Corc, Conall mac Luigthig)   Irish hero. This heroic Irish king was inaugurated into the throne of Cashel, in the southwestern PROVINCE of MUNSTER, by his FAIRY mother FEDELM; in the process of his INAUGURATION, his ear was magically singed red. He traveled to Scotland to meet the king of the Picts but had been treacherously set up for murder, for his shield had been blazoned with OGHAM letters calling for his death. An ally altered the message to one of welcome, however, and Corc wound up marrying the king's daughter and returning to Ireland to establish a dynasty.

Corineaus   British hero. This ancient warrior defeated the monstrous GIANT named GOG or Gogmagog; little else is known of him.

Cormac mac Airt (Cormac mac Art)   Irish hero. Among the dozens of Irish characters who bore the name of Cormac, the most important was Cormac mac Airt, king of TARA. The land's prosperity was contingent upon the rectitude of its sovereign, and in Cormac's time SALMON practically leapt out of the rivers, the land was heavy with grain, and the COWS gave so much milk there were not enough pails to hold it. FIONN MAC CUMHAILL, the great warrior and leader of the band of FIANNA, lived during Cormac's reign.

As is typical of heroes, Cormac's conception and birth were marked by mysterious signs and portents. When his father, ART MAC CUINN, was traveling toward his death at the battle of Mag Mucrama, he stopped overnight at the home of a SMITH who prophesied that any child conceived by his daughter ACHTAN would become a king. Art slept with Achtan, leaving her instructions that any resulting child should be fostered in CONNACHT. As she neared the time for her child's birth, Achtan traveled across Ireland to satisfy Art's request, but she went into labor during a thunderstorm and gave birth to the new king under a hedgerow. Suckled by a WOLF that adopted him while his mother sought for help, Cormac survived and thrived in the wilderness,

growing up to take the throne as predicted. First he had to wed MEDB Lethderg, the SOVEREIGNTY figure who was also said to have been married to his grandfather and father.

Although tempted away from his realm by the OTHERWORLD beauties offered him by the sea god MANANNÁN MAC LIR, Cormac resisted their blandishments and came back to this world bearing a magical golden cup that broke whenever lies were spoken in its presence but mended itself when truth was told. As great a king as he was, he was ultimately forced from the throne after being disfigured when another king came to Tara furious because Cormac's son CELLACH had raped his daughter. In the fight that ensued, Cormac's eye was put out. As a BLEMISHED KING was unacceptable, Cormac stepped down in favor of his son CAIRBRE Lifechair.

Sources: Cross, Tom Peete, and Clark Harris Slover, eds. *Ancient Irish Tales.* New York: Henry Holt and Co. 1936, p. 503; O'Rahilly, Thomas. *Early Irish History and Mythology.* Dublin: The Dublin Institute for Advanced Studies, 1946, p. 132.

Corn Dolly (Corn Maiden)   Scottish and Irish folkloric symbol. A roughly human-shaped figure constructed from straw at harvest time, the Corn Dolly was often crafted from the last sheaf cut at harvest-time. Its origins are obscure but clearly mythic or ritual. The Dolly is associated with two figures of arguable antiquity: the CAILLEACH or HAG, and BRIGIT or the Bride, who may have been the hag's maiden form. Often the Corn Dolly was stored in a house or barn from fall until spring, when it played a role in sowing or other rituals associated with new life.

Source: Meaden, George Terrence. *The Goddess of the Stones: The Language of the Megaliths.* London: Souvenir Press, 1991, pp. 204–205.

Cornouaille   Breton mythological site. This Breton kingdom was famous in myth and legend as the home of the dissolute princess DAHUT; it was also the land to which TRISTAN brought the fair ISEULT at the beginning of one of Brittany's most romantic tales.

cornucopia Mythic symbol. From the Mediterranean came this horn of plenty, an emblem of FERTILITY that was embraced by the Celts, to whom the concept of abundance was a central part of religion. Although most commonly associated with goddesses such as Arecura and EPONA, the cornucopia was sometimes graven with the image of gods, including CERNUNNOS.

Corotiacus British god. Little is known of this Celtic god honored at Suffolk; the invading Romans connected him with their war god MARS.

Corp Criadh (Corp Creagh) Scottish ritual object. In the Highlands until the 19th century, clay dollies were sometimes fashioned by those who wished to work ill upon their neighbors or revenge themselves upon false lovers. This object was stuck with pins or cut, then placed in a stream where the running water would slowly dissolve the clay. When the image was entirely gone, the intended victim—having suffered from the pricks and cuts inflicted on the Corp Criadh—would die. Should anyone see the dolly before its final dissolution, the spell was broken and the victim would recover.

Source: Henderson, George. *Survivals in Belief Among the Celts.* Glasgow: James MacLeose and Sons, 1911, p. 16.

Corra Irish heroine or goddess. The sky demon defeated by ST. PATRICK on the top of the mountain that now bears his name, CROAGH PATRICK, drowned in Lough Corra at the base of the mountain after Patrick threw his silver bell at her and brought her down from the air. Other versions of the legend say that Patrick chased her across the country until she drowned in LOUGH DERG, where the monster serpent CAORANACH (a related name) also lived; this may have given rise to the tale that Patrick drove the snakes from the isle, when in fact they never lived there (see SERPENT). Corra has been interpreted as a MOTHER GODDESS whose power was broken by the arrival of patriarchal Christianity.

Source: MacNeill, Máire. *The Festival of Lughnasa, Parts I and II.* Dublin: Comhairle Bhéaloideas Éireann, 1982, p. 503.

Corrgenn (Coincheann) Irish hero. The *DINDSHENCHAS*, the poetry of Irish place-names transcribed in the 12th century, say that Coincheann was the murderer who killed the god DAGDA's son, ÁED MINBHREC, for seducing his wife. He was then sentenced to carry his victim's body on his back until he found a stone of equal size beneath which to bury it. He finally laid his burden down at the famous HILLFORT of GRIANÁN AILEACH.

cosmology Celtic philosophy and spiritual wisdom was neither written down nor constrained by text but conveyed instead through oral narrative, poetry, art, and ritual. Thus scholars must piece together Celtic belief from archaeological and textual evidences often widely separated in time and place. What makes the study of Celtic religion even more complicated is that most texts derive from Ireland, which has few graven images; most images derive from the Continent, where there are few known Celtic texts. Because continental and insular Celts lived in lands where indigenous beliefs may well have been different and had varying impacts on Celtic life, comparison of text and image is difficult. Does a horned god found in France mean the same as a horned figure mentioned in an Irish text? How can one be certain?

An added difficulty arises because of the astonishing POLYTHEISM of the Celts. Few Celtic divinities appear in text or inscription more than once (see CELTIC PANTHEON). Whether this means that the Celts had a vision of ultimate divinity of which the multiple forms were only aspects, or whether there was no such abstract concept of divinity, we cannot know. Finally, many Celtic texts were written by Christian monks; we have no way to know whether, how, and how much they may have altered texts to bring them into congruence with their own beliefs.

Scholars have, despite these difficulties, attempted to find common threads among Celtic religious texts and artifacts. They speak of the Celtic worldview as based in the concept of an OTHERWORLD, a land of perfect if somewhat sterile beauty to which humans have occasional access. Such access comes at certain sacred times (such as BELTANE and SAMHAIN) or in liminal places (BOGS, ISLANDS). Residents of the Otherworld could pass into our world more readily than we could pass into theirs, and they commonly made raids on this world to acquire things and people they desired. BARDS and musicians were frequent visitors to the Otherworld, from which they brought back beautiful poems and songs.

The Celts were not dualistic in their view of the world, preferring to speak of balance rather than conflict between winter and summer, male and female, night and day. The goddess of SOVEREIGNTY symbolized abundance and prosperity, although she also had a dark aspect, in which she brought death and destruction. The heroic human king was her consort, hemmed about with sacred vows that kept the land fertile and the people safe (see KINGSHIP).

Despite arising originally from a nomadic background, Celtic religion was deeply rooted in place, with hundreds of divinity names known for SPRINGS and RIVERS, hills and promontories. Whether this is the result of coming into contact with nonnomadic people cannot be determined, but the sense of humans as guardians of the earth's sanctity was reflected in a belief that people and place were deeply connected.

countless stones Scottish and British folkloric motif. There is a common story told of the STONE CIRCLES erected by the pre-Celtic peoples of Britain: that one cannot ever correctly count the number of stones in the ring. Bad luck was said to afflict anyone who even tried to count the stones, especially the stones of STONEHENGE and of Stanton Drew. In some tales, a baker decides to break this spell by putting a loaf of bread upon each one of the stones in turn, but the loaves disappear as he continues around the circle, so that the stones remain uncounted.

Source: Grinsell, Leslie V. *Folklore of Prehistoric Sites in Britain.* London: David & Charles, 1976, p. 63.

couril Breton folkloric figure. The *courils* were evil, or at least mischievous, FAIRIES who congregated around ancient STONE CIRCLES, especially those of Tresmalonen, where they enjoyed dancing all night. Should a human wander near them in the darkness, they captured him and kept him dancing until he died of exhaustion. Or, if the hapless wanderer was a young woman, they enjoyed her favors and left her pregnant with a half-fairy child.

Source: Henderson, George. *Survivals in Belief Among the Celts.* Glasgow: James MacLeose and Sons, 1911, p. 73.

courtly love Literary and historical movement. In the lands of the continental Celts, a cultural movement began in the Middle Ages that glorified the service of a knight to a married woman (whose husband was sometimes the knight's lord). The knight pledged himself to his lady and then, through heroic service, tried to win the right to her heart—and presumably, to other parts of her as well although intercourse was forbidden to the courtly lovers. Courtly love existed primarily as a literary movement, with traveling poet/singers called troubadours and later trouvères praising the relationship between knight and lady, but there were also "courts of love" in the palaces of such notables as Eleanor

of Aquitaine, where women heard the complaints of those who felt their lovers had not acted in keeping with the elaborate rules of courtly love. Other famous "courts" were those of Eleanor's daughter, Marie of Champagne; the countess of Flanders, Elizabeth de Vermandois; and even the queen, wife of Louis VII, Alix de Champagne. The movement, with its emphasis upon at least spiritual and sometimes physical adultery, was never condoned by the Christian church but has been tied to ancient Celtic myths in which a younger lover gains the heart of a queen from an older king.

See DIARMAIT, GRÁINNE, and FIONN MAC CUMHAILL; LANCELOT, GUINEVERE, and king ARTHUR.

Source: Markale, Jean. *Courtly Love: The Path of Sexual Initiation.* Rochester, Vt.: Inner Traditions, 2000.

court tomb (court cairn) Mythological site. Relics of the pre-Celtic MEGALITHIC CIVILIZATION found throughout the Celtic lands include these early burial structures. Typically a paved semicircular courtyard stands in front of a CAIRN or stone mound, which covers a small interior chamber whose entrance faces east. The courtyard at the impressive court tomb at Creevykeel in Ireland's Co. Sligo could easily have held 50 people. Archaeologists speculate that, if the mounds were indeed gravesites, the courtyards could have been used for funerary ceremonies.

Source: Harbison, Peter. *Pre-Christian Ireland: From the First Settlers to the Early Celts.* London: Thames and Hudson, 1988, p. 47.

Coventina British goddess. Known from sculptures found at a sacred WELL in Northumberland, Coventina was portrayed as a reclining woman pouring WATER from an urn, or as a woman surrounded by plants, who emptied her water-vessel onto them. Although primarily a British goddess, especially ruling the Carrawburgh River,

Coventina has also been found in Spain and France with titles like Augusta and Sancta, "high" and "holy," that emphasize her importance. She may, like other Celtic water goddesses, have had a HEALING aspect.

Source: Allason-Jones, Lindsay. "Coventina's Well." In Billington, Sandra, and Miranda Green, eds. *The Concept of the Goddess.* Routledge: London and New York, 1996, pp. 107–119.

cow Symbolic animal. BULL and cow were significant Celtic symbols for the feminine and masculine powers, the bull representing warrior strength, the cow indicating abundance and prosperity. Used in ancient Ireland as a way of calculating wealth, the cow was a provider of MILK and BUTTER, two vital foodstuffs. Many goddesses were associated with cows, including BRIGIT, BÓAND, and the MÓRRÍGAN. But the cow itself could be divine, as in the case of the GLAS GHAIBHLEANN (in Scotland, Glas Ghaibhnann), a magical white cow spotted with green who walked about the land, providing milk from her inexhaustible udder to anyone who wished it. Wherever she passed, the grass grew greener and sweeter, the farmers grew wealthier. These associations indicate to many scholars a connection with cow-cults in other Indo-European lands.

All cows in Ireland were said to be the descendants of the OTHERWORLD cows that arose from the western ocean at the beginning of time: BÓ FIND, the white cow, and her sister Bó Ruadh and Bó Duh, the red and black cows respectively. Cows were, not surprisingly, associated with women, not only in legend but in reality, for women did the milking, made the butter, and tended the cows in their summer pastures.

Sources: O hEochaidh, Séan. *Fairy Legends of Donegal.* Trans. by Máire MacNeill. Dublin: Comhairle Bhéaloideas Éireann, 1977, pp. 265, 329; O'Sullivan, Patrick V. *Irish Superstitions and Legends of Animals and Birds.* Cork: Mercier, 1991, p. 10.

co-walker Irish and Scottish folkloric figure. Just before or after someone died, an exact replica was often seen walking about. A woman on her deathbed might be seen at church, or a recently deceased man at his own wake. These co-walkers were sometimes described as TWIN souls, freed with the approach of death, but they were also spoken of as FAIRIES disguised as the person who stood on the edge of the OTHERWORLD. It was important never to speak to these shades or fairies, who would ultimately depart and not be seen again, although it is unclear whether the danger was considered to be to the deceased or the living.

Craebhnat (Creevna) Irish heroine. Near Doneraile in the southwestern PROVINCE of MUNSTER, a sacred TREE was dedicated to this woman who, when confronted with the demand that she marry, tore out one of her eyes, hoping that her disfigurement would drive away her potential groom. The tree was an ASH, one of Ireland's magical trees. Another tree nearby was said to possess the power of keeping people afloat; anyone who carried the slightest shaving of its bark or wood could never drown. It is not clear whether the local people envisioned Craebhnat as a FAIRY or as one of the SAINTS.

Craiphtine (Craftine, Cratiny) Irish hero. One of those credited with the invention of the musical instrument most connected to Ireland, the HARP, this musician appeared in myths of the hero LABHRAIGH, whose fitful sleep he eased with his melodies. So powerful was Craiphtine's music that he was able to send entire armies to sleep with it, making him very useful to his ruler in times of war.

Crandelmass Arthurian hero. This minor character in the legend of king ARTHUR of CAMELOT was one of the early opponents to Arthur's rule.

crane Symbolic animal. The Celts believed that BIRDS, like TREES, stood in two worlds, belonging to the OTHERWORLD as well as this one. Birds like the crane—at home not only in air and on land but also in the water—were especially magical. Cranes typically represented the feminine force, especially when they appeared in THREES; because they stand upright, they were imagined to have originally been human. In folklore cranes represent bad will and miserliness.

One of the most significant Irish myths involving cranes is that of FLONNUALA and her brothers, the CHILDREN OF LIR, in which the evil sorceress stepmother AÍFE transformed the children into SWANS and was herself cursed to become a crane. A strange crane-like stance, in which a person stood on one leg while holding out one arm, was used in cursing; the goddess BADB assumed this position at DA DERGA's hostel when she cursed king CONAIRE for breaking his sacred vows. An ancient Irish taboo on eating crane's meat has suggested to some that the bird once had a totemic function, as an ancestral divinity or symbol.

Sources: Green, Miranda. *Symbol and Image in Celtic Religious Art.* London: Routledge, 1989, pp. 183, 279; MacCulloch, J. A. *The Religion of the Ancient Celts.* London: Constable, 1911, p. 38.

crane bag Irish mythological symbol. Texts disagree as to whether the AÍFE of this tale is the same as the evil stepmother of the story of the CHILDREN OF LIR. Some describe the jealous sorceress Aífe, after being turned to a CRANE for her malevolence in turning the children of Lir into swans, flying away to live on the sea, the domain of MANANNÁN MAC LIR; other tales appear to describe another woman of the same name. Despite her wickedness, she lived to the ripe age of 200 and died of natural causes, whereupon Manannán crafted a bag from her feathery skin in which to hold treasures, items of worth that had been lost in shipwreck. Another story has it that Aífe fell in love with a man named Ilbhreac, the beloved of the sorceress Iuchra, who cursed her rival and condemned her to become a crane.

Attempts to gain possession of the crane bag form the basis of several hero tales, including ones centered on FIONN MAC CUMHAILL.

Crannóg (Crannog)   Archaeological site. Early settlements in Celtic lands were often built on artificial ISLANDS in LAKES and were made of brush and surrounded by wattle fences; the lake provided protection for the residents of the crannóg as well as the necessary life-giving liquid. There is some evidence that the building of the circular dwellings on such lake settlements was invented in pre-Celtic times; they were used into the early Christian era, and indeed in some cases as late as the 17th century C.E. Some restored crannógs can be seen at historical parks, notably Cragganowen, near Ennis, Co. Clare, in Ireland.

Source: Aalen, F. H. A. *Man and the Landscape in Ireland.* London: Academic Press, 1978, p. 87.

creation   Cosmological concept. Most cultures have a myth that describes the creation of this world, usually from the chaos of an earlier world by a divine power, often a GODDESS. The Celts are among the few people who lack such a myth. Although several ancient authors including Strabo and Caesar refer to a Celtic cosmology, its creation myth either has been lost or never existed. Both Ireland and Scotland know creation stories centering on the great HAG, the CAILLEACH, who created the earth by dropping things (pebbles that became boulders, and the like) from her apron, but the Cailleach, although absorbed into the lore of the Celts, appears to have been pre-Celtic.

Créd   Irish heroine. Two famous breast-shaped mountains, the PAPS OF DANU in the southwestern province of MUNSTER, are associated with this FAIRY QUEEN or legendary heroine, who demanded that, to become her lover, a man had to compose a splendid praise-poem describing her heavily guarded palace—without ever seeing it. CÁEL, a seer as well as a poet, penetrated her defenses with his inner vision, composed the requisite poem, and won Créd's love. "Wounded men spouting heavy blood would sleep to the music of fairy birds singing above the bright leaves of her bower," were the words that won her heart. To protect her beloved, Créd made him a magical battle-dress; nonetheless he was killed in the service of his king, whereupon Créd threw herself into his grave and died. Créd was a poet herself, and one of her songs is included in the *COLLOQUY OF THE ELDERS.*

Either the same figure or another heroine of the same name was the daughter of legendary king GUAIRE and ancestral mother to the O'Connors. She too died tragically when, although married to another king, she fell in love with the warrior poet CANO MAC GARTNÁIN. Cano was visiting from Scotland, where his home was once so cheery that 50 fishing nets were rigged so that whenever fish were caught the bells chimed out. His father had been murdered, however, and Cano had escaped to the court of Créd's husband, where he was smitten with the queen. Créd, similarly stricken, gave everyone a sleeping potion except Cano, to whom she revealed her desire. Out of pride Cano refused to consummate his love with Créd until he had regained his patrimony. He gave her his EXTERNAL SOUL—a stone containing his essence—as a pledge of his love. The meddling of Créd's stepson brought such torment that Créd killed herself, crushing the stone of Cano's soul as she did so; Cano died several days later.

Creiddylad (Cordelia, Creudylad)   Welsh goddess. The springtime feast of BELTANE was dedicated in parts of Wales to Creiddylad, in whose honor a great contest was held between two contenders for her hand, GWYTHYR FAB GREIDAWL and GWYNN AP NUDD. Such May contests between winter and summer are known in other Celtic lands as well. Creiddylad was transformed into Cordelia, daughter of Lear in Shakespeare's play, but in Welsh mythology she was not the daughter of LLYR the sea god but of the the hero LLUDD; Shakespeare, who drew on the works of Geoffrey of Monmouth in writing his play, confused the two.

Creidne (Crédne)   Irish god. One of the artisan gods of the magical race called the TUATHA DÉ DANANN, Creidne "the brazier" specialized in precious metals like bronze and GOLD. Together with GOIBNIU and LUCHTAR, he was one of *na trí dée Dána*, the three craft gods of the Tuatha Dé. Danann Creidne made the weapons his people used in their battle against their terrifying enemy, the FOMORIANS. Some tales claim he was the SMITH who crafted the silver hand for king NUADA when the latter was injured in battle while other tales credit DIAN CÉCHT. Legend says that Creidne was drowned while attempting to import gold from Spain. Another Creidne was one of the WARRIOR WOMEN who fought with the famed FIANNA.

Crimthann   Several kings of Ireland were called by this name, as was the Christian saint who became the missionary scholar Colum Cille. The most important figures named Crimthann were:

- **Crimthann of Tara,** fosterling of king DIARMAIT; his charms caught the eye of queen BECFHOLA, but his unwillingness to travel on Sunday, when she was available for a tryst, ended their affair prematurely.
- **Crimthann Mór mac Fidaigh,** brother of the supernatural MONGFHINN and father of the cannibal woman EITHNE Úathach, was recorded as a historical king of TARA but exists at the margin between myth and history, as his relatives indicate.
- **Crimthann Nia Náir,** whose father was the striped man LUGAIDH Riab nDerg, and whose mother was also his grandmother, the incestuous CLOTHRA. Probably the incest motif here points to Clothra's position as goddess of SOVEREIGNTY, married in turn to each of the

kings of her land. He lost his life in the battle of the INTOXICATION OF THE ULSTERMEN, as did his fierce foster mother, the satirist RICHIS.

Croagh Patrick   Irish mythological site. In the west of Ireland, in Co. Mayo, a dramatic triangular mountain rises from sea level to 2,500 feet. Often wrapped in clouds, the mountain has been sacred for millennia, for pre-Celtic ruins have been found on its summit that date to the Neolithic period. It was once called Cruachan Aigle after AIGLE, a man who died there after carrying rocks in his pockets up its slopes; it now goes by the name of Croagh Patrick, after the saint who Christianized Ireland. It was there that ST. PATRICK fasted for 40 days and 40 nights in emulation of Christ's desert sojourn, then wrestled with the powers of pagan Ireland and finally defeated them in the form of CORRA, a demon who drowned in a LAKE at the peak's base.

The powers of PAGANISM did not stay thoroughly defeated, however, for the ancient festivals reemerged in new, albeit Christian dress. Such was the case with LUGHNASA, the ancient harvest festival that was converted to the still-extant Christian ritual of climbing Croagh Patrick, locally called The Reek, on the last Sunday in July. As many as 60,000 pilgrims—including, on one occasion, Princess Grace (Kelly) of Monaco—annually ascend the mountain, some barefoot, some on their knees. Climbing hills on Lughnasa was standard Celtic practice. More remnants of paganism cling to the festival in its local name, Domhnach Chrom Dubh or CROM DUBH's Sunday, after another pagan divinity that Patrick defeated in his struggle for Ireland's soul.

Source: Dames, Michael. *Mythic Ireland.* London: Thames and Hudson, 1992, pp. 167–188.

Crobh Dearg (Crove Derg)   Irish goddess. "Red claw" was an Irish goddess of the southwestern PROVINCE of MUNSTER, sometimes said to be the sister of LATIARAN, a Christianized goddess of the region, as well as the important local saint Gobnat. Possibly a form of BADB, Crobh Dearg is associated with a holy WELL on or near the famous PAPS OF DANU. Local tradition involved visiting the well and its nearby FAIRY MOUND, Cahercrovdarrig, on BELTANE; CATTLE from the vicinity were driven there for purification until recent times.

Source: MacNeill, Máire. *The Festival of Lughnasa. Parts I and II.* Dublin: Comhairle Bhéaloideas Éireann, 1982, pp. 272–274.

Crochan (Cruacha)   Irish heroine or goddess. The pregnant servant of the runaway queen of TARA, ÉTAIN, Crochan gave birth to the great queen and goddess MEDB in a cave in CONNACHT called variously OWEYNAGAT, the Cave of the Cats, or Síd Sinche, the fairy mound of Sinech (an otherwise unknown personage whose name means "large breasts"). Although the cave looks like a hole in the earth, Crochan saw the mystical site as a beautiful FAIRY palace and lived there even after her daughter built a palace on a rath or HILLFORT and named it CRUACHAN in her honor. Her name means "vessel"; she is sometimes called Crochan Crocderg or Croderg, "the blood-red cup."

crodh mara   Scottish mythological animal. The Highlanders of Scotland believed that, out in the ocean deeps, the FAIRIES kept hornless supernatural CATTLE that could come ashore to mate with mortal COWS, bettering the herds of earth. They were often RED, like many fairy creatures, but they were also sometimes seen as gray or dun.

Crom Cruach (Crom Crúaich, Cenn Cruaich, Cromm Cruaich)   Irish god. There is no known narrative regarding the activities of this deity, but he is recorded in several ancient sources as the primary god of the ancient Irish. He was worshiped, it is said, in the form of stone idols to which children were sacrificed. King TIGERNMAS worshiped Crom Cruach in this way every SAMHAIN, smashing the heads of first-born children against his ghastly image—believed to be the Killycluggan Stone with its scowling face, now on display in the National Museum of Ireland. Such stone images of the divine were said to have been destroyed by ST. PATRICK, following in the footsteps of such continental exemplars of piety as St. Martin of Tours, who demolished hundreds of Celtic and Roman statues in his attempt to purify the land of pagan influences. Many STANDING STONES, STONE CIRCLES, and other sacred images nonetheless escaped uninjured. Some have connected Crom Cruach to the DAGDA, the "good god" who provided abundance to his children; the early Irish scholar Vallancey claimed Crom-eocha was a name of the Dagda.

In the *DINDSHENCHAS*, the place-poetry of ancient Ireland, Crom Cruach is described as a war-inducing idol, at the base of which the blood of first born children had to be poured. So long as one-third of all children were sacrificed to him, the cruel deity would provide MILK and corn for the surviving people. The place where his GOLD idol stood, ringed by twelve fierce stone figures, was called Mag Slecht, believed now to be in northeast Co. Cavan.

Source: Gwynn, Edward. *The Metrical Dindshenchas.* Royal Irish Academy, Todd Lecture Series. Dublin: Hodges, Figgis, and Co., Ltd., 1906–1924, pp. 21–23.

Crom Dubh   Irish god or hero. This obscure figure appears in legends of ST. PATRICK as a pagan king who grew angry at Patrick for failing to sufficiently thank him for the gift of THREE BULLS; the saint had only said "thanks to god" with the arrival of each gift. When Patrick wrote his words on three slips of paper and had their weight calculated against that of the bulls, they were revealed to be identical, and Crom Dubh immediately was converted. Crom Dubh's name remains current as the title of the annual cele-bration at Croagh Patrick in Co. Mayo. Patrick's kingly adversary is sometimes called CROM CRU-ACH, suggesting that the "king" was a humanized version of an ancient god.

Cromlech See DOLMEN, MEGALITHIC CIVILIZATION.

Crón Irish goddess or god. Obscure ancient Irish divinity mentioned in several texts as "the swarthy one" or "the dark one" and connected with a giant SERPENT, perhaps the one also known as CAORANACH. She was said to live in an enchanted valley called Crón's Glen.

Crónánach Irish hero. Despite an impres-sively ugly appearance, this OTHERWORLD piper from the FENIAN CYCLE played marvelously, and when morning light struck his features, he was transformed into a handsome man who could pass for a king.

crooker British folkloric spirit. Travelers to the Derwent River in the English Peaklands were cautioned to beware of this haunting spirit.

crossing water Folkloric motif. In some Celtic lands, including on the Isle of Man, it was believed that FAIRIES could not cross running water; thus if one were pursued by the WILD HUNT, running across a stream offered protec-tion. Standing water was no substitute, as fairies were often said, especially in Ireland, to live on ISLANDS in or under the waves of LAKES.

crow Symbolic animal. One of the most mythologically significant BIRDS of Celtic lands, the black-feathered crow was usually connected to the goddess in Ireland, although in Wales it is the god/hero BRÂN THE BLESSED who bears a crow-name, for Brân means raven or "carrion crow." Black-winged MÓRRÍGAN and the scald-

crow BADB both took crow forms, as did the con-tinental Celtic CATHUBODUA; all were connected with battle, and some have described the shriek-ing black-robed DRUID women of ANGLESEY as enacting the part of the crow goddess as battle raged. War, death, and foreboding were associ-ated with the crow goddess, who flew over the battlefield searching for carrion rather like the Scandinavian Valkyries.

Perhaps because they hover over dying beasts as though predicting death, crows were believed to have premonitory or divinatory powers (see DIVINATION). Continental Celts believed that crows could reveal where a town would best be situated. They could be trusted to settle disputes wisely; complainants had only to set out similarly sized piles of food and let the birds either eat or scatter one claimed in advance by the more truthful contender. In Ireland it was considered ill-fortune to have a crow look down your chim-ney, for that would indicate a coming death.

Sources: MacCulloch, J. A. *The Religion of the Ancient Celts.* London: Constable, 1911, p. 247; O'Sullivan, Patrick V. *Irish Superstitions and Legends of Animals and Birds.* Cork: Mercier, 1991, p. 25.

Cruachan (Crogan, Rathcrogan, Cruachain, Crúachu, Rathcruachain, Bri Ele) Irish mytho-logical site. In the eastern part of the western PROVINCE of CONNACHT was its capital, Cruachan, the seat of its great queen and god-dess, MEDB. Now anglicized as Rathcrogan and close to the tiny town of Tulsk in Co. Roscommon, Cruachan was one of Ireland's most important ancient sites, the regional equiv-alent of EMAIN MACHA in ULSTER and TARA in MEATH. Replete with earthworks and antiquities, some 49 in all, it can still be visited today.

The land around it rises gradually, so that even the relatively small raths and other earth-works on the site command a grand view over the province and out to the midlands. The cen-tral rath (see HILLFORT) after which the complex

Cúchulainn

is named, rises to 4 meters in height and is 88 meters in diameter. Other earthworks in the area include Dáithi's Mound, topped with a tall STANDING STONE; avenues that resemble those at Tara; and most important, the CAVE of the CATS, OWEYNAGAT.

The figure most closely associated with Cruachan was Medb. She was born there, in the cave of Oweynagat, to a woman named CROCHAN Crocderg who gave her name to the entire area. At Cruachan Medb lived with her husband AILILL. Nothing remains of Medb's supposed fort except the unexcavated steep-sided rath near the center of the archaeological site, ringed about by five concentric circles. Also on the two-mile-square site are the Rath of the Bulls, whose name recalls the most significant story set at Cruachan, the *TÁIN BÓ CUAILNGE* or *Cattle Raid of Cooley*, an expedition that set out for ULSTER from Cruachan on SAMHAIN. Samhain was also the time of the other great epic set at Cruachan, the *Echtra Nerai*, the *Adventures of NERA*, in which one of Ailill's men descended to the OTHERWORLD through Oweynagat.

Sources: Dames, Michael. *Mythic Ireland*. London: Thames and Hudson, 1992, pp. 237–242; Gwynn, Edward. *The Metrical Dindshenchas*. vol. III. Royal Irish Academy, Todd Lecture Series. Dublin: Hodges, Figgis, and Co., Ltd., 1906–1924, pp. 349–355; Hull, Eleanor. *The Cuchullin Saga in Irish Literature*. London: David Nutt, 1898, pp. 111 ff; Raftery, Brian. *Pagan Celtic Ireland: The Enigma of the Irish Iron Age*. London: Thames and Hudson, 1994, p. 70.

Crudel Arthurian hero. When the Jewish merchant JOSEPH OF ARIMATHEA arrived in Britain bearing the GRAIL, the cup that Jesus Christ had used at his Last Supper, he was met by the pagan king Crudel, who imprisoned the visitor until he was released by Christian warriors.

Crunniuc (Cronnchu, Crunnchu) Irish hero. A mortal man selected by the goddess (or FAIRY QUEEN) MACHA, who lived with him on his farm, bringing prosperity and wealth to man and land. When Crunniuc announced his intention of traveling to the Assembly of ULSTER, a pregnant Macha attempted to dissuade him, but to no avail; he would brook no opposition. So she settled for a promise that he would not discuss her with anyone, nor even mention her presence in his life.

Crunniuc was unable to keep his promise and, even worse, boasted that Macha was faster than the king's swiftest horses. A race ensued, which Macha won. She collapsed at the finish line, however, giving birth to TWINS as she died and cursing the entire region with the famous DEBILITY OF THE ULSTERMEN. Nothing is said of Crunniuc after his wife's death, although he cannot have been a popular person thereafter.

Cuailnge (Cooley) Irish mythological sites. This lush peninsula juts out into the Irish Sea on the east coast of Ireland, just below Carlingford Lough, a narrow bay named for a Viking called Carling who plundered the area in historic times. The name of the peninsula is now usually anglicized to Cooley. To the north, across the bay, rise the blue-gray Mountains of Mourne, while along the spine of the Cooley peninsula run the low forested Cooley mountains. The region is famous in Irish myth, for it was to this narrow strip of land, home to the magical bull DONN CUAILNGE, that the great TÁIN or CATTLE raid was launched by queen MEDB from her stronghold in CRUACHAN.

See *TÁIN BÓ CUAILNGE*.

Cúchulainn (Cuhullin, Cú Chulainn, Cuchullin) Irish hero. Irish legend has no hero to match him, nor any stronger or more renowned in battle, although the mighty FIONN MAC CUMHAILL comes close. Cúchulainn appears most prominently in the ULSTER CYCLE, which tells how he was born magically when his mother, DECHTIRE, drank water with a worm in it; the same magical conception story is told of Cúchulainn's king CONCOBAR MAC NESSA, so the two are mythic doubles. Concobar was either Dechtire's brother or father, and when the unmarried woman began to show her pregnancy, rumors circulated that the child was the result of incest. Dechtire married, but her shame caused Cúchulainn to be born prematurely; he lived nonetheless, bearing the name of SÉTANTA.

All the heroes of Ireland argued over who would foster the brilliant young man, but his mother decided that each should offer a special gift. Thus Cúchulainn gained all the best ancient Ireland had to offer: the poetry of AMAIRGIN, the eloquence of Sencha, the wealth of Blaí Briuga. The powerful FERGUS MAC RÓICH served as his tutor in the manly arts, while kindly FINDCHÓEM nursed him; CONALL CERNACH was his foster brother and Concobar, his foster father.

Variants claim Cúchulainn was the son of SUALTAIM MAC ROICH, an otherwise unknown ULSTER chief usually called his foster father; or of the god LUGH, conceived when Dechtire was in the enchanted form of a bird. All the tales agree that Cúchulainn showed his warrior nature early. At five years old, he went along to the great court at EMAIN MACHA, challenging all the boys there to a contest with child-size weapons, which he won handily.

When king Concobar traveled to CUAILNGE— a place that would play such an important part in Cúchulainn's later life—the boy Sétanta was left behind playing. He caught up with the royal party at the home of the SMITH, CULANN, which was guarded by a vicious dog that Cúchulainn easily killed in order to enter. The host deplored this wanton killing, but the gracious seven-year-old promised to serve as Culann's hound until he found a suitable replacement. Thus the boy earned his adult name, for Cú means "hound," and the hero was the "hound of Culann."

We next hear of the boy hero when he grew furious at his hurling companions and brained them all, going into such a contortion of fury that he became virtually unrecognizable. He raged back to Concobar's fortress, still swollen with fury—for when he fought, Cúchulainn went into what was called the "warp-spasm,"

with one eye retreating into his skull while the other protruded, and with columns of blood and light projecting from his head. It took several huge vats of water to cool his fury.

When he grew old enough to court a woman, Cúchulainn settled upon the fair EMER, who had all the finest attributes of womanhood as he did of manhood. Emer's father, FORGALL MANACH, did not approve of the match and sent Cúchulainn on what he thought was a fool's errand: to study with the WARRIOR WOMAN SCÁTHACH in Scotland. There Cúchulainn convinced the skilled warrior to teach him her secrets, which resembled the kind of astonishing feats seen today in martial-arts movies. One impressive maneuver, however, he seems to have invented himself: the SALMON-leap, a kind of frisky pounce that made Cúchulainn virtually unstoppable in battle.

While in Scotland, and despite his promise to be true to his intended Emer, Cúchulainn had a dalliance with the warrior AÍFE, who conceived a son by him. When he was grown to young manhood, Aífe gave their son CONNLA Cúchulainn's ring and sent him to Ireland. The boy refused to identify himself to his father, and so Cúchulainn unknowingly and unwittingly killed Connla. Despite ultimately marrying Emer, Cúchulainn had many affairs, including one with the fairy queen FAND, who stole him away from human life. None, however, resulted in another son.

Cúchulainn's most famous adventure was his single-handed defense of Concobar's Ulster against the CATTLE RAID initiated by queen MEDB. His chief weapon was his spear, GÁE BULGA. As Cúchulainn was not actually an Ulsterman, he did not suffer the debility brought on by the dying curse of MACHA, wherein the men of Ulster would fall down in something resembling labor pains for four days and five nights whenever their land was attacked. While the Ulstermen were writhing in pain, Cúchulainn fended off one hero after another, killing them all in single combat, including his beloved foster brother FERDIAD. (For a complete description of Cúchulainn's feats in that epic battle, see TÁIN BÓ CUAILNGE.)

Cúchulainn died when he violated his GEIS or sacred vow never to eat DOG meat. Various versions of his death are given in ancient texts, but one constant is his refusal to meet death in any other way than standing. To assure that he would do so, Cúchulainn had himself chained to a pillar, where he was attacked by javelins and other weapons even long after his death. Only when the carrion CROWS, servants of the goddess BADB, flew down to peck at his eyes, was the hero acknowledged to be gone.

Cúchulainn has inspired much literature after the heroic period. Yeats wrote several plays about him, including *The Only Jealousy of Emer*, about his affair with the fairy queen Fand, and *On Baile's Strand*, about his unwitting murder of his only son. Morgan Llywelyn's historical novel *Red Branch* details the Cúchulainn saga.

Sources: Cross, Tom Peete, and Clark Harris Slover, eds. *Ancient Irish Tales.* New York: Henry Holt and Co., 1936, pp. 134–153; Hull, Eleanor. *The Cuchullin Saga in Irish Literature.* London: David Nutt, 1898, pp. 15, 253.

Cucullatus See *GENIUS CUCULLATUS.*

Cuda British goddess. An obscure goddess, found in Cirencester, ancient capital of the Celtic Dobunni tribe; she was depicted seated and holding an egg, apparently a symbol of fruitfulness and potential.

Cuilenn (Cullen, Culann) Irish hero. This FAIRY king gave his name to a unique feature of the Northern Irish landscape, the Ring of Gullion, a huge circle of mountains created by ancient volcanic action. A mountain in the center, SLIEVE GULLION, was said to be his home—although local folklore also named the CAILLEACH as the occupant of the mountain, living beneath the CAIRN that crowns its summit. Near the summit of the mountain is a LAKE, said to turn gray anyone who swims in it.

FIONN MAC CUMHAILL tried his luck by swimming there, having been challenged by the FAIRY QUEEN ÁINE's lustful sister MILUCRA to do so. Because Áine had pledged never to sleep with a man with gray hair, and because she wanted Fionn for himself, Milucra set about making him unattractive to her sister. She built and bewitched a little lake on the summit of the mountain, where she tricked Fionn into swimming. He emerged silver-haired, aged, and bent. His men, the FIANNA, captured Milucra and forced her to give their leader a restorative potion from her golden CORNUCOPIA, but in doing so she made sure his hair remained silver. Some texts say it was Cuilenn came to Fionn's rescue by offering him a drink from a golden cup, which also endowed the hero with wisdom.

Sources: Joyce, P. W. *Ancient Celtic Romances.* London: Parkgate Books, 1997, pp. 351 ff; MacNeill, Máire. *The Festival of Lughnasa, Parts I and II.* Dublin: Comhairle Bhéaloideas Éireann, 1982, p. 164.

Cuirithir See LIADAN.

Culann Irish hero. A SMITH who forged the weapons for CÚCHULAINN's foster father, CONCOBAR MAC NESSA, he was entertaining the men of ULSTER when the boy SÉTANTA arrived late and wantonly killed his favorite dog. Culann was angry, and Sétanta offered to serve in the hound's stead until a canine replacement could be found, thus becoming Cú Chulainn, "hound of Culann." Some texts conflate Culann and Cuilenn, who may be the same or derived from the same figure.

Culhwch See KULHWCH.

Culhwch ac Olwen See KULHWCH AND OLWEN.

cumbal See MILK.

Cumhall (Camall, Camhall) Irish hero. Father of the great hero FIONN MAC CUMHAILL, whom he sired upon the unwilling MURNA, after abducting her from her father TADG mac Nuadat and causing enmity between his family, the CLAN BAÍSCNE, and hers, the CLAN MORNA. Although legends of Cumhall's death vary, he is commonly held to have been killed by Tadg's ally, CONN of the Hundred Battles, king of TARA.

Cunedda Welsh hero. In some mythological texts, this man is one of the original settlers of Wales, who arrived with his eight sons to found the Celtic kingdoms there. The dynasties of Gwynedd were named for him.

Cunobelinus (Cunobeline) British hero. The figure upon which Shakespeare built his tragic hero Cymbeline was a southern British warrior whose 40-year leadership of the Catuvallaunians ended with the invasion of the Romans.

Cunomaglus See APOLLO.

Cunrie (Kundrie, Kundry) Arthurian heroine. The name of the LOATHY LADY in some Arthurian texts; she is a form of the goddess of SOVEREIGNTY.

cup See GRAIL.

curad-mír (*curadmir*) See CHAMPION'S PORTION.

Cú Roí Irish hero. As CÚCHULAINN was the great hero of ULSTER, the northern PROVINCE of Ireland, so was Cú Roí to MUNSTER in the southwest; possibly the hero stood at the center of a lost epic cycle of which only tantalizing bits remain. Even the meaning of his name is unknown—the first part means "hound," a common name for heroes, but the last part is unclear, as is his connection to the mythological ancestor DÍRE, of

whom he was sometimes said to be the son but sometimes appeared to be the double. Similarly, Cú Roí's relationship to the various figures named LUGAIDH is confusing, although the latter is sometimes mentioned as the former's son.

Like Cúchulainn, Cú Roí first revealed his prowess as a child, becoming a fighter at a precociously early age. After reaching maturity he embarked upon many adventures and campaigns, being king at TARA according to some texts and therefore subject to the kind of GEIS that such kings as CONAIRE also endured. He was said to have traveled to the OTHERWORLD in the company of Cúchulainn to steal away its treasures, including the magical woman BLÁTHNAT, three Otherworldly COWS, and a CAULDRON of abundance. The agreement was that the booty would be evenly split—how three cows can be evenly divided among two heroes is not revealed, though the parallelism of woman and cauldron is notable—but Cúchulainn reneged on the deal. Cú Roí, in retaliation, buried Cúchulainn so that only his head stuck out of the ground, then shaved his erstwhile companion entirely bald and covered him with cow dung.

Bláthnat became Cú Roí's queen, but she betrayed him by conspiring with Cúchulainn, whom she had taken as a lover, to reveal the circumstances that would permit her husband to be killed: If a SALMON, his EXTERNAL SOUL, was killed, Cú Roí would meet his doom. And indeed, upon the slaying of the magical salmon, Cú Roí lost his strength and was easily killed. Cú Roí was avenged when his loyal poet FERCHERTNE grabbed the traitorous woman and leapt off a cliff to his death—causing hers at the same time.

Cú Roí had many adventures before that unfortunate end, including one in which he disguised himself as a herdsman to create dissent among Cúchulainn and two other heroes, CONALL Cernach and LÓEGURE BÚADACH. Urging them each to cut off his head, in return for which he would cut off theirs, Cú Roí was twice decapitated and twice rejoined head to body, but both Conall and Lóegure refused to fulfill the entire bargain. Only CÚCHULAINN offered his own neck after the third decapitation and miraculous recapitation, and so Cú Roí announced him as the chief of all heroes.

Unlike his human Ulster counterpart, Cú Roí appears to have been originally a deity transformed into a hero, for he lived in a rotating OTHERWORLD fortress whose entrance disappeared after sunset; the site is variously locked in the Slieve Mish mountains of Co. Kerry or at Temair Luachra, an untraceable place that probably refers to TARA in Co. Meath. Within that castle he kept his magical CAULDRON, so huge that 30 oxen fit inside it; thus he resembles the fertility deity called the DAGDA. Some have found in Cú Roí an ancestral deity of Munster, others a figure of the sacred king who brings good fortune with an honest reign (see SACRAL KINGSHIP).

Sources: Cross, Tom Peete, and Clark Harris Slover, eds. *Ancient Irish Tales.* New York: Henry Holt and Co., 1936, p. 328; Gantz, Jeffrey. *Early Irish Myths & Sagas.* New York: Penguin, 1981, p. 219. O'Rahilly, Thomas. *Early Irish History and Mythology.* Dublin: The Dublin Institute for Advanced Studies, 1946, p. 321.

curse Cosmological concept. The Celts, because they believed fiercely in the power of the word, took both blessing and cursing very seriously. A special power and responsibility of the BARD was to ensure that the king was generous and responsible. Should a king prove stingy, as was the case of BRES mac Elatha, it was the poet's job to level a sufficiently dreadful curse upon him that he would become physically blemished. Since a BLEMISHED KING could not retain the throne, such a curse would bring new leadership.

Other famous curses in Celtic mythology include the one that AÍFE, stepmother of the CHILDREN OF LIR placed on her stepchildren, which turned them into SWANS; the retaliatory curse leveled upon her by the children's grandfather, the magician BODB DERG, which turned Aífe into a CRANE; and the curse of MACHA that brought down the men of ULSTER every time

they were invaded (see DEBILITY OF THE ULSTERMEN). Curses were not easily undone, for they required someone more powerful than the original speaker to change their outcome. They could also be long-lasting; Aífe's curse on the Children of Lir lasted almost a thousand years.

Humans as well as divinities employed verbal curses. In Ireland a person visited a designated spot—a holy WELL or CURSING STONE—and spoke the words, sometimes while engaging in some ritual, such as turning round stones against the sun (counterclockwise). The interruption in the expected order would be carried forth together with the words to bring destruction to the victim. In Cornwall pins stuck into apples or potatoes caused harm to the intended victim, and it was believed that verbal curses became ineffective if spoken aloud rather than muttered in a low tone.

cursing stones Irish ritual object. Around Ireland, one can still find stones that are reputed to carry curses farther and faster and to make them stronger than if the same curse is uttered without the help of the stones. Typically they are small round stones in a graveyard or other sacred site. Often a specific ritual is attached to the use of the cursing stones. In Ballysummaghan and Baroe, in Co. Sligo, for instance, one has to be barefoot for the curse to work. Undoing the curse is difficult, if not impossible. In the Sligo case, the cursed person has to agree to be temporarily buried while charms against the curse are recited. In Co. Clare, at Kilmoon between Killeany and Lisdoonvarna, some famous cursing stones led in the 18th century to a murder after the victim was believed to have been "turning the stones against" the attacker.

cú síth Scottish mythological being. Unlike other FAIRY creatures, the Highland fairy DOG was neither black (see BLACK DOG) nor RED with white ears, but dark green and the size of a small BULL. It made enormous footprints, the size of a large man's, and always moved in a straight line as it traversed the world hunting for prey, including other dogs.

Custennin Welsh hero. This minor figure in the story of *KULHWYCH AND OLWEN* was the herdsman to Olwen's father, the GIANT YSPAD-DADEN PENKAWR.

c'wn annwn (cwn annwfn) Welsh mytholog-ical beings. The hounds of the OTHERWORLD of Welsh mythology were, like many other FAIRY creatures, RED with white ears, although they could also look like normal beagles. But they did not act like normal DOGS, ranging through the world baying in terrifying voices. Their presence was believed to portend death.

See BLACK DOG, GABRIEL HOUNDS.

Cycle of the Kings (Historical Cycle) Mythic story sequence. There are several major sequences of Irish mythology, centering on dif-ferent figures, geographic areas, and eras. The ULSTER CYCLE revolves around the heroes of that province, CÚCHULAINN and CONCOBAR MAC NESSA, as well as FERGUS mac Roich, who joins their great opponent MEDB. The FENIAN CYCLE centers on FIONN MAC CUMHAILL and the band of warriors he leads, the FIANNA, including OISÍN and DIARMAIT. The MYTHOLOGICAL CYCLE includes stories of the gods themselves, including the great divinities of the TUATHA DÉ DANANN.

The HISTORICAL CYCLE, sometimes called the Cycle of the Kings, includes tales of the kings of TARA, including CONN of the Hundred Battles and NIALL of the Nine Hostages, as well as ART MAC CUINN and the mad king SUIBHNE. Many of the myths incorporated in this cycle focus on the king's righteousness or lack thereof and its results. Some of the kings are known to historical record, but the stories told of them are exagger-ated and magical. Like other Irish mythological texts, these tales reveal something of the past, but exactly what is highly questionable.

Cyhyreath See CAOINTEACH.

Cymidei Cymeinfoll Welsh heroine. A Welsh giantess and wife of the similarly gigantic LLASSAR LLAESGYFNEWID, she owned the CAUL-DRON of regeneration that gave rise to much of the action of the second branch of the *MABINO-GION*. She herself gave birth to innumerable armored warriors, once every six weeks; her name has been translated as "big bellied battler."

Source: Gantz, Jeffrey, trans. *The Mabinogion.* New York: Barnes & Noble Books, 1976, pp. 72, 75, 87.

Cymon Welsh hero. He plays a minor role in the story of OWEIN, the hero who married the lovely LADY OF THE FOUNTAIN, for he set Owein's quest in motion when he unsuccessfully fought against the Black Knight who was belea-guering the lady's domain.

Cymru Welsh term. The people of Wales were not originally called Welsh, which means "strangers" in the tongue of their British neigh-bors. In their own language, still in use, the peo-ple are called "brethren" or "friends." Cymru is the land, Cymri the people, and Cymric the lan-guage they speak.

Cynan Welsh hero. The brother-in-law of the quasi-historical king MAXEN, Cynan helped Maxen become the western Roman emperor. He was rewarded for his service by being allowed to take control of Brittany, where he mutilated the local women by cutting out their tongues, in order to preserve his own warriors' Welsh lan-guage by eliminating any potential competition. Like Maxen, Cynan is probably fictional rather than strictly mythological, invented to serve a political purpose rather than linked with ritual and worship.

D

Da Derga (Da Dearga, Ûa Dergae) Irish god or hero. One of the most significant Irish narratives dealing with the ancient Celtic vision of KINGSHIP is set in the hostel or inn of this obscure character. When the king of TARA, CONAIRE, arrived at Da Derga's hostel on the magical feast of SAMHAIN (November 1) after breaking a series of sacred vows (see GEIS), he faced his doom within it. First a HAG came to him demanding entrance; when he denied it, she stood on one leg like a CRANE and cursed him. Immediately, Conaire developed an all-consuming thirst, which no water from any source in Ireland could quench, and died of it. Da Derga made no attempt to help him, implying that he was in agreement with the punishment.

The identity—indeed even the name—of Da Derga is unclear. Some texts give him as Ûa Dergae, "the nephew of the red goddess," while others call him Da Derga, "the red god." If the former is correct, he could be related to MEDB or Flaith, goddesses of SOVEREIGNTY, a reasonable enough connection given that the story's main point is the punishment of the king for not maintaining his sacred vows as the earth goddess demanded. If the latter, he may have been a god of the OTHERWORLD, for the color RED is commonly linked to that realm. Da Derga has virtually no personality and little role in the story named for him.

Sources: Cross, Tom Peete, and Clark Harris Slover, eds. *Ancient Irish Tales.* New York: Henry Holt and Co., 1936, p. 93; Dillon, Myles, ed. *Irish Sagas.* Cork: The Mercier Press, 1968, p. 105; Gantz, Jeffrey, ed. and transl. *Early Irish Myths and Sagas.* New York: Penguin Books, 1984, pp. 60 ff.

Dagda (Daghdha, Dagdae, Dagda Mór, Cera, Samildanach) Irish god. This ancient Irish divinity was called "the good god," because he was good at everything; while other gods of the TUATHA DÉ DANANN were specialists, the Dagda was an artisan and a diviner, a husbandman and a warrior and a wise king, all at once. He was also benevolent, the god of abundance and fecundity. The Dagda owned a magical CAULDRON that could never be emptied and a mallet (whose phallic meaning is unmistakable) so huge it had to be be dragged along on a cart. He also had a pair of magical PIGS that could be eaten again and again but always revived themselves, as well as an orchard that, no matter the season, was always filled with fruit. The Dagda was thus not only an ideal of masculine excellence but also a god of the earth's FERTILITY.

He was no handsome swain; far from it. The Dagda was portrayed as an almost comic character, wheeling his huge mallet along, dressed in a too-short tunic that left his privates exposed, indulging his extreme and excessive appetites whenever he desired. Yet he was invariably helpful, a force of fertility that could not be ignored or avoided. He was called by several alternative names that stress his benevolence: Eochaid Ollathair, "father of all," and Ruad Rofhessa, "lord of great knowledge." Some scholars connect him with the mysterious god named CROM CRUACH, citing as evidence the Dagda's untranslated title Crom-eocha. He was also one of the multivalent gods who were called by the title of Samiladanach, "many-skilled man."

The Dagda had many mates among the Irish goddesses, including the black-winged MÓRRÍGAN, whom he encountered at the River Unshin (Unius) in CONNACHT, standing with one foot on each bank and washing the clothes of those about to be killed in battle (see WASHER AT THE FORD). True to form, when the Dagda saw the enormous goddess bending over the stream, he was overcome with desire and engaged her in intercourse. So satisfactory did she find their encounter that she agreed to support his side in the next day's battle at MAG TUIRED, singing her magical chants from the sidelines as the Tuatha Dé Danann fought their mortal enemies, the monstrous beings called the FOMORIANS, and finally drove them from Ireland.

Most often, the Dagda is described as the consort of BÓAND, another deity of abundance. Among their many children were the goddess of inspiration, BRIGIT, and the god of poetry and beauty, AONGHUSÓG; thus poetry is, symbolically, the offspring of an abundant life. The Dagda's other children included the FAIRY king MIDIR and the great magician BODB DERG. As consort to Bóand, the Dagda was associated with the great BRÚ NA BÓINNE, the vast ceremonial earthworks on the Boyne, the river named for Bóand, which later became his son Aonghus's palace. Because the Dagda had consorted in secret with Bóand, who was at the time the wife of the god NECHTAN, he is sometimes called the foster father of Aonghus. He was sufficiently devoted to his son that, when Aonghus wanted to marry, the Dagda provided the bride-price: clearing 12 great

plains overnight so that Aonghus might have his beloved.

Another of the Dagda's many children was ÁED MINBHREC, who was killed in a jealous rage by a man named CORGENN. Despite his power, the Dagda could not revive his beloved son, but he put a sacred vow (see GEIS) on Corgenn, forcing him to carry his victim's body on his back until he found a stone the exact size and weight of the deceased. Only then could Corgenn rest. Thus the man hauled the body around Ireland until he found a place for it: the ancient HILLFORT of GRIANÁN AILEACH in Co. Donegal.

Although the force of fertility itself cannot be killed, the Dagda was said to have died in the second battle of MAG TUIRED. He fought valiantly, even heroically, but a woman named CETHLION, wife of the Fomorian king BALOR, killed the Dagda. Afterward he continued his reign from the afterlife of the OTHERWORLD, where he enjoyed his four great palaces and ate his fill from his magically abundant cauldron and ever-fruiting orchard.

Sources: Gwynn, Edward. *The Metrical Dindshenchas.* Royal Irish Academy, Todd Lecture Series. Dublin: Hodges, Figgis, and Co., Ltd., 1906–1924; MacCulloch, J. A. *The Religion of the Ancient Celts.* London: Constable, 1911, pp. 74–77 ff.

Dagonet   Arthurian hero. Although originally only king ARTHUR's jester, Dagonet showed his bravery in battle after being knighted as a joke.

Dahut (Dahud, Ahés, Ahé, Keben)   Breton heroine or goddess. The most renowned Breton folktale tells of a princess whose great city of YS gleamed behind its seawalls off the coast of La Raz, at the tip of the peninsula of Brittany, or perhaps in the port of today's city of Douarnenez. Daughter of the Christian king GRADLON, Dahut herself followed the old religion and worshiped the old powers of the land. With the help of the sea magicians called the *KORRIGANS*, Dahut set about building the world's most magnificent city. Great walls were erected so that marshy land could be reclaimed from the deep; the walls were so cleverly painted by DWARFS that they appeared to be GOLD. Only Dahut had the key to the gates that kept back the waters, and she wore it on a chain around her fair neck. She built herself a beautiful palace, with stables whose marble floors matched the colors of the horses they housed. Her wealth came to her from the sea, for she had captured and harnessed sea DRAGONS, which daily brought her riches from abroad.

Magnificent homes rose within the new city, which became so renowned that it would one day be said that Paris itself was only a reflection, like Ys (par-Ys, a false etymology) but not so grand. But the people of Ys grew hard and selfish; they would not endure beggars or even working people in their beautiful city, accepting only those who were wealthy and beautiful. Despite the miserliness of her people, Dahut's city rang day and night with music and song, while Dahut received in her own palace entourages of princes and nobles from around the world.

That palace harbored a dark secret, for each night Dahut selected the most handsome of her visitors and secretly gave him a mask that, she whispered, would allow him to pass unseen to her tower bedroom. And so he did, slipping excitedly past the guard and into the waiting arms of the princess. After a night of pleasure, as the swallows flying past the tower windows alerted them to dawn's arrival, the chosen man would put on the mask again to retrace his steps. But this time the mask would grow tighter and tighter until it squeezed the very breath out of the unfortunate young man, after which a servant would haul the body to an abyss between Huelgoat and Pualoauen.

One night Dahut met her match, however. Dancing at a ball with a prince whose attractive demeanor set her thinking about that evening's pleasure, she was surprised to hear him call for a certain tune on the pipes. As she danced, she found herself whirling faster and faster, unable to stop. The people around her, too, danced

faster and faster, growing more and more terrified at their inability to stop either the music or their response to it. Then the stranger—for this was not really a prince but CADO, a sea demon who wanted Dahut in his own realm forever; or perhaps it was the DEVIL himself—slipped his hand into Dahut's secret neck-pouch and extracted the silver key to the great seawalls. As the horrified residents danced on and on, they saw him open the sluices, saw the water begin to pour into the city, saw it rush into the ballroom and rise around their dancing feet.

Only the Christian king Gradlon was able to get away, led off by St. Coretin (or GUÉNOLÉ in some versions), who provided a horse for him. The king rode into Dahut's palace to rescue her, but as soon as she mounted behind her father, the horse refused to move. The saint called to Gradlon to push his daughter into the water, and, desperately, he did so, pushing Dahut into the turbulent sea. Then, in a great leap, the horse moved again. It struck the Rock of Garrec on the Breton coast, where its hoofprint can still be seen. Some tales say that Dahut was thrown into the very abyss where her victims rested, the Abyss of Ahéz. Others claim that Dahut did not die but lives on, as a MERMAID floating above her sunken city, still luring men to their doom.

The story of Dahut may well have its basis in ancient Celtic myth, but with the coming of Christianity, condemnation of ancient pagan rites was so interwoven with the tale that it is impossible to know what elements are original and what were added to make it an instructional parable. In the beginning of the story, Dahut lives at one with nature and the elemental spirits, who make possible her regal life in her crystalline city. That she brings death as well as life to the city suggests that she was based on a misinterpretation of an ancient divinity of life's cycle.

Sources: *Breton Folktales*. London: G. Bell & Sons, 1971, p. 198; Guyot, Charles. *The Legend of the City of Ys*. Trans. and illus. by Deirdre Cavanagh. Amherst: University of Massachusetts Press, 1979.

Dáire (Dara)   Irish hero. Like ÁED and AILILL, Dáire is a name found frequently in Irish mythology and mythological history. Meaning "fertile" or "fruitful," it is sometimes anglicized as Dara; but the name Dara may also derive from *doire*, which means "oak" or "oak grove." Some scholars contend that although the various figures bearing this name appear to be different and have different regional associations, they spring from the same root, perhaps a god like the DAGDA who ruled FERTILITY. In addition to several minor figures in the FENIAN CYCLE, the most important figures bearing this name are:

- **Dáire, father of** LUGAIDH Laíghde and his four brothers (also named Lugaidh); Dáire heard a prophecy that his son Lugaidh would become king of Ireland. Hedging his bets, Dáire gave that name to all his sons.
- **Dáire, son of** FIONN MAC CUMHAILL (sometimes recorded as CONÁN), who was swallowed by a monstrous worm that he killed from within to free himself.
- **Dáire of the Poems,** BARD and musician of the band of heroes called the FIANNA, who was known for the beauty of his songs.
- **Dáire Derg,** "red Dáire," a one-eyed villain whose children, the Fothads, were adversaries of FIONN MAC CUMHAILL.
- **Dáire mac Dedad,** ancestor of the Érainn people, an early race in Ireland, perhaps an ancestor god euhemerized or demoted into a mortal.
- **Dáire mac Fiachan,** owner of DONN CUAILNGE, the great brown BULL sought by queen MEDB in the epic *TÁIN BÓ CUAILNGE*. Dáire originally agreed to give the Donn to Medb in exchange for her "friendly things" (one of the epic's most famous phrases), but when he heard Mebd's men boasting of how Dáire's acquiescence was irrelevant as they would take the bull in any case, he decided to fight rather than be perceived as weak. This decision set in motion the CATTLE RAID on his territories, in what is now the Cooley peninsula in Co. Louth.

Source: MacNeill, Máire. *The Festival of Lughnasa. Parts I and II.* Dublin: Comhairle Bhéaloideas Éireann, 1982, pp. 434–436, 451–452.

Daireann (Doirend, Doirinn)   Irish heroine. The sister of the better-known heroine SADB, Daireann took a fancy to the great warrior FIONN MAC CUMHAILL, who did not return the interest. In revenge, she poisoned him—not with a death potion but with an enchanted elixir that drove the great man insane. Most of Fionn's followers, the FIANNA, abandoned him during his insanity, but they returned when his wits did. Daireann's pride took another blow when Fionn had a child with Sadb, who became his favorite follower, the poet OISÍN.

Dáirine   Irish heroine. This Irish princess, daughter of the minor king Tuathal Techtmar, caught the eye of the king of Ireland's eastern province, LEINSTER. But that king, Eochaid, was forced by Tuathal to marry Dáirine's older sister FITHIR instead. Eochaid outwitted his father-in-law, however; he claimed that Fithir had died and promptly wed the younger sister. He did not have much happiness with her, for Dáirine happened upon the place where Fithir was being held captive and thus discovered her husband's perfidy.

Dame du Lac   See LADY OF THE LAKE.

Dames Vertes   French folkloric figures. In areas of modern France that were once Celtic territory, we find folktales about these "Green Ladies" who lurk in the forests, luring travelers into ravines by their beauty and their sweet voices, then tormenting them by holding them upside down over waterfalls and laughing at their terror. Such elemental spirits are found in many cultures; in the case of the Dames Vertes, they were especially associated with the wind, on which they traveled across the land, making plants grow with their breath. They could also take human form, always being dressed in

GREEN, a color known in Ireland to be the favorite choice of the FAIRY people.

See also GREEN LADIES.

Damona Continental Celtic goddess. Among the countless goddesses of Celtic Gaul we find Damona, whose name appears to mean "divine COW" and who thus may be a goddess similar to the Irish BÓAND; she has also been interpreted as a goddess of sheep. She was described as the consort, variously, of the gods BORVO and APOLLO Mortitasgus, both relatively obscure divinities; she may have been polyandrous, having both husbands at once.

Dana See DANU.

dancing lights See FAIRY LIGHTS.

dancing stones see MERRY MAIDENS.

Danu (Dana, Anu, possibly Donand, Danann) Irish goddess. Since there was once a goddess of this name in Ireland, it is possible that one appeared in other Celtic countries as well. Although no myths about her still exist, there are many place-names that bear her name; the Dane Hills, home of the HAG named BLACK ANNIS; the great river Danube of eastern Europe; and the famous PAPS OF DANU in Ireland's southwestern province of MUNSTER, two rounded breast-shaped hills topped in prehistory with rock CAIRNS in the position of nipples. Most significantly, we find an Irish divine race, thought to represent the gods of the Celts, called the TUATHA DÉ DANANN, the people of the goddess Danu; they were later called the *daoine sídhe*, anglicized as Dana O'Shee or FAIRY-folk, after being demoted and diminished from divinity into folktale figures.

Danu's name has been derived from the Old Celtic *dan*, meaning "knowledge," and she has been linked to the Welsh mother goddess DÔN. Some texts call her the daughter of the mighty DAGDA, the good god of abundance, a connection that supports the contention that she was an ancient goddess of the land's fertility. She may be the same as Danann, daughter of the wilderness goddess FLIDAIS in some texts. She is sometimes said to be the mother of the SONS OF TUIREANN.

See also ANU.

Source: Condren, Mary. *The Serpent and the Goddess: Women, Religion and Power in Ancient Ireland.* San Francisco: Harper & Row, 1989, p. 57.

Daoine sídhe Irish folklore figures. One of the many euphemisms for the FAIRY people of Ireland, this term means "folk from the mound," for these diminished deities were believed to live in the ancient BARROWS, HILLFORTS, and other prehistoric monuments of Ireland (see FAIRY MOUND). Many other cordial and flattering terms were used, presumably to elicit the good will of the amoral and sometimes mischievous fairies: The Good Folk (*daoine maithe*), The Gentry (*daoine uaisle*), and simply Them.

darkness and light Cosmological concepts. Today we see dawn as the beginning of the day, which ends in night, but to the Celts, day began with evening and ended with afternoon, just as the year began with fall and ended in summer. Thus Celtic holidays fell on what we would consider the night before the actual feast day: for example, SAMHAIN, November 1, is still celebrated as Hallowe'en on October 31. Although any Celtic creation myth has been lost, this pattern suggests that our sunlit world was preceded by another, more shadowy one. The mythological idea of the OTHERWORLD, that separate but connected place from which objects in this world derive power, points to the same idea. The Celts did not see darkness and light as antagonists, in the way that the Persian philosophy of Manichaeism, for instance, did; rather, they were complementary parts of a single whole.

Source: Rees, Alwyn, and Brinely Rees. *Celtic Heritage: Ancient Tradition in Ireland and Wales.* London: Thames and Hudson, 1998, pp. 83 ff.

Dark Rosaleen See ROISIN DUBH.

Darlughdacha (Darludacha) Irish heroine. When the Celtic goddess BRIGIT was converted into a Christian saint of the same name, monkish writers provided her with a human biography: She was abbess of the great religious center at KILDARE. In these Christian texts, Darlughadacha—whose name means "daughter of (the Celtic god) LUGH"—was described as St. Brigit's boon companion, who shared a bed with her. When Darlughdacha deliberately burned her feet to mortify the flesh after gazing lustfully at a warrior, Brigit miraculously healed her. Although there may have been a historical woman of this name who was the companion of a Christian abbess in Kildare, scholars argue that it is more likely that Darlughdacha was an otherwise lost Celtic goddess translated into a Christian nun.

Source: Condren, Mary. *The Serpent and the Goddess: Women, Religion and Power in Ancient Ireland.* San Francisco: Harper & Row, 1989, p. 71.

Dathí (Dathi, Daithí) Irish hero. The last pagan king of Ireland, Dathí was reputedly buried in CONNACHT's great provincial capital at CRUACHAN, where a STANDING STONE (which far predates his alleged reign in the fifth century C.E.) is said to mark his grave. Dathí, a nephew of NIALL of the Nine Hostages, reigned in Connacht for 23 years before succeeding to the throne at TARA. There is some evidence that the historical Dathí was never a king at all but merely a successful warrior who invaded the Continent and was promoted in rank by later annalists.

Daui Irish hero. Two minor figures in Irish legend held this name: Daui Dalta Dedad, a king of TARA who kept his brother from becoming king by blinding him; as a BLEMISHED KING could not rule, this proved an effective way to gain power, but Daui was assassinated only seven years later. Another king, Daui Ladrach, was similarly ambitious and willing to kill to gain the throne, but the warrior LUGAIDH Laíghde was cleverer, using Daui's ambition to clear the path for his own ascension.

Davy Jones Scottish and Welsh folkloric figure. "Davy Jones's Locker," a common name for the ocean, appears to derive from a Celtic god who entered his OTHERWORLD kingdom through WATER. Although most RIVERS in Celtic lands were named for goddesses, a few in Britain (Tavy, Tay) have been derived from the Celtic root word *taff*, "stream," which could have been Christianized into Davy. This might explain the first name, but what about Jones? Scholars point to a Scottish god of the ocean with the slightly similar name—SHONEY, who lived in the Otherworld where he imprisoned those who drowned. Thus the familiar Davy Jones may descend from a Celtic divinity whose lockup was the briny deep. Alternatively, Davy Jones may combine the most common first and last names found in Wales, where David is sometimes spelled Davydd; the presumed god of the deep, in this interpretation, is simply a conversational image for the ocean, used by Welsh sailors who brought the phrase into currency.

Source: Spence, Lewis, *The Minor Traditions of British Mythology.* New York: Benjamin Blom Inc., 1972, p. 15.

dead hand Irish folkloric object. An old Irish belief held that a hand cut from a dead person—especially a victim of murder, an executed criminal or a child—held great magical power. Thieves could not be caught if they were carrying a dead hand; cream need only be stirred nine times for huge amounts of BUTTER to form.

Deae Matres Continental Celtic goddesses. "Divine Mothers" is the translation of the Latin name given to one of the most common goddess images found in Celtic lands. The sculptures sometimes show two mother figures, but more often there are THREE, the number that represented intensification to the Celts. Typically the Mothers are shown seated; often they appear to be of different ages (young maiden, fertile mother, and aging crone), but they are also sometimes depicted as identical triplets. They hold sacred objects: sacrificial knife, offering plate (PATERA), foodstuffs, bread, FISH. Since many, if not most, Celtic divinities are connected to the FERTILITY of the land and the people who depend upon it, it is not surprising that these goddesses are associated with food and abundance. In addition to the figure commonly called DEA NUTRIX, the "nourishing goddess," we also occasionally find the Mothers in the form called the "pseudo-Venus" or false VENUS, a single voluptuous woman holding symbols of fertility. There is no historical indication of the ritual practices connected with these goddesses, who seem to have been absorbed into the Roman religious framework early in imperial times.

Dealgnaid (Delgnat, Elgnat, Elgnad) Irish heroine. When the invader PARTHOLÓN arrived in Ireland, he brought his wife Dealgnaid. After successfully establishing his people on fertile land, he set about conquering additional territory—leaving his wife alone with only a handsome servant, Togda, to keep her company. And keep company the servant did, right into the bedroom. When Partholón returned to find his wife in another man's arms, he did not blame her but himself because, knowing his wife's desires, he should not have abandoned her. The couple reconciled, and Dealgnaid bore the ancestors of the Partholonian people.

Dea Nutrix (pl., Deae Nutrices) British and continental Celtic goddesses. Excavations in a number of temples of Roman Britain have yielded dozens of small pipe-clay statuettes of three similar figures holding fruit, eggs, grain, children, and other symbols of abundance and FERTILITY; they may be similar to the DEAE MATRES, the triple Divine Mothers. Sometimes the same goddess is depicted singly, in which case she often nurses an infant; both forms of the divinity emphasize their relation to food. The name the Celts used of these divinities has been lost, and so they are called by a Latin term meaning "nourishing goddess." The cult of Dea Nutrix seems to have been widespread, for her figure has been found in England, France, and southern Germany, sometimes in temples, sometimes in graves, sometimes thrown as offerings into sacred springs.

Source: Straffon, Cheryl. *The Earth Goddess: Celtic and Pagan Legacy of the Landscape.* London: Blandford, 1997, pp. 26, 29, 108.

death Cosmological concept. Archaeological evidence suggests that the Celts believed in permeable boundaries between this world and the next, with certain locations such as the hearth and burial grounds perceived as places where the dead could reenter this world after their demise. Caesar claimed that the continental Celts believed in REINCARNATION, while other writers of his era expressed their belief that the impressive bravery of Celtic warriors stemmed from their belief that they would live to fight again. Whether this represents actual Celtic belief is a subject of scholarly dispute.

Burial practices are often used as evidence in determining a culture's view of death. In the late centuries B.C.E., the continental Celts buried their dead, often with significant "grave goods" like mirrors and weapons; some of the greatest archaeological finds come from such early Celtic graves. But then the Celts began to practice cremation, burning the bodies of their dead; it is not known whether this indicated an alteration in their beliefs or adoption of Roman customs. Among the insular Celts, by contrast, there is no evidence of burial until the first century B.C.E. suggesting that cremation or excarnation (exposure) was practiced. There is also evidence in myth that some human remains, especially the HEAD, may have been preserved, especially in the case of those killed in battle.

The dead did not occupy a realm separate from this world, like the Christian Heaven or Hell, but continued their relationship to those left behind—a relationship that could be either happy or destructive, depending on the events of physical life. In the Scottish Highlands it was believed that the dead could return to wreak physical vengeance on the living who had harmed them; thus death was not a termination but a transubstantiation, a change in form.

The Celtic conception of the OTHERWORLD where gods and FAIRIES lived was later melded with the Christian realm of the dead. Similarly, the dead became confused with the fairies; such was the case with the Irish farmer who, kidnapped AWAY from his cabbage garden, found himself surrounded by people, dead for years, who spoke hollowly in an unknown tongue and whom he banished by speaking the name of God. Even modern people occasionally confuse the dead with the fairies, for both sneak across to our world in order to work mischief. Like the land of the fairy, the land of the dead was often positioned out in the western sea, often floating as an unstable ISLAND (although Spain is mentioned in one Irish text as the home of the dead, something that may be SATIRE). Just as readily, the dead were imagined resting quietly in their graves, ready to come forth when occasion demanded or the season was right.

Although the contention is controversial, some have seen the likelihood of a belief in reincarnation in Celtic myths and traditions. A belief in reincarnation would explain the lack of interest in where the dead reside. In addition, Celtic warriors were renowned throughout the ancient world for their fearlessness, because they believed that death was a passage to another life.

Before finding another body, the dead could return to this world for a certain reason or on a certain day. Thus we find Irish folktales of young mothers who return nightly to nurse their left-behind infants and of lovers who come back to watch over a beloved; sometimes the deceased return for nothing more than to sit by the fire and smoke a pipe or otherwise engage in the comforting activities of the life left behind. Most commonly, the dead returned on the festival of SAMHAIN on November 1, when the veils between the worlds were thin. On Samhain, a murdered person could return to exact vengeance just as readily as a thankful family member could grant a boon. Relationship between living and dead, therefore, seems to have been imagined as continuing after the transition of death.

Sources: Cunliffe, Barry. *the Ancient Celts.* Oxford: Oxford University Press, 1997, pp. 208 ff; Dorson, Richard M., ed. *Peasant Customs and Savage Myths: Selections from the British Folklorists.* Vol. II. Chicago: University of Chicago Press, 1968, p. 29; MacCulloch, J. A. *The Religion of the Ancient Celts.* London: Constable, 1911, pp. 165 ff; Ross, Anne. *Folklore of the Scottish Highlands.* London: B. T. Batsford, Ltd., 1976, p. 40.

death coach (dead coach) Irish folkloric object. On foggy nights in Ireland, a black coach could sometimes be seen drawing up to a home. Black HORSES drew the coach, which had no coachman nor occupants. Or perhaps there was a driver, but he had no head; the horses too might be headless. This coach was sent from the land of the dead to fetch someone from this life. It would never leave this earth empty; if someone not scheduled to die were to stand in the coach's way, he would become the victim, so it was best to avoid such a coach and, certainly, never to attempt to stop it from picking up its intended passenger. Sightings of the death coach foretold death, just as did the cry of the BANSHEE.

Sources: Evans-Wentz, W. Y. *The Fairy-Faith in Celtic Countries.* Gerrards Cross: Colin Smythe Humanities Press, 1911, p. 221; Westropp, T. J. *Folklore of Clare: A Folklore Survey of Country Clare and County Clare Folk-Tales and Myths.* Ennis, Co. Clare: Clasp Press, 2000, pp. 10–12.

Debility of the Ulstermen (es Nóinden Ulad; Ceisnoidhe Uladh) Irish mythological theme. The men of the province of ULSTER were cursed because of a man's mistreatment of his wife. The pregnant goddess MACHA warned her mortal husband, the farmer CRUNNIUC, not to mention her when, against her will, he went to the Assembly of Ulster. But speak of her he did; indeed, he boasted that she was swifter than the king's best horses. At that, a race was proposed, and Macha was brought forth from her home. Pointing out how near to term she was, Macha begged not to be forced to run, but the king hoped her size would slow her down, so the race went forward. Macha, powerful and swift even in advanced pregnancy, was around the track before the king's horses had made it halfway. But the exertion brought on labor pangs, and she died giving birth to TWINS.

As she died, Macha called down a CURSE on the men who caused her death: that, whenever an enemy attacked, the Ulstermen would fall to the ground for four days and five nights with pain such as she endured in her labor, for nine times nine generations. This Curse of Macha played an important part in the Irish epic *TÁIN BÓ CUAILNGE*, for the hero CÚCHULAINN, who was not born in Ulster and therefore not susceptible to Macha's curse, had to hold off the entire army of CONNACHT while the Ulstermen writhed in agony with their "debility."

Sources: Condren, Mary. *The Serpent and the Goddess: Women, Religion and Power in Ancient Ireland.* San Francisco: Harper & Row, 1989, pp. 31–32, Cross, Tom Peete, and Clark Harris Slover, eds. *Ancient Irish Tales.* New York: Henry Holt and Co., 1936, p. 208.

decapitation See HEAD.

Decca (Deoca) Irish heroine. In the mythological story of the CHILDREN OF LIR, one of the THREE SORROWS OF IRELAND, this historical MUNSTER princess of the seventh century C.E. married the king of CONNACHT. Hearing a tale of singing SWANS—the enchanted maiden FION-NUALA and her four brothers, whose human voices remained despite their transformed bodies—Decca demanded to see them. When her husband refused, she left him; he gave in and had the swans brought to their palace, where Decca was able to see them just as they turned into human beings again, only to die of advanced age and turn to dust before her eyes.

Dechtire (Dechtere, Deichtine, Dectora) Irish heroine or goddess. The mother of the great Irish hero CÚCHULAINN conceived her child in miraculous fashion. One day, Dechtire and her 50 maidens simply vanished from EMAIN MACHA, the great capital of ULSTER where she lived with her brother (or father), king CONCOBAR MAC NESSA. Nothing was heard for years, but then a flock of 51 birds appeared on the fields around the capital. They were appallingly hungry, eating everything they found until the fields were barren, not even a blade of grass left. Faced with famine, the people of Ulster tried to follow the birds in chariots; hunting them, they believed, would provide some food for the starving people, as well as ending their depredations. All the great warriors of Ulster rode out on the hunt: manly FERGUS Mac Roich, bitter-tongued BRICCRIU, sweet-singing AMAIRGIN, and finally king Concobar himself. When the hunting party found the flock, they noticed that the birds flew in pairs, each joined by a silver chain, while at their head flew one wearing a yoke of silver. But try as they might, the men could not catch up with the birds, which led them steadily southward.

Growing weary, Briccriu and Fergus went in search of lodging and found a spacious house where a man and a woman welcomed them. The next day a wondrous child was found. Legend offers several variations on how Cúchulainn (then called SÉTANTA) was conceived and born. Most commonly his conception, like that of other heroes, was miraculous in needing no father. Spying a tiny worm in a glass of wine, Dechtire recognized an opportunity to give birth to a hero and drank it down; or perhaps she was impregnated by the god LUGH, either while she was in bird form or in her human body, in a dream or in real time. When she was ready to give birth, Dechtire vomited out the child, thus remaining virgin while becoming a mother. Discovering the miraculous child, the warriors of Ulster argued over who should raise it. Finally, the land's greatest heroes decided to share the boy's upbringing, each offering his special gifts to Dechtire's son. At that point, Dechtire disappears from the story; some scholars believe that her ability to give birth parthenogenetically points to a pre-Celtic MOTHER GODDESS who was absorbed into the pantheon when the Celts arrived in Ireland.

Sources: Dexter, Miriam Robbins. *Whence the Goddesses: A Sourcebook.* New York: Pergamon Press, 1990, p. 89; Hull, Eleanor. *The Cuchullin Saga in Irish Literature.* London: David Nutt, 1898, p. 15.

Dé Danann (De Danaan)   See TUATHA DÉ DANANN.

Dee (Deva)   British goddess. "The goddess" is the meaning of this name, which was borne by the British RIVER believed to be, like most rivers in Celtic lands, a feminine divine force. The River Dee was believed to need feeding with human victims at regular intervals; a folk rhyme tells us that "Bloodthirsty Dee, each year needs three; but bonny Don, she needs none." The Romans called Dee by a variation of their own word for "goddess," Deva.

deer   Symbolic animal. The Celts saw the fleet-footed woodland herds as the wild equivalent of their own domesticated herds of CATTLE. Like cattle, whose herds were guided by a strong BULL, the deer herds had a virile leader, the STAG; both animals were associated with gods of masculine power, ESUS and CERNUNNOS, respectively. Similarly parallel were the doe and the COW, and

their goddesses FLIDAIS and BÓAND both symbolized maternal love and abundance. Deer offspring also appear in mythology, most memorably in the story of the transformed SADB who gave birth to her fur-faced son, OISÍN the BARD, whose name is still used in Irish to mean "fawn."

In the Scottish Highlands, we find stories of GIANT goddesses who tended vast herds of deer; the island of Jura (from the Norse for "deer island") was occupied by Seven Big Women who ran with the deer. Similarly, the CAILLEACH named Beinne Bhric was a HAG who could shapeshift into a gray deer (see SHAPE-SHIFTING). Unlike the hesitant SEALS or SWANS, shy beings that could be caught and tamed, the deer women of legend were eager to mate with human men. Such folklore has led some to theorize an ancient cult of the deer, in which the animal was viewed as sacred, perhaps even totemic or related to humanity as distant ancestors. Traces of such a religious vision are fainter in Ireland and Wales, which may indicate that the cult died out earlier there or that it was exclusively Scottish.

Source: McKay, John G. *More West Highland Tales.* Vol. 2. Scottish Anthropological and Folklore Society. Edinburgh: Oliver and Boyd, 1969, pp. 408, 500.

Deimne (Demna, Demne)   Irish hero. This was the childhood name of the hero FIONN MAC CUMHAILL, whose adult name means "fair" or "brilliant."

Deiotaros   Continental Celtic god. Known from the Celtic people called the Galatae in Asia Minor this god's name means "the BULL-god" or "the divine bull," suggesting that he may be similar to TARVOSTRIGARANUS of Gaul.

Deirdre (Derdriu, Deridriu)   Irish heroine. She is called "Deirdre of the Sorrows," and the story of this tragic heroine certainly fulfills the promise of her title; together with the tales of the CHILDREN OF LIR and of the SONS OF TUIREANN, the story of Deirdre and the SONS OF UISNEACH is called one of the THREE SORROWS OF IRELAND.

The tale begins at Deirdre's birth, which happened to coincide with a feast that her father, the poet and storyteller Fedlimid mac Daill, was hosting for the king of Ulster, CONCOBAR MAC NESSA. In attendance at the feast, and therefore at the girl's birth, was the druid CATHBAD, who immediately foresaw her future: that the girl would grow to be the most beautiful woman ever known, and that she would cause the destruction of the kingdom. Most of the Ulstermen grew pale with horror at the prophecy and demanded that the child be put to the sword to spare the kingdom, but the lustful king Concobar refused. Determined to be the one who enjoyed that phenomenal beauty, Concobar decided to have the infant reared as his private prize. Entrusting Deirdre to LEBORCHAM, the wise woman (occasionally called a wise man), Concobar returned to his palace at EMAIN MACHA and turned his attention to other matters, trusting that when the girl had grown to womanhood, he would take her for his own.

But such was not to be. As she neared the end of her maidenhood, Deirdre saw a RAVEN fly down to drink the blood of a calf spilled on snow. She turned to Leborcham and whispered that she would love a man with skin that white, lips that red, hair that black. Leborcham knew immediately who was her fated partner: Concobar's nephew NOÍSIU, son of the warrior UISNEACH. So she arranged, despite her promise to the king, that the two young people should meet.

Instantly they fell in love. Unable to live without each other, they ran away, accompanied by Noísiu's brothers Ardán and Ainnle. Concobar, furious at losing his prize, pursued them around Ireland, but finally the four escaped to Scotland, where they lived a rugged but happy life in the woods near Loch Etive. Deirdre and Noísiu may have had children, for a son Gaiar and daughter Aíbgéne are mentioned in some texts. But Deirdre's beauty once again

attracted the attention of a king—this time, the Scottish king in whose woods they were living. When he decided that the beautiful Deirdre must be his wife, she and the sons of Uisneach fled again, this time to a remote island where, they thought, they could finally live in peace.

Back in Ulster, however, Concobar had not ceased tormenting himself about the loss of his gorgeous prize. He lured the couple back to Ireland by vowing that he had lost interest in Deirdre; Noísiu, homesick, agreed to return. Despite premonitions of doom, Deirdre reluctantly agreed, and with the three sons of Uisneach sailed for Ireland under an ominous blood-red cloud. Immediately upon landing, Noísiu and his brothers were set upon by Concobar's warriors, who killed them without offering them a chance to defend themselves. Hauled back to Conobar's court in chains, Deirdre bitterly reproached the king for his deceit and violence.

Once he had Deirdre, Concobar decided he no longer wanted her. So, to humiliate her further, the king gave her away to one of the men who had killed her lover. As the murderer bore her away in his chariot, Deirdre leapt from it and was killed, her head smashed against a stone. Because of his lust and deceit, many of Ulster's finest warriors became disgusted with Concobar and abandoned his kingdom to serve under queen MEDB of CONNACHT, who then launched a war on Concobar that is the basis of the most significant Irish epic, the *TÁIN BÓ CUAILNGE*.

Sources: Dillon, Myles, ed. *Irish Sagas.* Cork: The Mercier Press, 1968, pp. 53 ff; Hull, Eleanor. *The Cuchullin Saga in Irish Literature.* London: David Nutt, 1898, pp. 23 ff.

Delbáeth   Irish goddess. This obscure Irish goddess, "fire-shape," is mentioned in the *BOOK OF INVASIONS* as the mother of DONAND, believed to be the same as the important goddess of earth, DANU. Another figure of this name was a DRUID associated with the mystical hill of UISNEACH, where he was said to have built a great FIRE from which FIVE points of light streamed out.

Delbacháem Irish goddess or heroine. An ancient Irish ADVENTURE tale tells of this woman of the OTHERWORLD, held captive in a high tower by her mother, the fierce WARRIOR WOMAN COINCHENN, who had been cursed that she would die if her daughter ever wed. To prevent this, Coinchenn challenged every suitor to battle, invariably besting them all. But one finally came who could win over her: the king of TARA, ART mac Cuinn. He had been placed under a GEIS by his stepmother, the self-willed and wanton FAIRY BÉ CHUMA, that he could not eat until he had stolen Delbcháem from her magical island. Bé Chuma thus plotted against both, for she was angry at Art for resisting her advances and for showing interest when she disguised herself as the beautiful Delbacháem; she hoped that both would die in the attempted rescue. But Art, with the assistance of beautiful and mysterious women, discovered how to free Delbcháem safely, causing her mother's death as predicted. Upon returning to Tara, Art banished the troublesome Bé Chuma.

Delga Irish hero. This obscure ancient character lives on today, for the name of his palace DÚN Delgan remains in the important city name Dundalk. Little is known of Delga; even his race is disputed, for some tales call him a FOMORIAN, while others say he was a member of the FIR BOLG, both legendary groups of Irish invaders.

deosil See DIRECTIONS.

derbfine See FINE.

Derbforgaill (Dervorgilla, Devorgilla) Irish heroine. Several mythological Irish heroines bear this name, which is also that of an historical Irish woman Derbforgaill of LEINSTER, who in the 12th century C.E. married the Ua Ruairc (O'Rourke) chieftain of Breffni near Sligo. While her husband was on a pilgrimage, she ran off with or was kidnapped by DIARMAIT mac Murchada (Dermot MacMurrough). The resultant war between her husband and her lover led to the arrival of Norman warriors and to their settlement of Ireland, which in turn brought about the destruction of the Celtic way of life and the eventual claim of ownership of Ireland by England. Derbforgaill is often derided as an adulteress or blamed for Ireland's later woes, but she acted in keeping with ancient Irish beliefs that a woman had the right to choose her consort rather than being held captive in marriage.

A mythological woman of this name was a SHAPE-SHIFTING daughter of king Ruad who conceived a passion for the hero CÚCHULAINN and transformed herself and her maidens into SWANS to fly to him. But when he saw the great white birds, Cúchulainn did not react as Derbforgaill hoped: He threw rocks at her until he brought her to earth. As she fell, Derbforgaill turned back into a woman, and the shocked hero, hoping to save her life, fell to his knees and sucked the stone from her flesh. Although Derbforgaill was healed, Cúchulainn's action made them blood kin and thus thwarted her ambition of sharing his bed. Derbforgaill then married LUGAIDH Riab nDerg, a friend of Cúchulainn's. She died when, in a contest to see who could shoot urine the farthest, Derbforgaill so overwhelmed the other women that they fell upon her and killed her. To avenge her death, Cúchulainn massacred 150 women of the family, causing Derbforgaill's husband to die of grief at the slaughter.

Source: Hull, Eleanor. *The Cuchullin Saga in Irish Literature*. London: David Nutt, 1898, p. 82.

dergfhlaith Irish ritual drink. Combining the words for dark RED (*derg*) and SOVEREIGNTY (*flaith*) as well as that for ALE (*laith*), this term means "the dark-red ale of sovereignty" and is used to describe the drink offered to the king by the earth goddess to seal their union. This Irish INAUGURATION custom is believed to have continental Celtic antecedents but may have evolved from the union of Celtic invaders with an earlier, goddess-centered culture; scholars disagreed on the subject. Acceptance of the red ale bonded the king to the land, encircling him with sacred vows and responsibilities (see GEIS and BUADA) specific to his region, in addition to the demands of GENEROSITY and nobility required of all Irish kings. Some myths connect the red ale specifically to MEDB, goddess of sovereignty who was humanized into the great queen of CONNACHT; it is also associated with other goddesses of the land, including ÉRIU and Flaith.

Dér Gréine (Dia Griene)   Irish and Scottish heroine or goddess. "Tear of the sun" is the name of a heroine in several Irish and Scottish tales; she may have originally been a goddess, daughter of the sun deity or the sun itself. In Ireland she was the daughter of a king, given to the hero LAOGHAIRE Mac Crimthann as a reward for his service to her father in killing the fierce GIANT named GOLL MACMORNA. In Scotland this figure's mythological roots show through the folktale in which, held captive in the Land of Big Women, Dia Griene was freed by a young man named Brian (a generic folktale name) with the assistance of the CAILLEACH in disguise as a FOX. As Dia Griene and her charming, if bumbling, male companion attempted their escape, the Cailleach sacrificed herself to permit their safe return.

Source: Monaghan, Patricia. *O Mother Sun: A New View of the Cosmic Feminine*. Freedom, Calif.: The Crossing Press, 1994, pp. 76–78.

Derravaragh (Lake Derravaragh, Darravaraugh)   Irish mythological location. On the shores of this scenic lake in Co. Westmeath, FIONNUALA and her brothers, the CHILDREN OF LIR, were turned into SWANS by their evil stepmother AÍFE.

destruction (*togail*, togla)   Irish mythological text. Among the various categories of heroic tales in Ireland, which include visions (see AISLING) and VOYAGES as well as CATTLE RAIDS and WOOINGS, is the class of tales called destructions. As the title indicates, the tales concern the destruction, often by fire, of a building. The most famous of these tales, the *Destruction of DA DERGA's Hostel*, describes a king's failure to observe the sacred vows that his role required (see GEIS) and his resulting death.

Deva   See DEE.

Devil   Christian cosmological concept. The Celts had no image of an evil force that resembled the Christian DEVIL. The Celtic worldview was instead ambiguous and non-dualistic, with dark balancing light rather than warring with it. Christianization meant that some Celtic divinities were redefined in the new religion as negative forces; this is not uncommon, for the gods of one religion often become the devils of the next. The continental Celtic god of wilderness, CERNUNNOS, was the main inspiration for Christian iconography of the devil, with his horns and partially animal body. When goddesses were demonized, they were sometimes described as the DEVIL'S MOTHER.

Source: Grinsell, Leslie V. *Folklore of Prehistoric Sites in Britain*. London: David & Charles, 1976, p. 20.

Devil's Father (Duveruckan, Duvephucan)   Irish folkloric figure. Unlike the DEVIL'S MOTHER, a figure that draws on ancient goddesses and mythological monsters of pagan Ireland, the Devil's Father seems to have been entirely invented after Christianization of Ireland. The Devil's Father haunted wakes, where he hoped to meet his son stealing the soul of the deceased. He could be recognized easily, for he had THREE legs, a RED tail, and a phallus-shaped walking stick.

Devil's Mother (Kiraghna, Keeronagh)   Irish goddess or heroine. Just as male gods sometimes appear in Christian thought and iconography as the DEVIL, so goddesses were occasionally transformed into demonic forces by those who wished to deter their continued worship. In Ireland such goddesses were sometimes called the Devil's Mother, a name borne by a large squat mountain in northern Connemara, in Ireland's western province of CONNACHT. Two characters who were said to have battled the arriving ST. PATRICK—the bird-fiend CORRA and the fearsome serpent CAORANACH—also bear this name.

Source: MacNeill, Máire. *The Festival of Lughnasa, Parts I and II.* Dublin: Comhairle Bhéaloideas Éireann, 1982, p. 400.

Devona (Divona)   Continental Celtic Goddess. A Celtic goddess of whom little is known, she may be the same as SIRONA, the Gaulish goddess of HEALING. SPRINGS, especially thermal or hot springs, were believed to have healing powers (modern science is finding some support for this belief), and Devona may have been a spring goddess, for the second part of her name seems to derive from the Celtic root for "stream," while the first syllable means "goddess."

Diana   Roman goddess. Her name appears on many sculptures found in Celtic lands occupied by Rome, but like the Greek goddess ARTEMIS, Diana was not originally a Celtic goddess. An ancient Italic goddess of the open sky, Diana became a lunar divinity of the hunt in Roman times; her name was then carried to Celtic lands by invading legionnaires, who renamed apparently similar goddesses after the Diana of their homeland. Many Celtic goddesses were absorbed under her name, their personal names lost to history; often it is not possible to tell whether or in what ways the original Celtic goddess was similar to the Roman import. Several goddesses of the wilderness kept their own names and identities, however: ABNOBA, the goddess of the Black Forest; ARDUINNA, the boar goddess of the Ardennes forest; the CAILLEACH, pre-Celtic Scottish goddess of wildlife; the bear goddess ARTIO of Britain and Gaul; and the Irish woodland maiden FLIDAIS.

Sources: MacCulloch, J. A. *The Religion of the Ancient Celts.* London: Constable, 1911, pp. 42, 177; MacNeill, Máire. *The Festival of Lughnasa, Parts I and II.* Dublin: Comhairle Bhéaloideas Éireann, 1982, p. 417; Straffon, Cheryl. *The Earth Goddess: Celtic and Pagan Legacy of the Landscape.* London: Blandford, 1997, p. 31.

Dian Cécht (Dian Chect, Diancécht)   Irish god. When members of the magical race called the TUATHA DÉ DANANN were ill or wounded, they called for Dian Cécht, their master of leechcraft, who knew the location of a SPRING called the Well of Slaine that healed every wound except beheading. HEALING gods were common among the Celts; Dian Cécht appears to be an Irish corollary to the healing water gods known on the continent as APOLLO, although that name was not Celtic but applied through the INTERPRETATIO ROMANA by invading Roman legions to local healing gods, most of whom were connected to healing waters.

Despite his powers and his knowledge of the secret spring, Dian Cécht was not invariably successful. He failed to heal NUADA, king of the Tuatha Dé Danann after a battle with the monstrous FOMORIANS on the plain of MAG TUIRED. An enemy cut one arm completely off, and a severed limb was beyond even Dian Cécht's skill to heal. Because a BLEMISHED KING could not reign, Nuada was forced to yield the throne of TARA to the evil half-Fomorian BRES mac Elatha. Bres created havoc in the land, and so the Tuatha Dé Danann pleaded with Dian Cécht to try again.

This time, Dian Cécht created a completely functional arm of silver for Nuada, who henceforth was known as Nuada of the Silver Arm. But that was still not sufficient, for although he could fight strongly with his metal arm, Nuada was still too physically damaged to rule. Dian Cécht's son MIACH, a healer like his father, finally healed Nuada completely by magically helping him grow skin over the silver prosthesis.

Furious at being outshone by his offspring, Dian Cécht killed Miach. Miach's devoted sister AIRMID, tending his grave, found hundreds of herbs growing, one for every part of the human body, one for every day of the year. As she was sorting them and creating a system for their use, Dian Cécht crept up on his daughter and destroyed her careful work; with that action the secrets of healing were taken from this earth. Dian Cécht was humanized into MAC CÉCHT, husband of the land goddess FÓDLA, one of the three land goddesses who greeted the invading Celts.

Source: O'Rahilly, Thomas. *Early Irish History and Mythology.* Dublin: The Dublin Institute for Advanced Studies, 1946, p. 66.

Diarmait (Dermot, Diarmuid) Irish hero. Many Irish heroes bear this name, which also appears in surnames like MacDermott, Donn, MacDiarmuid, Gwynne, and Gwynn; these are borne by people who claim descent from one or another of the mythological Diarmaits. The most important Diarmaits are:

• **Diarmait, king of** TARA, who plays a minor role in the tale of his wife BECFHOLA; unhappy with Diarmait, she desired his foster son CRIMTHANN, and when Crimthann disappointed her, she traveled instead to the OTHER-WORLD with the fairy king FLANN ua Fedach.

• **Diarmait mac Murchada** (MacMurrough, McMurrow), the historical prince of LEIN-STER who eloped with the feisty DERBFOR-GAILL, or kidnapped her from her husband, the chieftain of the Ua Ruairc (O'Rourke) clan of Connaught; that she took her dowry with her suggests that she was functioning under the old law that encouraged women's freedom in selection of a mate and assured

their financial well-being when they changed marriages. History meets myth in this tale, for its combination of love, politics, and betrayal has attracted many poets and storytellers over the centuries. Whether Derbforgaill was raped or seduced or, as some contend, was the seducer, her one-year residence with Diarmait led to lasting consequences. Her husband called for vengeance, gathering his forces together with those of the high king, Tairdelbach Ua Conchobair (Turlough O'Connor), and Derbforgaill was promptly returned to the wilds of Breffni, the Ua Ruairc stronghold. But Diarmait was unwilling to concede defeat; he went abroad and gathered an army of Normans under Richard de Clare, Earl of Pembroke, popularly known as Strongbow, who married Diarmait's daughter Aífe to tie himself more closely to the cause. Landing in Waterford, Strongbow marched on and took Dublin, beginning a long period of Norman and later British control over the island.

• **Diarmait Ua Duibne** (Diarmait Ó Duinn, Dermot O'Dyea), descendant of the obscure goddess Dubinn; he was the most famous of the mythological heroes of this name. Diarmait was the fated lover of beautiful young GRÁINNE who was betrothed to the aging FIONN MAC CUMHAILL. Diarmait was said to have a "love spot" (see BALL SEIRC) on his forehead, given to him by a magical woman who told him that it would make him irresistible to any women who saw it. Some tales describe Diarmait as hiding his love spot under bangs or otherwise keeping it covered, so that he might proceed with a normal life unhindered by women's desires.

At a feast in Fionn's hall, however, a breeze lifted Diarmait's hair. Gráinne spied the love spot and fell hopelessly in love. Diarmait was unwilling to elope with the espoused wife of his host and leader, but Gráinne was unwilling to live without him. When she learned that her beloved was under a GEIS that forbade him to refuse a woman who came neither mounted nor on foot, neither in the night nor the day, she came to him riding a mule, just at sundown, thus fulfilling the demands of the geis. They set off together, but Diarmait still refused to sleep with her because of his fear of Fionn or his loyalty to his leader. And so the couple lived in the forest chastely—much to Gráinne's annoyance—until a mysterious invader threatened Gráinne in the night, whereupon she shamed Diarmait into becoming her lover.

Thereafter they traveled through Ireland, endlessly pursued by Fionn and the FIANNA; the stones on which they slept, actually prehistoric DOLMENS, are still called "beds of Diarmait and Gráinne." Legend has it that there are exactly 366 dolmens in Ireland because the year they spent running from Fionn was a leap year. When Fionn finally caught up with the pair in Co. Sligo's forest of Dubros, Diarmait hid in a HAZEL tree. Fionn, suspecting Diarmait's hiding place and knowing the young hero's weakness for the game called FIDCHELL, sat down beneath the tree and called for his board. He called as well for OISÍN, Diarmait's friend, to be his opponent.

Fionn's instinct was shrewd, for Diarmait could not resist helping Oisín win. With perfect aim, he threw hazelnuts down from the tree, straight at the space where Oisín should move next. Instantly Fionn knew he had found his prey and pulled Diarmait out of the tree. The pursuit did not end with the recapture of the lost bride after all, for Gráinne remained with Diarmait, who returned to the Fianna. (Some legends say that they retired to Co. Leitrim and raised a family.) Fionn had the last word, however, by withholding treatment when Diarmait was injured while hunting wild BOAR beneath BEN BULBEN in Sligo and allowing his rival to die in agony.

Sources: Campbell, J. F. *Popular Tales of the West Highlands*. Vol. III. Edinburgh: Edmonston and Douglas, 1862, p. 81; Cross, Tom Peete, and Clark Harris Slover, eds. *Ancient Irish Tales*. New York: Henry Holt and Co., 1936, p. 370; Dillon,

Myles, ed. *Irish Sagas*. Cork: The Mercier Press, 1968, pp. 135 ff; Gregory, Lady Augusta. *Gods and Fighting Men: The Story of the Tuatha De Danaan and of the Fianna of Ireland*. New York: Oxford University Press, 1970, pp. 269 ff; MacCulloch, J. A. *The Religion of the Ancient Celts*. London: Constable, 1911, pp. 365–366.

díchetal do chennaib   Irish divination ritual. Among the many forms of DIVINATION used by the ancient Irish, this one remains mysterious. Described as "composing on the fingertips," it is unclear whether it was a form of psychometry (divining information about a person or object through touch) or a kind of INCANTATION (perhaps using fingertips as mnemonic devices for memorizing words or syllables). It may have been a form of prophecy in which BARDS and seers among the DRUIDS drew meaning from a kind of automatic uncomposed flood of speech. Despite its basis in Celtic religious practice, ST. PATRICK allowed its continued use when other divinatory practices were forbidden, because this ritual did not involve invoking the names of the old gods.

Dígne (Dige, Dighe, Duibne)   Irish goddess. Goddess of the land of MUNSTER in southeast Ireland, she was later merged with the HAG goddess CAILLEACH. The Dingle peninsula in Co. Kerry, reputed to be Ireland's most scenic area, bears her name. Inscriptions in OGHAM writing have been found there bearing Dígne's name; she has therefore been interpreted as the ancestral goddess of the region.

Díl   Irish heroine. This obscure figure is known only from the *BOOK OF INVASIONS*, which says that she was the wife of the equally mysterious DONN; she drowned as her people, the MILESIANS, arrived in Ireland.

Dinadan (Dinaden)   Arthurian hero. The satirist of the ROUND TABLE, Dinadan is a relatively obscure figure who appears as a prankster in several Arthurian tales. He fought a tournament with LANCELOT, who wore a dress for the occasion; when Dinadan lost, he had to don women's attire.

Dindraine Arthurian heroine. The sister of PERCIVAL, this minor character in Arthurian legend was a generous woman who gave her blood to heal a woman of leprosy.

Dindshenchas (Dinnshenchas, Dinsheanchas) Irish mythological text. Usually translated as "poetry of place," these ancient Irish texts describe the myths associated with various places in the landscape. The date of their composition is unknown; the *Dindshenchas* may have been recited orally before being written down in the 12th-century *Book of Leinster* and in other medieval manuscripts.

Each of these place-poems gives the myths related to a site, which often explain the place-name. Many ancient Irish stories come down to us through the *Dindshenchas*. Often the poems do not actually tell the story but allude to it, so although they represent a major source of information on Celtic mythology, it must sometimes be supplemented by other texts. Given the late and post-Christian date of transcription, it is unclear whether the poems are reliable, but in many cases, the *Dindshenchas* is the only source for a myth or mythological figure.

See also PLACE-LORE.

Sources: Gwynn, Edward. *The Metrical Dindshenchas.* Royal Irish Academy, Todd Lecture Series. Dublin: Hodges, Figgis, and Co, Ltd, 1906–1924. Reprinted Dublin Institute for Advanced Studies, School of Celtic Studies, 1991; Ó Murchadha, Diarmuid, and Kevin Murray. "Place-Names." In Buttimer, Neil, Colin Rynne, and Helen Guerin, eds. *The Heritage of Ireland.* Cork: The Collins Press, 2000, pp. 146–155.

Dinny-Mara (Dooinney Marrey, Dunya Mara) See MERMAN.

Dinomogetimarus Continental Celtic god. Only one inscription exists naming this Gaulish god, whom the Romans identified with their warrior divinity MARS.

Dìreach See FACHAN.

directions (*aiats, deosil, tuathal*) Cosmological concept. The Celts did not have four directions, but five: NORTH, SOUTH, EAST, WEST, and center. The fifth direction makes clear the relativity of the rest, which are judged from the position of the speaker. The center is not only a directional marker but a spiritual or philosophical conception, for as the speaker moves, so does the center from which all directions are measured. The radically place-based nature of Celtic religion seems linked to this concept of direction.

This elusive fifth direction appears in the mythological division of Ireland into five PROVINCES. Four provinces existed on the earthly plane: LEINSTER in the east, MUNSTER in the southwest, CONNACHT in the west, and ULSTER in the north. The fifth province, the center, could not be limited to a single place. Although a central province called MIDE or Meath was designated in medieval times, the original fifth province was a moveable, even multiple, site. Each province had a center (CRUACHAN, KNOCKAULIN, EMAIN MACHA, KNOCKAINY), and the island as a whole had two centers, the hills of UISNEACH and TARA. Upon Uisneach, an even more central center was found: the STONE OF DIVISIONS, a huge boulder that was said to show the map of Ireland. Thus the center is, in Irish mythological thought, both many places and no place.

In addition to the directions of the compass, another set of directions was important to the Celtic worldview. This was the difference between *deosil* and *tuathal*—the first meaning to move southward in a circle, the second to move northward. Today we would say clockwise and anticlockwise or counterclockwise, but these Irish words come from a time when the Sun, the

Moon, and the stars were the only timepieces known. Clocks rotate as they do because the sun moves in that direction around the horizon, always moving toward the south; indeed, south is defined as the direction of the sun at noon from the Northern Hemisphere, for despite our perception that the sun stands overhead, it is in fact always to the south. Thus to move *deosil* (*deiseal, desiul*) is to move in the direction of natural order, while to move *tuathal* is the opposite, to go against nature. This belief continues among contemporary NEO-PAGANS who believe that to go *widdershins*, or counterclockwise, in a ritual circle brings bad luck.

Sources: Dames, Michael. *Mythic Ireland.* London: Thames and Hudson, 1992; Hull, Eleanor. *Folklore of the British Isles.* London: Methuen & Co. Ltd., 1928, pp. 72–80; MacCulloch, J. A. *The Religion of the Ancient Celts.* London: Constable, 1911, pp. 193, 237.

Dirona   See SIRONA.

Dis Pater (Dispater, Dis)   Continental Celtic god. This Latin name, given by Julius Caesar to an unknown god he believed was the primary divinity of his Gaulish enemies, means "Father of Hell." The Celts had no conception of an underworld in an afterlife or in a place of torment, so Caesar may have gotten it wrong. This would not be the only time he did so, as he also imagined that his Celtic foes had a pantheon resembling that of Rome, with a centralized administration and an order of precedence, although in fact the Celts had no such bureaucratic organization of their divinities.

What god Caesar and his legions renamed Dis Pater is impossible to know, although three gods have been nominated: the one sculpted with a hammer who goes variously by the names of SUCELLUS and TARANIS, the horned god CERNUNNOS, and the woodland god ESUS (called by the Romans by the name of their parallel divinity, SILVANUS). This god may have been a divinity of the OTHERWORLD, the Celtic domain of the gods and later of FAIRIES, which faintly resembles the Roman underworld. But far from being a distressing place, the Celtic Otherworld was beautiful beyond measure, timeless, and populated by gifted immortals.

Díthorba   Irish hero. In the tale of MACHA Mong Rua (Red-Haired Macha), Díthorba was the name of an allegedly historical king of ULSTER with whom Macha's father, ÁED RUAD, shared rulership in seven-year cycles; the third king in the team was CIMBÁETH. Magical NUMBERS appear consistently in this tale, for in addition to the three kings with their seven-year reigns, we find the arrangement sustained by seven DRUIDS, seven BARDS, and seven nobles, suggesting that the story is not historical but mythological.

Díthorba opposed Macha—sometimes described as his niece—when, after her father's death, she took his place in the kingly cycle. She went to war for her rights and killed Díthorba, whose sons escaped to the Burren, the rocky lands of Co. Clare. Macha hunted them down there and, disguised as a HAG, approached them. Each in turn attempted to rape her; each in turn she overpowered. When all were tied together, she led them back to EMAIN MACHA, the Ulster capital, where she forced them to dig the impressive HILLFORT still visible today.

Divano   Continental Celtic god. This obscure god was identified by the Romans with their warrior divinity MARS.

divination   Celtic ritual. Attempting to see into the future was an important duty of the DRUIDS among both the insular and the continental Celts. Early documents, all written by their Mediterranean enemies, depict the Celts as superstitious to the extreme. Tactitus claimed the Celts regularly read the still-pulsing entrails of sacrificed men, and Strabo agreed, but both were Romans who had reason to paint their enemies as barbarians, so this evidence for HUMAN SACRIFICE is arguable. Other comments are less controversial, including the use of ANIMALS in divination rites and the reading of auguries in the flight of BIRDS.

A great deal of evidence from Ireland, untainted by Roman influence but possibly affected by the Christian faith of transcribers, shows that the druids, and especially the BARDS, used divination often. They had several elaborate and complex mechanisms for entering the altered states necessary to speak prophecies: chanting of incantations (see *DÍCHETAL DO CHENNAIB*), psychometry or reading the auras of objects (see *TEINM LAEDA*), trance (see *IMBAS FOROSNAI*), and use of letters (see *OGHAM*). Plants too had their uses in divination; the wands carried by druids have been interpreted as divining rods. Some texts suggest that a kind of yoga was practiced by druids who, holding themselves in specific postures, spoke their prognostications. The most elaborate and complex ritual of divination was that used to determine a new king; after devouring raw meat, a poet was wrapped in a recently slaughtered BULL-hide to dream of the new king (see BULL-SLEEP).

Although specialists were required for the most complex issues, divination was also practiced by ordinary Celtic people who, like people before and after them, desired to know what life held in store for them. On several pivotal days during the year, especially SAMHAIN on November 1, the future could be read in OMENS and dreams even by ordinary folk.

Source: MacCulloch, J. A. *The Religion of the Ancient Celts.* London: Constable, 1911, p. 247 ff.

divination through incantation See *DÍCHETAL DO CHENNAIB*.

divination through letters See *OGHAM*.

divination through touch See *TEINM LAEDA*.

Dobharchú (Dorraghow, Dobharchu, Otter-King) Irish folkloric figure. The unsleeping black-and-white striped king of the OTTERS was, in Irish legend, a supernatural being who hunted and killed humans. The king was difficult to kill, for he was vulnerable only to silver bullets. Not only that, but hunting him was dangerous, even fatal, for a successful hunter was likely to die within a day. Even such an extreme penalty might be worth risking to obtain the hide of the Dobharchú, for even the smallest piece of the hide of the king otter protected its holder from drowning. Into historical times, bits of non-kingly otter fur were sold by unscrupulous merchants to sailors, who had great need of protection from death by water. Several families claimed descent from otters, most significantly the McMurrows.

dobie (*dobbin*) British folkloric figure. A kind of BROWNIE, the *dobie* was known for being rather simple, if well-meaning; thus its name became slang for a dim-witted person. Some *dobies* were ghosts rather than FAIRIES; both kinds haunted houses and could be sent away (see LAYING THE FAIRIES) by giving them gifts. The name is also applied to RIVER spirits with the power of SHAPE-SHIFTING, as well as to HOLED STONES found on riverbanks, which were believed to be excellent protective AMULETS.

dog Symbolic animal. Dogs appear frequently in the myth and folklore of Celtic lands: as the ANIMAL form of a divinity, usually a goddess; as a companion to heroes, usually male; and as spirit-beings associated with the OTHERWORLD. The connection of dogs with religion may be very ancient in Celtic lands, because remains of their bones, found in early sites, appear to indicate they were killed sacrificially. The disgust that even contemporary people in the ancient Celtic lands feel toward eating dog meat, not shared by people of many lands, may be a long-lasting memory of a taboo against consuming the flesh of a sacrificial victim.

The first category of dog imagery is exemplified in the sculpted altars dedicated to the goddess NEHALENNIA, who was invariably shown with a small lapdog gazing up worshipfully from beside her feet. Like other Celtic goddesses, she had no more frequent animal companion. Fruit and eggs also appear on such altars, suggesting that the dog symbolized FERTILITY and abundance. Or dogs may have been seen as healers, for they accompany such goddesses as the continental HEALING goddess SIRONA. Dogs lick their wounds until they heal; this may have led to the common (if mistaken) belief in Celtic countries that dogs can heal human wounds through licking. It is also possible that Roman visions of the dog as healer found their way into Celtic iconography, for the sculptures of healing goddesses with dogs date from the period when Celtic lands were occupied by the legions of imperial Rome.

Not all dogs are healing companions; the dog who accompanies the massive goddess on the GUNDESTRUP CAULDRON, found in Denmark but apparently illustrating Celtic myth and ritual, seems connected with death, an association found as well in the folkloric BLACK DOG. But death, in the Celtic worldview, led to rebirth, so the dog images buried in graves may have represented the promise of future life. Similarly dog and corn appear together on statues of the goddess, suggesting that the Celts connected the death of the seed with new growth, and both with the dog as healer and psychopomp or leader of the souls of the newly dead. Connections of dogs with the Otherworld appear in the stories of the Irish goddess BÓAND, drowned with her little lapdog Dabilla, and LÍ BAN, who was turned into a MERMAID together with her unnamed pet dog.

Several gods are associated with dogs, notably NODENS. But more commonly the male figures associated with the dog are heroic warriors; indeed, the Irish word for "hound," *cú*, becomes the first syllable in the name of the great heroes CÚCHULAINN and CÚ ROÍ. Just as goddesses had lapdogs, heroes had hunting hounds, many of whose names come down to us in legend: ADHNÚALL, BRAN, and SCEOLAN, dogs of FIONN MAC CUMHAILL; the Welsh Drudwyn, hunting dog to the hero KULHWCH; and Failinis, hound of the god LUGH. These dogs appear merely to intensify the masculine strength of their owners and rarely—with the exception of Fionn's Bran—had personalities of their own. Yet through their hunting, they embodied the life-and-death cycle, bringing food to the human table that entailed the death of birds and other animals; thus these hunting hounds may have associations similar to those of the companions of goddesses.

Also straddling the line between life and death was the ambiguous FAIRY dog or Black Dog, a fearsome apparition with burning eyes and a terrifying howl. Seen in Germany and Britain as well as Ireland, the Black Dog warned of death and war; at the outbreak of World War II, there were many sightings in Europe of this mythological beast. Irish superstition connects such dogs with the BANSHEE or death-warning fairy woman; dogs howling near the home of a sick person were believed to predict death, while the first note of the traditional funeral dirge was said to replicate the howling of the Black Dog.

The *CÚ SÍTH* or fairy dog was distinguished from the Black Dog by the color of its coat, which was dark green. It moved soundlessly, always in a straight line, so it was easy to tell from other dogs that followed scent-trails in big loping circles. The *Cú Síth* could bark, and loudly, but only three times. On the third, it sprang forward and devoured anyone nearby. On the Isle of Lewis in the Hebrides, it was believed that a survivor of such an attack was able to extract a tooth from the *Cú Síth*, which served as a local ORACLE until it emigrated, with its owner, to Canada, where it is presumably still to be found.

In Scotland even dogs entirely of this world were credited with having some supernatural powers. When they howled at the moon or growled at nothing in particular, it was believed that they were alerting their human keepers to the presence of supernatural or fairy powers. Dogs were also believed to see ghosts of the dead, witches, or other persons only visible to people with SECOND SIGHT.

Sources: Campbell, John Grigorson. *Witchcraft and Second Sight in the Highlands and Islands of Scotland.* Detroid: Singing Tree Press, 1970, p. 163; Green, Miranda. *Symbol and Image in Celtic Religious Art.* London: Routledge, 1989, pp. 28 ff, 89, 144; MacGregor, Alasdair Alpin. *The Peat-Fire Flame: Folk-Tales and Traditions of the Highlands & Islands.* Edinburgh: The Moray Press, 1937, pp. 37 ff; Whitlock, Ralph. *The Folklore of Wiltshire.* London: B. T. Batsford, Ltd., 1976, p. 129.

Dòideag   Scottish heroine. This allegedly historical WITCH of the Isle of Mull off Scotland was blamed—or given credit, depending on the politics of the speaker—for the destruction of the Spanish Armada when it invaded England. Such control over the weather is typically attributed to the HAG named the CAILLEACH, on whom Dòideag seems to be patterned.

dolmen   Symbolic structure. Doorways of stone leading nowhere stand in fields and pastures, on rocky hills and in verdant valleys, throughout Celtic lands. The Breton word for these structures is dolmen, meaning "table of stone," although one would have to be a GIANT to eat off most dolmens; contemporary archaeologists prefer the term portal tomb, while in Wales the same structures are called cromlechs (from words meaning "bent" and "flat stone"). These distinctive and memorable structures are also called DRUID altars, but they were built thousands of years before the Celts and their priests arrived in the land.

Perhaps as many as 6,000 years have passed since the stone uprights were capped with their huge crossbeams, yet the engineering of these mysterious prehistoric people was so exact that hundreds of these structures are still standing today. Indications of burials have been found in recesses under dolmens, leading archaeologists to call them tombs, but burials were few in comparison to the population. Those whose remains (sometimes cremated elsewhere) rest beneath the dolmens may have been victims of HUMAN SACRIFICE, or they may have been people of high status who were considered worthy of a distinguished burial. But this does not mean that the placement and building of dolmens may not have had purposes other than the funereal; similar structures found in the Canadian arctic serve both as geographical markers and as shamanic doorways to another world.

The Celts, arriving long after the dolmens were built, created many tales about them. In Ireland the stone structures are called "beds of DIARMAIT and GRÁINNE," for the eloping couple were said to have slept together on a different one each night, as they fled her furious intended husband, FIONN MAC CUMHAILL. This legend connects the dolmens to FERTILITY and sexuality, as does the frequent folklore that claims the stones either cause sterility and barrenness, or that they increase the likelihood of conception. Such lore may encode pre-Celtic understandings of these pre-Celtic monuments, may be Celtic in origin, or may represent Christian interpolations into Celtic legend.

dolorous blow   Arthurian motif. In stories of the FISHER KING, this is the name of the accidental blow struck to his groin by his brother BALIN, which caused the land to become barren.

Domnall (Donal, Domnal, Dónal, Donald, sometimes Daniel)   Irish or Scottish hero. Popular in both Irish and Scottish tradition, this name was carried by a number of minor heroes and kings, most significantly Domnall of TARA, who succeeded the mad king SUIBHNE; and Domnal Míldemail, the Scottish king to whose lands the hero CÚCHULAINN was sent by the father of his intended bride, EMER, who feared for his daughter's virtue.

Domnu (Déa Dumnu)   Irish goddess. This obscure Irish goddess is mentioned in the *BOOK OF INVASIONS* as the ancestral mother of the monstrous FOMORIANS, who were defeated by the magical TUATHA DÉ DANANN. As the Tuatha Dé have been often interpreted as gods of the arriving Celts, while the Fomorians represent an earlier people, Domnu may have been an ancestral goddess of the early Celtic or pre-Celtic Irish. Domnu's name has been translated as "deep," which suggests that she is a goddess of the ocean depths or the misty depths of the OTHERWORLD. Inver Domnann (Broadhaven) in Co. Sligo may derive its name from her.

Dôn Welsh goddess. Just as the Irish divinities are called the TUATHA DÉ DANANN, the tribe of the goddess DANU, so the gods of Wales were called the Children of Dôn after this otherwise little-known goddess. Among Dôn's many children, several figure prominently in the Welsh legends transcribed in the *MABINOGION*. Her daughter was the virgin mother ARIANRHOD, who was nominated to serve as footstool to Dôn's brother, king MATH. Of Dôn's four sons, three represented important social roles, while the last was a trickster who eludes definition: GWYDION the BARD, GOVANNON the SMITH, the farmer AMAETHEON, and the troublemaking GILFAETHWY.

Dôn herself played little role in Welsh mythology. Her name, however, connects her to a number of other divinities connected with the land's FERTILITY. In Ireland both Danu and the related ANU encouraged prosperity; on the Continent, a hypothesized Danu was a goddess of the watercourses whose name was reflected in the important river system, the Danube. Support for this theory comes from the occurrence of Welsh rivers with names similar to Dôn's: Trydonwy and Dyfrdonwy, the latter also being the name in the TRIADS of one of the THREE WELLS in the ocean.

Alternatively, Dôn may be another form of the name DOMNU, believed to be the goddess of the ocean and ancestral mother of the FOMORIANS, whom some describe as early Celtic settlers in Ireland. Finally, some texts show Danu's children as children of the goddess BRIGIT, leaving open the possibilities that they may represent the same divine force, that they may originally

have been the same, or that they were confused by the storyteller.

Like the Tuatha Dé Danann, the Children of Dôn bear the name of their mother, while no father is mentioned. Their inheritance was thus matrilineal, or traced through the maternal line (see MATRILINY). Not only that, but Dôn's children continue the tradition, for her brother Math was succeeded not by his own son but by his nephew, Dôn's son Gwydion; then Gwydion was succeeded by his sister Arianrhod's son, LLEU LLAW GYFFES. These matrilineal successions have given rise to the theory that the deities derived from a time when humans, too, traced ancestry through the mother-line. Those who argue this interpretation of the myths also suggest that matriliny may have been a pre-Celtic tradition carried over into Celtic times when indigenous women bore children to the invaders; the myths would then describe the "inheritance" by half-Celtic children of their mothers' lands. Others point to the consistency of matrilineal descent in Celtic myth from various lands as providing evidence that the Celts themselves once traced lineage in this fashion.

Sources: Dexter, Miriam Robbins. "Queen Medb, Female Autonomy in Ancient Ireland, and Irish Matrilineal Traditions." In Jones-Bley, Karlene, Angela Della Volpe, Miriam Robbins Dexter, and Martin E. Huld, eds. *Proceedings of the Ninth Annual UCLA Indo-European Conference.* Washington, D.C.: Institute for the Study of Man, 1998, pp. 95–122; Dexter, Miriam Robbins. *Whence the Goddesses: A Sourcebook.* New York: Pergamon Press, 1990, pp. 42–46; MacCulloch, J. A. *The Religion of the Ancient Celts.* London: Constable, 1911, p. 103; Rhys, John. *The Welsh People.* London: T. Fisher Unwin, 1906, p. 37; Spence, Lewis. *The Minor Traditions of British Mythology.* New York: Benjamin Blom, Inc., 1972, p. 21.

Donagha Irish folkloric character. In the far southwest of Ireland, folklore tells of a married couple—Donagha, a lazy man, and his carping wife VARIA—who fought constantly and viciously. Granted two wishes by the FAIRY folk, Donagha was so lazy that he wasted one of them asking that the load of wood he was carrying should walk home by itself; it grew legs and did so. When her lazy husband arrived home with his strange companion, Varia upbraided him for the waste of a good wish. Thereupon Donagha wished her far away. Her cabin instantly flew off to Teach na Vauria in Co. Kerry, while he himself flew off to Teach an Donagha—Donaghadee, near Belfast, in Co. Down—on the other end of the island.

Donand Irish goddess. This obscure Irish goddess is noted in the *BOOK OF INVASIONS* as the mother of the three heroes BRIAN, IUCHAIR, and IUCHARBA (see SONS of TUIREANN). She is usually considered to be identical to DANU, although she may originally have been a separate goddess.

Donn Irish god. The shadowy Irish god of the dead, whose name puns on "brown" and "king," appears in few myths and is often confused with or absorbed into other mythological characters. Donn lived at Tech Duinn, the House of Donn, a rocky island off the southwest coast of Ireland; he is also connected with Donn Well in Co. Donegal. He was often conflated with the DAGDA, the benevolent god of abundance and fecundity, but they in fact had little in common aside from residence in the OTHERWORLD. Donn represented isolation and death, especially death by drowning, for from his seaside home he brewed up storms to cause shipwrecks, the better to draw more souls to his realm.

Donn Bó Irish hero. Famous for his sweet singing, this young Irish warrior was slain and, as was customary, decapitated by his killer. But when his HEAD was taken to the victory banquet and displayed on a pillar, it began to sing such a piercingly beautiful melody that everyone in the hall was reduced to tears.

Donn Cuailnge (Don Cooley, Donn Tarb) Irish mythological beast. The great Brown BULL of Cuailnge was the only animal in Ireland that matched FINNBENNACH, the great White Bull. One lived in ULSTER, in the fields of the minor king DÁIRE; the other in CONNACHT, in the fields of the provincial queen MEDB's consort AILILL mac Máta. When Medb and Ailill argued over who owned more, the queen was discouraged to discover that her herds had no equal to Finnbennach. Sending her warriors to Dáire, Medb asked for a year's loan of Donn Cuailnge, offering a fortune and her own "friendly thighs" to cap the deal; she hoped that during his stay in Connacht the Donn would impregnate one of her cows with a splendid calf, thus making her the equal of Ailill in possessions.

At first Dáire was quite willing, especially given the rental fee, but when he heard some of Medb's men boasting that they would take the Donn whether his owner approved or not, he became enraged and refused Medb's offer. Thus began the cattle raid that makes up the greatest of Irish epics, the *TÁIN BÓ CUAILNGE*.

It was, in fact, not a mere bull that Medb sought. Donn Cuailnge was the reincarnation of a man named FRIUCH, who had once worked as a swineherd for the magician BODB DERG. Another man, RUCHT, worked nearby for a man named Ochall. The two fought over everything and, after they died, continued as they reincarnated in many forms (see REINCARNATION). They fought WORMS, STAGES, RAVENS, warriors, and phantoms before reincarnating as the splendid bulls, a SHAPE-SHIFTING that is otherwise only seen in gods and BARDS. Medb had her way and brought the Brown Bull to Connacht, but as soon as Finnbennach and the Donn were in the same pasture, their aeons-long combat began again. Donn Cuailnge killed Finnbennach, but died of his wounds shortly thereafter.

Source: MacNeill, Máire. *The Festival of Lughnasa, Parts I and II.* Dublin: Comhairle Bhéaloideas Éireann, 1982, pp. 152–159.

Donn Fírinne Irish fairy king. Within the mountain of KNOCKFIERNA (Cnoc Fírinne, the hill of Fírinne) in Co. Limerick was the SÍDHE or FAIRY palace of this king of Ireland's magical race, the TUATHA DÉ DANANN. Donn Fírinne, one of the best-known fairy kings of the land, sometimes kidnapped mortal women to join him in his fairy dances. Because they would never be seen again in the surface world, this figure may be connected to the obscure OTHERWORLD king of the dead, DONN.

Donn Ua Duibne (Donn O'Duin, Donn Ó Duibhne) Irish mythological beast. This wild BOAR killed the romantic hero DIARMAIT Ua Duibne, but it really was not a boar at all but a SHAPE-SHIFTING human. The boar was Diarmait's half brother, borne by his mother COCHRANN to her lover, a shepherd. When Diarmait's father, also named Donn, discovered that his wife had given birth to another man's child, he killed the infant by crushing it. The child's father, however, knew magic: He waved a HAZEL wand over the mangled body, and the child came back to life but transformed into a wild PIG. The unfortunate Donn lived only to wreak vengeance and, when Diarmait came upon him on the legendary hill of BEN BULBEN, knew that his chance had come. Although Donn lost his life to Diarmait, he was able to prick the hero with one of his needle-sharp whiskers, and Diarmait bled to death.

dooinney-oie (night-man) Manx folkloric figure. This kindly Manx water spirit warned sailors and farmers of storms by calling, howling, or sounding a horn.

Dornoll (Dornolla) Irish heroine. The powerful but unattractive daughter of Domnall Míldemail, king of Scotland, Dornoll was a DRUID and WARRIOR WOMAN who fell in love with the hero CÚCHULAINN. But he spurned her to study with another Scottish amazon, SCÁTHACH.

Dorraghow See DOBHARCHÚ

dove Symbolic bird. Among the continental and British Celts, the dove was associated with HEALING and with ORACLES, a connection that may have arisen because the ill are often eager for insight into the future.

Dowth See BRÚ NA BÓINNE.

dracae Scottish folkloric figure. The *dracae* are evil water FAIRIES who attempt to lure passersby by SHAPE-SHIFTING into the forms of desirable golden objects that appear to be floating just out of reach in LAKES and RIVERS. When the traveler reaches, the GOLD cup drifts slightly away until the victim falls into the water and drowns. One captive of the *dracae* found herself beneath the waves in a beautiful land where she was enslaved as a MIDWIFE to the FAIRIES. At last released, she discovered that because she had touched her eye with FAIRY OINTMENT, she perceived the *dracae* pretending to be normal men and women, walking unnoticed among us.

dragon Mythological beast. Breathing fire, eating maidens, scorching villages—the dragon of medieval legend was an enormous scaly monster, sometimes winged, often snaky, that demanded a hero. In Britain, ST. GEORGE or ST. MICHAEL rescued the land by slaying the evil being, who was sometimes said to be the DEVIL himself. In Ireland, ST. PATRICK was the favorite dragon-killer of storytellers, for he fought and killed the monstrous CORRA, CAO-RANACH, and OILLIPHEIST, all described as monstrous beings. Indeed, despite the fact that snakes never existed in Ireland, these fearsome creatures were described as serpentine. A number of interpreters have found in these images a coded message about the extirpation of pagan beliefs by the new Christian religion, an interpretation that has been applied as well to the George/Michael motifs.

In Britain, however, saints were not required; regular heroes could step in when necessary to fight WORMS—called that not because they were small or insignificant, but because *worm* was the Norse and Saxon word for "dragon." Famous English dragons included those of Unsworth and Wantley, the latter having seven heads and three times that many sets of eyes. In the 12th century the famous Linton Worm ravished Roxburghshire with its poisonous breath; it was killed when a local hero shoved a blazing brand down its throat. Even as late as 1614, a dragon was allegedly sighted in West Sussex. While some reports touched on standard characteristics such as breathing fire, eating sheep and maidens, and the like, others described dragons as beautiful, especially when curled up to sleep, their scales looking like shining jewels.

Killing dragons was not easy, for those shining scales protected them. One Scottish dragon had to be lured out of her lair, where she was nursing several dragonets between destructive forays around the countryside. Finally one Charles the Skipper hit on the clever stratagem of building a bridge of empty barrels, covered with iron spikes. When the dragon ventured onto the bridge, the spikes impaled her. Meanwhile, back at the cave, her children were being smoked to death by her erstwhile prey. In despair at losing her brood, the dragon flailed herself with her massive tail until she died, on a rock still called Dragon Rock.

Although often described as based in Celtic belief, dragon tales are in fact of unknown origin. They occur most frequently in Wales, a nation symbolized by a red dragon; the Welsh hero who became king ARTHUR's father bears the provocative name of UTHER PENDRAGON, which may mean "dragon's head." Some writers have imaginatively linked dragons with underground RIVERS, others with earth energy; their most famous contemporary appearance is in the work of American-born Irish writer Anne McCaffery, whose fantasy civilization of Perth is described in *Dragonhold, Dragonflight, The White Dragon*, and many other works.

Sources: Douglas, George. *Scottish Fairy and Folk Tales*. West Yorkshire: EP Publishing, 1977, pp. 77 ff; Harland, John, and T. T. Wilkinson. *Lancashire Legends*. London: George Routledge and Sons, 1873, pp. 63 ff; MacDougall, James. *Folk Tales and Fairy Lore in Gaelic and English*. Edinburgh: John Grant, 1910, p. 97.

dreams Cosmological concept. In addition to the AISLING, a traditional form of Irish poetry in which supernatural encounters occurred while the poet was in a dreaming state, the dream had significance in Celtic religion as a place that could provide access to the OTHERWORLD. Myths emphasize this connection, for FAIRY people are able to visit human dreamers, as the fairy queen FAND did when she seduced the hero CÚCHULAINN and as the unnamed fairy of the western isle did when she lured BRAN mac Febail away to her realm. Such beliefs are also reflected in the form of DIVINATION called the *tarbhfleis* or BULL-SLEEP, in which a BARD, glutted with the meat of a newly slaughtered bull, slept wrapped in the bloody hide in order to dream the identity of the new king.

Dreco Irish heroine. A sorceress of the FOMORIANS, the mysterious people described as monstrous in the *BOOK OF INVASIONS*, Ireland's mythological history, Dreco used a poison draught to kill 20 warriors sent against her. The exact site of the slaughter, Nephin (Nemthend) overlooking Lough Conn in Co. Mayo, is known from Irish place-name poetry, which describes Dreco as a BARD as well as a magician.

Source: Gwynn, Edward. *The Metrical Dindshenchas*. Royal Irish Academy, Todd Lecture Series. Dublin: Hodges, Figgis, and Co., Ltd., 1906–1924, p. 15.

druid Celtic social role. Members of the priestly class among the Celts were called druids, from a word interpreted variously as meaning "oak" or "wise." Although the druids did not write down their beliefs, which were transmitted orally to the chosen initiates, we have some textual documentation from other sources. Early Roman writers including Caesar described a priesthood of magicians and poets, philosophers and lawyers—for the druids played all of these roles in Celtic society. Caesar reported that an elected chief druid presided over an annual meeting at the center of the Celtic territories in Europe, where they discussed and disputed and settled difficulties.

Both men and women served as druids, although possibly in different ways; the Irish word *bandrui*, woman druid, emphasizes the fact that the priesthood was not limited to one gender. Whether male or female, the druid went through an extensive period of training before assuming the office's authority and responsibility. It is not clear whether the role was hereditary or whether, like Asiatic shamans, Celtic druids were called to their vocation by an inward leaning.

Once the period of training had passed, the druid served as a seer who used various means of altering consciousness in order to forecast and advise the people. Oracular traditions including incantation (*DÍCHETAL DO CHENNAIB*), psychometry (*TEINM LAEDA*), writing (*OGHAM*), or trance (*IMBAS FOROSNAI*) were employed to discern the correct path for an individual or a tribe; in this sense, druids served as political advisers as well as counselors. They also conducted SACRIFICE, both seasonally and when their divinations showed it necessary; because they foresaw the future, they were important adjuncts to the work of all members of the society, from herdsman to king.

Finally, druids were educators; many young people studied with them for a time, learning the history of their people, religious concepts, mathematics, astronomy, writing, and other subjects before returning to life in the other classes of society. Since all education was through memorization, the training that future kings, warriors, and craftsmen received was instantly accessible to them in later life.

Druids and BARDS were connected, although there is scholarly contention as to whether they formed a single order or separate orders. Certainly their duties overlapped, for poets entered an altered state of consciousness to compose verses and were expected to have SATIRES ready should a king prove ungenerous. Both druid and bard relied upon magic, for the magic of words was an important part of Celtic belief; although poets specialized in verbal magic, they also took part in other magical rites such as the *tarbhfleis*, the BULL-SLEEP, in which they attempted to dream the identity of the new king. The duties of both bard and druid so overlapped with those of the BREHONS, the legal experts, that it is difficult to discern clear lines of distinction between these groups.

Several writers have suggested a connection between druidical practice and shamanism, an arctic religion based in the belief that other worlds above and below the visible world can be accessed through altered consciousness (see CELTIC SHAMANISM). The druids indeed practiced ways of entrancing themselves; they ate acorns before prophesying, confined themselves to darkened rooms, chanted incantations, and otherwise attempted to strain their senses to see visions. This view of the druid as shaman has gained advocates in recent years, although some scholars limit the term to religions derived from the spiritual practices of Siberian magicians.

The religious ceremonies conducted by the druids are all but lost to our knowledge. They were apparently conducted in the open air, probably in sacred groves called *NEMETONS*; as OAKS were especially sacred, it is highly likely that oak groves were favored locations for ritual. Whether HUMAN SACRIFICE was part of these rites is fiercely debated; Caesar spoke of men and animals being burned in wicker cages, but Caesar was an enemy of the Celts and might have consciously or unconsciously painted them as cruel barbarians.

With the coming of Christianity, the druids disappeared. In some cases their power had already been broken, for when the Romans invaded, they put to the torch the druids' sacred groves on the Continent and, in a slaughter still remembered by history, on the sacred isle of ANGLESEY in the Irish Sea. With their sanctuaries destroyed, the druids' power waned. Some druids may have become Christian monks or otherwise adapted to the new religion, but it is certain that many died with their memorized knowledge still sealed in their minds. A number of druidical revivals have been seen in the last few centuries, ranging from the Gorsedd poetic competition in Wales, established in 1792, to the various Celtic shamanic societies functioning today.

Sources: Brunaux, Jean Louis. *The Celtic Gauls: Gods, Rites and Sanctuaries.* London: Seaby, 1988, pp. 57–65; Lonigan, Paul R. *The Druids: Priests of the Ancient Celts.* Contributions to the Study of Religion, No. 45. Westport, Conn.: Greenwood Press, 1996; Lonigan, Paul, "Shamanism in the Old Irish Tradition." *Eire-Ireland,* Fall 1985; MacCulloch, J. A. *The Religion of the Ancient Celts.* London: Constable, 1911, pp. 287 ff, 305 ff; O'Curry, Eugene, "Druids and Druidism in Ancient Ireland," in Matthews, John. *A Celtic Reader: Selections from Celtic Legend, Scholarship and Story.* Wellingborough: Aquarian Press, 1991, pp. 15 ff; Ross, Anne. *Pagan Celtic Britain: Studies in Iconography and Tradition.* London: Routledge & Kegan Paul, 1967, p. 52.

druid's egg   See SERPENT STONE.

druid's fog (*féth fiada,* ceó druídecta)   Symbolic object. One of the powers that DRUIDS were said to possess was the ability to wrap themselves in mist and thus to pass by their enemies (or even their friends) undetected. This invisibility may have actually been a form of SHAPE-SHIFTING—the passing druid might become a veil of mist, just as he or she could become an animal or a bird—rather than a fog conjured by and separate from the druid. As possessors of this magical fog, druids were like gods or FAIRIES, who were also said to have such power; the TUATHA DÉ DANANN received the druid's fog as a consolation prize after losing Ireland to the MILESIANS. ST. PATRICK was similarly believed to have made himself invisible to the eyes of those who would harm him; in the famous poem "St. Patrick's Breastplate," he and a companion passed by dangerous druids, who saw only a fawn and a deer.

druid's glass   See SERPENT STONE.

druineach   Scottish folkloric figure. Not frequently encountered by humans, this Highland spirit appears in spring to beat upon the ground, an activity that brings forth the first green growth.

Dryantore   Irish hero. The hero FIONN MAC CUMHAILL and his warrior band, the FIANNA, killed Dryantore's three sons as well as the husband of his sister AILNA. This GIANT then set out to punish the murderers. After snaring them in a DRUID'S FOG that Ailna created, Dryantore captured Fionn and his harper, the sweet-singing DÁIRE, and imprisoned them in his OTHERWORLD palace. The rest of the warriors found and freed them, and Dryantore was killed in the ensuing battle.

Drystan   See TRYSTAN.

duality   Cosmological concept. The concept of duality can be understood in two different ways. Some writers use it as a synonym for dualism, the philosophical division of the world into two opposing sets of categories: black and white, light and dark, male and female. One of the most prominent philosophical dualists was the Christian bishop Augustine of Hippo, who was a fervent follower of the Persian sage Mani in his youth and continued to espouse an either/or philosophy after his conversion. Augustine waged an ardent and ultimately successful campaign against a competing philosophy, that of the presumably Celtic monk Pelagius (see PELAGIANISM), founder of the "happy heresy" that the natural world was created just as God wished. Augustine, by contrast, rejected the physical and especially sexual world as a hindrance to gaining admittance to heaven, a view that lasted long after the teachings of Pelagius were forgotten. Later Church Fathers, heavily influenced by neo-Platonic ideas that the "ideal" world is better than the "real," continued to support a dualistic vision of sin and salvation.

The double vision of the Celts was not dualistic in this sense. From its earliest period, Celtic art showed a fascination with forms that were both one thing and another (the RAM-HEADED SNAKE, for instance), or that were meant to be seen from two different angles. Divinities were often double or even multiple, or could change forms at will. Celtic dualism suggests a vision of the world as filled with complementary dyads, so that rather than light and darkness, or male and female, as opposing each other, they can be seen as part of a great whole.

Source: Ross, Anne, "The Divine Hag of the Pagan Celts." In Venetia Newall, ed. *The Witch Figures.* London: Routledge & Kegan Paul, 1973, p. 146.

Dub (Dubh, Dubhlinn, Dublind)   Irish heroine or goddess. The capital city of the Republic of Ireland, Dublin, is named after this famous BARD and DRUID woman, for it was originally *Dubh-linn* or "the pool of Dub," a deep pool in the mouth of the River Liffey, into which dub fell after being killed by a slingshot. The shot was cast in revenge after Dub drowned a woman with whom her husband was consorting, making the tale a tangle of betrayals and vengeance. Because *dubh* also means "dark" and the name of the city is often translated as "dark pool," this heroine may have been invented to explain Dublin's name. The town was originally founded by Norsemen, who called it Dyflinasrski; in Irish, the town is called Baile Átha Cliath, the town on the wicker ford, in remembrance of the wicker bridge built by the bitter-tongued BARD named AITHIRNE.

Dubinn   Irish goddess. This obscure goddess is known through her descendent, DIARMAIT Ua Duibne, Ireland's most romantic hero.

Dubthach (Dugall Donn)   Irish hero. Christian legend provides this as the name of the pagan chieftain father of St. BRIGIT who consorted with her Christian mother, one of the slaves in his court. Several significant anecdotes

in the life of St. Brigit revolve around disputes with her father: when she gave away his bejeweled sword to a beggar; when, to prevent him from finding her a husband, she caused her EYES to pop out of her head and dangle down her cheeks on bloody threads. In Scotland, Brigit's father was Dugall Donn.

duck   Symbolic bird. The animal of SEQUANA, goddess of the source of France's river Seine, who was often depicted sailing in a boat whose prow was shaped into a duck's head. BIRDS are often symbols of Celtic divinity, especially of goddesses.

Duibne   See DÍGNE.

dullahan (*dúlachan, dulachan*)   Irish folkloric figure. The headless horseman of Irish tradition, the *dullahan* was sometimes described as the driver of the DEATH COACH; elsewhere he was a phantom who rode a horse that had lost its own head. A masculine and lesser-known form of the BANSHEE, the wailing FAIRY that predicted death, the *dullahan* carried news of impending death to anyone who saw him riding past—though they may have seen nothing after he struck out their eyes with a flick of his whip.

Dumaitis   Continental Celtic god. An obscure god from Gaul, identified by the invading Romans with their god MERCURY, Dumaitis is known only from a single inscription.

Dumbarton   Scottish mythological site. One of the most significant historical sites of Scotland is a huge two-peaked basalt rock northwest of Glasgow, a reminder of ancient glacial action. Given its prominence and ease of defense, the rock of Dumbarton has been a fortress since prehistory. Although its most significant legend describes it as the site of ST. PATRICK's objection to Roman soldiers when they attempted to enslave some of his congregation, not all local legend is pro-patrician; another tale has it that the huge rock dropped there as witches were throwing stones at St. Patrick to drive him from Scotland. Such stories of landscape creation through rock-casting are typically told of the CAILLEACH, an ancient goddess who could easily be imagined as wishing the departure of the arriving Christians.

Source: Straffon, Cherly. *The Earth Goddess: Celtic and Pagan Legacy of the Landscape.* London: Blandford, 1997, p. 172.

Dún Mythic location. In Irish and Scottish Gaelic, this word means "fortress." It is used of many mythological sites, including:

• **Dún Ailinne,** a great HILLFORT in Co. Kildare established in Neolithic times but taken over as a provincial capital by the Celts around the seventh century C.E.; eastern corollary to CRUACHAN in CONNACHT and EMAIN MACHA in ULSTER. It is now called KNOCKAULIN Hill. Recent excavations at Dún Ailinne have revealed several banks—among the largest earthworks in the land—and a wide causeway; foundations of ancient structures have also been uncovered at the site. The site is named for ALEND, an obscure goddess.
• **Dún Aonghusa** (Dún Angus), a fort on the Aran Islands that uses a sheer cliff as protection on one side, while the rest is stone. Legend has it that the FIR BOLG, the second mythological race to arrive in Ireland, built the fort and named it after Angus, their chief.
• **Dún Bolg,** legendary place of battle where the warriors of LEINSTER showed their objection to the bórama or COW-tribute they were forced to pay to the king of TARA. The story, reminiscent of that of the Trojan Horse, tells how disguised warriors erupted from baskets hanging from the cow-tribute's backs and battled the king's men into submission.
• **Dún Delgan,** named for the FOMORIAN chief DELGA, this fortress became CÚCHULAINN's

home; the modern Irish town of Dundalk is named after it.
• **Dún Scaith,** the fortress of the warrior woman SCÁTHACH, on the Isle of Skye near Isleornsay. The same name appears on the Isle of Man as a portal through which Cúchulainn's warriors invaded the OTHERWORLD to gain possession of its magical CAULDRON of abundance.

Sources: Condren, Mary. *The Serpent and the Goddess: Women, Religion and Power in Ancient Ireland.* San Francisco: Harper & Row, 1989, p. 66; Raftery, Brian. *Pagan Celtic Ireland: The Enigma of the Irish Iron Age.* London: Thames and Hudson, 1994, p. 71.

Dun Cow (*Y Fuwch Frech*, Y Fuwch Laethwen Lefrith) British and Welsh folkloric figure. Like the GLAS GHAIBHLEANN in Ireland, the great Dun Cow wandered the British and Welsh land, giving milk to anyone who asked. Unable to respect their good fortune, some evildoers killed the cow to make stew, or attempted to milk her into a sieve, which killed the ever-giving cow. In Lancashire she is said to have died at a farm called "The Old Rib," where her whale-sized rib bone was long displayed. In Wales she was called *Y Fuwch Frech,* "the freckled cow," and Y Fuwch Laethwen Lefrith, "the milk-white milch cow"; she was said to have borne two long-horned OXEN called the Ychen Bannog, who killed the monstrous *AFANC.*

Another Dun Cow was a magical ever-fruitful beast that belonged to an Irish SAINT who, upon the cow's death, had it tanned and made into vellum so that it could become a book. In the *Book of the Dun Cow* many of Ireland's great myths were recorded, including the epic *TÁIN BÓ CUAILNGE,* the story of a great cattle raid.

Sources: Harland, John, and T. T. Wilkinson. *Lancashire Legends.* London: George Routledge and Sons, 1873, pp. 16–19; Parry-Jones, D. *Welsh Legends and Fairy Lore.* London: B. T. Batsford, Ltd., 1953, p. 135.

dunnie *(doonie)* British folkloric figure. In Northumbria this mischievous sprite disguised itself as a midwife's horse when a woman was in labor, then disappeared, leaving the midwife stranded; it did the same to plowmen who went to hitch up the team, only to find themselves alone in the barn. In Scotland the same creature, called a doonie, often appeared in the shape of a horse but could also seem to be an old woman or man; the same wicked and sometimes dangerous teasing was attributed to the doonie as to its southern relative.

Source: Spence, Lewis. *The Minor Traditions of British Mythology.* New York: Benjamin Blom, Inc., 1972, p. 92.

dunter   See *POWRIE.*

Durgan   Irish heroine. This unfortunate Irishwoman was destroyed by her own truth-telling. Herccad, Durgan's mother, was sleeping with one of her slaves, and Durgan reported this to her father. Herccad then arranged to have her daughter killed, to cover her disgrace.

dwarf   Folkloric figure. Dwarfs or little people found in most Celtic lands were immigrants from Scandinavia or Germany, where they were common folkloric characters resembling trolls. In Irish lore dwarfs were either FAIRIES or simply short people like the harpist of FIONN MAC CUMHAILL, Cnú Deiréil; the creatures in the former case were not true dwarfs but shapely small versions of normal-sized humans. Legends of pint-sized people inspired one of the great SATIRES of the English language, Jonathan Swift's *Gulliver's Travels,* whose human hero was a GIANT among the diminutive Lilliputians.

Dyfed   (Dyved)   Welsh region. Much of the action of the *MABINOGION* is located in this region of southwest Wales; Dyfed is thought to take its name from the tribal name of the Demetae, a Celtic tribe that dwelled there. Dyfed's king was PWYLL, husband of the goddess or heroine RHIANNON; it was in Dyfed that she bore his child PRYDERI and was punished for her perceived betrayal. There, too, ARAWN, lord of the OTHERWORLD, reigned for a year, having exchanged rulerships with Pwyll so that the human lord could rid ANNWN of the king's most resolute opponent. Historically, the region gave rise to the first codification of Celtic law in Wales, called the laws of HYWEL DDA after the king who encoded them.

Dylan   (Dylan Son-of-Wave, Dylan Eil Ton) Welsh hero or god. In order to become the ceremonial footholder to king MATH of Wales, ARIANRHOD was asked to submit to a test to ensure that she possessed the requisite virginity. But when she stepped over Math's wand, a baby dropped from her womb (despite the fact that she was unaware she was pregnant) and fled immediately to the sea. He is sometimes called Dylan Ail Ton, "son of wave" or Ail Mor, "son of the sea," and so he has been interpreted as being Arianrhod's child with a sea god or MERMAN. (Arianrhod second child, born on the same occasion, was LLEU LLAW GYFFES.) Certainly the sea was Dylan's element, for he swam like a fish and took great pleasure in feeling the waves under his body. But he was killed by his uncle, the rapist GILFAETHWY, whose assault on Math's previous footholder had set in motion the entire story.

Dyfr   (Dynwir)   British heroine. At king ARTHUR's court at CAMELOT, we find three figures known as the THREE SPLENDID WOMEN: Dyfr the golden-haired, the challenging ENID, and the virtuous TEGAU EURFRON. Dyfr is the only one with little legend connected with her, except the acknowledgment of Glewelwyd Gafaefawr, a knight, as her lover.

Eachlach Urlair (Eclock Urleer, Eachrais ùrlair, Creeper on the Floor, Trouble-the-House) Scottish folkloric figure. This feminine spirit—a BOGIE or WITCH—was believed to live near castles and to provide unspecified, even mysterious, service to their residents. Her name came to mean any domestic servant, but in Highland folklore she is described as having originated not in the human world but in the OTHERWORLD.

Eachtach Irish heroine. The loyal daughter of the Irish hero DIARMAIT Ua Duibne and his beloved spouse GRÁINNE, she attacked her father's lord, FIONN MAC CUMHAILL, when Fionn refused to help Diarmait as he fought to the death with an enchanted BOAR.

each uisce *(each uisge)* See WATER HORSE.

Eadán (Edán) Irish hero. Eadán arrived in Ireland with the MILESIANS, the last wave of invaders and the victors at the battle of Tailtiu over the magical TUATHA DÉ DANANN, the tribe of the goddess DANU. Among the Tuatha Dé was FÓDLA, one of the three primary goddesses of the land, together with BANBA and ÉRIU. Eadán killed Fódla in battle. Not all of Fódla's people were killed, however. Many of them moved to an OTHERWORLD, from which they continued to have influence on the world they left behind.

eagle Symbolic animal. This large bird of prey, once relatively plentiful in Celtic lands, is far less so now. Despite its impressive size and fierceness, the eagle did not hold much symbolic power among the Celts, who used it primarily to indicate comprehensiveness in a list of a mythological figure's alternative identities. Thus Ireland's one-eyed SALMON of wisdom sometimes appeared as FINTAN, an ancient invader who shape-shifted into many forms, including the eagle; in British legend, a magical PIG named HENWEN gave birth to eaglets as well as bees and WOLVES. Only the Welsh hero LLEU LLAW GYFFES was solely identified with the eagle, into which form he changed after he was treacherously murdered by his wife. The eagle's appearance was sometimes associated with ORACLES or interpreted as an OMEN of things to come; the eagle could also be a form worn by a SHAPE-SHIFTING magician or BARD.

Apart from mythology, there are folkloric vestiges of a belief in eagles' might, for they appear in Wales as having the power of DIVINATION. There it was believed that eagles who lived on Mount Snowdon were oracular and had the power to control weather; those whose ancestors had eaten eagle flesh were thought to have extraordinary psychic powers, to the ninth generation.

Easal (King of the Golden Pillars) Irish hero. In one of the THREE SORROWS OF IRELAND, the tale of the SONS OF TUIREANN, Easal was a king who helped the young warriors. Condemned to perform a dozen near-impossible feats as retribution for murdering their father's enemies, the three men would have died had not Easal given them food from magical PIGS that, killed each day and devoured each evening, were found foraging happily and in fine health the next morning. Eating the flesh of these magical beings also inoculated one against any disease. Easal may have been a reflection of the great god of abundance, the DAGDA, who was also said to possess miraculous self-restoring pigs.

east   Cosmological concept. In the mythological directions of the ancient Irish, east was the direction of commerce and wealth, opposite to the western province of wisdom. The direction of sunrise, and thus, metaphorically, of beginnings and openings, the east is the location of the PROVINCE of LEINSTER, connected with youthful vigor and enterprise.

See DIRECTIONS.

Easter   Non-Celtic festival. The Christian feast of Easter appears in Celtic lands as a substitute for BELTANE, the spring festival that similarly celebrated resurrection and returning life. The most famous Easter story in Ireland confuses the two festivals, having ST. PATRICK lighting an "Easter fire" on the top of SLANE hill near TARA, in direct competition with the high king's fire on the latter hill. Since pagan Ireland did not celebrate Easter, the fires must have been those of Beltane. Other spring and Beltane traditions were transferred to Easter after Christianization, including the idea that the sun danced on that day and that holy WELLS hold greater efficacy for cures on that day.

Source: MacNeill, Máire. *The Festival of Lughnasa, Parts I and II*. Dublin: Comhairle Bhéaloideas Éireann, 1982, pp. 88, 354.

Eba   Irish heroine. This obscure mythological character appears in the *BOOK OF INVASIONS* as a

healer who went to sleep on a shore called Traig (Trá) Eba, where she was drowned by the rising tide. She may be the same as Abba, the companion of the first settler to reach Ireland, the woman CESAIR.

Éber   (Eber, Ébir)   Irish hero. In the *BOOK OF INVASIONS* several characters bear this name, which may be derived from the similarly named Eber (Heber) in the biblical Book of Genesis. The most important was Éber Finn, chief of the MILESIANS and son of the eponymous Míl Despaine (Mil of Spain or the Spanish soldier). After his people's defeat of the magical race, the TUATHA DÉ DANANN, Éber was granted the southern half of the country, while his brother ÉREMÓN was awarded the north; Éber, unhappy with the division and believing his portion to be smaller than Éremón's, mounted an unsuccessful war in which he was killed. Another character of this name, Éber Donn, was Éber Finn's envious older brother; he played but a small role in Irish myth and was often conflated with the king of death, DONN. The figures are easily confused and may have originally been one.

Ebhla   Irish heroine. Daughter of the evil druid CATHBAD and his wife Maga, Ebhla was the granddaughter of the god of poetry, AONGHUS Óg. Her children were the fated SONS OF UISNEACH.

Ébhlinne   (Evlinn, Ébliu, Éblenn, Eblinne)   Irish goddess. In Co. Tipperary, near the borders of Co. Limerick in Ireland's southwest province of MUNSTER, this mountain goddess was honored in the range called the Twelve Mountains of Ébhlinne (also called Slievefelim Mountains, the Keeper Hills, and the Silvermine Mountains). The highest peak in the range is MAUHER SLIEVE (Máthair-Shliabh), the mother-mountain, where MIDSUMMER celebrations in Éblinne's honor, marking the Celtic harvest feast of LUGHNASA, continued until recent times. As is common with ancient goddesses adapted into a new culture, Ébhlinne was euhemerized into a queen of the region.

From the *DINDSHENCHAS*, Ireland's geographical poetry, we learn that Ébhlinne was the daughter of GUAIRE, king of the BRÚ NA BÓINNE, the pre-Celtic mound city on the River Boyne in eastern Ireland. Married to the king of Cashel, Ébhlinne eloped with her stepson, but the escaping lovers were drowned in the waters of Lough Neagh. The motif of a woman leaving an older king for a younger man is found frequently in Celtic mythology, the most famous being the love triangles of GUINEVERE, LANCELOT, and ARTHUR in Britain; TRISTAN, ISEULT, and MARK in Cornwall; and GRÁINNE, DIARMAIT, and FIONN MAC CUMHAILL in Ireland. Contemporary scholars link such stories to the figure of the goddess of SOVEREIGNTY, who kept the land fertile by marrying consecutive kings.

Sources: Gwynn, Edward. *The Metrical Dindshenchas.* Part II. Vol IX. Royal Irish Academy, Todd Lecture Series. Dublin: Hodges, Figgis, and Co., Ltd., 1906–1924, p. 22; MacNeill, Máire. *The Festival of Lughnasa, Parts I and II.* Dublin: Comhairle Bhéaloideas Éireann, 1982, pp. 214, 428.

Echtach (Echta) Irish heroine or goddess. This obscure figure was pictured as a spectral OWL who haunted the region of east Co. Clare, where her sister, the cannibal woman ECHTHGE, lived. It is unclear whether she is the same figure as the similarly named EACHTACH. Some sources have Echtach as Echthge's rival rather than her sister.

Echthge (Aughty, Echtga, Eghchte) Irish goddess. In the area around the low, rolling Irish hills called Sliabh na Echthge (Slieve Aughty, mountains of Echthge) in east Co. Clare, the connection of the land's name to a mysterious goddess of the TUATHA DÉ DANANN is still remembered. Daughter of the god NUADA of the Silver Hand, Echthge received the lands now named for her as her dowry after she slept with

the man who owned them. Little is known of her except epithets or titles—"the awful one" and "awful daughter and terrible goddess"—and a fragmentary legend about her killing and eating her own children.

Because many place-names in her region are derived from the name of the CAILLEACH, the pre-Celtic HAG goddess, the Celtic Echthge may have absorbed or become absorbed into that older divinity. The Slieve Aughty area is best known in recent times as the home of the famous White Witch of Clare, BIDDY EARLY, of whom stories are still spun; much of the earliest published Irish folklore derives from the area, which bordered upon Coole Park, the demesne of Lady Augusta Gregory, near which poet William Butler Yeats wrote of "fair Eghte of the streams."

Source: Gwynn, Edward. *The Metrical Dindshenchas.* Vol. III. Royal Irish Academy, Todd Lecture Series. Dublin: Hodges, Figgis, and Co., Ltd., 1906–1924, pp. 201–213.

echtra See ADVENTURE.

Ecne Irish hero or god. Grandson or great-grandson of the ancestral Irish goddess DANU, Ecne was an early divinity of poetry, WISDOM, and inspiration. He plays little part in myth.

Ector (Ector de Maris, Ector of the Forest Sauvage) Arthurian hero. Several figures connected with the great knight LANCELOT bear this name. Ector de Maris was Lancelot's brother and joined him as a knight of the ROUND TABLE; Ector of the Wild Forest was Lancelot's foster father.

eel Symbolic animal. Fish do not play much role in Celtic legend, with only the SALMON having a significant mythological association. Almost as frequently, we find the eel, but only in Ireland, where the eel was a plentiful source of food during its annual spring migration. Said to grow out of horsehairs left too long in the water, eels were believed to have the ability to reincarnate themselves; they were sometimes said to travel across land to graveyards, where they slithered underground and ate the corpses. In Co. Clare, near LISCANNOR, a monster eel called an OLLIPHEIST or eascú crawled up from the water to sneak into graveyards and feast. It was pursued across the country by the outraged residents and finally killed near the CAIRN called Conn Connachtach in Kilshanny, some miles distant from the sea.

Eels appear in myth as well as folklore: The fearsome goddess MÓRRÍGAN appeared as an eel to the hero CÚCHULAINN, perhaps in her role as a foreteller of doom; the monstrous CAORANACH fought with saints and heroes from the depths of LOUGH DERG ("dark red lake," called so after her blood shed copiously at her death).

Efnisien (Evnisien, Efnissien) Welsh hero or god. The evil brother of the hero BRÂN THE BLESSED, Efnisien was the cause of the war between Wales and Ireland that forms the centerpiece of the second branch of the collection of epic tales called the *MABINOGION*. When Brân agreed to the proposal of the Irish king MATHOLWCH to wed their sister, the sweet BRANWEN, Efnisien used the occasion to stir up trouble (his usual role in Welsh myth) by mutilating the Irish HORSES. Such sacrilege—for horses partook of divinity as well as being cherished by warriors for their usefulness in battle—ignited a war between the two previous allies. This resulted in deep unhappiness for his sister, who was held a virtual prisoner in Ireland and forced to endure humiliation and deprivation at her husband's hands. When Brân heard of this, he marched into Ireland with his armies.

The Irish had a weapon in this war. Because of Efnisien's troublemaking, Brân had given Matholwch a magical CAULDRON in which dead soldiers could be placed and which would revive them as zombie-like killing machines. Matholwch brought out the cauldron to keep his

troops strong against the mighty forces of Brân. Efnisien redeemed himself, however, by leaping into the cauldron. As it could reinvigorate only the dead, his living body caused it to burst apart.

Source: Gantz, Jeffrey, trans. *The Mabinogion.* New York: Barnes & Noble Books, 1976, pp. 77–79.

egg Symbolic object. Eggs appear in the iconography of Celtic goddesses of abundance like SIRONA. An obvious symbol of potential life, they may also have conveyed the promise of rebirth, for they are found among grave goods. Some eggs had magical properties—for example, the crimson eggs of CLÍDNA's birds, which bestowed the power of SHAPE-SHIFTING on those who ate them. A magical egg-shaped object called the SERPENT'S STONE may have represented an egg.

egret Symbolic bird. Waterbirds were important religious symbols to the Celts, for they lived comfortably in various elements: in air, in water, on land. The egret was the special symbol of the continental Celtic god ESUS, although the CRANE also appears in his iconography.

Eiddilig Gor British mythological figure. One of the Three Enchanters of Britain, this DWARF could escape any pursuer by changing his form into any being of earth, air, or water.

Eire (Érie) See ÉRIU.

Éirinn (Eirinn) Irish heroine or goddess. In some texts, this name is given as that of the mother of the three goddesses of the Irish land: ÉRIU, BANBA, and FÓDLA. As her name is formed from that of Ériu, the titular goddess of the island, it is likely that Éirinn does not represent a real myth but a poetic tradition.

Eiscir Riada (Eisgir Riada) Irish mythological site. The Irish word *eiscir*, which means a series of low ridges, has become *esker*, the internationally recognized term for such relics of the glacial era. Ireland was relatively late in seeing the prehistoric glaciers melt, for until approximately 10,000 years ago, most of the island lay under ice. Because it is a relatively young land, Ireland has many glacial features besides the esker, including drumlins (small, moundlike hills) and erratics (large boulders).

One of the most impressive of Ireland's glacial vestiges is a band of eskers that divides the island almost exactly in half, running from Dublin to Galway. Called the Eiscir Riada, it marks the mythological border between the lands of the southern king (variously ÉREMON or EÓGAN MÓR) and the king of the north (ÉBER Finn or CONN of the Hundred Battles). In ancient times it formed a road across the boglands. The Esker Riada crosses the Shannon River, the main waterway into the Irish interior, near the hill of UISNEACH, mythologically important as the central point where the land's four PROVINCES meet.

Éis Énchenn (Ess Euchenn) Irish heroine. When the great hero CÚCHULAINN traveled to Isle of Skye, off Scotland, to learn martial arts from the WARRIOR WOMAN named SCÁTHACH, he was opposed by three strong men who were no match for the Irish hero. Cúchulainn struck off their heads and proceeded on his journey. On his way back, he had to travel along a narrow road that ran along the edge of an abyss. As he crept along, he encountered a frail HAG who asked him to step aside and let her pass. As there was room for but a single traveler on the narrow road, Cúchulainn obligingly hung out over the abyss, clinging by his toes. But the crone—who was Éis Énchenn, the mother of Bir, Blicne, and Ciri, the warriors that Cúchulainn had killed—stomped on his hands, hoping to send him tumbling to his death. Instead, Cúchulainn did his famous SALMON-leap and struck off Éis Énchenn's head, killing her.

Source: Hull, Eleanor. *The Cuchullin Saga in Irish Literature.* London: David Nutt, 1898, p. 79.

Eisirt Irish folkloric figure. Just as FAIRY communities have their FAIRY QUEENS, so they have BARDS that are even more powerful than human poets. Eisirt was one of the OTHERWORLD's most significant poets, servant of king IUBDAN. He caused trouble when, challenged to make good on his claim that ULSTER was populated by GIANTS, he traveled there and returned with the court DWARF—who was still monstrous by comparison with fairy folk. Fascinated, king Iubdan himself went to Ulster, with his tiny wife BEBO, who attracted much male attention.

Eisteddfod Welsh festival. Perhaps the longest-sustained Celtic festival (although that claim is sometimes challenged by Ireland's PUCK FAIR), this bardic competition is held each year at various venues in Wales, near the ancient feast of LUGHNASA on August 1. Many scholars believe the festival began in Celtic times or shortly thereafter, when BARDS steeped in oral tradition engaged in poetical combats. The current assembly was reestablished in 1860 as a national event, but it can be traced by historical references to 1176. Both poetry and song are featured at the events of the National Eisteddfod, with the Welsh language almost exclusively used.

Eiteag Scottish folkloric figure. This FAIRY was said to live in the remote and beautiful Glen Etive, a valley that bore her name; she may be a folkloric echo of a land goddess.

Eithne (Ethna, Ethne, Ethné, Annie) Irish heroine or goddess. This common Irish name, which means "sweet nutmeat," was borne by dozens of queens, heroines, and goddesses in Irish mythology, the most common being:

• **Eithne, daughter of BALOR.** The king of the monstrous FOMORIANS, Balor of the Evil Eye, had one beautiful daughter, Eithne (sometimes called Eri), mother of the hero LUGH. There are several versions of how she came to conceive. One, apparently older, says that her father had been granted a prophecy that Eithne's child would kill him. To ensure that the prophecy would not be fulfilled, he shut his daughter up in a tower in his remote kingdom on Tory Island, off the northwest coast of Ireland, assuming that a girl who never sees a man could never have intercourse with one.

Unfortunately, prophecies are not so easily thwarted, and Balor's own actions led to his undoing. Coveting the GLAS GHAIBHLEANN, the cow who never ceased giving milk and who lived on the mainland in the care of a human named CIAN, Balor stole it. But Cian would not let the magical being escape without a fight. He dressed himself as a woman and, with the help of a woman DRUID named BIRÓG, slipped into the tower and lived with Eithne until she had borne triplets, including Lugh. Balor, still attempting to outwit the prophecy, threw the children into the sea, but Lugh survived to kill his grandfather at one of the most famous of Ireland's mythological battles, the second battle of MAG TUIRED.

Myth being nothing if not inconsistent, there are variants to the story: One has Cian's name as MacInelly; another gives the name of the physician god DIAN CÉCHT as Eithne's lover and father of Lugh; yet another names as her lover Mac Cennfaelaid, the brother of the cow's owner, Gaibhlín, and states that Mac Cennfaelaid fathered the SEAL-people upon Eithne's 12 handmaidens; yet another says that Eithne, offered by her Fomorian people as a pledge of friendship to their enemies the TUATHA DÉ DANANN, became the wife of their king NUADA and therefore the ancestress of the hero FIONN MAC CUMHAILL. Some scholars have found early evidences of Eithne as a virginal goddess who lived only on the milk of a sacred COW and was guarded from male intercourse by demons; that hypothetical figure is presumed to have become degraded into the Eithne of folklore. A late legend describes Eithne leaving the Otherworld and meeting ST. PATRICK, only to die a fortnight later; this story seems to confuse the divine Eithne with the quasi-historical princess (below).

- **Eithne, wife of** ELCMAR, an alternative name for the RIVER goddess BÓAND.
- **Eithne the Fair,** a human woman so charming that she was noticed by FINNBHEARA, king of the MUNSTER FAIRIES, who cast a spell over her, causing her to slip slowly into a sleep from which she could not be awakened. In her dreams she visited the OTHERWORLD, a land so beautiful that upon awakening, she found this world frightful and ugly. Despite a guard placed upon her, Eithne escaped from her husband and traveled to Finnbheara's FAIRY MOUND at KNOCKMA in Co. Galway, at a place called the Fairies' Glen. Her pursuing husband overheard the fairies gossiping about how happy Finnbheara was with his beautiful prize and how he could never be thwarted until sunlight entered the center of his mound.

  Brokenhearted but persistent, Eithne's husband set to work digging into the mound. He dug and dug but found nothing, until he heard voices murmuring that he must throw salt upon the ground. As soon as he did so, he could see Eithne in the fairy court, from which he pulled her. But at home, she remained in a comalike swoon, unable to communicate. Finally Eithne's husband discovered a tiny fairy PIN holding a sash, and when he removed it, Eithne awakened—believing she had been away but one night, when in fact she had been asleep a year.

- **Eithne Aittencháithrech** ("having furze hair"), sister of the great queen MEDB and, like all her sisters, wife of king CONCOBAR of ULSTER. She does not appear significantly in legend, being outshone by her sisters.
- **Eithne Ingubai,** wife or mistress of the hero CÚCHULAINN in occasional texts, although the more common name for his wife is EMER and for his mistress, FAND.
- **Eithne of** TARA, sometimes called Eithne Tháebfhota or Long-Sides, daughter of king CATHAÍR MÓR and wife of several kings of Tara, including CONN of the Hundred Battles

and his grandson, CORMAC MAC AIRT, to whom she bore a son, CAIRBRE Lifechair; while she reigned at Tara the fields bore three crops each year, showing that she was a form of the goddess of SOVEREIGNTY.

- **Eithne Úathach or Eithne the Horrible,** a cannibal woman who became more beautiful the more infant flesh she devoured.
- **Eithne of CONNACHT,** a quasi-historical princess who, with her sister FEDELM, left the great capital of CRUACHAN one morning to bathe in the little spring called OGALLA. There they met white-clad men whom they mistook for DRUIDS. In fact, the men were monks, including ST. PATRICK, whom they asked to explain the new religion. "Who is your god?" the girls asked, "Is he manly? Does he have beautiful daughters? Is he the sea and the sky?" Patrick, cleverly ignoring the question about god's daughters, converted the girls, who instantly died in order to go to heaven with unstained souls. This transparent piece of Christian propaganda is interesting in the questions that the princesses put to Patrick, which reveal the animism of the Celts before Christianity.

Sources: MacNeill, Máire. *The Festival of Lughnasa, Parts I and II.* Dublin: Comhairle Bhéaloideas Éireann, 1982, pp. 320, 403–404, 551–552; Wilde, Lady. *Ancient Legends, Mystic Charms and Superstitions of Ireland.* London: Chatto and Windus, 1902, p. 42 ff.

Elaine (Elayne, Elain, Elane) Arthurian heroine. In the room where she was held captive by a curse, Elaine of Astolat (the Lady of Shalott) wove magnificent tapestries that permitted her to see the events of the outer world without leaving her castle. On one of those tapestries a handsome knight appeared, and Elaine fell in love with him. Finally she could bear it no longer, and although she knew it would mean her death, she set off in a boat for CAMELOT and the handsome LANCELOT, dying along the way of her love for

him. This powerful and evocative story was the invention of Sir Thomas Malory in his *Morte D'Arthur;* but, like so much Arthurian material, it was derived from earlier Celtic legend.

The original Elaine may have been the siren of Scotland's Clyde River. There she lived on a rock-built castle on the rock of DUMBARTON, staring into a magic mirror in which she could see all that went on in the world—a mirror that has been interpreted to mean the waters itself, whose mirroring surface could be "cracked" by storms. She may be related to the Welsh FAIRY ELEN.

Another Elaine had what her namesake desired: She slept with Lancelot and bore his son, GALAHAD. Daughter of the FISHER KING, Elaine arranged to have accomplices get Lancelot so drunk that he thought he was sleeping with his beloved GUINEVERE; thus he remained pure despite his physical adultery. Yet another figure of this name Elaine of Garlot, played a very minor role in Arthurian legend as a half sister to king ARTHUR; unlike two other sisters, MORGAN and MORGAUSE, who turned against the son of their mother's deceit, Elaine assisted Arthur by marrying one of his enemies, NENTRES, thus forging an alliance.

Source: Spence, Lewis. *The Minor Traditions of British Mythology.* New York: Benjamin Blom, Inc., 1972, p. 18.

Elatha (Elada, Eladha, Elotha) Irish hero. The first residents of Ireland, the FOMORIANS, were terrifying monsters, say the early Irish texts. But there were a few upon whom one could look without loathing; a few were even beautiful. EITHNE, daughter of the Fomorian king BALOR, was such a beauty. So was the king Elatha, whose name means "craft" or "skill," who mated with the land goddess ÉRIU, whose people, the TUATHA DÉ DANANN, ultimately displaced the Fomorians from their Irish lands. She was already married, but who could resist a golden-haired man wrapped in a cloak all embroidered with gold thread? (In some variants, it was Eithne who received Elatha in this fashion.)

After their tryst, Elatha gave Ériu a golden ring and prophesied that she would bear a son. And so she did, but their son BRES mac Elatha was not popular among the Tuatha Dé, and so Ériu sought help among Elatha's people. Her liaison finally led to the famous battle of MAG TUIRED, when the Fomorians were evicted from Ireland, for the half-Fomorian Bres, elected king, proved a stingy and unreliable one, and he was ousted by the Tuatha Dé king NUADA. Some read these complex myths as encoding the continuing struggles between various waves of Celtic immigrants to Ireland's shores, who had to jockey for rulership with the island's earlier residents.

Elcmar Irish god or hero. This shadowy figure appears in legends connected with the famous BRÚ NA BÓINNE, the neolithic monument on the banks of the River Boyne in north central Ireland. He was said to be the husband of the RIVER goddess BÓAND (sometimes, in this context, called EITHNE) who cuckolded him with the DAGDA; variants have it that Bóand's husband was NECHTAN or NUADA. When the son of Bóand and the Dagda, AONGHUS Óg, was born, he evicted Elcmar from the Brú by reciting a charm at a feast his father was hosting—the same charm used to expel the early mythological race called the FIR BOLG from Ireland by the TUATHA DÉ and, in turn, by the MILESIANS who drove the Tuatha Dé into the OTHERWORLD.

elder Symbolic tree. In most Celtic lands, it was considered very unlucky to burn the wood of an elder TREE (genus *Sambucus*), because the spirits of FERTILITY were thought to live within it. If a desperate situation arose that demanded use of elder wood, it was important to ask permission of the tree and its spirits; even with appropriate begging, the branches might bleed when you cut them. The tree's name hints at a connection with the ELF people; it was called the eller tree in the north of Britain where, until quite recent times, rags were offered to these trees to bring good luck. In the Cotswolds, elders were associated

with WITCHES; an elder tree might be a transformed sorceress or carry malign power, so it was avoided in building furniture, especially cradles. In Ireland and on the Isle of Man, the elder was one of the trees most often connected with the FAIRIES and with GIANTS. Despite its frightening reputation, the elder tree was used to make berry wine and flower tea.

Sources: Briggs, Katharine M. *The Folklore of the Cotswolds.* London: B. T. Batsford Ltd., 1974, pp. 13, 120; Spence, Lewis. *The Minor Traditions of British Mythology.* New York: Benjamin Blom, Inc., 1972, pp. 107–108.

Éle Irish heroine. One of the lesser-known sisters of the great queen and goddess of Ireland, MEDB, Éle's name seems to indicate that she was of the FAIRY or elfish race.

Elean nam Ban (Eilean nam Ban Móra) Scottish folkloric site. Highland folklore tells of an "Isle of Women," located somewhere off the coast, on which a green WELL marked the edge of the world. Such mysterious ISLANDS, not tied down in time or space, are a common motif in Celtic folklore and represent portals to the OTHERWORLD. Sometimes the island is called Eilean nam Ban Móra, the Island of the Big Women, suggesting that the residents were GIANTS; the name was sometimes applied to an actual island, the Isle of Eigg.

Source: McKay, John G. *More West Highland Tales.* Vol. 2. Scottish Anthropological and Folklore Society. Edinburgh: Oliver and Boyd, 1969, p. 48.

Elen (Elen of the Hosts, Ellen, Helen, Ellyll, Ellyllon) Welsh heroine or goddess. Scores of churches in Wales are dedicated to St. Helen, mother of the emperor Constantine. What was a Roman matron doing in Wales? Folklore claims that she was Welsh herself, daughter of COEL

Hen, "old King Cole." The Welsh pseudo-saint Helen was a Christian version (or conversion) of the earlier Welsh mythological figure Elen, whose name seems to mean "sprite" and who was the wife of the great magician MERLIN. Elen also appears in the Welsh *Dream of Maxen:* The epic's conquering hero became emperor of Rome but returned to Wales to seek the lovely maiden of his dreams; marrying Elen, he fortified the country with the help of her brothers and returned to Rome to conquer it once again. Yet another—or perhaps the same?—Elen appears as a builder of magical highways that she used to transport her armies across the country when they were needed, for which she was dubbed Elen of the Hosts.

Elen's name may be derived from the Welsh word for ELF or ghost, *ellyll* (pl., *ellyllon*), which in turn recalls several Irish FAIRIES who bear the name Aillén. The small, transparent ellyll was usually a SOLITARY FAIRY, but the ellyllon sometimes gathered under the rulership of their queen, MAB, to dance about as TROOPING FAIRIES. Often the ellyll acted like a BROWNIE, working around the house until discovered, at which time it instantly took its leave. But they were also creatures of great magic who lived in wild areas, eating toadstools for dinner.

Sources: Evans-Wentz, W. Y. *The Fairy-Faith in Celtic Countries.* Gerrards Cross: Colin Smythe Humanities Press, 1911, pp. 233 ff; Straffon, Cheryl. *The Earth Goddess: Celtic and Pagan Legacy of the Landscape.* London: Blandford, 1997, pp. 71, 144.

elf (elves, elven, elfin folk)   This name for the people of the OTHERWORLD came into Britain from Scandinavia with Viking raiders and immigrants; it soon became naturalized and is found as often as such words as FAIRY and BROWNIE.

elf-locks   Folkloric motif. When a FAIRY visited a sleeping human, he or she often dreamed of a blissful romantic encounter. But the one seduced in dream awakened to find that his or her hair was hopelessly tangled, impossible to comb out. Such mischief was common when fairies and humans interacted whether in sleep or waking life.

elf-shot (elf-smitten)   Folkloric motif. When fairies attacked a beast or a person, they had more than magic to use as a weapon. They also had tiny arrows that they flung with great force so that, despite being almost invisible, they caused great damage. A single elf-shot could bring down a COW, so folklore tells us. Those injured by these darts fell into partial or full paralysis, still called by its old name of FAIRY STROKE.

Elgnad   See DEALGNAID.

Elidyr (Editor)   Welsh hero. Many stories are told of people who have gone to FAIRYLAND, but few are as famous as that of this man, recorded in the 12th century by the Welsh geographer and historian Giraldus Cambrensis. As a child, Elidyr encountered two little men who took him to the OTHERWORLD, where he lived in ease and joy. All was beautiful there—bountiful land, beautiful people, endlessly sunny weather. Elidyr stayed for a few hours and then realized his mother would be worrying over his absence and so, regretfully, departed for home.

It was a squalid poor home, and when he told his mother of the lovely land he had visited, she sent him back to get something they could use. Back he went, into the hole on the riverbank where he had descended before. And the Otherworld was just as he remembered it. Remembering his errand, he found a little gold ball that he thought no one would miss. No one, however, can steal from the FAIRIES, so when Elidyr attempted to leave he was caught by the fairies, who were angry and disappointed at his actions. They did not punish him but allowed him to go back to the surface world, free and safe. But thereafter, no matter how he sought,

Elidyr could never find that riverbank entrance to fairyland.

Elin Gow   Irish hero. There are many mythological and folkloric versions of the Irish story of the GLAS GHAIBHLEANN, the magical COW that gave forth milk so abundantly that no one who owned her ever went hungry. The cow belonged to a SMITH, who was sometimes said to be the god GOIBNIU, other times described as a mere man, Elin Gow (Elin the smith). Despite his lowly status, Elin had attempted to marry the daughter of the king of Spain, who owned the Glas at the time. To earn the princess's hand, Elin had to tend the magical cow—which was difficult, because the cow moved so fast that no one had ever been able to keep up with her for a single day. If Elin failed, as so many had before him, he would not only lose the cow and the princess but his life.

To everyone's amazement, the Irish smith managed what no man had done before him, keeping pace with the cow for seven whole years. But when he brought the cow (nothing more is said about the princess) back to Ireland and hired a man named CIAN to care for it, his helper grew weary and went to sleep, allowing the cow to be stolen by the evil FOMORIAN king BALOR. If all's well that ends well, the story has a happy ending, for not only did Cian get the cow back, but he stopped for a tryst with Balor's imprisoned daughter EITHNE and left her pregnant with the hero LUGH.

Source: Curtin, Jeremiah. *Hero-Tales of Ireland.* New York: Benjamin Blom, 1894.

elm   Symbolic tree. As with other sacred TREES, the Irish and British alike believed it would bring misfortune to cut down elms (genus *Ulmus*), trees with a graceful vase-like form that must have appealed to the aesthetic sense of the Celts as much as to people today, who plant elms by the hundreds in cities despite the tree's vulnerability to disease. There is evidence that the kind of blight that destroyed most American elms in the last century occurred in the history and prehistory of Celtic lands, for there are periods when the pollen record lacks elms, while at other times they are plentiful. It is possible that the folklore regarding protection of standing elms recognizes their genetic fragility.

Elphin   (Elffin)   Welsh hero. The foster father of the legendary great Welsh poet TALIESIN was a bumbling sort of fellow who tended to get into trouble. His own father recognized that when he discovered that Elphin was spending his inheritance with no concern for the future. Elphin's father sent him down to a fish-weir, telling him that his fortune would thereafter have to come from the water. That very day the reborn Taliesin—who as a servant boy in the home of the goddess CERIDWEN had accidentally sipped a magical fluid that made him incomparably wise—was hauled out of the sea, where he had been thrown at birth. Elphin took the child home and raised him tenderly, and Taliesin repaid him with filial devotion. But Elphin never completely reformed and occasionally needed to be rescued by his foster son, who willingly obliged.

Elysium   See FAIRYLAND.

Emain Ablach   (Eamhain, Emhain; Abhlach) Irish mythological site. One of the greatest Celtic visions of the OTHERWORLD was that of Emain Albach, the Isle of Apples, a beautiful place of everlasting summer whose handsome residents danced the sun-drenched days away. It was to Emain Albach that the hero BRAN mac Febail traveled, lured there by a dream-woman who left him a silver branch that tantalized him with memory of her loveliness. When he finally reached it, he found her there and lived happily for uncounted years until he grew homesick for earth. His lover, NIAMH of the Golden Hair, reluctantly let Bran leave for home, together with a group of other visitors to her land. But when they reached the shores of Ireland, one sailor was so moved that he leaped ashore. In the Otherworld, time passes more slowly than does ours, and the eager man could not endure the transition to earthly time; all his years caught up with him, and he died and faded to dust within an instant. Bran, saddened by the choice between death and exile, sailed away again; presumably he still sails between this world and the other.

Emain Albach was said to lie somewhere off the coast of Scotland or Ireland; many such entrances to the Otherworld were depicted as seagirt green ISLANDS. Its capital was Cruithín na Cuan, and its king MANANNÁN MAC LIR, the Irish god of the sea for whom the Isle of Man was named; occasionally that real island was called Emain Albach. The name may have been the origin of AVALON, the Arthurian Otherworld.

Emain Macha (Emania, Navan Fort) Irish mythological site. A late Bronze Age HILLFORT in Co. Armagh, identified with the mythical capital of the ancient PROVINCE of ULSTER. The name of Armagh in today's Northern Ireland derives from *ard Macha*, "the heights of MACHA." A goddess of the magical race called the TUATHA DÉ DANANN, Macha came to this world to live with a farmer named CRUNNIUC. As long as she lived with him, he was blessed with ample crops and fine health among his herds—suggesting that Macha was acting as the goddess of SOVEREIGNTY. Despite his new wealth, Crunniuc grew restless and decided to attend the Assembly of Ulster at the court of king CONCOBAR MAC NESSA. Macha strongly advised against it, but when she saw he was determined to go, she begged him at least to keep her presence in his life a secret. Off he went, giving her the promise she desired.

Once he got to the Assembly, Crunniuc forgot his promise. Indeed, he did just the opposite, bragging that his wife was such a speedy runner that not even the king's best horses could win a race with her. Hearing the boasts, king Concobar grew infuriated and demanded that

Crunniuc prove that he spoke truly. Brought forth from her home, Macha implored the king to let her be, for she was heavily pregnant. Hoping that her pregnancy would slow her steps, Concobar commanded the race to begin.

Quick as a flash, Macha was around the course, but as she crossed the finish line her labor pains began. So hard and fast did they come on that Macha died from the tearing pain and loss of blood. Before she died she cursed the men of Ulster, promising that, every time the land was invaded, they would fall down writhing with pangs like hers (see DEBILITY OF THE ULSTERMEN). Macha died giving birth to TWINS, from which the place of Assembly was henceforth called Emain Macha, supposedly meaning "the twins of Macha."

Another etymology is also provided in Irish myth. Once again the central character is Macha, but this time Macha Mong Rua, "red-haired Macha," a WARRIOR WOMAN who went to war against her father's colleagues when they refused to honor her ascension to the throne to replace him upon his death. She killed one of her opponents, CIMBÁETH, but his five cowardly sons ran from the battlefield. She pursued them across Ireland to the rocky Burren, where she found them camped out under the stars. Disguising herself as a loathy HAG, she crept near them, and despite her effective and revolting disguise, every one of them in turn attempted to rape her. As they did, she overpowered them and tied them up, dragging them back to Ulster and using a brooch from her neck (*eo-muin*) to mark out a vast hillfort that she forced them to build for her.

That mythological fort still stands, not far outside today's Armagh city. The ancient sacredness of the place is still apparent from the unusual number of churches in the town, for the early Christians often built their churches on ground that had already been held sacred by the Celts. Called Navan Fort, the Hillfort is an archaeological dig and heritage site, equivalent in stature to the other great capitals of ancient Ireland, such as CRUACHAN in CONNACHT, TARA in MEATH, or KNOCKAULIN in LEINSTER.

Research at the site has dated it to 700 B.C.E., rather earlier than the time of the first Celtic invasion; either Emain Macha was originally a settlement of the pre-Celtic peoples, or Celtic Ireland must be moved back 300 years from its current beginning point. Over the next 800 years, nine rebuildings took place, with less than a century between each. This could indicate a land in the grip of war, or regular rebuildings for other reasons (ritual or cultural), or a mixture of destruction and rehabilitation. One structure of log and stone seems to have been built specifically for the purpose of being burned and buried. Emain Macha continued to be an important political and cultural capital until approximately 500 B.C.E.

Only Tara figures more importantly in Irish myth than Emain Macha, which in turn is followed closely by Cruachan. It may be that Emain Macha is so well remembered because the ULSTER CYCLE (also called the Red Branch Cycle for the hall of treasure at Emain Macha) is the best-preserved sequence of stories from ancient Ireland. Emain Macha was the palace of king Concobar and the place where the exploits of the hero CÚCHULAINN occurred and were retold; it was toward Emain Macha that the great queen MEDB marched her armies on the cattle raid described in the epic *TÁIN BÓ CUAILNGE*. Perhaps myths as extensive as these originally existed for the other capitals of Ireland, but only the Ulster Cycle remains to suggest what glorious narratives might have been lost.

Sources: Gwynn, Edward. *The Metrical Dindshenchas.* Part II. Vol IX. Royal Irish Academy, Todd Lecture Series. Dublin: Hodges, Figgis, and Co., Ltd., 1906, pp. 125 ff; Raftery, Brian. *Pagan Celtic Ireland: The Enigma of the Irish Iron Age.* London: Thames and Hudson, 1994, pp. 74 ff.

Emer (Eimher, Emer Foltchaín, Emer of the Fair Hair) Irish heroine. For almost two millennia, the name Emer has been synonymous with the ideal of womanhood, for she possessed in equally high measure each of the six gifts of femininity: a sweet voice, fine speech, beauty of form and feature, wisdom, chastity, and skill in needlework. This paragon of femininity became the wife of the epitome of masculinity, the hero CÚCHULAINN—although not as quickly as either of them could have wished. Cúchulainn found his way to Emer's side after his king, CONCOBAR MAC NESSA of ULSTER, became concerned that so many of the women of his household had become obsessed with the handsome hero. He sent off to find the best woman in the land for Cúchulainn to marry, figuring that the hero's marriage would quell the lustful feminine fires (it did not, neither for them nor for him). After a year and a day, the men returned to Emain Macha, capital of Ulster, with the news that they had found no one perfect enough for the hero. So Cúchulainn himself set off, for he had heard that FORGALL MANACH had a daughter whose wisdom and beauty all admired.

When Cúchulainn arrived, he found Emer teaching needlework to all the women of the house. He exchanged some riddling words with her, and she matched him, word for word and wit for wit. "I am," she told him, "a TARA among women, the whitest of maidens, one who is gazed at but gazes not back; I am the untrodden way." Almost immediately the well-suited pair fell in love, but Forgall placed two things in opposition. One—the fact that Emer's older sister Fial was not yet married—was beyond Cúchulainn's control, but the second—that he was not yet well enough trained in the manly arts—he could do something about.

So Cúchulainn set off for Scotland, to learn from the greatest teacher of the arts of war: a WARRIOR WOMAN named SCÁTHACH. As they separated, Emer and Cúchulainn vowed to be true to each other. She was; he was not. Within a short time he had conceived a son with Scáthach's daughter (or sister, or double), ÁIFE. And that was not the only affair the hero would have, while Emer remained invariably monogamous.

As the ULSTER CYCLE, to which the story of Emer belongs, was transcribed by Christian monks, it is likely that the figure of Emer was tamed, if not created, by them to model behavior expected of Christian women, for mythological Celtic women of earlier periods were as ready to act upon their desires as their men were, with the goddesses of the land being especially fickle in their relationships with human kings. It is impossible to say if the figure of Emer was derived from a more self-sufficient earlier goddess or if she was always a human woman.

After his return from Alba, Cúchulainn naturally expected to marry Emer. But Forgall continued to refuse, and he imprisoned Cúchulainn in the fortress of Lusca (now Lusk, Co. Dublin). But he did not realize how much Cúchulainn had learned from Scáthach, for the hero made his improbably high SALMON-leap and freed himself, killing several dozen men along the way. Forgall himself leapt to his death while Cúchulainn departed with Emer and other treasures of the house—several cartloads of gold and silver—to his own home at DÚN Delgan (now Dundalk).

As he had before their marriage, so Cúchulainn acted afterward, taking lovers when he willed. But Emer knew her own worth and refused to be jealous of any woman whom the hero bedded. Only once did Emer become concerned, and that involved no human woman at all but FAND, one of the greatest of FAIRY queens, wife of the sea god MANANNÁN MAC LIR. FAIRY LOVERS took their mates away to another realm, leaving them impotent to love the merely human.

When Cúchulainn had been gone a month with Fand—which must have seemed like moments in the OTHERWORLD—Emer decided that she had no recourse but to murder Fand. She hid herself near where the illicit couple was making love, ready to spring and kill. When she saw how tender and beautiful their desire was, she decided to leave them to each other and to their pleasures. Fand, however, discovered Emer and, realizing how much Emer loved her husband, returned to the Otherworld while the human couple drank a potion of forgetfulness. Emer, loyal to the last, died with Cúchulainn on the Pillar Stone to which he affixed himself so that he would die standing upright after his last battle.

Source: Hull, Eleanor. *The Cuchullin Saga in Irish Literature*. London: David Nutt, 1898, pp. 7, 57 ff.

Enid (Enide) Arthurian heroine. In several Arthurian romances, Enid appears the epitome of womanly virtue, one of the THREE SPLENDID WOMEN of CAMELOT, together with DYFR and TEGAU EURFRON. To prove his worthiness to marry the beautiful Enid, the knight Erec set off on a series of adventures, one of which involved hunting for a mysterious white STAG. Having proven his strength and bravery, Erec retreated to the joys of Enid's company—which soon proved so delightful that he retired utterly from his knightly duties. After a time, courtly gossip that Erec was no longer worthy of his wife, because he had grown lazy with too much love, reached Enid's ears. Afflicted to her soul by the rumors, Enid arranged that Erec should overhear them. Outraged, Erec set out to redeem his reputation—this time bringing Enid along for company. The two had many adventures and returned to court successful and renowned. In the Welsh version of the same story, Enid's overattentive husband is called GEREINT. References to Enid as the model of perfection in a wife appear from time to time down to the present.

Eochaid (Echid, Eoachaidh, Echuid, Echaidgh) Irish hero. Irish mythology knows innumerable heroes and kings of this name, which means "horseman." The various figures of this name may ultimately derive from the same original and represent mythological beings, or some originally human men may have been absorbed into the ancient divinity, a hypothesized sun god. The most important figures with this name are:

• **Eochaid Airem,** "horseman plowman," was husband of the queen of TARA, ÉTAIN, of whom Ireland's most beautiful love story is told. Wishing to ascend to the position of Tara's king and with enough successful combats to show his worthiness, Eochaid scheduled his INAUGURATION. But the people of Ireland would not accept a king without a queen to represent the SOVEREIGNTY of the land. So he set out to find the most beautiful woman in Ireland and found her in Étain— who was the reincarnated lover of the FAIRY king MIDIR.

In many incarnations after being cursed by a jealous rival, Étain had forgotten her identity, so she went willingly to Tara to become Eochaid's wife, but Midir had not forgotten. He wagered with Eochaid and won Étain back, taking her to his great palace under the hill at BRÍ LÉITH. Étain was pregnant before leaving Tara, and she gave birth to a daughter whom Eochaid unwittingly married (see ÉSA); their own incestuously conceived daughter, MESS BUA CHALLA, became the mother of king CONAIRE. It has been argued that incest motifs hide myths of origin, for in the beginning of time, incest would have been the only way to populate the globe. Thus this complex myth may describe a time of world creation.

- **Eochaid Fedlech,** king of Tara and father of superlative daughters: MEDB, CLOTHRA, EITHNE, ÉLE, and MUGAIN. He had four sons as well: Furbaide and three boys, all named Finn, who went by the collective name of FINN Emna. Having brothers with the same name seems to have been a family trait, as this Eochaid was the brother of Eochaid Airem, above. He may actually have been the same person, since both were said to have been married to Étain.
- **Eochaid Iúil,** god of the OTHERWORLD and, in some texts, husband to the fairy queen FAND.
- **Eochaid mac Eirc,** husband of the goddess TAILTIU and ideal king of early legend during whose realm the land bore abundantly, rain fell so softly as to seem like dew, and no man ever lied. It may have been he, or Tailtiu's next husband, Eochaid Gargh, who established the LUGHNASA fair at TELTOWN in her honor. A

member of the early race called the FIR BOLG, he fought the arrival of the magical TUATHA DÉ DANANN but was killed at the first battle of MAG TUIRED.
- **Eochaid Garbh,** second husband of the land goddess Tailtiu and probable founder of the famous Lughnasa fair at Teltown.
- **Eochaid Mugmedón,** quasi-historical king and father of NIALL of the Nine Hostages by the British princess CAIRENN; he is one of the great ancestral figures of Irish history, from whom several ruling families traced descent.
- **Eochaid Ollathair,** "all-father," a name for the DAGDA.

Sources: Cross, Tom Peete, and Clark Harris Slover, eds. *Ancient Irish Tales.* New York: Henry Holt and Co., 1936, p. 508; Dames, Michael. *Mythic Ireland.* London: Thames and Hudson, 1992, pp. 240–242, 17, 139.

eó fis   See SALMON.

Eógan (Owen) Irish hero. Several quasi-historical Irish kings bore this name, which means "yew tree," including:

- **Eógan mac Néill** (mac Neíll Noígiallaig), son of the great king of TARA, NIALL of the Nine Hostages and himself the founder of the kingdom of Tyrone (Tir Eógan) in the PROVINCE of ULSTER; he is said to have established a kingship at the impressive stone fort of GRIANÁN AILEACH in the fifth century C.E.
- **Eógan of CONNACHT,** a king who asked to be buried upright, facing the land of his enemies, so that his spirit could continue to defend his land; but his enemies exhumed his body and buried it facing the other way.
- **Eógan Mór** (Eógan Taídlech, Eógan Fitheccach, Mug Nuadat), quasi-historical king of the southwestern province of MUNSTER and husband of BEARE, the legendary Spanish princess who gave her name to the Beare peninsula and who probably disguises an ancient god-

dess of the land. Eógan waged unrelenting war upon CONN of the Hundred Battles at the border of their two lands. When Conn invaded, Eógan fled to Spain; he returned to fight again, but he was again defeated and finally slain by his longtime enemy Conn.

- **Eógan, son of** AILILL Olom, grandson of Eógan Mór and legendary founder of the historical Eóganacht (Owenacht) dynasty of southern Ireland. Eógan was resting once with his foster brother, LUGAIDH mac Conn, when they heard marvelous music. They traced its source to a yew tree (the meaning of Eógan's name) where a harper, FER í (which also means "yew"), eluded their attempts to speak to him. From that moment, despite the hypnotic harmony of the music, the brothers were at war. Lugaidh's manservant Do Dera took his master's place in the field and was killed by Eógan, who believed momentarily that he had killed his brother; but then he saw familiar legs fleeing and realized that Lugaidh had escaped. The brothers met again later, and that time Lugaidh brought with him a DRUID, Dil Maccu Crecga, who enchanted Eógan. With the foresight that druids were known for, he first arranged that Eógan should make love to his daughter, Moncha, knowing that her children would then become kings of Munster. After fathering a son on Moncha, Eógan was killed in the battle.

- **Eógan mac Durthacht,** the man who killed the romantic hero NOÍSIU in the tragic story of DEIRDRE of the Sorrows, one the THREE SORROWS OF IRELAND and a centerpiece of the ULSTER CYCLE of stories. When king CONCOBAR MAC NESSA finally realized that the beautiful Deirdre would never willingly be his, he angrily gave the heroine to Eógan, from whose chariot she threw herself, preferring suicide to life without her lover. Eógan appears in several other legends in supporting roles.

Eógobal Irish god. This obscure figure was the father (or perhaps grandfather) of two god-

desses or FAIRY QUEENS of the southwestern province of MUNSTER, ÁINE and GRIAN, who were not raised by Eógabal but by the sea god MANANNÁN MAC LIR.

Epona Continental Celtic and British goddess. Among people whose vision of divinity was so polytheistic that the same name of a god or goddess is rarely found more than once, Epona is an exception, for statues and altars to her have been excavated across continental Europe, the center of her worship, and in Britain—more than for any other god or goddess of the Celts. Yet little is known of this goddess except that she was connected with HORSES. Her name means "horse," from the Gaulish *epos*, and she was depicted astride a horse (usually a mare), surrounded by horses, or even occasionally lying naked on the back of one.

The greatest concentration of inscriptions to Epona are found in Roman Gaul, especially in Burgundy, and in the Metz-Trier and Meuse valley regions of Germany, where great numbers of images and altars have been found. She was worshiped in Britain as well, but that expansion of her domain may have occurred after Roman occupation, for she was a popular goddess with the legions, who may have brought her across the North Sea with them. The soldiers also brought Epona back to Rome, for she is the only Celtic goddess granted a feast day (December 18) there. She is, however clearly not Roman, for there were no such equestrian goddesses in their pantheon. Often Epona carried a plate, called a *PATERA*; sometimes she bore symbols of abundance, like sheaves of wheat and ears of grain, a SERPENT, or a CORNUCOPIA.

Such a prominent goddess, adopted wholesale by the invading armies, was likely to have been associated with prestige and power; it is believed that her worship was especially strong among the horse-riding warrior elites, whom others may have wished to emulate. As kings typically rose from this class, Epona may have had a regal association.

Epona's worship may have been spread by soldiers, but her appeal was considerably broader, for small personal altars to Epona have also been found, presumably made for the home. Many of these show Epona as a maternal force, either feeding horses from her hand or accompanied by a mare suckling her foals. She is also shown surrounded by unsaddled horses; indeed, any depiction of horses with a goddess points to Epona in her role as goddess of the FERTILITY of the land and of the animals that graze upon it. Occasionally she is referred to in the plural, as the Eponas, emphasizing her reproductive powers.

Yet Epona was not herself an animal power, like CERNUNNOS the stag god; she was rarely herself shown embodied in a horse but only riding or accompanied by them. And although that emblematic horse was forceful and vigorous, Epona was sometimes linked, like other MOTHER GODDESSES, with images of death. She was depicted with the funerary bird, the RAVEN, or with that OTHERWORLD creature, the DOG; or she carried KEYS, suggesting her power to open the entrance to the Otherworld. She may have been seen as a companion or guardian on the trip to the next world.

As Celts commonly associated horses with the SUN, this connection of abundance and death could refer to the sun's daytime powers of increasing vegetative growth, on which the herds rely, and its evening journey beneath the earth, often called the night-sea-journey. Such an interpretation is supported by her connection with hot SPRINGS, believed to be warmed by the sun's passage on the earth's nether side; as goddess of thermal springs, Epona was connected with APOLLO and SIRONA.

Popular as Epona was on the Continent and in Britain, there is no evidence of her in Ireland and little in Wales, where, however, we find the horse goddesses MACHA and RHIANNON respectively. Apparently similar divinities were often found among the insular and continental Celts, with images found nearest Rome and myths and legends found furthest away. Such is the case with the horse goddesses: We have images of

Epona from the Continent and stories of Macha and Rhiannon from Ireland and Wales. It is unclear how closely connected such figures might be; scholars argue about how best to interpret the connections among them.

It is similarly debated how and whether to connect Epona with the mare that figures in an ancient rite of the INAUGURATION of kings, as described by Giraldus Cambrensis, who claimed it was practiced in Ireland in Celtic times. The man to be inaugurated, he said, had to eat a stew made from the meat of a freshly slaughtered mare and drink a broth made from her blood; only after engaging in that ritual was a man believed to be wed to the land goddess. This appears to echo an Indo-European rite from India, where horses also figure in a marriage-inauguration ritual that solidified a king's SOVEREIGNTY over the land.

The most famous horse monument of Britain, the 360-foot-long WHITE HORSE OF UFFINGTON, has been dated to the Celtic era by archaeologists, who nonetheless hesitate to connect the flowing white chalk figure with Epona. Whether named Epona or not, the White Horse is thought to have been first carved into its hillside on the Berkshire downs in 50 B.C.E., after Celtic settlement but before the Roman invasion that brought Epona's worship to Britain. Since there is no evidence for a male divinity of horses among the Celts, the White Horse, if not Epona herself, may represent a British corollary whose name was lost with the arrival of the popular Gaulish goddess. Vestiges of such a horse goddess can also be traced in the folkloric figure of Lady GODIVA and the mysterious white-horse-riding woman of Banbury Cross who appears in nursery rhymes.

Sources: Green, Miranda. *The Gods of Roman Britain*. Aylesbury: Shire Publications Ltd., 1983, pp. 23, 54; Green, Miranda. *Symbol and Image in Celtic Religious Art*. London: Routledge, 1989, pp. 16 ff; Ross, Anne. *Pagan Celtic Britain: Studies in Iconography and Tradition*. London: Routledge & Kegan Paul, 1967, p. 206.

equinox   Calendar feast. The Celts did not celebrate the solstices, the year's longest and shortest day, nor the equinoxes, those two days (approximately March 21 and September 21) when day and night are of equal length. Instead, the Celtic calendar focused on the points between those solar indicators (see IMBOLC, BELTANE, LUGHNASA, SAMHAIN). However, pre-Celtic people in Celtic lands did note the equinoxes and solstices, as the great megalithic sites like the BRÚ NA BÓINNE, LOUGHCREW, and STONEHENGE indicate (see MEGALITHIC CIVILIZATION). Some vestiges of their calendar feasts may survive in festivals like NOLLAIG (which may, however, be derived from the Christmas holiday of the birth of Jesus) and St. John's Day or MIDSUMMER.

See also AUTUMN EQUINOX.

Érainn   Historical people of Ireland. In the late centuries of the last millennium B.C.E. a Celtic people that the ancient geographer Ptolemy called the Iverni settled in southwestern Ireland; these people are generally called the Érainn. They were not Ireland's first settlers, the unknown people of the MEGALITHIC CIVILIZATION; nor were they the last to migrate there, for the Lagin and Féni peoples followed. Scholars have suggested that the mythological FOMORIANS and FIR BOLG people, who preceded the magical TUATHA DÉ DANANN on Irish soil, may be a memory of these early people.

Erc   Irish hero or heroine. A number of minor characters in Irish mythology, both male and female, bear this name, which means "salmon" or "speckled." One was a WARRIOR WOMAN who fought with the great hero FIONN MAC CUMHAILL as one of the members of his band, the FIANNA. Another was the brother of the loving ACHALL; she died of grief at his murder.

Erce   British goddess. An obscure goddess, called the "mother of earth," Erce is known from early British verbal formulae called CHARMS; her name has been interpreted to mean "exalted one." She may have been Germanic rather than Celtic, although the distinction is difficult to make where those historical peoples lived and worshiped closely together.

Éremón   (Heremon, Eremon)   Irish hero. The MILESIANS or Sons of Míl were the last wave of invaders of Ireland, according to the book of legends called the *BOOK OF INVASIONS*. Leading the invasion were two sons of Míl himself, Éremón and ÉBER Finn, who fought the magical forces of the TUATHA DÉ DANANN for control of the island and were victorious; their myth is thought to encode real historical memory of a final wave of Celts who, arriving in Ireland, took political control from earlier Celtic and indigenous non-Celtic peoples.

After their victory the two brothers disagreed on who should rule the land, so the wise poet AMAIRGIN divided it in two along the low glacial hills that stretch from today's Dublin to Galway, the EISCIR RIADA, with Éremón getting the north, Éber Finn the south. Éber Finn remained disgruntled and waged unrelenting war upon Éremón until the latter was forced to kill his brother. Now king of a united Ireland, Éremón established the kingship at TARA, naming the sacred hill after his wife, TÉA.

Source: Gwynn, Edward. *The Metrical Dindshenchas.* Part II, Vol. IX. Royal Irish Academy, Todd Lecture Series. Dublin: Hodges, Figgis, and Co., Ltd., 1906–1924, p. 22.

éric   (*eric, éraic, dire-fine, lóg n-enech*)   Irish legal tradition and mythological motif. "Honor-price" is the usual translation of this word that describes an ancient Irish legal demand for recompense for crimes according to the social standing of the victim. In Celtic Ireland, there was no police force or court of law. Rather, each person had an honor-price according to rank, due upon murder or injury to the TUATH or tribe. If one man murdered another, for instance, the murderer and his kin would owe an éric of gold, cattle, slaves, and other valuables to the victim's kin, according to his rank. Other crimes, such as slander and rape, were also punished with the éric. As the entire kinship group was responsible for such debts, the legal requirement had an inhibiting effect on hotheaded youth most prone to violence.

Many Irish myths revolve around the collecting of an honor-price, as when the SONS OF TUIREANN had to perform impossible feats as punishment for killing their father's enemy CIAN. "Every éric is evil," stated the *SENCHAS MÓR*, the great collection of legal documents and commentaries, on the grounds that it almost inevitably led to more bloodshed.

Ériu (Éire, Erin) Irish goddess. The green island at the far western periphery of Europe bears the name of its earth goddess, Ériu. That we do not call Ireland FÓDLA or BANBA is explained by the myth that, when the final wave of invaders, the MILESIANS, arrived on Ireland's shores, they encountered three sisters, all goddesses of the land, each of whom asked that the island be called after her. The sorceress Banba made her demand from the top of her favorite MOUNTAIN; so did Fódla, when the invaders arrived at her mountain. Each stalled the Milesians in their attempt to reach the center of Ireland, and to each the same promise was given. But at the center the invaders found the resplendent Ériu, who made the same demand as the others. Because Ériu promised greater prosperity than did her sisters, the chief BARD of the Milesians, AMAIRGIN, decided to call the island after Ériu (Érinn being the genitive of her name, meaning "of Ériu"). The names of Fódla and Banba are still sometimes used as poetic names for Ireland.

It was at the sacred central mountain, UIS-NEACH, that Ériu greeted the invaders. One, Donn mac Míled, replied to her demands with insults, and Ériu calmly sentenced him to death; he drowned shortly thereafter, indicating that Ériu had control over the seas as well as the land.

She may have been a cosmic goddess, for she is described as decked in rings, while her name, which derives from the word for "round," suggests that she originally may have been a solar or lunar goddess whose domain included the sky. Usually seen as a massive woman, Ériu was sometimes a long-beaked gray CROW. She was also embodied in her sacred mountain, which slowly grew as she aged.

As goddess of the center, Ériu was the one who ceremonially married the king in the INAU-GURATION rite, the *banais ríghe*, that tied his fortunes to those of the land. She established the ÓENACH or festival at Uisneach every BELTANE (May 1), which involved markets and games as well as more sacred events, including the lighting of TWIN fires on the hilltop.

A member of the magical TUATHA DÉ DANANN, Ériu is described in different texts in various relationships to the other divinities: as daughter of ERNMAS, a mother goddess; as the mother of the half-Fomorian king BRES mac Elatha; as the wife of the obscure god MAC GRÉINE (son of the sun), also called Cethor; as the lover of ELATHA, to whom she bore Bres; and as the queen of SOVEREIGNTY who is mistress to the hero LUGH. Like so many other deities of the Tuatha Dé Danann, she was killed at the fierce battle of TÁILTIU by the very Milesians she had welcomed. Her grave on Uisneach hill is marked by the STONE OF DIVISIONS, a huge glacial boulder that reputedly shows the map of Ireland on its cracked surface.

Source: MacAlister, R. A. Stewart. *Lebor Gabála Érenn: The Book of the Taking of Ireland, Part 5.* Dublin: Irish Texts Society, 1956, p. 35.

Erne Irish heroine or goddess. The place-name poetry of Ireland, called the *DINDSHEN-CHAS*, records the story of how the important RIVER Erne and the LAKE from which it rises gained their names. A noblewoman named Erne—described as "chief among the maidens of CRUACHAN," the great capital of the PROVINCE of

CONNACHT—traveled there with a group of women, all of them frightened away from their own home by the sound of a gigantic voice issuing from the tiny opening of the cave called OWEYNAGAT or Cave of the Cats. Taking with her the COMB (symbol of feminine potency) of her mistress, the great queen MEDB, Erne took her party northward to a lake in which they all drowned. The motif of the woman drowned in an important water-source usually indicates an ancient goddess of the watershed.

Source: Gwynn, Edward. *The Metrical Dindshenchas.* Vol. III. Royal Irish Academy, Todd Lecture Series. Dublin: Hodges, Figgis, and Co., Ltd., 1906–1924, pp. 461–467.

Ernmas (Éirinn) Irish goddess. This relatively obscure Irish MOTHER GODDESS is best known for her offspring, the three goddesses of the land, FÓDLA, BANBA, and ÉRIU; the name of this goddess is also given in some ancient texts as Éirinn. Ernmas also appears as the mother of the triple war goddesses, MACHA, BADB, and the MÓR-RÍGAN; her name is connected with the modern Irish word *embas* ("death by iron" or "death by weapons").

Erriapus Continental Celtic and British god. Inscriptions in Gaul describe this deity, connected by the Romans with their god of commerce, MERCURY; in England horned gods like CERNUNNOS have been linked with this obscure figure.

Ésa (Esa, Ess) Irish heroine. A minor figure in Irish mythology, Ésa was the daughter of the beautiful ÉTAIN, a FAIRY woman reborn as a mortal, and the human king of TARA, EOCHAID Airem. When Étain's first love, the fairy king MIDIR, came from the OTHERWORLD to reclaim her, she was pregnant with Eochaid's daughter Ésa. Eochaid later unwittingly married this same daughter, having been tricked into imagining Ésa to be Étain. The daughter of Ésa and Eochaid Airem was the madwoman and later queen, MESS BUACHALLA.

Source: Gwynn, Edward. *The Metrical Dindshenchas.* Part II, Vol. IX. Royal Irish Academy, Todd Lecture Series. Dublin: Hodges, Figgis, and Co., Ltd., 1906–1924, p. 22.

Esus (Hesus) Continental Celtic god. Not much is known of this Gaulish god, whose name has been translated as meaning "strength" or "rapid motion" or even "anger." There is the provocative mention in the Roman author Lucan of "uncouth Esus of the barbarous altars," who was worshiped with human sacrifice in which DRUIDS read the future from the streams of blood running down victims hung in trees. Comments from other early authors link Esus to the Roman gods MERCURY and MARS, presumably indicating that he was a god of merchants and warriors.

We have as well inscriptions and altars showing Esus in the company of BULLS and CRANES or working as a woodcutter. And there are names that seem to derive from his: the Breton town of Essé, thought to have been a center of his worship; the people called the Esuvii in the same region of France; and the personal names Esugenos, "son of Esus," and Esunertus, "strong as Esus." Evidence of his cult has been found in England and Switzerland as well as France.

From this scant information—some coming from the pens of Celtic enemies and therefore suspected of the taint of bias—scholars have attempted to reconstruct the character and worship of this clearly important continental Gaulish divinity. That his victims were hung in TREES, taken together with images of Esus cutting wood, suggests a deity of vegetation whose powers were to be seen in the strong trees of the forest. The suggestive similarity between his name and that of the Christian Jesus, as well as the image of a victim hung on a tree, has led to some imaginative interpretations, most recently in the popular novel *Daughter of the Shining Isles* by Elizabeth Cunningham.

Esyllt (Essellt) Welsh heroine. The original of ISEULT, the romantic figure of Arthurian legend, Esyllt was described as the wife of king March (who became king MARK in the Arthurian cycle) and the lover of his nephew TRYSTAN (who similarly became TRISTAN). Her name is believed to derive from a phrase meaning "the one gazed upon" and may be Germanic rather than Celtic in origin. But the story of her elopement with a young man, leaving behind her aging husband, recalls Celtic myths of the SOVEREIGNTY goddess.

Étain (Etaine, Aideen, Édain, Edain, Achtan) Irish heroine or goddess. The many Irish mythological figures who bear this name are easily confused, because their myths so often involve reincarnation, disguise, and false identification. They may, indeed, all ultimately descend from or be connected with a single early source, possibly a sun goddess. The meaning of her name ("swift one") and the early epithet Echraide ("horse-rider") connect her with such equine goddesses as the continental Celtic EPONA, the Welsh RHIANNON, and the Irish MACHA. The Celts connected HORSE with the SUN, pictured as a steed that no one could outrun. There are several mythological renderings of this goddess, most notably:

• **Étain, lover of MIDIR**, was an OTHERWORLD woman whose affair with the FAIRY king Midir aroused the ire of his wife FUAMNACH, a DRUID and sorceress, who turned Étain into a fly. In this miserable form she flew about the world for many years until she fell into a cup of wine held by an ULSTER princess who, drinking down the cup with the insect-Étain within it, became pregnant. (Impregnation by drinking insects is a common motif in Irish mythology.) The princess gave birth to a girl whom she named Étain and who grew up to be the most beautiful woman in Ireland. When EOCHAID Airem wished to be king at TARA, he was unable to proceed with his INAUGURATION until he married, for part of the

inaugural festivities demanded a queen to enact the part of the goddess of the land. Searching through the land for the most appropriate mate, he found the beautiful Étain, who had forgotten her earlier life and agreed to marry him. Their wedding and Eochaid's inauguration were celebrated in high style, and nothing seemed to suggest a happy future would not unfold.

But if Étain had forgotten Midir, Midir remembered Étain. First he came to Tara disguised as AILILL Anglonnach, her husband's brother, feigning illness and claiming that only the touch of Étain's hand could soothe him. Étain reluctantly agreed to make love with him to save his life. The tangled story sometimes describes Midir as only taking on Ailill's identity to spare Étain's honor while having access to her. In most versions Midir is ultimately rejected by the honorable Étain.

He then conceived of a new plan to win back his love. Coming to Tara in his own identity, he challenged Eochaid to play FIDCHELL, a game like cribbage. Eochaid believed himself to be a fine player, but he had never played against the forces of the Otherworld—or of true love. Midir won. They wagered again, and this time Eochaid's determination to win was so strong that he put up Étain as the prize. Midir won again, and when he kissed Étain, all her memory of their former life together returned. Transforming themselves into beautiful SWANS, they flew out through the skylight at Tara, once again together in love.

The king pursued them as they fled to CRUACHAN, the capital of CONNACHT, where Étain's maid CROCHAN gave birth to the great goddess and queen MEDB (often described as a double of Étain). Then they went to Midir's home, the FAIRY MOUND at BRÍ LÉITH, which Eochaid stormed in an attempt to get his wife back. But Midir was not about to lose Étain again. He sent out 50 enchanted women, all looking exactly like Étain, and dared Eochaid to chose the right one. Most of them were fairies but there were some humans among them, and Eochaid chose one of them. To his sorrow, it proved to be his own daughter, ÉSA, with whom Étain had been pregnant when she fled with Midir. Eochaid did not, however, find this out until he had sired a granddaughter on this daughter. While some variants say that Étain broke through the fairy GLAMOUR herself and returned to Eochaid, most versions of the tale end with her living happily ever after with her fated love Midir.

- **Étain, lover of Eochaid Fedlech**, was the daughter of the king ÉTAR. She bore Étain Óg to the brother of EOCHAID Airem, whose name was Eochaid Fedlech. Such duplication of names is not uncommon in early Irish literature.

- **Étain Óg,** daughter of the Étain above, married a king, Cormac, and bore him a daughter, for whom she had great ambitions. Because Cormac had a baby daughter from an earlier relationship, Étain Óg arranged to have the baby killed. The warriors assigned to do the dire deed were, however, so charmed by the child that instead of killing her, they abandoned her in a cowshed, hoping that she would be found. And indeed, the cowherd who used the shed adopted her, and so she was called MESS BUACHALLA, the herdman's fosterling. In some variants Mess Buachalla is the daughter of ÉSA rather than of Étain Óg.

- **Étain, lover of EÓGAN** Mór, was a FAIRY woman who rescued her lover, the king of MUNSTER, after his defeat at the hands of CONN of the Hundred Battles. Her home was Inis Grecraige or Beare Island in Bantry Bay; there she took care of her lover and his men until they were recovered enough to return to the fray.

- **Étain of the Fair Hair** (Fholtfhild), a fairy woman who lived within the Hill of Howth near Dublin, called BENN ÉTAIR after her father, ÉTAR; married to a mortal, she died of grief when he was killed. The same name was given to another fairy woman whose domain was the sea, where she lived with her father, the sea god MANANNÁN MAC LIR, and her sister, CLÍDNA of the waves.

- **Étain, mother of CORMAC MAC AIRT**; usually called ACHTAN. When the Irish hero ART MAC CUINN, lodging with a SMITH on the night before a battle, was told that any child of this Étain was fated to be king at TARA, he slept with the girl in hopes of conceiving such a son. Leaving instructions that any child conceived should be fostered by a friend in the distant province of CONNACHT, Art went to battle and to his death. Étain did conceive and, as instructed, traveled to Connacht to give birth in the foster father's home, but a great storm forced her to take cover, during which her labor began. Wandering off to find help after giving birth to Cormac, Étain returned to find the child gone, for a female WOLF had adopted him. Cormac's wolf-mother raised him to boyhood, and he and Étain were reunited when he claimed the throne of Tara.

Sources: Cross, Tom Peete, and Clark Harris Slover, eds. *Ancient Irish Tales.* New York: Henry Holt and Co., 1936, pp. 93 ff; Dames, Michael. *Mythic Ireland.* London: Thames and Hudson, 1992, pp. 233–238; Dillon, Myles, ed. *Irish Sagas.* Cork: The Mercier Press, 1968, p. 15; Gregory, Lady Augusta. *Gods and Fighting Men: The Story of the Tuatha De Danaan and of the Fianna of Ireland.* New York: Oxford University Press, 1970, p. 88; Gwynn, Edward. *The Metrical Dindshenchas.* Part II, Vol. IX. Royal Irish Academy, Todd Lecture Series. Dublin: Hodges, Figgis, and Co., Ltd., 1906–1924, p. 22.

Étan Irish goddess. Often confused with ÉTAIN, this name identifies a goddess of crafts, daughter of the healer god DIAN CÉCHT and wife of OGMA, god of eloquence. Several other minor figures, including a mistress of the hero CÚCHULAINN, also bear the name.

Étar (Étair, Eadar) Irish hero. A minor figure in legends of the beautiful romantic heroine or goddess ÉTAIN, Étar is sometimes described as Étain's father in her human reincarnation. In other versions of the story, she is conceived immaculately by a queen who drinks up a worm in her wine, and Étar is her stepfather or foster father. Étar gave his name ("great") to the Hill of Howth near Dublin, called in Irish BENN ÉTAIR. He is said to have been the mate of ÁINE, the sun goddess who was daughter or lover of the sea god, MANANNÁN MAC LIR. For her wedding gift to him, Áine gave Étar a golden chain that protected him both against drowning and against human weapons. He was not protected against dying of love, however, and when he died of a broken heart after Áine rejected him, he was buried at Howth. In some texts, Étar appears as a woman who similarly died of love, but whether this indicates another being or an original androgynous god is not known.

Ethal Anbuail Irish hero. The father of the romantic heroine CÁER, beloved of AONGHUS Óg, the god of arts, Ethal Anbuail was described as a FAIRY king of CONNACHT.

evil eye See EYE.

Excalibur Arthurian symbol. The most famous sword in European history, Excalibur belonged to king ARTHUR of CAMELOT, to whom it was given by the mysterious and magical LADY OF THE LAKE. Excalibur is often confused with the unnamed sword that Arthur, as a youth, extracted from a massive rock in which it had been magically embedded by the great magician MERLIN. A prophecy that the man who could withdraw the sword would become Britain's king brought many knights to make the attempt, but all failed until the young Arthur withdrew it as easily as though it had been in butter. When he later broke that sword in combat, Arthur was given Excalibur, made by the magical SMITH WAYLAND. The special property of Excalibur was that its scabbard protected its possessor from all wounds.

But Arthur's sister MORGAUSE (sometimes, MORGAN), in league with his son/nephew and enemy MORDRED, stole the scabbard from Excalibur, leaving Arthur vulnerable. Wounded in his final battle, Arthur heaved the sword into a lake, from which a mysterious womanly hand emerged, presumably that of the Lady of the Lake. Should Arthur reappear to lead his land again, it is said that the great sword will be ready for his hand.

The name Excalibur is a corruption of the Welsh Caladfwlch, which became Caliburn and, through a false connection with Latin, finally Excalibur. Connections have been drawn with CALADBOU, or "hard fighter," the sword wielded by the great Irish hero FERGUS mac Róich.

Source: Evans-Wentz, W. Y. *The Fairy-Faith in Celtic Countries.* Gerrards Cross: Colin Smythe Humanities Press, 1911, p. 222.

external soul Symbolic object. Some cultures have believed that the soul could exist outside the body: in a stone, for instance, or a tree. Several Celtic myths allude to this belief: The queen CRÉD fell upon and crushed the soul of her beloved CANO MAC GARTNÁIN; the hero CÚCHULAINN killed his rival CÚ ROÍ by catching a SALMON that hid his soul. In addition, folklore describes moths or butterflies—and occasionally, BEES—which appear after a person's death and which hold their escaping soul.

Source: Henderson, George. *Survivals in Belief Among the Celts.* Glasgow: James MacLeose and Sons, 1911, pp. 76 ff.

eye Symbolic object. A common and complex symbol, the eye has spiritual significance both around the world and in Celtic lands. An earlier (probably Neolithic or New Stone Age) European cult surrounding an Eye Goddess is detected behind the carved eye-like spirals that peer from rocks throughout the Celtic lands; that pre-Celtic goddess may have influenced the conception of the CAILLEACH, noted for her single eye. Many such one-eyed beings are interpreted as solar powers. As a SUN goddess, the Cailleach would represent the weaker sun of winter, for she is invariably associated with the storms of that season; her alternative form is found in Scotland as Bride, the summer maiden, but whether that figure is connected with the Irish goddess of spring's awakening, BRIGIT, is difficult to determine. The evil-eyed FOMORIAN king, BALOR, is similarly associated with the winter season, when his single eye blighted vegetation.

Irish Brigit's connection with the eye, and therefore potentially with the sun, is greatly strengthened by the dedication of many Irish holy WELLS to her. While offering HEALING powers against many diseases, the wells were held to be especially effective in curing eye diseases. While the ritual varied slightly from region to region, typically one was to rise at dawn, perform the well's PATTERN or prescribed ritual actions, then bathe the eyes in the well's water. Diseases that might cause blindness, such as glaucoma and diabetes, were equally likely to be cured by the water of holy wells.

Irish belief in the magical powers of sight included SECOND SIGHT, the ability to see things at a distance or before they happened, and the evil eye, in which a spiteful person could curse another merely with a glance. The envious could, it was believed, gain possession of an object by looking at it with ill intent. Squinting—common among the nearsighted—was sometimes interpreted as casting a CURSE. Precautions against the evil eye, including verbal CHARMS and protective gestures, were common in rural Ireland into the 19th century. In Scotland, too, there was a fear of the power of the evil eye, which was believed to result from covetousness or envy; someone looking upon another's fortune with resentment could destroy that good luck. "Envy splits the rocks," a Scottish proverb warned. Healthy animals could die, people be struck down by an illness impossible to diagnose, houses burn to the ground—all from a mere glance. To assure oneself of protection against such ill fortune, Scottish people took precautions: not allowing animals into the barn with full bladders, putting sixpence in a bowl of water, wearing RED thread around the neck.

Sources: Campbell, John Grigorson. *Witchcraft and Second Sight in the Highlands and Islands of Scotland.* Detroit: Singing Tree Press, 1970, p. 59; Carmichael, Alexander. *Carmina Gadelica: Hymns and Incantations.* Hudson, N.Y.: Lindisfarne Press, 1992, pp. 136–147; Crawford, E. G. S. *The Eye-Goddess.* Chicago: Delphi Press, 1994.

F

fachan (*athach*) Scottish folkloric figure. This one-legged, one-eyed monster haunted the wilder districts of Scotland. In its one hand, which grew from its chest, it held a flail covered with iron apples, with which it struck out at passersby while hopping about on its single leg. One form of the *fachan* was called the *ATHACH*; another, called the dìreach, haunted the lonely Glen Eitive. As a DRUID cast curses by standing on one leg with an arm in the air (see *GLÁM DÍCENN*), some believe the stories of the *fachan* derive from fear of that posture's power.

Fachtna Irish hero. Several heroes bear this name, but only one has any importance in Irish legend. The king of ULSTER, Fachtna Fáthach, married the studious girl whose original name had been Assa ("gentle") but who turned into the warrior NESSA ("ungentle") after the evil DRUID CATHBAD had killed her beloved tutors in an attempt to ravish her. Whether Cathbad succeeded is difficult to know, because although Nessa did bear a son, he came forth carrying a WORM in his hand. Nessa explained that she had conceived after drinking from a glass in which two worms were swimming, thus becoming magically impregnated. Her son bore her name, becoming CONCOBAR MAC NESSA, but was reared by Fachtna and took over the throne of Ulster from him.

Faerie (Fairy, Feri) Contemporary religion. The tradition in contemporary American neo-paganism that bears this name can be considered part of the CELTIC REVIVAL, although it is only marginally related to Celtic worldviews, deriving instead from folkloric images of the diminished gods of the FAIRY realm. (See NEO-PAGAN.)

Faifne Irish hero. In Irish place-lore, this poet was the brother of the "noble and skillful" maiden AIGE, who was transformed into a doe by evil FAIRIES. Fleeing from the hunters and their dogs who relentlessly pursued her, Aige finally lost her life when trapped by the minor king Meilge, apparently an enemy of her family. Fulfilling the duty of a BARD, her brother then cast a SATIRE so strong it raised blemishes upon the murderer, thus ending his kingship (see BLEMISHED KING). Meilge's warriors then turned upon the poet and killed him.

Source: Gwynn, Edward. *The Metrical Dindshenchas. Part II.* Vol. IX. Royal Irish Academy, Todd Lecture Series. Dublin: Hodges, Figgis, and Co., Ltd., 1906, pp. 67–71.

fairy (faery) Celtic folkloric figure. Celtic fairy lore is vast, with some form found in every Celtic land. While there are many regional variations, there are also similarities among the fairies found in Ireland, Scotland, Wales, Cornwall, the Isle of Man, and Brittany. Many scholars argue that the fairies are degraded versions of ancient gods, both Celtic and pre-Celtic, whose power remained active in the people's minds even after they had been officially replaced by later religious beliefs. Other theories are that fairies were the faded memory of indigenous people replaced by later immigrants, or elemental spirits of nature. Finally, folklore sometimes fails to distinguish fairies from the dead, nor is it possible to determine if the Celts themselves originally blurred the distinction between the two or whether that is a later confusion. Fairies are described as stealing people from this world (see FAIRY KIDNAPPING), and the difference between death and this sort of kidnapping is difficult to discern.

Most fairies lived in great cities, where they danced and feasted constantly; when they traveled to another fairy court, they did so in a great throng that caused a huge wind (see FAIRY BLAST). When such TROOPING FAIRIES encountered people on these expeditions, they snatched up and took AWAY those they favored; for this reason rural people warned against walking near FAIRY MOUNDS and other liminal places at night, when the fairies were most likely to be about. Other fairies were SOLITARY FAIRIES, including the shoemaking LEPRECHAUN and the tippling *CLURICAUNE*. They lived alone, often busying themselves about some craft or industry. Such farmyard familiars as the BROWNIE and the BUCCA were helpful to humans unless sent away by being showered with gifts. But some solitaries were more frightening, such as the BANSHEE and her sister, the FAIRY LOVER; encounters with either led to death or disappearance.

In appearance fairies were typically small, about $3\frac{1}{2}$ feet tall, and red-haired; indeed, RED hair was not only construed as indicating fairy blood in humans but in animals as well. Short people with red hair would not be mistaken for fairies unless they wore the distinctive fairy colors of red and GREEN. Most fairies were exceedingly comely, with long hair like silk and glowing complexions that, even when green, were a delight to behold.

Fairies were immortal, or perhaps appear to have been so because of the difference between our world's time and theirs (see FAIRY TIME). Tales describe wizened old fairies or a fairy funeral, but such stories are rare. More commonly fairyland is described as a place without death or pain, where even fairy battles have no mortal consequences.

The fairies were immoral as well as immortal, for they stole away married men and women from their spouses, drank hard liquor to excess and punished anyone who brewed his own and did not share it with them, and otherwise broke the bonds of normal society. But they had their own morality and code of behavior. They demanded respect for their privacy and punished anyone who spied upon them. Beyond that, the fairies demanded qualities that make social intercourse pleasant: no boasting or coarse language on the one hand, but no gloominess or lack of generosity on the other. They were fanatical about neatness and punished anyone who was slatternly enough to offend their sensibilities. Finally, although they thought nothing of stealing from our world, they would not endure anyone stealing from theirs, and they punished such theft ruthlessly.

They were both respected and feared. "Their backs towards us, their faces away from us, and may God and Mary save us from harm," was a prayer spoken whenever one ventured near their dwellings. The tendency to speak of them in euphemisms such as The Gentry and The Good Neighbors hid a fear that they might retaliate against anyone who did not flatter them in this fashion.

The word *fairy* itself is not in any way Celtic or from any of the Celtic lands. It is a derivation from the Roman *fatae*, the powers or goddesses of fate, through the French *faerie*. The word first became *fays*, and *fay-erie* meant being under the power of the fays (see GLAMOUR). It is a slippery term used by various writers to refer to different beings of the OTHERWORLD: diminished goddesses, elves, even ghosts.

Sources: Briggs, Katherine M. *The Personnel of Fairyland*. Cambridge: Robert Bentley, 1954; Briggs, Katherine. *The Fairies in Tradition and Literature*. London: Routledge & Kegan Paul, 1967; Evans-Wentz, W. Y. *The Fairy-Faith in Celtic Countries*. Gerrards Cross: Colin Smythe Humanities Press, 1911; Keightley, Thomas. *The Fairy Mythology*. London: H. G. Bohn, 1870; Kirk, Thomas. *The Secret Commonwealth of Elves, Fauns, & Fairies*. London: David Nutt, 1893.

fairy (Irish) Once they were divine: the TUATHA DÉ DANANN, the children or people of the goddess DANU. According to the mythological history of Ireland, the *BOOK OF INVASIONS*, the Tuatha Dé were the penultimate invaders of the island, wresting control from the sturdy dark FIR BOLG and the fierce FOMORIANS. When the final invaders came, the Tuatha Dé went the way of their enemies, being defeated in the great battle of TAILTIU by the Sons of Míl or MILESIANS.

The Milesians did not evict the defeated race from Ireland; instead, a deal was made that the Tuatha Dé would take the underside of the world while the Milesians ruled the surface. Through this curious treaty the ancient race remained within the hills, under the bogs, and in other liminal areas of Ireland, where they were transformed into the fairy people. Sometimes the story of their fall from power was connected to the Christian story of the angels' fall from heaven, and the fairies were thus described as fallen angels.

Some divinities of the Tuatha Dé Danann appear in Irish fairy lore, such as CLÍDNA, MACHA, and MIDIR, while others do not. Thus the mythological description of their banishment to FAIRYLAND is at odds with actual fairy lore, which survived largely through the oral tradition until it was collected by folklorists in the late 19th and early 20th centuries. Whether there were ever tales describing such divinities as the DAGDA and BRIGIT living under the local hill is a matter of conjecture.

The people of the OTHERWORLD were rarely referred to by speakers either as fairies or as Tuatha Dé Danann; fearing their power, their human neighbors called them by such Irish phrases as the Daoine Maithe (the Good People), the Áes Sídhe (People of the Fairy Mounds), and the Daoine Uaisle (the Gentry). Other names used were similarly euphemistic, such as the Wee Folk, the Hill Crowd, the Red Caps, and the Host of the Air, a phrase used by William Butler Yeats as the title of one of his most memorable early poems.

Sources: Croker, T. Crofton. *Fairy Legends and Traditions of the South of Ireland*. London: William Tegg, 1862; Curtin, Jeremiah. *Tales of the Fairies and of the Ghost World Collected from Oral Tradition in South-West Munster*. New York: Lemma Publishing Corp., 1970. Originally published, London: David Nutt, 1895; Gregory, Lady Augusta. *Visions and Beliefs in the West of Ireland*. Gerrards Cross: Colin Smythe, 1970; Lenihan, Edmund. "The Fairies Vs. the Money Economy." In Patricia Monaghan, ed. *Irish Spirit: Pagan, Celtic, Christian, Global*. Dublin: Wolfhound Press, 2001, pp. 122 ff; MacManus, Dermot. *The Middle Kingdom: The Faerie World of Ireland*. Gerrards Cross: Colin Smythe, 1959; O hEochaidh, Séan. *Fairy Legends of Donegal*. Trans. Máire MacNeill. Dublin: Comhairle Bhéaloideas Éireann, 1977; Wilde, Lady. *Ancient Legends, Mystic Charms and Superstitions of Ireland*. London: Chatto and Windus, 1902, pp. 37 ff.

fairy (other Celtic) Fairy traditions are found in other Celtic lands as well as Ireland, most notably in Scotland and on the Isle of Man. There is not, however, a single Celtic root-word that describes the fairies of different lands, leading some to question as to whether there was ever an overall Celtic fairy-faith or whether the fairies derive from pre-Celtic people's beliefs. On the Isle of Man, the fairies were called *ferrish*, a word that seems to derive from the English word *fairy*, which immigrated so long ago that it has become incorporated into place-names like Close ny Ferrishyn, "fairy hill." The *ferrishyn* (p1.) dressed in RED caps and GREEN coats, lived in the branches of nut trees, and traveled with packs of red-eared white hounds. They liked to disorient people who walked the hills in the evening, turning them around so that they do not know where they are headed (see PIXY-LED, STRAY SOD). In Wales the fairies were called the *twlwyth teg* or "fair family"; in Cornwall the *spyrys* or "spirits"; in Brittany the *KORRIGANS* or "sea-fairies."

Sources: Douglas, George. *Scottish Fairy and Folk Tales.* West Yorkshire: EP Publishing, 1977, pp. 103 ff; Leather, Ella Mary. *The Folk-Lore of Herefordshire.* London: Sidewick & Jackson, 1912, pp. 43 ff; Parry-Jones, D. *Welsh Legends and Fairy Lore.* London: B. T. Batsford, Ltd., 1953; Rhys, John. *Celtic Folklore: Welsh and Manx.* Oxford: Clarendon Press, 1941, pp. 197 ff.

fairy animals Folkloric motif. In their beautiful FAIRYLAND, the fairies kept magical CATTLE (see FAIRY COW) as well as DOGS (see BLACK DOG) and CATS (see CAT SITH). All of these looked rather like their kin in our world. But there were other, wilder fairy animals, creatures that existed neither entirely in our world nor entirely in the OTHERWORLD. There were fairy HORSES that lived in the ocean (see WATER HORSE) and SEALS that were really people (see SILKIE). There were monstrous beings (see *AFANC*) as well as less terrifying but still unlikely beings (see KELPIE). Such beings were not necessarily under the command of the fairy folk themselves but were linked to the fairies by their Otherworldly natures.

fairy arrow See FAIRY DART.

fairy battle Folkloric motif. FAIRIES were generally considered to be immortal; thus battles to them were like sporting events to us, opportunities to engage in rough and sometimes risky play. The fairies of various PROVINCES of Ireland were believed to contest with each other in the way that hurling teams do today, traveling across the land to do night battle and then carrying their wounded home at dawn. Phlegm-like substances found on bushes in the early morning were believed to be the fairies' blood, shed in the endless battles.

fairy blast (fairy wind, elfin eddy) Folkloric motif. When TROOPING FAIRIES traveled together, the speed of their passage created a blast of wind discernible even in this world. Sometimes in the summer the traveling fairies could be seen, swirling up dust and straw on even the stillest day. But that dust devil hid the results of FAIRY KIDNAPPING, for as the troop passed, things disappeared from our world. If one threw a left shoe at the whirlwind, anything the fairies were stealing dropped from their hands. Men, women, children, animals, all were known to appear from within a fairy blast subjected to this treatment. Bonnets, knives, and earth from molehills could work as a substitute for the shoe, especially if the words "that's yours, this is mine" were spoken as the object was hurled into the whirlwind. But if the speaker attempted to trick the fairies out of something rightfully theirs, like one of their astonishing sets of bagpipes, the theft backfired when the human discovered the magical possession dissolved into dust or turned into woodland debris in his hands.

The fairy blast was strong enough to pick up adult humans and carry them long distances. Those who traveled at night were most subject to such kidnapping, as were those who wandered onto or who deliberately disturbed a FAIRY PATH. Tales are legion of people who found themselves far away from their starting point, dropped by the fairy blast in London or New York or an inaccessible region of ice. Occasionally these captives were returned to the place they left, but often they could not recognize the place because the wind had blown their wits away, or they returned so long after their disappearance that all was changed.

Source: McKay, John G. *More West Highland Tales.* Vol. 2. Scottish Anthropological and Folklore Society. Edinburgh: Oliver and Body, 1969, p. 18.

fairy boat Scottish folkloric motif. Off Scotland, a ghostly boat was sometimes seen by sailors whose boats were about to be struck by a storm. This warning permitted them, if they heeded it well, to haul into shore and survive the coming weather. Those who ignored the warning were likely to lose their lives at sea. This tradition is one of the many in which FAIRIES and the dead are hopelessly confused, for the fairy boat was often said to be crowded with familiar faces, the men of the area who had been lost at sea and were returning to warn their erstwhile friends of danger. In some regions of coastal Ireland, it was believed that no one ever really drowned; they were taken away to live with the undersea fairies. As bodies were often lost in the stormy sea, this comforting belief was rarely contradicted.

fairy bride Folkloric motif. Among humans prone to FAIRY KIDNAPPING, brides occupy one of the top categories. Many tales exist of women who, upon returning home in their bridal finery, fall into a swoon from which they cannot be awakened (see FAIRY SLEEP). Commonly, the groom had to locate the FAIRY MOUND into which the bride's soul had been stolen; there he found her dancing and had to steal her back. Even upon returning home, though, he found his bride still unconscious, in which case her clothing was searched for any tiny remnant (a PIN, a thread) of FAIRYLAND. Removing that swiftly brought her back to consciousness. Occasional stories exist of young men en route to their weddings being snared by FAIRY LOVERS, but brides were much more at risk.

Source: Kennedy, Patrick. *Legendary Fictions of the Irish Celts.* New York: Benjamin Blom, 1969, p. 111.

fairy circle Folkloric motif. When FAIRIES danced, they left their mark upon the dewy grass, which thereafter showed a perfect circle. These naturally occurring rings of green are in fact caused by biological agents such as fungus, but they were believed enchanted and even dangerous. Sleeping in a fairy circle was ill-advised, for the fairies might return and carry off the sleeping person (see FAIRY KIDNAPPING). CATTLE were guided away from the circles, which were believed (without reason) to be poisonous.

fairy colors Folkloric motif. Two colors were most often connected with the FAIRY folk: RED and GREEN. Their men wore red caps and green (though occasionally blue) breeches, while women donned green dresses. Because of their fondness for these colors, fairies were believed to take umbrage when humans wore them and could cause trouble for such miscreants. A century ago, many women in the Scottish Highlands refused to wear green on the grounds that it was unlucky; Dundee's defeat at Killiecrankie was explained by the rumor that he wore green on that fateful day. SOLITARY FAIRIES sometimes wore gray, as though to distinguish themselves from their TROOPING FAIRY kin.

Source: MacGregor, Alasdair Alpin. *The Peat-Fire Flame: Folk-Tales and Traditions of the Highlands & Islands.* Edinburgh: The Moray Press, 1937, p. 4.

fairy cow (fairy cattle, *crò sith*) Folkloric motif. FAIRIES were often openhanded to their human neighbors, and never more so than when they offered the use of their COWS. Fairy cows were almost invariably hornless RED cattle with white ears, or speckled red-and-tan. They gave prodigiously of milk and always had TWIN calves.

One story from Co. Donegal tells of a family with 10 children who were slowly starving in a lean winter. While the parents debated one night what they could do to scrabble together some food for their offspring, they heard the noise of lowing. Outside, in the dire storm, they found a red-speckled cow that they brought into the byre. The next day the cow gave birth to a female calf and began to give forth milk abundantly. Worrying over whose animal had wandered onto their land, the family asked around the region, but no cow was reported missing. The cow stayed with them for years, having a calf each year and filling the buckets with sweet milk. One day the man, exasperated at finding the cow munching in a field of new oats and forgetting to be grateful for his good fortune, raised his staff to her. Gathering all her little herd together, the cow disappeared and was never seen again.

Another form of fairy cattle was known under the name of CALAMITY MEAT. This was an animal that appeared to have died accidentally but that had actually been stolen by the fairies to swell their Otherworldly herds. In place of the cow in this world, the fairies left a piece of ALDER wood enchanted so that it appeared identical to the cow that had been "elf-smitten." Because of the belief that fairies kidnapped cattle, it was deemed important never to eat the flesh of an animal that died in an unusual fashion. Undersea fairies were believed to have their own cattle that grazed on the seaweed, appearing to us like SEALS or sea-lions.

Sources: Curtin, Jeremiah. *Hero-Tales of Ireland.* New York: Benjamin Blom, 1894, pp. 60, 121; MacGregor, Alasdair Alpin. *The Peat-Fire Flame: Folk-Tales and Traditions of the Highlands & Islands.* Edinburgh: The Moray Press, 1937, pp. 40 ff; McKay, John G. *More West Highland Tales.* Vol. 2. Scottish Anthropological and Folklore Society. Edinburgh: Oliver and Boyd, 1969, pp. 166 ff; O hEochaidh, Séan. *Fairy Legends of Donegal.* Trans. Máire MacNeill. Dublin: Comhairle Bhéaloideas Éireann, 1977, pp. 265, 329.

fairy crafts Folkloric motif. Generally FAIRIES lived simple, irresponsible lives devoted to dancing and feasting, but some fairies had jobs. The most familiar Irish fairy, the LEPRECHAUN, was shoemaker to the fairy world; a SOLITARY FAIRY, he industriously kept the dancing troops shod. Fairy women were often described as brilliant spinners and weavers; they were also quite critical of the skills of human women in those areas.

fairy dart (fairy arrow, saighead sithe) Folkloric motif. Miniscule arrows, perfectly shaped, were said to litter the ground around fairy haunts in Scotland and Ireland; it is likely the term originally described prehistoric flintheads. The fairy SMITH made these arrows specifically for use against humans, who could be greatly injured by the arrows despite their tiny size. A story from the Isle of Skye says that a couple reaping by moonlight found their tools falling from their bleeding hands, although they could find no reason for the wounds. They abandoned their work and, next day, found the tiny arrows the fairies had hurled at them when they got too close to the Good People's secret places. And a good thing they retreated, for Scottish tradition says that being struck by the dart was a form of FAIRY KIDNAPPING; the outer shell of the person remained (or appeared to die), but his or her true self lived in the confines of FAIRYLAND. Cows struck by the dart ate like other animals but gave no milk.

Said to have been made with hellish help, the dart was crafted by the fairy smith but sharpened and polished by the DEVIL. Both people and animals were targets of the tiny weapon thrown by the fairy folk, sometimes for spite, sometimes as retribution for treading on fairy property, and sometimes just to make mischief. People would typically not feel the darts, but their hands would soon swell with painful arthritis. The dart passed through the skin without puncturing it, so it was not always possible to accurately diagnose the fairy wound. Without treatment, however, that wound was invariably fatal.

There were several ways to cure the ill effects of a wound from a fairy dart. The most effective was to find the wounding dart and to take a drink of water while holding the dart below the water.

If the dart was too small to locate, the next recourse was the Mary Candle: a candle drawn three times around an animal's forelegs or a person's torso, then three times around the belly, then three times around the hind legs or thighs. Performed on a beast, this ritual required two people, who made the sign of the cross with every completed pass around the cow, then passed the candle along the cow's backbone and finished with the sign of the cross again, made between the horns. This ritual was only efficacious if the fairy dart had not pierced the animal's heart; if it had, death was inevitable.

Sources: Campbell, John Grigorson. *Witchcraft and Second Sight in the Highlands and Islands of Scotland.* Detroit: Singing Tree Press, 1970, p. 91; Dorson, Richard M., ed. *Peasant Customs and Savage Myths: Selections from the British Folklorists.* Vol II. Chicago: University of Chicago Press, 1968, p. 24; MacGregor, Alasdair Alpin. *The Peat-Fire Flame: Folk-Tales and Traditions of the Highlands & Islands.* Edinburgh: The Moray Press, 1937, p. 16; O hEochaidh, Séan. *Fairy Legends of Donegal.* Trans. Máire Mac Neill. Dublin: Comhairle Bhéaloideas Éireann, 1977, pp. 29, 79, 81; Wilde, Lady. *Ancient Legends, Mystic Charms and Superstitions of Ireland.* London: Chatto and Windus, 1902, p, 81–83, 200.

Fairy Flag Scottish folkloric motif. One of the most famous relics of FAIRYLAND to be seen in our world is the Fairy Flag of Dunvegan Castle, belonging to the MacLeod clan, on the Isle of Skye off Scotland. One fall night, it is told, a GREEN-clad woman was seen entering the nursery of the castle, where she found the infant heir sound asleep and his nurse napping. Such a caller would generally be suspected of planning a FAIRY KIDNAPPING, but the woman merely sat down and began to sing a beautiful air called "Taladh na Mna Sithe," or "Lullaby of the Fairy Woman." The nurse awakened but was immobilized by fright as she watched the fairy woman

carefully wrap the child in a silken garment. Then the woman disappeared, leaving the child safe and sound.

When the nurse carried the child down to the great banqueting hall to tell the strange tale to his parents, all eyes were captured by the mysterious fairy blanket. It became the special banner of the MacLeods, and it was said to protect all members of that clan when they went to war. (Every nurse to the MacLeods had to learn the lullaby of the fairy woman, too, as it was believed to weave a magical protective spell around the children.)

Other versions of the genesis of the Fairy Flag are that it came into the MacLeods' possession through a magical woman of the Holy Land, who claimed the unfurled flag would cast a GLAMOUR that made each soldier seem like an entire battalion. Finally, it is claimed that one of the chiefs of the MacLeods was wooed by a fairy woman who came to this world to be with him; she could not remain away from her home, however, and left the Fairy Flag behind when she abandoned him.

Source: MacGregor, Alasdair Alpin. *The Peat-Fire Flame: Folk-Tales and Traditions of the Highlands & Islands.* Edinburgh: The Moray Press, 1937, pp. 20 ff.

fairy food Folkloric motif. Fairy food was tastier than anything that one can find on earth, but FAIRIES preferred our grosser fare and snuck into our world to steal it. They especially desired our BUTTER, from which they stole the essence or *FOYSON*, for however tasty, fairy food offered little nourishment. Many charms to preserve butter are known, including putting mullein leaves or holy water in the churn. Fresh-baked bread was also a favorite of the fairies, who would steal it away if it were left unguarded.

By contrast, sometimes the fairies provided food from their own larders to help their human neighbors in time of need. Many stories of Ireland's Great Hunger of the 1840s and other hard times tell of food such as marvelous sweets being found in abandoned fields, saving a family from starvation. Generally, food discovered in such peculiar circumstances was thought to be cursed and should be avoided, but severe hunger seemed to make such foods available to humanity. As the fairies were reputed to be gifted bakers, their fairy cakes made of oatmeal and barley were especially tasty.

Many stories claim that however delightful to the senses fairy food appears, it is really only twigs and pebbles with a GLAMOUR or spell cast upon them. It was especially important never to eat when visiting FAIRYLAND, whether by choice or because one was the victim of FAIRY KIDNAPPING, for once a human devoured fairy food there, it was virtually impossible to return to earthly life.

fairy fort   See FAIRY MOUND.

fairy hill   See FAIRY MOUND.

fairy housekeeper (Toice bhrean bear tiqhe) Irish folkloric figure. At the bottom of the enchanted LOUGH GUR in Co. Limerick, a strange figure resides. Once every seven years the lake's water disappears, revealing the fairy housekeeper who walks over to a stone chair, sitting there for a few hours before disappearing with the reappearance of the lake.

fairy hunger   See HUNGRY GRASS.

fairy islands   Folkloric motif. Enchanted ISLANDS in the western ocean are a typical location for the OTHERWORLD or FAIRYLAND. Often these islands were said to drift around, not being tied down to any one place (or time) but appearing at intervals and in different sites. One such fairy island appeared every seven years to the southwest of Rathlin O'Birne island, off the coast of Co. Donegal. It was possible to settle such a land, to bring it into this world, by landing live embers on it.

fairy kidnapping   Folkloric motif. An important part of fairy lore is the idea that fairies regularly steal from humans. Of all the ways that FAIRIES could upset the human world, the most disturbing was the fairy kidnapping or snatching. This is to be distinguished from FAIRY THEFT, which does not involve the mysterious transportation of human beings; families could live more easily without their BUTTER than without their mother. Fairies would steal what is best in our world: the sweetest cream as well as the most brilliant musician. Thus many rituals and verbal formulae were designed to avert the attention of the fairy world. One of these was the bestowal of nicknames, under the belief that hearing the real name of a beloved person would alert the fairy kidnapper to a potential victim.

Anyone could be taken by the fairies, but certain categories of humans were most vulnerable. As fairy babies were both rare and, when born, exceedingly ugly, our own charming infants were greatly at risk. Sometimes they would be simply snatched away; at other times, a substitute would be placed in the cradle, either an enchanted rock or stick or, worse yet, an ugly fairy (see CHANGELING). For this reason, new mothers in the Isle of Man made certain that a pair of their husband's trousers was always in their bed, for the pants would scare the fairies away. Beautiful young people were also highly desired; brides on their wedding day might be snatched away before the marriage could be consummated (see FAIRY BRIDE), and handsome young men could wander away on the arm of a RED-haired girl, never to be seen again (see FAIRY LOVER). Finally, musicians and poets of genius were sometimes stolen away for their talents, forced to entertain the fairy throng at one of their endless balls, and then discarded when the fickle Good Folk had had their fill.

Generally, one discarded by the fairies pined for the beautiful land left behind and died not long after returning to mortal life. Some sturdier sorts were condemned in a different fashion, if they accidentally or purposely stole the magical salve that let them see the fairies with their mortal eyes (see FAIRY OINTMENT).

Sources: Henderson, George. *Survivals in Belief Among the Celts.* Glasgow: James MacLeose and Sons, 1911, p. 59; MacGreogor, Alasdair Alpin. *The Peat-Fire Flame: Folk-Tales and Traditions of the Highlands & Islands.* Edinburgh: The Moray Press, 1937, p. 5.

fairyland Folkloric or mythological site. The land of the OTHERWORLD beings known as FAIRIES was not entirely of our world but not entirely separate. Sometimes just called fairy, it existed just beyond reach, on a floating ISLAND out in the western ocean or beneath a grassy mound (see FAIRY MOUND), on a bleak wet BOG or floating in the air. There were portals or gates between the worlds through which the fairy folk came forth and through which humans could pass to visit them. However, for most people, the passage was one way, for it was rare for humans to return from fairyland—although they might return so far distant in time or place (see FAIRY TIME) that they found nothing familiar to great them.

Fairyland was beautiful, in a static and unchanging sort of way. Trees there bore blossoms and fruit simultaneously, the sun always shone, and the weather was always mild and fine. There was no death in fairyland, nor disease, nor pain of any kind. Food there tasted better than any food on earth, and the wine brought a pleasant sensation without ever causing drunkenness. The fairies spent their time in merrymaking, dancing, and flirting and making love without ceasing.

Paradoxically, despite (or perhaps because of) the perfection of their world, fairies lusted for what our world holds. They made frequent raids on this side of the veil, stealing away people and BUTTER and shiny objects. Some stories claim that they always returned what they borrowed, but fairy borrowing, FAIRY KIDNAPPING, and FAIRY THEFT are generally indistinguishable to the human eye. There are many NAMES FOR FAIRYLAND, most of which stress its beauty and distance from the surface world of humanity.

fairy lights Folkloric motif. When TROOPING FAIRIES traveled from one of their OTHERWORLD dance halls to the next, they went in great processions, carrying torches above their heads. As the fairy race is smaller than the human race, people saw such parades as twinkling lights, streaming along invisible but always-straight pathways.

fairy lover (fairy mistress, lianan sidhe, *la belle dame sans merci*) Irish, Scottish, and Breton folkloric figure. Many stories of FAIRYLAND centered on this ravishingly beautiful woman—for it was almost always a woman—who stole away the most brilliant poet or the most handsome man from this world and made him her lover. Not that it required much work on the fairy woman's part, for these gorgeous beings made the most beautiful mortal woman seem coarse and unattractive. The fairy mistress called to her chosen mate through dreams that haunted him until he sought her out, living on her charmed ISLAND in the western sea or beneath some ancient mound. Once he tasted her charms, he rarely attempted to leave her, since she was not only magnificent to look upon but was utterly wanton. Because time passed differently in fairyland than in our world, a single night with the fairy mistress crept by pleasantly while centuries slipped away on this side of the veil. When, as occasionally happened, the human lover grew homesick, he returned to find his home dissolved in the mists of time and usually lost his fairy lover to boot. Such was the case with the great BARD, OISÍN, who was stolen away from this world by the beautiful NIAMH of the Golden Hair. Despite his joy with Niamh; he became homesick and begged to be allowed a brief visit home; she warned him to remain upon his magical horse while he looked upon his beloved Ireland, but when he leaned down to touch the soil, he fell from astride his mount and instantly dissolved into dust.

Fairies were notoriously fickle, so sometimes a fairy woman discarded her human husband and send him unceremoniously back into this world.

Rarely could such a man recover to lead a normal life. More commonly, he pined away and died soon after his return, longing for the beauties he saw in fairyland. Occasionally, as with THOMAS THE RHYMER, he survived and finally returned to his fairy lover, to live happily in the Otherworld thereafter.

Some described the fairy lover as the sister of the BANSHEE, the spirit of life and beauty as distinguished from the foreteller of doom. But both took the human lover from this life, although in different ways. Several goddess figures appear in both guises, as does ÁINE of the magical lake LOUGH GUR, who became the bride of a human earl and bore his son before abandoning him; she is said to serve as banshee or death-warner for local families in Co. Limerick.

Occasionally fairy kings stole human maidens away, often on their wedding day (see FAIRY BRIDE); in addition, there are tales in Scotland and Ireland of male fairies who seduced young women (see GANCONER). But it is much more common to find the fairy lover in female form. Her image has inspired many artists, including the English poet John Keats, who immortalized her as "La Belle Dame Sans Merci," the beautiful woman who has no mercy.

Sources: Briggs, Katherine. *The Fairies in Tradition and Literature.* London: Routledge & Kegan Paul, 1967, pp. 123 ff; Wilde, Lady. *Ancient Legends, Mystic Charms and Superstitions of Ireland.* London: Chatto and Windus, 1902, p. 134.

fairy midwife Folkloric motif. Like the bride, the baby, and and the musician, the midwife was a category of human almost irresistible to fairies. They were apparently unskilled in this medicinal art themselves, so when a difficult birth was occurring in FAIRYLAND, they had to send for help from their human neighbors. Rarely did they do as humans did, however, hiring a midwife or asking a friend to serve in that capacity. They simply took what they needed, kidnapping the best midwife they could find. Sometimes they left an enchanted stick or elderly fairy in her place, but often she just vanished. Once the child had been safely born, the midwife was returned to home and family, often with a fine reward for her help—unless she had unwittingly rubbed her eye with salve (see FAIRY OINTMENT), in which case she was blinded in punishment.

One of the most famous fairy midwives was the Irishwoman Biddy Mannion of the island of Inishshark, who was stolen away by no less than the king and queen of the fairies to care for their sickly child. Biddy served well, leaving a thriving fairy infant behind when she returned home, where she discovered that a GLAMOUR or spell had been cast upon a fairy substitute so that not even her own family had realized her absence.

Sources: Briggs, Katherine M., and Ruth L. Tongue. *Folktales of Britain.* London: Routledge & Kegan Paul, 1965, p. 38; Kennedy, Patrick. *Legendary Fictions of the Irish Celts.* New York: Benjamin Blom, 1969, p. 106; Parry-Jones, D. *Welsh Legends and Fairy Lore.* London: B. T. Batsford, Ltd., 1953, p. 53.

fairy mist Irish folkloric motif. Like the DRUID'S FOG that hid people from sight, the fairy mist appeared suddenly and without warning. It was especially dangerous at night or on bogs and similar wild places. Some legends claim that being surrounded by the fairy mist was an OMEN of impending death.

fairy mound (fairy fort, fairy hill) Folkloric site. Throughout the Celtic lands we find traces of a race even more ancient than the Celts—the unknown people of the MEGALITHIC CIVILIZATION who lived approximately 5000 B.C.E. and built thousands of structures of stone. Some, like STONEHENGE and BRÚ NA BÓINNE, are internationally renowned, but such monumental structures are less common than the PASSAGE GRAVE, the DOLMEN, and the other vestiges of a people who spoke an unknown language, worshiped unknown gods, and disappeared for an unknown reason. Their influence continued, however, for the incoming Celts recognized the sanctity of their monuments and reinforced it with tales of fairies who lived within the BARROWS and under the dolmen arches.

Small natural hills and drumlins might also, although rarely, be labeled as fairy mounds. More often ancient barrows were said to cover diminutive cities where the fairies danced the endless days away. Walking past such mounds at night or on the turning points of the year (BELTANE on May 1 and SAMHAIN on November 1) was considered very risky, for the otherwise invisible door might open and the passerby might be lured into an at-first pleasurable, but endless and inescapable dance. Such fairy mounds are called in Irish SÍDHE; the fairies who lived within them thus became the DAOINE SÍDHE, the people of the fairy mounds. Early texts say that they were originally the TUATHA DÉ DANANN, the ancient magical race condemned to live beneath the earth when the MILESIANS invaded Ireland.

Sources: Evans-Wentz, W. Y. *The Fairy-Faith in Celtic Countries.* Gerrards Cross: Colin Smythe Humanities Press, 1911, pp. 99 ff; MacCulloch, J. A. *The Religion of the Ancient Celts.* London: Constable, 1911, p. 66; Ross, Anne. *Pagan Celtic Britain: Studies in Iconography and Tradition.* London: Routledge & Kegan Paul, 1967, p. 41.

fairy music Folkloric motif. Irish FAIRY folk, like Irish human folk, were renowned for their love of music. They could not get enough of a good tune and were known to kidnap a fine musician (pipers and harpers were especially at risk), keeping them overnight to play at their fairy dances, then returning them to earth. Usually the payment for a job well done was a haunting melody full of what the great harper Turlough O'Carolan called *PLANXTY*, a hypnotizing irregularity of rhythm or tone that distinguishes fairy music from music composed by mortals. O'Carolan spoke from experience, for

he was a harper of ordinary ability until he slept one night on a FAIRY RATH or within a FAIRY RING. When he awoke, he was filled with wild music that he played until he died.

Fairy music was sometimes heard at night; the period between midnight and dawn was the most common time for such events. Usually the music came from FAIRY MOUNDS, but sometimes the source was invisible, surrounding the night traveler, coming from all directions at once, with the sound of laughter echoing within it. A dark spot on a BOG might open suddenly into FAIRYLAND, or the side of a big boulder, or a bit of wild field, or the weedy patch beneath a FAIRY TREE. Peering into the opening, one saw a tiny world filled with celebrating fairies. Rare was the person who managed to escape without being overwhelmed with desire to join the dance, from which few humans ever returned.

Fairy music was never somber. Their tunes made the feet tap and the body sway in dance. Many tales are told of how fairy music so possessed a human that he or she was unable to stop dancing. If one were in FAIRYLAND, that presented no problem, for the years slipped away during these endless dances while everyone remained strong and young. Here on earth, someone cursed to dance endlessly died from the exertion.

There is some contention as to what the favorite musical instrument of the fairies was, some saying the bagpipe, some saying the HARP. Some legends speak of fairyland as a kind of music school where talented pipers and harpers learned their trade; others describe it as a kind of ancient musical award, for only the very best musicians disappeared without a trace and were understood to have been taken AWAY.

Those who built their homes on fairy-haunted places were often disturbed in their sleep by the music emanating from them (in other legends, their possessions were scattered by the FAIRY BLAST). In Scottish folklore we hear of a man who built his house on an ancient HILLFORT and never got a wink of sleep until he moved—but he learned several tunes by heart before being forced to relocate.

Sources: Bord, Janet, and Colin Bord. *The Secret Country: An Interpretation of the folklore of ancient sites in the British Isles.* New York: Walker and Co. 1976, p. 169; Grinsell, Leslie V. *Folklore of Prehistoric Sites in Britain.* London: David & Charles, 1976, pp. 31, 50; Killip, Margaret. *The Folklore of the Isle of Man.* London: B. T. Batsford, Ltd., 1975, pp. 37, 38; MacGregor, Alasdair Alpin. *The Peat-Fire Flame: Folk-Tales and Traditions of the Highlands & Islands.* Edinburgh: The Moray Press, 1937, pp. 13, 29 ff; O hEochaidh, Séan. *Fairy Legends of Donegal.* Trans. Máire Mac Neill. Dublin: Comhairle Bhéaloideas Éireann, 1977, p. 119; Wilde, Lady. *Ancient Legends, Mystic Charms and Superstitions of Ireland.* London: Chatto and Windus, 1902, pp. 29 ff.

fairy ointment   Folkloric motif. A kind of salve made in FAIRYLAND, possibly from the oil of four-leafed clovers or SHAMROCKS, fairy ointment permitted the viewer to see things as they really are. The fairy ointment appears often in stories of midwives who were taken AWAY to attend to the birthing mothers (see FAIRY MIDWIFE); instructed to apply the ointment on the eyes of the newborn, the midwife unwittingly rubbed her own eye and deposited some of the ointment there, suddenly seeing a ruined shack where a palace had appeared the moment before, and a wizened old thing where a charming babe had been.

Such fairy ointment permanently bestowed a change in vision, permitting the viewer to see through any fairy GLAMOUR or spell set up to hide portals to fairyland. The fairies themselves were stripped of their invisibility and could be seen stealing about the land, taking the essence from food, kidnapping brides, and working other mischief. This power infuriated the fairies, who punished theft of the fairy ointment harshly; even if the ointment was taken unwittingly, the fairies blinded the thief.

Source: Curtin, Jeremiah. *Hero-Tales of Ireland.* New York: Benjamin Blom, 1894, p. 156.

fairy path   Folkloric motif. In rural Ireland it was considered very important not to build a house so that it crossed the paths that FAIRIES took in moving from one region to another. Unlike humans, fairies followed straight paths wherever they went, even when that meant traveling over lakes or bogland or even the sea. Because their unbending paths went straight through obstacles, havoc was likely to be created by the continual passage of fairies through a house built in their way; anything built in the fairies' path will be either destroyed or become uninhabitable because of trouble within the place. Frequently the fairies punished unwary builders by tossing things around inside an offending house with the FAIRY BLAST of wind, or by carrying off the culprit to another space or time. Because fairies were believed to live in the western regions, BUILDING TO THE WEST was discouraged where there was evidence of fairy haunting.

Source: Danaher, Kevin. *Folktales from the Irish Countryside.* Cork: Mercier Press, 1967, pp. 251–252.

fairy queen   Folkloric figure. FAIRYLAND was imagined as a monarchy, ruled by a beautiful queen. Some fairy kings are mentioned in literature and legend, but by far the most frequent royalty of the OTHERWORLD is a goddess figure like ÁINE, CLÍDNA, or FAND. It was upon this tradition that two important authors drew: Edmund Spenser, who lived in Ireland while writing his allegorical poem *The Faerie Queene*, and William Shakespeare in his creation of TITANIA, mate to OBERON in *A Midsummer Night's Dream*.

fairy rath   Folkloric site. The Celts erected walls of earth, called raths or HILLFORTS, to protect their hilltop palaces, and these circular walls can be seen across the ancient Celtic lands even today. One reason so many raths are still extant—never having been leveled by farmers or built upon by householders—is the insistence of folklore that such places were openings to

FAIRYLAND and were therefore off-limits to development. Fear of the punishment that came of meddling with anything belonging to the fairies also extended to FAIRY TREES and FAIRY MOUNDS. Many of Ireland's most significant ancient monuments have remained to this day because of these beliefs, sometimes derided as superstitious but serving an admirable purpose in preserving the past.

Source: Evans-Wentz, W. Y. *The Fairy-Faith in Celtic Countries*. Gerrards Cross: Colin Smythe Humanities Press, 1911, pp. 32–37.

fairy ring   Folkloric motif. Sometimes one sees, on a grassy field, a circle of a darker green. Such a pattern has long been believed to mark the place where FAIRIES frolicked in their circle dances around their beautiful queen. These fairy rings were believed enchanted even when the fairies were not using them as dance floors; livestock were kept from grazing on them, and they were protected from the plow as well. Tales of plagues that struck cattle after a farmer unthinkingly or deliberately allowed his herds to graze on a fairy ring are legion. Other stories tell of people who unwittingly or arrogantly stepped into a fairy ring and found themselves dancing frenetically without the ability to stop; some even danced themselves to death. Someone outside the circle could save the unfortunate dancer only by grabbing some clothing that reached outside the circle, for anyone reaching within it would be struck by the same wild need to dance.

fairy sleep   Folkloric motif. Someone who was the victim of FAIRY KIDNAPPING might not disappear entirely—although that often happened—but might lapse into a coma-like sleep from which he or she could not be awakened. A woman of the Burren in west Co. Clare was once found in such a state, but when her rescuer overheard the fairies speaking among themselves about still possessing the tablecloth she had been wrapped in when kidnapped, he reclaimed the cloth and restored the woman to consciousness. Often, the clothing of a person who visited FAIRYLAND was pierced by a tiny PIN; until it was removed, the person slept without waking.

fairy-stricken cattle   See CALAMITY MEAT.

fairy stroke   Folkloric motif. We still speak of someone who loses control over part or all of his body as having suffered a stroke. The full or partial paralysis that we now know to be caused by an interruption of blood to the brain or a clot therein was believed in the past to be a punishment for offending the FAIRIES. They could punish anyone who angered them—by cutting down a FAIRY TREE, for example, or allowing cattle to graze in a FAIRY RING, or stealing anything that belonged to them—simply by touching the offender. The stroke of a fairy hand, powerful enough to paralyze even the strongest man, was greatly feared. Many sites of legendary importance, such as FAIRY MOUNDS, were protected for generations by this belief.

fairy theft   Folkloric motif. For all their sensitivity to humans stealing from them—a misdemeanor that they punished with all their might—the FAIRIES thought nothing of stealing from humans. Food was their favorite target, for their own FAIRY FOOD was not as nourishing as ours. They did not actually carry the food away; they drained its essence (called *FOYSON* or *toradh*), leaving it stale and dry and useless. They stole a lot of BUTTER, and they also stole MILK by making the drinker spill it, then lapping up its essence. Strong drink, too, was often taken AWAY. Anything, in fact, could draw their attention and be spirited away from our world, including human beings (see FAIRY KIDNAPPING).

fairy time   Folkloric motif. Time passed differently in FAIRYLAND than on earth. It sped by here, while there it was endless. An evening passed at a fairy dance might be the equivalent of centuries of human time. Many stories tell of people lured or kidnapped into fairyland who stayed what seemed to be a short time and who, returning, found everything changed. The most famous of these stories is the tale of the poet OISÍN, a member of the heroic band called the FIANNA and lover of the beautiful NIAMH of the Golden Hair. His time with her was endlessly loving and beautiful, but he finally grew homesick for earth. Despite Niamh's discomfort with the idea, he traveled back to visit his old friends, but found everything changed. Pagan Ireland was gone; church steeples rose everywhere. Confused, he forgot Niamh's warning not to touch the soil of earth. Leaning off his horse, he fell from the saddle. Immediately all the years he had lived came upon him, and he withered, died, and turned to dust all in an instant.

Source: Briggs, Katherine M. *An Encyclopedia of Fairies: Hobgoblins, Brownies, Bogies, and Other Supernatural Creatures.* New York: Pantheon Books, 1976, pp. 398 ff.

fairy tree   Folkloric motif. The TREE was one of the most important religious symbols to the Celts; virtually all species of trees were deemed magical in some ways. None was more tightly linked to the FAIRY world than the THORN or hawthorn, whose spiky thorns, white blossoms, and distinctive RED haws or berries were said to have been favored by the Good People. All individual hawthorns shared in the fairies' general beneficence toward their species, but certain thorns marked fairy lands: those that grew from the top of ancient mounds or raths (see FAIRY MOUNDS); those that grew alone in a stony field; those that grew in a group of THREE; and those that grew together with an OAK and an ASH to make the most magical of all groves.

Stories of the misfortune that befell those who dared cut down a fairy tree are legion, including one from the 20th century regarding a planned hospital in Kiltimagh, Co. Mayo. The only available field had two fairy trees in it, but no one in the area would agree to cut either down. When a man was found willing to risk the deed, no one was surprised when he suffered a stroke (see FAIRY STROKE) the next day. The hospital, however, went up without difficulty. The same is not true of an American-owned factory built in Ulster some 20 years ago; perhaps the most popular current tale about fairy thorns is that of the ruin of the DeLorean car company, whose factory was built over the sacrificed roots of a fairy tree.

Belief in fairy trees has not entirely died out in Ireland. In 1999 a famous fairy thorn tree in Co. Clare gained worldwide attention when a local schoolmaster, Eddie Lenihan, waged a campaign to have a road redirected that would otherwise have been built over the grave of the tree. The fairy thorn of Newmarket-on-Fergus still stands on the main road from Shannon Airport, testimony to the ongoing strength of reverence for the fairy folk in Ireland.

Source: Lenihan, Edmund. "The Fairies Vs. The Money Economy." In Patricia Monaghan, ed. *Irish Spirit: Pagan, Celtic, Christian,* Global. Dublin: Wolfhound Press, 2001, pp. 122 ff.

Falias   Irish mythological site. The magical race called the TUATHA DÉ DANANN or tribe of the goddess DANU came from four sites, of which Falias was one. Ireland's INAUGURATION STONE, the LIA FÁIL, came from Falias, whose ruler was named MORFESSA.

Fand (Fann)   Irish folkloric or mythological character. The most famous of Ireland's FAIRY queens was Fand, "tear," beautiful wife of the sea god MANANNÁN MAC LIR who, like other FAIRY LOVERS, stole away the heart of a mortal. And it was no mere man she captivated but the greatest of Irish heroes, CÚCHULAINN. She came to him in a vision in which she whipped him senseless; he fell into a lovesick stupor in which he lingered for a year. When the year had passed and the great feast of SAMHAIN came, at which time passage to the OTHERWORLD is possible for mortals, he went to Fand, leaving behind his loyal wife EMER, the paragon of Irish womanhood. Although Emer had endured his other affairs, she could not bear to lose him to FAIRYLAND, so she followed him. When she saw how deeply Fand loved him, and he her, Emer offered to step aside. Fand, not to be outdone, offered the same and returned to her own husband, who wrapped her in his magical cloak to make her forget the human hero. On earth, Cúchulainn and Emer drank a potion of forgetfulness and returned to their earlier state.

Far Darrig (Fear Darrig; pl., Fir Darrig) Irish folkloric figure. RED is the color of FAIRYLAND, and thus the Far Darrig ("red man") is one of the mysterious beings who inhabited that world. Dressing characteristically in red, he was a mischievous and rather ugly, short, and annoying Irish FAIRY who believed his practical jokes were entertaining, when in fact they were appalling and cruel. It was considered unlucky at any time to refuse a request from the Far Darrig, who could be quite imaginative in his punishments. The Far Darrig sat by the fire, smoking a pipe and thinking; he would eat a repast left by a friendly family but did not like to be spied upon. His presence in a house brought good fortune.

Far Gorta (Fear Gorta; pl., Fir Gorta) Irish folkloric figure. The "hungry man" of Irish legend may be the GHOST of someone who died of famine or a wraith from the OTHERWORLD; he stood by the roadside begging and rewarded those who gave him alms with good fortune.

See HUNGRY GRASS.

Far Liath   See GRAY MAN.

fasting (in Irish, *troscad;* in Welsh, *ymprydio*) Celtic ritual. To "fast against one's enemy" was a traditional form of protest in ancient Ireland and Wales. When a wrong had been done, the victim would sit upon the doorstep of the oppressor, taking no food and telling passersby of the crime committed. Those who were of elevated rank (kings and BARDS, for instance) could avoid paying the *ÉRIC* or honor price for someone they had injured; in such cases fasting was the injured person's only form of reprisal. An effective form of protest that often resulted in the situation being rectified, the hunger strike is described in several ancient mythological texts. The tradition never entirely died out, being revived at intervals as a form of nonviolent protest.

Source: Kelly, Fergus. *A Guide to Early Irish Law.* Vol. III. Dublin: School of Celtic Studies, Dublin Institute for Advanced Studies. Early Irish Law Series, 1988, pp. 182 ff.

Faughart   Irish mythological site. The small town of Faughart in Co. Louth is renowned as the birthplace of St. BRIGIT, a Christianized version of the Celtic goddess of the same name. A holy WELL there is reputed to have special healing powers over eye diseases.

fawn   See DEER.

Fea   Irish goddess. The sister of BADB, Fea was an Irish war goddess of whom little is known.

feast *(féis)*   Celtic ritual. The great feasts of the ancient Celtic world were often literally so, with much food and drink being shared among the participants. But the word has a deeper meaning than simply a party, for the feasts were held on seasonally significant dates: SAMHAIN (November 1), the beginning of winter; IMBOLC (February 1), spring's awakening; BELTANE (May 1), the start of summer; and LUGHNASA (August 1), the harvest feast. Little is actually known about how the Celts celebrated these festivals, although analysis of folklore and tradition offers some suggestions about ancient beliefs.

Fedelm (Fidelma, Feidhelm, Feithline) Irish heroine or goddess. Several heroic Irish women bear this name, including:

- **Fedelm, seer of CRUACHAN**, a poet and DRUID who met queen MEDB as she was about to launch the CATTLE RAID that forms the basis of the great Irish epic, the TÁIN BÓ CUAILNGE. Fedelm cut a dashing figure, armed and mounted in a chariot, her golden hair falling past her waist and her eyes bright with three irises each. Asked by Medb if she had the *IMBAS FOROSNAI*, the prophetic light of foresight, Fedelm said that indeed she did. But when Medb, hoping for victory, asked what the future of her enterprise would be, Fedelm predicted, "I see crimson, I see red." Her words proved true, for the raid had a bloody conclusion, and many of Medb's best warriors were killed.
- **Fedelm, princess of CONNACHT**, who with her sister EITHNE was met one morning while bathing in the sacred SPRING of OGALLA by white-clad men they mistook for DRUIDS; the men were, in fact, ST. PATRICK and his followers. Fedelm and Eithne asked a series of questions of Patrick that tell much about the pantheism of ancient Celtic religion, including asking if their god resided in NATURE or not. The story ends with the girls accepting baptism from Patrick and dying instantly, in order to ascend to heaven in perfect purity. Given that Eithne and Fedelm are powerful goddess names of the region, it is difficult not to see this legend as propaganda.
- **Fedelm the Nine-Times Beautiful** (Fedelm Noíchrotach, Fedelm Noíchride or Fresh-Heart), a WARRIOR WOMAN of great beauty (as her name emphasizes) who chose the heroic CONALL Cernach over her husband, CAIRBRE Nia Fer, and may have accepted the even greater hero CÚCHULAINN as her lover as well.
- **Fedelm of Munster,** FAIRY caretaker of the future king of Cashel, CORC MAC LUIGTHIC, who was marked by fire during a ritual celebrated by Fedelm and her sisters.

The name Fedelm may have been a generic term for a woman prophet, for a related name (Gaulish *Uidula*) can be seen in an early Celtic inscription, found in a woman's grave, that describes a college of sorceresses or seers. The text is difficult to interpret but appears to refer to a magical sisterhood.

féis See FEAST.

féith na filíochta Irish folkloric motif. The "vein of poetry" was believed to be located in the rear scalp of BARDS who, when they began composing, felt blood surge through the vein in exactly the meter necessary for the poem.

Fenian Cycle Cycle of Irish myths. Enduringly popular, the cycle of tales about the hero FIONN MAC CUMHAILL and his merry band of heroes, the FIANNA, include some of the most famous characters of Irish myth: DEIRDRE of the Sorrows, the fated lovers DIARMAIT and GRÁINNE, OISÍN the poet, and the heroic Fionn himself. The divinities of Celtic times are cloaked in human form in these quasi-historical tales centered on the southern lands of Ireland, LEINSTER and MUNSTER, as another great heroic cycle centers on the PROVINCE that provides its name, ULSTER. The cycle exists in written form, both in ancient and more modern texts, as well as in the form of innumerable oral tales that exaggerate the warrior antics of the Fianna.

fenodyree See *GLASTIG*.

feolagan Scottish folkloric figure. A dangerous and elusive FAIRY that was said to plague sheepherders, especially on the islands of the Hebrides—and most especially those pastured around Kebock Head on the Isle of Lewis. Larger than the usual fairy, the *feolagan* paralyzed sheep by walking across their backs. Immobilized, unable to either eat or drink, the animals soon died. There was only one way to break the spell of the *feolagan*, which was to capture him and force him to walk across the sheep's back again, in the opposite direction. It was important that the *feolagan* be the very one that originally bewitched the sheep, or the attempted cure only brought more paralysis to the animal. When a great number of sheep were affected, one could imprison the guilty *feolagan* in a jar of salt, grains of which could then be used to cure the sheep.

Source: MacGregor, Alasdair Alpin. *The Peat-Fire Flame: Folk-Tales and Traditions of the Highlands & Islands.* Edinburgh: The Moray Press, 1937, p. 131.

Ferchertne (Fercetrniu) Irish hero. This BARD served the heroic king CÚ ROÍ, who abducted the woman BLÁTHNAT from the OTHERWORLD; she conspired with his enemies to cause his death, whereupon the loyal Ferchertne leapt from a cliff in MUNSTER, pulling Bláthnat over the side with him and causing both their deaths.

Ferdiad (Ferdia, Fear Diadh) Irish hero. One of the most famous single combats in Irish epic literature is that between Ferdiad and his beloved foster brother, the hero CÚCHULAINN, with whom he trained on the Isle of Skye with the warrior woman SCÁTHACH. When the DEBILITY OF THE ULSTERMEN—the result of a curse that the goddess MACHA laid on the warriors of that province after its boastful and competitive men had caused her death—struck, just as the massed armies of queen MEDB were marching toward the border between ULSTER and her province of CONNACHT, Cúchulainn was left to single-handedly hold the line until the crisis passed; because he was not Ulster-born, Cúchulainn was not subject to the curse. One after another he challenged and beat the heroes of the Connacht army. Perhaps the last best chance of Medb in her campaign was Ferdiad, whose tough skin (for which he was sometimes called Conganchness, "horn-skinned") might have offered protection against

Cúchulainn's weapons. But Ferdiad refused to fight his foster brother, for such a fight would have to be to the death.

Cúchulainn stood at the ford that ultimately bore Ferdiad's name (now Ardee, Co. Louth), gaining glory and wreaking havoc, killing one warrior after another in single combat. Finally Medb promised her fair daughter FINNABAIR to Ferdiad if he would fight, and he reluctantly agreed. For three days the well-matched pair fought, neither gaining the upper hand. But at last, Cúchulainn used his magical spear, GÁE BULGA, to kill his foster brother, although to win in such circumstances caused him great sorrow.

There is some evidence that the figure of Ferdiad derives from an earlier, possibly divine, original, perhaps an ancestral god of the people around the river ford where Ferdiad was said to have been killed. Such minor ancestor figures were frequently swept into larger narratives, being both preserved and altered by such action.

Fergus (Feargus) Irish hero. There is no more virile a name than this in Irish tradition, for it means "male potency" or "manhood" (sometimes translated simply as "semen"). Dozens of figures bear the name, including 10 members of the heroic band of warriors, the FIANNA; because there are so many it has been suggested that Fergus was not an individual name but was derived from a title of kingship. Most of the characters are minor; most are related to the northern province of ULSTER; all may descend from the same original. The most important mythological figures with this name are:

- **Fergus Fínbél,** the Fianna's poet, who although not as skilled nor as important as the beloved OISÍN, was an advisor to FIONN MAC CUMHAILL, who in some sources is Fergus's father.
- **Fergus Foga,** an early king of Ulster who invented the spear.
- **Fergus Lethderg,** one of three sons of the mythological settler NEMED and ancestral father to the British people.

- **Fergus Mòr** (Fergus mac Eirc), an ancestral figure of Scotland who asked to be crowned in his own kingdom while seated on the famous INAUGURATION STONE from the hill of TARA, the LIA FÁIL. Ireland's great stone was sent across the water for the occasion, but then Fergus Mòr refused to send it back.

- **Fergus mac Léti** (mac Leide, mac Leda), an Ulster king whose fantastic adventures are thought to have been the inspiration for Jonathan Swift's satirical masterpiece, *Gulliver's Travels.* Once when he was out sailing, Fergus was set upon by small water sprites who intended to steal his possessions and drown him. He turned the tables and snatched them up, holding them until they agreed to grant his three wishes. Fergus made only one wish in three parts: He wanted to be able to swim underwater in ponds, lakes, and the ocean. The fairies agreed, but restricted his powers by saying he could not submerge himself in Lough Rudraige in Ulster—where, of course, he was soon tempted to swim. There he encountered a water monster called a muirdris, which frightened him so much that his head turned around to face his back. He survived, but his DRUIDS faced the difficult question of whether this change made him a BLEMISHED KING and therefore unfit to reign. Through some loophole of interpretation, they determined that having one's head on backward was not a blemish, but to keep Fergus from knowing what had happened, they covered all the mirrors in EMAIN MACHA, the great royal residence of Ulster. And so Fergus lived happily enough for seven years, until a woman he had mistreated revealed the truth. Fergus returned to Loch Rudraige and killed the muirdris, but fell dead of exhaustion afterward, his head still facing backward.

- **Fergus mac Róich** (mac Roech, mac Roth, MacRoy), the greatest of heroes by this renowned name. He was king of Ulster—the province most associated with the regal name of Fergus—when he married NESSA, the WARRIOR WOMAN whose son bore her name: CON-COBAR MAC NESSA. She agreed to wed Fergus on the terms that her son ascend to the throne for a year, so that thereafter his progeny would be royal. Fergus willingly agreed, but when the year was over he discovered that Nessa had plotted with his nobles to keep him from returning. Fergus went south from Ulster and gathered allies at TARA, but Concobar resisted the army and maintained control of Fergus's former kingdom.

Fergus made peace with his usurper, but Concobar's continual treachery finally turned him into an enemy. When the fated beauty DEIRDRE was born and a prophecy revealed that desire for her would destroy the land, Concobar refused his druids' advice that the infant be killed to spare the land bloodshed. Instead he sent her away to be raised to womanhood, with the intention of having her beauty for himself. She found her own lover, however, and escaped with him to Scotland. From there Deirdre, her lover NOÍSIU, and his brothers, the SONS OF UIS-NEACH, were lured back with a promise of safety, which Fergus guaranteed with his honor. But no sooner had Fergus departed the court than Concobar had Noísiu killed and took Deirdre for himself—although she outwitted him by choosing death over life without her love. Fergus, infuriated that his honor had been besmirched by Concobar's devious plan, raided the royal court at EMAIN MACHA and burned it to the ground. (Archaeological excavations have, indeed, found evidence of a huge conflagration at Emain Macha in the dim prehistorical past.)

Fergus took his warriors and headed west, to the court of queen MEDB at CRUACHAN, the western equivalent of Emain Macha. There, according to many texts, he became her lover. They were well matched, for both were sexually voracious. His manhood was so impressive that the seven-foot-tall stone pillar on Tara called the LIA FÁIL is also called Bod Fhearghais, "Fergus's phallus." His surname may imply his father was a stallion, appropriate to such a well-endowed hero.

As Medb's lover, he may have fathered a child called Ciar, who gave his name to Co. Kerry in the southwest of Ireland. Fergus served Medb well in the CATTLE RAID related in the Irish epic *TÁIN BÓ CUAILNGE*, dispatching hundreds of his former countrymen with his enormous sword CALADBOLG. He would even have killed his enemy Concobar had not the king's son successfully opposed him. The great epic telling of these deeds might well have been lost, for Ireland's poets fell on hard times with the loss of SOVEREIGNTY of the Celtic kings. But several BARDs went to Fergus's grave and, using an ancient formula for invoking the dead, brought back his ghost. Fergus recited the entire ancient tale, retrieving it for new ages to enjoy.

Fergus got into that grave because of his affair with Medb. Although Medb praised her husband, AILILL mac Máta, for his lack of jealousy, even the patient Ailill could not help but make a bitter comment when he saw his wife frolicking nude with Fergus in a lake (either one near Carrickfergus in Co. Antrim or Lough Carrowmore in Co. Mayo). Ailill's faithful friend, the warrior-poet LUGAIDH, killed Fergus, pretending he had mistaken him for a STAG. This confusion may indicate that Fergus was originally a god, perhaps a horned god like the continental CERNUNNOS, which his love affair or marriage with the woodland goddess FLIDAIS also suggests.

Sources: Cross, Tom Peete, and Clark Harris Slover, eds. *Ancient Irish Tales*. New York: Henry Holt and Co., 1936, p. 471; Dillon, Myles, ed. *Irish Sagas*. Cork: The Mercier Press, 1968, pp. 40 ff; MacCulloch, J. A. *The Religion of the Ancient Celts*. London: Constable, 1911, p. 336.

Fer Í (Fer Fi)   Irish hero. Possibly originally a god, this magical harper of MUNSTER played so beautifully that no one who heard him could resist responding; if he played a sad song, all wept; a happy song, and all would laugh with joy; a lullaby, and everyone would fall sound asleep.

He unwittingly caused the enmity between the foster brothers LUGAIDH mac Conn and EÓGAN when they overheard him practicing outdoors and fell to disputing at whose court he should play. That argument led to a bitter feud that ended with Eógan's death. Fer Í, in the meantime, became the father of two important fairy queens of Munster, ÁINE and her TWIN sister GRAIN, suggesting that he was a FAIRY king or diminished god himself.

He was described, in the region around the magically important LOUGH GUR in Co. Limerick, as a RED-haired DWARF and brother of Áine. He played *suantraighe*, "sleep music," on his THREE-stringed HARP, which put not only people but the world to sleep, so that the springs that fed Lough Gur froze up and looked like stones beneath the glassy surface. He could also play *gentraighe*, "laughter music," melodies so light that those who heard them burst into delighted laughter.

ferrish   See FAIRY (OTHER CELTIC).

fertility   Cosmological concept. To people who live close to the land, the question of fertility is the most compelling one they face. Should the land grow sterile, should the herds grow barren, should the rivers not run flush with fish, death from starvation can soon follow. The Irish linked the fertility of the land to the king's righteousness; they believed that if the king behaved generously and honorably, the goddess of the land's SOVEREIGNTY, the king's spouse, would be happy and bear abundantly. Fertility was thus neither in the domain of the feminine nor of the masculine but existed in the balance struck between them. Among the continental Celts, images of abundance—the CORNUCOPIA and the EGG—are found with both gods and goddesses.

festival   See CALENDAR, FEAST.

fetch (feach)   Scottish and Irish folkloric figure. Each of us was thought to have a kind of detachable aura, like a shell, around us. It looked exactly like us and could wander like a ghost in places distant from our bodies. Encountering one's fetch had various meanings: If you met yourself in the morning, it meant good luck was coming; but if you ran into your exact image in the evening or near a graveyard, death was on the way. Those with SECOND SIGHT could see the fetches of other people as well as their own. The fetch was apparently distinct from the CO-WALKER, which could be a FAIRY or ghost rather than an aura.

féth fiada   See DRUID'S FOG.

Féthnat   Irish goddess. This obscure member of the magical race, the TUATHA DÉ DANANN, was a gifted musician.

Fflur   Welsh heroine or goddess. This obscure figure appears in the Welsh TRIADS as the beloved of the hero CASWALLAWN, who fought with Julius Caesar for her hand. Her name suggests that she may be related to the flower-maiden BLODEUWEDD; the contention of two rulers points to a connection to the goddess of SOVEREIGNTY; but Fflur's legend and its meaning are virtually lost.

Fiacclach mac Conchinn (Fiacail, Fiachu mac Conga)   Irish hero. The vigorous foster father of the Irish hero FIONN MAC CUMHAILL, Fiacclach provided Fionn a magical sword that never missed its mark.

Fiachna   Irish hero. Common in Irish mythology, possibly meaning "raven," this name borne mostly by minor heroes. The exceptions are:

- **Fiachna of MUNSTER,** an incestuous king who fathered a son on his daughter MUGAIN.
- **Fiachna mac Báetáin,** whose wife CAÍNTIGERN bought a victory for him by sleeping with the sea god, MANANNÁN MAC

LIR, who so desired her that he arranged for Fiachna to win the battle in return for his wife's favors. This Fiachna may be a historical king, though his genealogical background—he was thought to have been conceived parthenogenetically by his mother—suggests a divinity or totem ancestor.

- **Fiachna mac Dáire,** to whom a WORM spoke when he snagged it while fishing in Cuailnge, in the northern PROVINCE of ULSTER. The miraculous talking worm made an odd prediction: that war would be waged over a BULL from the region. Unlikely as the prediction seemed, the worm had reason to know its truth, because it was the reincarnated soul of a swineherd who would later take the shape of the great Brown Bull, DONN CUAILNGE. This bull would become the object of the CATTLE RAID launched by queen MEDB in CONNACHT, who had been advised by another worm (the swineherd's most bitter enemy, who would become the White Bull of Connacht, FINNBENNACH) to marry AILILL mac Máta, thus setting the stage for the epic battle between the two bulls.

Fiachra   Irish hero. Several minor mythological characters have this name, most notably one of the doomed CHILDREN OF LIR.

Fial   Irish goddess. Goddess of the River Feale, which empties into the great Shannon and which bears her name, Fial was a typical Celtic RIVER goddess, associated not only with the water but with the entire watershed, thus being a divinity of FERTILITY and abundance. The name is also given to the daughter of the goddess MACHA, who died giving birth to Fial and her twin brother Fall.

Fianna (Fenians, Fiana)   Irish heroes. Although the name is used generically to refer to any group of armed warriors wandering the Irish countryside (and thus used of revolutionaries in several eras), the usual mythological reference is to the group that served under the leadership of the great hero FIONN MAC CUMHAILL. The stories of the FENIAN CYCLE are among the best known of Ireland's ancient tales.

There may be an historical aspect to the stories, for there were indeed such roving bands who made their skills and weapons available to various kings. They were not exactly mercenaries, although they certainly required payment for their services, sometimes taken in booty from those they defeated, for they were fiercely loyal to their chosen king and did not readily change sides. Texts indicate that such bands found a place in Irish society in the early Middle Ages and may well have existed before then. Not tied to a single TUATH or kingdom, these fianna seem to have fought to keep invaders like the Vikings out of Ireland. The rough-hewn social organization seems to have disappeared by the time of the Normans' arrival in the 12th century.

Standing on the outskirts of society, the fianna were a meritocracy, with membership based upon skill and strength rather than noble blood or wealth. Thus the fianna can be seen as a means of social advancement for those who possessed the requisite abilities. Such raw talent was shaped into warriors through an exhausting boot-camp or initiation. The applicant was, for instance, placed in a deep hole and given a shield; the members of the fianna then threw spears from which a less-than-able applicant could suffer dire wounds—or worse. The applicant would be chased through the woods and, if caught, wounded as well as rejected for membership. On top of all this, the new member was expected to be a poet, able to thrill the fianna with compositions and recitations.

Women were not excluded from the fianna, although more typically the warriors are said to have been men. There are stories of WARRIOR WOMEN like Creidne and ERC, both members of Fionn's Fianna, as well as other women who fought solo rather than with a band of warriors. That there is some likely historical referent for such figures can be found in Roman writers who deplored the fact that Celtic women fought alongside their men.

Thus it is possible to see the Fenian Cycle as glamorizing the exploits of an exemplary band of warriors, living in the wildwood, ready to fight for the sake of glory, to avenge an insult or to protect Ireland's high king. These tales are among the most continually popular of Irish myths and include not only tales of glory but also romances like the story of ÉTAIN, reborn to rejoin her fated lover MIDIR, as well as poetic philosophies like the story of OISÍN the BARD, stolen away from earth by a FAIRY QUEEN, who later returns to a world from which paganism had been driven.

fidchell Irish game. This ancient game was rather like today's cribbage, in which pegs (probably of wood, as the name means "wood wisdom") were moved about a board. *Fidchell* also apparently resembled chess in being a game of strategy whose intention was the taking of the opponent's pieces. No examples of the gameboard have been found, but the game appears frequently in mythology, most memorably in the wager by the fairy king MIDIR against the king of TARA, EOCHAID Airem, with the queen ÉTAIN as the prize.

Fideal Scottish folkloric figure. This Highland siren figure lured handsome young men into lakes and ponds, then drowned them; she is a species of *VOUGH*.

Fiecal Irish heroine. One of the wise women who reared the hero FIONN MAC CUMHAILL, she plays a minor role in the cycle of stories devoted to him.

fifth province See MIDE.

Figgy Dowdy (Madge Figgy) Cornish folkloric figure. In Cornwall old tradition uses this name for the spirit of a holy WELL at Carn Marth, where dolls were baptized in an unusual ritual. As most such places were originally ruled by goddesses, some find in Figgy Dowdy's peculiar name a misapprehension of the Cornish words for "the reaper goddess" or "the good goddess of the scythe." She may be related to the legendary witch MADGY FIGGY.

fili (*file*; pl., *filid*, *filidh*) Celtic social role. In early Ireland poets, or *filid*, were highly trained members of a hierarchical profession with seven levels, of which the ollam was the highest. Families of filid, like the Ó Daillaighs of Co. Clare, organized schools and trained their kin and other apprentices in demanding, rigorous memorization. Hundreds of pieces had to be memorized before a new composition was attempted; in addition, there were techniques of DIVINATION to learn as well as other magical rituals. It can be hard to distinguish the *fili* from the BREHON, or lawyer, and the BARD, or singer, as there is some overlap among their fields; similarly, in very early times the DRUID and *fili* were interchangeable, for poetry was believed to be a magical art. No more clear a connection between them can be found than the position of SATIRE, whose stinging words were demanded of the poet whenever a king needed to be chastened. The magic of the *fili's* words would disfigure the wrongheaded king, thus causing him to lose his right to rule (see BLEMISHED KING). As Celtic Ireland waned, the power of the poets became more mundane; they attached themselves to powerful chieftains whose praises they sung. Even after the great poetic schools had ceased to function, the status of the poet remained high, as it does in Celtic lands today.

Find Irish divinity. This word, which means "white," appears in the names of many mythological figures and folkloric heroes. There is some evidence of an early divinity by this name, possibly a god who prefigures the hero FIONN MAC CUMHAILL or a goddess related to BÓAND, the white COW goddess whose name is carried by the River Boyne. The geographer Ptolemy, in the second century C.E., spoke of a divinity

called Bouvinda, whose name is cognate with the magical cow BÓ FIND, who is in turn possibly an aspect of Bóand. It is unclear whether this word is a name or a title, and whether it refers to a specific figure or to the radiant nature of divinity itself.

Findchóem (Finnchaem, Fionnchaomh) Irish heroine or goddess. Like other Irish mythological women, Findchóem chose an unusual way to conceive: When she found a WORM in a glass of water from a holy WELL, she drank the water down, worm and all, in the hopes that she would conceive a hero. She did, bearing the hero CONALL Cernach; but her foster son CÚCHULAINN was even more powerful. Such unnatural conception is found in other lands as well, for example in mythological stories of ancestral mothers of Chinese dynasties, and may reflect a period when lineage was traced through the mother. Evidence of such MATRILINY is found in much early Irish mythological material, with several kings bearing their mother's names; AILILL mac Máta of CONNACHT, named for his mother, the obscure Máta; and the king of ULSTER, CONCOBAR MAC NESSA, named for his mother NESSA—who was also Findchóem's mother. Findchóem herself may be a double of her own mother, who conceived in exactly the same fashion. Such duplication is common in Irish and other Celtic mythology.

Findias (Finias, Findrias) Irish mythological site. A mysterious city of the magical TUATHA DÉ DANANN, it was ruled by a master of WISDOM named USCIAS. The unerring sword of king NUADA came from Findias.

fine (*derbfine*) Irish social role. The "kin group," or *fine*, was a major form of social organization in ancient Ireland. Those who were descendants of the same great-grandfather, called *derbfine* or "true kin," shared land that could not be sold by any member without the consent of the others; less closely related people constituted the *fine*. The individual was responsible to the group for his good behavior, since the entire kin group was held responsible for any *ÉRIC* or honor price due for the injury or killing of a member of another kin group. Conversely, if a member of the *fine* was killed or injured, the whole group shared in the honor price, which was usually paid in COWS. Heads of kin groups, chosen by election, negotiated for the group and represented them in public gatherings.

Source: Kelly, Fergus. *A Guide to Early Irish Law.* Dublin: School of Celtic Studies, Dublin Institute for Advanced Studies. Early Irish Law Series, Vol. III, 1988, pp. 12–13.

Fíngein   Irish hero. Common in Irish narratives, Fíngein is the name of several significant healers and some minor kings.

Finn   Irish hero. This name, which like FIND means "white" or "fair" and refers to WISDOM rather than skin tone, was a common name for heroes both male and female; it is a variant of the name given to the greatest of Irish heroes, FIONN MAC CUMHAILL. The most prominent Finns were the three identically named triplet brothers who were known as the Three Finns of Emain Macha or Trí Finn Emna, despite their given names of Bres, Nár, and Lothar. Together they impregnated their sister-lover, CLOTHRA of CONNACHT, with a son who was born with red stripes dividing the portions of his body inherited from each of his fathers. They then took up arms against their father, king EOCHAID Fedlech of TARA, but were defeated by him, whereupon he died of sorrow at their loss.

Finnabair   (Findabar, Fionnúir)   Irish heroine or goddess. The beautiful daughter of MEDB of CONNACHT may be a double of that goddess-queen, for she has many of the same qualities, including a steely sense of her own worth. She loved the hero FRÁECH and agreed to a tryst with him on an island surrounded by a deep pool. Fráech, swimming naked out to her, had to fight off a fierce sea-monster, which attempted to remove that which would have made their tryst enjoyable. Despite his bravery and his desire for Finnabair, Fráech could not fulfill the dowry demands of Medb and AILILL mac Máta, her parents, who coveted the CATTLE of the OTHER-WORLD that were part of Fráech's fortune. Many adventures ensued before Finnabair and her lover were united. They were soon parted again when the girl was captured and dragged to a fortress in the Alps, from which Fráech freed her.

During the CATTLE RAID on the northern PROVINCE of ULSTER, recorded in detail in the epic *TÁIN BÓ CUAILNGE*, Medb offered Finnabair to various warriors in return for their willingness to fight against the hero CÚCHULAINN, who was single-handedly holding off the Connacht army. Like other heroes, Fráech took up the challenge; like other heroes, Fráech was killed. Finnabair then died of a broken heart. This heroine is very likely a diminished goddess, as are others who share the name—GUINEVERE in the Arthurian cycle, as well as the Welsh heroine Gwenhwyfar and the Cornish Jennifer.

Finnbennach   (Findbennach, Fionn Bheannach)   Irish mythological beast. This splendid white-horned BULL began his existence as a swineherd named RUCHT, who served a man called Ochall Ochne and who argued constantly with another swineherd, FRIUCH. Their enmity was so deep-seated that every time they died, they were reborn as enemies. They were RAVENS, fighting in the air; they were STAGS, fighting in the woodlands. Finally they were reborn as water-WORMS in different streams and in distant parts of Ireland. It was difficult for them to wage war upon each other in this lowly form, to say nothing of the miles between them. So they set about preparing to continue their warfare in another incarnation. Rucht whispered to queen MEDB of CONNACHT that she should wed AILILL mac Máta; Friuch similarly whispered to the king of

Cuailnge that he should prepare for war that would be waged over a bull. Then the two worms wriggled themselves into position to be drunk up by two COWS, thus impregnating them so that they could both be reborn as bulls.

The reborn swineherd became the most magnificent bull in Connacht. Born into Medb's herd, he felt it beneath him to be owned by a woman and thus joined her husband Ailill's, making him one bull richer than she was. As this dramatically altered her legal relationship with Ailill, Medb set about finding a bull as superb as Finnbennach, locating the other reborn swineherd in the powerful body of the brown bull DONN CUAILNGE of ULSTER. Medb's CATTLE RAID finally brought together the bitter enemies, who immediately set upon each other in a fierce battle in which Finnbennach was killed—but in the process, he gored Donn Cuailnge so that the other bull died as well. This cattle raid was chronicled in the Irish epic TÁIN BÓ CUAILNGE.

The SHAPE-SHIFTING and REINCARNATION that mark this curious story suggest that the two swineherd/water-worm/bulls were originally gods or BARDS, the two categories of beings most prone to such behavior. If that is so, the explanatory referents are lost, leaving just a vigorous tale of war and battle.

Finnbheara (Finvarra, Fin Varra, Fionvarra, Finbar). Irish hero. FAIRYLAND was more often spoken of as ruled by a queen rather than a king, but Finnbheara is an exception. From his FAIRY MOUND at KNOCKMA near Tuam in Co. Galway, he ruled all the fairies of the western province of CONNACHT—or, some say, all the fairies of Ireland. Although he had a fairy wife, ÚNA, Finnbheara specialized in stealing beautiful women, lulling their suspicions away with the soothing music of fairyland and then snatching them from this world. In the bright beauty of Finnbheara's palace, these women forgot their earthly lives and danced and sang without sadness or sorrow. Sometimes, as in the story of EITHNE the Fair, the woman's body remained behind and

she seemed to be in a coma from which she could not be aroused; sometimes she simply vanished. Both Lady Gregory and William Butler Yeats collected tales of Finnbheara; he appears in several of Yeats's plays and many of his poems as a symbol of the beautiful OTHERWORLD.

Source: Wilde, Lady. *Ancient Legends, Mystic Charms and Superstitions of Ireland*. London: Chatto and Windus, 1902, p. 43.

Finnéces Irish hero. When the great hero FIONN MAC CUMHAILL was a small boy, he lived as a student with the DRUID Finnéces. Some say they lived near the mouth of the River Boyne in the east, some say near the falls of ASSAROE in the west. In either case, they lived near a pool over which magical HAZEL bushes hung, dropping their nuts into the water and nourishing the SALMON that swam there. For seven years Finnéces had been waiting for just the right moment to gain the WISDOM that the salmon held within itself. When the time was right, the druid caught the FISH, who came to his line as though by prearrangement.

Finnéces set the fish to cook, leaving the boy Fionn to watch it and warning him not to touch it or taste it. But the salmon sizzled and spattered onto Fionn's thumb, which he stuck into his mouth to ease the pain. Immediately wisdom flooded him—the very wisdom that the old druid had been hoping to attain. Almost the same story is told of the great Welsh BARD TALIESIN, but it is the CAULDRON of the goddess CERIDWEN that holds wisdom in that tale; the name of the boy who steals wisdom in that story is GWION, cognate to Fionn. Given the similarity of the names Finnéces and Fionn, some have suggested a doubling of one figure; additionally, the salmon is often sometimes called FINTAN, another similar name.

Source: O'Rahilly, Thomas. *Early Irish History and Mythology*. Dublin: The Dublin Institute for Advanced Studies, 1946, p. 326.

Finnen (Fennel, Finnine, Fininne) Irish goddess. One of the FAIRY QUEENS or goddesses of the significant archaeological region around LOUGH GUR in eastern Co. Limerick, Finnen bears a name meaning "white" or "brilliant," parallel to other mythic figures including the great hero FIONN MAC CUMHAILL. She forms a pair with another local goddess, ÁINE, "the bright one," suggesting an ancient TWIN sun goddess.

Finn McCool Irish and Scottish folkloric figure. Legends and tales of this GIANT abound in Ireland (especially in the northern province of ULSTER) as well as in Scotland. Although a degraded form of the great Irish hero FIONN MAC CUMHAILL, Finn is also a figure in his own right, a kind of Paul Bunyan, full of reckless energy. The most famous stories told of him are that he created the GIANT'S CAUSEWAY, a renowned basalt rock formation, by dropping stones, and that he bested the giant BENADON-NER through trickery; other variants say Finn slew the giant who built the causeway.

Fintan Irish hero or god. "The white ancient" is the meaning of this name, which is worn by several important mythological figures:

• **Fintan the salmon,** also known as GOLL Essa Ruaid ("the one-eyed one of the red waterfall"), who swam in the pool at the source of one of Ireland's rivers, variously the Boyne and the Erne, nibbling the HAZEL nuts that dropped from magical bushes that surrounded the water. He was caught by the DRUID FINNÉCES and eaten, accidentally, by the great hero FIONN MAC CUMHAILL, who thereby gained immense WISDOM.
• **Fintan mac Bóchra,** the most ancient of Irishmen, the only one to survive the flood that brought the seafaring queen CESAIR and her 50 women to Ireland. The women were accompanied by only three men, two of whom "perished of embraces," according to the *BOOK OF INVASIONS*, while Fintan, to save himself,

fled. He then transformed himself into many shapes, including the one-eyed SALMON GOLL Essa Ruaid as well as an EAGLE and a hawk. Such SHAPE-SHIFTING is seen also in BARDS such as AMAIRGIN and TUAN MAC CAIRILL, as well as in the stories of several divinities.
• **Fintan, son of NIALL Nioganach,** who plays a minor role in the tale of the INTOXICATION OF THE ULSTERMEN.

Fiongalla Irish heroine. This obscure figure is connected with the southwestern PROVINCE of MUNSTER, where the "fair-cheeked one" was bewitched by the powerful woman DRUID Amerach from ULSTER, who grew no older despite the passing years. She made Fiongalla vow never to sleep with a man until one brought her magical YEW berries, HOLLY boughs, and marigolds. Amerach lost her power over Fiongalla when a hero named Feargal performed the almost impossible task.

Fionn Cycle See FENIAN CYCLE.

Fionnghal nam Fiadh (Flora of the Deer, Sorch an O-rfhuil, Clara of the Golden Hair, the Crazed One of the Mountains) Scottish heroine. In a story that resembles the Irish tale of the wild woman MIS, the beautiful maiden Fionnghal was jilted by her lover, who took his ambitious mother's advice to marry a richer woman. Fionnghal went mad, running into the mountains naked and screaming. She lived there among the DEER, growing hair so that she looked like a member of the herd, who accepted her as one of their own.

Eventually all her kinsmen and other pursuers gave up the chase, save her once-beloved, who kept tracking her despite her madness. At last one day he found her, naked and asleep, in his own campsite. He covered her with his cloak and waited. When she awoke she was sane and thankful but told him that she was dying and, indeed, did so soon thereafter. Her lover brought her body down from the mountains and, as soon as he had delivered it to her kin, died himself. From their adjoining graves, two great weeping willows grew up and entwined themselves.

Source: Carmichael, Alexander. *Carmina Gadelica: Hymns and Incantations.* Hudson, N.Y.: Lindisfarne Press, 1992, p. 657.

Fionn mac Cumhaill (Finn Mac Cool, Finn Mac Cumhal, Demne Máel)   Irish hero. There are two great heroes in Irish mythology, each the center of a cycle of myths and connected with an era and a PROVINCE. The great warrior CÚCHULAINN of the ULSTER CYCLE is the first; he is described as living at the height of Celtic Ireland's power (presumably the fifth and sixth centuries C.E.) and is associated with the northwestern province. A later hero is FIONN MAC CUMHAILL, whose warrior band, the FIANNA, recalls the unattached bands of protective warriors common in Ireland through the early Middle Ages. Because their center was at the Hill of Allen (see ALMU) in Co. Kildare, the Fianna and their leader are linked to the southeastern province of LEINSTER.

Fionn bears the name of his father, CUMHALL, who died when he was young. Legend varies about why he was left fatherless at an early age. In one tale, Cumhall raped the noble MURNA and was killed in retaliation by the hero CONN of the Hundred Battles, leaving the unfortunate Murna pregnant with Fionn. In another, Cumhall was innocent of wrongdoing but fell into conflict with an opposing clan; the conflict between Cumhall and Fionn's CLAN BAÍSCNE with their antagonists, CLAN MORNA, is the basis for much legend in the FENIAN CYCLE. Other variants exist as well, all of which emphasize the early demise of Fionn's father and the importance of feminine energy in his early life, for it was through his mother Murna that Fionn claimed divine descent from her ancestor NUADA of the Silver Hand, king of the mythological TUATHA DÉ DANANN. The most significant influence on Fionn's childhood was his aunt and foster mother, the DRUID BODHMALL, who nursed him and began his education, which was furthered by LUATHS LURGANN, a WARRIOR WOMAN who trained Fionn in the martial arts and whom he accidentally killed.

As is the case with all such heroes, Fionn's power was evident early; while still a boy, he acquired all the world's WISDOM and revealed his great skill as a fighter. Sent by his aunt to study with the hermit druid FINNÉCES, Fionn (then called Demne Máel or "druid's tonsure") was left to watch a SALMON turning on a spit. That salmon was no ordinary fish but the renowned salmon of wisdom, sometimes called FINTAN, a BARD who had lived in many incarnations and thus gained all possible wisdom. Finnéces had been watching for seven years—not coincidentally, since the time of Fionn's birth—for the salmon to rise in the waters of the sacred WELL (see ASSAROE), and when it did, he captured it neatly and set it to cook, intending to devour it and thus gain all of Fintan's vast vision. But the salmon splattered onto Fionn's thumb, and he stuck it in his mouth to salve the pain. Thus did Fionn gain all the salmon's wisdom; from then on, all he had to do was suck on his thumb and he would enter an altered, visionary state in which he could see past, present, and future. As all the names of the characters in this story are connected, the salmon has been seen as a triplication or intensification of Fionn himself.

Not only wisdom was Fionn's from childhood but also strength and skill with weapons. His name derives from his first fight to the death, when after winning an athletic competition he was challenged as victor by a rival, whom he killed, whereupon he was dubbed "the fair boy" or Fionn, a name that stuck. To it was added his father's name, so that the hero went by the full name of Fionn mac Cumhaill, Fionn son of Cumhall.

From that point, as with all such heroes, Fionn was sent to study his craft further and chose the warrior woman BÚANANN, who is parallel to the Scottish amazon SCÁTHACH who trained Cúchulainn. But he had a male tutor as well, the warrior CETHERN MAC FINTAIN. By the time he entered manhood, Fionn had all the necessary skills for fame and glory: He was the world's fastest runner, he never missed the mark with his spear, he could swim across any body of water, and he had the added advantage of being able to suck his thumb and know the whereabouts and weaknesses of his enemy.

Like king ARTHUR gathering the knights of the ROUND TABLE, Fionn gathered a band of warriors to defend his province, Leinster. Such fianna seem to have been a real feature of ancient Irish life; rather than maintaining standing armies, kings relied upon such groups and their leaders for protection against invaders, but they also fought among themselves, as the continual disputes between Fionn's Clan Baíscne and the opposing Clan Morna show. Among Fionn's dearest companions in the Fianna were his hunting dogs BRAN and SCEOLAN. Many Fenian legends describe Fionn's prowess in battle, as when he becomes the only hero powerful enough to subdue the monstrous AILLÉN TRENCHENN, who regularly burned the palace at Tara.

Fionn is now generally believed to have originally been divine, a status made clear in legends that he created the countryside as part of his activities. He is said to have cut mountains in half with his sword and left scratches where he clung to rocks as he climbed. More often the Fenian stories tell of adventures in the human realm. A typical story tells of a slovenly man who approached Fionn when he was traveling in Scotland and gained employment as a carrier of the hero's baggage. The man revealed a superhuman strength that impressed even Fionn. Not only that, but he could hunt, and every morning caught a deer for breakfast; beyond that, the man could cook, always having the deer nicely grilled by the time warriors of the Fianna were awake. One member of the Fianna was envious and bitter; this man, CONÁN, challenged the slovenly servant to a race to the Hill of Howth and back again, with the loser to be decapitated. The man refused to permit Conán to wager his head but accepted the challenge.

They set off, with the slovenly servant stopping to take pebbles from his shoe and to cut his long trailing cloak. He still reached the goal before Conán, however, and he struck Conán such a blow that his head turned around on his neck. Fionn demanded that Conán's head be set right, and the servant agreed, but only if Fionn would take him to his home. As they arrived, the servant was transformed into a prince, for the curse he had been laboring under could only be lifted if he entered his home with Fionn mac Cumhaill. Such folktales, which probably were drawn into the orbit of the Fenians from their disparate original sources, are typical of those connected to Fionn in the oral tradition.

The Fenian Cycle places an unusual emphasis on courtship and love for such an apparently masculine sequence of tales. Because Fionn has no single wife, he is linked to one woman after another: SADB, who was turned into a DEER, so that Fionn's brilliant son OISÍN was born with fawn's fur for brows; ÁINE, by whom he had two sons; the poetess CRÉD; the unnamed daughter of the king of Greece; the married Maer and the unfaithful Maigneis; and many others. As he grew older, Fionn remained desirous of women but became less desirable himself. In his dotage he was betrothed to the beautiful GRÁINNE, who preferred the young hero DIARMAIT; the saga of their elopement and pursuit by Fionn does not show the elder hero in the best of lights, especially when he refused to heal his wounded rival, but it is full of realistic drama.

The story of how Gráinne became Fionn's betrothed is told in the place-lore legends of the CAIRN-crowned hill SLIEVENAMON. Desiring a young partner, Fionn volunteered to impregnate the strongest, speediest girl in MUNSTER—the winner to be determined by a footrace. Standing on the cairn atop Slievenamon, Fionn gave a signal, at which point all the young women of the province ran toward him. Competitive and strong, the king's daughter Gráinne outran everyone and reached the hilltop first. But she never, the story says, bore the heroes she had been promised, although some variants say that after her lover's dcath, Gráinne agreed to fulfill her duties as Fionn's wife and bore him several children.

Just as there are multiple versions of the story of Fionn's birth, so there are variants of how Fionn died. Most commonly the hero's antagonists of the Clan Morna are blamed; the head of that clan, the one-eyed GOLL MAC MORNA, dealt the death blow. Fionn's death is said to have happened at numerous locations around both Ireland and Scotland. He may have been reborn as the hero MONGÁN. Or perhaps Fionn did not die at all, but rests with the Fianna, sleeping in a cave somewhere in Ireland until his land needs him again, like the once and future king ARTHUR of Britain.

Sources: Almqvist, Bo, Séamus Ó Catháin, and Páidaig ó Héalaí. *The Heroic Process: Form, Function and Fantasy in Folk Epic.* Dublin: The Glendale Press, 1987, p. 76; Cross, Tom Peete, and Clark Harris Slover, eds. *Ancient Irish Tales.* New York: Henry Holt and Co., 1936, pp. 260 ff; Curtin, Jeremiah. *Hero-Tales of Ireland.* New York: Benjamin Blom, 1894, pp. 407, 438, 463; Kennedy, Patrick. *Legendary Fictions of the Irish Celts.* New York: Benjamin Blom, 1969, pp. 222–223; MacKillop, James. *Fionn mac Cumhaill: Celtic Myth in English Literature.* Syracuse, N.Y.: Syracuse University Press, 1986; McKay, John G. *More West Highland Tales.* Scottish Anthropological and Folklore Society. Vol. 2. Edinburgh: Oliver and Boyd, 1969, p. 69; Ó hÓgáin, Dáithí. *Fionn mac Cumhaill: Images of the Gaelic Hero.* Dublin: Gill & Macmillan, 1988.

Fionnuala (Finola, Finnguala, Fionnuala, Fionguala, Finnuala, Fionnula) Irish heroine. One of the most famous Irish myths centers on this girl, child of king LIR and his beloved first wife ÁEB, who was the daughter of the magician BODB DERG. Lir and Áeb were happy together and delighted when Fionnuala and her twin brother ÁED were born. But then Áeb died giving birth to her second set of twin sons, FIACHRA

and CONN, and Lir married his wife's foster sister AÍFE, hoping to make a happy home for his motherless children.

Aífe was jealous of her charges, however, and plotted against them. Convincing Lir that she was desperately ill and needed the attentions of her foster father, Aífe set off with the children to Bodb Derg's home in the west. Along the way, she turned on them and transformed them into SWANS, cursing them to remain so for 900 years.

Even Bodb Derg's magic was not enough to undo the damage—although he turned his foster daughter into a demon of the air (in some versions, a CRANE) in retaliation for her action. But the CHILDREN OF LIR were left as swans with human emotions and human voices to sing of their woes. They spent 300 years on Lough Derravaragh in the center of Ireland, then 300 years on the frigid Sea of Moyle to the north, and finally on an island in the far west, off Co. Mayo (although local legend in west Co. Cork also claims they lived there). There the enchantment finally wore off, but the years they had lived caught up with them instantly, and they aged, died, and turned to dust, to be buried in the old way, standing upright in the grave.

Sources: Gantz, Jeffrey, ed. and trans. *Early Irish Myths and Sagas.* New York: Penguin Books, 1984, pp. 147 ff; Gregory, Lady Augusta. *Gods and Fighting Men: The Story of the Tuatha De Danaan and of the Fianna of Ireland.* New York: Oxford University Press, 1970, pp. 124 ff; Joyce, P. W. *Ancient Celtic Romances.* London: Parkgate Books, 1997, pp. 1–32; Kennedy, Patrick. *Legendary Fictions of the Irish Celts.* New York: Benjamin Blom, 1969, p. 27; Markale, Jean. *Women of the Celts.* Rochester, Vt.: Inner Traditions, 1986, p. 242; Squire, Charles. *Mythology of the Celtic People.* London: Bracken Books, 1996, p. 142.

Fir Bolg (Gáilióin, Fir Domnann) Irish mythological race. The legendary history of Ireland tells of many invasions—indeed, it is called the *BOOK OF INVASIONS*. Although the magical and sometimes monstrous races described are clearly mythological, the text does reflect the historical truth that Ireland was settled in multiple migratory waves. Some of these were non-Celtic people, including the unknown earliest settlers and the later Picts. Then came the Celts, not all at one time but in several waves. The earliest were people whose dialect was called P-Celtic; later-comers spoke a Q-Celtic language. It has not been established beyond dispute how many migrations took place, or what tribes came, nor from what area they originated. What is clear is that Ireland was not settled all at once by only one people; nor was there always a peaceful reaction to new people arriving in already occupied lands.

Among these early immigrants or invaders were some that have come into legend as the Fir Bolg; earlier scholars derived their name from the presumed connection with the word for "bag" and called them "men of the bags," but the current understanding is that their name is related to the tribal names Builg or Belgae, the same Celtic tribes that gave their name to Belgium. These peoples may have traced their descent from a hypothesized ancestral divinity named Bolg or Bulg, possibly the ruler of thunder; thus their name would mean "sons of the god/dess Bolg" and would be corollary to the later TUATHA DÉ DANANN, "children of the goddess DANU."

Legend has it that the Fir Bolg were descended from the children of NEMED or Nemedians, another mythological race who had lived in Ireland generations before the Fir Bolg. Cast out by the fierce FOMORIANS, Nemed's son STARN found himself in Greece, where his descendants were enslaved for 230 years, carrying bags of dirt to build up hills. Eventually they turned these bags into boats and escaped, returning to their ancient homeland.

They arrived on the harvest feast of LUGHNASA under the leadership of Dela, who divided the island among his sons: the southwestern PROVINCE of MUNSTER went to Gann and Sengann; SLANE took the eastern province of LEINSTER, and Rudraige, ULSTER to the north.

Dynasties were established and kings began to rule. Among the Fir Bolg kings of note were EOCHAID mac Eirc, who ruled the middle province with his famed wife TAILTIU; Rinnal, who invented spear points; and DELGA, who built the great fort of DÚN Delgan, now Dundalk in Co. Louth. Other renowned members of the Fir Bolg were the healer Fíngein Fisiochda and the hero SRENG. Curiously, there is no mention of the monstrous Fomorians who drove out the Fir Bolg ancestors, although they reappear ultimately to combat the Fir Bolg's own conquerors.

The Fir Bolg ruled for only 37 years before the Tuatha Dé Danann arrived, the most magical of Ireland's mythological races. In the great combat called the first battle of MAG TUIRED, the Tuatha Dé Danann king NUADA drove the Fir Bolg from Ireland, although he lost his arm and his right to the throne in the process (see BLEMISHED KING). Like later (and possibly earlier) conquered peoples in Ireland, the Fir Bolg retreated to the distant reaches of the Celtic world: the Aran Islands off Ireland's west coast, where their king Aonghus built the great fort of Dún Aongusa; to islands off the Scottish coast; and to wild Connemara, where their king was said to be named Bola, a possible derivative of their tribal name.

Irish place-names refer to this mythological race: Dún Bolg in Co. Wicklow, Moherbullog in Co. Clare, Moyboulogue in Co. Cavan. If they do represent a Celtic people who were driven to the geographical fringes by later Celtic invaders, it is likely that the inhabitants of those areas descend from the Fir Bolg.

Sources: MacAlister, R. A. Stewart. *Lebor Gabála Érenn: The Book of the Taking of Ireland, Part 4.* Dublin: Irish Texts Society, 1941, pp. 1–90; O'Rahilly, Thomas. *Early Irish History and Mythology.* Dublin: The Dublin Institute for Advanced Studies, 1946, pp. 16, 42.

fir chlis   Scottish folkloric figure. The "nimble man" personified the northern lights or aurora borealis in Scottish folklore.

Fir Dea   See TUATHA DÉ DANANN.

Fir Domnann   See FIR BOLG.

fire   Symbolic element. The force of fire is different from the other major elements in that it is not constant. Water is available in rain as well as rivers and oceans; the earth is everywhere beneath our feet; air surrounds us continually. But fire is found in only two ways: in the domestic hearth and in the flames of wildfire, which are often set by lightning. More distantly, fire can be imagined as existing in the SUN, often pictured as a ball of flame; there is evidence that the Celts connected the earthly and solar fires.

Fire deities are found in Celtic mythology, typically with wildfire divinities being male and those of the hearth fire, female. TARANIS, the continental Celtic thunder god, was associated with lightning and with the fires that typically followed its strikes. LUGH appears to have served the same function in insular mythology. Honoring the hearth fire was a belief shared by the Celts with their Indo-European kin from areas as diverse as Lithuania and India; the ritual was most notable in the cult of the Roman Vesta, served by a college of priestesses. A similar college appears to have served the Irish goddess BRIGIT; interpreters argue that the Christian sisterhood of Kildare replicated the Celtic tradition in which an ashless, ever-burning fire was tended by one sister each night for 19 nights, the 20th being left for Brigit herself. Under Christianity, that flame blazed for more than 10 centuries, to be extinguished by a Protestant bishop; the holy flame was relit in 1994 by members of the Brigidine order, the continuation of that established by St. Brigit.

Given the preponderance of female hearth-fire divinities and the association of that fire with the sun, the likelihood of the sun being perceived as a goddess seems high. However, a longstanding belief that all cultures honored the sun as a masculine force has kept this question from being examined until recently. In the last several decades, evidence has mounted that sun goddesses were more common than previously proposed. Many scholars now offer evidence that the Celts saw the sun as a feminine force, as nurturing as the hearth goddess; others suggest a double rulership of the sun by both god and goddess.

In Ireland fire was connected with a number of festivals. Those of MIDSUMMER may be displaced from celebrations of LUGHNASA, the Celtic summer festival, or may hearken to a pre-Celtic past. St. John's Eve, celebrated on June 23, just two days after the year's longest day on the summer SOLSTICE, was called Bonfire Night in many regions of Ireland. Celebratory blazes, always circular, were lit near holy WELLS and at other sacred sites, and dances were held through the night. Neglecting the fires might mean that FISH would not come into the rivers nor fields bear grain and potatoes. In Co. Limerick, there was a tradition of striking dancers with a recently cut reed to protect them against illness; the reeds were then tossed into the fire, the potential contagion thus being burned away. The bravest dancers leapt over the fire, whose ASHES were used in blessings on crops, stock, and homes.

In Scotland fire was construed as both protective and purifying; fire carried around a house in a sunwise direction protected building and occupants from harm. Into recent times in Scotland, the NEED-FIRE was practiced when famine or epidemic threatened; all hearth fires in an area were extinguished, then a group of men created a new fire by rubbing planks of wood together until a flame burst forth. Those attending the ceremony took a flame of the new fire to their home, while the original fire was doused with water and the ashes smeared on cattle for protection.

Sources: Danaher, Kevin. *The Year in Ireland.* Cork: Mercier Press, 1922, p. 135; MacCulloch, J. A. *The Religion of the Ancient Celts.* London: Constable, 1911, pp. 261 ff, 199 ff; McCrickard, Janet. *Eclipse of the Sun.* Glastonbury: Gothic Image, 1994, p. 22; Ross, Anne. *Folklore of the Scottish Highlands.* London: B. T. Batsford, Ltd., 1976, p. 98.

Fir Ghorm (Fir Gorm) See BLUE MEN OF THE MINCH.

Fir Gorm See BLUE MEN OF THE MINCH.

first footer (qualtagh) Scottish folkloric figure. In Scotland and on the Isle of Man, the first person (or being of whatever species) met on the road when on the way to a christening or a wedding was traditionally offered bread and cheese, to buy the goodwill of the spirits for the new year. More important was the first person to enter a home on January 1. Called the *qualtagh* among the Manx and the first footer in Scotland, this person should be a dark-complected man of hearty good health. On the Isle of Man, RED-headed people were feared as first footers, for that coloring was thought to be connected to the FAIRY realm, while in Scotland redheads were acceptable. It was important for the first footer to bear a gift, for an empty-handed caller indicated poor fortune for the year. In return, the first footer was offered something, usually food or drink.

fish Symbolic animal. The preeminent Christian symbol had significance to the Celts as well. The fish was emblematic of WISDOM, especially in the form of the SALMON or trout that was believed to swim in holy WELLS and other water sources. These fish were said to be speckled, with the same number of spots as the HAZEL nuts they had devoured from the magical bushes that surrounded the well.

Fisher King British or Arthurian hero. In GRAIL legends, especially in stories concerning the pure knight PERCIVAL, we find the image of a king who, injured almost unto death, sits in his boat and fishes while the land about him withers and dies. Once a virile and vital young man, he had unwisely attacked a mounted stranger who, before he died, left a portion of his sharp lance in the young king's groin; on the lance tip were

the words, "The Grail." Kept alive, but not well, by a magical stone, the king waited in agony for someone to lift the enchantment.

Although some disclaim any Celtic influence on this figure, others point to the motif of the BLEMISHED KING, in which the land and its ruler are seen as a married couple, with the earth reliant upon the king's health to be fruitful. The earth goddess could not be fructified by the Fisher King, who needed the curative power of the Grail to revive himself and the land. In addition to works based upon the Grail legends, this figure appears in T. S. Eliot's "The Waste Land" and in the film comedy *The Fisher King*.

In some texts Alain le Gros appears as Percival's father, called the Fisher King because he reproduced a biblical miracle, feeding a throng of people with only one fish, then building the castle of CORBENIC as a home for the Grail. Other names for the Fisher King include Anfortas ("infirmity"), Alain, Bron, Pelles, and Rothniam.

Fithel (Fítheal, Fíothal, Fithil) Irish hero. A wise judge or BREHON of Irish tradition, he adjudicated the disputes of the warrior band, the FIANNA, who served under his brother FIONN MAC CUMHAILL; he eventually departed to serve under king CORMAC MAC AIRT at TARA.

Fithir Irish heroine. When the beautiful Fithir drew the eye of the king of LEINSTER, the girl's father Túathal Techtmar refused her hand to the king, forcing him to wed her older sister DÁIRINE instead. But then Dáirine mysteriously died, or so the king reported when he returned once again to ask for Fithir's hand. This time his wish was granted, but when Fithir discovered that her sister was actually imprisoned with her handmaidens in a high tower in a thick dark woodland, she died of shock and shame.

five Cosmological number. The most significant numbers to Celtic peoples were THREE, representing intensification, and five, representing a natural order, as witnessed by the five fingers of each hand and the toes of each foot. Five may have formed the basis of the early Irish counting system, for the number appears in many mythological contexts (the five-pointed spear of the CONNACHT king AILILL mac Máta, the five sacred names of the hill of TARA, the five warriors who simultaneously killed the hero FIONN MAC CUMHAILL). In addition, there was a social context, for the smallest family unit, called the *geilfine*, comprised five people. Ireland applied the number geographically, dividing the island into five mythological PROVINCES, of which the central one, MIDE, was a magically situated center around which the other four were located. Thus five can be seen as a magically enhanced version of four, the number of wholeness, as well as a naturally occurring number that has its own innate power.

Source: Rees, Alwyn, and Brinley Rees. *Celtic Heritage: Ancient Tradition in Ireland and Wales.* London: Thames and Hudson, 1998, pp. 118 ff, 186 ff.

Flaith (Flaithius)   See SOVEREIGNTY.

Flann   Irish hero. Several minor figures of Irish mythology bear this name, which means "blood-red." The two most prominent may be versions of the same figure, for both are renowned lovers: Flann mac Díma, lover of MUGAIN, wife of DIARMAIT mac Cerbaill, who burned down Flann's house and caused him to drown, thus bringing a curse upon himself; and Flann ua Fedach, the FAIRY KING who eloped with the queen of TARA, BECFHOLA.

Flidais (Flidas, Fliodhas)   Irish goddess. Many European cultures had a woodland goddess like Flidais, who resembles the Greek ARTEMIS, the Roman DIANA, and the continental Celtic ARTIO. Flidais represented the force of FERTILITY and of abundance. As goddess of wild beasts, whose very name means "doe," she rode in a chariot drawn by DEER; as goddess of the domestic herds, she

possessed a magical COW that gave enough MILK to supply 30 people each night.

Her animal nature was also revealed in her sexual behavior, for she was as voracious as her consort, the randy FERGUS Mac Róich; if Flidais was not interested, Fergus made do with seven normal women. Flidais was sometimes said to be married to the fairy ÁDAMMAIR, about whom nothing else is known. Her daughters had temperaments similar to hers: BÉ CHUILLE, evicted from FAIRYLAND for her promiscuity; another wanton woman of whom little legend remains, Bé Téite; and finally FAND, the wild FAIRY who stole away the hero CÚCHULAINN from his admired wife EMER.

Source: Clark, Rosalind. *The Great Queens: Irish Goddesses from the Morrígan to Cathleen Ní Houlihan.* Irish Literary Studies 34. Gerrards Cross: Colin Smythe, 1991, p. 31.

Florence   Arthurian hero. The great knight GAWAIN had several illegitimate sons, including Florence, who was killed when LANCELOT, trapped in queen GUINEVERE's bedroom, fled with sword flying.

foawr   Manx folkloric figures. These GIANTS were said to live at sea and to amuse themselves by throwing boulders at passing sailors. They are occasionally thought to be derived from the mythological Irish race, the FOMORIANS.

Fódla (Fodla, Fodhla, Fóta)   Irish goddess. Three goddesses of the magical race, the TUATHA DÉ DANANN, met the mortal MILESIANS when they staged the final invasion into Ireland recorded in the mythological *BOOK OF INVASIONS*. The goddesses each offered to let the invaders pass if they would name the land for her. The Milesians cavalierly promised they would do so, and so she stepped aside. Fódla met the invaders at Slieve Felim, a mountain in Co. Limerick, or on nearby MAUHER SLIEVE, otherwise dedicated to an obscure goddess named ÉBHLINNE, which may be another name for Fódla.

BANBA met the invaders on her mountain, Slieve Mis; she offered them the same arrangement, and they made the same agreement with her. But it was ÉRIU, goddess of the central mountain of UISNEACH, who was the most impressive and wealthy, and so Ireland (Érinn) is named for her. Some versions of the *Book of Invasions* claim that it was not Ériu who owned Uisneach but Fódla; the three goddesses of the land are sometimes conflated in this fashion. Fódla was married to MAC CÉCHT, a warrior of her tribe. She was killed by EADÁN at the battle of TAILTIU—which marked the victory of the Milesians over the Tuatha dé Danann.

fod seachran   See STRAY SOD.

fogou   Cornish mythological site. Underground stone chambers found in Cornwall, believed to have been built between between 500 B.C.E. and 500 C.E., *fogous* appear to have been places of ritual. As there is evidence of occupation by Celts during the latter part of that period, it is possible that the *fogous* were built by or used by them, although evidence suggests a pre-Celtic spiritual vision. An important clue is the alignment of many of the *fogous* to the summer SOLSTICE sunrise, which betrays a different CALENDAR than that used by the Celts; some have suggested that the stone chambers are late revivals of the MEGALITHIC CIVILIZATION that inspired STONE-HENGE. Legends link the *fogous* with unearthly women, possibly goddesses. The beehive-shaped *fogous* often have secret chambers within them; imaginative reconstructions center on the idea of initiation or other ceremonies being held in the small chambers.

Sources: Bord, Janet, and Colin Bord. *The Secret Country: An interpretation of the folklore of ancient sites in the British Isles.* New York: Walker and Co., 1976, pp. 76, 20; Straffon, Cheryl. *The Earth Goddess: Celtic and Pagan Legacy of the Landscape.* London: Blandford, 1997, pp. 20, 84–85.

Fomorians (Fomoire, Fomhóire, Fomoré) Irish mythological race. Lurking in the background in Ireland's mythological history are monsters, which prey upon the various settlers and wage unrelenting war until they are at last defeated by the magical TUATHA DÉ DANANN. As there is general agreement by scholars that the myths of Ireland's settlement related in the BOOK OF INVASION and other texts are based in ancient history, the question has arisen as to who, then, these demonic beings could be. Certainly it is unlikely that they had but one leg, and one arm coming out of their chests, as early descriptions have it. But there is little evidence to determine who they really were. Earlier interpretations of them as sea monsters or pirates have been discounted as based on false etymology, for the *mor* in their names is not the word for "sea" but for "phantom." More commonly they are now interpreted as the remnant ghosts of ancient divinities whose people, subjugated in early invasions, remained in Ireland and intermingled (and intermarried) with the invaders.

While the earliest narratives do not distinguish one Fomorian from the next, in later mythological texts they are individually portrayed. They seem the peers of the Tuatha Dé Danann, with whom they frequently intermarry; the Tuatha Dé goddess ÉRIU, after whom Ireland is named, took as her husband the Fomorian king ELATHA; their son BRES Mac Elatha became king at TARA for a short time. The gigantic and evil Fomorian King BALOR, too, was related to the Tuatha Dé through his daughter, the fair EITHNE, whose son was the half-breed LUGH. Such alliances were not stable, and the Tuatha Dé finally met the Fomorians in the greatest combat in Irish mythology, the second battle of MAG TUIRED, at which Lugh killed his grandfather Balor and the Fomorians were driven forever from the island and into the sea.

Forgall Manach   Irish hero. He was father to the beautiful EMER, the most accomplished woman in Ireland and therefore the fit wife for the hero CÚCHULAINN; Forgall's main role in the ULSTER CYCLE is to thwart Cúchulainn's desires. Forgall, whose surname means "the wily one," sent the hero away to train with the WARRIOR WOMAN SCÁTHACH on the Isle of Skye, thereby ensuring that his daughter's husband would become the greatest of Irish heroes, as Scáthach ran the world's best martial arts academy.

Fortuna Roman goddess. Not a Celtic goddess, the Roman divinity of fortune is found nonetheless throughout Britain with her rudder, her wheel, and her CORNUCOPIA, all symbols of her power to steer the faithful through life's changes and to offer them abundance. Celtic goddesses of abundance were typically earth deities, but Fortuna was honored more in urban areas; she was, however, associated with a plentiful harvest during her June festival, the Cerealia, celebrated in rural Britain until the 19th century.

Fortunate Isles Mythological site. Various ISLANDS just off the shores of Ireland and Scotland have been called by this name, which refers to the belief that FAIRIES or the gods of the TUATHA DÉ DANANN lived on beautiful floating islands in the western sea.

fosterage Irish social custom. Noble children in ancient Ireland were not reared by their own families but by unrelated people, in a system called fosterage. The practice created bonds between families and territories, so intense that the bond of fosterage was held to be five times stronger than that of blood. The children received training—in druidic arts, in war, in householding—together with their food and lodging, which was provided in accord with the child's family's social status. Children raised in the same household became foster brothers and sisters to each other without being related by blood. Some of the most intense relationships in Irish mythology are those between fosterlings, and unquestionably the most poignant single scene in the many Irish tales is the combat

between the hero CÚCHULAINN and his beloved foster brother FERDIAD, which after three days ended in Ferdiad's death.

Myth suggests that fostering by the mother's brother—the child's uncle—was particularly common. Thus Cúchulainn was fostered in the court of his uncle, king CONCOBAR MAC NESSA. Such reliance upon the maternal uncle suggests that despite emphasis in Irish law on strict limitation of women's rights, the matrilineal line was considered significant (see MATRILINY). The legal relationship between uncle and fosterling was almost as strong as that between parent and child; it was a fosterling's duty to care for his foster parents in their age. The bonds created by such fostering were thus not only emotional but legal and financial.

Fothad Canainne Irish hero. One of three brothers, he was connected with two PROVINCES, the western region of CONNACHT and the eastern one of LEINSTER. Most of his legend has disappeared or been absorbed into that of the warrior hero FIONN MAC CUMHAILL, but he is interpreted as a diminished ancient divinity, possibly a fire god.

Fourknocks Irish mythological site. Among the many relics of the MEGALITHIC CIVILIZATION in the Irish midlands, Fourknocks is outstanding for its size. While most other PASSAGE GRAVES are so small that only a few people can comfortably fit within their inner chambers, the huge mound at Fourknocks could hold several dozen with ease. Lintels engraved with zigzag designs are part of this impressive site's decorations.

four-leafed clover See FAIRY OINTMENT.

fox Symbolic animal. In the Cotswolds, the wily fox was connected with a similarly canny human—the WITCH, who could assume the fox's shape in order to steal BUTTER from her neighbors and otherwise wreak havoc on the region. As foxes are known in farming communities for their nighttime raids on valuable chicken flocks, the connection of evil witch and thieving fox seemed easy to those searching for a target for their anger.

foyson Folkloric motif. Within every substance on earth is its *foyson* or *toradh* ("essence"). The *foyson* of food is its nourishment, and it was this, Irish folklore contends, that the FAIRIES stripped from food when they stole it. The MILK might remain there, creamy in the milk pail, but without its *foyson*, it had no nourishment left. Many rituals and verbal CHARMS existed to protect the *foyson* of foodstuffs from being stolen AWAY by fairies.

Fráech (Fraoch, Fraich, Fróeach) Irish hero. The romantic hero beloved of FINNABAIR, daughter of queen MEDB of CONNACHT, Fráech was the son of the goddess BÉBINN and thus was half-divine. His appearance was entirely divine, for he was the most handsome man in Ireland. His reputation preceded him to Medb's court at CRUACHAN, and Finnabair fell in love with Fráech just from the descriptions of his masculine glories. Her desire was only heightened by his actual presence. Happily, he fell just as much in love with her. Finnabair gave him a little ring, a gift from her father AILILL mac Máta, and suggested that he ask for her hand in marriage.

Whether from greed or because he opposed the match, Ailill set a dowry that Fráech could not meet, demanding that the young man bring the magical red-eared COWS of his goddess-mother to Cruachan. This seemed impossible, so Fráech resigned himself to the loss of Finnabair. But Ailill was not assured that the young man would not elope with his love, so he stole Finnabair's ring from Fráech while the latter was swimming, tossing it into the water, where a SALMON ate it. Then he challenged Fráech to gather the magical healing berries from a ROWAN tree growing on an island; the tree was guarded by a DRAGON that almost killed Fráech, but he defeated the dragon in single combat. Fráech was so badly wounded that it took all the nurses of the OTHERWORLD to bring him back to health, whereupon he returned to earth, caught the ring-swallowing salmon, returned to Cruachan, and demanded Ailill agree to his courtship of Finnabair. This time, he also agreed to bring his magical cows to Ailill, and so an agreement was finally struck.

After happy years with Finnabair, Fráech returned home one day to find her, their children, and his magical cows gone. He traced them to a stone castle in the high Alps, from which an Irish spirit helped him free them. But their reunion was short-lived, for in Ireland Medb was mustering her armies for a CATTLE RAID on ULSTER, which Fráech joined immediately upon their return. Facing the greatest of Irish heroes, CÚCHULAINN, at a ford in the River Dee, Fráech lost his life in combat, and Finnabair died of grief.

This mythological story migrated from Ireland to Scotland, where it lodged in a romantic ballad about the "daughter of Donald" loved by the handsome Fraoch, who swam across Lough Luaim to get her the berries she desired.

Sources: MacCulloch, J. A. *The Religion of the Ancient Celts.* London: Constable, 1911, p. 377; McKay, John G. *More West Highland Tales.* Vol. 2. Scottish Anthropological and Folklore Society. Edinburgh: Oliver and Boyd, 1969, p. 115.

Fraechnat Irish heroine or goddess. One of the women who arrived with the first boatload of invaders into Ireland, according to the place-lore called the *DINDSHENCHAS*, was Fraechnat, who died and was buried on a mountain that bears her name, Slieve Fraech. She does not, however, appear on the list of CESAIR's companions in the *BOOK OF INVASIONS*, so she may have been a local divinity adapted to the tale.

framing spell Scottish magical belief. Crossing two threads, in the way they would be interwoven on a loom, was an occasional spell in Scotland.

Friuch   Irish hero. The swineherd of the supernatural magician BODB DERG had such antagonism toward his competitor RUCHT, swineherd to the farmer OCHALL OCHNE, that whenever he died, he reincarnated in a form that matched Rucht's. Their combat went on lifetime after lifetime, in the air and on the land and in the sea, as they wore various animal and human bodies. Finally they contrived to be reborn as the strongest BULLS in Ireland—Rucht as the white-horned bull FINNBENNAC and Friuch as the brown bull DONN CUAILNGE. The two great bulls of course fell upon each other in combat, each killing the other. The story of their endless cycle of REINCARNATION is part of the background to the great Irish epic, *TÁIN BÓ CUAILNGE*.

frog   Symbolic animal. While it is relatively rare for frogs to be described as magical in Celtic folklore, there is a Scottish tradition of the King Frog, who wore on his head a jewel that had great power for HEALING. The only way to obtain the stone was to locate the King Frog, who hid in a fen or BOG, then let down a tame OTTER into the water in hopes of scaring the frog to the surface. When he appeared, one rapped him on the head, thus dislodging the stone, which had to be grasped quickly lest it disappear beneath the water's surface.

Fuamnach   Irish heroine. This DRUID was the jealous wife of the FAIRY king MIDIR. When Midir sought to replace her with the beautiful ÉTAIN, Fuamnach struck back. With a potion she received from her foster father, she poisoned Étain, who was transmuted into an insect. (Romantic versions of the story call the transformed Étain a butterfly, but others more baldly call her a worm or a fly.) Some versions say that Fuamnach waved a branch of ROWAN, a magical tree, thereby turning Étain into a puddle of water, a worm, and a fly; another wave of the wand created such a wind that the fly was blown clear out of Midir's palace. Fuamnach did not ultimately prevail, however, for Midir sought out Étain after her rebirth as a human once again and, though she was queen of TARA, brought her back to his OTHERWORLD home.

fuath   See *VOUGH*.

Fuinche   See MURNA.

funeral rites   Ritual observance. Not much is known about ancient Celtic funerary rituals, but burial rather than cremation or exposure appears to have been the norm. Stones carved with OGHAM writing are thought to have been erected to mark some graves, although not necessarily for those of lower status. Grave-goods—items deposited in the grave, presumably to accompany the dead to the OTHERWORLD—are found in profusion: chariots, coins, ornaments, weapons. There is some evidence of HUMAN SACRIFICE at the graves of rulers, for skulls are found detached from the rest of the skeleton, pointing to decapitation.

There is both archaeological and textual evidence of a fear that the dead could return to haunt the living, and some funerary rites seem designed to forestall that, including binding the feet of corpses as though to assure they would not wander about. Later customs kept the feet free, apparently to speed the dead on their way to the Otherworld and prevent their hanging about to bother the living.

Source: MacCulloch, J. A. *The Religion of the Ancient Celts*. London: Constable, 1911, pp. 309, 337 ff.

Furbaide Ferbend   Irish hero. This ULSTER warrior, son of CONCHOBAR MAC NESSA, used his sling to kill the great queen MEDB of CONNACHT, his aunt. Furbaide's mother was Medb's sister, CLOTHRA, whom Medb killed at the very place (Lough Ree in the Shannon River) where Furbaide killed her.

furze Symbolic plant. One of the most common BOG plants of Ireland, the thorny furze is crowned with vanilla-scented yellow blossoms for much of the year. It has little value except as tinder, but it was described as feeding many NEED-FIRES and other sacred blazes, presumably because it was so plentiful. Fairy legends say that people under a GLAMOUR or spell will mistake the gold of furze for real metal and stuff their pockets with it before returning home to find a litter of petals. (See also GORSE.)

Fuwch Laethwen Lefrith   See DUN COW.

Fynnodderee Manx folkloric figure. The "hairy one" of the Isle of Man loved human women—so much so that he was evicted from the OTHERWORLD for missing too many FAIRY dances while pursuing non-fairy maidens. He roamed about, neither of this world nor the other, unable to settle down or to cut his long shaggy hair. Despite his loneliness, the fynnodderee was invariably kind to humans and could be as helpful as a BROWNIE.

Source: Keightley, Thomas. *The Fairy Mythology.* London: H. G. Bohn, 1870, p. 402.

Gabhair (Gavra, Gowra)   Irish mythological site. The great legion of warriors known as the FIANNA, followers of the epic hero FIONN MAC CUMHAILL, were almost invariably successful in battle. Even such warriors, however, finally meet their match, and so it was that the Fianna was finally routed at a great battle at Gabhair, said to be a plain near Garristown, Co. Dublin. The Fianna had grown arrogant and troublesome, so the high king CAIRBRE Cinn-Chait decided to end their domination over the land. He was successful, but in doing so lost his life to Fionn's grandson, the warrior OSCAR—who himself was killed in the battle.

Gablach   Irish heroine. The GIANT woman Gablach was wooed by an equally huge man from Spain named Lutur. When Gablach's family met her fiancé, an army surrounded them and demanded battle, for the human hero Fuither had set his sights on winning Gablach's hand. His violent suit came to naught, for Lutur picked up a roofbeam and brained several dozen soldiers, which excited Gablach so that she joined in the fight, killing Fuither in her energetic defense of her betrothed.

Gabriel hounds (Gabriel ratchets, gaze hounds, lyme hounds)   British folkloric figures. In Britain spectral dogs (see BLACK DOG and POOKA) were thought to disguise themselves as migrating waterbirds, especially wild geese, and to fly overhead barking in voices that sounded like birdcalls. When they circled over a house rather than flying straight on, it portended death or other disaster. The antique name "ratchet," meaning a hunting hound, shows that the belief is an old one, probably related to such FAIRY figures as the BANSHEE and other foretellers of doom. The "Gabriel" to whom the hounds belonged is another name for GWYNN AP NUDD, the Welsh king of the OTHERWORLD, and does not refer to the Christian archangel.

Gadelus   See GOIDEL.

Gáe Assail   Irish mythic symbol. Ireland's magical race, the TUATHA DÉ DANANN, had four treasures: an inexhaustible CAULDRON that was owned by the beneficent god DAGDA, the INAUGURATION STONE called the LIA FÁIL that stood on the royal hill of TARA, the sword of the warrior king NUADA that always found its victim, and the Gáe Assail, a spear that returned to the hands of its thrower when it had finished its bloody business. If the thrower yelled the word for "yew" *(ibar)* while launching the spear, the result was certain death for the victim.

Gáe Bulga (Bolga, Bolg) Irish mythic weapon. The famous weapon of the Irish hero CÚCHULAINN was given him by his teacher, the WARRIOR WOMAN of the Isle of Skye, SCÁTHACH. The Gáe Bulga seems to have been a spear or javelin (*gáe*) that could slice through flesh, thus giving its bearer an immense advantage in battle. Cúchulainn used it to kill the two men most dear to him: his son CONNLA and his foster brother FERDIAD. Some scholars have derived the second part of the spear's name from the FIR BOLG, one of the ancient mythic races of Ireland.

Gaheris (Gaheris of Orkney) Arthurian hero. One of the sons of king LOT of Orkney and MORGAUSE, the half-sister of king ARTHUR who also gave birth to Arthur's illegitimate son and implacable enemy, MORDRED. Gaheris was one of those whom LANCELOT killed as he rescued queen GUINEVERE from execution by burning.

Gahmuret Arthurian hero. According to one text, the man who was later to be the father of the pure knight PERCIVAL joined the army of the Caliph of Baghdad, where he single-handedly rescued a besieged queen, Belkane of Zazamanc, from two armies. Entranced with her savior, Belkane married him and bore a son, Feirefiz, but even the glories of her realm could not keep the warrior from returning to Wales, where he found another woman ready to be won through battle: the fair HERZELOYDE, who became Percival's mother.

Gaiar Irish hero. In some texts, this otherwise obscure figure is the son of the doomed lovers DEIRDRE and NOISÍU.

Gaiblín See GAVIDA.

Gáilióin See FIR BOLG.

Gaine Irish heroine. In the place-poems of ancient Ireland, the *DINDSHENCHAS*, this other-wise unknown woman is named as "learned and a seer and a chief DRUID," although how she composed and prophesied is unclear, because she never spoke a word. Yet it was Gaine who named the central hill of the land UISNEACH, "over somewhat," because her student, the powerful druid MIDE, had cut off the tongues of Ireland's other druids, buried them on the hillside, and sat over them.

Source: Gwynn, Edward. *The Metrical Dindshenchas.* Part II. Vol. IX. Royal Irish Academy, Todd Lecture Series. Dublin: Hodges, Figgis, and Co., Ltd., 1906–1924.

Galahad (Gwalchafed) Arthurian hero. One of the chief knights of the ROUND TABLE, Galahad was the illegitimate son of LANCELOT and ELAINE of Corbenic. The young Galahad was king ARTHUR's perfect representative: the most pure, the most loyal, the most chaste of all his knights. As such, he offers a foil to the human and imperfect Arthur as well as to the noble but flawed Lancelot. Thus Galahad, in many Arthurian tales, became the one who found the mystical chalice called the GRAIL, after which the knight was never seen again; apparently, the con-tact of his pure soul with the powerful vessel sent him instantly to heaven. Although his name may have Celtic roots, suggesting a falcon of battle, and despite his FAIRY heritage as the foster son of the LADY OF THE LAKE and the son of Elaine, scholars agree there is no true Celtic analogue for this saintly figure; rather, Galahad seems a post-Christian invention grafted onto the leg-end's pagan rootstock.

Source: Evans-Wentz, W. Y. *The Fairy-Faith in Celtic Countries.* Gerrards Cross: Colin Smythe Humanities Press, 1911, pp. 315 ff.

Galahaut (The Haute Prince) Arthurian hero. A minor figure in the story of king ARTHUR and his knights of the ROUND TABLE, Galahaut was at first Arthur's enemy but, when the brave

LANCELOT defeated him, converted to the side of CAMELOT. So devoted was Galahaut to his erstwhile opponent that he died of grief when he heard that Lancelot had died.

Galatia Ancient Celtic land. This area of central Anatolia (now Turkey), settled by Celts in the third century B.C.E., was mentioned by the Christian St. Paul in his epistles to the residents of the region.

Galehodin Arthurian hero. The most outstanding knight of the ROUND TABLE, LANCELOT, had only one brother, Galehodin, who is otherwise obscure. A number of figures who surround Lancelot have similar names (GALAHAD, GALAHAUT), which may indicate that they derive from the same original.

Galióin (Gailioin, Gálian, Galioin) Irish mythological race. This tribe of Irish settlers of unclear heritage appears in two important mythological texts: the quasi-historical, the *BOOK OF INVASIONS* and the epic *TÁIN BÓ CUAILNGE*. In the former they are described as part of the invading FIR BOLG people; in the latter, their fierceness so intimidates queen MEDB that she considers having them killed rather than risk keeping them as allies, but her lover FERGUS mac Róich convinces her that, separated and spread among the troops, they would be an invaluable asset, as they prove to be. They are thought to represent an early Celtic tribal group.

Gallizenae Breton folkloric figures. These historical DRUID women lived off the west coast of Brittany, on the Isle de Sein (Sena) near Pointe de Raz, at a site usually connected to legends of the dissolute pagan princess DAHUT and her city of YS. They are believed to have been a college of priestesses rather like the one thought to have served the Irish BRIGIT, practicing DIVINATION and other forms of MAGIC without intercourse, social or otherwise, with men.

Galvia Irish mythological figure. The name of the contemporary county of Galway derives from this obscure figure, said to have been a princess drowned in the RIVER that bears her name. As the same story is told of two goddesses, SÍNANN and BÓAND, it is likely that Galvia was once an important goddess of the watershed.

Gamh (Gam) Irish mythological site. In Ireland's Co. Sligo, a holy WELL was known in medieval times as one of the Mirabilia Hiberia, Ireland's wonders. On the side of the hill of Tullaghan, opposite a sheer precipice, a half-salt, half-sweet well rises from a space among THREE flagstones. The well is now dedicated to ST. PATRICK, and the story is told that it sprang up when the saint, pursuing the demon called variously the DEVIL'S MOTHER and CAORANACH, became thirsty and prayed for water, whereupon the well broke through the rock. Patrick then hid nearby until the demon, also thirsty, came to drink; her blood caused the well's bitterness. The well's pagan history can still be found in the common tale that it harbors sacred SALMON, which, if caught and eaten, will nonetheless be seen frisking about the well the very next day.

The *DINDSHENCHAS*, Ireland's place-name poetry, name the region around the well Sliab Gamh, the mountains of Gamh, after a servant of the MILESIAN invader ÉREMÓN. Gamh was beheaded, but whether in battle or as punishment for some wrongdoing is not clear; the corrupted text seems to indicate that Gamh was killed because of failure to observe agricultural rituals. His head, thrown into the well, caused its sweet water to turn salty part of each day.

Sources: Gwynn, Edward. *The Metrical Dindshenchas*. Part II. Vol. IX. Royal Irish Academy, Todd Lecture Series. Dublin: Hodges, Figgis, and Co., Ltd., 1906–1924, p. 22; MacNeill, Máire. *The Festival of Lughnasa, Parts I and II*. Dublin: Comhairle Bhéaloideas Éireann, 1982, pp. 113–114.

ganconer (gean-cannah, gan-ceann, gean-canach, love-talker)   Scottish and Irish folkloric figure. Maidens in Scotland were traditionally advised to stay away from lonely country roads, especially those in mountain areas, for they might meet this handsome fairy—readily recognizable by his clay pipe—who would make them promises so sweet that, after he evaporated from sight, the girl was left to pine away and die. The *ganconer* was the male version of the much more commonly found FAIRY LOVER or mistress.

The same figure was found in Ireland, where he was called the *geancanach* and was said to especially favor milkmaids. The Irish poet Ethna Carbery wrote of him: "Who meets the Love-Talker must weave her shroud soon," for his love was destructive. The word used to be applied to human men who were excessively boastful about their sexual prowess.

Ganore   Occasional name for GUINEVERE.

Garaid   Irish hero. In the FENIAN CYCLE, we learn of this old warrior who the women of FIONN MAC CUMHAILL's court feared might make advances to them; therefore they tied his beard and hair to the walls of their home while he slept. Awaking with a start, Garaid tore off his scalp trying to free himself and then exploded with fury, burning the house—at Drumcree, near Mullingar—with all the women in it and laughing sadistically as they died.

Garb Mac Stairn   Scottish folkloric figure. This Scottish GIANT appears in a legend of the Irish hero CÚCHULAINN. Desirous of a BULL that the hero owned, Garb traveled to Ireland but, reaching Cúchulainn's house, found only a servant who claimed the house was empty except for his sick mistress. Nonetheless Garb demanded access to the house's owner and pushed his way into the sickroom. There he found the woman, lying wanly, suckling a large babe. The giant poked his finger into the baby's

mouth and Cúchulainn—for the large baby was he—bit down so hard he struck bone. Garb and Cúchulainn then began to fight to the death, and it took a week for the superhuman hero to win against the fierce Scottish giant. A similar story is told of FINN MCCOOL, the folkloric version of the hero FIONN MAC CUMHAILL.

Gareth (Gareth of Orkney, Beaumains, Gaheriet)   Arthurian hero. A minor hero of Arthurian romance, he was the nephew of king ARTHUR, son of his half-sister MORGAUSE and king LOT of Orkney. Because of his most notable physical trait, KAY named him Beaumains, "beautiful hands." Gareth was accidentally killed by his best friend LANCELOT, who was desperately struggling to save queen GUINEVERE from the executioner's flames.

Gargantua   Continental Celtic god. The great French satirist Rabelais based the most famous GIANT in French literature upon this obscure old Celtic god, perhaps originally named Gurgiunt or Gargam. A resident of the OTHERWORLD, he burst through occasionally to create landscapes by tossing around rocks or opening a cask so that floodwaters covered the earth.

Garland Sunday (Garden Sunday, Garlic Sunday)   See LUGHNASA.

Garravogue (Carravogue, Garbhóg, Ghearagáin, Garrawog, Garragh-Maw)   Irish folkloric figure. Two similarly named HAG-like beings appear in Irish oral folklore, both of whom may descend from the ancient goddess called the CAILLEACH. In Co. Sligo, the River Garravogue was said to be named for a WITCH who fell into it and drowned; the same story is told of the maiden GILE, whose drowning formed Lough Gill, so the two may have originally been the same figure in maiden and hag form.

In Co. Meath, and nearby Co. Cavan, the woman Garrawog broke the Sabbath by eating blackberries on the way to church, was turned into a giant SERPENT or cannibal, and dissolved when ST. PATRICK threw holy water at her. In other versions of the tale, Patrick threw his apostolic staff at her, whereupon she split into four pieces, one going up into the air, two off to the sides into LAKES, and the final piece disappearing underground beneath a large rock.

The fact that the hag split into pieces that travel to the four DIRECTIONS argues that Garravogue was an ancient goddess figure suppressed by Christian apologists, for cosmic goddesses whose bodies form the tangible world are often described in myth in this way. That the hag goddess was not entirely suppressed under Christianity is evidenced by the legend that Garrawog will rise again when enough people bearing her surname (Gargan or Garraghans) walk over her grave. A carved head in nearby Clannaphillip, once in the church but now installed behind the grotto of the Virgin Mary, is said to represent Garrawog.

Sources: Gwynn, Edward. *The Metrical Dindshenchas.* Part II. Vol. IX. Royal Irish Academy, Todd Lecture Series. Dublin: Hodges, Figgis, and Co., Ltd., 1906, p. 18; MacNeill, Máire. *The Festival of Lughnasa, Parts I and II.* Dublin: Comhairle Bhéaloideas Éireann, 1982, pp. 400–401, 517–522.

Gaul Ancient Celtic land. The Celtic lands now generally contiguous with the nation of France, as well as adjoining lands now part of the nations Belgium, Germany, and Switzerland, were brought under Roman domination by Julius Caesar, who wrote of them in his *Gallic Wars.* It is from Caesar that we learn much of what is known about the culture and religion of the continental Celts. But as Caesar sought political domination over the Celts, it is difficult to evaluate his truthfulness. What we do know is that the people Caesar called Gauls were not a single tribe but many disparate tribal peoples who shared a common language and roughly common beliefs and customs.

As with other Celtic peoples, the Gauls are believed to have mixed and mingled with the people who inhabited their lands before them, probably Old Europeans. They later moved on to the islands off the coast, so that Britain and Ireland received a culture already changed by encounters with the indigenous peoples of Gaul. In addition, the Germanic tribes slightly to the north are not easily separable geographically from the Celts of Gaul, so that religion and culture on the Continent were both complex and dynamic. Much of that richness has been lost through the reinterpretation of continental Celtic or Gaulish divinities into Roman categories and the application of Roman names to them in a process known as the INTERPRETATIO ROMANA. Thus we have MERCURY listed as the chief of gods and MINERVA following shortly after. In some cases, the original Celtic name of the divinity in question became a surname, but in many others, the original was lost.

Gavida (Gaiblín, Gaibhleen, Goibhleann) Irish hero. Brother of CIAN and uncle of the hero LUGH, Gavida fostered his nephew until he was old enough to meet his fate as the killer of his monstrous grandfather BALOR of the Evil Eye. Sometimes this figure is said to be identical to the SMITH god GOIBNIU.

Gavrinis (Gavr'inis) Breton mythological site. In the center of a small harbor off the coast of Morbihan in southern Brittany is an island upon which the fabulously engraved ritual chamber of Gavrinis is found. Far predating the Celts, the CAVE is linked by its SPIRAL iconography—deeply incised carvings decorating more than a score of enormous granite uprights—to Ireland's BRÚ NA BÓINNE and by its megalithic rock architecture to Britain's STONEHENGE. Although it is not possible to know for what purpose they were intended, such monuments are typically oriented toward some astronomical point; in the case of Gavrinis, the winter SOLSTICE sunrise, toward which it is oriented precisely.

Some have theorized that the rising SUN, as it begins its rebirth toward summer on that day, may have been thought to revivify the bones placed within, of which traces have been found.

Like other monuments of the MEGALITHIC CIVILIZATION, Gavrinis was probably known by the local Celtic peoples and may have been a ritual site for them, some 3,000 years after it was built. Other Breton megalithic sites appear in folklore as the place of OTHERWORLD happenings, so as was the case in Ireland, superstitious local lore may have protected such monuments long after their meaning was forgotten.

Source: Evans-Wentz, W. Y. *The Fairy-Faith in Celtic Countries.* Gerrards Cross: Colin Smythe Humanities Press, 1911, pp. 409 ff.

Gawain (Gawain of Orkney, Gawayne, Gavin, Gauvain, Gwalchmei)   Arthurian hero. Gawain is one of the best known of the knights of the ROUND TABLE who served the great king ARTHUR. He was Arthur's nephew, son of his half-sister MORGAUSE and king LOT of Orkney, and was one of Arthur's first supporters.

Hero of a famous early English romance, *Sir Gawain and the Green Knight* (c. 1370 C.E.) by "the Pearl Poet," which like other Arthurian literature draws heavily on Celtic themes, Gawain was challenged by a monstrous Green Knight. The hero fought fiercely and beheaded the stranger, but the Green Knight returned for the combat exactly one year later. Meanwhile, the wife of his host Bercilak had attempted three times to seduce the chaste Gawain, with no success save that she left her girdle with him. Inexplicably, instead of returning the incriminating piece of underwear, Gawain hid it.

When the beheaded and reheaded giant Green Knight reappeared, he struck three times at Gawain, the third one a crippling wound as retaliation for hiding the girdle. Several Celtic themes are found in the romance, especially beheading (see HEAD) and triplicity (see THREE). Some scholars have interpreted Gawain as a late

version of the Celtic SMITH god GOIBNIU, the Green Knight may be a literary counterpart to the British folkloric figure, the GREENMAN.

Gawain is also known from the tale of RAGNELL, a woman who had been bewitched so that she appeared ominously ugly. Beneath that terrifying exterior, however, Ragnell was a pure spirit who gained Gawain's love. Upon their marriage, she confided her secret to him, telling him that she could only appear as a young maiden for part of each day. Did he prefer, she asked, that she be a beautiful woman in the daytime, when his friends could admire her, or at night, when he could enjoy her charms? Gawain wisely offered the choice back to her, whereupon she revealed the solution to the riddle, "What do women want?," which he had been charged with answering. Women, she told him, want to be given the chance to choose their own life. The spell that held her captive was then broken, she became a beautiful young woman again, and Ragnell and Gawain lived happily together thereafter.

Source: Turner, R. C. "Boggarts, Bogles and Sir Gawain and the Green Knight: Lindow Man and the Oral Tradition." In Stead, I. M., J. B. Bourke, and Don Brothwell. *The Lindow Man: The Body in the Bog.* Ithaca, N.Y.: Cornell University Press, 1986, pp. 170–176.

Geali Dianvir   Irish hero. He was the eldest son of the king of the FIR BOLG, Irish invaders who may be mythological memories of early Celtic arrivals; his people were defeated by BALOR, king of the evil FOMORIANS, who similarly may reflect historical indigenous peoples. After the battle, the defeated Fir Bolg sailed away from Ireland, returning to the mysterious land of Gallowna, where they attempted to recoup their strength.

From Gallowna, Geali Dianvir was sent back to repair the damage to his people's reputation that Balor had dealt. When he arrived in Bantry, in western Co. Cork in the southwestern PROVINCE of MUNSTER, Geali Dianvir found the

Formorian queen surrounded by Balor's men, who every night applied venom to their swords so that they were unbeatable in battle. The venom was obtained from a WELL into which the warriors plunged their weapons; the Fir Bolg hero decided to eliminate their advantage by turning it from poison to clear water. To do this, he poured 20 measures of the MILK of the magical COW of abundance, the GLAS GHAIBHLEANN, into the well. The Fir Bolg hero was then able to gain the advantage over Balor's men and drive them to the outer reaches of the land.

Source: Curtin, Jeremiah. *Hero-Tales of Ireland.* New York: Benjamin Blom, 1894, p. 298.

Gebann   Irish god. This obscure god is known only as the father of the beautiful goddess CLÍDNA and as the chief DRUID of the sea god, MANANNÁN MAC LIR.

Gebrinius   Continental Celtic god. Identified by the Romans with their warrior divinity MARS, this god appears in several inscriptions in lands inhabited both by Celts and by Germans, so it is unclear which culture gave rise to him.

geis (*geas, geiss, ges;* pl., *geasa, gessa*)   Irish ritual vow. Magical vows or pledges were often required of kings and other heroes in Irish literature, apparently reflecting a real religious custom. In some cases, the reason for the geis is given, as when the king of TARA, CONAIRE, is instructed not to eat the flesh of birds, because his mother had been enchanted into that form at one point, making him kin to the birds. But more often the *geasa* seem frivolous, as with Conaire's vow not to ride around Tara with his right shoulder to the sea, nor to let THREE RED horsemen ride past him to the hostel of a red man, nor to be away from Tara more than eight consecutive nights.

Sometimes geasa are extraordinarily complicated, even exaggerated, as with DIARMAIT's vow never to refuse a woman who came to him neither in the day nor at night, neither on horseback nor on foot, neither clothed nor naked. Comic as they may seem, the *geasa* were deeply serious, so much so that breaking such a vow meant death. Geasa were not chosen by the man making the vow—for it was invariably a man—but were imposed by DRUIDS or by women, the latter often substituting for the goddess of SOVEREIGNTY.

Kings were especially subject to sacred geasa, which provided a mechanism to evaluate their integrity (see KINGSHIP). The land's FERTILITY depended upon the king's righteousness; thus a king who broke his geasa as Conaire did caused privation when the land became sterile. Heroes too were pledged to avoid taboo places, people, and foods, or to satisfy certain peculiar demands, their strength and even continued life depending upon their performance. *Geasa* are wound into the plot of many ancient Celtic legends and romances.

Sources: Dillon, Myles. *There Was a King in Ireland: Five Tales from Oral Tradition.* Texas Folklore Society. Austin: University of Texas Press, 1971, p. 21; Joyce, P. W. *Ancient Celtic Romances.* London: Parkgate Books, 1997, pp. 433–434.

Gelorwydd   Welsh hero. This obscure figure is named in some texts as a warrior who bathed the dying on battlefields with his own blood, bringing them great peace.

generosity   Cosmological concept. An ancient Celtic king faced many requirements or sacred vows (see GEIS), but the most important was generosity. An ungenerous king, such as the half-FOMORIAN BRES turned out to be, would be driven from his throne by SATIRES and might even die miserably in punishment for his greed and stinginess. The traditional expectation of royal generosity was translated in Celtic lands into a general requirement of hospitality, especially to strangers. In post-Celtic times, belief that the FAIRIES would punish the ungenerous kept alive the priority given to this value.

genius cucullatus (pl., *genii cucullati*) Continental and British Celtic god(s). Named for a
hood (in Latin, *cucullus*) attached to a cloak,
these "hooded spirits" are found across Celtic
lands on the Continent and in Britain; in the
former, they appear singularly, while in Britain
the *cucullati* are invariably triplets. Although
their exact function and meaning is not established, their form suggests that they were spirits
of FERTILITY, for they look like a group of small
phalluses; in some sculptures, indeed, removing
the hood reveals not the head of a man but that
of a phallus.

In Britain the *genii cucullati* were depicted as
DWARFS holding EGGS, further emphasizing their
connection to fertility. The distribution pattern
of these sculptures is identical to that of the
mother goddesses called the DEAE MATRES, with
whom they often appear; sometimes the goddess
they accompany is named CUDA.

genius loci (pl., *genii locii*) Continental Celtic
and British god(s). This Latin phrase, meaning
"spirit of the place," refers to the divinities that
embody and are embodied within special
natural places: mountains, WELLS, waterfalls,
even prominent glacial boulders. The Celts saw
NATURE as filled with divinity, each god or
goddess being connected with a specific site; for
this reason, few divine names are found in the
Celtic world more than once. RIVERS and MOUN-
TAINS tended to be seen as goddesses; ancient
TREES and some watercourses as gods.

Such place-deities had multiple functions,
guiding FERTILITY, prosperity, and death within
their region. With Roman settlement, names of
the invading gods were affixed to the native
ones—or, in some cases, the now-unnamed
native divinity was subsumed into the Roman
god (see INTERPRETATIO ROMANA). APOLLO and
MINERVA and MERCURY stood in for dozens, even
hundreds, of specific place-identified Celtic
nature gods and goddesses. Because altars to
unnamed deities of place were simply carved with
"*genius loci*," many specific names have been lost.

Such altars typically bore emblems of abundance
and fertility like the CORNUCOPIA, the turret
crown, and the *PATERA* or offering plate.

Sources: Green, Miranda. *Symbol and Image in
Celtic Religious Art.* London: Routledge, 1989,
p. 99; Ross, Anne. *Pagan Celtic Britain: Studies
in Iconography and Tradition.* London: Routledge
& Kegan Paul, 1967, p. 30.

Gentle Annie (Gentle Annis) Scottish folkloric figure. A supernatural HAG with blue-black
skin, Gentle Annie was the weather spirit who
brought raw winds down Cromarthy Firth in
Scotland. Her name, which is clearly a flattering
and mollifying one, has been connected to the
ancient goddess name ANU; her appearance and
personality resemble the CAILLEACH.

gentry See FAIRY.

Geodruisge Irish folkloric figure. This GIANT
from Co. Mayo had his palace on Downpatrick
Head, locally called Dún Geodruisge. He stole
CATTLE from a powerful WITCH who cursed him,
so that his palace broke off from the mainland,
sending the thieving giant out to sea.

George See ST. GEORGE.

Gereint (Keraint, Gereint fab Erbin) Welsh
hero. With his wife ENID, this Welsh hero is
described as presenting the perfect model of the
loving couple. Yet their legend is convoluted at
best and their relationship hardly seems ideal.
Described as cousin to king ARTHUR, Gereint
won Enid's hand through service to her kingly
father. After their marriage, he devoted himself
to leisurely pursuits with her, neglecting his
kingdom until both his subjects and Enid herself
began to complain. Rather than listening to the
criticism, Gereint punished Enid cruelly for
repeating comments about his unworthiness to

rule, even suspecting that her actions were an indication that she had been unfaithful.

Gereint then set out to prove the rumors wrong, almost dying in an attempt to prove his manly strength. He dragged Enid along, demanding that she remain completely silent. She did not, for she kept seeing disasters on the horizon; he ignored her, causing himself great trouble. Finally, however, they came to the castle of OWEIN. There, ignoring not only Enid's warnings but those of his host, he attempted to win at an enchanted game, held in a court surrounded by severed HEADS. Approaching a maiden sitting within the court, Gereint was assaulted by her protector, a fierce knight. In the ensuing fight, Gereint proved himself, killing the knight and ending the violent games forever. Thereafter, he reconciled with his loyal wife Enid.

Geróid Iarla (Gerald, Earl of Desmond; the Red Earl)   Irish hero. When Maurice, the Earl of Desmond in southwestern MUNSTER, saw the beautiful fairy queen ÁINE swimming in the form of a SWAN at the mouth of the River Comóg that flows into enchanted LOUGH GUR, he fell hopelessly in love with her. The only way to claim such a SWAN MAIDEN was to steal her cloak, which Maurice did. Thus did Áine come to live with him and to bear their child, the next earl, Geróid.

Maintaining a relationship with a FAIRY BRIDE, however, meant living with the prohibitions and taboos she set down. Áine required that Maurice never show surprise at anything their son might do, but the earl forgot himself when, at a banquet, Geróid leaped into a bottle and out again. The boy and his mother immediately disappeared into the LAKE—or perhaps Geróid transformed himself into the GOOSE that swam by at that moment. Every seven years on a moonlit night, Geróid rides forth from Lough Gur on a white HORSE.

Source: Evans-Wentz, W. Y. *The Fairy-Faith in Celtic Countries.* Gerrards Cross: Colin Smythe Humanities Press, 1911, p. 79.

ghost   Folkloric figure. Because the OTHERWORLD and the land of the dead blend together in the Celtic mind, it is difficult to distinguish the ghosts of dead humans from those diminished divinities called the FAIRIES. Often the two groups of beings were described as frequenting the same magical parts of the landscape (BOGS, LAKES, and ISLANDS); they had roughly the same habits of life; and ghosts, like fairies, could take humans away with them to the Otherworld.

Not all people became ghosts, but only those who suffered an interruption of the normal course of life, such as a young mother who died in childbirth and was concerned for the safety of her child; such an unsettled soul could come back to haunt house and family. Elders who died after a full life sometimes returned as well, however, taking a pipe by the fireside and otherwise keeping up the activities of a long settled life; this seems to be stirred more by habit than by desire to affect the lives of the living.

Those who died violent deaths could sometimes be seen haunting the location of their demise, as was the case when a headless ghost appeared in a small west Mayo town; such ghosts could be sent away with holy water or blessed candles. Ghosts appeared not only singly but en masse, as when the entire crew of a ship that went down at sea appeared just before another storm to warn their erstwhile fellows. Such gentle ghosts were the exception; more commonly, ghosts attempted to lure the living into the grave with them.

Sources: Jones, T. Gwynn. *Welsh Folklore and Folk-Custom.* London: Methuen & Co., Ltd., 1930, pp. 32–50; Ó Catháin, Séamus, and Patrick O'Flanagan. *The Living Landscape: Kilgallian, Erris, County Mayo.* Dublin: Comhairle Bhéaloideas Éireann, 1975, pp. 102, 119.

Gialla Deacair (Gilla Dacker)   See ABARTA.

giant (giantess)   Folkloric figure. The fact that huge rocks, bigger than anything that could be readily moved by humans, were deposited across the islands of Ireland and Britain by retreating glaciers meant that the landscape suggested huge beings powerful enough to build the other landscape features. Common tales tell of gigantic women who drop boulders from their aprons and of feuding giants who throw the boulders at each other.

Giant figures of men and animals are found carved into the chalk hills of southern England; sites like the LONG MAN of Wilmington and the CERNE ABBAS GIANT in Dorset that show large male figures are locally said to be the outlines drawn around giants killed on the hillsides. The date of origin of these figures is unknown, so it is difficult to say whether this represents a survival of a Celtic belief. Other English folklore similarly refers to giants who had to be slain in order to make the countryside safe for settlement; the hero Tom Hickathrift of the Norfolk marshes was said to have killed the Giant of Smeeth. Although most giants were threatening to humans, some of the race had positive qualities; Jack o' Legs from Herefordshire was a ROBIN HOOD character who redistributed the wealth of the local rich to the area's poor.

In Scotland the Great Cave (or Cave of Raitts) in Inverness was said to have been built by a giantess who carved the 70-foot cavern from the hillside while her companion giants quarried the stone used to prop up the cave's sides. Such landscape-forming legends are frequent in Scotland, where we find the story of giants who sought to marry the daughters of a human knight; the girls were saved by men who fought with a giant HAG who had the power to turn them to stone. Her curses could be lifted and the petrified returned to life, however, with the water from a WELL on the Island of the Big Women, a mythical land that appears in many Scottish folktales, apparently a specifically giant-occupied part of the OTHERWORLD.

In Wales we find the giantess Mol Walbee, who found a pebble in her shoe and tossed it to the ground, where it still stands as a huge boulder in a churchyard. She seems to be a form of the pre-Celtic CAILLEACH, credited throughout the islands as the creator of landscapes. A woman of gigantic proportions, the Cailleach formed mountains whenever she let slip pebbles from her apron. Not all earth-forming giants were female, however; in Cornwall there are stories of hurling matches between groups of male giants, their thrown pebbles forming mountains. In Ireland too we find the GIANT'S CAUSEWAY, a monumental series of basalt slabs that form what seem to be steps out to sea, said to be the creation of giant carvers.

The connection of giants with the formation of the landscape, as well as texts that describe them as resident before human occupation in various Celtic lands, suggests that they are recollections of ancient divinities displaced by later invaders or immigrants. Similarly, the naming of prominent hills for such non-Celtic divinities as the Cailleach suggests that she and her giant kin were honored by pre-Celtic people whose religious visions were accommodated and absorbed by the Celts.

Invaders often describe the divinities of the conquered as monstrous, and giants like the FOMORIANS of Ireland were said to occupy lands desired by historical people, who had to eliminate them in order to gain access to the land's wealth. In his *History of the Kings of Britain*, Geoffrey of Monmouth said that the first king of Britain (then called Albion), Brutus, arrived to find only a few inhabitants, all of them giants, including the monstrous GOG, who was defeated by the heroic wrestler Corineus; an image of the battle can still be seen in London's Guildhall, where the figures are inaccurately named Gog and Magog.

The most famous literary vestige of this Celtic folkloric tradition is Jonathan Swift's *Gulliver's Travels*, in which the eponymous hero finds himself variously a giant among tiny people and a mite among giants.

Sources: Briggs, Katherine M., and Ruth L. Tongue. *Folktales of Britain.* London: Routledge & Kegan Paul, 1965, pp. 68 ff; Campbell, J. F.

Popular Tales of the West Highlands. Vol. III. Edinburgh: Edmonston and Douglas, 1862, pp. 1 ff; Curran, Bob. *Complete Guide to Celtic Mythology.* Belfast: Appletree, 2000, pp. 94 ff; Dillon, Myles. *There Was a King in Ireland: Five Tales from Oral Tradition.* Texas Folklore Society. Austin: University of Texas Press, 1971, p. 39; Grinsell, Leslie V. *Folklore of Prehistoric Sites in Britain.* London: David & Charles, 1976, p. 27; MacKenzie, Donald A. *Scottish Folk-Lore and Folk Life: Studies in Race, Culture and Tradition.* Glasgow: Blackie & Sons, Ltd., 1935, pp. 99–117; McKay, John G. *More West Highland Tales.* Vol. 2. Scottish Anthropological and Folklore Society. Edinburgh: Oliver and Boyd, 1969, p. 28; Spence, Lewis. *The Minor Traditions of British Mythology.* New York: Benjamin Blom, Inc., 1972, p. 71.

Giant's Causeway Irish mythological site. One of the great natural wonders of the PROVINCE of ULSTER is a strangely shaped mass of basalt rocks near Portrush, Co. Coleraine. Folklore claims that FINN MCCOOL, the diminished version of the great mythological hero FIONN MAC CUMHAILL, killed the Scottish GIANT who built the step-shaped rocks as a first step in his invasion of Ireland.

Giants' Dance British mythological site. This name is given to STONEHENGE in the geographical commentary of Geoffrey of Monmouth in 1136 C.E. According to many legends, STONE CIRCLES were formed when WITCHES or other supernatural creatures danced on a Christian holiday (often Sunday) and were turned to stone for such frivolity; the enormity of the trilithons of Stonehenge may have given rise to the idea that the petrified beings were giants.

Sources: Grinsell, Leslie V. *Folklore of Prehistoric Sites in Britain.* London: David & Charles, 1976, p. 28; Spence, Lewis. *The Minor Traditions of British Mythology.* New York: Benjamin Blom, Inc., 1972, p. 84.

Gile (Gilla) Irish heroine or goddess. The LAKE beside the small and picturesque western Irish city of Sligo, Lough Gill, is named for this princess or diminished goddess, daughter of an otherwise unknown father named Romra. Gile was bathing in the waters of a spring when Omra, apparently her lover, approached. Unable to bear his looking upon her nakedness, Gile ducked her head under the water and accidentally drowned.

Her foster mother, finding the girl's body, began to weep so vigorously that the spring and her tears joined to form the "vast and stormy lake," as the place-name poetry, the DINDSHENCHAS, describes Lough Gill. Romra and Omra then fell into battle, each killing the other; burial CAIRNS are said to have been erected over them, although the text is unclear as to whether those are the renowned ones atop nearby Carns Hill. Given that the names of father and lover differ only by one letter, they may be connected figures or TWINS. Like much of Ireland's place-name poetry, the story of Lough Gill seems a fragmentary myth dislodged from its explanatory context.

Source: Gwynn, Edward. *The Metrical Dindshenchas.* Royal Irish Academy, Todd Lecture Series. Dublin: Hodges, Figgis, and Co., Ltd., 1906–1924, p. 18.

Gilfaethwy (Gilvaethwy) Welsh hero. Violent brother of the Welsh poet-hero GWYDION and son of the mother goddess DÔN, Gilfaethwy conceived a lust for the virgin GOEWIN who served his uncle, king MATH, as ceremonial footholder. According to the Welsh compilation of mythology, the MABINOGION, Goewin did not respond to Gilfaethwy's desire. Refusing to attend to her refusal, he assaulted and raped Goewin. In punishment Gilfaethwy was turned into a DEER, PIG, and WOLF, consecutively.

Gillagréine (Giolla Gréine) Irish goddess or heroine. Although relatively obscure, this ancient figure has left her name across the landscape of east Co. Clare in Ireland. In despair at learning that, although her father was human, her mother was a sunbeam, Gillagréine leaped into the water of Lough Gréine or Lough Graney ("lake of the sun"), floated down to Daire Gréine ("sun's oak grove"), and finally came to rest at Tuam Gréine or Tuamgraney ("the sun's tomb"). She may have been an early SUN goddess of the region.

Gille Dubh (Ghillie Dhu) Scottish folkloric figure. In relatively recent times—at the end of the 18th century—this FAIRY man appeared in the region around Loch a Druing in the Scottish Highlands. A rather seedy-looking person, he wore nothing but moss and leaves, and his unkempt black hair fell about him like a cloak. He was a silent, kindly sort, ready to rescue the lost and care for those in need. Nonetheless he was made the object of sport by some local lairds, who decided to use the poor fairy for target practice. He made himself scarce; a full night's hunting did not scare him up, nor was he ever seen afterward.

Gillian (Jillian) British folkloric figure and site. In England, mazes called Gillian Bowers were cut into turf. In springtime the young men ran races through these turf mazes, while a woman impersonating the otherwise unknown folkloric figure Gillian was "imprisoned" at the center of the maze and "freed" by the race's winner. Such mazes are also found in Scandinavian countries, where they go by the unexplained name of Troy Towns. A ritual of freeing the SUN maiden from her winter captivity seems implied by the game. A goddess named Gillian, perhaps ruling the springtime, may have given her name to these sites.

Source: Monaghan, Patricia. *O Mother Sun: A New View of the Cosmic Feminine.* Freedom, Calif.: The Crossing Press, 1994, pp. 108–110.

Giona (Giona mac Lugha) Irish hero. Despite being a grandson of the great hero FIONN MAC CUMHAILL, Giona was a lazy fellow and could not control his warriors, who found him an uninspiring leader. Fionn took the young man under his tutelage and formed him into a great hero of the FIANNA.

glám dícenn Irish ritual posture. When a BARD or a DRUID wanted to cast a truly effective CURSE in ancient Ireland, he or she would assume a particular position: standing on one leg, holding out one arm, and closing one eye. This fearsome position intensified the power of the verbal curse so that its power was impossible to avoid. The HAG who destroyed king CONAIRE, in the story of DA DERGA's hostel, assumed the *glám dícenn* before she cursed him for breaking his sacred vows (see GEIS).

glamour Folkloric motif. A glamour is a spell, cast by a FAIRY or a WITCH (occasionally, a gypsy), that caused humans to imagine things that are not there and to see things as they are not. Originally a Scottish word, the word passed into international usage stripped of its magical meaning and now indicates only fascinating personal attractiveness. In the past, glamour was never sought after but was rather to be avoided or broken—the latter by using FAIRY OINTMENT or holding up to one's eyes a bit of four-leafed clover or SHAMROCK (which may have been the main ingredient in fairy ointment). The clover's power would permit the viewer to see reality rather than fairy fantasy; thus a visitor to FAIRYLAND would see a miserable CAVE rather than a gorgeous ballroom, and the people there would be old and wizened rather than firm and young.

Glanlua Irish heroine. A minor figure in one of the tales of the heroic FIANNA, this woman assisted their leader FIONN MAC CUMHAILL in escaping from the imprisonment of a GIANT named DRYANTORE.

See AILNA.

Glas Ghaibhleann (Glas Ghaibhnann, Glas Gavlen, Glas Gownach, Glas Gainach, Glas Gaunach; Fuwch Leathwen Lefrith) Irish mythological figure. Irish folklore and mythology tells of a great COW whose MILK was so plentiful that it could feed multitudes; because of the 100% cream content, its milk made copious BUTTER as well. The cow was so strong that she could wander through three of Ireland's four PROVINCES in a single day; thus place-names across the land (usually beginning with Glas, as in Glasnevin, although also occurring in such forms as Knockglas, "mountain of the Glas") bear testimony to her passage. (Her name became a common noun for SPRING or stream, so at times it is difficult to distinguish the original intent of such place-names.) As she traveled, she gave milk to anyone who needed it, filling whatever vessel they carried, no matter how large or small. It is possible that the Glas is an ancient image of the Irish land itself, for Ireland is occasionally called Druimin Donn Dilis, "the faithful brown white-backed cow."

The Glas did not have to have a calf in order to give milk. Indeed, as much as five years could pass without the cow calving, yet her milk flowed unceasingly. Some stories say that she was a FAIRY beast, belonging to the king of the Land Under Wave or the OTHERWORLD; other stories suggest she was the goddess BÓ FIND, who took the form of a white cow.

Usually the cow was said to be guarded by a SMITH named Gaivnin Gow, Gavidin, or simply Gavin; in Ireland, the smith was said to live among the rolling hills of Co. Cavan. The smith kept the Glas's halter, to which she came unfailingly every night; some legends say that the Glas was the smith's enchanted sister or stepsister. In Ireland place-names associated with the cow are often found near sites named for the smith. Some versions of the story name the smith god GOIBNIU as the owner of the Glas.

Many legends center on plots set in motion by greedy people who wished to steal the Glas for their exclusive enrichment, but she invariably escaped or was freed, bringing her abundance back to the people. In one story the Glas was confined by a man within Glen Columkille in Co. Donegal, but she levitated into the air and, clearing the high ridges around the glen, disappeared into the sky. Since that time, legend claims, there has been no free milk in Ireland.

Other legends claim that a wicked woman tried to milk the Glas into a sieve and, angered, the cow disappeared from earth. Another tale, from the rocky region called the Burren, says that someone tried to milk the Glas into a swallow-hole called Poll na Leamhnachta ("hole of sweet milk"), but when even the Glas's immeasurable milk could not fill the endless cavity, the exhausted cow disappeared, and she has never again been seen on the Burren, previously her favorite pasturage.

The Glas appears in Britain, Scotland, and Wales under the name of the DUN COW, whose mythological background is made clear in descriptions of her impossible abundance. As in Ireland, the British Dun Cow was killed by greed: A WITCH tried to milk her into a mesh, killing the miraculous beast; a whale rib in Kirkham, Lancashire, was long said to have been one of the Dun Cow's bones. In Wales the cow was called Fuwch Leathwen Lefrith; she wandered the country, generously giving forth milk until she reached a valley, Towry, where the residents saw her as potential steak-and-kidney pie. Before they could slaughter her, she disappeared, taking all her abundance with her.

The cosmological and cosmic significance of this magical cow is reinforced by scholars who trace the motif to the Indo-European mythologies of India, where we find cloud cows who rain milk down upon earth and who, according to the *Rig Veda*, were stolen by the demon Vritra, who wished to bring drought and famine to earth. This connection of the cow not only with milk but with water is found in the figure of the river- and cow-goddess BÓAND, after whom the River Boyne is named. The connection between cow and river is further reinforced by descriptions of the cow's meandering course across the land, never traveling less than six miles a day.

The Glas figures prominently in the story of the magical conception of the hero LUGH, grandson and killer of the monstrous FOMORIAN king BALOR of the Evil Eye. After Balor had been driven to the periphery of Ireland by the fierce warriors of the FIR BOLG, he reigned from a frightening fortress on Tory Island off Co. Donegal. Opposite him on the mainland, at Druin na Teine, lived the smith with his magical cow. Balor conceived a powerful desire to own the cow—thus removing it from Ireland, where it nourished the people—but the smith watched it incessantly, only taking his eyes off it when he worked at the forge; while he was working, the Glas was closely guarded by a man variously named CIAN, MacInally, or Fin son of Ceanfaeligh. He had to follow along behind the Glas—never in front of her—as she meandered through the island, keeping up with her strenuous pace. She moved so fast and so far that it was no wonder that Cian finally grew inattentive and took a nap.

At that point Balor struck. He stole the Glas and packed her aboard a boat that sailed for Tory Island, stopping en route at the little island called Inishbofin (Inis Bó Find, "island of the white cow"), where she drank from a WELL called Tober na Glaise ("gray cow well"); when they landed at Tory it was at Port na Glaise ("gray cow port").

The smith, furious to find his magical cow gone, threatened Cian with death unless she was returned in three days. So Cian traveled to Balor's realm, where the king gave him impossible tasks to fulfill in order to earn back the cow. While there, however, Cian spied Balor's beautiful daughter EITHNE, trapped in a high tower because Balor feared the prophecy that her son would kill him. Balor reasoned that, if Eithne never saw a man, she could not bear a child, thus providing her father with immortality.

Disguised as a woman, Cian slunk into Eithne's lodgings and seduced her; the child she bore was Lugh, who was later to kill Balor in battle, fulfilling the prophecy. Cian returned the cow to the smith but died at Balor's hands in retaliation for his seduction of Eithne.

The cow of abundance is connected in myth and legend to various figures, most commonly BRIGIT, who as Ireland's St. Brigit was said to have a cow that gave copious milk and filled the abbey's storehouses with butter. This connection of Glas and Brigit extends to Britain; a sculpture of the saint as milkmaid can be found in GLASTONBURY.

Sources: Curtin, Jeremiah. *Hero-Tales of Ireland.* New York: Benjamin Blom, 1894, pp. 283, 296; Hull, Eleanor. *Folklore of the British Isles.* London: Methuen & Co., Ltd., 1928, pp. 150–153; MacNeill, Máire. *The Festival of Lughnasa, Parts I and II.* Dublin: Comhairle Bhéaloideas Éireann, 1982, pp. 163–165.

Glass-ben (Glass) Irish heroine. The nurse of the hero OSCAR, she died when she learned that her fosterling was killed in battle.

glastig (*glaistig, glaistic, glaisein, glaishrig*) Scottish and Welsh folkloric figure. A FAIRY of Scotland and Wales, "the gray-handed one" was a gray thin woman (sometimes, a GIANT) whose long yellow hair hit the ground behind her; like others of her race, she wore the preferred fairy color, GREEN, from which she was sometimes known as the green *glastig.* Rarely seen in company (although sometimes a pair could be spotted together), the *glastig* hung around farms where there were COWS; she was also found around people of friendly demeanor but low intelligence, whom she loved and cared for.

The *glastig* had a preternaturally loud voice that could be heard many miles away. As a spirit of the MILK cattle, she demanded an offering of the first milk taken each morning; failure to observe this politeness resulted in her drying up the milk or otherwise punishing the stingy dairyman. If offered regular libations of milk, left in pitcher or bowl on the doorstep, the *glastig* stayed for some time. As a householding spirit like the BROWNIE, she cleaned especially well whenever guests were on the way, so awakening to a sparkling clean house was an immediate signal to look out for visitors. As with other laboring spirits, it was important never to speak of the *glastig* or, even worse, to compliment her labor, for that forced her to move away to another farm.

In the Isle of Man the fenodyree was a figure similar to the *glastig*; she lived in the mountains but snuck down to the farmlands to tend to the fields and to help secretly about the house. Like similar fairy figures, she refused to accept payment or recompense for her work and disappeared if it was offered.

Source: MacKenzie, Donald A. *Scottish Folk-Lore and Folk Life: Studies in Race, Culture and Tradition*. Glasgow: Blackie & Sons, Ltd., 1935, pp. 176–194.

Glastonbury British mythological site. Considered by some to be the site of the OTHERWORLD island of AVALON, the small southwestern English city of Glastonbury has many mythical and legendary associations. Below its pyramidal hill, the TOR, lie the ruins of several significant Christian sites, including Glastonbury Abbey, beneath which king ARTHUR and queen GUINEVERE are said to be buried, and the renowned Chalice WELL, also called the Blood Spring, with its iron-red waters. The legend of JOSEPH OF ARIMATHEA says that he built the first Christian church in Britain there. As Christian chapels and churches were often established on older Celtic and pre-Celtic sacred sites, it is no surprise to find that Glastonbury was held in legend to be the entry to ANNWN, the Welsh Otherworld, where the fairy king GWYNN AP NUDD reigned; there is evidence of Iron Age, probably Celtic, settlement on the Tor, which may point to a Celtic origin for that folkloric character. Thus the site remains connected in legend to the sacred even if the original monuments and myths have been lost.

glastyn (*glashtin*) Manx folkloric figure. On the Isle of Man lived this form of the spectral WATER HORSE, who appeared as a handsome man with curly hair, beneath which, if carefully examined, were ears that looked remarkably like those of a horse. Handsome he might be, but he was also dangerous. He snuck into the homes of young women when they were alone—their families having gone to market or out fishing—and dragged them into the sea to their deaths.

Glen Lyon Scottish mythological site. In an astonishing survival of ancient, possibly Celtic, ritual, a Scottish region continues an age-old tradition centered on summer's beginning at BELTANE on May 1. Located in the Grampion mountains of Tayside near Fortingall is a small valley called Glen Lyon. Within the small valley are many place-names associated with the ancient goddess, the CAILLEACH or HAG: Glen Cailliche (Hag's Glen), Allt Cailliche (Hag's Stream), and Tigh nam Cailliche (Hag's House), the last being a pile of water-smoothed rocks of roughly human form. The largest, a bit over a foot in height, is named the Cailliche; two smaller stones go by the names of the Bodach (old man) and Nighean (daughter). Some small unnamed rocks represent the old woman's babies. Each Beltane, a local resident washes the stones and replaces them in a traditional spot; each SAMHAIN the hag and her family are put away into a small stone house.

The connection of the ritual appearance and disappearance of the stone family with the Celtic holidays may indicate that it derives from Celtic times, although the hag goddess herself is believed to reach back even deeper into prehistory and represent a cosmic goddess of the pre-Celtic people. Legends in the area say that the Irish hero, FIONN MAC CUMHAILL, once lived there.

Sources: Clarke, David, with Andy Roberts. *Twilight of the Celtic Gods: An Exploration of Britain's Hidden Pagan Traditions*. London: Blandford, 1996, pp. 66 ff; Straffon, Cheryl. *The Earth Goddess: Celtic and Pagan Legacy of the Landscape*. London: Blandford, 1997, p. 177.

Glewlwyd Gafaelwar   Welsh hero. This warrior and guardian figure of Wales was absorbed into Arthurian legend as the watchman at the gates of king ARTHUR's court at CAMELOT.

gnome   Folkloric figure. Not a Celtic creature at all, the gnome found in Celtic lands derives from medieval science and alchemy that imagined creatures appropriate to each of the four elements: salamanders (fire), nereids (water), sylphs (air), and gnomes (earth). The gnomes were thought to live under the earth, working perhaps as miners; the word itself may derive from *genomus*, "earth-dweller." They are easily confused with such truly folkloric creatures as FAIRIES and KNOCKERS, but have no real legends attached. The DWARFS familiar to modern children from the tale of Sleeping Beauty are a variation of the gnome.

goat   Symbolic animal. There is evidence that the goat was among the animals considered sacred to the Celts and therefore useful for SACRIFICE. Because of a CURSE, goats were forbidden near the Christian abbey in KILDARE, originally a site of Celtic worship. As the sanctuary was sacred to women, and men were barred from it, the goat may have represented the male force; the horned god CERNUNNOS was often depicted with goat's legs, though with stag's horns. The sexuality of the male goat is legendary; in Christian imagery, derogation of the male sexual force is indicated by showing the DEVIL as a goat-footed being. Perhaps this connection explains why ST. PATRICK was so often described as a goatherd: a symbolic way of describing Christianity's control over male sexual instinct. In folklore the same energy is personified as PUCK or the POOKA, a FAIRY being.

The most notable remnant of ancient regard for the animal is the still-extant PUCK FAIR, a harvest festival in the town of Kilorglin in southwestern Ireland, where a white male goat is crowned as king, fed fresh cabbage, and displayed aloft on a platform while festivities go on beneath it. The fair's name comes from the Irish word *poc*, meaning "he-goat." The fair traditionally lasts three days in mid-August: Gathering Day, when the goat is installed as king; Fair Day, when festivities abound; and Scattering Day, when the goat is taken from his perch and sold at auction or released into the wild. Documented evidence shows that the fair has been continually held since at least 1613, although it is believed its earliest date is much earlier; some, however, contend that the obvious pagan symbolism of the rite would have caused its eradication during the period of Christianization and claim it is a medieval or Norman invention.

Sources: Condren, Mary. *The Serpent and the Goddess: Women, Religion and Power in Ancient Ireland.* San Francisco: Harper & Row, 1989, p. 74; MacNeill, Máire. *The Festival of Lughnasa, Parts I and II.* Dublin: Comhairle Bhéaloideas Éireann, 1982, pp. 290–300, 414.

goayr heddagh   Manx folkloric figure. The Isle of Man is haunted by this FAIRY creature or GHOST that takes the form of a GOAT.

Goban Saor   (Gobhan Saor, Gubawn Seer) British and Irish folkloric figure. In parts of Britain and Ireland where Vikings lived, we find vestiges of the divine SMITH, WAYLAND, in this folktale character. An amoral figure, he once put an old woman into his furnace so that he could hammer her into a young maiden. He is said to have served as architect on many significant churches. It is often difficult to tease out the various cultural strands in tales of Goban Soar, who like the Celtic smith god GOIBNIU is sometimes described as the owner of the great cow of abundance, the GLAS GHAIBHLEANN.

goblin   (hobgoblin)   British folkloric figure. A general name for evil FAIRIES, "goblin" indicates a being who is at best mischievous and irritating, at worst dangerous. Goblins came in various guises, including the VOUGH and the POOKA, the BOGIE and the WATER HORSE; all have roots in the Celtic vision of the OTHERWORLD; they are thus distinct from GNOMES, which belong to the lore of medieval alchemy. English poet Christina Rossetti used aspects of traditional fairy lore in her long poem "Goblin Market," linking the image of leering, evil goblins with the motif of FAIRY KIDNAPPING to create a frightening vision of emotional distress.

Gobnat (Gobnait, Cobnat, Abby, Abigail) Irish heroine, saint or goddess. A Christian shrine in Ireland's Co. Cork, at the town of Ballyvourney, shows a SHEELA NA GIG, a self-exposing HAG whose image has been linked to ancient MOTHER GODDESSES. The resident spirit of the shrine is said to be St. Gobnait, patroness of BEES, who may be a Christianized version of an ancient goddess of the locality. The bees served as her watchdogs, warning her against any danger that approached.

She is said to have been one of three sisters, the others being the more clearly mythological CROBH DEARG (or LASAIR) and LATIARAN. In early February the beginning of spring in Ireland and the time of the Celtic feast of IMBOLC are devoted to Gobnait, suggesting that she was the first of a triad of seasonal goddesses, for her sisters are also linked to dates in the ancient calendar. A famous shrine to her is located at what is now Kilgobnet (church of Gobnat) in Co. Kerry.

Source: Straffon, Cheryl. *The Earth Goddess: Celtic and Pagan Legacy of the Landscape.* London: Blandford, 1997, p. 73.

Goborchinn Irish mythological race. A branch of the ancient mythological Irish race known as the FOMORIANS, the Goborchinn were ruled by EOCHAID Echchenn, "horse-head." As the Fomorians were consistently associated with the sea, the Goborchinn may have some connection to the mythological WATER HORSE. Those who interpret the *BOOK OF INVASIONS*, in which the Goborchinn appear, as a mythological record of actual immigrations into Ireland suggest that the Fomorians represent a pre-Celtic people of which the Goborchinn were part.

god (gods) Cosmological concept. It is impossible to speak of the "God of the Celts," for the Celts were polytheistic in the extreme; they did not believe in one but in many gods. Unlike the Romans, who conquered the Celts and reinterpreted their religion even as they recorded it (see INTERPRETATIO ROMANA), the Celts did not arrange gods in a hierarchical order. Despite Caesar's announcement that MERCURY was the chief Celtic god, there seems to have been no such head of a ranked pantheon.

In particular, the Celts did not believe that male gods took precedence over goddesses; there is significant evidence that the reverse was true. While goddesses seemed to represent stable parts of the landscape (mountains and RIVERS and the like) as well as the force of FERTILITY and many human arts, gods more typically lent their energies to the changeable aspects of life: the surging sea, the transformations of MAGIC, the burgeoning of vegetative and animal life. Often gods were seen to reflect the life of human men, as with ploughman gods and hunters, although even those could also indicate the cycle of fertility that led to abundance.

goddess (goddesses) Cosmological concept. The prominent role played by the goddess in Celtic lands has been noted by virtually all scholars of the subject, although whether that prominence translated into greater freedom or power for actual women is a subject of fierce contention. Similarly, there is debate about whether the strong goddess figures found in Celtic lands were adopted from earlier, presumably matrilineal, cultures such as the Picts, or whether they represented the Celtic worldview. Whichever is true, Celtic goddesses had in common with Celtic gods their special link to place; most goddesses are found in only one place and seem to have been envisioned as intertwined with its powers. Goddesses are particularly connected with fresh water, both in the form of SPRINGS (usually called WELLS) and of RIVERS; with ANIMALS, especially the COW; and with MOUNTAINS, especially high peaks.

Celtic goddesses had several functions: They were maternal, caring for the earth itself as well as for individual children; they were prophetic, especially foretelling death; and they were transformational, connected with poetry and smithcraft and healing. The domain of the various MOTHER GODDESSES included the entire lifecycle, from birth through adolescence and the FERTILITY of maturity. Such maternal goddesses were envisioned as protective forces, providing the necessities of life—especially food—to their huge families of human children. These maternal goddesses are often envisioned as being the earth itself; round mountains were envisioned as the breasts of the great mother goddess, and rivers were imagined alternatively as her blood and her nourishing MILK.

Images of the mother goddess are ubiquitous throughout the Celtic world; probably they were used as protective AMULETS as well as objects of worship. The strength of the mother goddess has led many scholars to propose that the Celts had a matrilineal social organization in which descent was traced through the mother-line; others, however, contend that vestiges of such a social structure represent the heritage of pre-Celtic groups like the Picts, as does the practice of polyandry or multiple husbands so common in Celtic mythology. Yet others deny all indications of the importance of the ancestral mother as feminist propaganda and propound the idea that the Celts were completely patriarchal and patrilineal.

In addition to the mother goddess, we find the feminine divine associated with PROPHECY throughout the Celtic world. In many cases she seems a goddess of death, predicting rather than bringing about the inevitable end of life. Finally, we find goddesses associated with transformation: with the INAUGURATION of kings (see SOVEREIGNTY) and with SHAPE-SHIFTING, as well as with POETRY, with smithcraft, and with HEAL-ING. Some contend that all are aspects of maternity, but goddesses associated with prophecy and transformation are not usually described as having children, which suggests that the domains were separate.

Sources: Condren, Mary. *The Serpent and the Goddess: Women, Religion and Power in Ancient Ireland.* San Francisco: Harper & Row, 1989, pp. 175–176; Green, Miranda. *Symbol and Image in Celtic Religious Art.* London: Routledge, 1989, p. 9; MacCullogh, J. A. *Celtic Mythology.* Chicago: Academy Publishers, 1996, pp. 93, 224; Sjoestedt, Marie-Louise. *Celtic Gods and Heroes.* Trans. Myles Dillon. Mineola, N.Y.: Dover Publications, Inc., 2000, pp. 24–37.

goddess-king marriage   See SOVEREIGNTY.

goddess of sovereignty   See SOVEREIGNTY.

Godiva (Godgifu, Dame Goode Eve) British heroine. In 1967, on the reputed 900th anniversary of Lady Godiva's death, the town of Coventry held a celebration in her honor. Her apparently historical story incorporates so many Celtic mythological motifs that it is difficult to discern the truth behind the legend. Both she and her husband, Leonfric earl of Mercia, are mentioned in medieval chronicles, which praise her generosity and record details of her famous ride.

When Leonfric piled such ruinous taxes upon his vassals that the land was groaning and people were starving, Godiva pleaded for mercy. But Leonfric refused to alleviate the people's woes. Cruelly, he taunted his wife that only if she rode naked through Coventry town would he ease the tax burden on his people. The brave lady took up the challenge, but to preserve her modesty she asked that the windows of the town be shrouded with fabric on the day of her ride. Then, dressed only in her long HAIR, she rode through the empty streets.

Only one person—Peeping Tom—ignored her request, and he was struck blind at the sight of her resplendent body.

The region around Coventry was home to the Celtic tribe called the Brigantes, who recognized the HORSE goddess either as EPONA or under another name. Their own tribal name indicates that they honored BRIGIT, a goddess known in other contexts to have the power both to blind and to restore sight. The image of a mounted woman clad only in her hair is known in Ireland from the story of the forthright heroine GRÁINNE. Finally, female nakedness as a Celtic cult practice to increase the FERTILITY of the fields is known from classical sources, including the Roman author Pliny; Lady Godiva's ride had the effect of providing more abundance for her impoverished people. Thus the legend of Lady Godiva both disguises and preserves the image of an ancient goddess protector.

Source: Davidson, Hilda Ellis. "The Legend of Lady Godiva." In *Patterns of Folklore.* Totowa, N.J.: Rowman & Littlefield, 1978, pp. 80–94.

Goewin Welsh heroine or goddess. Chosen to perform the ceremonially important office of footholder to king MATH of Wales, whose feet were never to touch the ground—a common indicator of a sacred king—Goewin had the misfortune to inspire lust in the heart of one of Math's nephews. Aided and abetted by his brother, the trickster poet GWYDION, GIL-FAETHWY raped Goewin. He was punished severely for the crime, but Goewin lost both her virginity and her position, for only an untouched girl was permitted to hold the king's feet. As partial recompense, Math married her and made her queen.

Gog (Gogmagog, Gigmagog) Cornish folkloric figure. This Cornish GIANT was described by Geoffrey of Monmouth as attacking the British king Brutus during his INAUGURATION ceremonies, only to be soundly defeated by the warrior Corineus. The legendary figure later developed into two threatening beings, Gog and Magog, who attacked Londinium (London) during the reign of king Vortigen.

Goibniu (Goibne, Gaibnenn, Gobnenn) Irish god. The SMITH of the TUATHA DÉ DANANN, the tribe of the goddess DANU, Goibniu was one of the three gods of craft who created a new arm for their king NUADA when his arm was struck clear off in battle. As a BLEMISHED KING, it appeared Nuada would be forced to resign his rulership. Goibniu set to work, crafting a silver arm so perfect that, attached to the stump, it began working like a real arm. (Some versions say the god of healing, DIAN CÉCHT, crafted the silver arm.) Nuada of the Silver Arm was still not considered unblemished, and so the stingy and evil half-Fomorian BRES mac Elatha ascended to the throne, only to be driven out not long after. The situation was resolved when the gifted physician and magician MIACH sang incantations that made skin grow over Nuada's silver arm, making him whole once again. With that bionic arm, Nuada was able to lead his people to victory in the second battle of MAG TUIRED, which established the Tuatha Dé's dominion in Ireland.

Before the battle, the son of Bres and BRIGIT came to spy upon Goibniu and steal his magical secrets. Goibniu killed the lad, RUADÁN, which caused his mother to invent the wild sound of KEENING to express her grief. For himself, Goibniu was able to heal his wounds by traveling to the sacred WELL on SLANE hill.

Every smith was a magical figure in ancient Ireland, turning raw stone first into metal and then into beautiful and useful objects such as jewelry and weapons. Such high prestige carries over to the mythological sphere as well. Sometimes named as the owner of the GLAS GHAIBHLEANN, the COW of abundance, Goibniu was said to live in Co. Cavan, where the name of the Iron Mountains suggest an early mining industry. This connection with abundance is also emphasized by the myth that Goibniu possessed a

CAULDRON from which his guests could endlessly drink and, instead of becoming intoxicated, grow ever younger and more healthy. In folklore Goibniu survived as GOBAN SAOR, a sharp and clever smith who appears in many tales.

Goidel (Gadelus, Gaedhal, Gael, Gaedel Glas, Gathelus) Irish hero. It is probable that this figure is a literary invention rather than a real divinity; he is named as the ancestor of the Goidelic (Gaelic) Celts of Ireland, Scotland, and the Isle of Man. In a complicated and clearly Christianized text, he is said to have been the grandson of an Egyptian Pharaoh, healed of a childhood illness by the biblical Moses. English poet and propagandist Edmund Spenser described Goidel or Gathelus as the son of Cecrops of Argos, a mythological Greek king, who married a princess of Egypt and took her to Spain, where they became the ancestors of the Irish race. Goidel may be the same as the figure who otherwise appears as Míl (see MILESIANS), although he is also called one of Mil's sons or grandsons. His ancestor RIFATH SCOT was the one who, in the chaos of the biblical Tower of Babel, became a speaker of Scots Gaelic; Goidel himself created the Irish language by joining words from the other 72 languages he knew.

gold Symbolic metal. Gold was a valuable metal to the Celts, who were renowned as metal-workers, but its value was based as much in myth as in commerce. It was associated with the SUN and, as such, with prosperity brought about through the growth and abundance of summer's vegetation. This association made gold a sought-after metal for personal ornamentation; TORCS or neck-rings of twisted gold are among the treasures of ancient Celtic design and craftsmanship. Ritual objects, like the golden BOAT found in Broighter BOG, also attest to the importance of gold to the Celts, both insular and Continental.

The Celtic reverence for gold was noted by ancient authors. Diodorus Siculus noted that the Celts had "a strange and peculiar custom in con-

nection with the sanctuaries of the gods; for in the temples and sanctuaries which are dedicated throughout the country a large amount of gold is openly placed as a dedication to the gods." The openly displayed gold would not be stolen, for that would bring on unshakable bad fortune; the same tradition can be found in the placing of COINS in sacred spots in Ireland and Britain today, which similarly tend to remain undisturbed.

Gold was also linked with the GODDESS and her diminished form, the FAIRY QUEEN, for such beings were often described as having long golden HAIR. ÁINE and ÉTAIN are described as combing their golden locks with a golden COMB. The lights of FAIRYLAND are often said to be gold, and human greed could be tempted by the apparent wealth of gold found there, though stolen pocketsful would reveal themselves to be only the butter-colored flowers of the GORSE when the visitor returned to earth.

In degraded form after the decline of Celtic religion, this magical substance became nothing but money, as when leprechauns were sought for their pot of gold and the treasure of the goddess was transformed into the "Money Hole" of MUNSTER, a place of inexhaustible wealth lost somewhere on the slopes of the Loughfennel mountains. Thistles were sometimes said to grow at locations of buried FAIRY gold.

Sources: Dames, Michael. *Mythic Ireland.* London: Thames and Hudson, 1992, pp. 91–98, 118–119; Ó Catháin, Séamus and Patrick O'Flanagan. *The Living Landscape: Kilgallian, Erris, Country Mayo.* Dublin: Comhairle Bhéaloideas Éireann, 1975, pp. 111 ff; Raftery, Brian. *Pagan Celtic Ireland: The Enigma of the Irish Iron Age.* London: Thames and Hudson, 1994, pp. 23–25; Ross, Anne. *Pagan Celtic Britain: Studies in Iconography and Tradition.* London: Routledge & Kegan Paul, 1967, p. 19.

Goleuddydd Welsh heroine or goddess. The legend of this Welsh princess, whose name means "bright day," probably disguises an ancient goddess of FERTILITY, who may derive either from Celtic or pre-Celtic sources. She married a prince, CILYDD, but was unable to conceive by him, causing consternation among her people, who both wished for an heir to the throne and worried over the symbolism of a barren couple on the throne. Unfortunately, when she finally became pregnant, Goleuddydd went mad and refused to live indoors, raging through the wilderness instead (the same motif is found in the Irish tale of MESS BUACHALLA). When the time of her labor came, she went to the sty of a swineherd and there bore her son, thereafter called KULHWCH or "pig." Like RHIANNON, the Welsh HORSE-goddess who bore a colt, we have here a transparent disguise for an ancient PIG goddess of fertility.

Goll mac Morna (Aed, Aodh mac Fidga) Irish hero. This one-eyed warrior was the traditional enemy of the great Irish hero FIONN MAC CUMHAILL. He was a hero originally named Aed ("bright"), son of Morna (hence, mac Morna). His father may have been a GIANT of the FIR BOLG people, who are associated with the province of CONNACHT, also Goll's domain. When Aed lost an eye in combat with a man named Luchet, he became Goll ("the one-eyed"). Other versions of the tale say that Goll's opponent was CUMHALL, Fionn's father, whom Goll promptly killed and beheaded. This initiated an endless feud between Goll's family, the CLAN MORNA, and Fionn's, the CLAN BAÍSCNE.

Goll was not always Fionn's enemy, for he rescued the hero from the clutches of three powerful HAGS who held him captive in the cave of Keshcorran, and Fionn rewarded him by giving Goll his daughter in marriage. Nor was Fionn always Goll's foe, for he once found him sleeping by the Shannon River and, sheathing his sword, let the weary one-eyed warrior rest. Thus many see Fionn and Goll as part of a mythological cycle in which each relies upon as well as opposes the other. Ultimately, however, enmity rules: Fionn, freed from Keshcorran, promptly killed

Goll's grandson FER í, which began the cycle of violence again. Ultimately driven to the edge of Ireland, Goll lived without food or water for 30 days, becoming wild with despair and hunger before dying at the hands of a minor member of the FIANNA, Mac Smaile. Goll's death did not end the feud, which continued until the Fianna was finally overcome at the battle of GABHAIR. Some legends say that after his death Goll found a new home in one of the magical ISLANDS of the western sea, on whose shores he had met his doom.

Goll also appears in the legend of LUGH, the half-FOMORIAN, half-TUATHA DÉ DANANN hero best known for killing his grandfather, the fierce and evil BALOR. One version says that Lugh was killed by Goll, while in another Lugh killed Goll after the great second battle of MAG TUIRED. Goll himself is easily confused with the Fomorian king Balor, who had one evil EYE that killed with a glance. Finally, a minor tale describes Goll's death at the hands of the young warrior LAOGHAIRE mac Crimthann, who won the hand of his beloved DÉR GRÉINE as a result of his successful battle against the gigantic Goll.

Goll mac Morna may be connected with, or identical to, another one-eyed figure, the SALMON who swam in the pool near the famous waterfall of ASSAROE and sometimes named FINTAN, who also bore the name of Goll Essa Ruaid. This identification further links Goll to Fionn, for it was the salmon of Assaroe that, cooked and accidentally eaten by Fionn (see FINNÉCES) that gave Fionn his magical insight and WISDOM. Finally, Goll mac Morna has been linked to another one-eyed hero, Goll mac Carbada, killed by the ULSTER hero CÚCHULAINN in a fight that echoes Fionn's with Goll.

Source: MacNeill, Máire. *The Festival of Lughnasa, Parts I and II.* Dublin: Comhairle Bhéaloideas Éireann, 1982, p. 186.

Golwg (Golwg Haffddydd) Welsh heroine. In some early Arthurian legends, this is the name of the maidservant to ESYLLT, who later became the lover of a friend of TRYSTAN's. When the story evolves into that of Tristan and ISEULT, the maid's name is given as BRANGIEN.

Good God, The See DAGDA.

goose Symbolic bird. Both the tame and the wild goose (see BARNACLE GOOSE) had mythological and symbolic significance to the Celts. The barnyard goose, a notoriously aggressive being, was seen as an image of the warrior divinities, both male and feamle. Stone geese lined the temples of Gaul, while Brittany produced bronzes of war goddesses with goose-head helmets. Given this symbolism, it is ironic that the Celtic siege of Rome was ended when the geese of the goddess Juno Moneta's temple set up such a commotion that the defenders were roused and the invading Celts defeated. So strong was the identification of Celtic people with the goose that the animal was a taboo food among the Britons, used for DIVINATION and eaten only on ritual occasions. Some FAIRY beings could change by SHAPE-SHIFTING into geese, as could the waterbird-hero Geroid Iarla.

Goreu (Goreu fab Custennin) Welsh hero. A relatively obscure character, Goreu appears as a hidden child in the story of KUHLWCH AND OLWEN—hidden because a GIANT, OLWEN's father YSPADDADEN PENKAWR, had eaten his 22 earlier-born siblings. Freed by king ARTHUR, Goreu became a member of the court of CAMELOT and ultimately slew his family's gigantic enemy.

Gorgon Greek goddess. A familiar icon to the Romans was the decapitated HEAD of the Gorgon Medusa, whose image from Greek mythology was taken over by them and used as an apotropaic or warning sign. When the Roman legions arrived in Celtic lands, they found a well-established cult of the head; the Gorgon seemed a familiar emblem and was adopted into some Romano-Celtic temples, most notably that of SUL at the famous thermal springs or AQUAE SULIS at Bath in southwestern Britain. While Medusa was a goddess, the Celtic sacred head was typically a male one; thus the "male Gorgon" found in the temple of Sulis is a unique melding of Greek, Roman, and Celtic meanings in one image.

Gorias Irish mythological site. Somewhere in the OTHERWORLD was the magical city of Gorias, from which the TUATHA DÉ DANANN received one of their great treasures, the spear of LUGH.

Gorlois Arthurian hero. IGRAINE, one of the most beautiful women in Wales, was married to the duke of Cornwall, Gorlois, and was the mother of several daughters, including the magical MORGAN and the doomed MORGAUSE. Although she was happy with her husband, Igraine caught the attention of the heroic UTHER PENDRAGON, who wished to take her to bed. Igraine was a faithful wife, however, and so Uther conspired with the magician MERLIN to appear to Igraine in the body of her husband. Igraine did not know that Gorlois was already dead by Uther's hand when she conceived ARTHUR, the once and future king of Britain.

Gorm (Gorm the Grim) British mythological site. The image of a GIANT of this name is carved into the side of the gorge of the River Avon. Gorm probably descended from a local divinity made monstrous by the interpretations of Celtic (possibly Viking) religion by Christian priests. The image was said to represent a cannibal; vestiges of belief in a figure with this name are also found in Orkney.

gorse Symbolic plant. A hardy plant found throughout Ireland and Britain, gorse grows in harsh as well as fertile conditions. In spring the tough prickly bushes burst out with velvety fragrant yellow flowers, some of which remain through the summer. It had two major uses: as a fuel, for it is plentiful and burns at an intense heat; and as the mainstay of hedges, for CATTLE hesitate to approach its spiny, dense growth. In Wales, a sprig of gorse was worn as protection against WITCHCRAFT. (See also FURZE.)

Govannon (Gofannon, Gafannon) Welsh god. The Welsh SMITH god, a parallel deity to the Irish GOIBNIU, was a great artificer linked with the magician king MATH. Smithcraft was considered almost magical in early times, when the refining of metal was still a new and rare process. The divine smith had agricultural powers as well, for it was he who cleaned the plows at the end of planting, to ensure that the tools of abundance would serve another year.

Govannon appears in the collection of myths called the *MABINOGION* as the accidental murderer of the goddess ARIANRHOD's magical son DYLAN, who was mourned by the very waves of the sea. In folklore Govannon was renamed GOBAN SAOR and described as the builder of early churches. In addition to his role as god of craftsmanship, Govannon had power over the elements and the weather; some have found in him an ancient thunder divinity like TARANIS.

Gradlon (Gradlon Muer, Grallon, Garallon, Gralon) Breton hero. In one of the most dramatic stories from the Celtic region of France—Cornuoille or Brittany—we learn of the king Gradlon and his beautiful pagan daughter, DAHUT. He was a loving father who indulged his daughter's every wish, including attending her nightly balls and other diversions within the walls that protected the low-lying city from the surging sea. A monk, GUÉNOLÉ, warned him about his daughter's allegedly evil proclivities, but Gradlon would hear nothing against Dahut. Yet the beautiful city of YS was doomed, for Dahut attracted the attention of CADO, a sea god or sea monster who wanted to drag the princess down to the undersea world with him. The monk saved Gradlon, for the king had accepted Christianity despite his daughter's more tradi-

tional beliefs; in some variants, Guénolé forces Gradlon to sacrifice Dahut to the sea in order to save himself, while in others the two simply escape as the deluge pours into the magnificent city of Ys.

Gradlon appears in several other tales from Brittany, which show him as a model of the Celtic regional king who made his land wealthy and who protected it by defeating the Vikings on the Loire river. In some texts, his name is said to have been borne by later kings of the region.

Grail (Holy Grail) Symbolic object. Generally pictured as the sacred cup from which the Christian savior Jesus drank at his Last Supper in Jerusalem, the Grail is also sometimes said to be the platter on which he was served his bread or paschal lamb at the Passover dinner he shared with his disciples on the night before he died. A third alternative holds that the Grail was a cup that caught the blood of Jesus as he lay dying. After his crucifixion and resurrection, JOSEPH OF ARIMATHEA, a merchant at whose house the Last Supper was held, transported the Grail to Britain. Thus the Christian emblem of the mystery of transubstantiation—the change of common bread and wine into the body and blood of Jesus—became grafted onto a series of legends and myths of Celtic origin to become a complex yet compelling tale that continues to inspire poets and thinkers.

The Grail quest was set in motion by a young knight of the ROUND TABLE, PERCIVAL, who found himself in a dead kingdom ruled over by a king who had been wounded in his groin, the symbol of his FERTILITY, and so could do nothing but fish in the land's increasingly empty LAKES, for which reason he was called the FISHER KING. The king welcomed Percival to his castle, where a banquet was prepared.

There the young knight was presented with strange visions: Before his eyes appeared a floating chalice and a bleeding lance that hovered in midair while the court sat in silence. Percival chose to remain silent in the face of these marvels, never asking what they signified. The vision then evaporated, as did the palace and the king and all his court.

And so the quest began. The Grail quest took a different form for each knight who embarked upon it, for each was granted the quest appropriate to his character. Various endings are proposed in various texts: The thinly disguised Christian hero GALAHAD receives the Grail and is transfigured into sanctity; LANCELOT finds the Grail Castle but falls into a trance and does not enter; Percival returns to the Grail Castle, asks the relevant questions—whose is the cup, why does the lance bleed, and what does it all mean?—and thus heals the king and restores the land, after which he himself is elevated to the KINGSHIP.

The story of the quest for the Grail includes several Celtic motifs. The Fisher King is the BLEMISHED KING of Celtic tradition, which held that any king with a physical blemish could not rule. The Grail itself is the CAULDRON that appears in many forms in Celtic myth: It is the Welsh goddess CERIDWEN's cauldron wherein WISDOM was brewed, the cauldron of rebirth of the Welsh hero EFNISIEN, and the great ever-abundant cauldron of the Irish god DAGDA. The symbolic meaning of the Grail fluctuates, but it is connected generally to fertility, although in some Christian tellings it appears to represent the opposite, being linked with the refusal to accept sexuality and thus with sterility.

Sources: Cowan, Tom. *Fire in the Head: Shamanism and the Celtic Spirit.* San Francisco: HarperSanFrancisco, 1993, p. 164; Evans-Wentz, W. Y. *The Fairy-Faith in Celtic Countries.* Gerrards Cross: Colin Smythe Humanities Press, 1911, pp. 311–325.

Gráinne (Grania, Grainne, Grace)   Irish heroine or goddess. The story of this fiery woman and her lover DIARMAIT Ua Duibne is one of the most famous of the entire FENIAN CYCLE, told and retold in many variants. It begins with a race up the sides of the MUNSTER mountain called SLIEVE-

NAMON, "the mountain of the women." When the aging hero FIONN MAC CUMHAILL announced that he would wed the fastest woman in Ireland, the self-possessed princess Gráinne decided that the honor should be hers. Fionn sat on the CAIRN atop the mountain, and at a signal all the women raced toward him. Fleet of foot and fierce of heart, Gráinne reached the prize first. And so the wedding was set.

Various texts claim that Gráinne was a princess of ULSTER, of Munster, or of TARA. Most agree that the wedding feast was held on the royal hill of Tara, where a monument called Rath Gráinne still stands. But before the wedding festivities had ended, Gráinne had noticed that her new husband was considerably older than she was. Restlessly, she looked around.

Among the gathered heroes of Fionn's band, the FIANNA, was Diarmait Ua Duibne, a young man who had many clearly visible attractions but whose most irresistible was under cover. Either a cap or bangs always covered Diarmait's forehead, for there was a dimple or birthmark called a *BALL SEIRC*—a beauty mark that caused any woman who saw it to grow crazy with love. At the festival, Diarmait was playing with Fionn's dogs, and as he did so he happened to toss his hair from his forehead, and the *ball seirc* was revealed. Instantly Gráinne fell hopelessly in love with him. (This theme of fated love occurs as well in the Celtic-inspired story of TRISTAN and ISEULT, but there the fated affair is launched through mistaken sharing of a love elixir.)

Diarmait had no desire to run off with the new wife of his leader, one of Ireland's fiercest warriors. But he did not reckon on Gráinne's willfulness. Gráinne learned that Diarmait was under a GEIS, a sacred vow, never to refuse a woman who came to him neither clothed nor unclothed, neither afoot nor on horseback, in neither daylight or dark. And so Gráinne arrived veiled in mountain mist or catkin down, mounted on a GOAT, just at sunset, and thus found a way to force him to run away from Fionn with her.

In some versions of the tale, Gráinne drugged the entire Fianna—including her intended husband, but sparing the man she desired—and convinced Diarmait to elope with her. The couple ran toward the Shannon River that cuts Ireland in half, sleeping there in what became known as the Wood of the Two Tents, for Diarmait feared to sleep in the same tent with Gráinne, knowing that Fionn was on their trail. Once again Gráinne prevailed, mildly mentioning to Diarmait—after a narrow escape from a monster—how nice it was to know something, at least, found her desirable. Shamed, Diarmait joined Gráinne in her tent.

Fionn was indeed behind them, together with the entire Fianna. The couple kept a step ahead of their pursuers, Gráinne wrapped in a cloak of invisibility while Diarmait leaped stupendous lengths to stay out of danger's reach. Each night they slept on a different stone bed, so that the DOLMENS that mark the Irish countryside are now known as the "beds of Diarmait and Gráinne." They ran so far and so fast that they never slept two nights in one place nor ate a cooked supper— but they ran far and fast together.

Finally, however, they grew exhausted by their constant travel and took refuge with a giant named SEARBHAN, who let the couple hide in his magical ROWAN tree, warning them however to leave the berries strictly alone. But hungry Gráinne could not resist, and Diarmait killed Searbhan so that the two could eat the magical fruit. Unfortunately, Searbhan's dying screams revealed the couple's location to the pursuing Fionn.

Climbing quickly up the tree, Diarmait and Gráinne hid from her former suitor, his former leader, but Fionn suspected where they were. He sat beneath the tree and began to play FIDCHELL, a cribbage-like board game that had been Diarmait's passion, against his friend OISÍN the BARD. Unable to resist indicating the best move to his chum, Diarmait dropped berries onto the board from above, thus revealing his location to Fionn. And so the pursuit began again, until the god AONGHUS óg pleaded the lovers' cause to the pursuing Fionn, and the pair was restored to favor. They did not return to Fionn's abode at the fort of Almu, rather, they retired to Gráinne's rath near the magical cave of Keshcorran in Co. Sligo.

Fionn finally had his revenge: He lured Diarmait into a wild BOAR hunt atop the legendary peak of BEN BULBEN, knowing that the young man was under a geis never to hunt boar and realizing that Diarmait would have a hard fight against the boar, Gulben, who was a man whom his father had killed, enchanted into that fierce form. When the magical boar lay dead with no injury to Diarmait, Fionn again taunted his rival, forcing him to pace out the length of the corpse. A sharp bristle stabbed him and Diarmait fell down, near death from unquenchable bleeding. He begged Fionn to bring him water, and the old man did so, but then let it trickle away as the dying Diarmait watched, remarking that Gráinne should see his beautiful body like that, all covered with gore and blood.

Because of her name, which hides the word for SUN within it, Gráinne has been often interpreted as a diminished goddess of SOVEREIGNTY, whose selection of Diarmait over the failing Fionn meant the passage of her power to the younger man. Similarly, the circuit of Ireland by the loving couple recalls the king's circuit of his lands with the goddess as well as the daily movement of the sun across the landscape.

Sources: Campbell, J. F. *Popular Tales of the West Highlands.* Edinburgh: Edmonston and Douglas, 1862, pp. 39 ff; Dillon, Myles, ed. *Irish Sagas.* Cork: The Mercier Press, 1968, p. 135; Gregory, Lady Augusta. *Gods and Fighting Men: The Story of the Tuatha De Danaan and of the Fianna of Ireland.* New York: Oxford University Press, 1970, pp. 269 ff; MacCullogh, J. A. *Celtic Mythology.* Chicago: Academy Publishers, 1996, pp. 150, 254.

Grana Irish heroine. In Co. Limerick, at Carrigogunnel ("rock of the candle"), a light shone every night, killing whoever cast eyes upon it. Grana was the name of the WITCH or FAIRY who lit the smiting candle; she may be a diminished form of GRÁINNE or GRIAN, goddesses associated with that area. One of the valiant FIANNA, Regan, donned a cap of invisibility and snuffed Grana's candle, thereby destroying her power.

Grannos (Grannus) See APOLLO.

Gray Man (Far Liath, Liath Mhor) Scottish folkloric figure. A GIANT specter who haunted the Scottish shores as well as those of Ireland, the Gray Man is thought to personify the sea mist in which travelers can be lost and, thereafter, drowned. He looked especially for boats carrying RED-haired people and women but would attack any other boats at whim.

Sources: Curran, Bob. *Complete Guide to Celtic Mythology.* Belfast: Appletree, 2000, pp. 126–127; Douglas, George. *Scottish Fairy and Folk Tales.* West Yorkshire: EP Publishing, 1977, pp. 94 ff.

green Symbolic color. Together with RED, this was the color most favored by the FAIRY races who inhabit the ancient Celtic lands. Many humans, especially in Scotland, traditionally refused to wear this color so as not to offend their fairy neighbors; indeed, some Scottish families considered it fatal to don the color. Common associations between the color green and flourishing vegetation point to the fairies' earlier incarnation as spirits of FERTILITY and abundance.

Green Children British folkloric figures. Mythology and history collide in the tale of the Green Children, a girl and boy with GREEN skin and hair who abruptly appeared in Suffolk in the 12th century. They spoke no known language and, although clearly ravenous, refused to eat the meat they were offered. Although the boy died shortly after the pair crawled out of a hole under a downed tree, the girl lived to learn enough human speech to tell her rescuers that she and her brother came from a race that lived beneath the earth. She called her home St.

Martin's Land, which she described as a land of constant rain that otherwise closely resembled the upper world. The girl explained that she and her brother had become lost while tending their flocks and had accidentally come up to the surface world. The girl later married, but she kept frequenting the place of her emergence and one day disappeared, presumably to find her way home. Recent theories hold that the children were not FAIRIES at all—as their coloring suggested—but that their green hue was the effect of malnutrition, and that they were simply lost children from a war-torn area of England who had reached the unfamiliar "surface" by traveling through abandoned mineshafts.

Source: Keightley, Thomas. *The Fairy Mythology.* London: H. G. Bohn, 1870, pp. 381 ff.

Green Isle Scottish mythological site. One of the FORTUNATE ISLES, the Green Isle was a part of FAIRYLAND filled with orchards of magical fruit, especially APPLES. The Green Isle was sometimes called the Isle of Apples and imagined to be inhabited only by women.

Green Ladies British folkloric figures. Like the identically named DAMES VERTES in France, these FAIRY maidens were thought to haunt fresh water—WELLS and LAKES and pools—in Britain. They were sometimes destructive, luring people to their death like MERMAIDS, but could be jovial and pleasant as well.

Green Man British folkloric figure. Found carved in stone and wood in English medieval art, this figure of a man's face peering out from leaves and branches—or perhaps composed of those leaves and branches—is one of the most evocative and mysterious evidences of folk belief in Celtic lands. Although known by no other name than the Green Man, he has been interpreted as representing a guardian spirit of the corn, a masculine force of abundance. Most faces have a mild or even benevolent look, although a few look angry or threatening; some seem intoxicated.

A similar figure is found outside England as early as Roman times, when a male Medusa was sometimes used as an ornament; whether the head had religious significance is unknown, although he may have represented the woodland god SILVANUS. But the male mask in Britain is distinct in that the leaves are not a decoration but part of the face, which either emerges from them or dissolves into them.

If there was a myth or legend that defined the meaning of the Green Man, it has been lost. It is possible, however, that vestiges remain in literature and folk tradition. The Knight that GAWAIN meets in the poem *Sir Gawain and the Green Knight* is often interpreted as a literary reflection of this figure. The dancer called JACK-IN-THE-GREEN, who wears a leaf-covered mask in some British festivals on BELTANE (May 1), may be a living representative of the Green Man.

Sources: Basford, Kathleen. *The Green Man.* Ipswitch: D. S. Brew, Ltd., 1978; Bord, Janet, and Colin Bord. *The Secret Country: An interpretation of the folklore of ancient sites in the British Isles.* New York: Walker and Co., 1976, p. 76; Ross, Anne, and Michael Cyprien. *A Traveller's Guide to Celtic Britain.* Harrisburg, Pa.: Historical Times, 1985, p. 121; Spence, Lewis. *The Minor Traditions of British Mythology.* New York: Benjamin Blom, Inc., 1972.

Grian Irish goddess. Although many commentators find evidence of SUN gods among the Celts, there is equal or stronger evidence that the sun was seen as a goddess, at least in Ireland where a goddess with the clearly solar name of Grian ("sun") is found. As her name is pronounced like "green," some places that include this syllable, like Pallas Green near the FAIRY hill of KNOCKAINY, may refer to Grian; some have posited the derivation of that word from the solar power to bring forth plants.

Although no myths remain of Grian in Ireland, she is found in place-names like Tuamgraney and Lough Graney, which are also described as locations important to the obscure figure GILLAGRÉINE. Grian is described as the sister or twin of another goddess with solar attributes, ÁINE, the goddess or FAIRY QUEEN of the magical lake LOUGH GUR. As Áine was associated with summer rituals, it has been proposed that Grian ruled the winter sun. Whether there is any connection between Grian and the vibrant heroine GRÁINNE is not established. Many goddesses were called Grian as a kind of title; thus Macha is called "sun of womanfolk."

Sources: Condren, Mary. *The Serpent and the Goddess: Women, Religion and Power in Ancient Ireland.* San Francisco: Harper & Row, 1989, p. 35; O'Rahilly, Thomas. *Early Irish History and Mythology.* Dublin: The Dublin Institute for Advanced Studies, 1946, p. 289.

Grianán Aileach (Greenan Elly, Aileach, Oileach; Ailech Néit; Aleach Ned) Irish mythological site. An impressive, huge stone triple-walled HILLFORT in Co. Donegal goes by this name, which means the "sunroom" (*grianán*) of the otherwise unknown Aileach, said to be a woman or a goddess buried under the structure. But the vast circle of stone is no sunroom, and Aileach has also been defined as the name of the land or the tribe of its builders. Thus while the structure itself speaks eloquently of past importance, the name is more puzzling than explanatory. Occasionally it is said to have been named after GRIAN, the hypothesized SUN goddess, but that is true only insofar as the word *grianán* derives from that of the sun.

Aileach is listed in early texts as the capital of the PROVINCE of ULSTER after the fall of EMAIN MACHA, thus putting it on the same level of such important sites as TARA and CRUACHAN. Legend has it that the TUATHA DÉ DANANN, the mythological tribe of the goddess DANU, built Grianán Aileach and held it against the MILESIAN invaders; their king, NUADA of the Silver Arm, is said to be buried beneath its walls. The site was also the special home of the beneficent god DAGDA, who buried his son ÁED Minbhrec there. Grianán Aileach was one of the last forts to be held by the historical rulers who descended from the Celts, for it remained the seat of the Ui Néill dynasty, descendants of NIALL of the Nine Hostages, until the 13th century.

Griflet (Jaufre) Arthurian hero. This young man, one of the first knights of the ROUND TABLE was the lover of BRUNISSEN.

Grimes Grave Goddess British goddess. Because it is difficult if not impossible to date rock, the cultural origin of the tiny figure that goes by this name cannot be unquestionably established. The goddess was found in Norfolk, England, in the area of prehistoric (4000 B.C.E.) flint mines called Grimes Graves, where pit-mines as deep as 50 feet were dug with only deer antlers as shovels. Roughly shaped from white chalk, the goddess figure is squat and smirking, possibly pregnant; she reminds many observers of the SHEELA NA GIG, controversially labeled a goddess figure. That the Grimes Goddess was deliberately deposited in the mine is argued by the offerings found with it: a chalk phallus and several small chalk balls, a chalk lamp, flint blocks, and antlers. The original name of the goddess has been lost, and her meaning can only be a subject of conjecture.

Grisandole See AVENABLE.

groa'ch Breton folkloric figure. In Brittany we find a folkloric figure that may be related to the Scottish and Irish *GRUAGACH*, but which had an evil disposition in contrast to the *gruagach's* helpful one. Once, it was said, there was a boy and a girl, promised as spouses to each other at birth but orphaned and left to grow up as best they could. When he came of age the boy, Huarn, went off to seek his fortune. His intended, Bellah, gave him three TALISMANS: a

bell that would ring when he was in danger; a knife that would free him from any bonds; and a staff that would take him wherever he wanted to go. Off Huara set, walking until he reached the Isle of Lok, where a FAIRY woman lived surrounded by the waters of the LAKE. She took him beneath the water and showed him a palace, all built of seashells with crystal and coral decorations that made soft music as he passed. A garden of water plants grew around it, and within it people were celebrating merrily.

Inside the palace the *groa'ch* lay down upon a golden bed, her GREEN dress clinging to her voluptuous body and coral ornaments winking from her silky black hair. She urged the boy to stay with her, promising him the riches of the sea, for her lake opened into it through a secret passage, and all her treasure was gathered from ships that sank in the ocean. Huach almost forgot himself in the splendor of this FAIRYLAND, but back home Bellah heard the bell ring and, disguised as a boy, came rushing to save her promised lover. As they escaped together, the sea drowned the palace of the tempting but destructive water-WITCH.

Source: *Breton Folktales*. London: G. Bell & Sons, 1971, pp. 117 ff.

Gromer Somer Joure Arthurian hero. The beautiful maiden RAGNELL was turned into a HAG by this evil magician.

Gronw Pebyr Welsh hero. After the Welsh poet-hero GWYDION had created a woman of flowers for his son/nephew LLEU LLAW GYFFES, the flower-wife BLODEUWEDD grew tired of her husband and fell in love with the hunter Gronw Pebyr. The two conspired to kill Lleu, with Blodeuwedd providing the secret information about her husband's vulnerability and Gronw Pebyr striking the fatal blows.

grove See NEMETON.

gruagach (*grogan, grógach*) Scottish and Irish folkloric figure. This figure may descend from Celtic guardian divinities who watched over specific families and may originally have been divine ancestors. In Scotland the *gruagach* was a FAIRY woman who watched the CATTLE like a barnyard BROWNIE; she required frequent libations of MILK, preferably poured into special hollowed-out stones (see *BULLAUN*) called *leacna gruagach*. She dressed in GREEN, as was the fairies' habit, and had long golden HAIR, another indication of her OTHERWORLD nature. Even on sunny days, she was often drenched, as though she had been out in a downpour, and quietly asked humans who encountered her if she could stand beside the fire and dry herself.

The *gruagach* could also be male; in Co. Donegal, an immigrant Scottish family reported seeing a small man hanging about the farmstead, dressed only in his long RED hair (a sure sign of fairy blood). When the farmer was later injured while threshing oats, the little naked fellow took over and kept a steady pace of work despite his lack of appropriate attire. The woman of the place, apparently suspecting her laborer was a fairy, avoided speaking to him or thanking him for his work (see LAYING THE FAIRIES). But after several days of work by the *gruagach*, the woman took pity upon his nakedness and knit him a tiny sweater. That was all it took; the little guy disappeared the next day. The *gruagach's* name has been connected with terms for "hair," with which they were believed to be spectacularly endowed.

Sources: Kennedy, Patrick. *Legendary Fictions of the Irish Celts*. New York: Benjamin Blom, 1969, p. 136; MacCullogh, J. A. *Celtic Mythology*. Chicago: Academy Publishers, 1996, p. 245; MacDougall, James. *Folk Tales and Fairy Lore in Gaelic and English*. Edinburgh: John Grant, 1910, pp. 217–221; O hEochaidh, Séan. *Fairy Legends of Donegal*. Trans. Máire MacNeill. Dublin: Comhairle Bhéaloideas Éireann, 1977, p. 89.

Guaire Irish hero. The father of the mountain goddess ÉBHLINNE of MUNSTER, Guaire lived in the great BRÚ NA BÓINNE, the prehistoric stone complex on the banks of the River Boyne, far to the north of his daughter's land. Another Guaire was an historical king of CONNACHT, renowned for his GENEROSITY; he even provided meals to anchorites in the nearby mountains by having the food whisked through the air. Guaire's castle at Kinvarra in Co. Galway, which can still be visited today, was the site of the challenge to the BARD Senchán, which resulted in the return of the lost epic, *TÁIN BÓ CUAILNGE*, from the OTHERWORLD.

Source: MacNeill, Máire. *The Festival of Lughnasa, Parts I and II*. Dublin: Comhairle Bhéaloideas Éireann, 1982, pp. 327–328.

guee Manx curse or prayer. On the Isle of Man, it was traditional to both pray and CURSE while kneeling; cursing was called "wishing upon the knees." One strong traditional curse was called the Skeab Lome or "naked broom," in which a broom was invoked as a power to sweep away evil (or one's enemies).

Guénolé (Guénole, Gwénnolé, Winwaloe) Breton hero. This Breton SAINT was the abbot of YS, the beautiful doomed city of the pagan princess DAHUT. It was Guénolé who saved GRADLON, Dahut's father, while sentencing Dahut to die beneath the waves of the sea. Such figures, interpolated into Celtic myth with the coming of Christianity, sometimes have at their root an ancient elemental divinity, transformed and humanized. As Guenole is connected with the sea, he may have taken on some aspects of an ancient sea god; conversely, he may simply represent the intrusion of Christian morality into Celtic culture.

Guid Folk See NAMES FOR THE FAIRIES.

Guinevere (Guenièvre, Gwenhwyvar, Gwenhwyfar, Ganore) Arthurian heroine or goddess.

The theory that the stories of the quasi-historical king of Britain, ARTHUR, derive from Celtic mythology is strongly supported by the central position of Guinevere in the tales. If, as many agree, Arthur's "wife" is a thinly disguised Welsh goddess, the sad tale of her betrayal of the aging king for the noble younger man becomes a variant of the common story of the king's marriage to the goddess of SOVEREIGNTY—a goddess who married one king after another, for she was the land itself. In offering herself to the manly knight LANCELOT, by this interpretation, Guinevere enacted the traditional role of the goddess.

Variants in which Arthur married three women, each named Guinevere, further strengthen the identification of this queen with the THREE-fold goddess, as does the derivation of her name (gwen, white; hwyvvar, FAIRY or spirit) from words that link her to the OTHER-WORLD and to the Irish goddess/heroine FINNABAIR. Similarly, her marriage to Arthur on the festival of summer's beginning, BELTANE, points to a ritual drama rather than merely a dynastic alliance.

The story of Guinevere's marriage to an aging king and her later love for a handsome knight almost exactly parallels the Irish story of fair GRÁINNE and her young lover DIARMAIT, who ran away from the aging FIONN MAC CUMHAILL; there are also parallels in the forced marriage of the the young heroine ISEULT to king MARK of Cornwall despite her love for the younger TRISTAN. Like Diarmait, Lancelot at first attempted to maintain his loyalty to his king while sleeping next to the woman he loved, placing a sword between them to deter intimacy, just as Diarmait pitched two separate tents.

Ultimately, however, love conquered caution, and the resulting affair between Lancelot and Guinevere split the loyalties of Arthur's knights of the ROUND TABLE. Many of them went off on hopeless quests, including that for the GRAIL. Guinevere finally determined that she could no longer live with Arthur and arranged an abduction, instructing her maidens to dress in GREEN—the color of FAIRYLAND—on the morning of Beltane, further support for the idea that she was herself from the Otherworld. Some versions of the story describe a decision by Arthur to execute Guinevere for her unfaithfulness, with Lancelot rescuing her at the last minute from the flames.

Her escape, however, was followed by an eventual return to Arthur. By then the court of CAMELOT was in ruins and its king was in combat with his mortal enemy and bastard son, MORDRED. Although in many tellings Guinevere is blamed for the shambles that Camelot became, it was Arthur who had planted the seed of its downfall. Arguments for interpretation of Guinevere as the goddess of Sovereignty point to early legends that Mordred carried off and married Guinevere in an attempt to solidify his claim to Camelot's throne, suggesting that she, rather than Arthur, held the keys to the kingdom. Contemporary renderings of the tale, including Marion Zimmer Bradley's wildly popular *Mists of Avalon*, attempt to redeem centuries of disdain for Guinevere.

Sources: MacCullogh, J. A. *Celtic Mythology.* Chicago: Academy Publishers, 1996, p. 123; Markale, Jean. *Courtly Love: The Path of Sexual Initiation.* Rochester, Vt.: Inner Traditions, 2000, p. 116.

Guinglain   Arthurian hero. A minor figure in the tales of CAMELOT, Guinglain was the son of the transformed HAG, RAGNELL, and the exemplary knight of the ROUND TABLE, GAWAIN.

Gundestrup Cauldron   Archaeological treasure. In 1891 a great silver CAULDRON was found in a Danish peat BOG, where it may have been either ritually deposited or hidden in a time of crisis. Bas-reliefs across the face of the vessel, which is believed to date from the 2nd or 1st century B.C.E. show enigmatic scenes that appear to be rituals, and figures that appear to be divine. Because the site where the treasure was found is of ambiguous history, it has sometimes been argued that the cauldron represents Germanic rather than Celtic material, but most scholars agree that the cauldron either was of Celtic manufacture or was influenced by Celtic belief. A goddess being conveyed on a cart and a horned god resembling the one known elsewhere as CERNUNNOS are among the most important figures on the vessel.

gunna Scottish folkloric figure. A CATTLE-herding BROWNIE of the Scottish islands, the *gunna* hung about small farms making sure the cows did not trample the garden. As with many such helpful sprites, he went naked despite the weather. Any attempt to provide clothes drove the *gunna* away (see LAYING THE FAIRIES).

Gutuatros (pl., Gutuatri) Continental Celtic social role. This name was born by certain continental Celtic DRUIDS who served at specific temples. As the name appears to mean "speakers," they may have practiced DIVINATION.

Guy Fawkes British folkloric belief. The 1605 failure by Roman Catholics to destroy the English Houses of Parliament, led by a man named Guy Fawkes, led to an annual festival, supposedly in honor of the conspirators' execution. The date of the festival, November 5, is suspiciously close to the old Celtic feast of winter's beginning, SAMHAIN, on November 1. In addition, the typical celebration involves bonfires, which may have replaced the festival fires traditional to Samhain.

Guyomard Arthurian hero. The lover of king ARTHUR's half sister, the sorceress MORGAN, Guyomard was an untrustworthy knight who so angered Morgan that she cursed a valley in the magical forest of BROCÉLIANDE. Any knight who wandered into that PERILOUS VALLEY after being unfaithful to his mistress would be trapped there forever, surrounded by imagined demons and insurmountable obstacles. LANCELOT, who was ever true in his heart to his beloved Guinevere, finally broke the enchantment.

guytrash See TRASH.

Gwalchmei (Gwalchmei fab Gwyar) Welsh hero. In Arthurian legend, Gwalchmei appears as the world's speediest runner and as one of the advisers to the mythological king ARTHUR.

gwartheg y llyn Welsh folkloric figures. Most Celtic lands have tales of FAIRY COWS that recall the supreme importance of their herds to the ancient Celts. In both Scotland and Ireland these cattle of the OTHERWORLD were imagined as having the typical coloring of fairy beings: RED body and white ears. In Wales the pattern changed slightly, for the gwartheg were completely white like GHOSTS. They could interbreed with the stock of earthly farmers, much to the advantage of the mortal COWS visited by a stray white fairy BULL. Alternatively, a fairy cow might decide to settle down on this side of the veil, producing prodigious amounts of MILK until, like the mythical cow of abundance called the GLAS GHAIBHLEANN, she was driven away by greed. One farmer who attempted to slaughter his fairy cow found her and all her progeny called AWAY by a LAKE-maiden.

Gwawl Welsh hero. A minor character in the Welsh MABINOGION, he was a suitor for the hand of the goddess/queen RHIANNON against the heroic king PWYLL. Through trickery, Gwawl forced Pwyll to step back from his suit, but Pwyll returned the favor by tricking Gwawl into crawling into a bag, which he then used like a football with his warriors.

Gwendydd (Gwendolyn, Gwendolena, Gwenddydd, Gwyneth, Ganieda, Venotia) Welsh heroine. This Welsh woman was the sister of the renowned magician MERLIN—perhaps his TWIN, perhaps his lover, perhaps both. It was to her that Merlin passed on his magical powers and his knowledge, once the seductive VIVIANE had trapped him in her magical forest. In tales that describe her as Merlin's wife, Gwendydd married the generous king RHYDDERCH HAEL after Merlin went mad.

Gwenfrewi (Winefride) Welsh heroine. The quasi-historical 7th-century Gwenfrewi was assaulted by a local prince, whose attempt on her virtue she managed to escape. He came after her and, drawing his sword, decapitated her as punishment for her self-control. Rolling down a hill, her HEAD came to rest in a little valley, where a healing WELL immediately burst forth. Bueno, a minor SAINT and Gwenfrewi's uncle, put her head back on her shoulders, where it instantly knit together, leaving only a small thin scar across the throat as evidence of the crime.

Gwern Welsh hero. The child of the Welsh princess BRANWEN and her Irish husband, king MATHOLWCH, did not live long. His uncle EFNISIEN mutilated Matholwch's horses without reason, which gave the king cause to hold Branwen a prisoner in Ireland, during which time she bore Gwern, who was named king of the land in his infancy. Efnisien killed Gwern by burning him alive when he was only three years old, causing the great battle in which most of the Welsh heroes and all the warriors of Ireland were killed.

Gwidion See GWYDION.

Gwion (Gwion Bach) Welsh hero. The name of the great Welsh bard TALIESIN in his first incarnation was Gwion, whose adventures began when he was a little boy hired by the great HAG goddess CERIDWEN to tend to household tasks. An important one was to stir the CAULDRON in which Ceridwen brewed herbs for a year and a day, intending to make her ugly son AFAGDDU wise, in order to make up for his appearance.

Warned not to taste the brew, Gwion tried to follow orders, but the stuff bubbled out and seared his skin. The boy popped his finger into his mouth and, therefore, absorbed all the WISDOM intended for the goddess's son. In a series of transformations, Ceridwen pursued him until he turned himself into a grain of wheat that, transformed into a hen, she gobbled up. It impregnated her so that she gave birth to a reborn Gwion, who became the great poet Taliesin.

gwrach y rhibyn Welsh folkloric figure. Like the WASHER AT THE FORD, this BANSHEE-like FAIRY woman warned of imminent death, usually by standing at a crossroads or near a bend in a stream. She was huge and hideous, with coarse RED hair, a massive nose, and eyes that shone red.

gwragedd annwn Welsh folkloric figure. While most FAIRY women were dangerous to humans, luring men to FAIRYLAND to enjoy and discard, the Welsh LAKE maidens or *Gwragedd Annwn* were a different breed, for they enjoyed settling down with human men and made excellent wives. However, there was a firm taboo against ever lifting a hand to such a lake maiden. Even a blow struck in jest caused them to leave husband and children behind, taking all their fairy wealth—which could be substantial—and plunging into the nearest lake.

Gwri Welsh hero. This name was given to the kidnapped hero PRYDERI by his foster father, after the boy had miraculously appeared from out of the night sky one BELTANE.

Gwyar (Anna) Welsh goddess. The story of this ancient Welsh goddess, wife of the god of heaven, is fragmentary. All that is left is the meaning of her name ("gore"); her relationship to king ARTHUR, said to have been her brother (at other times the name given for Arthur's sister is MORGAUSE or MORGAN); and the information that she had two sons, one good, the other bad.

Gwyddno (Gwyddno Garanhir)   Welsh hero. A minor figure in the story of KULHWCH AND OLWEN, he was said to have a basket that was magically filled with food at all times—a basket that Kulhwch had to steal in order to gain his beloved Olwen.

Gwydion (Gwidion, Gwydion ab Dôn) Welsh hero. The son of the great Welsh mother goddess DÔN, Gwydion figures importantly in the great compilation of myths called the MABINOGION. Although he is central to the action, he plays a secondary role to the more active parties: his brother GILFAETHWY, his uncle MATH, his sister ARIANRHOD. When Gilfaethwy conceived a lustful fixation upon the maiden GOEWIN, ceremonial footholder to king Math, Gwydion helped him find an opportunity to rape her. In punishment, Math turned the brothers into DEER, PIGS, and WOLVES consecutively. When he gained his human form back, Gwydion proposed that, as the deflowered Goewin could no longer be footholder to Math, Arianrhod take her place.

But Arianrhod failed to pass a magical test of virginity, giving birth to a wriggling lump of flesh that leapt into the sea to become DYLAN Son-of-Wave and another unformed child whom Gwydion nursed in a chest until he was old enough to claim arms and a name from his mother. Arianrhod, still angered by Gwydion's connivances, refused, but Gwydion found a way to trick her into naming the boy LLEU LLAW GYFFES. Next, with Math's help, Gwydion formed a woman, BLODEUWEDD, from flowers to be the boy's bride. That, too, ended poorly, with the girl attempting to murder her husband, who turned into an EAGLE. Gwydion, always ready with MAGIC, brought Lleu back to human form and sent Blodeuwedd away in the form of an OWL.

Other tales show Gwydion changing fungus into horses and creating seagoing ships from thin air. Under the name of Gwion, he was imprisoned in the OTHERWORLD, where he became a BARD as a result of the inspiration he received. He may have brought back more than poetry from the Otherworld of ANNWN, for one text refers to him as a thief who stole magical swine and brought them to the surface world. This magician, poet, and trickster is believed to be a diminished version of an earlier Welsh god, one whose domain included both the stars, where he lived in the Milky Way (Caer Gwydion), and the underworld of Annwn.

Source: Evans-Wentz, W. Y. *The Fairy-Faith in Celtic Countries.* Gerrards Cross: Colin Smythe Humanities Press, 1911, p. 378.

gwyllion   Welsh folkloric figure. In Wales strange female spirits were said to haunt lonely roads. With her apron thrown over her shoulder, trudging wearily along carrying a wooden milk-pail, this ancient HAG wore ash-colored rags and an oblong four-cornered hat. There is no record of her attacking those she met on the roads, but her appearance was fearsome enough to frighten lonely travelers. Like other members of the FAIRY races, she feared metal, especially IRON, and vanished instantly if confronted with a knife or other piece of cutlery.

Gwynn ap Nudd (Gwyn ap Nudd, Herne, Herne the Hunter, Gabriel)   Welsh hero. The Welsh king of FAIRYLAND, "White One, son of the Dark," was said to reside under GLASTON-BURY TOR, the small pyramidal hill that is southwestern England's most significant feature. Gwynn reigned over the folk called the TYLWYTH TEG, beautiful tiny people who wore blue and danced all night in the fashion of Irish FAIRIES. His special feast was spring's beginning, BELTANE, when he led the WILD HUNT to raid the land of the living. His name means Gwynn, son of Nudd; his father was king of a Hades-like Otherworld called ANNWN. He could materialize at will, surrounded by his beautiful host playing FAIRY MUSIC. His queen was the daughter of LLUDD, CREIDDYLAD, on whom Shakespeare based the character of Cordelia in *King Lear.*

Alternative names used of Gwyn ap Nudd are Herne the Hunter, the frightening figure who skulks around Windsor Forest in England; and Gabriel, known best for his vicious fairy hounds.

Sources: Evans-Wentz, W. Y. *The Fairy-Faith in Celtic Countries.* Gerrards Cross: Colin Smythe Humanities Press, 1911, pp. 152 ff; Lonigan, Paul R. *The Druids: Priests of the Ancient Celts.* Contributions to the Study of Religion, No. 45. Westport, Conn.: Greenwood Press, 1996, p. 169; Spence, Lewis. *The Minor Traditions of British Mythology.* New York: Benjamin Blom, Inc., 1972, p. 109.

Gwythyr fab Greidawl   Welsh folkloric figure. This warrior was one of two contenders for the hand of the maiden of springtime, CREIDDYLAD, in Welsh folk ceremonies that marked the BELTANE season. Representing the summer, Gwythyr always won, defeating the winter king, GWYNN AP NUDD.

Gyre-Carling   See HABETROT.

Habetrot (Habitrot, Gyre-Carling, Gy-Carlin)   British folkloric figure. A spinner goddess diminished after Christianization to a FAIRY spirit, Habetrot was a healing spirit. Those who could induce her to weave them a garment never suffered from illness. She appeared in some areas of Britain as a FAIRY QUEEN (Gyre-Carling or Gy-Carlin) who stole any flax left unspun at the end of a year.

On the Scottish border the tale is told of a lazy girl who, instructed by her mother to finish spinning seven hanks of yarn, hurt her fingers. Wandering in search of a stream in which to soothe her hands, the girl encountered an old spinning woman who gave her seven lovely soft hanks spun by ghostly women with twisted mouths. The silky thread attracted a handsome lord who married the girl for her spinning skills. The girl brought her husband to Habetrot, who showed him the deformed spinners and predicted that his new lady would soon look that way. Shocked, the lord forbade his wife to spin—permitting her to live the idle happy life she preferred.

Source: Douglas, George. *Scottish Fairy and Folk Tales.* West Yorkshire: EP Publishing, 1977, pp. 109–110.

Habondia (Abundia, Abunditia)   Germanic or Celtic goddess. The name of this obscure goddess became the word *abundance*, suggesting an earth or harvest divinity. Habondia was found in Celtic lands but may be Germanic; she was noted by medieval WITCH-hunters as the particular divinity of their prey.

Hafgan (Havgan)   Welsh mythological figure. In Welsh mythology Hafgan ("summer song") was one of two rival kings of the OTHERWORLD who battled constantly. His opponent was the better-known king ARAWN of ANNWN. Hafgan was magically endowed with the ability to recover from any blow once he had received a second; thus his opponents had but one chance to lay him low. In the collection of Welsh myths called the *MABINOGION*, Arawn asked the human prince PWYLL to be his substitute for a year and to battle Hafgan for him. Magically switching their appearances, Arawn went forth to rule Pwyll's land for a year, while Pwyll descended to Annwn to take Arawn's throne for the same time; at the end of the year, Pwyll defeated Hafgan in single combat.

hag   Irish and Scottish folkloric figure. Old, blind or one-eyed, humpbacked, with rheumy eyes and hairy chin, the hag of Irish and Scottish legend was not beautiful at first look. But kiss her, and she became a gorgeous maiden in full bloom of youth. This unlikely reversal is found in many stories of the great goddess of SOVEREIGNTY, of war goddesses like the MÓRRÍGAN and MACHA, and the pre-Celtic creator goddess, the CAILLEACH. In Arthurian legend the hag appears as the LOATHY LADY, who spurs on the quest for the GRAIL, and as RAGNELL, who leads her husband to understand what women really want.

Sources: Clark, Rosalind. *The Great Queens: Irish Goddesses from the Morrígan to Cathleen Ní Houlihan.* Irish Literary Studies 34. Gerrards Cross: Colin Smythe, 1991; Condren, Mary. *The Serpent and the Goddess: Women, Religion and Power in Ancient Ireland.* San Francisco: Harper & Row, 1989; Moane, Geraldine. "A Womb Not a Tomb: Goddess Symbols and Ancient Ireland." *Canadian Women's Studies: Les cahiers de la femme.* Vol. 17, 1997, pp. 7–10; Ross, Anne, "The Divine Hag of the Pagan Celts." In Venetia Newall, ed. *The Witch Figures.* London: Routledge & Kegan Paul, 1973, pp. 139–164.

Hag's Glen (Coom Callee)   Irish sacred site. In the southwestern province of MUNSTER, traditionally associated with the powerful figure of the HAG named the CAILLEACH, the scenic valley of Coom Callee (Hag's Glen) forms part of MacGuillycuddy's Reeks, Ireland's highest mountains. Local legend has it that a hag in that glen cared for a small child and that a rock was imprinted with their footprints. In the mid-19th century an old woman living alone in the Glen was given the name of the Cailleach, furthering the identification of the valley with the mythological hag.

hair   Symbolic object. Hair was an important ritual and spiritual symbol to the ancient Celts. Warriors wore their hair long and their mustaches untrimmed when they went into battle, sometimes treating them with lime to create a fearfully wild appearance. Women's hair was long as well, often braided or otherwise dressed;

hair was considered a mark of their sexual power. DRUIDS wore a special tonsure or haircut that distinguished them from others in the tribe.

Folklore records many superstitions that emphasize the continuing importance of hair as a symbol. People were careful never to throw cut or combed hair into fire, for fear that they would come down with fever; this is typical of magical part-equals-whole thinking. RED hair was considered especially significant, for it showed that FAIRY blood ran in the person's veins. MERMAIDS lured sailors by combing their hair, and according to the principle of SYMPATHETIC MAGIC it was dangerous for girls to COMB their hair when their brothers were at sea. Animal hair also had power, especially that of HORSES, which could come alive if put in water. Should a person, especially a child, be bitten by a DOG, the wound had to be bound with hair from the animal to ensure healing.

Hairy Jack   British folkloric spirit. A BLACK DOG from the Lincolnshire region, he haunted wild places in the region and turned himself into a little lame man in order to pass unnoticed among the neighbors.

Hallowe'en (Hallowmas)   See SAMHAIN.

Hallstatt   Archaeological site. At this important site, near Saltzburg in Austria, a great treasure of ancient Celtic artifacts was found. Dated from approximately 700–600 B.C.E. (after the URNFIELD period but before the LA TÈNE), the artifacts included weapons and tools of bronze and IRON, as well as some ritual objects. Buried with their presumed owners, the design of the objects suggests a cultural change from earlier times, when less decorated objects had been the norm. A parallel change from cremation, only a few generations earlier, to earth entombment suggests a change in the worldview of these very ancient Celts, for how people treat their dead tells a great deal about what life (if any) was presumed to lie ahead.

These Hallstatt-era bodies were laid out on four-wheeled wagons and encased in a tomb of OAK that was then covered with earth. Bronze vessels, iron spears, and traces of meat and poultry were found buried with them, presumably indicating the beginnings of Celtic belief that the OTHERWORLD of death required sufficient grave goods (weapons, tools, ornaments) for the soul's happiness.

The fact that a great SALT-mining region is located near Hallstatt gives rise to the theory that the early Celtic wealth was derived from mining and trading in salt, an extremely valuable commodity in the days before refrigeration. Salt was used to preserve meats, and as the Celts were a CATTLE-raising people, such a preservative had great value in keeping people fed through the long winters. Buried saline deposits were mined and the salt pulverized for transportation and use.

hammer Celtic symbol. The "god with the hammer" was a common image of divinity among the continental Celts; variously called TARANIS, DIS PATER, SILVANUS, and SUCELLUS, he was depicted as strong, mature, and bearded. As a symbol of the force and energy of such gods, the hammer is sometimes interpreted as representing storm and thunder, although there is no definite indication of such a meteorological meaning. Indeed, other interpretations connect this god to the earth's FERTILITY rather than to the sky; the fact that the god often carries a cup, common symbol of earthly energy, supports this interpretation. Finally, some commentators see the hammer as representative of the blighting force of winter, although that remains a minority view. The club or MALLET carried by the DAGDA may be an Irish form of the hammer.

Handsel Monday (Di-luian an t-sainnseil) Scottish festival. The first Monday after HOGMANY (New Year's Day) was a day for DIVINATION or forecasting futures through games of chance and trial; on the Isle of Skye this day was the first in a sequence of 12 days whose weather predicted that of the following 12 months. The holiday's name is anglicized from the Scottish *sainnseal*, the gift offered to every visitor on this day.

hare Symbolic animal. The hare, in Ireland, was believed to be a WITCH in disguise, perhaps because the animal was mythically connected to that witch-like being, the CAILLEACH. When a hare was injured, a witch in the neighborhood would sport an identical injury. The same belief is found on the Isle of Man, where a wounded hare would always get away unless shot with a silver bullet; the transformed witch would thereafter be found, either alive or dead, with an identical wound.

In Scotland it was believed that witches took the form of hares in order to steal MILK—a common target of magical theft. Disguising herself as a hare, the witch would sneak into a barn and suckle the milk from a COW's udder. If caught, the hare would instantly turn back into human form. Hares seen in unusual places, including in regions where they were not typically found, were similarly believed to be disguised witches. If pursued, such hares would run into houses, revealing the witch's habitation. If one found a group of hares together, it was clearly a gathering of a witches' coven.

The fierce temperament of hares was sometimes assigned to the FAIRY Rabbit, a bold being that tried to drown people at sea; if the potential victims were carrying earth from their home, or from legendary Tory Island, they could survive even the onslaught of this malicious spirit.

Such folklore may be a late recollection of an earlier religious meaning for the hare. Caesar recorded that eating the flesh of the hare was taboo to continental Celts, which suggests that the animal was seen as sacred or ancestral; Dio Cassius mentioned a DIVINATION using hares that was employed by the Celtic warrior queen BOUDICCA before she entered battle. Such fragments of ancient lore suggest that the SHAPESHIFTING character given to hares in folklore may be a vestige of ancient religious imagery.

Sources: Campbell, John Grigorson. *Witchcraft and Second Sight in the Highlands and Islands of Scotland.* Detroit: Singing Tree Press, 1970, pp. 8, 33; O hEochaidh, Séan. *Fairy Legends from Donegal.* Trans. Máire Mac Neill. Dublin: Comhairle Bhéaloideas Éireann, 1977, p. 247; Ó hÓgain, Dáithí. *Irish Superstitions.* London; Gill & Macmillan, 1995, p. 57; O'Sullivan, Patrick V. *Irish Superstitions and Legends of Animals and Birds.* Cork: Mercier, 1991, p. 76.

harp   Symbolic object. The stringed instrument that today symbolizes Ireland was associated in ancient times with the beneficent god DAGDA, at whose call it would fly across the land, killing anyone that stood in its way. The Dagda harp had only THREE melodies: sleep, grief, and laughter. A similar legendary harp can be found in the Welsh tale of KULHWCH AND OLWEN.

See also CRAIPHTINE.

harvest dollies   Celtic folkloric figures. Until the relatively recent past, the harvest celebration in Celtic lands was replete with mythological and folkloric significance. On the Isle of Man we find straw images called *mheillea* ("harvest") or *baban ny mheillea* ("doll of the harvest"), which were decorated with ribbons to form dresses and referred to as "maidens," feminine figures probably derived from an ancient goddess of the abundant harvest. Approximately four inches tall, these figures were often crafted from the final sheaf harvested. Such harvest dollies were kept near the hearth until replaced by a similar doll after the next year's harvest. In Scotland a similar "harvest maiden" was thought to protect farms against fairy mischief if suspended somewhere within the house.

hawthorn   See THORN.

Haxey Hood Games   British folkloric festival. In the small town of Haxey in Humberside, a traditional midwinter game takes place on Twelfth Night, the last day of the old Christmas holidays. In medieval times, legend says, the scarlet hood of a local noblewoman, Lady de Mowbray, was blown off her head as she rode to church, and a dozen men sprang forward to save it for her. Delighted, she granted the village a plot of land—the Hoodland—whose produce provided a hood for a contest among 12 villagers, still held each year under the guidance of the RED-dressed gobbans (boggins, boggans). A fool begins the ceremony in the wee hours of the morning by giving an oration in the town square. As he finishes with the words "House against house, town against town, if you meet a man knock him down, but don't hurt him," a fire is lit at his feet; this is called "smoking the fool."

When the fool's part has finished, the games proper begin. The King Gobban throws 12 hoods into the air, and everyone scrambles for one. Anyone who manages to get away with a hood to the safety of a village inn gets free drinks. Some have argued that the origins of this rite are far more ancient than the medieval period and have seen in it the memory of a ritual of HUMAN SACRIFICE.

hazel   Celtic sacred tree. One of the most revered trees among the Celts, the hazel (genus *Corylus*) was thought to produce nuts of WISDOM when it grew at the sources of great RIVERS; the nuts made the flesh of fish (especially SALMON) speckled, with one spot appearing for each nut eaten. Thus the most speckled fish brought the most wisdom to the eater. Stories of both the Boyne and the Shannon rivers include descriptions of the magical hazel groves that fed the fish that swam at the river's source. Uneaten nuts turned into bubbles of inspiration, readily seen in the Shannon's source in Co. Cavan, which bubbles from underground SPRINGS feeding the pool. Hazel trees were said to shade CONNLA'S WELL somewhere in Co. Tipperary; anyone eating their nuts would become a brilliant BARD and scholar.

The connection of hazelnuts with wisdom is also found in Celtic mythology that requires bards to carve their staffs from hazel wood and in the taboo against burning the wood of the hazel tree. Hazel twigs are still said to guide water-witches to underground streams. In the Americas the unrelated witch-hazel tree (genus *Hamamelis*) is thought to have the same power. Hazel, like THORN, is one of the traditional trees believed to be inhabited by FAIRIES. In Ireland Tara was once described as a hazel grove; in Scotland the word *Carlton* (from the ancient Celtic word *Calltuinn*) designates an area where a sacred hazel grove once thrived.

Source: Hull, Eleanor. *Folklore of the British Isles.* London: Methuen & Co., Ltd., 1928, pp. 128–129.

head Celtic symbol. Sculptural and literary references to the head appear throughout the ancient Celtic world, so much so that early scholars used to speak of the "cult of the head," although that phrase is currently out of academic fashion. Sculptured heads without torsos—thus interpreted as severed from the body—have been found in many sites, dating as far back as the earliest proto-Celtic culture of the URNFIELD period. At times, such disembodied heads are inhuman, having three faces; occasionally a sculpture combined the head with the phallus to produce a double image of potency. Religious sculptures of the head of a sacred animal have also been found; thus the sacredness of the head was not necessarily limited to the human. The sacred head was used over the entire Celtic area for many centuries, making it the single most important and common Celtic religious symbol.

Myths as well as ritual objects emphasize the importance of the head: The head of Welsh hero BRÂN THE BLESSED (whose name has been connected to *pen*, the Welsh syllable meaning "head") continued speaking for years after his death, as did the Irish MAC DATHÓ and CONAIRE Mór, although the Irish heads' capacity for posthumous speech did not last as long. After the young musician and warrior DONN BÓ was killed

in battle, his head was brought to a feast where, asked to sing, it produced such a piercing melody that the music reduced everyone to tears. The speaking (or singing) severed head, neither entirely of this world nor fully in the OTHER-WORLD, was believed to have oracular powers and could be consulted to learn the future.

In folklore this ancient mythological vision survived in stories of GIANTS with the power to replace their severed heads on their bodies and go on as before; thus it was imperative for their opponents to keep head and body far apart until both were blue with cold and the danger of recapitation was past. Similar magical powers were granted to the decapitated head in tales that it could, of its own volition, become a weapon and attack the warrior who severed it from its body.

Such stories recall ancient Celtic traditions. Warriors traditionally cut off and displayed the heads of defeated enemies, for the head was seen as the place where personality or essence was most condensed or pure, rather like the contemporary American image of the heart. The Roman author Livy described the Celtic Boii warriors placing the severed head of an enemy chieftain in a TEMPLE, while lesser warriors' heads were strung from the bridles of those who defeated them, presenting a fearsome appearance to enemies. Greek historian Diodorus Siculus similarly described warriors beheading those they killed in battle and strapping their heads to horses' bridles or nailing them upon houses. Poseidonius speaks of being sickened by the sight of so many heads on display around a Celtic chieftain's home, but he adds that familiarity dulled his horror. Distinguished enemies' heads were embalmed in cedar and kept in a special box, to be proudly displayed when talk turned to exploits of war.

These historical records are reflected in Irish myth that tells of the hero CÚCHULAINN returning from battle carrying nine heads in one hand, 10 in the other, and of his wife EMER's acceptance of the heads of his own 10 slayers upon the hero's death. The heads of defeated enemies were called "the masts of MACHA," a poetic phrase that otherwise referred to acorns on which PIGs feasted. Other Irish sources speak of warriors taking out the brains of their defeated victims and mixing them with lime to form a "brain ball" that could be used as a weapon or displayed as a trophy; it was the brain ball of the hero Meisceadhra that was hurled at Meisceadhra's killer, king CONCOBAR MAC NESSA, lodging in Concobar's head and eventually causing his death.

There is evidence that the Celts connected their reverence for the head with that for WATER, since skulls and metal replicas of heads have been found in sacred SPRINGS and WELLS. The reverence offered the "heads" of RIVERS—their sources—such as that which holds sacred the round pool at the source of the Shannon River, may combine these two symbolic meanings into one.

Sources: Chadwick, Nora. *The Celts.* New York: Penguin Books, 1971, pp. 161 ff; Green, Miranda. *The Gods of Roman Britain.* Aylesbury: Shire Publications Ltd., 1983, p. 66; Green, Miranda. *Symbol and Image in Celtic Religious Art.* London: Routledge, 1989, p. 211; MacCulloch, J. A. *The Religion of the Ancient Celts.* London: Constable, 1911, pp. 240 ff; Ross, Anne. *Pagan Celtic Britain: Studies in Iconography and Tradition.* London: Routledge & Kegan Paul, 1967, pp. 61 ff, 104, 120.

healing Traditional healing took several forms, including herbal remedies, spells, and rituals. The efficacy of some ancient herbal remedies has been upheld by contemporary biochemistry, while other remedies are untested or have been proven ineffective. Many of our common modern drugs derive from plant sources, like aspirin (salicylic acid) from willow (plants of the genus *Salix*), which is known in many lands as an effective remedy against pain. In Scotland, St. John's Wort *(Hypericum pulchrum)* was known as an herb useful for keeping away FAIRIES who might steal people from their beds; this suggests

that what we now call depression was earlier described as FAIRY KIDNAPPING.

Other forms of healing required magical rituals, as when trailing pearlwort *(Sagina procumbens)* was attached to the skins of animals and people to protect them against the evil EYE. Even such rituals may have resulted in healing; modern medicine knows the so-called placebo effect, whereby people given sugar pills show improvements similar to those in patients given real medicines. Scientists continue to explore the connection of body, mind, and spirit.

In Ireland water from holy WELLS was sprinkled on or fed to sick animals and people; in Scotland chanted spells assisted in the healing of minor injuries and ailments like sprains and boils. Various regions also had specific healing rituals; often these involved visiting places held sacred by pre-Celtic people, such as SPRINGS and STONE CIRCLES. Some of these places may have induced healing by purely physical means, as with thermal springs that may have relieved the pains of arthritis, but more commonly the location has no detectable biological effect. The gathering of herbs sometimes required specific rituals (cut with material other than IRON, gathered at specific times of day, rewarded with drinks of wine) of apparently magical intent and import.

Many healing techniques were widely known and used by ordinary people. In some cases, however, local herbalists or WITCHES might be called upon; these were often older women who earned a modest living from consulting with their neighbors in times of need, but such power could backfire if such a person were suspected of using her powers for ill and was accused of WITCHCRAFT.

Sources: Campbell, John Grigorson. *Witchcraft and Second Sight in the Highlands and Islands of Scotland.* Detroit: Singing Tree Press, 1970, pp. 103 ff; Carmichael, Alexander. *Carmina Gadelica: Hymns and Incantations.* Hudson, N. Y.: Lindisfarne Press, 1992, pp. 377 ff; Kavanagh, Peter. *Irish Mythology: A Dictionary.* Newbridge, Co. Kildare: The Goldsmith Press, Ltd., 1988, pp. 42–53; MacCulloch, J. A. *The Religion of the Ancient Celts.* London: Constable, 1911, p. 206.

healing stones   Celtic ritual object. Boulders and pebbles with holes in them were honored in many Celtic lands as healing stones; the tradition, often associated with stone monuments of the MEGALITHIC CIVILIZATION, may reach back into pre-Celtic times. In Brittany newborns were passed through the hole in the healing stone at Fouvent-le-Haut to protect them from the ailments of infancy and from the spells of malevolent WITCHES; in Amance money was tossed through a HOLED STONE as a substitute for the child to be protected. In Cornwall the round rock at MEN-AN-TOL, near Madron, was thought to prevent and cure rheumatic ailments if one crawled naked through the stone or was pushed through by others while repeating a spell a magical number of times (usually THREE or nine).

In England similar rites have been recorded. The Long Stone of Gloucestershire was said to cure children with measles, whooping cough, and other contagious diseases, while those who could safely drop through a large holed stone in Dartmoor, called the Tolmen, into the North Teign River below would be cured of arthritis. In Ireland children suffering from the limb-twisting vitamin deficiency called rickets were passed through the Cloch-a-Phoill in Co. Carlow in hopes of a cure. Another huge (10 × 9-foot) stone, located at a triple crossroads in Co. Sligo and called either Clochbhreach (Speckled Stone) or Clochlia (Gray Stone), has an apparently natural small (2 × 3-foot) perforation through which children with measles were passed. Holed stones from Ireland were revered through England and Scotland as being especially efficacious healers. Indeed, one Irish rock in Northumberland was never permitted to touch English soil, to preserve its healing powers; it was held to work best if applied by a person of Irish blood or ancestry.

In Scotland stitch-stones relieved skin ailments and other chronic complaints; they were kept by the healed individual until called for by someone else, whereupon the most recently affected delivered the stones for use. The Stones of Stenness on Orkney were considered curative of many ailments if one walked around them three times *deosil* (in the direction of the SUN, or clockwise).

Sources: Bord, Janet, and Colin Bord. *The Secret Country: An interpretation of the folklore of ancient sites in the British Isles.* New York: Walker and Co. 1976, pp. 41–47, 60; Grinsell, Leslie V. *Folklore of Prehistoric Sites in Britain.* London: David & Charles, 1976, pp. 15, 25; Meaden, George Terrence. *The Goddess of the Stones: The Language of the Megaliths.* London: Souvenir Press, 1991, p. 186.

hearth   Symbolic site. The Celts connected the center of home with the OTHERWORLD. The hearth, where the cooking fire blazed—a FIRE that, in most cases, provided heat for the home as well—was a significant spiritual symbol. Early archaeological sites show an emphasis on the hearth, which was found decorated with divine symbols like those on the ram's-head andirons found in Gaul.

It is believed that sacrifices to the family's ancestors were made at each home's hearth. It was a liminal space, not entirely of this world but opening out to that of the spirits. FAIRIES and GHOSTS were attracted to the hearth, especially at pivotal days such as SAMHAIN, the beginning of winter on November 1; on that night, ghosts of the deceased would sometimes be seen warming themselves by the hearth-fire or sitting in their accustomed place, calmly smoking or knitting.

heather   Symbolic plant. Common in Ireland and Britain, the low-growing heath or heather is a tough BOG plant that blooms with charming pink or purplish flowers that carpet wild areas in summer. BEES love heather and make from it a honey that is a favorite food in parts of Scotland. In Ireland heather was classed as a "peasant" tree, but it nonetheless is included in the TREE ALPHABET.

Heathrow British archaeological site. Now the name of an airport near London, Heathrow was originally a pre-Roman Celtic settlement from the fourth century B.C.E., which included an impressive square earthworks originally topped by a timber TEMPLE and surrounded by a colonnade of posts. Such a square-within-a-square design has also been noted in temple buildings in other Romano-Celtic regions, suggesting that the design has roots in Celtic religious views.

heaven Cosmological concept. The Celts generally did not imagine heaven and earth as opposed to each other; nor did they describe them as a complementary pair. There is, for example, no myth of the marriage of heaven and earth, nor of their forced separation, as occurs in some other cultures. Instead, fragmentary myths suggest that the Celtic worldview was similar to that found in shamanic cultures (see CELTIC SHAMANISM). While in Judeo-Christian cosmology heaven is usually seen as the abode of the dead and of the divine forces, the Celts located both in the OTHERWORLD, which could be found out to sea, under a hill, or in an invisible universe parallel to ours, but never in the sky.

Hedessa British folkloric figure. This spirit of the small SPRING in the Peaklands that bears her name (Hedess Spring) may derive from an ancient water goddess.

Hefydd Hen (Hefaidd Hen, Heveidd Henn) Welsh hero or god. Hefydd the Ancient or Old Hefydd was the father of RHIANNON, the mythological horsewoman who appears to be a diminished goddess. Thus Hefydd himself may have been an ancestral Welsh divinity, although no recorded story explains his mythical function.

Heilyn Minor Welsh hero. When BRÂN THE BLESSED waged his fierce war on Ireland in the Welsh epic *MABINOGION*, only a few warriors survived the battles. Heilyn was one; he opened the magic door through which the survivors escaped.

Hellawes Arthurian heroine. A sorceress, Hellawes attempted unsuccessfully to seduce the great knight LANCELOT.

Hellyas Arthurian hero. This minor figure in Arthurian legend was an ancestor of the ROUND TABLE knight LANCELOT.

Hengroen (Llamrei) Arthurian figure. This name is given in the Welsh TRIADS to king ARTHUR's horse in the final battle at CAMLAN.

Henky Scottish folkloric figure. In the islands off Scotland, Orkney and the Shetlands, FAIRY people could be detected because they limped ("henked") when they danced, although the reason for this handicap is not explained in folklore. Thus Henky was a common name for a fairy person in that region.

Henwen British goddess of abundance. In British mythology this magical sow-goddess ("old white one") came forth early in creation to give life to the world. As she roamed the hilly countryside, she gave birth to litter after litter. Instead of piglets, however, Henwen produced a grain of wheat and a BEE; a grain of barley and a bee; a WOLF cub, an eaglet, and a kitten, each strange litter in a different part of the country.

Hen Wife (Cailleach nan Cearac) Scottish folkloric character. On farms in the Scottish Highlands, a woman who kept chickens was believed to have magical powers and thus to be associated with WITCHCRAFT. The same was not true of a man who operated the same business. The character of the Hen Wife appears in a number of folktales and may be connected with the CAILLEACH as goddess of animals, or it may simply derive from the perceived power of women who earned their own living through the sale of EGGS and meat.

herbs   See HEALING.

Hercules   Romano-Celtic god. Celtic artists did not typically depict gods in human form; with the arrival of the invading Romans around 200 B.C.E., however, they adapted their style to reflect classical figure modeling. In addition, the INTERPRETATIO ROMANA—the renaming of Celtic gods and goddesses with the names of Roman divinities—encouraged artists to carve deities with classical as well as Celtic attributes and to label them with Roman names. Thus the Greco-Roman hero Hercules appears frequently in Celtic art, particularly on the Continent, as an altered version of Celtic gods, some of whose names are known, while others are lost. SEGOMO, BORVO, and SMERTRIUS are all shown as brawny, powerful gods bearing Herculean clubs, but what these gods meant to their people is not entirely clear; Borvo's connection with the healing springs at Aix-les-Bains suggests that he may have fought disease rather than other gods. According to the second century C.E. Greek writer Lucian, the god of eloquence, OGMIOS, was depicted as Hercules because verbal talent was a kind of strength among the Celtic people.

Herla   British folkloric or mythological being. In Herefordshire it was believed that a king of ancient times, Herla, still haunted the land in the form of a tiny half-animal man astride a large GOAT. Trapped in the OTHERWORLD centuries ago, Herla was doomed to lead the WILD HUNT, called Herla's Rade, on moonlit nights—although some sources say that he transferred this duty to the English king and thereafter rested in the Otherworld.

Hermes   See MERCURY.

Herne   British folkloric figure. In *The Merry Wives of Windsor*, Shakespeare speaks of Herne as a hunter who hanged himself from an oak tree and was thereafter forced to haunt the woods where he died. Herne the Hunter appears in various legends as a horned spirit, suggesting that he may have originated as a woodland deity like CERNUNNOS. One tale from Windsor Forest describes Herne in language typical of FAIRIES, for he was said to shoot his victims with invisible darts if they intruded upon magical places. (See GWYNN AP NUDD.)

heron   Symbolic animal. Several BIRD species had specific symbolic value in Celtic tradition. One of these was the heron, which as a waterbird existed in several elements (air, land, water), thus becoming an emblem of OTHERWORLD power. Herons appear in contexts similar to that of CRANES, typically representing the feminine force. An exception is the story of the bitter satirist AITHIRNE who sought to steal the herons of the FAIRY MOUND of BRÍ LÉITH. These herons represented the sinful quality of inhospitality.

hero's portion   See CHAMPION'S PORTION.

Herzeloyde   Arthurian heroine. This princess of Wales did not want to marry just anyone; she demanded a man who was truly heroic. And so she let it be known that whoever won a tournament would win her hand as well. After years of adventuring in the east, the warrior GAHMURET arrived on the scene just in time to claim the prize. Gahmuret was rather footloose and, after impregnating his bride, left for the east once again, where his luck ran out and he was slain. Heartbroken, Herzeloyde moved to a small woodland cottage, where she gave birth to her son, PERCIVAL, whom she intended to keep from all knowledge of his heritage. His heroic blood found its way out when Percival was old enough to join king ARTHUR at CAMELOT.

Hibernia   Celtic land. This ancient name, which meant "winter country," was used by Greek and Roman writers to refer to both Ireland and, occasionally, Britain. To Mediterranean peoples, the rainy chill of Ireland apparently seemed a perpetual winter.

high king *(ard rí, ard ri, ard righe)*   Irish social role. The question of what power the king of TARA had over other Irish kings is far from settled. Because a king's power came from the TUATH (his people and their land) and from his union with the goddess of the land, there seems little likelihood that Tara's king held centralized political authority. While it is easy today to imagine a group of lesser kings who reported to the high king, that was not the case. The high king held a ceremonial and religious office rather than a political one. He could not demand that other kings follow his orders, but he had the responsibility of keeping Ireland fertile and blooming by following his *BUADA* and *geasa* (see GEIS), his sacred vows and taboos. Many high kings figure prominently in mythology, including NIALL of the Nine Hostages, CONN of the Hundred Battles, and CONAIRE.

hill   See FAIRY MOUND.

hillfort (rath, ráth, dun, dún, lis, cashel) Celtic archaeological site. Across Ireland, and to some extent in Britain as well, remains of Celtic settlements still stand, their various names all describing a high wall of earth, usually atop a hill, and usually circular. Some archaeological evidence suggests that over these permanent foundation walls, buildings of wood were erected; some archaeological evidence has been found supporting that theory. Built from approximately 700 B.C.E. through the early Middle Ages, the hillforts are connected to Celtic settlement and seem to have been locations for trade, government, and ceremony.

That Ireland was a populous land in the first century of the common era is suggested by more than 30,000 surviving hillforts, each of which would have housed from several dozen to several score residents. Many towns today still carry the name of the hillfort of the area: Rathangan, Lisdoonvarna, Lisadell, Dunmore. Cashels are somewhat larger than other hillforts and, like the town that bears that name in Tipperary, were usually built on high, easily defensible ground. In all cases, the earthen walls of the hillforts appear to have been constructed to simplify defense of the site. Some hillforts important in myth include GRIANÁN AILEACH, EMAIN MACHA, TARA, and CRUACHAN.

Sources: Aalen, F. H. A. *Man and the Landscape in Ireland.* London: Academic Press, 1978, pp. 81 ff; Raftery, Brian. *Pagan Celtic Ireland: The Enigma of the Irish Iron Age.* London: Thames and Hudson, 1994, pp. 38 ff.

Hill of Allen   See ALMU.

Hill of Tara   See TARA.

Hill of Uisneach   See UISNEACH.

Hill of Ward   See TLACHTGA.

Historical Cycle (Cycle of the Kings)   Irish mythological texts. Several sequences of Irish myths appear in ancient manuscripts, generally divided, in roughly chronological order of the supposed occurrences, into the MYTHOLOGICAL CYCLE, the ULSTER CYCLE, the FENIAN CYCLE, and the Historical Cycle. The last includes stories whose events would have occurred between late Celtic and early Christian times (third to 11th century C.E.). Many tales appear based in historical reality, but they have been embellished with mythological motifs and descriptions of supernatural happenings. The stories often revolve around the important ritual and political center at TARA and concern the Celtic concept of SOVEREIGNTY or right rulership. Among the kings who appear in the Historical Cycle are

CONN of the Hundred Battles, CORMAC MAC AIRT, MONGÁN, and GUAIRE.

hoard Archaeological site. Celtic hoards, found in BOGS and similar hiding places, include gold TORCS, embellished CAULDRONS, and lunae or moon-collars. Scholars believe that the treasures were deposited in the bogs to protect them against theft by invaders, perhaps Vikings. Hoards were also intended as SACRIFICE, perhaps in cases of epidemics or other disasters, either threatened or actual.

hob (Hobtrust, hobtrush, hobgoblin) British and Scottish folkloric figure. The syllable *hob*, frequently found in words related to FAIRIES, is believed to be a diminutive for Robert, a name given to English BROWNIES or helpful household spirits; the flattering name ROBIN GOODFELLOW comes from the same stem. In northern Britain the hob was a kindly spirit, helpful to local people when they needed HEALING or farm work. As with similar beings, it was important never to reward the hob in any way, for that would scare him off (see LAYING THE FAIRIES).

Less kindly hobs were also known in folklore, such as Hob Headless, a scary being who haunted a road near the River Kent. Confined under a rock for 99 years, Hob Headless trapped passersby who rested upon his rock, gluing them down so that they could not rise and escape. Hob Headless is typical of the hobgoblin, a generic name for malicious spirits. In Scotland hobgoblins caused distress and mischief just for their own sake. They took on ominous forms to terrify people walking at night; even a haystack could become a threatening apparition, coming alive in the night and frightening the traveler into an exhausting run or a useless fight against the invisible foe. Variant legends say that to encounter such an apparition indicated coming death.

Sources: Campbell, John Grigorson. *Witchcraft and Second Sight in the Highlands and Islands of Scotland.* Detroit: Singing Tree Press, 1970,

p. 131; Clarke, David. *Ghosts and Legends of the Peak District.* Norwich: Jarrold Publishing, n.d., p. 36; Spence, Lewis. *The Minor Traditions of British Mythology.* New York: Benjamin Blom, Inc., 1972, p. 90.

hobbyhorse British folkloric figure. Many folkloric events are believed to be remnants of early religious ceremonies, degraded by the passage of years. One of these is the hobbyhorse, a puppet of a horse worn by a man in parades at British festivals. As the syllable *hob* usually indicates a connection with the OTHERWORLD, the hobbyhorse is thought to derive from Celtic practice, perhaps related to the horse goddess EPONA.

Hogmany (Hagmany) Scottish festival. The last day of the year in Scotland (sometimes called "the night of the candles" or "the night of the pelting") was celebrated with many traditional activities, some of which have roots in the Celtic worldview. Candles were kept lit all night. Houses were decorated with HOLLY, branches of which were used to whip boys for their own protection, with each drop of blood drawn assuring them of a year of good health.

A man dressed in a cowhide bellowed through the streets, followed by men and boys throwing snowballs and striking him with a switch to create a loud boom. This rowdy procession followed the sun's course (see DIRECTIONS) THREE times around the village, striking each house for good luck, demanding treats or money or both, and repeating a nonsense rhyme. Upon being admitted to a home, the Hogmany party offered the *caisein-uchd*—a sheep's breastbone on a stick—to the household, to be placed in the fire and held to the noses. Such peculiar traditions have their roots in protective rituals intended to keep the participants healthy through the new year and may earlier have been used for DIVINATION.

Sources: Campbell, John Grigorson. *Witchcraft and Second Sight in the Highlands and Islands of*

Scotland. Detroit: Singing Tree Press, 1970, p. 230; Carmichael, Alexander. *Carmina Gadelica: Hymns and Incantations.* Hudson, N.Y.: Lindisfarne Press, 1992, pp. 76–78, 579; Ross, Anne. *Folklore of the Scottish Highlands.* London: B. T. Batsford, Ltd., 1976, p. 122.

holed stones   Symbolic object. In addition to their uses for healing (see HEALING STONES), large rocks with holes in them were used in all the Celtic lands to seal marriage vows. Loving couples clasped hands through the natural holes while pledging their troth. In some regions a church wedding was not considered valid unless vows were also spoken at the holed stone. In Britain the term *DOBIE* Stone is applied to these natural formations, connecting them with the FAIRIES of that name.

hollow hill   Irish folkloric site. The idea that some hills are hollow, the better to accommodate the FAIRY palaces within them, is typical of Irish images of the OTHERWORLD as a region close to our world yet not part of it.

holly   Symbolic plant. Its red berries and shiny evergreen leaves made the common holly (genus *Ilex*), a small TREE or shrub, especially visible in snowy woodlands, and thus it became associated with the Christian midwinter feast of Christmas. The name comes from Middle English and is associated with the word *holy*. Before Christianization, however, the tree had been sacred to the Celts as the emblem of the ruler of winter, the Holly King, whose opponent was the OAK King; a vestige of this seasonal combat may be found in the Welsh myth of combat between the kings HAFGAN and ARAWN. The holly is symbolically paired with the IVY, the first representing the masculine force, the second symbolizing the feminine; the connection remains familiar through the holiday song, "The Holly and the Ivy," whose melody and lyrics date to the medieval period.

holy wells   See WELL.

honor-price   See *ÉRIC.*

hooper (hooter)   Cornish folkloric figure. A helpful but sometimes vindictive Cornish weather spirit like the Scottish GRAY MAN, the hooper was a dense fog that blocked out all vision, or a cloudy curtain from which a central light shone. Anyone who saw the hooper stayed ashore, for its appearance was invariably followed by fierce storms. One legend tells of a sailor who jeered at the hooper and took out his crew despite the warning; his boat passed into the gloom and was never seen again.

horn (antlers, horned god, horned goddess) Symbolic object. One of the primary symbols of the god of male potency, horns or ANTLERS are frequently found on Celtic divinities. Two major forms of the horned god have been cataloged. The first wears the antlers of a STAG and sits cross-legged, staring forward. This Gaulish god is usually dubbed CERNUNNOS, "the horned one," after an inscription found on a sculpture of this type in Paris; he is thought to represent a force of prosperity. Occasionally this figure is depicted as having THREE HEADS, although it is possible that such sculptures indicate the connection of Cernunnos with other gods. Gaulish MERCURY and COCIDIUS are also occasionally shown wearing horns, although the symbol is not always associated with these divinities of wealth.

The second type of horned god showed horns of domestic animals, usually those of BULLS, attached to the heads of male deities. Although many such divinities have been found, they have no distinctive symbols save the horns to tell us what they represent. As horned helmets have been found, presumably originally worn by warriors or leaders, the horns may represent leadership and power.

Goddesses are also found with horns, although less often than gods. Usually the goddess wears antlers, which are found on the heads of some female DEER, although occasionally bulls' or goats' horns crown a goddess's head. Such goddesses are believed to indicate a force of animal nature and a link between female fecundity and the animal world.

A peculiarly Celtic religious symbol was the RAM-HEADED SNAKE, which was translated in Christian times to an image of evil rather than of power. The Christian DEVIL with its ram's horns is a direct descendant of this powerful Celtic divinity.

Some folkloric celebrations seem to encode ancient rituals of the horned god; see ABBOTS BROMLEY.

Sources: Green, Miranda. *The Gods of Roman Britain.* Aylesbury: Shire Publications Ltd., 1983, pp. 64 ff; Green, Miranda. *Symbol and Image in Celtic Religious Art.* London: Routledge, 1989, pp. 27, 87, 96; Ross, Anne. *Pagan Celtic Britain: Studies in Iconography and Tradition.* London: Routledge & Kegan Paul, 1967, pp. 18, 127, 132.

horse Symbolic animal. One of the most important animals to the Celts was the horse, not only for religious and symbolic reasons but also for practical ones. The Celts were known throughout ancient Europe for their horsemanship, especially in warfare. Horses were central to the Celtic way of life as a means of transportation and as an indication of nobility. Celtic nobles rode in chariots instead of on horse back, while less honored warriors formed the mounted cavalry. Nobles were often buried with their horses and gear, indicating a connection in life that was not ended by death.

The funerary use of horses in Celtic lands may derive from their association with the solar power; the SUN is seen in many cultures as bearing the dead away at sunset and into rebirth at dawn. Celtic COINS with solar and equine emblems suggest a connection between horses and the sun, the spoked wheel, a double image of sun and horse-drawn chariot, was especially linked to the goddess EPONA, champion of the Celtic cavalry under Roman occupation, whose cult spread into Rome itself. Some have found in the nursery rhyme "Ride a cock horse to Banbury Cross, to see a fine lady upon a white horse" a faint folkloric echo of Epona; similar connections have been drawn to the quasi-historical figure of Lady GODIVA, who rode naked on horseback to protest her husband's oppressive taxation policies.

On the Continent the widespread cult of the goddess Epona (whose name means "horse" or, because it is feminine in gender, "mare"), passed from the Celts to the Roman legionnaires, for whom she became the cavalry goddess. Many Romano-Celtic sculptures and reliefs show Epona seated on a horse, surrounded by horses or foals, or offering feed to horses. Because of the reverence due the horse and to Epona, the Celts did not eat horseflesh, a taboo that has passed into contemporary European cuisine. The taboo was lifted on sacramental occasions when horses were sacrificed, as at the midsummer festival.

In Ireland the horse was connected with the goddess of SOVEREIGNTY through the *banais ríghe*, the sacred marriage of king and land goddess that the early geographer Geraldus Cambrensis claims included the sacramental mating of the king with a white mare; the mare was then killed and cooked into a broth that the king drank. This curious ritual, recorded in no other text, has corollaries in other parts of the Indo-European world, most notably in India, but there is scholarly debate over whether the HORSE SACRIFICE was indeed part of Irish royal INAUGURATION.

An Irish corollary to Epona is found in MACHA, who proved herself faster than the king's team in a horse race that ended in her death. Also in Ireland, connection between horses and humans appears in the post-Christian folktale that Noah brought animals two by two into the ark, except for the horse; he accidentally brought only a mare, which was impregnated by one of Noah's sons, so that all horses today have a distant human ancestor. This peculiar tale seems to dimly reflect the same alleged kingship ritual mentioned above.

Irish folklore credited horses with SECOND SIGHT, especially with the ability to see GHOSTS of the dead—possibly a connection to the animal's ancient funerary symbolism. According to legend, a rider who looked between the ears of a mount shared the horse's ability to see ghosts. Horses were sometimes stolen and ridden by FAIRIES; in the early morning the animals were lathered with sweat as though they had spent the night galloping despite being confined to their stalls. Only one horse could not be stolen by the fairies, and that was the *fíorlár* or true mare, the seventh consecutive filly born of a mare. Where the true mare was born, a four-leafed CLOVER called Mary's Clover sprang up, imbued with curative powers. Such a rare horse protected her rider from any harm, of this world or another, and could never be beaten in a race. Other superstitions also emphasized the protective power of horses; burying a horse's head in a building's foundation kept its occupants safe.

In Wales the horse is associated with the figure of RHIANNON, a goddess who appears in the first branch of the *MABINOGION* riding an impressively speedy white horse and surrounded by endlessly singing birds. After she married king PWYLL, Rhiannon gave birth to a son who was kidnapped under mysterious circumstances; she bore the blame, and until her name was cleared, she had to carry all visitors to the palace on her back, thus reinforcing her connection to the horse.

In England horse figures are found carved into the turf of chalky lands such as Berkshire and Wiltshire. Eleven white horses are cut into the sides of hills, dated according to their style to the late 18th or early 19th century and interpreted as regimental emblems. However, some of these horses may have been carved over earlier, possibly Celtic, horse figures. Apparently unchanged for many centuries is the renowned WHITE HORSE OF UFFINGTON, whose slender, graceful body stylistically resembles horses from Celtic coins. Archaeologists are hesitant to provide a date for the Uffington horse, although excavations measuring the rate of slippage down the hillside have calculated its age as consistent with Celtic occupation of the region.

"Scouring" the horses—removing the turf that would have grown over them if not regularly weeded—was a community affair that often coincided with a fair or market; the seven-year cycle of scouring the Uffington horse continued into recent centuries, with more than 30,000 people recorded as having attended the ceremonies and festival in 1780. The English novelist Thomas Hughes set his 1889 book, *The Scouring of the White Horse*, at the festival; the book is considered an adequate source for folklore of the region.

Sources: Dexter, Miriam Robbins. *Whence the Goddesses: A Sourcebook.* New York: Pergamon Press, 1990, pp. 92–93; Green, Miranda. *The Gods of Roman Britain.* Aylesbury: Shire Publications Ltd., 1983, p. 23; Green, Miranda. *Symbol and Image in Celtic Religious Art.* London: Routledge, 1989, pp. 146; Ross, Anne. *Pagan Celtic Britain: Studies in Iconography and Tradition.* London: Routledge & Kegan Paul, 1967, p. 321.

horse sacrifice   Irish ritual. The early traveler to Ireland, Giraldus Cambrensis, wrote an account in the early sixth century C.E. of a ritual HORSE sacrifice that many scholars have accepted as accurate, despite the absence of any similar accounts. According to Giraldus, the INAUGURATION of the Irish HIGH KING at TARA, the *banais ríghe*, required that the candidate have intercourse with a white mare, who was then killed, cooked up into broth, and devoured by the king. Often described as a "barbaric" rite, this unusual ritual might be disregarded as unlikely, save that it echoes another Indo-European inauguration, in which the queen was to wear the hide of a newly slaughtered mare for ritual coition with the king.

Source: Dexter, Miriam Robbins. *Whence the Goddesses: A Sourcebook.* New York: Pergamon Press, 1990, pp. 92–93.

hospitality Symbolic ritual. In Celtic Ireland the king's duty included the redistribution of wealth through endless feasting and open-door hospitality. Should a king fail to provide for guests, he could lose the throne, as happened when the beautiful half-FORMORIAN king BRES fed a BARD poorly and was forced from power as a result.

Hospitality was not only required of kings. Other members of society were expected to open their doors to the needy and to travelers. Those who set up households at crossroads thereby showed their willingness to feed and house the passerby. Largesse was equal to the person's means; thus an impoverished person could offer meager food, while a wealthy one was expected to spread an impressive table. Cuts of meat and other foods were offered according to the caller's social rank; only a few visitors could expect honey wherever they went. Thus Celtic expectations of hospitality were a form of resource reallocation.

hot water Irish folkloric motif. Irish lore warned against throwing hot water outside at night, for fear that it might strike and harm the FAIRY folk who lingered in the farmyards after hours. In the days before drains were installed in cottage kitchens, the housewife threw the cooking and cleaning water onto the stones of the haggard or courtyard, thus cleaning the yard with the used water. Cries warning the fairies against the coming boiling splash ("Towards ye! Towards ye!") would also have been useful in keeping any unobserved humans safe from inconvenient drenching.

Hu (Hu Gadarn, Hu the Mighty) Neo-pagan god. The prime deity of some cults of contemporary NEO-PAGANS who claim to be practicing DRUIDS, this agricultural divinity appears to date to the Middle Ages, although he may be a vestige of an earlier god.

Hulac Warren (Hector Warren) British folkloric site. A great rock called the Warren Stone near Buxton was once a GIANT of this name. When he tried to rape the maiden HEDESSA, she turned into a spring, while he was petrified into stone. The story, which recalls tales of the Greek Apollo's attempts on innumerable nymphs, may be a combination of classical and indigenous stories.

human sacrifice Celtic ritual. According to Roman sources, both the continental and the insular Celts practiced human sacrifice. Julius Caesar described a ritual in which victims were trapped, together with scores of animals, in a gigantic human form made from wicker, then burned alive; Diodorus Siculus, Strabo, and Tacitus agree that the Celts sacrificed human beings to their gods. The latter claimed that the Celtic priesthood of DRUIDS "deemed it a duty to cover their altars with the blood of captives and to consult their deities through human entrails." The murderous assault on the Celtic sanctuary at ANGLESEY was explained as necessary to exterminate a priestly class that Tacitus said worshiped at altars "soaked with human blood."

Later writers, friendlier to the Celts, argued that the Romans slandered their most powerful European enemies. Contemporary evidence suggests that human sacrifice may indeed have been practiced, although probably not regularly, by the druids. Such sacrifices may have been an ancient form of capital punishment, reserved for criminals and other prisoners. Because the Celts are thought to have believed in REINCARNATION, the taking of a human life would have had a different meaning for them than for those who believed in a single lifetime.

Sacrificed humans may not have suffered a tortuous death in Caesar's WICKER MAN. Bodies found in BOGS in circumstances that suggest sacrifice of people with fine nails and skin and full stomachs, perhaps individuals of a high, perhaps even royal, class who were well treated before death. Some, such as the LINDOW MAN, appear to have suffered the THREEFOLD DEATH of strangling, cutting, and drowning. Some myths, such as that of the HIGH KING CONAIRE, who was burned to death in the hostel of DA DERGA, support the idea of human sacrifice as a Celtic practice.

Sources: Lonigan; Paul R. *The Druids: Priests of the Ancient Celts.* Contributions to the Study of Religion, No. 45. Westport, Conn.: Greenwood Press, 1996, pp. 100 ff; Piggot, Stuart. *The Druids.* London: Thames and Hudson, 1968, pp. 110 ff.

hungry grass Irish folkloric site. Folklore is never static; significant historical moments find their way into folktales. This was the case with the Irish Famine, called in Irish *An Gorta Mór*, The Great Hunger. English occupation of the island denied Irish farmers the right to own land, so most lived as impoverished tenants of often absent landlords. What made this possible was an agricultural import from South America: the potato, which thrived in the rainy Irish climate. A small patch of land, even one measuring less than an acre, when planted with potatoes could provide enough sustenance to support a farming family.

Combined with limited access to other food, such monoculture provides the conditions for famine when disease or poor weather strike. Such was the case in 1848–50, when an airborne fungus caused the potatoes to turn into black slime immediately after harvesting. There was still ample food available, in the form of CATTLE being readied for market, but most livestock belonged to the landlords, and so millions of tenant farmers starved. That Ireland continued to export food throughout the Famine years led to continuing bitterness and political strife.

Although the blight passed within the decade, the effects of the Famine were felt for years thereafter; Ireland's population today is still only half what it was before the Famine struck. Actual morbidity figures are unknown, especially given the poor records kept during the disaster, but it is generally agreed that between one and one-and-a-half million people died from starvation and disease, while approximately the same number were forced to emigrate.

From this tragic sequence of events came the legend of the hungry grass, patches of soil that are so infected with memories of the Great Famine that anyone who steps on them is instantly stricken with insatiable hunger, and soon dies even though well fed. Sometimes it is said that hungry grass grows over the unmarked graves of Famine victims, other times that it springs up wherever people died—by the roadside or in hovels—of hunger. Animals are less affected by hungry grass than humans, although there are stories of cattle that died mysteriously after eating it.

hungry man (féar gortach, far gorta) Irish folkloric figure. A variant of the legends of the HUNGRY GRASS that causes insatiable hunger in anyone who treads upon it, the hungry man is an insistent vision of a starving beggar who stands by the roadside with his hand silently out for alms; giving the hungry man food brings good luck. Like the hungry grass, this figure is assumed to have arisen after the Famine of the 1840s, although it may have tapped into earlier folkloric traditions.

Hy-Brâzil (Hy-Brazil, Hy-breasal, Hy-brasil, I Breasil) Irish mythological site. Somewhere in the ocean, the Celts believed, was a magical island of peace and plenty ruled over by a king, BRES, or a FAIRY QUEEN, NIAMH of the Golden Hair, or occasionally MANANNÁN MAC LIR, the sea god. The ISLAND appeared every seven years, usually in a different place, always in the west. Several islands off the west coast of Ireland laid claim to be Hy-Brâzil, including Inisbofin off the Galway coast. In 1908 many people claimed they had spotted Hy-Brâzil in the Atlantic off the west coast of Ireland, floating in an area of the ocean where no island had previously been seen.

Belief in the existence of Hy-Brâzil was strong and long-lasting; the land appears on medieval European maps as a real island, usually located off Ireland. When European sailors reached South America, they believed the rich lands there to be the mythological land of plenty; thus one of that continent's major countries still bears the name of the Celtic magical island.

Hy-Brâzil is sometimes confounded or conflated with Otherworldly sites like TIR NA NOG ("the land of youth") and MAG MELL ("the plain of delights"), but each has its own distinctive qualities.

Source: Löffler, Christa Maria. *The Voyage to the Otherworld Island in Early Irish Literature.* Salzburg Studies in English Literature. Salzburg, Institut Für Anglistik und Amerikanistik, Universität Salzburg, 1983, pp. 306 ff.

Hyperboreans Celtic people. The ancient Greeks recorded the existence of a people they called the Hyperboreans, a name meaning "beyond the north wind," a semi-mythological people with magical powers. These peaceful vegetarians worshiped APOLLO, it was said, in a huge stone circular TEMPLE associated by some with STONEHENGE, although most ancient geographers placed the Hyperborean homeland in Europe rather than on the island of Britain. By the fourth century B.C.E., Greek authors were saying that the alleged Hyperborean homeland was populated by the people they called Celts, adopting one of the names the Celts themselves used, which meant "the lofty ones" or "the warriors."

Hywel Dda (Howel Dda)   Welsh hero. In the southwestern Welsh kingdom of DYFED in the 10th century (ca. 910 to 950 C.E.), king Hywel Dda (Hywel the Good) created an impressive body of law codified in the late 12th (some sources say 13th) century as Cyfraith Hywell or the Laws of Hywel, the first unified body of law in the land. This legal code is often described as the Welsh parallel to the Irish BREHON laws.

Ialonus Continental Celtic god. This obscure divinity who ruled cultivated fields was identified by the Romans with MARS, now conventionally described as a war god but originally a divinity of fertility.

Iarbanel Irish hero. In the legendary history of Ireland, the BOOK OF INVASIONS, the hero NEMED was the father of Iarbanel, who was in turn ancestor of the gods known as the TUATHA DÉ DANANN, or tribe of the goddess DANU; from Iarbanel's brother Starn descended the Tuatha Dé's enemies, the FIR BOLG. It is not clear if Iarbanel was the consort of Danu, as this genealogy implies, for she is not linked with any god.

Ibath, Ibcan Minor Irish heroes. Descendants of the hero IARBANEL, they were called NEMEDIANS after Iarbanel's father, their grandfather NEMED.

Iberia Celtic location. The peninsula today called Spain and Portugal was, in ancient times, a Celtic stronghold. Myth connects Iberia with Ireland, for one group of mythological migrants described in the BOOK OF INVASIONS were the MILESIANS, or the Sons of Míl; its alternative name, Hibernia, derives from this word. The name of Míl Despaine, mythological forebear of these migrants, translates into "Spanish soldier."

I Breasil See HY-BRÂZIL.

Icauna Continental Celtic goddess. To the Celts, both continental and insular, RIVERS were invariably goddesses who ruled both the waters and the lands of the watershed. Icauna was the tutelary goddess of the Yonne River in northern France.

Icovellauna Continental Celtic goddess. Inscriptions to Icovellauna have been found at Metz and Trier in Germany, but little is known about her meaning or cult. As the first syllable *(Ico-)* of her name means "water," she is presumably a WATER divinity, probably the HEALING goddess whose octagonal shrine was excavated at the SPRING of Sablon.

Source: Green, Miranda. *Symbol and Image in Celtic Religious Art*. London: Routledge, 1989, p. 40.

Igerna See IGRAINE.

Igraine (Egraine, Yguerne, Igrayne, Ygerna, Igerna, dgerne, Eigr, Ingraine) Welsh and Arthurian heroine. When the beautiful Igraine caught the eye of heroic UTHER PENDRAGON, he was overcome with desire to have her as his consort although, already partnered with GORLOIS,

Duke of Cornwall, Igraine had no desire for Uther. Conspiring with the magician MERLIN, Uther changed his appearance so that Igraine believed herself to be sleeping with her husband although her companion was in fact the bewitched Uther. From their mating the future king ARTHUR was conceived; after news of Gorlois's death reached Igraine, she married Uther, who had resumed his original appearance.

Igraine had several other children by Gorlois. Two have similar names and may derive from the same original: MORGAUSE and MORGAN are frequently confused in legend. The other was ELAINE of Garlot.

Source: Ellis, Peter Berresford. *Celtic Women: Women in Celtic Society and Literature.* Grand Rapids, Mich.: William B. Eerdmans Publishing, 1995, pp. 61–62.

Ilberg Irish god. When the god of fertility, the DAGDA, decided to relinquish his leadership of his people, the ancient Irish gods called the TUATHA DÉ DANANN, Ilberg was a contender for the post. Son of the sea god MANANNÁN MAC LIR, Ilberg did not get the nod and thereafter retired to his palace at the magical waterfall of ASSAROE.

Ildathach Irish mythological site. When the OTHERWORLD was envisioned as a floating ISLAND, it sometimes bore this name, which means "many-colored land," in reference to its gorgeous and unearthly hues.

Ile (Eila, Yula) Scottish goddess. One of the largest of the Hebrides, a string of islands off Scotland's west coast, the isle of Islay was named for this goddess. Sometimes she is described as a queen or princess named Yula of Denmark. Although Ile, even in diminished form, is an obscure figure, the island that bears her name is less so, for it was the inaugural site for the Lords of the Isles, who in a typical Celtic INAUGURATION rite stepped on a stone impressed with footprints to receive their office. See INAUGURATION STONES.

Source: Straffon, Cheryl. *The Earth Goddess: Celtic and Pagan Legacy of the Landscape.* London: Blandford, 1997, p. 147.

images Cosmological concept. Celtic artists traditionally employed a decorative and ornate abstraction for ritual objects whose spiritual or religious meaning can only be guessed at. Most engravings, sculptures, or other images of continental Celtic gods and goddesses date to the Roman era, with the exception of severed HEADS that date to as early as the eighth century B.C.E. and occasional rough-hewn wooden planks with graven heads and flat bodies.

After the Roman invasion, Celtic artists on the Continent and in Britain began to produce (sometimes mass-produce) human-formed divinities that show skill in modeling and follow classical patterns; clearly it was not lack of ability that discouraged representation of gods in human form. The fact that the most popular divinities sculpted were those that would appeal to wealthy members of society suggests that these Romanized Celtic divinities were made either for Roman residents of the provinces or for well-off Celts wishing to emulate their new masters. The connection of such images to Roman influence is made clear not only in the classical draperies that shroud them but in the fact that they are not found in Ireland, where the Roman legions never invaded.

Why the Celts originally declined to show their divinities as men and women is not well understood, for in myth the gods and goddesses move about, fall in love, engage in battle, and do other things that seem to require bodies. Celtic art, rather than being representational, tended to be decorative and abstract, even art that had spiritual meaning. In some cultures, such as Islam, it is forbidden to depict the divine as human, but we have no documented evidence for such a philosophy among the Celts, who in any case turned to such depictions with great ease after Roman contact. See INTERPRETATIO ROMANA.

Sources: Piggot, Stuart. *The Druids*. London: Thames and Hudson, 1968, pp. 79–86; Straffon, Cheryl. *The Earth Goddess: Celtic and Pagan Legacy of the Landscape*. London: Blandford, 1997, p. 29.

imbas forosnai *(imbus forosna, himbas forosnai)* Divination system. Among the Irish DRUIDS, this form of DIVINATION was used to discover the location of hidden or stolen objects or to learn secrets kept from public knowledge. The term, "illumination between the hands," refers to the second stage of the ritual. First the BARD or seer chewed on raw meat, which was then offered to the powers of the OTHERWORLD. The answer to the query was supposed to come into the seer's mind by the next day, but if that did not happen, the second stage began: After speaking incantations into his or her hands, the seer slept with palms on cheeks and dreamed the answer to the queries.

Imbolc (Imbolg, Óilmelc, Oímelg, Olmec, Candlemas) Celtic holiday. The Celtic year was broken into four parts, and the points between the equinoxes and solstices were celebrated as major festivals. Imbolc, on February 1, was the day on which winter ended and spring began. Its name means "in the belly," presumably because cattle and sheep were pregnant with spring's young at this time; it has also been connected with a word meaning "to wash," presumably referring to ritual purification. The alternative name of Óilmelc refers to the lactation of ewes that also occurs around this time.

Yet although it was described as spring's awakening, the weather at this time was generally more wintry than not. Thus weather MAGIC and DIVINATION were common to the day. The Manx said the "Old Woman of the Spells," a form of the CAILLEACH, tried to find dry sticks on Imbolc in order to build a fire, thus making herself comfortable enough to prolong winter; such traditions may form the basis of the American Groundhog Day. In Ireland the day was dedicated to St. BRIGIT, the Christianized version of the Celtic goddess of the same name, whose feast day this became; many folkways celebrate her, including plaiting swastika-like crosses fashioned of reed and rush to invite Brigit into the home.

On the Isle of Man, the day is called Laa'l Breeshey, the day of Brigit. Manx customs included leaving the front door open so that Brigit (or in some cases, the FAIRIES) might feel welcomed and enter, or sweeping out the barn and leaving a lit candle to burn there beside a table on which ale and bread (the "Brigit supper") was offered to the visiting spirits, whether saintly or fey. As in other Celtic lands, the Isle of Man saw weather divination practiced on this day. One tradition said that as far as the sunbeam reaches on Imbolc, that far will the snow come before BELTANE on May 1; thus, as in other places, a bright Imbolc was thought to promise a lengthened winter. A similar belief had it that when Imbolc was sunny, a wet or snowy spring was in the offing. A rainy or snowy Imbolc, by contrast, would force the Cailleach, the weather-controlling HAG, to stay indoors rather than gathering more wood for her fire. Without laying in an additional stock of fuel, she would be forced to end winter early.

In Britain seasonal symbolism outweighed weather divination. As in other Celtic lands, Imbolc was associated in the Cotswold hill-country with candles that represented the increasing strength of the sun being lit throughout the house to celebrate the day. Tea was traditionally to be served without any artificial light, for on Imbolc the sun's light was supposed to be strong enough to illuminate the table spread with the feast.

In Scotland rush or reed figures of Brigit were constructed and dressed in bits of cloth, with a shell called "the guiding star" placed on the chest. This poppet was carried from house to house, usually by young women, or put to bed with lullabies. Ashes strewn on the doorstep would be checked in the morning to see if Brigit had honored the household with a visitation, which was thought to bring good luck for the year. Sometimes a piece of peat was put inside a sock, then hit upon a step while a verse was recited asking that SERPENTS not come forth.

Ireland's various regions had different traditions for this day. The day was generally a holiday when rural work stopped, although farmers might plow a ceremonial furrow in the spring fields or put a spade into the earth as a ritual invocation for good harvest. Strips of cloth or ribbons were placed outdoors, to catch the first light of the sun on Imbolc or the dew of the dawn; called a Brat Bríde or Brigit's cloak, the cloths were used for healing throughout the year. The faithful visited (and still visit) holy WELLS dedicated in Brigit's name. In KILDARE a rush swastika cross was plaited; hung over the door, it protected against fire until the next Imbolc, when the dried cross would be stored in the rafters while another green one took its place. In western Connemara a straw rope plaited from rye straw cut by hand was formed into a circle (the *crios bridghe* or Brigit cross) and carried from door to door so that people could leap through it while praying for health and good fortune. In southwestern Co. Kerry mummers dressed in white imitated Brigit begging from door to door. Both of these latter customs have been revived in recent years, most significantly at Kildare, a town traditionally associated with the figure of Brigit transmogrified into the Christian saint; there the celebration of Imbolc has become an important local festival.

Sources: Berger, Pamela. *The Goddess Obscured: Transformation of the Grain Protectress from Goddess to Saint.* Boston: Beacon Press, 1985, p. 70; Briggs, Katharine M. *The Folklore of the Cotswolds.* London: B. T. Batsford Ltd., 1974, p. 19; Callan, Barbara. "In Search of the Crios Bhride." In Patricia Monaghan, ed. *Irish Spirit: Pagan, Celtic, Christian, Global.* Dublin: Wolfhound Press, 2001; Carmichael, Alexander. *Carmina Gadelica: Hymns and Incantations.* Hudson, N.Y.: Lindisfarne Press, 1992, pp. 583–584; Paton, C. I. *Manx Calendar Customs.* Publications of the Folk-lore Society, reprinted.

Nendeln/Liechtenstein: Kraus Reprint Limited, 1968, p. 35; Ross, Anne. *Folklore of the Scottish Highlands.* London: B. T. Batsford, Ltd., 1976, p. 126.

immortality Cosmological concept. Although some writers describe the Celtic gods as immortal, tales such as that of battles of MAG TUIRED describe the deaths of many of them. Gods and goddesses are occasionally victims of treacherous murder, as when MEDB was struck down while bathing. Thus it is not clear that the idea of immortality—in the sense of never suffering death—was part of the Celtic vision of divinity. Some Irish legends speak of a food that, when eaten by the gods, kept them young and hale: the PIGS of the sea god MANANNÁN MAC LIR, the contents of the ever-full CAULDRON of the smith GOIBNIU, and APPLES from the OTHERWORLD. The myths suggest that, without such magical food, divinities might age and die just like mortals, but existing texts and oral tales do not describe any deaths from old age among the gods.

Some ancient sources refer to a Celtic belief in the immortality of the human soul, which passed through various bodies; this is more properly termed REINCARNATION or metempsychosis. Some argue that rebirth in different bodies was not a Celtic vision of the afterlife but a classical misinterpretation, and that the Celts instead believed in the soul's reawakening in an Otherworld that resembled this one point for point, except for being timeless. Death, in either case, was a change in form instead of an ending; such a belief may explain the fearlessness that ancient writers ascribed to Celtic warriors.

Sources: Evans-Wentz, W. Y. *The Fairy-Faith in Celtic Countries.* Gerrards Cross: Colin Smythe Humanities Press, 1911, p. 503; MacCulloch, J. A. *The Religion of the Ancient Celts.* London: Constable, 1911, pp. 158, 376.

immovability (automatic return) Folkloric motif. The great stone monuments of the pre-Celtic people must have impressed the new settlers, for many superstitions accrued to the sites, which preserved them against desecration even millennia after the builders had passed away. One of these beliefs—recorded as far back as the early British historian Nennius—was that such stones would, if moved from their sacred location, return the next day of their own power. Sometimes the thief would be hurt or killed in the stone's return.

Source: Grinsell, Leslie V. *Folklore of Prehistoric Sites in Britain*. London: David & Charles, 1976.

imp   British folkloric figure. An old word for a cutting from a tree is *imp* or *ymp*, and the term came to be applied during Puritan times to FAIRY people as offshoots of the DEVIL. The concept is entirely a Christian one; pre-Christian residents of Celtic lands did not believe in a specific force of evil, much less that the people of the OTHERWORLD were the evil one's children.

imram   See VOYAGES.

inauguration   Celtic ritual. Although little is known of inauguration rituals among the continental Celts or those in Britain, there is significant evidence of the ritual's form in Celtic Ireland. The king was not an all-powerful person whose word was law, but rather a man chosen—often by inspired poets using complex DIVINATION methods, although possibly through feats of arms—to be married to the goddess of the land. The *banais ríghe*, the feast of inauguration, celebrated the marriage of the goddess of SOVEREIGNTY with her chosen king. The site of the ritual was a sacred hill such as TARA or a holy WELL; as there were hundreds of kings in ancient Ireland, their inauguration presumably was held at the most sacred place in their territory.

What exactly happened at this ritual is unclear. Giraldus Cambrensis relates a complex ritual involving the king's mating with a mare; the mare was then killed and cooked, and the king was given its broth to drink (see HORSE SACRIFICE). Although that ritual finds echoes in other Indo-European lands, there is no further evidence that it occurred in Ireland.

More commonly, it is believed that the ritual included two main elements: the offering of a drink (possibly water from the sacred well, although red ALE is also mentioned) and intercourse with the goddess, or a woman representing the goddess. Again, it is not known how widespread such practices were or whether the coition was symbolic or actual.

After inauguration it was the king's duty to follow many ritual requirements (see *BUADA*). If he did so, the goddess offered the reward of abundant food and fine weather, while a king's failure to please the goddess would result in famine and disease and eventual removal from office. To assure that the king did his utmost to provide for his people, his life was bounded by sacred taboos and promises called geasa (see *GEIS*). See also MEDB, KINGSHIP.

Sources: Brenneman, Walter, and Mary Brenneman. *Crossing the Circle at the Holy Wells of Ireland*. Charlottesville: University of Virginia Press, 1995; Green, Miranda. *Symbol and Image in Celtic Religious Art*. London: Routledge, 1989.

inauguration stones   Celtic sacred object. Both literary and historical evidence support the idea that Celtic kings were invested with their office while standing upon a sacred stone. The most famous such stone was the LIA FÁIL, reputed to have been brought from the OTHERWORLD to stand upon the Irish hill of TARA. (Some legends say that the stone visible there in ancient times was not the real Lia Fáil; the real stone remained forever in the Otherworld while a replica was sent to this world.) The stone, that stands today at the same site, often described as resembling a phallus, is not the original.

According to one legend, the original Lia Fáil, also called the Stone of Destiny, was moved to Scotland in ancient times and used as an inaugural stone for 34 kings of Scotland. In 1296 this stone (now called the Stone of Scone) was removed from Scotland by order of Edward I and installed beneath the English coronation chair in Westminster Abbey in London; there it witnessed the inauguration of every British monarch, including today's Elizabeth II, with the single exception of Mary I. The Stone of Scone was, however, returned to Scotland in 1996, leaving open the question of whether the next British monarch will travel there to be crowned upon the sacred stone.

Evidence that the Stone of Scone is not the original Lia Fáil can be sought in traditions that the Lia Fáil screamed when the true king touched it. There is no historical evidence for the Stone of Destiny screaming upon the coronation of either Scottish or English monarchs.

The Stone of Scone is not the only inaugural stone known in Celtic lands. The stone upon which seven 10th century Saxon kings were crowned can still be seen beside the Guildhall in Kingston-upon-Thames. The Black Stone of Iona stood in the cathedral at Strathclyde until 1830, when it was lost; prior to that, it was used by highland chiefs as a witness in contracts and oaths. Finally, the Stone of the Footmarks on the Scottish island of Islay was recorded as the site for inauguration of the chiefs of the Clan Donald; the incoming ruler stood barefoot, feet in the footprints graven in the stone, to take his oath of office. That inaugural stone, however, was deliberately destroyed in the 17th century.

Ireland, too, had inaugural stones other than the mythological Lia Fáil. Near Belfast, the O'Neills were inaugurated while sitting in a stone chair that was last heard of in 1750, when purchased for use as a garden ornament; it has since disappeared. Another stone chair, called the Hag's Chair, can be seen on the heights of the CAIRN-studded hill of LOUGHCREW, but its legendary connection with inauguration is slight.

Sources: Bord, Janet, and Colin Bord. *The Secret Country: An interpretation of the folklore of ancient sites in the British Isles.* New York: Walker and Co., 1976, pp. 66 ff; Salvin, Michael. *The Book of Tara.* Dublin: Wolfhound Press, 1996, pp. 17 ff.

incantations   See DIVINATION, *IMBAS FOROSNAI.*

incest   Mythic theme. Tales that involve incest, especially that between brother and sister, have been interpreted as representing creation myths, because at the beginning of time the only way to populate the world would have been through incest. Implications of sexual congress between brother and sister appear in several Celtic myths, most prominently that of ARIANHROD, who bore two sons when asked to magically prove her virginity; sources imply that the father of these children was her brother Gwidion. King ARTHUR, too, had a child with his sister, the magical MORGAUSE. Such incestuous unions are often used to argue the original divinity of figures that have been diminished or euhemerized into human form.

Inchiquin   Irish mythological site. Near the small town of Corofin on the Burren, a wild rocky area of west Co. Clare, the tiny gray LAKE of Inchiquin is said to have a magical past. Three beautiful women lived there in underground caves, coming forth each night near a sweetwater SPRING. The lord of the area heard of them and, spying upon them, found one to his liking. He stole her from her sisters and took her to his fortress. She did not object, becoming his wife and bearing him several children. But she forbade him to ever invite company home—FAIRY women who agree to marry humans typically exact some such promise—and he pledged to her that he would not. Intoxicated while out with friends one night, he broke his promise, but when he arrived home with the company, he found his wife and children departing for the spring from which she had come. The errant lord could never recapture her, for the spring's waters rose until it became today's lake, forever hiding the entry to the fairy realm.

Sources: Kennedy, Patrick. *Legendary Fictions of the Irish Celts.* New York: Benjamin Blom, 1969, p. 282; Westropp, T. J. *Folklore of Clare: A Folklore Survey of County Clare and County Clare Folk-Tales and Myths.* Ennis, Co. Clare: Clasp Press, 2000, pp. 4–5.

Indech   Irish god. In the great Irish tale of the second battle of MAG TUIRED, this FOMORIAN hero wounded the god OGMA of the opposing army, the tribe of the goddess DANU called the TUATHA DÉ DANANN. Indech was the son of Domnu, a goddess of fertility who has been described as a version of Danu herself. The ancestry of Irish mythological figures is often quite tangled in this way. Some scholars argue that the various "tribes" of divinities represent the many waves of immigrants to the island; intermarriage among these immigrants led to interconnections among their divinities.

Inghean Bhuidhe   Irish goddess. One of THREE related goddesses known in the southwestern province of MUNSTER, "the yellow-haired girl" was the SISTER of LATIARAN, apparently an ancient fire goddess, and the mysterious CROBH DEARG or "red claw," perhaps another fire deity; the third sister is sometimes said to be LASAIR. Christianized into a SAINT, Inghean Bhuidhe was honored on May 6 with rituals around a sacred WELL. She is an obscure figure, known and honored within a small geographical region but with little legend to describe her powers.

Inis Glora   Irish mythological site. The last of three places to which the enchanted CHILDREN OF LIR were condemned, Inis Glora (now Inish Glora) is a small island off the west coast of Co. Mayo.

Intarabus   Continental Celtic god. An obscure god, the meaning of whose name cannot be determined, Intarabus is known from several inscriptions from Germany and Belgium. The Romans identified him with their own warrior god MARS, suggesting a connection with war or defense of land.

Interpretatio Romana ("Roman interpretation")   Cosmological concept. When the invading Roman legions arrived in Celtic lands, they confronted a complex group of divinities that only faintly resembled those they had left behind in Italy. Most disturbingly, there was no tightly organized pantheon with a hierarchical organization (see CELTIC PANTHEON). Nor did the Celts assign divine duties—ruler of the birth chamber, for instance, or god of the field boundaries—to specific gods as did the Romans. Instead, there was a clutter of gods and goddesses, some of whom seemed to be honored in only the smallest of regions, for Celtic divinities tended to be linked to specific places rather than to abstract meaning.

So the Romans set to work making order out of perceived chaos. Where there was a healing goddess, she was renamed MINERVA, or a healing god, APOLLO; where there was a powerful god, he became MARS. Gods of commerce or prosperity became MERCURY. Sometimes the old Celtic names were joined to the new name, so that SUL becomes Sulis Minerva (Minerva of the sun) in the town of healing springs now called BATH, and Mars Lucetius (Mars of light) in the same place. In other places, however, the old name was stripped away, so that we have dozens of inscriptions and sculptures to the Roman god JUPITER, shown dressed in Celtic garb and sometimes even wearing a neck ring called a TORC. What such gods' original names were is lost to history.

The Celts did not traditionally depict their divinities in human form, nor did they worship indoors. Thus the building of TEMPLES, for instance, to the HORSE goddess EPONA and the creation of temple sculptures of her riding a mare were an innovation in Celtic lands, brought by the Roman soldiers but ultimately embraced by the conquered Celts. Both temples and sculptures were inspired by classical originals, although retaining some native features. Continental Celtic peoples provide most of the inscriptions, temple ruins, and sculptures, while the island of Britain also offers a significant number; Ireland, however, because it was never invaded by the Romans, has no tradition whatsoever of interpreting native divinities as Roman ones.

The reinterpretation of indigenous divinities continued under the Rome-based Christian church, which learned from the legions that people resist having their ancestral divinities stripped from them. Instead of interpreting Celtic gods and goddesses as aspects of the trinitarian god, Christian evangelists took Pope Clement's advice to leave undisturbed the ancient holy places and to adopt old gods into the new religion as saints. Thus many Celtic saints, notably BRIGIT, have pagan origins.

intoxication   Mythic theme. Ancient Greek and Roman writers refer frequently—and disparagingly—to the Celtic love of intoxication. Although some of these accounts were simply derision of another culture, there is also evidence that the Celts, both continental and insular, took to drinking with the same gusto they showed in other aspects of life. Celtic leaders often offered their warriors liquor before battle, in order to free them from fear of injury and death. The sight of blue-painted warriors, wild with drink, charging across a battlefield is described as terrifying by more than one ancient writer. Drink also figured in Irish INAUGURATION rituals, which involved the new king's drinking the ALE of the goddess of the land. Whether the king drank enough to become tipsy is not known, nor is it established what the drink symbolized, whether the potential intoxication of power or the absorbing of some spiritual essence.

Irish literary sources invariably describe drunken behavior as occurring around the fall feast of SAMHAIN; the doors to the OTHERWORLD were said to open that night, and strong drink

may have either protected against or enhanced the likelihood of seeing into it. Archaeologists have found huge Celtic brewing vats but few storage vessels, suggesting that extra grain was used for brewing, which supplied binge drinking; once the cauldrons were empty, such excessive drinking would come to a halt until the next Samhain.

Intoxication of the Ulstermen (Mesca Ulad) Irish literary text. In the tale of this title from the great ULSTER CYCLE, king CONCOBAR MAC NESSA convinced his foster sons, the heroes CÚCHULAINN and FINTAN, to let him rule their lands for a year. At the end of that time, the king went off to celebrate restoration of their lands to their original rulers, intending to spend the first part of the evening with Fintan in the west, the second part in the eastern part of the territory with Cúchulainn. Halfway through the night the warriors were so intoxicated that they could not find Cúchulainn's fortress, winding up instead at that of their enemy, CÚ ROÍ, who attempted to trap them in an iron house that he set on fire. Cúchulainn, realizing that his expected guests were missing in transit, found and freed them, after which the Ulstermen destroyed Cú Roí's palace. Like other texts involving drunkenness, the *Intoxication of the Ulstermen* is described as occurring at SAMHAIN, the winter feast on November 1.

Sources: Cross, Tom Peete, and Clark Harris Slover, eds. *Ancient Irish Tales*. New York: Henry Holt and Co., 1936, pp. 215 ff; Gantz, Jeffrey, ed. and trans. *Early Irish Myths and Sagas*. New York: Penguin Books, 1984, pp. 188–218.

invasions   See *BOOK OF INVASIONS*.

Iona   Scottish mythological site. Best known now as the center of Celtic Christianity founded by St. Columcille, this tiny island in Scotland's Inner Hebrides is thought to have been the site of a Celtic shrine to a goddess, IOUA, whose name the island originally bore and who has been interpreted as a divinity of the MOON. Others connect the island's name to a word for YEW, a tree associated with sacred places and with death. The island's holy WELL was said to have risen directly from the magic CAULDRON of the TUATHA DÉ DANANN, the mythological tribe of the goddess DANU; its name, Tobar na h'oige or "fountain of youth," suggests that it conveyed the cauldron's powers of IMMORTALITY to the surface world. Those looking into the well at dusk or dawn, or on the night of the full moon, would see visions and receive healing. Although as a Celtic site it was open to both men and women, under Christianity women (except for nuns) were barred from residing on Iona; nonetheless one of the island's churches is home to a pregnant, self-exposing female figure called a SHEELA NA GIG.

Sources: Ross, Anne, and Michael Cyprien. *A Traveller's Guide to Celtic Britain.* Harrisburg, Pa.: Historical Times, 1985, p. 68; Straffon, Cheryl. *The Earth Goddess: Celtic and Pagan Legacy of the Landscape.* London: Blandford, 1997, p. 176.

iorasglach (*iorsglach-úrlair*)   Scottish folkloric character. A beggarly woman in threadbare clothing appears as a seer in some Highland folktales, typically striking the ground where she sits before uttering her prophecies to the lord and the court. This strange figure may be a faint folk memory of a Celtic or pre-Celtic ritual of DIVINATION.

Source: McKay, John G. *More West Highland Tales.* Vol. 2. Scottish Anthropological and Folklore Society. Edinburgh: Oliver and Boyd, 1969, p. 496.

Ioua   Scottish goddess. Ancient Scottish MOON goddess who gave her name to the famous sacred island of IONA.

Iovantucarus   Continental Celtic god. The name of this god has been translated as "the one who loves the young," suggesting a god of children or adolescents. The Romans interpreted him as both the warrior god MARS and the god of commerce and eloquence, MERCURY.

Irnan   Irish heroine. The goddess CONARAN of the TUATHA DÉ DANANN had THREE daughters, all skilled in the magical arts. Sent to capture some members of the heroic band of warriors called the FIANNA, they spun a magical web that held the men fast until the hero GOLL MAC MORNA appeared to do battle with them. He killed Irnan's two sisters, but the web held until he threatened Irnan too with death. She agreed to break the spell but instead turned into a monster and demanded that the three Fianna warriors fight her, in the traditional Celtic fashion of single combat. Fearful of her power, the heroes— OISÍN, OSCAR, and Celta—all refused, leaving their leader FIONN MAC CUMHAILL himself to do battle. Goll stepped in instead, killing Irnan. The story is a curious one, not tied to any of the major myth cycles, but it reflects a common theme of heroes killing HAG-monsters that may hide an ancient creation tale in which a goddess is killed in order to make the earth. See GARRAVOGUE.

iron   Folkloric motif. FAIRY folk dreaded iron more than any other substance, so it was considered wise to carry nails in one's pocket if one was passing a fairy rath, to put nails in the bottom of MILK pails to keep fairies from stealing milk, and to hide a nail in the bed where a mother was giving birth to assure the child would not become a CHANGELING. Iron crosses were believed effective as fairy repellents, and iron scissors could serve the purpose if held open to form a cross.

The source of these traditions, found across the Celtic lands, is unclear. The Celts were among the earliest Europeans to successfully work iron; their metalwork was justly renowned and provided wealth through trade with their neighbors. Indeed, the very word *iron* comes from a Celtic word, *iarn*, which was adopted into Latin and thereby spread through Europe. If, as some contend, the fairy people were originally the gods of pre-Celtic peoples, their reputed fear of iron might reflect a historical conflict.

Sources: Dorson, Richard M., ed. *Peasant Customs and Savage Myths: Selections from the British Folklorists.* Vol II. Chicago: University of Chicago Press, 1968, p. 25; O hEochaidh, Séan. *Fairy Legends of Donegal.* Trans. Máire MacNeill. Dublin: Comhairle Bhéaloideas Éireann, 1977, p. 167.

Is   See YS.

Iseult (Isolt, Isolde, Essyllt, Essellt)   Cornish or Breton heroine. The great romance that pairs Iseult with her lover TRISTAN, in opposition to her husband King MARK, parallels the even more famous British love triangle of GUINEVERE, LANCELOT, and ARTHUR. Mark, king of Cornwall (occasionally, Cornuaille in Brittany), found a single strand of golden HAIR so gorgeous that he immediately fell in love with the woman from whose head it came, and he dispatched his handsome young nephew Tristan to Ireland to find Iseult. On the return voyage, becalmed at sea and thirsty, Iseult offered Tristan a drink that her mother had brewed for the wedding night. Fearful that her daughter would live in a loveless if politically expedient marriage, the mother had used arcane herbal knowledge to make a potion that caused intense and boundless love. Meaning to assure her daughter's happiness, she instead destroyed it, for Iseult was hopelessly bound to Tristan from the moment they shared the magical drink.

Despite her feelings, Iseult did not yield herself physically and continued her journey, becoming the bride of Tristan's uncle and king. Her maid BRANGIEN, taking pity upon Iseult and feeling guilty for having served the magic potion, took her mistress's place in bed with Mark on their honeymoon, but eventually Iseult had to do her wifely duties. She tried to remain faithful to her wedding vows but began to meet Tristan in secret. Her suspicious husband subjected Iseult to a magical test of her purity; she was to cross a stream that, were she impure in any way, would drown her. Just as the test was to begin, Tristan arrived disguised as a beggar and helped Iseult cross the stream. The queen was thus able to honestly say that no man had touched her save her husband and the helpful beggar. Ultimately, however, the pain of their deceit caused the lovers to separate, although they lived miserably without each other's loved and loving presence. Tristan married a woman with Iseult's name (see ISEULT OF THE WHITE HANDS), but he died of a broken heart upon hearing a false report that the first Iseult was dead or would not come to him, and Iseult lived in sorrow until she too died.

Many commentators detect in this tale of doomed love a typically Celtic motif: the selection of the king by the goddess of SOVEREIGNTY, without whose approval no man can hope to rule. In addition to the tale's Arthurian echo, its love triangle is found in Ireland in the story of FIONN MAC CUMHAILL and his bride GRÁINNE, who eloped at their wedding with the handsome DIARMAIT; but in the Irish tale the heroine is far less a victim of circumstance and male lust, and much more an active party to the romance.

Sources: Bedier, Joseph. *The Romance of Tristan and Iseult.* Trans. Hilaire Belloc. New York: Vintage Books, 1965; Markale, Jean. *Courtly Love: The Path of Sexual Initiation.* Rochester, Vt.: Inner Traditions, 2000, p. 77.

Iseult of the White Hands   Cornish or Breton heroine. After TRISTAN had finally been separated from his fated lover ISEULT, he married another woman of the same name, called Iseult of the White Hands. Her happiness was short-lived, however, as Tristan, hearing of the original Iseult's death, pined away and died. The duplication of Iseult's name in the story suggests a hidden meaning connected to the role of the original Iseult as a goddess of SOVEREIGNTY: that Tristan replaced MARK in the favor of the goddess, suggesting that the older man was no longer fit to rule as king.

island Mythological site. The Celts considered islands to be liminal places, neither quite here nor quite in the OTHERWORLD, and thus useful as gateways for passing between worlds (see LIMINALITY). Islands share this marginality with natural sites such as BOGS, STONE CIRCLES, hills, and SPRINGS, and human-constructed sites such as HILLFORTS and HEARTHS as well.

There are many mythological islands in Celtic tradition, including AVALON, the Isle of Apples, to which king ARTHUR was guided by the LADY OF THE LAKE; the Isle of Women, an island or islands in the western ocean ruled by a beautiful queen and inaccessible except by her will (see TIR NA MBAN); and HY-BRÂZIL, a magical island that was visible only once every seven years. There are also actual islands around which tales and myths accrue; one of these is the small Isle of the Living in Ireland's southwestern province of MUNSTER, near Roscrea, where no person had ever died or ever would die; another is Inisbofin off the Connemara coast, where the mythological white COW appears every seven years. In Scotland the Hebrides are called the Isles of the Blessed; they are described as lands where budding and harvest occur simultaneously, which though not factually correct does correspond to descriptions of FAIRY islands.

Sources: Kennedy, Patrick. *Legendary Fictions of the Irish Celts.* New York: Benjamin Blom, 1969, pp. 219; Löffler, Christa Maria. *The Voyage to the Otherworld Island in Early Irish Literature.* Salzburg Studies in English Literature. Salzburg, Institut Für Anglistik und Amerikanistik, Universität Salzburg, 1983; Ross, Anne, and Michael Cyprien. *A Traveller's Guide to Celtic Britain.* Harrisburg, Pa.: Historical Times, 1985.

Island of Pigs Irish mythological site. This name was given to Ireland by the invading MILESIANS, because the magical residents called the TUATHA DÉ DANANN had cast a cloud of enchantment over the land, causing it to seem like a small pig-shaped island rather than the generous green island it truly is.

Isles of the Blessed See FORTUNATE ISLES.

Isolde See ISEULT.

Íte (Ita, Íta, Mo-Íde, Míde) Irish saint. A Christian woman of whom legends are told that are studded with pagan motifs, the historical Íte lived in the sixth century C.E. and founded a convent called Cill (church of) Íte, now Killeedy, Co. Limerick. Like the KILDARE nun BRIGIT, Íte seems almost mythological, possibly because her name was that of a goddess with whom she was conflated. Íte's chamber shone as though on fire, she cured a man by removing his horse's ears, and most important, she owned the mythological COW of abundance, the GLAS GHAIBHLEANN. Her miracles involved controlling the weather and the flight of birds, thus connecting her to earth goddesses of the MUNSTER region where she lived.

Source: Ó hÓgain, Dáithí. *Myth, Legend and Romance: An Encyclopedia of the Irish Folk Tradition.* New York: Prentice-Hall Press, 1991, p. 259.

Íth Irish hero. This minor character makes an appearance in the *BOOK OF INVASIONS*, where he is the first of his tribe, the MILESIANS, to spot the green island of Ireland on the horizon. He led a group of his people there but was quickly killed by the residents, the magical TUATHA DÉ DANANN. His nephew Míl Despaine avenged his murder by leading the Milesians in a successful invasion of Ireland.

Iubdan (Iubdán)   Irish hero. In the early Irish ADVENTURE tale *Eachtra Fhergus Mac Léide*, we meet Iubdan, the tiny boastful king of a people called the Faylinn, and his tiny queenly wife BEBO. His poet, EISIRT, tried to contain Iubdan's excessive bragging by telling him that nearby ULSTER was populated by giants—and proved it by traveling to Ulster and inviting back the poet Áeda who was in fact a dwarf. Then Eisirt put a GEIS, an unshakable demand, on Iubdan that he must taste the porridge of FERGUS mac Léti, the king of Ulster, before the next dawn. Taking his wife Bebo along, Iubdan set off to satisfy the geis—but the couple fell into the porridge and would have been drowned had they not been rescued and fished out. The tiny queen caught the fancy of king Fergus, who kept her as his mistress for a year and a day, after which Iubdan bought their freedom with a pair of flying shoes. The adventure tale of Iubdan has been cited as a source for the famous Lilliput section of Jonathan Swift's satirical commentary on humanity, *Gulliver's Travels.*

Iuchair (Iuchar)   Irish divinity. He was one of the THREE sons of the primal goddess DANU, who were known as the SONS OF TUIREANN and who were given a series of impossibly difficult tasks after killing their father's enemy CIAN. Iuchar may have been an ancestral divinity, and like his brothers BRIAN and IUCHARBA, he is sometimes said to have been the father of ECNE, a divinity of wisdom and inspiration. Because the brothers are so confused in the tales, some scholars have seen them as a triplication of one figure; others identify them with the three important TUATHA DÉ DANANN kings called MAC CUILL, MAC CÉCHT, and MAC GRÉINE.

Iucharba   Irish divinity. This minor god was one of the SONS OF TUIREANN and had little role separate from his brothers.

Iupiter   See JUPITER.

ivy   Symbolic plant. The ivy (genus *Parthenocissus*), a vining plant that grows quickly, almost rampantly, symbolized summer to the Celts; the Ivy King was described as opposing the Holly King in the endless flux of the seasons. At other times, the ivy was described as a feminine plant, opposed to the masculine HOLLY.

Iwein   See OWEIN.

Iweriadd   Welsh heroine. In some sources, Iweriadd is given as the name for the mother of the heroes BRÂN THE BLESSED and MANAWYDAN; in other texts, the heroes' mother is PENARDDUN, otherwise given as the name of the mother of their sister BRANWEN.

J

Jack-in-Irons British folkloric figure. In the northern English region of Yorkshire, travelers at night sometimes heard the sound of clanking chains and saw a strange looming figure called Jack-in-Irons. Jack said nothing, threatening or otherwise, but his presence was nonetheless said to be quite frightening.

Jack-in-the-Green British folkloric figure. In some rural British communities where spring festivals descending from the Celtic spring feast of BELTANE continued until recent times, a masked young man dressed in a costume of leaves danced through the streets. He is thought to be connected with Celtic tree-cults or with the mysterious figure called the GREEN MAN found in some architectural contexts in Britain.

Jack-o-Lantern See TINE GHEALÁIN.

Janiform See JANUS.

Januaria Continental Celtic goddess. A figure of a goddess by this name is known from a single HEALING shrine in Burgundy, in southwestern France. She is shown playing a pipe, which has been interpreted as indicating that music was used in her healing rituals.

Source: Green, Miranda. "The Celtic/Goddess as Healer." In Billington, Sandra, and Miranda Green, eds. *The Concept of the Goddess.* Routledge: London and New York, 1996, pp. 28 ff.

Janus Roman god. Rome had a god, Janus, who had two faces that looked in different directions; his name comes down to us in "January," the month that looks both forward to the new year and back to the old. In Celtic lands the Romans encountered occasional two-faced statues of unnamed gods and called them after their familiar god; scholars sometimes call these figures Janiform, "having the same form as Janus." The original Celtic meaning of the figures is lost, although they have been connected both with the reverence for the HEAD as symbol of essence and power and with the assignment of special power to TWINS.

Jeannie of Biggersdale British spirit. In the North Riding of Yorkshire, this dreadful spirit was said to live in Musgrave Woods where, like other BOGIES or boggarts, she threatened passing travelers. One farmer who attempted to drive her out of the region lost his horse when Jeannie cut it in two; the man was lucky to escape with his life.

Source: Briggs, Katherine M. *An Encyclopedia of Fairies: Hobgoblins, Brownies, Bogies, and Other Supernatural Creatures.* New York: Pantheon Books, 1976, p. 239.

Jenny Greenteeth British water spirit. A boggart or threatening sprite known until the 19th century, Jenny was said to haunt the streams of Lancashire, seeking to drown passersby. Such spirits may descend from early WATER divinities and may encode a faint folk memory of HUMAN SACRIFICE. Some scholars theorize that Jenny was only a nursery tale told to quiet unruly youngsters; the threat of a green-toothed monster hiding in pools would have kept adventurous children away from potential danger.

Source: Spence, Lewis. *The Minor Traditions of British Mythology.* New York: Benjamin Blom, Inc., 1972, p. 13.

Joan d'Arc (Jeanne-d'Arc) French heroine. There have been consistent attempts, both fictional and otherwise, to associate the historical figure of Joan d'Arc with residual Celtic beliefs in the French countryside from which she came. Joan was born ca. 1412 C.E. in the northern region of Lorraine, in a rural area where ancient beliefs remained as superstitions despite Christianity.

Early in her life Joan began to hear voices— two female, one male—that she understood to be SAINTS revealing her destiny. At the age of about 15, dressed in male garb, she traveled to meet the Dauphin, the embattled heir to the French throne, and announced herself as his general. Aware of the propaganda value of the girl's oddly charismatic quest, the Dauphin and his advisers agreed and were surprised by Joan's quick and accurate grasp of military strategy. At the head of her soldiers, Joan fought the English at Orléans, driving through their ranks to lift the city's siege and earning the title "Maid of Orléans."

Within a year, she had won the throne for the Dauphin, crowned as Charles VII with Joan at his side. Despite her prowess, Joan was captured

by French allies of the British, who sold her to the enemy. A trial for WITCHCRAFT followed in which Joan refused to deny her "voices," the sources of her inspiration. She was burned at the stake in 1431, apparently before she had turned 20. Only 25 years later she was granted a posthumous "trial" and declared innocent; in 1920 she was canonized by the Roman Catholic Church.

In addition to coming from an historically Celtic part of France, Joan responded to Otherworldly powers and embodied an ancient Celtic image of the woman as warrior that had been submerged for centuries. Several contemporary novelists, notably Anne Chamberlin *(The Merlin of St. Giles Well, The Merlin of the Oak Wood)*, draw inspiration from the Celtic motifs in the historical story of Joan. That this interpretation has deep historical roots is suggested by the fact that her inquisitors asked Joan what knowledge she had of the FAIRY faith or those who practiced it. Joan herself had no doubts that her inspiration was Christian; she answered, in all cases, that she was responding to the voices of saints, not those of fairies.

Source: MacCulloch, J. A. *The Religion of the Ancient Celts.* London: Constable, 1911, p. 263.

Joseph of Arimathea Arthurian hero. Although he figures but slightly in the Christian Bible, the merchant Joseph of Arimathea has a significant role in the story of the GRAIL. It was at his house that, on the night before his death, the savior Jesus had his Last Supper, in which the Grail was used as part of the dinner service. Whether it was a chalice or a platter, the object was sanctified with the miracle of transubstantiation, when bread and wine are turned into the body and blood of the Christian god's son.

Joseph was the only one of Jesus' disciples (and possibly, his uncle) with enough money to bury his master after the crucifixion on Mount Golgotha, the mountain of the skull. In return for his services, Pontius Pilate—the Roman provincial official who had sent Jesus to his death—gave him the Grail. (The story is self-contradictory at this point, because Joseph should not have needed to be rewarded with his own cup or platter.) He then set off on a prolonged journey around the Mediterranean, bearing the Grail and converting people to the new religion of Jesus. Finally he came to rest in Britain, where he had once traveled with Jesus when the savior was a boy. Joseph had many occasions to travel to the rich tin mines of Cornwall, but he passed up that region to settle in GLASTONBURY. There he thrust his staff into the ground on Wearyall Hill, and it burst into bloom despite the wintry weather. Assured by this miracle that he was to remain, Joseph built the first Christian church in Britain there.

Jowan Chy an Hor (John of Chyanhor) Cornish folkloric figure. The Celtic language of Cornwall in the far southwest of the island of Britain has little written literature; indeed, the only known folktale in the language is that centered on this heroic peasant and his exploits, which parallel those of similar folkloric heroes who adventure about the countryside showing their shrewdness and resiliency.

Jupiter (Iupiter, Jupiter, Jove) This Roman name was applied to various Celtic gods, including the relatively obscure Brixianus, Ladicus, Latobius, and Poeniunus. Under the INTERPRE-TATIO ROMANA, Celtic divinities were identified with similar (or presumed similar) Roman gods. In the process, the original names of some gods

were preserved as a surname to Jupiter's; other gods, however, were obliterated by this Roman habit, their individual significance disappearing into the mighty figure of the sky-lord.

Despite Caesar's contention that the Celtic Jupiter ruled the heavens, it is impossible to know whether the Celtic god was connected to the sky, as was the Roman original. The fact that many images carry a WHEEL, often a solar symbol, has led some to call the Celtic Jupiter a SUN god, although he is more convincingly described as a god of abundance and FERTILITY. Sculptures and reliefs show a mature, bearded man with curly mustache and beard; usually he is naked, showing him to be well-muscled and strong. He can be depicted carrying a thunderbolt, in which case the Celtic Jupiter is often called TARANIS, after the name of the thunder god of the continental Celts.

In addition to the images just described, we also find the Celtic Jupiter depicted as a mounted horseman fighting a monstrous SERPENT; the Roman Jupiter was never depicted astride a HORSE. The god was also honored with the so-called Jupiter columns, tall four-sided (or eight-sided) pillars found on the Continent. These pillars were carved in the form of a tree, and their attachment to Jupiter suggests he may have been connected with the Gaulish tree god ESUS.

Sources: Green, Miranda. *The Gods of Roman Britain.* Aylesbury: Shire Publications Ltd., 1983, p. 46; Green, Miranda. *Symbol and Image in Celtic Religious Art.* London: Routledge, 1989, p. 117; MacCulloch, J. A. *The Religion of the Ancient Celts.* London: Constable, 1911, p. 29.

K

Kay (Kai, Cai, Cei, Sir Kay) Arthurian hero. The kindly and sometimes buffoonish Kay appears in a number of Arthurian stories as ARTHUR's companion, foster brother, and seneschal (steward). He may have originally been a Welsh god of war, for the Welsh tale of *KULHWCH AND OLWEN* describes Kay as being able to go without sleep for nine days and stand underwater for the same length of time, to stretch himself as tall as the tallest tree, and to warm his comrades in cold weather simply with the heat of his body—all more than mortal powers. If Kay put a pack on his back, it became invisible; if he went into battle, no fewer than a hundred warriors would fall to his sword.

One of the most significant stories in which Kay appears is that of the kidnapping of queen GUINEVERE by the king named MELEAGANT. With Lancelot, Kay trailed Meleagant to his castle, where Kay was injured in an attempt to free the queen. Lancelot sneaked into the room where the injured Kay was sleeping; Guinevere was in the same room, and Lancelot went to her bed, leaving bloodstains on the sheets. The next day, Kay was accused of taking advantage of the queen, but Lancelot did battle to reclaim his friend's honor.

Some scholars believe that Kay was a god of Celtic peoples who were traditional enemies of Arthur's tribes; thus the connection of the two heroes in legend is interpreted as a folk memory of political links forged in reality.

Source: MacCulloch, J. A. *The Religion of the Ancient Celts.* London: Constable, 1911, pp. 122 ff.

keening Irish ritual. In Ireland ritual mourning for the dead was apparently a pre-Christian rite that survived into historical times despite clerical opposition. Keening was invented, legend has it, by the goddess BRIGIT after her son RUADÁN was killed in battle. It was a women's ritual, for they were the ones who screamed and clapped their hands over the body. Usually keeners were women of the village who were skilled in creating the woeful melodies, but wives and daughters could also join in the keening (from Irish *caoin*).

kelpie Scottish spirit. In Scotland storms at sea were believed caused by these mischievous, sometimes destructive, beings. Usually they appeared as blue men, although they could also assume the fearsome shape of a WATER HORSE. The BLUE MEN OF THE MINCH made waters constantly turbulent, discouraging all navigation; other kelpies stirred the waters only when they wished to cause trouble, so that even a smooth river or pond could turn treacherous once a traveler stepped into it. Kelpies were said to be able to leap up onto a horse passing over a ford, driving it mad with fear and endangering the rider. Boats could fall into the hands of malevolent kelpies—unless the skipper could complete rhyming couplets and force the kelpie away from the vessel. Kelpies have been described as a Scottish version of the Breton KOR-RIGAN, but the latter is more typically a lustful maiden, while the kelpie is not so highly sexed.

Sources: Evans-Wentz, W. Y. *The Fairy-Faith in Celtic Countries.* Gerrards Cross: Colin Smythe Humanities Press, 1911, p. 28; MacGregor, Alasdair Alpin. *The Peat-Fire Flame: Folk-Tales and Traditions of the Highlands & Islands.* Edinburgh: The Moray Press, 1937, p. 116.

Kenneth of the Prophecies (Brahan Seer, Kenneth MacKenzie, Cainnech, Coinneach Odhar Fiosaiche) Scottish hero. This folkloric figure can be described as the Scottish Nostradamus, a man with supernatural powers to predict the future. An echo of the Celtic BARD as prophet and diviner, Kenneth MacKenzie is alleged to be historical, but his story is filled with mythological motifs. His mother, napping near an ancient sacred site, dreamed of GHOSTS who described to her a powerful blue STONE. She found it and gave it to her son, who saw the future whenever he held it. Some tales say that Kenneth foresaw the tragedy of the Highland Clearances, when people were moved off the land to make more profit for landlords; others that he foresaw the destruction of the ancient clan system. An unfulfilled prophecy says that the entire Isle of Lewis and Harris will be destroyed in battle. Kenneth's magic blue stone is said to lie since his death beneath the waves of Lough Ussie, rather like the similar drowned blue power-object of a parallel Irish figure, BIDDY EARLY.

Source: *Folk-Lore and Legends: Scotland.* London: White and Allen, 1889, pp. 5–8.

Kerhanagh (Kiraqhna) Irish monster. In the Irish western province of CONNACHT, a mythical

beast of this name—which means "fire-spitter"—was said to have been driven by ST. PATRICK from the sacred mountain called CROAGH PATRICK. The demon then traveled across the land, poisoning holy WELLS with its fetid breath, as Patrick followed in hot pursuit, nearly losing the trail in Sligo. When the saint struck his staff on a rock near the hill of Tullaghan, sweet water poured forth, permitting Patrick to quench his thirst and reenter his battle with the monster, from which he emerged victorious. Such stories of Patrick and his battles with monsters have been variously interpreted as indicating Christian extirpation of earlier pagan, possibly Celtic, cults, or as showing Patrick stepping in for an earlier mythological hero who drove away threatening spirits. The Kerhanagh may be the same figure as CORRA and/or CAORANACH, although the legends differ. She is sometimes called by the English name, the DEVIL'S MOTHER.

Source: MacNeill, Máire. *The Festival of Lughnasa, Parts I and II.* Dublin: Comhairle Bhéaloideas Éireann, 1982, p. 515.

Keshcorran Irish mythological site. A cave near this small Irish town in the western province of CONNACHT was said to be the dwelling-place of three frightening HAGS. Reputedly, the caves of Keshcorran were connected by an underground passage to the most mythically important natural cave in Ireland, OWEYNAGAT (Cave of the Cats) where the phantom queen MÓRRÍGAN lived. There is, however, no actual connection between the caves, despite stories that a woman was led between them by a calf, to whose tail she was clinging. To explain the discrepancy between fact and fable, local people say that the DEVIL stopped up the passage.

The cave appears in the story *Buidhean Chéise Corainn* or the *Fight of Keshcorran*; the great hero FIONN MAC CUMHAILL was held captive there by powerful hags or goddesses, described as members of the TUATHA DÉ DANANN, the ancient divinities of the land. Fionn is associated with the cave in other tales of the FIANNA that call it his original home, while other stories claim that it was the abode of a magical SMITH. The goddess ÁINE was also said to live there, disguised as a hag, unusual behavior for this divinely radiant figure. Although the stories are confusing and confused, they offer evidence that Keshcorran had deep mythological significance.

Sources: Dames, Michael. *Mythic Ireland.* London: Thames and Hudson, 1992, p. 238; MacNeill, Máire. *The Festival of Lughnasa, Parts I and II.* Dublin: Comhairle Bhéaloideas Éireann, 1982, p. 186.

key Celtic symbol. Several goddesses including the horse goddess EPONA and the mother goddesses called the DEAE MATRES were depicted holding keys, usually interpreted as indicating a happy passage from this life to the OTHERWORLD of death.

Kildare Irish mythological site. Its name derives from words for "church" and "OAK," and this important town and district, in the eastern PROVINCE of LEINSTER, draws together important symbols of Celtic and Christian spirituality. It is especially associated with the figure of BRIGIT, a Christian saint presumed to have derived from a Celtic goddess, whose central sanctuary was there. The most significant day in the region is February 1, the old Celtic feast of IMBOLC, still celebrated as Lá Féile Bhríde, the day of Brigit.

killeen Irish sacred place. Across Ireland, "children's burial grounds" or killeens are found, carefully marked on maps and preserved against destruction. These small bits of field or grove were used for the burial of fetuses that were miscarried as well as babies who were born prematurely or who otherwise died without Christian baptism. As such, the babes were forbidden burial in Christian cemeteries, so the bereaved parents put them to rest in places held sacred before Christianity came to Ireland. Few of the original divinities to which these sacred grounds were dedicated are known.

King of Ireland's Son (Mac Rígh Éireann) Irish hero. In one of the richest of Ireland's orally transmitted tales, the eponymous hero shot a RAVEN in winter. Seeing its red blood and black feathers against the stark white snow, the King of Ireland's Son was inspired to seek out a woman with the same coloring (the same motif appears in the more literary story of DEIRDRE). Thus he embarked upon a long series of adventures, including taking care of the estate of a poor man whose debts would have denied him burial if the king's son had not worked to pay them. In doing so, the king's son won the gratitude of the dying man, which was later to be helpful in his quest.

As he searched for his beloved, the king's son found helpful servants. One was a GREEN MAN who desired a kiss from the intended bride; another, a man whose ears were so acute he could hear grass growing. Other servants appeared: a man who kept one finger always to a nostril so that his strong breath would not blow down houses; a speedy runner who kept one foot tied down; and a strong man. All were helpful in the tests set by the GIANT who held the king's son's beloved in enchanted bondage. When the princess was duly won, the little Green Man demanded his fee of the first kiss and further demanded to be locked alone with the princess when he collected it. His demands were met, and raging SERPENTS appeared that would have killed the king's son had he been alone with his bride, but the Green Man killed them. The sturdy Green Man was revealed as the grateful dead man whose debts the king's son had paid, and all lived happily ever after. The numerous folkloric motifs that appear in this story make it a favorite among those who categorize and analyze such tales.

Source: Hyde, Douglas. *Beside the Fire: A Collection of Irish Gaelic Folk Stories.* London: David Nutt, 1890, pp. 19 ff.

Kings, Cycle of the   See HISTORICAL CYCLE.

kingship   Sacred role. Although our current image of a king is that of a man with absolute power, to the Celts kingship was an office of responsibility and limitation. Upon INAUGURA-TION, the king entered a sacred marriage with the goddess of SOVEREIGNTY, possibly embodied in the queen as representative of the goddess of the land. So long as the king lived righteously, the land was fertile, the crops plentiful, the people well fed. As one text puts it, in the reign of a righteous king, "It was not possible to travel (Ireland's) forests easily on account of her fruit; it was not easy to travel her plains on account of the amount of her honey." But should the king fail to satisfy the goddess with his rectitude, the crops would fail and famine threaten.

Some scholars have interpreted the Celtic king's role as sacral (see SACRAL KINGSHIP). Such scholars contend that the king was less a leader than a priest, pointing to duties *(BUADA)* and taboos (see *GEIS*) that had little do with politics or military might, being instead symbolic actions that showed the people that the king lived with what was called in Ireland "the prince's truth," *fírinne flatho*. According to a seventh-century C.E. text, the king was never to oppress anyone by force of arms and was never to listen to unwise supporters.

Righteous behavior included HOSPITALITY, for it was part of the king's role to provide food and shelter for all who needed or desired it. In addition, the king was hedged around with sacred vows that varied from region to region; the king of TARA, for instance, was never to remain abed when the sun was up, while the king of CONNACHT was forbidden to ride a gray-speckled horse to CRUACHAN while wearing a gray-speckled robe. In Wales the mythological king MATH could never let his feet touch the ground but had to always have them in the lap of a virgin. Peculiar as such rules may seem, they parallel the taboos imposed upon royalty in other lands and seem intended to continually remind the king that he was not free to live as other humans are but must be always aware of the responsibility of his office. Several myths tell of the resulting chaos when kings broke their *geasa* or failed to satisfy the demands of hospitality. Thus the beautiful BRES was forced from Tara's throne when he fed a poet meager scraps; the king CONAIRE died horribly in the hostel of DA DERGA when he unwittingly broke the sacred vows of his office.

The rigors of Irish kingship have led some to hypothesize a Celtic vision of the king as a sacrificial priest whose life might be ended should his behavior bring on famine and disease. Sources for the responsibilities of the Celtic kings outside Ireland are relatively rare. Similarly, it is difficult to discern what the specific duties of the various levels of kingship were and how they related to each other. Irish law describes kings of a tribe (*rí tuaithe*), kings of several tribes (*rí ruiri*), provincial kings (*rí cóicid*), and finally the HIGH KING (*ard rí*). In early times the apparently "higher" offices of provincial and high king seem to figure more prominently in myth than in history; only after the Middle Ages does the high king's role seem to become political and strategic.

Source: Kelly, Fergus. *A Guide to Early Irish Law.* Dublin: School of Celtic Studies, Dublin Institute for Advanced Studies. Early Irish Law Series, Vol. III, 1988, pp. 17–21.

klippe   Scottish folkloric being. In Forfarshire in Scotland the klippe was a brown-skinned dwarfish FAIRY who haunted the moors and the roads.

Knight of the Glen   (O'Donohue of the Glen) Irish folkloric figure. The FAIRY king of the upper lake of Killarney in the southwestern Irish province of MUNSTER was the Knight of the Glen, Daniel O'Donohue. One of several stories told of this supernatural figure was that he stole away a local man, John Connors, bewitching a log to look like the man's body while he kept the man himself asleep in the OTHERWORLD. The enchanted log was duly waked and buried, with great mourning and ceremony, while the real John slept on in FAIRYLAND. When John finally roused and returned home, he frightened family and friends out of their wits and could barely convince them he was not a GHOST.

Source: Curtin, Jeremiah. *Hero-Tales of Ireland.* New York: Benjamin Blom, 1894, p. 17.

knitting Folkloric motif. The creation of fabric by twisting yarn together using two needles was an important craft in Celtic lands, especially Ireland and Scotland. It is believed to have been invented in the eastern Mediterranean, making its way over trade routes to the islands off Europe, where it was quickly adopted as a way of creating strong garments from sheep's wool. Specific designs and combinations of patterns evolved— the Jersey, the Guernsey, the Aran, the Shetland, the Fair Isle—that are still in use today, although no longer specific to village and regions. The common sight of a woman knitting soon gained archetypal or symbolic importance; the goddess ÁINE or her substitute, the FAIRY HOUSEKEEPER known as TOICE BHREAN, was said to sit beneath the waves of magical LOUGH GUR knitting, and other folktales similarly show the knitting woman as having magical or prophetic powers.

Source: Dames, Michael. *Mythic Ireland.* London: Thames and Hudson, 1992, pp. 109–110.

Knockainy (Cnoc Áine) Irish mythological site. Near the enchanted waters of LOUGH GUR in Co. Limerick is this low mountain topped with a single stone CAIRN, the home or SÍDHE of the FAIRY QUEEN named ÁINE. She may have originally been the regional goddess ANU or DANU, whose children were the gods called the TUATHA DÉ DANANN. Some interpret Áine as a SUN goddess, for a sun-WELL near Knockainy bears her name. Knockainy was especially important as a festival site at MIDSUMMER or at the harvest feast of LUGHNASA on August 1,

when processions of people bearing *clars* or straw torches drove their herds up the slopes of the hill with prayers for Áine's protection. The hill was once called Collkilla or "hazel-wood"; as the HAZEL marked sacred spots where wisdom could be gained, this ancient name may further point to the significance of Áine's hill.

Knockaulin (Cnoc Ailinne, Knockawlin) Irish mythological site. The kings of the eastern PROVINCE of LEINSTER once called Knockaulin (originally known as DÚN Ailinne) their royal seat, equivalent to TARA in the magical central province of MIDE and EMAIN MACHA in ULSTER. Recent excavations have revealed Celtic earthworks on the hill, supporting local legend about the hill's significance. Located near Kilcullen in Co. Kildare, the low hill is often confused with the nearby Hill of Allen (see ALMU), seat of the great hero FIONN MAC CUMHAILL.

knocker (knacker) Cornish folkloric figures. In Cornwall strange knockings were sometimes heard on mineshaft walls. Nobody appeared after the unearthly rapping, for the invisible knockers were the ghosts of long-dead miners (possibly Jews, who indeed worked in the Cornish mines, but more likely FAIRIES), still hard about their work.

The knockers were not dangerous but helpful, their knocking growing louder when miners came near a rich vein of ore. They did not bother with mined-out tunnels; they only haunted rich mines, preferably those where a fortune could be made extracting tin. Hearing a knocker was a sign of good luck, but if one said rude things about them, these spirits could turn vindictive. Knockers did not like crosses, so miners traditionally were careful not to wear them or to leave tools crossing each other when leaving work at night. They also did not like whistling, although singing in mines was acceptable.

Occasionally knockers haunted WELLS and CAVES, as other fairies might, but they tended to specialize in mines and related most strongly to miners. They were private creatures who did not appreciate being spied upon. One man who did so, by the name of Barker, managed to learn their fairy language sufficiently to hear them express their annoyance at his presence, and their plan to leave their fairy tools on his knee. Thereafter, the man suffered immense pain and stiffness in his knees, hence the Cornish proverb, "stiff as Barker's knee."

Source: Courtney, M. A. *Cornish Feasts and Folklore.* Penzance: Beare and Son, 1890, p. 138.

Knockfierna (Cnoc Fírinne, Knockfeerina) Irish mythological site. The "hill of truth" forms a twin to KNOCKAINY, the sacred hill only seven miles away; it offered an opening to the OTHER-WORLD and was the traditional site of LUGHNASA gatherings. Near several other important hills in Co. Limerick connected with the FAIRIES, Knockfierna was said to be the residence of an important fairy king, DONN FÍRINNE, whom some connect with the king of the Otherworld, also named DONN.

Knockgrafton Irish mythological site. On this mountain, in the Glen of Aherlow at the base of the Galtee Mountains, a hunchback overheard FAIRIES singing a monotonous song that went, "MONDAY, TUESDAY." His quick-witted ability to extend the fairy song thrilled them, and they cured his deformity. The story is a common one in Celtic lands.

Knockgraney (Cnoc Gréine) Irish mythological site. A hill near KNOCKAINY, not far from the small town of Pallas Green, is dedicated to the sister, TWIN, or double of ÁINE named GRIAN, "sun."

Knockma (Cnoc Meadha, Cnoc Mheadha) Irish mythological site. A hill near Tuam in Co. Galway, Knockma bears the name of MEDB but is better known as the mound of FINNBHEARA, FAIRY king of the western province of CONNACHT, who

lived there with his fairy bride ÚNA (also called NUALA). The site is now called Castle Hackett.

Knocknarea (Cnoc na Ria) Irish mythological site. Above the small northwestern town of Sligo rises a high mountain that was topped, some 6,000 years ago, with a mound and a rock CAIRN. According to legend, the cairn (*Miosgán Méabha*, or "Mebh's lump") covers the grave of the most famous of Ireland's queens, MEDB of CRUACHAN. But medieval texts say the cairn was erected by Eógan Bél, Connacht's last pre-Christian king, and Medb is said to have been killed many miles away, on the shores of Lough Ree on the River Shannon. Local tradition in Sligo holds that those ascending the mountain should carry with them a small stone or pebble to add to the cairn; conversely, it is very bad luck to take any stones away.

Knockshegowna (Cnoc Sídhe Úna) Irish mythological site. Over the rolling countryside of north Co. Tipperary, in an area replete with stories of magical FAIRY MOUNDS, rises this impressive hill, said to be the SÍDHE or palace of ÚNA, an Irish FAIRY QUEEN. She was said to have appeared there in the form of a calf one evening when a piper, Laurence Hoolahan, would not stop annoying her with his ceaseless drunken tweetings. When she spoke to him in human language, he was most surprised and was easily convinced to mount on her back. Within a second, the pair was at the River Shannon, 10 miles away, having flown through the air to get there. Úna was surprised that the piper was not terrified, but perhaps he was too intoxicated to show it. Because of his apparent courage, she leaped back and agreed to let him continue playing on the hillside as long as he wished. The story may be a fanciful one deriving from the misunderstanding of the hill's name as Fairy Calf Hill.

Knowth Irish mythological site. Near the better-known ancient site of Newgrange are two other mounds, Knowth and Dowth, all on hills overlooking a bend in the River Boyne and together called the BRÚ NA BÓINNE, the palaces of BÓAND, the river goddess. The great mound of Knowth and its companions were built some 6,000 years ago by an unknown people of great engineering skill and astronomical sophistication; the huge CAIRN of Knowth was oriented toward the point of sunrise on the spring and fall EQUINOXES, the times when day and night are equal. Knowth, which was under excavation for almost three decades, was opened to the public in early 2002, so it is now possible to view the impressive rock carvings, considered to be the most beautiful and expressive of all megalithic art in Europe.

Source: Eogan, George. *Knowth and the Passage-Tombs of Ireland.* London: Thames and Hudson, 1986.

korrigan (corrigan, ozeganned)   Breton folkloric figures. In Brittany the sea, RIVERS, and SPRINGS were said to be inhabited by lovely lustful golden-haired women who tried to lure men into their beds—and to a watery death. Such water sirens are common folkloric figures, found in almost every land. What distinguishes the Breton version is their association, in oral folklore, with ancient worshipers of earth goddesses or with women DRUIDS, from whom the *korrigans* are said to be descended. The persecution of earlier faiths by Christianity resulted in a fierce folkloric enmity between the *korrigans* and celibate priests, who were subject to endless lascivious temptation by the spirits. The *korrigans* play an important part in the story of the pagan princess DAHUT, for they built her beautiful city of YS.

Korrigans were small FAIRIES, less than two feet tall, and had translucent wasp-like wings. Lovely woodland grottoes with running streams (in French, *grotte aux fées*, or in Breton, *feunteun ar corrigan*) were especially attractive to *korrigans*, who made their homes in such places. If contacted there, they could sometimes tell the future. Seeking them out could bring danger, however,

for *korrigans* like other fairies were immoral and might as readily steal a person or child as tell a fortune. Some Breton legends speak of the *korrigans* as doomed human souls, unhappily trapped through tragic death to wander the earth, but more typically they are seen as nonhuman. In Breton folklore the term *korrigan* is often used as a synonym for the entire fairy race.

Korrigans are said to be less visible in even-numbered than odd-numbered centuries (the 2000s will see rather less activity than the 1900s, for instance). They are more likely to be seen at twilight than in the daytime, as is typical of such liminal beings. Some *korrigans* spent their time guarding buried treasure, while others made mischief for humans, tickling horses and causing nightmares. They derived most pleasure from circle dances within or near the pre-Celtic STONE CIRCLES and megalithic shrines still found in Brittany, singing "MONDAY, TUESDAY, Wednesday, Thursday, Friday" (*Di Lun, Di Merh, Di Merhier...*) but never mentioning the days of the weekend, for to do so caused magical deformation such as a lump on the back.

Kulhwch (Culhwch, Kilhwch)   Welsh hero. The hero of an important literary tale from Wales, Kulhwch was a cousin of the legendary king ARTHUR and may have descended from an ancient Welsh divinity.

See also KULHWCH AND OLWEN.

Kulhwch and Olwen   Arthurian tale. The late 12th-century Welsh tale *Kulhwch and Olwen* reaches back into Celtic myth and forward into the legends of the quasi-mythological king of Britain, ARTHUR. The hero Kulhwch was born of a princely man, CILYDD, whose wife GOLEUDDYDD went mad after becoming pregnant. While passing a PIG shed, she went into labor, whence the child was named Kulhwch or "pig-run." When Goleuddydd died, the boy's ambitious father gained a new wife through murder, killing the king of a neighboring land and carrying off the queen to become stepmother to the orphaned Kulhwch. The new queen hoped that Kulhwch would marry her own daughter, but when he failed to show interest, she cursed her stepson: that he would never marry until he won the daughter of the fearsome GIANT YSPAD-DADEN PENKAWR. Other versions say that the mother, Gilydd, survived her trauma and, remarried to a new husband, encouraged her son to seek the woman of his dreams, OLWEN.

When he grew up, Kulhwch hoped to win Olwen, the giant's daughter, and sought the help of his cousin Arthur to win her hand. He entered the court of CAMELOT and recited his distinguished heritage right back to the goddess DÔN and thus won Arthur's aid. They set out with a team of warriors and traveled until they met Kulhwch's aunt, sister of his long-dead mother, who warned them that no one ever left the giant's castle alive. Undeterred, Kulhwch and Arthur approached the castle. There Kulhwch met Olwen, and the two fell instantly in love. The maiden refused to leave without her father's blessing. That blessing could only be won if the hero performed 40 impossible tasks, one of which involved the capture of a scissors, razor, and COMB from a terrifying pig named TWRCH TRWYTH. Kulhwch completed the tasks—the tale grows very lengthy at this point—and thus won his beloved Olwen.

The text has been interesting to Celtic scholars because it occupies a middle ground between myth and legend, being composed of mythological motifs familiar from other Celtic lands as well as heroic names and personalities. Many magical and OTHERWORLD characters and objects are woven into the tale.

Kundry   See CUNRIE.

Kyteler, Alice   Irish heroine. Unlike Europe, including England and Scotland, Ireland did not experience a WITCH-burning hysteria. Only one woman was ever executed for WITCHCRAFT, and that was Petronilla, maid to the wealthy merchant Alice Kyteler of Kilkenny. Accused, together with 11 friends and members of her family, of witchcraft and heresy in 1324 by Bishop Richard Ledrede of Ossory, Alice escaped to England, where she lived out her life without history making note of her again. The accusations against her represented the first time that witchcraft was described as a heresy based in non-Christian beliefs.

Source: Davidson, L. S., and J. O. Ward. *The Sorcery Trial of Alice Kyteler.* Binghamton, N.Y.: Medieval and Renaissance Texts & Studies, 1993.

La Belle Dame sans Merci   See FAIRY LOVER.

Labhraidh Luathlam ar Cleb (Labriad) Irish hero or god. Ruler of MAG MELL, the "plain of honey" where the trees were always loaded down with magical fruit and vats of mead could never be emptied, Labhraidh arranged for the hero CÚCHULAINN to spend time with Labhraidh's wife's sister, the lovely FAIRY QUEEN FAND. In return for this dalliance, Cúchulainn had to fight and defeat three warriors who were troubling Labhraidh. This bargain set in motion a love triangle, because Fand was the only companion who tempted Cúchulainn to break faith with his wife, the peerless EMER. The story is told in an ancient text called *Cúchulainn's Sickness*, which formed the basis for the play by William Butler Yeats, *The Only Jealousy of Emer.*

Labhraigh (Labraid) Irish hero. Mythical and possibly historical ancestor of the people of the eastern province of LEINSTER, Labhraigh was said to have invaded Ireland in the second century B.C.E. besting an opponent named Cobhthach to gain his territory. A longer version of his legend reveals two kings, both called Labhraigh. The first, Labhraigh Lorc, had an evil brother (or uncle) named COBHTHACH, who yearned to be king over Leinster in the place of AILILL Áine, the true king. Cobhthach pretended to be near death, and when Labhraigh leaned over in grief, stabbed him to death; then Cobhthach poisoned Ailill. Ailill left a son, one who was called Moen ("speechless") because he never spoke. At least, he did not until struck by a ball when playing football one day, whereupon his playmates gave him the name of Labhraigh Moen ("the speechless one speaks").

Labhraigh Moen grew to be a kindly and generous nobleman, so much so that he attracted the attention of the evil usurper Cobhthach—who promptly banished him to the wilds of MUNSTER, far to the southwest, where the people were called the Fir Morca. There the king's daughter, the lovely MORIATH, fell in love with the exile. Stealing into court with his harper, the magnificent CRAIPHTINE, Labhraigh Moen waited until the magical music put the court to sleep, then seduced Moriath. When, the next morning, her mother heard Moriath sigh in a knowing satisfied way, she instantly guessed the truth, but the parents did not attempt to stand in the lovers' way. Labhraigh was welcomed by the king, and together the couple went east to win back Labhraigh Moen's kingdom.

First they captured the fort at Dinn Ríg, once again using Craiphtine's magical music—this time to put the defenders to sleep, while the attackers kept their ears carefully covered against the sleep-inducing music. Then

Labhraigh Moen set about making a trap for the usurper. He built a great hall, all of IRON, and once Cobhthach had entered, locked the door and heated the building up with bellows until the evil king and his entire army died.

In another version of the story, Moen became speechless when Cobhthach forced him to eat the hearts of his father and grandfather. Banished to Brittany, he heard the music of Craiphtine and, immensely moved, broke his silence to praise the harper. Thereafter, he raised an army and defeated the usurper Cobhthach at Dinn Ríg, the fort of kings.

Various interpretations have tried to discern the historical truth behind these fanciful narratives. The speechlessness of the king has been understood as an indication that he did not speak the language of the country or that he was in some way blemished (see BLEMISHED KING). In a variant of the legend, it was not Labhraigh who was dumb but anyone who saw him without hair covering his ears—for the king had the ears of an ass. (Anyone who did not keep silent was killed.) Then a young barber whispered the dreadful secret to a TREE, which was cut down and used to make a HARP for Craiphtine, and which then sang out the secret entrusted to it. Shamed, Labhraigh revealed his unsightly ears for all to see.

Ladra (Adra)   Irish hero. In the *BOOK OF INVASIONS*, we read of the earliest arrivals in Ireland: the lady CESAIR, with her 50 handmaidens and a scant three men. Ladra, the ship's pilot and Cesair's brother, was one of the three. Once he had brought them safely to land, Ladra demanded more territory than Cesair was willing to give. He set off to found his own kingdom, but he died trying to satisfy the many women who had accompanied him there, or perhaps from an oar that penetrated his buttocks. It is unclear from the multiple texts whether this figure is the same as ADRA or a separate character.

Lady of the Fountain (Laudine)   Arthurian heroine. The mysterious Laudine, the Lady of the Fountain, may descend from an ancient Celtic goddess of SPRINGS, for she ruled a splendid pool called BARENTON in the center of Brittany's magical forest of BROCÉLIANDE. Because Barenton's waters had the power to stir great storms, it was fiercely guarded by Laudine's husband, the Black Knight named Esclados le Roux. CYMON, a knight from king ARTHUR's court, tried to slay the guardian, only to be driven away. Returning to CAMELOT, Cymon related his story and inspired the young knight OWEIN to seek out the place and take on the Black Knight in single combat.

This time, the young adventurer had assistance, in the person of a maiden named LUNED, who told him the secret way to slay the Knight. Once that task had been accomplished, Luned helped Owein win the heart and hand of Laudine, who was quite willing to be wooed and won by such a brave knight. For a year the couple lived happily and contentedly together, but then Arthur and his knights happened by. Owein's lady entertained them splendidly, then was heartbroken when her husband begged to be allowed to accompany them on their adventures. Laudine agreed, only to be abandoned by her thoughtless knight.

War and adventure held so much appeal that Owein forgot to return to the Lady of the Fountain as the seasons passed and a new year began. When the maid Luned arrived at the king's company, Owein was shamed in front of the ROUND TABLE knights by her revelation of his betrayal. He went mad, roving the forest like a wild beast. Befriended by a lion and later by Luned, Owein followed the maidservant's suggestion and slipped up to Laudine's fountain in the dark of night. There he began sprinkling its water on the steps around it, causing great storms to ravish Laudine's land. Her maid told her of the Knight of the Lion—Owein in disguise—who could save her, so long as she would help him reconcile with his beloved lady. Desperate to save her land, Laudine agreed, and when Owein was revealed to be the savior knight, she kept her promise as he had not.

Source: Markale, Jean. *Courtly Love: The Path of Sexual Initiation*. Rochester, Vt.: Inner Traditions, 2000, p. 112.

Lady of the Lake Arthurian heroine. The mysterious Lady, sometimes called NIMUE or MORGAUSE although also differentiated from those characters, gave the king-to-be ARTHUR the magical sword EXCALIBUR. In early texts she is a FAIRY, a semidivine being who exists in a world parallel to ours, the Celtic OTHERWORLD, called in her case the Land of Women (see TIR NA MBAN). The Lady lived on a magical LAKE surrounded by her maiden servants; she captured LANCELOT and raised him to be her protector, for which he was called Lancelot of the Lake. In some sources, Lancelot was the Lady's lover and, by her, the father of the pure knight GALAHAD.

Later texts demoted the FAIRY QUEEN to a mere sorceress, who created an illusory lake to keep people away from her land. Her power in the Arthurian legends remained firm, however, for she protected Arthur throughout his life, and it is to her that Arthur returned at the end of his life. Giving back Excalibur to the lake's depths, the wounded king was then conveyed away—to where, no one knew—by the Lady. Her connection with Arthur has been described as parallel to that of the Irish goddess MÓRRÍGAN and the hero CÚCHULAINN.

Source: Evans-Wentz, W. Y. *The Fairy-Faith in Celtic Countries*. Gerrards Cross: Colin Smythe Humanities Press, 1911, p. 327.

Láeg (Laeg, Lóeg) Irish hero. Charioteer to the greatest of ULSTER's heroes, CÚCHULAINN, Láeg saved his master by taking a spear intended for him.

Lair Derg Irish goddess. This name or title, which means "red mare," was used of ÁINE, goddess or FAIRY QUEEN of southeastern Co. Limerick. RED is generally an OTHERWORLD color, and HORSES had associations with death; the title thus seems to point to Áine as a goddess of death who takes us on a ride to the afterlife.

lake (lough) Symbolic site. Celtic religion saw WATER as sacred, so it is not surprising that lakes were seen as potent symbols of the OTHERWORLD. Tales of cities beneath lake waters are found in many Celtic lands (see INCHIOUIN, LOUGH REE), as are stories of magical beings who dwell either under the lake's waves (see LÍ BAN) or on magical ISLANDS (see LADY OF THE LAKE).

The religious meaning of the lake as a passageway to the Otherworld seems to reflect ancient Celtic rituals in which treasures were offered to lakes; the great horde of objects found in the shallows (LA TÈNE) of Switzerland's Lake Neuchâtel were probably deposited ritually, perhaps to drive away plague or with an equally serious intention. Similar offerings were made at holy WELLS, which were commonly used for seasonal festivals, while lakes seem to have been more commonly visited ritually in times of great need. Records show that offerings to a lake near Toulouse in southern France preceded the end of a pestilence; the unreliable warrior Caepion then stole the treasures. When he was killed in battle soon after, this was taken as a sign that he had been punished for his greed. Such legends did much to protect lake deposits from thieves, and recent excavations at LOUGH GUR revealed significant and valuable artifacts.

lake maidens Celtic folkloric characters. Throughout the Celtic lands, LAKES were seen as entrances to the OTHERWORLD. In those lakes lived FAIRY women whose enchanted palaces under the waves could sometimes be seen from shore. These lake maidens—who sometimes appeared as SWAN MAIDENS—made wonderful wives for human men, but they were hard to capture. One had to steal something from the lake maidens; when she appeared as a SWAN, it must be her robe of feathers; at other times it could be her COMB or another personal object. Then she would come meekly to shore and become as industrious and pleasant a wife as a man could wish.

However, such maidens invariably placed taboos around their husband's behavior; the husband of ÁINE of LOUGH GUR could express no surprise at anything their son did, while MELUSINE's husband could not see her on Sundays. The Welsh lake maiden Nelferch extracted from her husband the agreement that he should not strike her without reason; she set a limit of THREE mistakes. They lived happily except for his tendency to tap her when he wanted to get her attention. Despite the good intentions behind his actions, she still considered it breaking her rule, and upon the third incident she disappeared. Whenever a lake maiden's rule was broken, she instantly disappeared, returning to her watery home, sometimes taking her children with her but just as often leaving them orphaned.

Source: Rhys, John. *Celtic Folklore: Welsh and Manx.* Oxford: Clarendon Press, 1941, pp. 2, 23.

Lambton Worm   British folkloric figure. The word WORM may seem to indicate an insignificant being, but in fact it was the Norse and Saxon word for DRAGON. One of the most famous British dragon stories concerns the worm that haunted the northern region around Lambton Castle. Its presence among humans began with an unruly 14th-century lord who went fishing on Sunday morning instead of going to church—and in full view of the chapel at that. His luck was bad until, just as the church bells stopped, something bit at his line. He hauled in a strange creature, a sort of EEL with nine mouths. Appalled and frightened, he threw it down a WELL—still locally called Worm's Well—and set about to reform his life. He even went to the Crusades. Meanwhile, in the well, the worm was growing larger and larger, until it emerged a true monster to ravage the countryside and kill all the knights sent to combat it.

When the lord returned from the Holy Land, he found his lands in disarray and his peo-

ple in fear. Realizing his guilt, he pledged to kill the worm. A wise woman advised him that he must have a SMITH make spiky armor and that he must fight the worm from the rock in the middle of the River Wear. In addition, she warned, he must kill the first creature he met upon his victorious arrival home. Planning ahead, the lord arranged to have a DOG let out the moment he approached his castle, then set off to do battle with the monster. It was a fierce struggle, but the worm finally impaled itself upon the spikes of the lord's armor and died. Alas, in the excitement of the lord's return home, his aged father ran to congratulate him. The lord immediately killed the dog that had, indeed, been let out as the designated victim, but it was not sufficient to meet the conditions set out by the old woman, and as a result no lord of Lambton died in his bed for nine generations.

Lammas   See LUGHNASA.

Lamorack de Galles   Arthurian hero. King PELLINORE's son, he was a famous warrior of the ROUND TABLE. He killed the husband of king ARTHUR's half-sister MORGAUSE, and her sons, who included GAWAIN, killed him in retaliation.

Lancelot   (Lancelot of the Lake, Lancelot du lac, Lanceloz, Lanzelot von Arlac)   Arthurian hero. The handsomest and bravest knight of the ROUND TABLE, he became the lover of ARTHUR's queen GUINEVERE, thus creating a fatal triangle that serves as the central dramatic conflict in the Arthurian cycle. The connection of Celtic mythology with the MATTER OF BRITAIN—the tales relating to king ARTHUR and his knights of the Round Table—has been widely argued, with general agreement that there is a connection but less agreement on specifics. Thus in the character and actions of the heroic knight Lancelot we may find Celtic themes and motifs, as we do in the other primary characters of the narrative, Arthur and Guinevere.

Lancelot's background is not clear from the texts; the fact that he is called "of the lake" suggests a relationship to the mysterious LADY OF THE LAKE, which in turn has led some to speculate that Lancelot was of the FAIRY people, although many texts claim that the Lady was only his foster mother and that his father was the French king Ban of Benoic, of whom little more is known. Other tales say he was the son of king Pant of Genewis and his wife, Clarine, from whom the infant Lancelot was stolen by the Lady of the Lake while Clarine was nursing her husband's battle wounds. The Lady then raised him in ignorance of his true family, which Lancelot learned as a young man.

He came to CAMELOT then, drawn by the fame of the great king and his beautiful queen. From the first he and Guinevere were drawn to each other. In the interests of her virtue and the court's harmony, however, both resisted their attraction. When Guinevere finally spent a night in the forest alone with Lancelot, the upstanding knight put a sword between them, to assure that he would not yield to fleshly temptation. Arthur, finding them sleeping virtuously beside each other and separated by the sword, took the sword with him, thus ensuring that the couple would realize they had been observed. Lancelot departed the court, intent upon seeking glory in the field of battle, and left a heartbroken Guinevere behind. (A similar incident occurs in the parallel Irish tale of GRÁINNE and DIARMAIT, but Gráinne was a more forthright and sexually demanding partner.)

One story, told by Chrétien de Troyes as *Le Chevalier de la charrette* or *The Knight of the Cart*, says their affair began when Guinevere was stolen away from Camelot by the giant or king MELEAGANT. Lancelot set out in pursuit of the kidnapped queen, but he soon lost the track and had to rely upon a strange DWARF who was dragging a cart full of condemned prisoners. When the dwarf told Lancelot that the only way he would ever see his beloved again was to join the criminals in the cart, Lancelot did so willingly. Approaching Meleagant's castle, Lancelot was confronted by two bridges: one that went beneath the moat, smooth and straight; the other, made of a sword blade, that went above the water. Desperate to find Guinevere, Lancelot took the shorter route, wounding himself dreadfully in the process. Locating the queen in a bedroom where the seneschal KAY slept, himself wounded, the bleeding Lancelot joined his beloved in her bed. The next day, when bloodstains were found on Guinevere's sheets, Kay was accused of seducing her, and Lancelot had to fight for his friend's honor.

When Guinevere returned to Camelot, it was as Lancelot's mistress as well as the land's queen. His fall from perfection meant that when he went on the quest for the sacred GRAIL, he was unable to attain his goal. Their affair was kept secret in the court, and Lancelot performed many noble deeds in Guinevere's honor. He freed the many knights held captive in the PERILOUS VALLEY, part of the forest of BROCÉLIANDE that king Arthur's half-sister, the sorceress MORGAN, had enchanted. Because she had been betrayed, she made sure that any knight who had ever wronged a woman would become trapped by her magic, seeing the trees as great battlements guarded by fire-breathing dragons. Many knights were trapped there, including the seemingly pure GAWAIN, until Lancelot—ever true to his queen and lover—freed them all.

The beginning of their affair was also the beginning of Camelot's downfall. Lancelot was not to blame, nor the hopelessly smitten queen, for Arthur's own past rose up to destroy his ideal kingdom. Guinevere was convicted of treason and sentenced to death by burning, but Lancelot arrived just in time to save her, and in the commotion killed his own best friend, the upright knight GARETH. Arthur's own illegitimate son MORDRED, conceived upon MORGAUSE, began a war on Camelot that ended with the deaths of all the heroes except Arthur, who was taken away by the mysterious Lady of the Lake—perhaps to rise again as Britain's "once and future king." According to some sources, Lancelot died in that final battle, although others say that he survived to become a saintly hermit in his castle, while his beloved Guinevere retired to a convent.

The Arthur-Guinevere-Lancelot love triangle echoes two more clearly Celtic romances: one from Ireland, that of the heroic leader FIONN MAC CUMHAILL, his young follower Diarmait, and the lady Gráinne; the other from Cornwall, that of the aging king MARK, the fair knight TRISTAN, and his fated lover ISEULT. In spite of some similarities, the stories have significant differences. The assertive Gráinne put a GEIS or sacred vow upon Diarmait that he must carry her off and later taunted him into sleeping with her, while Guinevere was less forthright in expressing her desire for Lancelot; some have seen the influence of Christianity in her hesitation. The Arthurian material lacks the magical motifs of that of Tristan and Iseult, who fell hopelessly in love after drinking a MAGIC potion intended for the bride to share with king Mark on her wedding night. Thus magically entangled, the couple fought unsuccessfully against their love; the trials of Iseult parallel those with which Guinevere's virtue was tested.

The similarity of these three stories, all from different Celtic lands, has led scholars to suggest that all derive originally from a myth in which the goddess of SOVEREIGNTY transfers her love to a new and younger king and thus authorizes his kingship. Lancelot, like Tristan and Diarmait, is selected by the goddess-queen as her next lover. If this were indeed a story of dynastic change, the goddess's choice would have indicated that a new king was to be installed. From this mythological outline, three Celtic cultures elaborated their own intensely evocative human tales.

In some texts Lancelot is the lover of the Lady of the Lake and, by her, the father of the pure knight GALAHAD. In other tales he was the accidental lover of ELAINE of Corbenic, by whom he conceived Galahad when, intoxicated, he believed he was sleeping with his beloved Guinevere. Some Arthurian tales do not show Lancelot as Guinevere's lover but as a faithful servant of the king; this has suggested to scholars that the love triangle was a late development of the myth.

Source: Markale, Jean. *Courtly Love: The Path of Sexual Initiation.* Rochester, Vt.: Inner Traditions, 2000, pp. 69, 116.

Land of Promise   See TÍR TAIRNGIRI.

Land of Women   See TIR NA MBAN.

Land of Youth   See TIR NA NOG.

Land Under Wave   See TIR FO THUINN.

Laoghaire (Loegaire, Leary)   Irish hero. This name is common among Irish heroes, including:

- **Laoghaire, son of NIALL** of the Nine Hostages. Quasi-historical high king of Ireland, during whose reign St. Patrick lit the BELTANE fire on SLANE hill; upon hearing the preaching of Patrick, Laoghaire was instantly converted.
- **Laoghaire Buadhach,** "Laoghaire the victorious," a hero of the ULSTER CYCLE who died rather than let a poet, Aodh, be killed by the angry king CONCOBAR MAC NESSA.
- **Laoghaire mac Crimthann,** consort of the heroine or sun goddess DÉR GRÉINE, whom he won by killing a fearsome GIANT named GOLL MAC MORNA. He was lured to the OTHERWORLD by a young FAIRY king, Fiachna, who came to beg his aid against an invader. Laoghaire was willing to help, but he found himself trapped, for once in FAIRYLAND he was unable to return to home, and he remained there forever.

Lasair   Irish heroine or goddess. In the province of ULSTER, this obscure figure is connected with a holy WELL called Tobar Lasair (Tobar Lastra) in Co. Monaghan, where she was celebrated with a festival on April 18. She is more significantly associated with MUNSTER, where she similarly is associated with a well that she shared with her sister, the otherwise unknown Ciar. As

Lasair's name means "flame," while Ciar's means "extreme darkness," the two may be TWINS that represent the important cosmological concept of balance or complementarity.

Lasair's name appears in several groupings of heroines or goddesses. She is said to have been the sister of LATIARAN and INGHEAN BHUIDHE, with whom she lived in a monastic cell at the little town of Cullen in Co. Cork. She later moved to nearby Killasseraugh (Cill Lasaire, "church of Lasair"), where she remains the patron SAINT of the parish. She was said to have had a holy well near Cullen, but its location has been lost, as has the date of her festival.

La Tène Period of Celtic culture. At the region called La Tène ("the shallows") in Lake Neuchâtel in Switzerland, one of the greatest of archaeological finds was made by amateur explorers in 1858: a huge deposit of thousands of objects, apparently thrown into the LAKE as part of a ritual, that ranged from golden TORCS to iron CAULDRONS, from elaborate silver brooches to sacrificed DOGS, PIGS, and CATTLE. The horde gave its name to the third period of the developing Celtic culture, the earlier ones being the URNFIELD and HALLSTATT; the La Tène period is now divided into three phases, I, II, and II.

Full of SPIRALS and whorling designs, the metal decorations on the art found in the horde, apparently created by a colony of artists on the lakeshore, represent masterpieces of ancient art. Old European or pre-Indo-European designs have been traced in the art of La Tène, as have Greek, Etruscan, Scythian, and even Persian designs, suggesting that the La Tène people were part of a wide network of cultural exchange in the Mediterranean world. Although the artists of La Tène only worked from ca. 500 B.C.E. until ca. 100 C.E., the style lasted until the Norman conquest of Ireland in 1169.

Latiaran (Lateerin, Lateeran) Irish goddess or heroine. In the tiny town of Cullen in northern Co. Cork, a strange monument is dedicated to Latiaran: a STANDING STONE in the rough shape of a heart, which stands near a diminutive holy WELL dedicated now to St. Latiaran, a holy woman unknown elsewhere. Local legend has it that she was a woman of such modesty that, when she was carrying some boulders (or hot coals) in her apron and a SMITH commented approvingly on the shapeliness of her ankles, Latiaran dropped her apron. The standing stone fell out of it, wedging itself upright in the ground, whereupon she disappeared beneath it. The stone, called Latiaran's heart, can still be seen in a patch of grass near the graveyard in Cullen.

Two aspects of this curious tale suggest an ancient goddess converted into a SAINT with the coming of CHRISTIANITY. The smith is elsewhere known as a magical being whose exemplar is the god GOIBNIU. The motif of rocks falling from the apron is otherwise found in tales of the world-creating HAG, the CAILLEACH. That Latiaran (whose name is untranslatable) was a fire goddess is suggested by the hot coals she carried, as well as the names of her two sisters: LASAIR ("flame") and INGHEAN BHUIDHE ("yellow-haired girl"). Or they may have been seasonal divinities, for they each ruled a different part of the growing seasons: Lasair, the first of spring; Inghean Bhuidhe, the beginning of summer; and Latiaran, the harvesttime, connected with that season by the local tradition that women should curtsy to Latiarin's heart as they passed during harvest and by the marking of Latiarin's feast day on the last Sunday in July, the old Celtic festival of LUGHNASA.

Even today the PATTERN or ritual to Latiaran brings rural people from around the region to celebrate the harvest. Latiaran Sunday is held on or just before July 25, her feast day. It was the first day for eating potatoes in that region, and the weather was reputed always to be fine.

Latiaran, whose name is found nowhere else but in Cullen, has been interpreted as corrupted diminutive form (from a hypothesized Laisrian) of the better-known Lasair. Both may be variants of the great figure of BRIGIT, who like Latiaran was said to have carried hot coals, in Brigit's case in the town of Ardagh, where she dropped them at "the little church of Lasair." As Brigit was a goddess connected with fire, it is possible that Lasair and Latiaran were originally titles or local names for her.

Sources: MacNeill, Máire. *The Festival of Lughnasa, Parts I and II.* Dublin: Comhairle Bhéaloideas Éireann, 1982, pp. 268 ff; Ó hÓgain, Dáithí. *The Hero in Irish Folk History.* Dublin: Gill & Macmillan, 1985, pp. 20–21.

Latis Continental goddess. Little is known of this obscure goddess, who has been interpreted as a goddess both of beer and of holy WELLS.

Latobius Continental Celtic god. A few inscriptions bear the name of this obscure god, whom the Romans associated with their warrior divinity MARS. His name has not been translated.

Laudine See LADY OF THE FOUNTAIN.

Launfal (Sir Launfal, Lanval) Arthurian hero. In the works of the 12th-century French poet Marie de France we find many Celtic motifs, perhaps derived from the folklore of Brittany. In one of Marie's most famous compositions, a puritanical knight of king ARTHUR's court, Launfal, hated the beautiful queen GUINEVERE, to whom he felt morally superior even before she fell in love with the glorious knight LANCELOT. At her wedding feast, Guinevere snubbed Launfal, prompting him to pack up and move back to his own castle, where he soon spent more than he had. He was in despair of what to do when a FAIRY LOVER named Tryamour came to his rescue, providing him with all the riches he needed in exchange for his love. Her one demand was that he never boast of her. He agreed, and they began to enjoy themselves together, he providing love in exchange for a great white horse, a hard-working squire, and an inexhaustible purse.

After seven years, Launfal returned to Camelot. To his surprise the hated Guinevere flirted with him. Once again Launfal became morally indignant and rebuffed her. Infuriated, Guinevere snarled that Launfal was so ugly no woman would ever look at him. Stung, the knight forgot his promise and began to brag to Guinevere of his lady's beauty and wealth.

As soon as he returned to his quarters, Launfal realized his mistake, for all his wealth had disappeared. To make matters worse, Arthur returned home to discover Guinevere, her clothing disheveled and torn, accusing Launfal of rape. When he explained his side of the story, he was set free for a year, with the demand that he produce his beautiful lady; after a year, Launfal had to return and await condemnation. Unlike every other story of a man who breaks his pledge to a fairy lover, Launfal was saved when Tryamour appeared and took him away to FAIRYLAND.

Source: Briggs, Katherine M. *An Encyclopedia of Fairies: Hobgoblins, Brownies, Bogies, and Other Supernatural Creatures.* New York: Pantheon Books, 1976, pp. 366 ff.

Lavaine Arthurian hero. A minor character in the tales of king ARTHUR, he was ELAINE's brother and a friend of Lancelot.

Law of the Innocents Celtic custom. One of the oldest extant laws in Scotland is the Law of the Innocents, which provides protection for unarmed civilians during warfare. Written in ca. 700 C.E. by the Christian cleric Adomnán, ninth abbot of IONA, the law penalized men who took advantage of war to rape women; some scholars have used this part of the law to argue that Celtic society, far from being fair to women, put them at grave risk with its warrior ways. Others, however, argue that women in Celtic lands did, in fact, have considerable power, which began to decline after Christianization and the arrival of Saxons and Vikings. In either case, the Law of the Innocents was used in the late 1990s by three women who protested against nuclear arms in Scotland by dismantling a Trident submarine control center; they were acquitted by an order to the jury by judge Margaret Gimblett.

Laying the Fairies Folkloric concept. There was only one way to get rid of FAIRIES: give them something. When fairies, especially BROWNIES, helped human beings, they did so for their own reasons, not to gain money or clothing. Some went naked and departed immediately upon being handed clothing (or hand-knit tiny sweaters). When fairies were driven off by this kind of misguided generosity, the former owner was said to have "laid" them.

Leborcham (Lavercam, Lebarcham, Levarcham, Lebharcham) Irish heroine. The nurse of the tragic heroine DEIRDRE of the Sorrows, she was born a slave but rose into the ranks of nobility by her wit and strength and finally became a BARD. Leborcham was so fleet of foot that she could run the entire length of Ireland in one day and be back by dawn to deliver news, a talent that brought her to the attention of the king of ULSTER, CONCOBAR MAC NESSA. When the doomed Deirdre was born and Concobar determined to raise her to become his concubine despite predictions that she would cause the downfall of the land, Leborcham was put in charge of the girl's upbringing and education. It was Leborcham who told Deirdre, struck by the sight of a RAVEN's blood against snow, of the man whose coloring resembled that sight: NOÍSIU, Deirdre's fated lover.

Leborcham remained loyal to her charge, and she tried unsuccessfully to warn the girl to leave Ireland after she and her lover had been tricked into returning from their Scottish exile. Unfortunately, Deirdre was already home and unwilling to go back into exile. Leborcham then tried another route: She went to Concobar and told him that her hard life in the wilderness had destroyed Deirdre's beauty, although she remained as radiant as ever. Alas for the girl, the king chanced to see her again and so realized Leborcham's deceit. When her lover was killed, Deirdre chose death over remaining as the king's enslaved consort.

Source: Dillon, Myles, ed. *Irish Sagas.* Cork: The Mercier Press, 1968, pp. 53 ff.

Lebor Gabála Érenn See BOOK OF INVASIONS.

Leherennus Continental Celtic god. Believed to be of pre-Celtic origin, Leherennus was worshiped in the mountain range of southern France, the Pyrenees; the Romans identified him with their warrior god MARS.

Leinster (Laighin, Galian) Irish province. One of the five ancient divisions of Ireland (with MUNSTER, CONNACHT, ULSTER, and MIDE), Leinster is the eastern PROVINCE, where today's capital city of Dublin is located. It was traditionally associated with prosperity and commerce, as well as nobility, good manners, and hospitality.

Leinster has historically been the richest of Ireland's provinces, constituting the "pale" of Anglo influence during the English occupation (the source of the expression "beyond the pale," which referred to regions that remained more Celtic). The name derives from an early Celtic people called the Lagin (Laigin, Laighnigh). Today, Leinster includes the counties of Dublin, Carlow, Kildare, Kilkenny, Laois, Longford, Louth, Meath, Offaly, Westmeath, Wexford, and Wicklow.

Len Irish hero. This obscure figure is known from several legends as the SMITH to the great magician BODB DERG. After him, the scenic lakes of Killarney in Co. Kerry are called, in Irish, Loch Lein.

Lén Línfiaclach Minor Irish hero. One of the several craft gods of ancient Ireland, Lén Línfiaclach lived in a LAKE where he devoted himself to crafting beautiful objects for FAND, daughter of the wilderness goddess FLIDAIS and one of Ireland's most powerful FAIRY QUEENS. To do his work, Lén Línfiaclach threw his anvil every night toward the east. As it traveled, it left three trails: one of water, one of fire, and one of purple jewels, which Lén Línfiaclach gathered for his creations.

Lenumius Continental Celtic god. Equated by the Romans with MARS, who was god of both war and agriculture, Lenumius is known from some inscriptions, but we have little other information about him.

Lenus Continental and insular Celtic god. In Gaul and parts of Britain, Lenus was invoked as the ancestral god of the Treveri tribe. Statues show him standing next to a large BIRD, perhaps a GOOSE; the juxtaposition may indicate his own powers or his partnering with a goose goddess.

Leodegrance Arthurian hero. This otherwise obscure character was the father of the great beauty GUINEVERE, who became the wife of his ally, king ARTHUR.

leprechaun *(leipreachán, lùracán, luchramán, luchragán, luchorpán, lupracánaig, lurikeen)* Irish folkloric figure. The most familiar Irish FAIRY is today depicted as a dwarfish man with GREEN clothing who knows the location of the pot of GOLD at the rainbow's end. One of many species of Irish fairy, the leprechaun was a solitary sort (see SOLITARY FAIRIES), encountered far less frequently than the more common TROOPING FAIRIES, who danced and sang and led travelers astray. Finding the leprechaun was only the first step to finding his treasure, for then one had to extract that information from him. The only way to do so was to trap and hold the little man, keeping him clearly in sight. The leprechaun's favorite trick to get out of such a trap was to claim that a monster approached, prompting his

captor to look up momentarily, whereupon the leprechaun disappeared.

The leprechaun's name comes from *leith brogan*, the maker of the brogan or shoe; he was the fairy's shoemaker (sometimes tailor), an industrious being rather like the Scottish and British BROWNIE, except that he rarely worked for anyone but himself, whereas the Brownie was a volunteer farm laborer. Of a somewhat surly disposition, the leprechaun could become downright malicious when crossed, so it was considered important to be polite when dealing with one.

There is some evidence that this fairy figure had a mythological antecedent: the important and all-talented god LUGH, sometimes called the shoemaker Lugh-chromain, "little stooped Lugh." As patron of the arts and of treasure, Lugh was diminished after Christianization (see CHRISTIANITY) and remained in this folklore figure. The BOOK OF INVASIONS also mentions a race of small-bodied monsters begotten by the biblical Noah's son Ham because his father had cursed him; these may have provided a mythic template for the leprechaun.

The leprechaun appears in some literary works, most notably the early 20th-century comic novel *Crock of Gold* by Dubliner James Stevens, which was the basis for the popular American musical (and later movie) *Finian's Rainbow*.

Sources: Evans-Wentz, W. Y. *The Fairy-Faith in Celtic Countries.* Gerrards Cross: Colin Smythe Humanities Press, 1911, pp. 241, 242; Keightley, Thomas. *The Fairy Mythology.* London: H. G. Bohn, 1870, pp. 371 ff; Kennedy, Patrick. *Legendary Fictions of the Irish Celts.* New York: Benjamin Blom, 1969, p. 130; Wilde, Lady. *Ancient Legends, Mystic Charms and Superstitions of Ireland.* London: Chatto and Windus, 1902, pp. 56 ff.

Leth Cuinn, Leth Moga Irish geographical divisions. Along the EISCIR RIADA, the great glacial ridge that divides Ireland from Dublin to Galway, the land was once divided between the leaders CONN of the Hundred Battles to the north and EÓGAN MÓR (under his name of Mug Nuadat) to the south. The northern region was called Leth Cuinn, while the southern region was Leth Moga. This is one of several ancient divisions of Ireland, the most common being the division into the five PROVINCES.

Lethderg Irish heroine or goddess. This name appears in the *DINDSHENCHAS*, the place-name poetry of Ireland, as the daughter of the great king of the province of ULSTER, CONCOBAR MAC NESSA. She was carried off by a party of warriors in the service of a minor king, Fothad. The obscure tale points to a form of the goddess of SOVEREIGNTY, who establishes a man in KING-SHIP when he mates with her. The name also appears as a compound name for MEDB, the great warrior queen whose connection to the sovereignty goddess has been well established.

Leucetius (Loucetius, Leucetius) Continental Celtic and British god. Known from a few inscriptions in continental Gaul and Britain, Leucetius was the consort of a better-known divinity, the goddess of sacred groves named NEMETONA. An inscription to the pair was found at the healing shrine of BATH, called by the Romans AQUAE SULIS, suggesting that Leucetius may have been a HEALING god. In Gaul, Leucetius was considered a form of MARS, perhaps as a healing divinity, for the warrior Mars was sometimes pictured fighting off disease. Leucetius's name includes the syllable for "bright" or "shining" and has been interpreted to mean "lightning."

ley lines Folkloric belief. The belief that there are invisible lines of power that run beneath the earth and connect ancient sites of power is a modern myth whose beginnings can be traced to the works of the writer Alfred Watkins, who charted in 1925 what he dubbed "the old straight path." Watkins believed that he had discovered an ancient form of geomancy or earth-energy tracking, indigenous to Britain. There is no mythological or other folkloric evidence of such a belief. In addition, the sites are so widely disparate in both time and place that few real "straight tracks" can be traced. There is no evidence that ley lines, under any name, were part of Celtic belief.

Liadan (Líadan, Liadhain, Lídain) Irish heroine. The BARD Liadan came from the Irish region most connected with music and song, the southwestern province of MUNSTER. Another poet, Cuirithir, fell in love with her while she was making a poet's circuit of the island, but she refused to interrupt her tour and declined his advances, instead inviting him to visit her at home in Co. Kerry. When he did not appear, she entered a convent. She soon regretted her decision but then found that Cuirithir had become a priest. This ended the possibility of consummation of their love, although their confessor suggested that they sleep together chastely as a proof of their holiness. When Cuirithir was exiled for seeking out Liadan, she died of grief at his praying stone. The story, although Christian, has many Celtic echoes, including the position of women as poets and the testing of the virtue of the lovers (also found in the story of LANCELOT and GUINEVERE) by having them sleep together without giving in to their passion.

Lia Fáil (Lia Fal) Irish mythological object. One of four great magical implements of the TUATHA DÉ DANANN, the people of the goddess DANU, the Lia Fáil or Stone of Destiny was a great STONE pillar that shrieked when touched by the true king. It came from the OTHER-WORLD, from the magical city of Fálias. (The Tuatha Dé's other magical objects, each from a different Otherworld city, were a spear that never missed, an invincible sword, and an inexhaustible CAULDRON.) The Lia Fáil was said to stand on the great hill of TARA in Ireland, where it was used in INAUGURATION ceremonies of the HIGH KING. A stone still stands on Tara hill, but there is some dispute as to whether it is the true Lia Fáil. For one thing, legends claim that the true Lia Fáil has been long resident in the OTHERWORLD, where it was taken when its owners were banished from the surface world, and that the stone in this world is a substitute. Other legends state that the true Lia Fáil is now in Scotland. In the sixth century C.E., Tara's king MUIRCERTACH MAC ERC loaned the Lia Fáil to his Scottish brother, FERGUS MÒR, who then refused to send it back; it became the Stone of Scone (Sgàin), which was stolen by the English king Edward I after the fall of Macbeth (1057) and installed under the throne at Westminster Abbey, serving for centuries as the INAUGURATION STONE and authorizing symbol of English monarchs (though not, reportedly, shrieking). The stone was returned to Scotland in 1996 after several earlier attempts by Scottish nationalists to recover it.

Still other versions of this story have it that the Scottish Stone of Scone is not the Irish Lia Fáil at all but a stone that came from Egypt. It had its own magical power, having been hallowed in ancient time when the biblical Jacob slept upon it and dreamed of angels ascending to heaven.

Lianan Sidhe (Liannan-Shee)   See FAIRY LOVER.

Liath

Irish hero. There are several figures in Irish mythology who bear this name. One was a member of the race of NEMED, who cut down all the trees on the hill of TARA so that corn could grow there, after which the hill was called Druin Léith in his honor. The other (who may be the same figure) loved a woman named BRÍ but was prevented by their deaths from wedding her; their names live on in the double name of BRÍ LÉITH, given to one of the great FAIRY MOUNDS of Ireland.

Liath Macha

Irish mythological animal. The "gray of MACHA" was the name of the favorite HORSE of the ULSTER hero CÚCHULAINN; the steed, which magically arose from a LAKE, was a gift from Macha, the primary goddess of Ulster.

Lí Ban (Liban)

Irish heroine. The story of the MERMAID Lí Ban ("finest of women" or "beauty of womanhood") was first recorded in the ANNALS OF IRELAND in the 17th century but was said to date to the 6th century. Variously described as the daughter of the king of Tara, AÉD ABRAT, or of the obscure Ecca (her mother is not named, but may have been ÉTAIN), Lí Ban was swept away by a flood that resulted from someone's failing to cover a sacred WELL. As a result, the well swelled and overflowed until it destroyed the kingdom of Aéd Abrat, drowning him and most of his family. Only Lí Ban survived, together with her little lapdog, both of whom were caught within an underwater bubble where they lived for a year. Watching the playful SALMON, so comfortable in the element that trapped her, Lí Ban prayed to become a FISH.

Her wish was granted: She was turned into a mermaid with a salmon's tail and a woman's torso and head. Her pet dog became an OTTER, and together the pair swam in the waters of LOUGH NEAGH for 300 years. During that time, Ireland became Christian—a common folkloric motif also found in the stories of another transformed maiden, FIONNUALA, and in that of OISÍN who lived in FAIRYLAND with the queen NIAMH of the Golden Hair.

At the end of three centuries, Lí Ban called out to a passing boat, entreating the men she saw to capture her and instructing them to meet her on the shores at Inver Ollarbha. In that boat was a priest, Beoc, who first went to Rome on an errand, then arranged for the mermaid's capture. She was hauled up and kept in a half-submerged boat, so that she could swim until it had been determined what should be done with this miraculous maiden. At first the local kings and priests argued over who had the right to claim her, but angels instructed them to wait until two OXEN (or STAGS) appeared—and then to trust that the beasts would haul the maiden to the territory in which she belonged. The miraculous oxen did, indeed, appear and carried Lí Ban to the church of the priest who had first found her, Beoc. There she asked to be baptized so that she might die

immediately and ascend to heaven, whereupon her wish was answered and she was named Murgen, "sea-born." Dying immediately, she became a SAINT and was regarded as a holy virgin.

This mixture of pagan and Christian elements shows how ancient divinities were brought into the domain of the new religion. Lí Ban was probably once a goddess like BÓAND and SÍNANN, two other divinities whose myths involve a well magically overflowing. Her original myth, however, is probably hopelessly lost under the accretion of Christian motifs.

Another (perhaps originally the same) Lí Ban was a FAIRY QUEEN, consort of the ruler of MAG MELL, "the honeyed plain," and sister of the great fairy beauty FAND; she and her husband, beset by monstrous FOMORIANS, set in motion one of Ireland's greatest love stories when they asked the hero CÚCHULAINN to save them. He did so, but he fell in love with Fand—the only love affair that threatened the durability of his marriage to the paragon of womanhood, EMER.

Source: Joyce, P. W. *Ancient Celtic Romances.* London: Parkgate Books, 1997, pp. 97 ff.

Licke British fairy. Licke is named, in several texts, as a small FAIRY who worked as a cook in the OTHERWORLD.

Lífe (Liffey) Irish heroine. The goddess of the River Liffey (see ANA LIFE) and of the plain (Mag Life) through which it flows, Lífe was described in the place-poetry of ancient Ireland, the DIND-SHENCHAS, as a sweet, hardworking, pleasant woman who died giving birth at Port Agmar in Aran, whereupon her consort, the otherwise unknown Deltbanna, son of Drucht, died of grief.

Another story says that Deltbanna was her husband, and that Lífe was a Pictish woman who crossed the lovely plain through which the Liffey now flows. The river was called at the time Ruitheach, "the flashy torrent," and Lífe said that its prospect was the most beautiful thing she had ever seen. Deltbanna immediately named the plain for her, and the river took its name from that affectionate act.

Sources: Gwynn, Edward. *The Metrical Dindshenchas.* Part II. Vol. IX. Royal Irish Academy, Todd Lecture Series. Dublin: Hodges, Figgis, and Co., Ltd., 1906, p. 61; Healy, Elizabeth, with Christopher Moriarty, Cerard O'Flaherty. *The Book of the Liffey: From Source to the Sea.* Dublin: Wolfhound Press, 1988.

liminality Cosmological concept. The Celts saw this world as impinging upon or existing parallel to an OTHERWORLD of spirits, FAIRIES, and divinities. Places that were not quite one thing, not quite another—twilight and dawn, the turning days of the year, geographical sites like BOGS and LAKES and misty ISLANDS—were the points of exchange between these two worlds. Such liminal (literally, "shadowy") places and times were very important in Celtic myth and ritual. On SAMHAIN and BELTANE, the year's most powerful days on November 1 and May 1, respectively, visitations from the Otherworld could be expected; passing at twilight near a FAIRY MOUND on either day amplified the liminality and thus made one subject to FAIRY KIDNAPPING.

Lindow Man Archaeological find. In the BOG near the British town of Lindow, one of the most important and baffling Celtic archaeological finds was made in 1984: a human body, preserved by the bog's tannic water, which appeared to be that of a HUMAN SACRIFICE who had suffered the THREEFOLD DEATH of Irish legend. Whether this man died in ancient times because of some offense or as an offering to remove famine or plague is impossible to determine, but the find has given rise to significant research.

Source: Ross, Anne. "Lindow Man and the Celtic Tradition." In Stead, I. M., J. B. Bourke, and Don Brothwell. *The Lindow Man: The Body in the Bog.* Ithaca, N.Y.: Cornell University Press, 1986, pp. 162–169.

Linton Worm   See DRAGON.

Lionel   Arthurian hero. This minor knight of the ROUND TABLE was a cousin of the superlative LANCELOT.

Lios   Irish mythological site. The term *lios* is often used to describe HILLFORTS and STONE CIRCLES in Ireland. One site of that name is especially renowned, as it is the largest stone circle in the land, with a circumference of almost 160 feet. Near the mythologically significant LOUGH GUR, the huge circle dates from as much as 4,000 years before the Celts arrived in Ireland. Like many such structures, it is astronomically aligned, in this case to the setting of the moon at MIDSUMMER.

Lir   (Lear)   Irish hero. The great Irish sea god MANANNÁN was called "mac Lir," meaning "son of Lir," but it is not entirely clear who Lir was. Some have described him as an earlier sea god who was absorbed into an invading people's mythology by being named as the antecedent or father of one of their own gods. Despite the similarity of names, Lir has nothing to do with the Shakespearean King Lear, who may be based on the Welsh god LLUDD, whom Shakespeare may have confounded with LLYR, another Welsh divinity. Lir may be the same as or distinct from the king of the same name, whose children were turned to swans (see CHILDREN OF LIR) by their evil stepmother, in one of the THREE SORROWS OF IRELAND. The story, one of the most familiar in Irish legend today, is not ancient but arrived from Britain or France in the Middle Ages; however, it has many motifs and themes that are typically Celtic, such as SHAPE-SHIFTING and magical incantations.

Lis   (Lios)   See HILLFORT.

Liscannor   Irish mythological site. In the small town of Liscannor near the renowned Cliffs of Moher, a holy WELL dedicated to the goddess turned-saint BRIGIT gathers the faithful on February 1, Brigit's feast day and the Celtic feast of IMBOLC or spring's awakening. A PATTERN of circular transits up and down a hillside precedes a visit to the well itself; the well's waters trickle down the rocky wall of the well house, which penetrates to within the hill, an unusual location that has led scholars to theorize that the original figure to whom the well was devoted was a goddess, rather than a saint.

That goddess was probably not Brigit, for the dedication of the well to her is relatively recent. Until the 1950s, the pattern day was on LUGHNASA, the old Celtic harvest feast on August 1. That day is associated with goddesses like TAILTIU who died while giving birth—a representation of the vegetation's death to provide life—and to the HAG of harvest, the CAILLEACH. The nearby cliffs are called, in Irish, Ceann na Caillghe, "the hag's head," reportedly because the hag MAL leapt from their top to her death. Some local legends connect this hag with the monster called the OLLIPHEIST.

Litavis   (Litavus)   Continental Celtic goddess. Not much is known of this goddess, whose name seems connected with words for "earth" or "broad," suggesting that she was a deity of the wide world. She was sometimes described as the consort of the god CICOLLUS, whom the Romans saw as similar to their god MARS, but she was not herself renamed by the invading legions.

liver   Symbolic food. Scottish Highlanders historically had a superstitious aversion to liver, which was considered inedible. Not even monsters like WATER HORSES ate their victims' livers, which were sometimes the only trace of the unfortunate human meal left at the scene of a disappearance.

Llacheau   (Lohot)   Arthurian hero. This obscure figure was said to have been an illegitimate son of king ARTHUR.

llamhigyn y dwr   See WATER-LEAPER.

Llassar Llaesgyfnewid (Llassar Llaes Gyfne-
wid) Welsh god. A relatively obscure Welsh
GIANT, he owned a CAULDRON that figures importantly in the collection of Welsh myths called the
MABINOGION, for it had the power to regenerate the
bodies of slain warriors. The evil Evnyssen
employed the cauldron's power in his people's
great but ill-fated battle with the Irish. Llassar's
wife, CYMIDEI CYMEINFOLL, was a cauldron of war
herself; every six weeks a fully armored warrior
sprang from her womb. Some interpreters claim
that the cauldron belonged to Cymidei rather than
to her husband.

Llefelys (Llevelys) Welsh hero or god. In
Welsh myth, this king ruled on the Continent
while his brother, LLUDD, ruled Britain. He came
to Lludd's aid in ridding Britain of three plagues.

Lleu Llaw Gyffes (Llew Llaw Gyffes)
Welsh god or hero. When the goddess ARIAN-
RHOD sought to become king MATH's footholder—an office previously held by the maiden
GOEWIN, whose rape rendered her unsuitable to
perform the sacred duties—she was tested to
ensure her virginity. To Arianrhod's surprise and
horror, as she stepped over Math's magical rod,
she bore two children. One, DYLAN, disappeared
immediately into the sea; the other, an unformed
ball of flesh, was snatched up by Arianrhod's
brother, the poet GWYDION, who put it in a magical chest where it formed finally into a child—a
boy, who may have been Gwidion's own son,
born of his love for Arianrhod.

It was a mother's right to name her children,
and Arianrhod angrily refused to name the pre-
mature babe born through trickery. So Gwydion
tricked his sister again, forcing her to grant the
name Lleu Llaw Gyffes—"bright one of the skil-
ful hand"—to the boy. Similarly, it was her right
to arm him with weapons, and here again
Gwydion tricked Arianrhod so that Lleu could

be outfitted as a warrior. Finally she cursed her
mysterious son, declaring that he should never
wed a human woman. Once again, Gwydion
tricked his sister, this time with Math's help. The
two men formed a woman out of flowers, and so
Lleu was married to BLODEUWEDD, the aptly
named "flower-face."

Unfortunately, Lleu had no happiness with
his wife. She soon took a lover and began to plot
how to be rid of him. Because Lleu was protected from harm by the strange fact that he
could never be killed when inside or outside,
while on horseback or afoot, Blodeuwedd challenged him to stand under a thatched roof by the
side of a river, with his foot on a deer. Lleu took
the dare. Standing in this unlikely position, Lleu
received his death-blow and sailed away in the
form of an EAGLE. His murderer did not go free;
she was turned into the nocturnal OWL.

Many scholars have seen Lleu as a parallel
divinity to the Irish LUGH, although the complex story has little in common with those told
of its alleged Irish cousin.

Lludd (St. Lludd) Welsh saint or goddess.
Christianity, employing the same adoption of
native divinities that the Roman legions earlier
practiced, "converted" many ancient divinities,
calling them SAINTS but keeping their symbols,
and sometimes even their narratives, intact.
Thus we find that when Lludd was decapitated
for her holiness, her head rolled down a hill;
where it stopped, a healing SPRING gushed forth.
The motif of the miraculous HEAD is typically
Celtic, as is the power ascribed to healing
WELLS. Behind this Welsh saint, therefore, an
early goddess may hide.

Lludd Welsh god or hero. Several figures in
Welsh mythology bear this name; they may be
aspects or echoes of each other or distinct fig-
ures, although it is difficult to disentangle them.
The most important is Lludd Llaw Ereint
(NUDD), an ancient British king whose brother
LLEFELYS ruled on the Continent; the two were

sons of BELI, god of death. According to the early historian Geoffrey of Monmouth, it was Lludd who built London, but the god behind this alleged king can be detected by Geoffrey's description of a temple dedicated to him (on the site of today's St. Paul's, near the old entrance to the city called Ludgate).

Three plagues struck Britain while Lludd was king: a race of demons called the Corianiad; two DRAGONS; and a GIANT magician. With his brother's help, Lludd defeated all three, setting poisonous insects lose on the Corianiad, getting the dragons drunk so that they were easy to kill, and killing the magician in mortal combat. It is believed that this ancient royal character inspired William Shakespeare in his play *King Lear*, but he confused Lludd's name with the similar Welsh figure LLYR.

Llwch Llawwyanawc (Llwch Lleminawc, Llwch Llenllawc) Welsh hero. This minor character in Welsh legend bore a flaming sword as he led king ARTHUR through the dim OTHER-WORLD.

Llyn Tegid   See TEGID.

Llyr (Lear)   Welsh god. Not much is known about this ancient god, who may be the same as the Irish sea god LIR. Some scholars interpret Llyr as an underworld or OTHERWORLD divinity, but as the Celts often described the Otherworld as an ISLAND in the sea or as a land beneath the waves, these two interpretations are not necessarily in conflict. The Welsh Llyr was father of the hero MANAWYDAN, with the great mother goddess DÔN's daughter PENARDDUN; he also sired the warrior BRÂN THE BLESSED and the love goddess BRANWEN, with the queen named Iweriadd (Ireland).

In some texts Llyr appears as a human king, Llyr Llediath, "Llyr of the foreign accent," while in later folklore he was Christianized as a SAINT who was buried under the River Sahr, an appropriate site for an ancient water divinity.

Geoffrey of Monmouth mentions a King Leir, on whom Shakespeare is assumed to have based his memorable mad king.

Loathy Lady   Arthurian heroine. The foul and ugly HAG who appears in some Arthurian tales is a form of the ancient goddess of SOVER-EIGNTY, who becomes a blooming young woman when kissed by the rightful king; she also recalls the great pre-Celtic figure of the CAILLEACH, the weather-controlling GIANT. In some legends of the sacred GRAIL, she appears as the figure who asks candidates the mysterious questions that test their purity. Variously known as Cundrie and as lady RAGNELL, the Loathy Lady inspired the medieval English poet Geoffrey Chaucer in his "Wife of Bath's Tale."

lob   British folkloric spirit. Like HOB, the syllable *lob* appears in many British FAIRY names. Lob-Lie-by-the-Fire was a big BROWNIE who did hard farm labor despite his lazy name. The term *lubber* (as in "landlubber") descends from this term and was used to describe people who were so distracted from ordinary life that they were clumsy and foolish.

Lóequre Búadach.   Irish hero. Minor figure in the story of the feast of BRICCRIU.

location of Otherworld   Cosmological concept. The Celtic OTHERWORLD was a place of the dead, the gods, and the FAIRY people, but it was neither above nor below our earth, where the Christian description locates heaven and hell. Rather it existed in a parallel universe, not entirely separate from our world but not within it either. This contiguous world was believed to be reached through portals in either time or space (see LIMINALITY). Temporally, the dates of SAMHAIN on November 1 and its opposite feast of BELTANE on May 1 were considered to be open to the Otherworld; in this world, borderland places like BOGS and ISLANDS served as the same kind of doorway. Within the Otherworld, time moved differently than in this world; people who spent a night there might return to discover a hundred years had passed on earth.

Locha Irish heroine. Handmaiden to queen MEDB of CONNACHT, she was killed in the great CATTLE RAID on ULSTER described in the Irish epic, the TÁIN BÓ CUAILNGE.

Lochlann (Lochlanns, Lochlannachs) Irish mythological site. In some texts, this appears as the name of the northern land of the FOMORIANS, the opponents of the magical TUATHA DÉ DANANN and several other mythological Irish races. Occasionally the Fomorians are called the Lochlanns or Lochlannachs. Some scholars have interpreted Lochlann as Denmark and lower Scandinavia; the Fomorian capital city of Berva, mentioned in some tales, is otherwise unknown and believed to be entirely legendary.

Source: Joyce, P. W. *Ancient Celtic Romances.* London: Parkgate Books, 1997, p. 430.

Loireag Scottish folkloric figure. This water FAIRY of the Hebrides, like the similar HABETROT, was a spinner, an appropriate skill for a matron spirit of a region where tweed-making was an important economic role for women. Loireag was small and plain but fierce, giving trouble if any rituals connected with spinning, warping, weaving, or washing were neglected. She was also a musician with a sweet voice—again, something to be expected in a region where women sang as they performed their textile labors, as can be seen in the famous "waulking songs" of Scotland, whose heavy rhythm accompanied the equally rhythmic work of preparing cloth.

lone sod See STRAY SOD.

Long Man (Long Man of Wilmington) British folkloric site. On Windover Hill in East Sussex, a figure of a man holding two immense staffs is carved into the white chalk soil. At 226 feet, it is even taller than the CERNE ABBAS GIANT (although it lacks that figure's notable sexual organ). The Long Man may represent some unknown god of the Celts or a pre-Celtic people. Local legend has it that the outline was traced around the body of a real GIANT after he was killed on the hillside by pilgrims; the tale may recall Christian opposition, which may also have resulted in the figure's emasculation.

Source: Newman, Paul. *Gods and Graven Images: The Chalk Hill-Figures of Britain.* London: Robert Hale, 1987, pp. 134–154.

Lorois Arthurian hero. A young knight of CAMELOT, Lorois encountered a court of mounted women while riding through the woods one day—beautiful damsels, entirely nude, with flowers in their hair. Riding beside them were their lovers astride strong HORSES. Behind that splendid party came another, more pitiful one: a hundred thin women dressed in black and riding scrawny horses, who were accompanied by thunder and snow as they rode, followed at a distance by a hundred men of similar appearance. The first group were those who had opened themselves to love, while the second group had refused it.

losses of the year Scottish and Irish ritual. At SAMHAIN, the Celtic festival on November 1 that marked the end of one year and the beginning of another, many rituals and games of DIVINATION sought to discover the "losses of the year": whether the coming year would be a happy one with few losses, or a difficult one with many losses. In Scotland the tradition moved to HOGMANY on January 1, when the evil of the past year was expunged by a thorough cleaning and the FIRST FOOTER foretold the coming year's luck.

Lot Irish heroine. A fierce WARRIOR WOMAN of the unearthly FOMORIANS, Lot led her people in their war against their enemy, the people of

PARTHOLÓN. As with most Fomorians, she was described as improbably ugly, with lips on her breasts and four eyes on her back.

Lot (Lotha)   Arthurian hero. A minor character in Arthurian legend, he was the husband of king ARTHUR's half sister MORGAUSE and father of the knight of the ROUND TABLE, GAWAIN. His part in the action is mainly through his sons, since he fell to the powerful king PELLINORE in Arthur's battle for the throne; the sons of the two kings feuded thereafter.

Loucetius   See LEUCETIUS.

Loughcrew (Sliab na Cailleach)   Irish mythological site. A great megalithic burial center in Co. Meath, near the center of Ireland, Loughcrew is connected in legend to the great HAG, the CAILLEACH, and its Irish name means "mountain of the hag." There are a number of PASSAGE GRAVES and other ritual sites on the several hills that make up the Loughcrew complex, one of Ireland's oldest and richest in graphic ornamentation—SPIRALS, starbursts, meanders, and other designs are carved into the granite rock. On the side of one hill is the Hag's Chair, a grouping of rocks that form a seat from which one can see several distant counties. Atop that hill is a decorated CAIRN oriented to the sunrise on spring and fall EQUINOX.

Lough Derg   Irish mythological site. The legends about Lough Derg in Co. Donegal claim that it was occupied by a great monster (or SERPENT) called CAORANACH, whose massacre by ST. PATRICK bloodied the lake waters (hence its name, "dark red lake"). Another LAKE of the same name is found in Co. Galway, where the great magician of the TUATHA DÉ DANANN, BODB DERG, was said to have had his palace.

Since Ireland became Christian, Donegal's Lough Derg has been the most significant place of pilgrimage, especially to St. Patrick's Purgatory on Station Island, where the saint was said to have descended through a CAVE to an OTHERWORLD in order to do battle with evil. The legend, however, does not date from early Christian times but to the medieval period. In the late 16th century pilgrims were housed in dormitories according to their PROVINCE, so that the island formed a microcosm of all Ireland. The site continues to attract pilgrims today.

Source: Dames, Michael. *Mythic Ireland.* London: Thames and Hudson, 1992, pp. 22 ff.

Lough Gur   Irish mythological site. This small LAKE in Co. Limerick, inhabited for almost 6,000 years, is surrounded by low hills, each of them connected with a goddess (see ÁINE) or god (see DONN FÍRINNE). Site of the largest extant STONE CIRCLE in Ireland, the Grange, the lake is believed to be an entrance to the OTHERWORLD, a belief common to Celtic lands where water was seen as the dividing line between this world and that of the FAIRIES.

The many legends connected with the lake emphasize a cycle of time, usually seven years. Each time that cycle passes, distinctive events occur. The lake empties of water, and passersby see a tree growing from its bottom, covered with a GREEN cloth; beneath it, a woman named TOICE BHREAN sits KNITTING. The goddess or fairy queen Áine is similarly seen at Lough Gur each time the seven-year cycle ends, as is her enchanted son GERÓID IARLA, born to her after her affair with Maurice, earl of Desmond, who saw her swimming in the form of a SWAN and stole her cloak in order to capture her. As with other such marriages, the groom was put under a taboo by the bride, in this case to show no surprise, no matter what their son might do. Maurice forgot himself when, at a banquet, the now-grown Geróid shrank himself into a tiny being and leaped into a bottle, then out again, resuming his regular size. The moment Maurice called out in amazement, Geróid disappeared into Lough Gur, appearing on its surface as a

GOOSE. Every seven years, he emerges from his fairy residence on the island named for him, Garrod Island, and takes on human form as he leaves the lake. He rides a white horse and leads the WILD HUNT across the land.

Other legends tell of a FAIRY HOUSEKEEPER who appears on the chair-shaped ancient monument called the Suidheachan or "housekeeper's seat" near the lake. The housekeeper once fell asleep when the dwarf harper, Áine's brother FER Í, stole her COMB (a female anatomical symbol, suggesting the theft might have been a rape), whereupon the housekeeper cursed the CATTLE of the region as well as the dwarf. Fer Í returned the comb, but to no avail, for the CURSE held and he died. The housekeeper, or another fairy woman, is believed to "steal"—drown—a human in the lake waters once every seven years. The lands around the lake are believed to be the territory of the fairy race, who frequently kidnap children from its shores.

Sources: Carbery, Mary. *The Farm by Lough Gur: The Story of Mary Fogarty*. London: Longmans, Green and Co., 1937; Croker, T. Crofton. *Fairy Legends and Traditions of the South of Ireland*. London: William Tegg, 1862, pp. 167 ff; Dames, Michael. *Mythic Ireland*. London: Thames and Hudson, 1992, pp. 73 ff; Evans-Wentz, W. Y. *The Fairy-Faith in Celtic Countries*. Gerrards Cross: Colin Smythe Humanities Press, 1911, pp. 78–79, 81 ff.

Lough Neagh Irish mythological site. This large LAKE in the northern province of ULSTER was originally a WELL, but when a careless woman left the lid off, the well waters exploded and formed the lake. In the process, the family of the maiden LÍ BAN drowned, leaving the girl alone beneath the waves with her little lapdog. Watching fish frolic about her, Lí Ban prayed to be turned into one; she was instantly transformed into a MERMAID with a SALMON's tail, and her little dog became an OTTER. Other stories from the region say that a magical city appears on clear days beneath the lake's waves, and that the folkloric FINN MCCOOL formed the lake when he scooped up a handful of dirt and threw it after an escaping GIANT, the lake being the hollow left by Finn's hand, and the Isle of Man, the clod of dirt he threw.

Lough Ree Irish mythological site. A LAKE by this name, formed by the great River Shannon, is said to have a city in its depths, visible on clear days. It was on its shores that the great queen and goddess MEDB was killed by her nephew FURBAIDE FERBEND in retaliation for her murder of his mother, her sister CLOTHRA.

loup-garou (loup-garow) See SHAPE-SHIFTING.

Luan Manx god. On the Isle of Man, the god known in other Celtic lands as LUGH or LUGOS was called Luan; he was an agricultural divinity whose feast was on the major Celtic holiday of LUGHNASA on August 1.

Luaths Lurgann Irish heroine. Her name means "speedy foot," and she was aptly named, for this WARRIOR WOMAN was the fastest runner in Ireland. She took in a nephew at whose birth she had been MIDWIFE, a boy who would grow up to become the hero FIONN MAC CUMHAILL, when he needed protection against those envious of his great potential. In her forest home, Luaths Lurgann trained the boy in the martial arts. Fionn was devoted to his aunt, but he accidentally killed her when, pursued by an enemy, he picked her up and ran to safety. Fionn ran so fast that the wind, tearing through the warrior woman's body, ripped her to shreds, leaving only her thighbones, which Fionn used to dig a LAKE, still called with her name, Loch Lurgann.

Lubbard Fiend British folkloric figure. Although not known from other sources, this character appears in the work of the great English poet John Milton, who in *L'Allegro* describes a "drudging Goblin" who threshed corn "that ten day-laborers could not end" before lying down by the fire to sleep off his labors until dawn, at which time he disappeared. This "fiend" seems a friendly BROWNIE or perhaps a lubber (see LOB), but the Puritan language of the time led Milton to describe his helpful FAIRY farmhand in negative terms.

lubber See LOB.

Lucan Arthurian hero. One of the most trusted members of king ARTHUR's court, Lucan served as his butler throughout his reign and was by his side at the battle of CAMLAN when Arthur was wounded. Despite that fatal cut, Lucan attempted to save his king and died doing so.

Luchtar (Luchta) Irish god. One of the minor gods of craftsmanship, Luchtar was the brother of the smith GOIBNIU. Ruler of carpentry, Luchtar crafted the spearshafts for the gods of the TUATHA DÉ DANANN, the people of the goddess DANU, in their fight against the monstrous FOMORIANS, in the mythological second battle of MAG TUIRED.

Lugaidh (Lugaid, Lughaidh) Irish hero. Several Irish heroes bear this name:

- **Lugaidh Laíghde** (Loígde), who had five brothers, all named Lugaidh. The brothers were out hunting when they encountered a HAG guarding a WELL, who demanded that one of them sleep with her. All but Lugaidh Laíghde pulled away in disgust, but he made love to her. Pleased with his abilities, the hag turned into a lovely young maiden who revealed herself to him as the goddess of SOVEREIGNTY.
- **Lugaidh mac Con Roí,** son of CÚ ROÍ and enemy of CÚCHULAINN. He is sometimes said to be the son of BLÁTHNAT and to have hated Cúchulainn because his mother betrayed his father for that hero. He gave Cúchulainn a fatal javelin-thrust, then allowed him to die with dignity, decapitating the dying hero as he propped himself upright against a pillar stone. Lugaidh was then killed by CONALL Cernach.
- **Lugaidh, friend of Ailill mac Máta,** who killed FERGUS mac Róich. The great warrior Fergus had incurred Ailill's enmity by becoming the favorite lover of queen/goddess MEDB, and Lugaidh and Ailill discovered the lovers swimming nude one day. Despite his blindness, the warrior-poet Lugaidh hurled his spear at Fergus and killed him.
- **Lugaidh Riab nDerg** (Lugaigh of the Red Stripes) was the son of CLOTHRA, MEDB's sister. Three brothers impregnated Clothra at the same time, and Lugaidh was the son of all three. Three red stripes across his body delineated which part of his body had been sired by which brother.
- **Lugaidh mac Conn,** foster son and enemy of the MUNSTER ruler AILILL Olom, who defeated Ailill's army at the battle of MAG MUCRAMHAN. Lugaidh later tried to apologize to the Munster king, but Ailill infected him with his poisoned breath, and the hero died.

Lugh (Lug, Luga, Lui Lavada, Lugh Lámfhoda, Lugh Samildánach) Irish god. One of the great heroes of Irish mythology, Lugh was the grandson of the frightening FOMORIAN king BALOR of the Evil Eye. A prophet had warned Balor that he would be killed by his grandson, but the Fomorian believed he could keep himself immortally safe by assuring that his daughter never saw a man, much less had intercourse with one. CIAN foiled that plan by dressing as a woman to sneak into the tower where Lugh's mother EITHNE was held captive. Eithne had triplet sons—a motif that suggests that Lugh was originally a multiple god—but only one lived. And that grandson Lugh did, indeed, kill his grandfather, because he had been raised among the TUATHA DÉ DANANN and fought on their side in the mythological second battle of MAG TUIRED.

Other sources call Lugh a son of the DAGDA, the great fertility god of Ireland. In the *BOOK OF INVASIONS*, we are told that Lugh gained his title of "many-skilled" when he arrived at TARA and entreated its king to permit him to join the Tuatha Dé Danann, proclaiming that he had already fostered with one of them, the sea god MANANNÁN MAC LIR. The Tuatha Dé were at first unwilling to accept Lugh. When they asked why they should accept him, he said he was a good carpenter, but they already had one of those. Lugh then said he was a SMITH, but there was already a smith in residence too. BARD, harper, historian, hero, magician—all of these already lived with the Tuatha Dé Danann at Tara. Did they have anyone who was skilled in all these arts, Lugh asked. The gods had to admit that they did not, and so Lugh was admitted to their company and dubbed Samildanch, "the one of many skills."

Lugh's second title, Lámfhoda, "of the long arms," came not because his arms dragged on the ground but because his weapons extended his reach beyond other warriors' abilities. Lugh's prowess with the javelin and sling made him a fierce opponent, as his grandfather Balor learned when they met in battle. The fact that Lugh was generally recognized as a harvest god suggests that this battle with Balor was part of a mythic cycle whose meaning is now lost but that may have depicted a seasonal change. For it was Lugh who led the Tuatha Dé against the Fomorians in that great final battle. After winning the campaign, Lugh decided to spare the life of the half-Fomorian king BRES, in exchange for agricultural information—another connection between Lugh and the seasonal cycle that culminates in harvest.

Lugh has been described as cognate with other Celtic gods: LLEU LLAW GYFFES in Wales and LUGOS in Gaul. He is sometimes described as a solar divinity because of the brightness of his face; some contend that his name is connected to the Latin word for light, *lux*. Lugh is more accurately described as a god of arts and crafts, his name probably deriving from the Celtic word *lugio*, for "oath," as Lugh oversaw the keeping of promises. He may have migrated from the Continent after the Celts had moved to Ireland, the story of his arrival at the door of Tara a mythic memory of his assimilation into the gods of the land.

Lugh's heritage runs through Irish mythology: he was the father of ULSTER's greatest hero, CÚCHULAINN, whom he sired on the human woman DECHTIRE. Lugh fought beside his son during the great TÁIN BÓ CUAILNGE, but as Celtic power in Ireland waned, so did Lugh's reputation. CONN of the Hundred Battles, king of Tara, waited within a DRUID'S FOG as Lugh prophesied the king's future, but thereafter Lugh disappeared from Ireland. Some believe he went undercover, appearing as the folkloric craftsman, the LEPRECHAUN, whose name has been translated as "little stooping Lugh."

Source: Curtin, Jeremiah. *Hero-Tales of Ireland.* New York: Benjamin Blom, 1894, pp. 296 ff.

Lughnasa (Lammas, Lughnasadh, Lughnasad, Garland Sunday, Crom Dudb Sunday, Bilberry Sunday; on the Isle of Man, Laa Lhuanys; in Wales, Calan Awst) Celtic festival. The four great FEASTS of the Celtic year ended with Lughnasa, the harvest festival on August 1; the next feast, SAMHAIN, marked the beginning of the new year. Named for the god LUGH, Lughnasa was noted among the continental Celts as the time when the great Council of the Gauls was held. In 12 B.C.E. the Roman emperor Augustus demanded that the great assembly meet at the altar dedicated to the god at Lyons (a town named for Lugh), thus both asserting his power over the subjugated Celts and implying that he could substitute for the great Lugh in Celtic worship.

In Ireland the festival was said to have been created by Lugh in honor of his mother, the goddess TAILTIU, who died on that day and in whose name an athletic contest was held. Some sources give the name of Lugh's mother as BALOR's daughter EITHNE and call Tailtiu his foster mother; yet other sources say that Lugh established the festival in honor of his two wives, Buí (a COW goddess) and NÁS (otherwise unknown, but connected with the word for "assembly"), a combination of words that together present a good picture of a CATTLE fair.

Primarily a harvest festival, Lughnasa was also a ritual of propitiation of awesome powers that might endanger the harvest, and it was celebrated with fairs and gatherings, some of which continue today. Although the actual date of the Celtic feast was August 1, the change of calendars from Julian to Gregorian in the Middle Ages affected Lughnasa more than the other festivals. Vestigial Lughnasa celebrations are still found in previously Celtic lands, stretching across a full month from late July through mid-August. Scholars occasionally argue over the designation of a festival as related to Lughnasa, but they have in common a focus on celebration of first fruits and the sale of livestock. In England Lughnasa festivals are found at Britford Fair at Warminster on August 11 and at Highworth Fair on August 13, both sheep fairs.

Lughnasa fairs were times at which contracts were established, possibly reflecting Lugh's ancient role as a sponsor and guarantor of oaths. One of these was the betrothal or marriage contract, including that kind of trial marriage called a TELTOWN marriage, whereby the couple plighted themselves until the following Lughnasa, at which point the bond could be made permanent or broken without consequences.

On the Isle of Man the great fair of Santon was celebrated on August 1, when people gathered to sell produce and livestock. Visiting of holy WELLS was also common, as was the climbing of MOUNTAINS; Snaefell Mountain was the favored destination, and tales abounded of indecent behavior that took place among young people enjoying the Lughnasa holiday there.

In Wales Lughnasa is called Calan Awst or "August Festival" and is traditionally marked by climbing hills to gather berries. A Welsh tradition claims that Lughnasa was the day that the biblical maiden, Jephtha's unnamed daughter, went to the mountains to bemoan that she would

be killed before losing her virginity; this story, like Manx rumors of sexual indiscretions, suggests that enjoyment of sexuality in the open air was part of the festival.

In Ireland the Sunday nearest that date is still traditionally celebrated as marking the harvest. Variously called Garland Sunday, Bilberry Sunday, and Crom Derg Sunday (after an early harvest god), the festival is called Reek Sunday in Co. Mayo after the "reek" or mountain, CROAGH PATRICK, where the greatest Lughnasa celebration is now held. As many as 60,000 pilgrims climb the pyramidal peak beside the sea on the Sunday nearest Lughnasa; local tradition has it that pilgrims are guaranteed heaven if they make the climb THREE times. Once they have ascended the peak, today's Christian pilgrims find not only a chapel dedicated to ST. PATRICK, who reputedly fought with forces of evil at that site, but ruins of neolithic structures, suggesting that the site was sacred to pre-Celtic people, while the designation of Lughnasa for the climb indicates that the mountain continued to be sacred to the Celts as well.

There are dozens of Lughnasa mountains around Ireland, including Mount Brandon in Kerry, where another significant ascent still takes place on Lughnasa. Near Brandon the oldest known Lughnasa celebration takes place: PUCK FAIR in the small town of Kilorglin. Now a street fair with booths and bands, Puck Fair is arguably ancient; some researchers contend that it dates back only several hundred years, but local tradition holds that it is of Celtic origin. The "puck" of the fair's title is a wild GOAT captured on a nearby mountainside and brought into town, where the small creature is displayed for three days (Gathering Day, Fair Day, and Scattering Day) on a high platform about the town's main street. The goat's reputation as a randy creature may reflect other associations of the Lughnasa festival with licentious behavior.

In Scotland the Lughnasa celebrations tend to group themselves around ST. MICHAEL's Day or Michaelmas on September 29, the archangel Michael having been substituted after Christianization for Lugh. Especially popular in the Highlands, Michael was the patron of HORSES, perhaps an odd role for an angel but enthusiastically celebrated with races. On the eve of Michael's feast, carrots were baked into a special bread pudding called a struan, and a cereal was made of all the grains grown in the area; carrots (the most phallic of vegetables) were also exchanged as tokens of affection, for which Michaelmas was sometimes called Carrot Sunday. Visitations to cemeteries and circuits of burial grounds indicated a somber side to the festival.

Sources: Cunliffe, Barry. *The Ancient Celts.* Oxford: Oxford University Press, 1997, p. 189; MacNeill, Máire. *The Festival of Lughnasa, Parts I and II.* Dublin: Comhairle Bhéaloideas Éireann, 1982; Paton, C. I. *Manx Calendar Customs.* Publications of the Folk-lore Society, reprinted. Nendeln/Liechtenstein: Kraus Reprint Limited, 1968, pp. 68 ff; Ross, Anne. *Folklore of the Scottish Highlands.* London: B. T. Batsford, Ltd., 1976, pp. 16, 140; Whitlock, Ralph. *The Folklore of Wiltshire.* London: B. T. Batsford, Ltd., 1976, p. 59.

Lugos (Lugus, Lugoves) Continental Celtic and British god. The god known as LUGH in Ireland and LLEU LLAW GYFFES in Wales appears in Gaul as Lugos (or, in several cases, as a group of three gods called the Lugoves). Sometimes regarded as a solar god, he is more accurately described as a divinity of crafts, as his connection by the Romans with their god MERCURY shows. As the Celts were widely known for their craftsmanship, the importance of this god cannot be understated. His name appears in many placenames: in France, Lyons, Léon, Loudan; in Holland, Leiden; in Britain, Lugavalum (modern Carlisle) as well as London (Lugdunum; alternative readings claim the word comes from Celtic for "wild place").

luideag Scottish folkloric figure. A monstrous female being who haunted a LAKE on the Isle of

Skye, the *luideag* was terrifyingly ugly and easily angered.

lunantishee Irish folkloric being. The FAIRY of the blackthorn tree (see THORN), one of the trees most beloved of the Irish fairy folk, the lunantishee was especially active on the feasts that begin summer and winter, respectively, LUGHNASA on August 1 and SAMHAIN on November 1.

lunar divinities See MOON.

lunastain Scottish folkloric custom. On LUGHNASA, the Celtic harvest feast celebrated around August 1, people in the Highlands and islands of Scotland made a special CAKE called the *lunastain*; alternate names are *luinean* when given to a man, *luineag* when the recipient was a woman. Such breads or cakes may have originated as propitiatory offerings or magical food to protect the eater or to bring good luck. A similar cake called struan was made and eaten on the feast of ST. MICHAEL.

Luned Arthurian heroine. This minor character in Arthurian romance served the mysterious and beautiful Laudine, the LADY OF THE FOUNTAIN; she effected a reconciliation between her mistress and OWEIN, her unreliable estranged husband, after a reformed Owein saved Luned from danger. Some of Luned's powers suggest that she was originally a FAIRY woman; the association of fairies—in Breton, KORRIGANS—with forest fountains strengthens this connection.

luridan Scottish folkloric figure. Recorded in 1665 as a BROWNIE-like FAIRY farmhand of the Scottish islands, the *luridan* also has much in common with the ancient Celtic conception of the GENIUS LOCI or spirit of a place, for he was tied to various sites, first in Wales and later on the large island of Pomonia in the Orkney islands. As with others of his fairy ilk, the *luridan* was a fine and diligent housekeeper, sweeping up and washing dishes at night, and rising early to stir the fire so that the house was warm when the family awakened.

lurikeen   See LEPRECHAUN.

Luter   Irish folkloric figure. In the *Book of Leinster*, we find mention of this Irish GIANT with 14 heads, who loved a woman giant named Goabal whose "charms" (not further defined) "extended over 80 feet."

Luxovius   Continental Celtic god. Known only from one inscription at a healing SPRING in eastern France, this god is believed to have been the consort of BRIXIA, a goddess sometimes linked to the important goddess BRIGIT.

Lyonesse   Arthurian site. British poets, especially those who worked with the Arthurian legends that make up the MATTER OF BRITAIN, believed there was an ISLAND of this name off Britain that had been drowned by the sea. Lyonesse has been located off Cornwall, near the Isles of Scilly, where a rocky outcropping called the Seven Stones is locally called "the city." The tradition combines the motif of the sunken city (see YS, INCHIQUIN) with that of the floating island of the Celtic OTHERWORLD. Alfred Lord Tennyson invokes the tradition when he speaks of the "sunset bound of Lyonnesse."

Mab (Mabb) Welsh folkloric figure. In Ireland the great goddess MEDB was diminished over time into a quasi-historical queen of the same name. In Wales the same process resulted in this FAIRY QUEEN who offers only a hint of earlier divinity. Queen Mab is best known from the reference in Shakespeare's *Romeo and Juliet*, where she appears as the "fairies' midwife," a role traditionally played by a human victim of FAIRY KIDNAPPING. Queen Mab's other duty, according to Shakespeare, was to bring night-mares—once again, a role rarely ascribed to Medb but common among mischievous fairies; her playfulness has led some scholars to derive her name from the Welsh term for child, *mab*, which also appears in the collection of myths called the *MABINOGION*. Shakespeare borrowed British and Welsh fairy lore at will; although vivid, his portraits of mythological beings are not necessarily accurate.

Mabinogion (Mabinogi) Welsh mythological texts. Much of what we know today about Welsh mythology comes from tales compiled as the four branches of the *Mabinogion*; another eight tales are sometimes counted as part of the collection. The stories are found in two sources: *The White Book of Rhydderch* (1300–1325) and *The Red Book of Hergest* (1375–1425). Although written after Christianization, the narratives are apparently based on the earlier oral literature of Wales and thus offer us a window into the Celtic past. The first English translation of the *Mabinogion* was not made available until 1838–49, when the work of Lady Charlotte Guest was brought to print.

The word *Mabinogion* was applied to the tales translated by Lady Guest; it is the plural form of the Middle Welsh word *mabinogi*, the term preferred by specialists today. The name of the collection has been derived from the obscure boy god MABON or MAPONUS, "son of the mother," and from the term for a young poet, *mabinog*; the latter suggests that the stories were a training manual for BARDS-to-be.

The *Mabinogion*'s tales concern the Children of Dôn, the descendants of an ancient and little-known goddess, DÔN; the Children of Dôn are parallel to the Irish divinities known as the TUATHA DÉ DANANN, the people of the goddess DANU, a name cognate to Dôn. Dôn's children's father is not mentioned, which has led some to assume that the *Mabinogion* dates from a period in which MATRILINY, the charting of descent through the mother rather than the father, was common. This interpretation gave rise to the imaginative retellings of the tales by Evangeline Walton in the mid-20th century.

The first branch of the *Mabinogion* centers on the prince of DYFED, PWYLL, who was convinced to exchange realms with the king of the

OTHERWORLD, ARAWN. His kingdom, ANNWN, was under siege by the mighty HAFGAN, who could only be killed if his opponent felled him with a single stroke. Pwyll agreed to the exchange of kingdoms as well as to the battle with Hafgan, whom he killed with a single thrust, freeing the kingdom and winning the everlasting gratitude of Arawn.

Soon after, Pwyll met the fair princess RHIANNON, whose speedy HORSE and Otherworldly beauty make her divine origin clear; after a struggle with GWAWL, a rival for her hand, Pwyll wed Rhiannon. Their wedded life was far from blissful. The disappearance of their newborn son on BELTANE night, plus traces of blood around the queen's mouth, led to accusations that Rhiannon had murdered and devoured the infant. Although her life was spared, Rhiannon was condemned to carry visitors to the palace on her back as though she were a horse. Fortunately, the infant prince was not dead but safe, having been carried off by a spectral creature who dropped the boy on a distant farm, where he was tenderly raised. When the young prince, PRYDERI, learned of his heritage and returned to the palace, his mother's innocence was revealed, and the land rejoiced.

The second branch of the *Mabinogion* describes the heroic journey to Ireland by the hero BRÂN THE BLESSED and his warriors, who set out to rescue the imprisoned princess BRANWEN. Brân and Branwen were children of LLYR, as were the hero MANAWYDAN and two half brothers, the kindly NISIEN and his evil TWIN, EFNISIEN. Brân and Manawydan, having accepted the proposal of the Irish warlord MATHOLWCH, sent Branwen off for what they hoped would be a happy and productive married life in Ireland. At the wedding, Efnisien performed a macabre surgery on Matholwch's horses, cutting off their tails, lips, and ears. This destroyed any hope of marital harmony for Branwen, who despite producing an heir to the realm, GWERN, was subjected to constant abuse. Finally she sent a starling back to Wales, to alert her brothers to her suffering; they mounted a war to free Branwen, succeeding only

in losing many lives. Branwen, freed and bound for home, died of a broken heart when she looked back and saw the island that had been her prison and that was her saviors' tomb.

The third branch of the *Mabinogion* concerns Branwen's brother, Manawydan, and the son of Pwyll and Rhiannon, Pryderi. At a double wedding ceremony, Manawydan wed the widowed Rhiannon, while Pryderi took as his wife the faithful heroine CIGFA. Not long after this happy day, the two couples found their land utterly barren and covered by a strange white mist. Nothing grew in the fields; the people were destitute. Their rulers eked out a living for awhile by hunting, finally giving up to become shoemakers in eastern Britain. Their work was so exquisite that other craftsmen became infuriated and threatened the group, whereupon they returned to Wales.

Worse was in store for them, for Pryderi and Rhiannon fell under an enchantment and vanished. After further hardships Manawydan and Cigfa learned that the curse was leveled by friends of Gwawl, the suitor for Rhiannon's hand who had been humiliated by Pryderi's father. Once peace had been made among the families, all the couples were reunited in happiness.

Finally, the fourth branch tells of the rape of GOEWIN, ceremonial foot-holder to king MATH, and the complications regarding her successor. Math's designated successor was his nephew GWYDION—another indication of matrilineal social organization—so it was natural that Gwydion's own sister ARIANRHOD would wish to serve as foot-holder. Before she could take the office, she had to prove her virginity. Math set up a magical test: If she could step over his magician's staff, her purity would be proven.

The test was a trick, and Arianrhod found herself giving hasty birth to two children of whose conception she had been unaware—DYLAN, son of the sea, and an unnamed bundle of unformed flesh that Gwydion took to himself. Angered at having been deceived, Arianrhod swore she would give that son neither a name nor arms—two prerogatives of the mother. Gwydion again tricked her into naming and arming her son, LLEU LLAW

GYFFES. In fury, Arianhrod cursed the boy, declaring that he would never have a wife from this earth. Yet again Gwydion and Math found a way around her, creating a bride for Lleu from a pile of flowers. The flower-maiden BLODEUWEDD proved treacherous and had her husband killed by her lover GRONW PEBYR.

In addition to these four branches, several other important Welsh mythological stories are often considered part of the full *Mabinogion*. These include the *Dream of MAXEN*, the romantic story of *KULHWCH AND OLWEN*, the adventure of OWEIN in winning the mysterious LADY OF THE FOUNTAIN, and the story of the reincarnated BARD named TALIESIN.

Source: Gantz, Jeffrey, trans. *The Mabinogion*. New York: Barnes & Noble Books, 1976.

Mabon (Mabon vab Modron, Mabon fab Modron)   Welsh hero. A relatively obscure figure, Mabon appears as a divine youth in the early Arthurian story of *KULHWCH AND OLWEN* as Mabon vab MODRON, "Son, son of Mother"; no father is mentioned, although whether that is to stress his matrilineal descent or because the father is insignificant is unclear. Another figure of the same name is known as Mabon vab Mellt; he may be the same Mabon bearing the patronym of his father MELLTS or a different god altogether.

Mabon's presumed earlier significance is alluded to in an early text that calls him "one of the Three Exalted Captives of the Island of Britain." That phrase refers to a story from the Welsh *MABINOGION* in which Mabon was rescued by the hero KULHWCH from the OTHERWORLD, where he had been held captive after being stolen from his mother in his infancy. So many years had passed that Mabon was the oldest living human. After his rescue, Mabon helped Kulhwch gain the hand of his chosen mate OLWEN. Two similarly named characters take minor roles in Arthurian literature—Mabonagrain and MABUNZ—both of whom are held captive, suggesting that the motif of captivity was basic to Mabon's myth.

Some have derived the name of the great collection of Welsh myths, the *Mabinogion*, from Mabon's name. Others connect him with the obscure god MAPONUS. Although presumed to have once been a significant figure, he is now a baffling puzzle.

Mabunz (Mabuz, Mâbûz)   Arthurian hero. In some texts, this name is given for the magician son of MORGAN, the sorceress sister of king ARTHUR. It may be a form of the name of the divine boy, MABON, whose mother is normally called MODRON, leading some scholars to connect these Arthurian figures with Welsh mythology. Mabunz is also described as the son of the LADY OF THE LAKE or of another Arthurian heroine, CLARINE.

Mac Cécht (Mac Cecht)   Irish god. This minor Irish divinity was a farmer and the husband of one of the goddesses of the land, FÓDLA, a member of the magical race called the TUATHA DÉ DANANN. Fódla's name means "divided" or "plowed" land, while Mac Cécht's parallel name means "plowman" or "son of the plow," suggesting that both were deities of agriculture. He may also have been a god of HEALING, for when the king of the Tuatha Dé lay dying, Mac Cécht walked across the parched land looking for water to revive him and was led by a wild DUCK to a SPRING; water was typically envisioned as a source of healing by the Celts. Mac Cécht was the son of OGMA, god of eloquent speech, and lost his life in combat with one of the invading MILESIANS. He and his brothers MAC CUILL and MAC GRÉINE, husbands of the three land goddesses made up a trio of parallel gods. Another Mac Cécht was a hero who championed the doomed king CONAIRE at DA DERGA's hostel, where he killed the man who decapitated Conaire and then offered the king's HEAD its last drink.

Mac Conglinne (Anéra meic Conglinne)   Irish hero. Not actually a mythological character but a figure from SATIRE, Mac Conglinne experienced a vision in an Irish AISLING poem of the 12th century. A poor BARD from Co. Roscommon, Mac Conglinne went on a POET'S CIRCUIT of the PROVINCE of MUNSTER, where he heard that poets were well treated—but where the king was suffering from the disease of uncontrollable gluttony. When Mac Conglinne arrived in Cork, however, he received no poet's welcome but was put up in a dingy hovel where he was eaten alive by fleas and lice. Furious, Mac Conglinne composed a satire so scathing that the abbot condemned him to be crucified. The night before the execution, he was tied to a STONE like the great hero CÚCHULAINN.

In the cold and dark, Mac Conglinne was attended by an angel who recited a long poem describing a land composed entirely of food—a vision that he knew was the missing secret to restore the ailing but gluttonous king to health. When day broke, the accused satirist demanded to be brought to the king, where he recited a luridly specific vision of the land of MILK and honey of which the angel spoke, while cooking haunches of meat before a manacled king. The suffering king finally vomited a demon from his mouth, who grabbed some of the food and disappeared. The satire combines references to ancient Celtic beliefs in the ancient requirement of HOSPITALITY and the prestige of the poet, as well as folkloric motifs of monstrous beings who can possess human bodies.

Source: Cross, Tom Peete, and Clark Harris Slover, eds. *Ancient Irish Tales.* New York: Henry Holt and Co., 1936, p. 551.

Mac Cuill   Irish god. The husband of the land goddess BANBA, the name of this minor divinity meant "son of HOLLY," a plant associated with winter, suggesting that he may have been connected with that season. With his brothers MAC CÉCHT and MAC GRÉINE, each of them the consort of one of the three important land goddesses, he belonged to a trio of parallel gods.

Mac Dathó (Mac Datho, Mes Roeda)   Irish hero. Hero of the ULSTER CYCLE tale *Scéla mucce Meic Dathó,* Mac Dathó was a warrior whose prize hunting hound AILBE was coveted by two kings, CONCOBAR MAC NESSA of ULSTER and AILILL mac Máta of CONNACHT. Unable to refuse either of the powerful rulers, he invited them and their warriors to a feast where he served an immense roasted PIG. As the finest champion was always given the best part of a feast (see CHAMPION'S PORTION), an argument ensued as to who would be so honored. In the melee that followed, the hound Ailbe was killed, providing Mac Dathó a solution to his problem.

Source: Dillon, Myles, ed. *Irish Sagas.* Cork: The Mercier Press, 1968, p. 79.

Mac Gréine (Mac Gréne)   Irish god. Mac Gréine was the husband of the important earth goddess who gave her name to Ireland, ÉRIU. With his brothers MAC CÉCHT and MAC CUILL he belonged to a trio of three parallel gods whose wives were land goddesses. His name means "son of the SUN," and although this is often cited as proof of an ancient Irish solar god, it may be a matrilineal name or title, the word for sun being feminine in Irish. It is clear that Mac Gréine does not bear his father's name, for he was, like his two brothers, son of the god of eloquence, OGMA. Mac Gréine lost his life to the warrior poet AMAIRGIN of the MILESIANS.

Macha   Irish goddess. The great capital of ancient ULSTER, the northernmost of the ancient PROVINCES of Ireland, was named EMAIN MACHA, "TWINS of Macha," after this goddess. She appeared from nowhere—or from the OTHERWORLD—at the door of the human farmer CRUNNIUC and made herself at home, helping him create bounty from the land and, ultimately, becoming pregnant by him. As with other FAIRY LOVERS, Macha placed a requirement on her husband: that he not brag about her. He could not keep silent when, at the Assembly of Ulster, he saw the king's HORSES and knew his supernatural wife could beat them in a race. Boasting of Macha's prowess, Crunniuc drew the attention of the king, who demanded that he prove his claim. Macha was dragged to the Assembly, where she pointed to her advanced pregnancy and begged not to be forced to race. The king, sure he would win because of Macha's perceived handicap, said that the race must go on.

Macha raced, handily beating the king's swift team but going into labor at the finish line. The effort killed her, and she died giving birth to her twins, a girl named FIAL and a boy named Fall. As she died, Macha cursed the men of the province (see DEBILITY OF THE ULSTERMEN), declaring that every time an enemy threatened, the warriors would become weak as women—some interpret this as ghost labor pains—for five days and four nights, for nine generations.

This is the most famous goddess named Macha, but there were two others, who may or may not have originally been the same. The first Macha was an obscure figure who was said to have been the wife of NEMED, one of the first settlers of Ireland. It was in her honor that the first plains of Ireland were cleared of thick forests. Macha, looking into the future and seeing the bloodshed that would afflict the country during the great CATTLE RAID of Cuailnge (TÁIN BÓ CUAILNGE), died of heartbreak. Like her more famous namesake, this Macha does not appear to be a goddess of war; both deplored men's war-making activities and, in the case of Macha wife of Crunniuc, brought difficulties to men who engaged in battle. The derivation of her name from words for "earth" or "field" also suggests a peaceful aspect to Macha.

Yet Macha is described by several ancient authors as a war goddess; the HEADS of fallen warriors were described as "the masts of Macha," a term that otherwise described the plentiful acorns on which half-wild PIGS fed. Macha is said to have been one of the "three Morrigna" or three goddesses of war (see MÓRRÍGAN). Her association with horses may have given rise to this connection, for Irish warriors went to battle either in chariots or mounted on horseback.

Although the two Machas discussed above had little to do with war, the third Macha was a true warrior. Macha Mong Rua (Mongruad), Red-Haired Macha, is alternately described as a form of the goddess or as an actual historical figure bearing the goddess's name. The *Annals of Ireland* describe a woman named Macha who was queen of the whole island in 377 B.C.E. Her father, ÁED RUAD, made a compact with two other kings—DÍTHORBA and CIMBÁETH—to share rulership of the land, each of them reigning for seven years. Their prowess as rulers was to be judged in three ways: Acorns ("mast") had to be abundant, thus providing good fodder for pigs; fabrics had to take dyes well; and women had to survive childbirth safely. All went well for many years under this shared rulership. The land was fruitful, the people were happy, and children were well fed.

When Áed drowned in a waterfall and Macha attempted to take his place in the succession, her corulers objected. So Macha waged war upon them, killing Díthorba and besting Cimbáeth before allying herself with him through marriage. When Díthorba's five sons escaped, she pursued them, disguised as an ancient HAG whom they attempted to rape. She overcame them all and marched them back to Emain Macha, where her warriors attempted to execute them. Macha, however, thought a better punishment was to force them to dig the massive earthworks now known as Navan Fort. The site includes a large artificial mound, several sacred WELLS, a racecourse, and other ritual sites. A new museum at Emain Macha includes holographic projections of the presumed stages of Emain Macha's ritual past.

Macha's connection with Ulster and with the tales of the ULSTER CYCLE have led some scholars to a rgue that she was the goddess of the region's SOVEREIGNTY; she would thus have been the peer of such important divinities as ÉRIU, after whom the island of Ireland was named, and MEDB, the goddess/queen of CONNACHT. That interpretation of Macha's significance is not, however, accepted without argument. Others interpret Macha as a pre-Celtic goddess who was assimilated into the social structure of the Celts.

Sources: Dexter, Miriam Robbins. *Whence the Goddesses: A Sourcebook*. New York: Pergamon Press, 1990, pp. 90–91; Hull, Eleanor. *The Cuchullin Saga in Irish Literature*. London: David Nutt, 1898, pp. 91 ff; Straffon, Cheryl. *The Earth Goddess: Celtic and Pagan Legacy of the Landscape*. London: Blandford, 1997, p. 36.

MacInelly   See CIAN.

Mac Moincanta   Irish god. A minor divinity of the TUATHA DÉ DANANN, he was called "father of the gods" after the beneficent DAGDA gave up that title. Later he was called a FAIRY king, but he was unseated as the head of the Irish fairies by the more important Fionnbharr.

Mac Roth   Irish hero. A minor hero of the TÁIN BÓ CUAILNGE, the great epic of the CATTLE RAID by queen MEDB of CONNACHT upon the adjoining PROVINCE of ULSTER, Mac Roth was the fleet messenger of Medb's consort, king AILILL mac Máta, and was said to have been able to cover all of Ireland's roads between sunrise and sunset of a single day. Another man of the same name was the minor king of Ulster who owned the great brown BULL, DONN CUAILNGE, whom Medb wished to borrow for a year, to impregnate one of her COWS and provide her with an offspring as good as one of Ailill's bulls. Medb offered a fortune in gold and her own fine favors as rent for the bull, which was quite sufficient for Mac Roth. But when he overheard Medb's warriors mocking him, saying that if he would not rent the bull, they would steal it, Mac Roth canceled the deal and the provinces went to war.

Madgy Figgy (Madge Figgy)   Cornish heroine. This renowned WITCH of Cornwall lived near Raftra, where she made her living scrounging debris from wrecked ships. Some believed she magically called up storms to cause such wrecks, sitting on a huge basalt rock off Land's End that has a level space on its top where she could invoke the weather spirits. Once she and her crew of wreckers found the body of a Portuguese lady on the shore, drowned in one of the storms Madgy Figgy had raised. The witch claimed the jewels the woman wore and hid them in a chest in her house. Every night thereafter, a strange light would be seen traveling to Madgy's cottage, until finally a stranger came to town and followed the exact path of the light. When he left, he had all the woman's jewels, and Madgy had a fortune in ransom. "One witch knows another, living or dead," she said sagely.

Source: Hunt, Robert. *Cornish Customs and Superstitions*. Truro: Tor Mark Press, n.d, p. 34.

madness   Mythological theme. In Celtic mythology, we find a number of figures who go mad—a state that generally leads to development of a prophetic or other paranormal skill. Male figures tend to go mad because of the horrors of war, suffering what we might call post-traumatic stress disorder today but was called "soldier's heart" in ancient Ireland, where the kings SUIBHNE and MUIRCERTACH MAC ERC both went mad from battle fatigue and died before being fully healed. In Welsh mythology, the warrior Myrddin (who becomes the magician MERLIN in the Arthurian material) went mad from the horror of the battle of Arfderydd and retreated to Scotland, where he both healed himself and discovered his prophetic powers.

The connection of madness with battle is reinforced by the presence in Irish mythology of the war goddess NEMAIN, "war-frenzy," whose name suggests that insanity was put to use in battle. Occasionally, female figures plagued with madness are found, most notably MESS BUACHALLA, whose insanity derived from her discovery that she had unwittingly committed incest with her father; and MIS, who went mad after drinking her own father's blood. Even in such cases, madness is typically a result of violence or bloodshed.

Source: McDowell, Patricia. "Soldiers' Heart." In Patricia Monaghan, ed. *Irish Spirit: Pagan, Celtic, Christian, Global.* Dublin: Wolfhound Press, 2001, p. 22.

Madrun   See MODRON.

Maedoc (Mogue, Maodhóg, Saint Maedoc) Irish legendary figure. Some of the early Christian SAINTS of Ireland have attributes or engage in activities that seem connected with the Celtic OTHERWORLD. Such is the case with Maedoc, associated with the eastern province of LEINSTER. He was said to have been born after his mother, queen EITHNE (also the name of a goddess), saw the MOON enter her husband's mouth at the very moment he saw a star enter hers. In 598 C.E. Maedoc set out on the back of a sea monster from Wales, where he had given the last rites to the land's patron saint, David. In Ireland he quickly converted the local chieftain and built a church, eventually becoming bishop of Ferns, then capital of the province.

Maelduin (Maeldun, Maeldúin, Maol Dúin, Mael Dúin, Maeldune)   Irish hero. One of the most famous VOYAGE poems of ancient Ireland, variously said to have been recorded in the ninth and the 11th centuries, concerns this young hero. Maelduin was born of violence after his father raped a nun, who then died giving birth to him. Maelduin's aunt raised him and told him the story of his conception and birth. In an epic story sometimes called the "Irish Odyssey," Maelduin then set off for the land of the Vikings to avenge his father, who had been killed by these invaders. Sixty warriors attended upon the young man, and their adventures constitute the major part of the tale. They met with giant ants, monster CATS, and other extraordinary beings before coming to an OTHERWORLD ISLAND

where they all found FAIRY LOVERS. Such mistresses were, however, notoriously difficult to leave, and Maelduin's group nearly remained their captives for eternity. In the end, however, they returned to the human world.

Source: Gregory, Lady Augusta. *Gods and Fighting Men: The Story of the Tuatha De Danaan and of the Fianna of Ireland.* New York: Oxford University Press, 1970, pp. 31 ff, 41 ff.

Maer   Irish heroine. This minor Irish heroine dabbled in the occult arts, bewitching nine nuts so that, when he ate them, the hero FIONN MAC CUMHAILL would come to her bed. Suspecting the curious gift, Fionn did not eat the nuts and thus thwarted Maer's plot.

Maeve   See MEDB.

Maga   See EBHLA.

Magdalenenberg   Continental Celtic archaeological site. A significant gravesite of the continental Celts was excavated in the early 1890s, and then again in the 1970s, at Villingen-Schwenningen in Germany, near the original source of Celtic culture. One of the largest burial mounds in the region, it covered more than a hundred graves, in which numerous ritual and personal artifacts were found.

magic   Cosmological concept. Magic is classically defined as actions or words performed or spoken with the intention of effecting a change, usually in the external world. The distinction is further made that magic is typically an individual pursuit rather than a communal one; when the group performs a ritual or chants special words, that is usually defined as religion rather than magic. In the case of the Celtic DRUIDS, the boundary between individual and communal pursuits becomes somewhat slippery, as individual action might be taken for a communal good. For example, a SATIRE might drive an ungenerous king from the throne; what seems an action of personal vengeance has at its base the social duty of the BARD to assure that wealth is redistributed through the king, the satire proving a corrective measure that promotes social harmony.

Individual Celts, like all other ancient peoples, practiced magic, both propitiatory (intended to keep bad events away) and intercessory (intended to draw good things near). AMULETS were used from earliest times to ward off evil; apparent amulets have been found in the early Celtic archaeological sites of LA TÈNE and HALLSTATT. Verbal magic is also known to have been used, especially in the form of CURSES, of which there is much evidence in the mythological texts.

Some Celtic magical practices survive in degraded form into the present, as superstitions; for instance, shortened versions of personal names—nicknames—are still used, though no longer with the intent of keeping loved ones hidden from OTHERWORLD eyes and thus safe from FAIRY KIDNAPPING. In addition, the ritual of leaving small rags at sacred WELLS or tied to TREES survives to this day; the rags, called *CLOOTIES*, have variously been described as left-behind prayers or as purgative rituals that condense within themselves negative influences to be discarded.

Many Celtic divinities had magical powers. This is especially true of deities associated with druids or bards. In Wales we find the magician-bard GWYDION, who was able with the help of his uncle MATH to turn flowers into a bride for his foster son LLEU LLAW GYFFES; in Arthurian legend derived from Welsh sources, we find the great magician MERLIN, whose powers included SHAPE-SHIFTING. In Ireland many deities had the power to change their shapes, most notably the sea god MANANNÁN MAC LIR.

Mag Mell (Magh Meall) Irish mythological site. The terms "plain of honey" and "plain of delights" appear in several Irish narratives as descriptions of the OTHERWORLD, where life is endlessly joyous and sweet, where trees bear blossoms and fruit at once, and where there is neither discomfort nor death. Although the name of this FAIRYLAND seems to imply that it is a level place on land, it is often described as a floating ISLAND, the domain of the sea god MANANNÁN MAC LIR.

Mag Mon See NAMES FOR THE OTHERWORLD.

Mag Mór (Mag Mor, Magh Mhór) Irish mythological site. The "great plain" was a place in the OTHERWORLD where the dead lived, walking incessantly over its level surface; it was seen as a kind of parallel dimension accessible from this world. Folklore suggests that the belief was found in Ireland as recently as 70 years ago.

Mag Mucramhan (Mag Mucrama) Irish mythological site. A field near the castle town of Athenry in Co. Galway is the reputed site of a great battle between the ruler of the province of MUNSTER, AILILL Olom, and his enemy and foster son, LUGAIDH mac Conn.

Mag Muirthemne Irish mythological site. The great hero of ULSTER, CÚCHULAINN, was sometimes said to live on the plain of Mag Muirthemne, south of contemporary Dundalk (DÚN Delgan in Irish), although that town is more commonly described as the site of his fortress.

Magog Irish and British hero. The name of a famous Cornish GIANT appears as well in the mythological history of Ireland. In the *BOOK OF INVASIONS*, Magog was said to have been the ancestor of PARTHOLÓN and NEMED, two early invaders; he was the ancestor as well of the Scythians, reputed to have been ancient relatives of the Irish. It is not known whether there is any connection between this Irish figure and the Cornish giant GOG.

magpie Symbolic bird. In Ireland it was considered an ill omen to see a magpie when setting out on a journey, while seeing a speckled horse or "magpie pony" was almost as unlucky. Four magpies in a row indicated a death in the family.

Mag Réin See NAMES FOR THE OTHERWORLD.

Mag Tuired (Moyturra, Mag Tuirid, Magh Tuireadh, Moytirra) Irish mythological site. Two great battles in Irish myth took place on the plain called Mag Tuired, both of which resulted in the victory of the TUATHA DÉ DANANN, the people of the goddess DANU, over another race in the struggle to rule Ireland. In the first battle of Mag Tuired, Tuatha Dé warriors under the leadership of their king NUADA wrested control of Ireland away from the earlier residents, the FIR BOLG, while in the second and more famous battle, the tribe of Danu drove out the FOMORIANS.

There is considerable contention about what actual location is referred to in the ancient legends. Although it is agreed that Mag Tuired was in the western province of CONNACHT, sites in Co. Mayo and in the adjoining Co. Sligo have been proposed. At the latter, megalithic remains are strewn about the area and could have given rise to the name, which means "plain of the pillars."

Maiden Castle British mythological site. In Dorset, a great HILLFORT was built during the Iron Age, presumably by the Celts, atop an earlier structure used by pre-Celtic people. In their turn, the invading Romans in the fourth century capped the hill with a temple of their own, dedicating it to DIANA. The site has thus been held sacred for as much as 6,000 years and seems to have been devoted to a wildwood goddess, if the Roman designation follows that of earlier peoples.

Source: Straffon, Cheryl. *The Earth Goddess: Celtic and Pagan Legacy of the Landscape*. London: Blandford, 1997, p. 97.

Maine (Maine, Mainí, The Manes) Irish heroes. These minor characters are the seven identically named sons of the great queen MEDB of CONNACHT and king AILILL mac Máta. One legend about the Maines says that Medb violently wished for the death of her enemy, king CONCOBAR MAC NESSA of ULSTER. A DRUID prophesied that her son Maine would kill him. Medb had no sons by that name, so she renamed them all.

One of the Maines, the one originally called Sin and later Maine Mórghor, went off with a band of warriors to Ulster to court the maiden Fearbh, daughter of Gearg. They were all enjoying the HOSPITALITY of Gearg when a strange wind blew up, which Maine's druid warned was a bad OMEN. Meanwhile a woman of the OTHERWORLD appeared to Concobar and led him to Gearg's home, where the host was slain as well as Maine Mórghor. Medb had a vision of what was happening but arrived too late to save her son.

Another hero of the same name was a Norse prince who did king Concobar mac Nessa's will when the errant hero NOÍSIU returned to Ireland with the beautiful but doomed DEIRDRE; Noísíu fell to Maine's sword.

Mairenn Irish heroine. A king of TARA had two wives, one of whom, Mairenn, always wore a gorgeous headdress of gold. The other, MUGAIN, was envious of her co-wife's jewelry but suspected that Mairenn was hiding something. Indeed she was, for Mairenn was bald beneath the gold, as the whole court might have seen when a bribed woman jester yanked the headdress off Mairenn's head. Mairenn cursed Mugain, but even as she did so, splendid golden locks covered her head so that no one saw her shame. As a result of her ill will, Mugain was forced to bear a lamb and a SALMON before she could give birth to a human child.

Source: MacNeill, Máire. *The Festival of Lughnasa, Parts I and II*. Dublin: Comhairle Bhéaloideas Éireann, 1982, pp. 326–327.

Mal Irish goddess. In the far west of Ireland is the scenic wonder called the Cliffs of Moher, known in Irish as Ceann na Caillghe, "the head of the HAG." The hag in question was called Mal—the nearby resort town of Miltown Malbay is named after her—and she was said to have given her name to the land after she died pursuing a handsome man across the country-side, intent upon making him her lover.

Mala Liath Scottish folkloric figure. In Ross and Cromary in Scotland, this name was given to a CAILLEACH or HAG figure who tended a herd of wild PIGS. The Cailleach in Scotland appears often in this form as a goddess of wild animals, especially DEER; in other lands she is more typically a weather divinity or creator goddess. She may descend from a pre-Celtic deity, since the word *cailleach* is not derived from any of the Celtic languages, although it has been adopted into several as a word for an old woman.

Maledisant Arthurian heroine. The name of this obscure character in Arthurian legend means "ill speech," and she derided a knight, BRUNO, until she fell in love with him, where-upon her speech became sugary and sweet.

Malekin British folkloric spirit. This FAIRY was said to haunt a castle in Suffolk after she was stolen away from her human family, who left her in the weeds while they worked in a nearby cornfield. Her story was recorded in the 13th century by Ralph of Coggeshall, an early collec-tor of such tales.

mallet Symbolic object. Several Celtic gods, especially SUCELLUS, carry a tool that resembles a HAMMER. Others lug about a much larger tool usually called a mallet, a kind of bat whose phal-lic symbolism is clear. The Irish god DAGDA was known for his enormous mallet, so big that he dragged it around on a wheeled cart.

Man (Isle of Man, Mannin, Ellan Vannin) Insular Celtic site. The small ISLAND between Britain and Ireland was settled in the fourth or fifth century C.E. by Irish sailors, who named it after the sea god MANANNÁN MAC LIR. Although not geographically remote, the Isle of Man was meteorologically so; boat travel to the island was hindered by frequent storms, so the Manx language slowly divided itself from its parent Irish. The residents of the island were fierce sailors who, in ancient times, counted as part of their realm the islands far to the north, the Hebrides; these were lost to Scotland at the bat-tle of Largs in 1263.

Many ancient customs continued into quite recent times on the island, including the longest-running parliament in Europe, the Tynwald; stories of mythological import long remained part of the oral tradition. The arrival of regular boat service in the 1830s, however, encouraged the decline of the Manx language against the favored English tongue; in 1974 the last native speaker of Manx died at the age of 74.

Manann (Manning) Folkloric figure. In Irish folklore this name is given to the pagan oppo-nent of ST. PATRICK, a figure who was said to have been confined to a pool in Co. Monaghan after being chased across the land by the saint. Transforming himself into a BIRD, a HARE, and a FISH, Manann was finally trapped when the saint prayed that, whatever he was, he would remain so until the end of time. As he was at that moment a fish, Manann never set fin outside water again.

Despite his confinement, Manann kept a great treasure with him in the pool, though no one could ever get it because of the magical pro-hibitions around it. When people tried to drain the pool, FAIRIES appeared and began piping until the workers—and the pool water, too—began to dance, frightening the workers away and ending the project. Manann has been described as a folkloric survival of the great sea god, MANANNÁN MAC LIR.

Source: MacNeill, Máire. *The Festival of Lughnasa, Parts I and II*. Dublin: Comhairle Bhéaloideas Éireann, 1982, pp. 166–168.

Manannán mac Lir (Manandan, Monanaun, Mananan, Oirbsiu) Irish god. An oceanic divinity, Manannán is described as the son of ("mac") LIR, an even older although obscure god of the sea. He never lived on land but made his home somewhere in the ocean, on an ISLAND variously called MAG MELL ("plain of honey"), TÍR TAIRNGIRI ("land of promise"), and EMAIN ABLACH ("island of apples"), the last of which has been occasionally connected with the Arthurian OTHERWORLD of AVALON.

A master of SHAPE-SHIFTING, Manannán was like the Greek Proteus (from whom we get our word *protean*, many-formed). He could grant this power to those he cherished and who cherished him, which made him a popular deity among BARDS and those who practiced DIVINATION. Manannán's magical powers were many. He traveled across the sea, faster than the wind could blow, in a magical self-propelling boat made of copper, drawn by a HORSE named Enbharr ("splendid mane" or "water-foam") whose HAIR was the froth of the waves. He could make a dozen men seem like an army; he could throw a handful of chips into the brine and make them look like an armada. He had a magic cloak that, when he shook it out, caused forgetfulness.

He was not originally one of the TUATHA DÉ DANANN, the most important deities of ancient Ireland, but by the 10th century he had been absorbed into their number. It was he, according to some tales, who gave the Tuatha Dé the idea of living under hills instead of leaving Ireland altogether, and for that he was accepted among them. In return he gave the tribe of DANU three gifts: the DRUID'S FOG or cloak of concealment; the feast of GOIBNIU where old age was kept at bay; and finally his own magical PIGS that could be killed each day, eaten each evening, and yet come alive again every morning.

Manannán sometimes appears in literature as a human figure, a sailor who never was lost at sea because of his uncanny celestial navigational skills; he is thus described in the works of the Irish scribe Cormac. In other stories from the oral tradition, he was a merchant mariner who, tired of Ireland, moved his base of operations to Scotland, where he appears in many folktales.

Manannán gives his name to the Isle of Man, where the sea's presence is always felt and where his grave can still be seen. Oral traditions about Manannán were scanty in other Celtic regions, but the long survival of the Manx tongue meant that traditions about the sea god survived on Man into relatively recent times. Until the 1830s, when regular boat service began, there was little regular contact between the Isle of Man and other lands, nor did the residents generally speak English. But the Manx language, a branch of Gaelic that was related but not identical to the tongues of Ireland and Wales, did not long survive the intensified contact with other lands, declining rapidly in the 19th century; the last native speaker of Manx died in the latter part of the 20th century.

Manannán was, according to legend, the first king of the island named for him; he lived in a castle on the top of Mount Barrule, where he is buried, although other stories claim his burial mound can be seen on the seashore beneath Peel Castle. A vantage point looking out to sea was called Manannán's Chair, from which he was said to keep watch. Manx fishermen claimed that, as they mended their nets, Manannán came to them, walking along the seashore followed by a curious being who seemed to have no head or torso but three legs—the symbol of the ever-moving sea and also the crest of the Isle of Man.

Manannán was associated with several goddesses and FAIRY women. Most prominent in literature was his daughter or wife FAND (called Fairyland's "pearl of beauty"), the only threat to the idealized marriage of the hero CÚCHULAINN and his paragon of womanhood, EMER. Manannán was also associated with the SUN goddess ÁINE, who left his watery bed to rise each morning; but other legends call her his daughter rather than his spouse. His children were the heroes Gaiar and MONGÁN.

Sources: Gregory, Lady Augusta. *Gods and Fighting Men: The Story of the Tuatha De Danaan and of the Fianna of Ireland.* New York: Oxford University Press, 1970, pp. 96 ff; Killip, Margaret. *The Folklore of the Isle of Man.* London: B. T. Batsford, Ltd., 1975, pp. 5, 43; Spence, Lewis. *The Minor Traditions of British Mythology.* New York: Benjamin Blom, Inc., 1972, p. 25.

Manawydan (Manawyddan, Manawydan fab Llŷr) Welsh god. From his name, it appears that Manawydan should be cognate to the Irish god of the sea, MANANNÁN MAC LIR, but in Wales this divinity was more associated with famine than with sailing. He remained, however, associated with the OTHERWORLD, which to the Welsh was more typically below ground than out to sea, as it appeared to the Irish.

Manawydan appears in several branches of the MABINOGION, the great collection of Welsh mythological tales that dates to the Middle Ages. In the second branch, Manawydan accompanied his brother, the gigantic hero BRÂN THE BLESSED, to Ireland to free their sister BRANWEN from an abusive marriage to king MATHOLWCH. When they got there, the king had set many traps for the rescuers, who fought so fiercely that only a few Irishmen survived—leaving Ireland empty except for five pregnant women. Manawydan accompanied the miraculous HEAD of his brother Brân back to Wales, as well as providing safe passage for their unfortunate sister Branwen, who died of sorrow at the bloodshed upon arriving safely home.

Manawydan went on to become the second husband of the miraculous queen (and probable goddess) RHIANNON, in a double wedding with her son PRYDERI and his beloved CIGFA. Shortly thereafter the land became strangely barren, all its people and animals disappearing into an Otherworldly mist. After attempting to eke out a living through hunting, Manawydan took the group east, where they worked as artisans.

Manawydan proved so talented as a shoemaker that other craft workers, fearing they would lose business, rose up and drove the group away. Back in Wales, things grew steadily worse, for Rhiannon and Pryderi fell under an enchantment and disappeared.

Living chastely with Cigfa, Manawydan ventured into the markets again, again to be driven back for his threatening excellence. He then turned to farming but constantly found his crops ravaged. Finally he caught several mice devouring his grain and made plans to ceremoniously execute them. As he prepared to do so, travelers arrived and bargained for the mice's safety—for the vermin were the disguised friends of an old enemy of Pryderi's father. Trading the rodents' lives for the freedom of his own family, Manawydan was able to reunite the two couples, who settled down to a happy life thereafter.

Sources: Gantz, Jeffrey, trans. *The Mabinogion.* New York: Barnes & Noble Books, 1976; Spence, Lewis. *The Minor Traditions of British Mythology.* New York: Benjamin Blom, Inc., 1972, pp. 25–26.

Manching Continental Celtic archaeological site. One of the largest and best-known Celtic settlements was excavated near the Bavarian town of Ingolstadt. A five-mile-long wall surrounded the many buildings of the settlement, and domestic and some ritual artifacts were found there; most of these are now housed in museums in Munich and Ingolstadt, although some remain at a small museum on the site.

Maoilin (Meeling, Miss Moylan) Irish heroine. Near the town of Duhallow in Co. Cork, there is a rock on which a shape like a handprint was long visible. It was said to have been left there by Maoilin, a girl who escaped from marriage to a man she did not love by rising into the air, flying across the valley, and disappearing into the rock. Another version of the story says that she was stolen away from her human bridegroom by a spectral one who took her to FAIRY-LAND. The rock was long visited on the harvest festival of LUGHNASA, when it was decked with flowers. Some believe Maoilin to be the vestige of an ancient goddess of the land or a FAIRY protector of its prominent families.

Source: MacNeill, Máire. *The Festival of Lughnasa, Parts I and II.* Dublin: Comhairle Bhéaloideas Éireann, 1982, pp. 210–211.

Maol Flidais Irish mythological figure. Like the great GLAS GHAIBHLEANN, the COW who gave endless amounts of MILK, the Maol Flidais was a symbol of abundance. Owned by the wildwood goddess FLIDAIS, this beast may have originally been a goddess, for she is described as equal to her mistress. Not only did she give milk copiously, but her gentle lowing could be heard across the land.

Maponus Welsh hero or god. A minor Welsh and British divinity, his name has been translated as "son of the mother" or "divine youth"; he is connected with the goddess MODRON, "mother." Known from several sculptures that show him as a naked lad holding a lyre, he may be the same as the similarly named god MABON. The Romans equated Maponus with APOLLO, suggesting that he was connected with the arts.

Marcassa Breton heroine. A traditional Breton folktale tells of the beautiful distant castle of the princess Marcassa, where a magical BIRD roosted who held the cure for the mysterious illness of the land's ruler. The bumbling hero, prince Luduenn ("little cinders"), set off to find the bird and thus speed the king's recovery, for his two strapping older brothers had gone forth and never returned. It did not take him long to find the brothers, who were living wildly and well in a distant city, where they stole his little money and turned him out. So Luduenn set off, poor but determined, to find princess Marcassa's palace. And indeed he found the palace, and within it a bird caged in gold, but first he was tempted to steal some magical self-replenishing bread and a kiss from the princess herself.

The kiss impregnated the sleeping princess, and when her son was a year old, she went in search of the father. Encountering the evil brothers, she realized that she was on the right path and that they had stolen her bread from Luduenn. When she reached the palace, she found her magical bird had been so fretful without her that he had worked no HEALING for the king. Once again in her presence, the bird sang joyously, and the king was soon well. When Marcassa told him what she had discovered about Luduenn's older brothers, the king had the dissolute boys killed and installed Marcassa and Luduenn as king and queen. This story has much in common with the Scottish folktale of Brian and DÉR GRÉINE.

Source: Luzel, F. M. *Celtic Folk-Tales from Amorica.* Trans. Derek Bryce. Dyfed, Wales: Llanerch Enterprises, 1985, p. 84.

March (March fab Merchiawn) Welsh hero. The Welsh corollary to king MARK of the legend of TRISTAN and ISEULT, March was called one of the "Three Seafarers of the Island of Britain," where he arrived on a boat from the land of the Norsemen to become his cousin king ARTHUR's occasional adviser.

mare Mythological animal. Although HORSES in general had mythological significance to the Celts, special importance was given to the female horse. The continental horse goddess EPONA was pictured riding on a mare or surrounded by fillies; the Irish goddess MACHA raced horses while pregnant, as though she were a mare herself; the Welsh goddess RHIANNON similarly rode on a magical mare. At UISENACH, the central sacred hill of Ireland, a rampart and ditch have been interpreted as being a horse temple, because beneath the outer ring were found tunnels in the shape of a stallion pursuing a mare.

Myth often diminishes into folklore and superstition. Thus it was with the sacred horse, who lived on after Christianization in the folk belief in the "true mare," the seventh consecutive filly borne to a mare. This lucky animal could not be kidnapped by the FAIRIES, and she could protect her owners from FAIRY KIDNAPPING as well. Where a true mare was foaled, SHAMROCKS grow in her honor.

Marie au Blè French folkloric character. Into Christian times in Valenciennes, at the time of the ancient Celtic harvest feast of LUGHNASA, a girl dressed in white was led through the streets by dancing young men. "Mary of the Wheat" was accompanied by an attendant who carried a white cloth upon which were displayed the first grains of harvested wheat. The festival, now abandoned, appears a late continental survival of Lughnasa.

Source: MacNeill, Máire. *The Festival of Lughnasa, Parts I and II.* Dublin: Comhairle Bhéaloideas Éireann, 1982, p. 387.

Mari Lwyd (Mari Llud) Welsh folkloric figure. In the period between Christmas and January 6—the old New Year's Day—an old HOBBYHORSE tradition was celebrated until relatively recent times in villages throughout South Wales. The head of a horse, said to be the MARE Mari Lwyd and decorated with ribbons and other finery, was carried from house to house by a group that, demanding entry with obscure words, were answered with more verses from within. The horse and her carriers were finally admitted, whereupon celebrations followed. Such "trick-or-treating" typically descends from earlier prophylactic or warding rituals, so the Mari Lwyd may have been a ritual of safety and propitiation of cosmic powers for the year. The modern Welsh poet Dylan Thomas knew of this folklore, which inspired his "Ballad of the Mari Lwyd."

Source: Straffon, Cheryl. *The Earth Goddess: Celtic and Pagan Legacy of the Landscape.* London: Blandford, 1997, p. 77.

Mark Cornish hero. The great romance of TRISTAN and ISEULT tells of a love triangle between that couple and king Mark of Cornwall (occasionally, of Cornouille on the Breton coast). When he was presented with a single strand of hair of dazzling gold, Mark decided that the woman from whose head the hair came was the world's most beautiful—and that he would have her for his bride. Discovering that the woman in question was the Irish princess Iseult, Mark sent his nephew Tristan to bring her to his court. On the journey home, the pair accidentally drank a potent liqueur that had the magical power to make people love until death. Thus bound, Tristan and Iseult could never be happy apart.

Nonetheless, Tristan dutifully brought his beloved to her new husband. When Iseult could not bear to spend her wedding night with Mark, she sent instead her handmaiden, BRANGIEN, who pretended to be the queen and was deflowered by Mark. The fated couple struggled against their love but finally left the court for several years to live together. When they returned, Mark took his wife back without complaint.

Mark is a relatively shadowy and passive figure compared to the active lovers. He is clearly parallel to two other Celtic heroes whose wives similarly left them for younger men: king ARTHUR of Britain, whose queen GUINEVERE preferred the young knight LANCELOT; and the aging Irish hero FIONN MAC CUMHAILL, whose forthright bride GRÁINNE ran off with his underling DIARMAIT. This recurrent plot has recalled to many commentators the motif of a goddess of the land's SOVEREIGNTY choosing a more virile and younger ruler as an older one fades.

Source: Bedier, Joseph. *The Romance of Tristan and Iseult.* Trans. Hilaire Belloc. New York: Vintage Books, 1965.

marriage Ritual and cosmological concept. The current understanding of marriage as a relationship between a man and a woman who have pledged sexual fidelity and economic interdependence for life is relatively new and, even today, limited to only certain regions of the world. As the Celtic world encompassed many lands with differing customs, it is not possible to categorically describe a single rite or tradition of marriage shared by all. A contemporary interpretation of some Celtic traditions as representing greater rights for women within marriage has both adherents and opponents; some believe that where such freedom is found, it derives from the customs of earlier settlers like the PICTS.

Mythologically, marriage often was used as a way of representing the relationship between a king and the land. Joined in a symbolic union with the goddess of the land's SOVEREIGNTY, the king was expected to live righteously, not breaking any of his sacred vows (BUADA) or taboos (see GEIS). Such rectitude would result, it was believed, in the land's being fruitful and the people, thus, well fed and happy.

Marrock Arthurian hero. A werewolf, Marrock could not assume human form unless he had human clothing. His wife, wishing to spend time with her lover, hid Marrock's clothes, forcing him to live as a WOLF in the hills. King ARTHUR encountered him and, realizing he was under an enchantment, brought him home, where Marrock was so friendly to his wife that she relented and returned his clothes. Thereupon, he resumed his humanity and his marriage.

Mars Continental Celtic and British god. When the Roman legions subjugated various Celtic tribal lands, they practiced the INTERPRETATIO ROMANA, calling local divinities by Roman names. Thus we have more than 60 versions of Mars, the Roman god of agriculture who, in later times, became a god of war—under the reasoning that Roman fields needed to be protected by warriors against invaders who might take them over. Whether the Celts saw their own Mars as similarly connecting war and agriculture is not clear, although some inscriptions and sculptures suggest as much, especially those in which Mars is depicted as wearing a warrior's attire but holding a CORNUCOPIA filled with the fruits of the harvest.

Mars is in some cases described as a protector of the people, identified with the god TEUTATES ("ruler of the people"), found in several sites. Other commentators suggest that the Celtic "Mars" may have been a god of the wildwood and/or of HEALING, the latter apparently arising from the image of a warrior fighting off disease.

Many inscriptions and altars to Mars are found through Celtic lands, suggesting that he was a popular divinity or that the divinities subsumed in the Roman god were so. Typical depictions of Mars show him in Celtic military garb, sometimes even wearing a twisted-metal TORC around the neck—an interesting decision given that the Celtic warriors had been defeated by the occupying Romans. In some cases Mars is shown naked, carrying a weapon, a clear reference to the tradition of Celtic warriors going to war without clothing or armor. Another Celtic motif appears in the occasional multiplication of Mars into THREE gods. Mars was never known as a triple god in Rome, but the Celts often emphasized divine power in this symbolic manner.

Mars figures are especially found in Britain and, on the Continent, among the Belgai and the Remi. In some cases a surname is provided for the Mars figure, which has been interpreted as originating in the original Celtic name for the regional or tribal divinity. Some of these names include:

- **Mars Alator.**
- **Mars Albiorix,** "world-king," tribal god of the Albici of Gaul.
- **Mars Beatucadrus,** "bright one" or "comely in slaughter."
- **Mars Braciaca,** possibly a god of grain or ALE.
- **Mars Camulos,** shown with an OAK crown or with ram's horns.
- **Mars Caturix,** "battle-king."

- **Mars Lenus,** a healing SPRING god of Trier in Germany.
- **Mars Lucetius,** "light."
- **Mars Mediocius,** found only in Colchester, England.
- **Mars Mogetius,** whose name appears on two inscriptions from Bourges and Seggau.
- **Mars Mullo** ("mule" or "wall"), a healer depicted with a horned SERPENT.
- **Mars Nabelcus,** known from several inscriptions in France.
- **Mars Rigisamus,** "king of kings."
- **Mars Smertrius,** whose name includes the same syllable for abundance as found in the goddess Rosmetra.
- **Mars Vesontius.**

Mary (Saint Mary)   Christian figure with Celtic resonances. When the Roman legions arrived in Celtic lands, they practiced the INTERPRETATIO ROMANA, whereby indigenous divinities were renamed with Roman names while keeping their original iconography and legends. In the same way, the Roman church adopted and adapted itself to the multiple indigenous religions of Europe by absorbing some of their spiritual visions into its own. Very useful in this project was the figure of the mother of Jesus, the virgin Mary, who assumed the symbols and stories of a number of Celtic and other European MOTHER GODDESSES.

In England a folk belief claims that the entire island was Mary's bridal dowry, provided by her brother, the merchant JOSEPH OF ARIMATHEA, who brought the GRAIL back to Britain after the death of Mary's son Jesus. In some legends Mary herself lived out her life in Britain after the resurrection.

Mary Candle   See MILKING CHARMS.

Mary Morgan (Morrigain)   Breton folkloric figure. This siren or MERMAID was said to haunt the shores off Brittany, singing sweetly to bring sailors to her dangerous rocks. She was especially associated with the Bay of Douaranez, where the legendary princess DAHUT was said to have built her crystal city of YS. Sailors were warned to carry a crucifix or other AMULET with them when sailing past Mary Morgan's rocks.

Math (Math fab Mathonwy)   Welsh hero or god. The fourth branch of the Welsh mythological texts called the *MABINOGION* bears the name of this mythological figure. In it we learn of king Math of Gwynnedd, whose ceremonial footholder GOEWIN was raped. Much of the action of the story revolves around Math's attempts to replace the girl with a qualified applicant, who had to be a virgin in order to keep Math magically safe. The apparently strange demand that Math never set foot on the ground was a common kind of kingly taboo or *GEIS* found in Celtic lands; in Ireland, for instance, the king of Tara was never to spend more than eight nights away from home.

Math's character is a rather shady and even unpleasant one. He was not above conspiring with his nephew GWYDION to reveal the secrets of Gwydion's sister ARIANRHOD; he also collaborated in the building of an artificial bride for Arianrhod's son, LLEU LLAW GYFFES, to thwart the curse that he would never find a wife. The fact that his heir was his nephew, rather than his son, gives support to the theory that MATRILINY, succession through the mother, predominated in ancient Welsh culture.

Source: Gantz, Jeffrey, trans. *The Mabinogion.* New York: Barnes & Noble Books, 1976.

Mathgen   Irish god. A minor member of the TUATHA DÉ DANANN, the magical tribes of the goddess DANU, Mathgen was a magician; he may be connected to the Welsh figure of the magician-king MATH.

Matholwch   Irish hero. In the second branch of the *MABINOGION*, the great compilation of

Welsh myths, we learn of an Irish king who tried to establish tighter bonds with the Celtic peoples across the Irish Sea in Wales, by marrying the beautiful young princess of the land, BRANWEN. Once they were back in Ireland, he treated her poorly because her evil half-brother EFNISIEN had attacked his horses. Despite Branwen's giving birth to their son, GWERN, Matholwch abused her physically and verbally, until her heroic brothers BRÂN THE BLESSED and MANAWYDAN brought an army to free her.

Matholwch set a trap, inviting the warriors from Wales to a banquet where warriors hid, disguised as sacks of grain, all about the dining hall. Efnisien intuited the danger, however, and killed the saboteurs. In the fighting that ensued, Brân and all but seven of the Welsh heroes were killed, though they took all the Irish warriors with them to the grave, including Matholwch. Arriving home in Wales, Branwen died of a broken heart at the carnage brought on by her unhappiness.

Matres See DEAE MATRES.

matriliny (matrilineality) One of the most contentious areas of contemporary research into the Celts is that of gender relations. Were Celtic women freer than others in their time, or is that a projection by scholars imagining a culture without strict gender stereotyping? Those who envision the Celtic world as one in which women had more rights (presumably, more obligations as well as greater power) point out that many mythological heroes in Celtic lands bear their mother's, not their father's, names. In Ireland we find the king of ULSTER, CONCOBAR MAC NESSA, son of his mother NESSA; the king of CONNACHT, AILILL mac Máta, son of the woman Máta; the romantic hero DIARMAIT Ua Duibne, whose name translates as "Dermot, descendant of the ancestral mother Dubinn"; and finally an entire race, the TUATHA DÉ DANANN, "people of the goddess DANU." In Wales we find MABON vab MODRON, "Son, son of Mother." In Wales we also find king MATH, whose throne was inherited by his sister's son (GWYDION,

son of DÔN), who was in turn succeeded by his sister's son LLEU LLAW GYFFES, all suggestive of a matrilineal inheritance.

The tracing of descent through the mother-line rather than patrilineal or father-line succession is not a clear argument for greater rights or powers for women, but it is suggestive of different gender relations during the periods in question. Because many of these figures date from an early mythological strata, it has been proposed that matriliny is a remnant of the cultural organization of the pre-Celtic people called the PICTS.

Source: Dexter, Miriam Robbins. "Queen Medb, Female Autonomy in Ancient Ireland, and Irish Matrilineal Traditions." In Jones-Bley, Karlene, Angela Della Volpe, Miriam Robbins Dexter, and Martin E. Huld, eds. *Proceedings of the Ninth Annual UCLA Indo-European Conference.* Washington, D.C.: Institute for the Study of Man, 1998, pp. 95–122.

Matrona British and continental Celtic goddess. Her name means "mother," and she was mother of the obscure British god MAPONUS, whose name seems to mean nothing more than "son of the mother." Matrona's name survives in the name of the river Marne in France, which formed the border between the settlements of Gaul and those of the Belgae. Celtic RIVER divinities were typically goddesses who embodied not only the life-giving force of the river's WATER but the FERTILITY of the land of the watershed. She may be the same goddess found in Wales as MODRON.

Matronae See DEAE MATRES.

Matter of Britain (Matière de Bretagne) Literary term. This term describes the Arthurian legends that, growing from presumed Celtic roots, became part of the literary heritage of England and, to a lesser extent, France, where some Arthurian material is found in Celtic

Brittany. The figures of LANCELOT and GUINE-VERE, the knights of the ROUND TABLE, the sorceress MORGAN and the magician MERLIN, and king ARTHUR himself are part of this cycle of tales, as are the motifs of the GRAIL quest and the love triangle that destroys a heroic court.

From medieval times, artists and authors have found inspiration in the Matter of Britain, but the Arthurian revival of the 19th century encouraged widespread use of the figures, narratives, and motifs of Camelot. Alfred Lord Tennyson wrote numerous pieces on the subject, notably *Idylls of the King*, while in America the satirist Mark Twain used Merlin as a central figure in *A Connecticut Yankee in King Arthur's Court*. The 20th century began with some relatively straightforward treatments of Arthur, including T. H. White's *The Once and Future King* and *The Sword in the Stone*, while the American poet T. S. Eliot relied upon the related Grail figure of the Fisher King in "The Waste Land." Later, a women's viewpoint was introduced in Marion Zimmer Bradley's popular novel, *The Mists of Avalon*, and its many prequels. Films inspired by the Arthurian material include *Excalibur* by John Boorman, who named his production company after Merlin.

Matus (Matunus)   British divinity. This BEAR deity—possibly a god, possibly a goddess—was honored at Risingham, just north of the great wall that emperor Hadrian built to keep Britain safe from the aggressive tribes of the north. It is possible that Matus was Pictish rather than Celtic.

Maughold (St. Maughold, Machutus)   Manx legendary figure. Early Christian legend on the Isle of MAN tells of this man who, after being converted by ST. PATRICK, was padlocked to a small boat and put out to sea; the key was thrown overboard, where a FISH ate it. Maughold was rescued, but the lock could never be opened until, many years later, a fish was caught and served to him, and it proved to contain the long-lost key. Unlocked at last, he rose to become

bishop of the island. Folkloric motifs in this story, as well as the celebration of Maughold's feast at the old Celtic harvest holiday of LUGH-NASA, suggest that a Christian legend absorbed an earlier pagan one.

Mauher Slieve   Irish mythological site. In the southwestern PROVINCE of MUNSTER, many mountains are named for goddesses (see ÁINE, MIS). In Co. Tipperary, in the center of a group of 12 mountains named for the otherwise obscure goddess ÉBHLINNE, rises a hill called Mauher Slieve, the Mother Mountain, which was a traditional site of celebrations for the Celtic harvest feast of LUGHNASA. Some versions of the *BOOK OF INVASIONS* say that the goddess of the Mother Mountain was FÓDLA, one of Ireland's THREE major earth goddesses.

Mauthe Doog   See BLACK DOG.

Maxen (Macsen, Macsen Wledig)   Welsh hero. An historical king, Maxen was originally a Roman soldier from Spain (possibly of Celtic origin, although that is unclear) who married a Celtic woman named ELEN (Helen) Lwddog after he moved to Britain in ca. 383 C.E. A fine warrior and general, he was proclaimed emperor Magnus Maximus of Rome by his legions, whom he led in an assault on the continental Roman lands and finally upon Rome itself. The emperor Valentinian II left the city when the usurping western emperor arrived, but Theodosius, emperor of the eastern part of the vast Roman territory, met Maxen in battle and defeated him, having him put to death on July 28, 388 C.E. His widow Elen was permitted to return to Wales, where she became the ancestral mother of several dynasties. Maxen appears in Welsh literature in the visionary 12th-century poem, *The Dream of Maxen*.

maypole   Folkloric object and custom. A strong straight sapling, cut down and reerected near the festivals of BELTANE, was a reminder of the life burgeoning in the woods and fields each spring. Dancers wrapped ribbons around the trees and performed elaborate synchronized dancing beneath them (see MORRIS DANCING). The maypole has been seen as a degraded form of the cosmic world TREE.

mead Symbolic drink. A wine made from honey, mead figures in a number of Celtic myths and legends as a drink favored by warriors. Its most consistent mythological association is with the goddess/queen whose name is the same as the drink, MEDB, and who represented the intoxication and danger of KINGSHIP.

Meath See MIDE.

Medb (Maeve, Medbh, Medhbh, Meave) Irish goddess and heroine. From her royal seat at CRUACHAN, the great capital of the western province of CONNACHT, a queen named Medb reigned with great vigor and power. Behind her stands the figure of a goddess, perhaps the goddess of the land whose marriage to the king granted him SOVEREIGNTY over her territory and hedged him about with sacred vows (see *GEIS*) at the same time. As a goddess, Medb is linked with the FIVE fierce figures known collectively as BADB or and sometimes including the MÓRRÍGAN.

At Medb's capital, now Rathcrogan near Tulsk in Co. Roscommon, more than 70 ritual and royal sites of the Celtic Iron Age are still visible, including the nearly circular main HILL-FORT on which it is believed that the local kings went through the ceremony of INAUGURATION. In a huge nearby CAVE with a tiny entrance called OWEYNAGAT, Medb was born of an otherwise obscure woman named CROCHAN Crocderg ("the blood-red cup" or "red cream"). Although originally from the royal hill of TARA, Crochan fled with her mistress, the reborn fairy queen ÉTAIN, from the king EOCHAID, Étain's human husband, who followed in hot pursuit. When

they reached Oweynagat, the pregnant handmaiden so admired the fairy palace or SÍDHE there that Étain made a gift of it and named the area around it after Crochan.

A flight from danger also appears in the story of the princess or priestess ERNE, after whom an important lake and river are named. Medb gave Erne several important treasures, notably her own COMB and casket (both feminine sexual symbols). Just then, a GIANT came from Oweynagat, terrifying Erne and her maidens, who fled as a group toward the mythological waterfall of ASSAROE. They drowned before they reached shelter, their bodies dissolving to become Lough Erne. The story is a common one, appearing near Cruachan in the story of the princess GILE who became Lough Gill, as well as in the stories of RIVER goddesses like BÓAND, SÍNANN, and GARRAVOGUE.

Medb's name means "mead" or "intoxication," which may refer to the cup she offers the king at his inauguration, and/or to the intoxication of battle (both figurative and literal, for mead was provided to Irish warriors before battle). In legend, Medb is fiery and self-willed, sleeping with whomever she chooses for her own pleasure or to gain political advantage through her "friendly thighs" (one of the most famous phrases in the *TÁIN BÓ CUAILNGE*, the great epic of her CATTLE RAID upon ULSTER). She was never without "one man in the shadow of another" (another famous phrase from the *Táin*), and although she kept AILILL mac Máta as her consort, her favored lover was the massively endowed FERGUS mac Róich, whose appetite matched hers and whose name indicates his manliness.

Fergus played an important role in Medb's cattle raid, which began with the so-called pillow-talk scene where Medb lay in bed with Ailill, praising herself and her possessions. Ailill claimed to have more than Medb—a claim that diminished Medb's social status according to BREHON law. When she found that Ailill did, indeed, have in his herd a splendid white BULL she could not match, Medb set out to find its equal. The only such equal was in Ulster, however, where the brown DONN CUAILNGE grazed on the lands of the minor king DÁIRE. (The two bulls were the reincarnations of bitter enemies, fated to cause trouble; see FRIUCH and RUCHT.)

First Medb tried to coax Dáire to loan her the great brown bull for a year, hoping that it would leave her COWS pregnant with astonishing offspring. Dáire overheard Medb's warriors boasting that his cooperation was irrelevant, for they intended to take back the bull even if he refused to lend it. Insulted, Dáire prepared for war. Medb marshaled her armies to march upon Ulster, taking advantage of the CURSE she knew would leave the men of the province unable to defend themselves (see DEBILITY OF THE ULSTERMEN)—a curse leveled upon them by the goddess MACHA in retaliation for their abuse of her during her pregnancy. Knowing her opponents would be writhing with the pains of a woman in labor for four days and five nights as soon as she launched the campaign, Medb set out from Cruachan, marching north and east. She traveled in an open cart with four chariots surrounding her, dressed in all her royal finery.

However, Medb made her plans without figuring on the strength of the hero CÚCHULAINN, who single-handedly defended Ulster against one great Connacht champion after another. While this combat was underway, Medb stole past and kidnapped the bull she needed. Soon the Ulstermen roused from their cursed state and began a massive battle against the forces of Connacht, who were finally driven off.

In perhaps the greatest anticlimax in ancient literature, the two bulls fell upon each other and fought—a fight of such magnitude that it extended across all the fields of Ireland. Although the brown Donn Cuailnge finally killed Ailill's white FINNBENNACH, he himself died not long after limping home to Ulster. Without the white bull, Ailill's possessions then matched Medb's, making her once again equal to her husband. Thus, from Medb's standpoint, the ending is a happy one.

Medb met her own end on the ISLAND of Clothrann in Lough Ree in the River Shannon, a place that was apparently sacred to her. On the island was a WELL in which Medb bathed each morning, apparently thereby renewing her youth and strengthening her power. Her nephew FURBAIDE FERBEND could not forgive Medb for killing his mother, her sister CLOTHRA. Although the island was far from shore, he practiced hurling stones from a slingshot until he was sure of his aim, then flung a ball of dried brains across the water to bring down the great Medb.

Medb may have died on Lough Ree, but she is said to be buried far away, in the great megalithic tumulus of KNOCKNAREA above the town of Sligo. Despite these connections with Connacht, she is also associated with the central province, MIDE, most notably with the hill of TARA, where Rath Medb may have been the site of ancient kingly inaugurations. Under the name of Medb Lethderg ("Maeve Red-Sides") she married one king of Tara after another, showing her to be the great goddess of Sovereignty so important in Irish myth.

Often described as a war goddess or warrior-queen, Medb indeed seems a strong battle leader, quite willing to put her champions in harm's way to gain her will. Her connection to battle is intensified by the fact that she is shadowed, throughout the *Táin*, by the even more frightening figure of the black-winged MÓRRÍGAN, a superhuman bird-woman who foretold the future of warriors as they began to fight. That Oweynagat, the Mórrígan's home, was at Cruachan suggests that the two figures were closely connected in the Irish mythological mind.

Sources: Dexter, Miriam Robbins. *Whence the Goddesses: A Sourcebook*. New York: Pergamon Press, 1990, pp. 91–93; Hull, Eleanor. *The Cuchullin Saga in Irish Literature*. London: David Nutt, 1898, p. liii; Kinsella, Thomas, transl. *The Tain*. Dublin: The Dolmen Press, 1969.

Medocius British god. Known from only one inscription in Colchester, Medocius may have been a local god of the land, a *GENIUS LOCI;* he is associated with the Roman god MARS, so he may have had a warrior aspect, possibly as protector of territory.

Medros Continental Celtic god. This obscure god connected with CATTLE may be a Celtic version of the Persian hero-god MITHRAS; the Persian god was popular among the Roman legionnaires, who brought him to Celtic lands.

megalithic civilization (megalithic culture) Pre-Celtic culture. Across all of the Celtic lands are found great structures made of rock, the work of a pre-Celtic people whose name and culture are obscured by the lack of written documentation. Called megaliths ("big rocks"), these structures give their name to the so-called megalithic civilization of approximately 5000 B.C.E. It is not known whether the monuments found in Ireland and Britain and in parts of the Continent (Brittany and, arguably, Malta) were built by waves of immigrants, possibly bringing new religious conceptions to the areas they invaded, or whether the style of architecture and its attendant religious conceptions spread among people of various cultures and languages.

Megalithic monuments range from a single upright STANDING STONE, called a MENHIR from the Breton word for such objects, to groups of stones that form a PASSAGE GRAVE, DOLMEN (from the Breton *tol men*, "table of stone"), or cromlech (from the apparently contradictory phrase "bent flat stone" in Welsh), to STONE CIRCLES that may surround or incorporate dolmens or menhirs. The size of megalithic structures ranges from the intimate to the immense, with STONEHENGE in Britain and the BRÚ NA BÓINNE in Ireland being the most famous if not the largest, an honor held by the great stone circle at LOUGH GUR.

Many of the monuments are decorated with symbols that have been variously interpreted as sunbursts and stars, water meanders, and other natural forms. Some archaeologists argue that these symbols form a consistent language that permits interpretation of the meanings of the structures—usually as goddess TEMPLES—but that theory is controversial.

Only two statements can be made of the megalith builders without argument. First, they were extraordinary engineers, creating the oldest remaining human structures out of worked and unworked rock. Second, they had an almost unsurpassed knowledge of the stars, for many of their monuments are precisely oriented to a specific constellation, MOON or SUN phase, or other such astronomical point. Thus the great tumulus at Newgrange admits the light of the winter SOLSTICE dawn through a stone transom that allows for the obliquity of the ecliptic, or the earth's wobble; on the same day, the lines of stones (*alinements*) at Carnac in Brittany point to sunrise. By contrast, the great open circle at Stonehenge is oriented toward the summer solstice dawn, and the CAIRN at LOUGHCREW opens to the dawn of both EQUINOXES.

The megalith builders were not Celts. Their monuments, apparently connected to their religious beliefs, were not designed by DRUIDS. Continuing misinformation about the sites' builders has led to demands by revivalist druid societies for access to Stonehenge for MIDSUMMER ceremonies, ceremonies that may not actually represent those of the Celtic priesthood.

If the Celts did not build the great stone structures, it is likely—although by no means proven—that they used them for ceremonies. If the impressive size and moving architecture of the monuments inspires contemporary worshipers, there is no reason to believe ancient peoples did not respond the same way. What is clear is that these great ancient sites became embedded in folklore in Celtic lands, where they were described as haunted by FAIRIES. Many folktales describe mystical events that happened within or around such monuments; it is impossible to tell whether such stories contain kernels of ancient lore from the time of the builders, actual historical experiences, or a fertile and poetic imagination.

The Celts, who honored deity out-of-doors and in multiple sites, would have found the megalithic monuments suitable for private or public rituals. That such religious behavior continued through Celtic times and into the period of Christianization is suggested by continued edicts of the church against such worship, together with traditionally Celtic rituals at WELLS and SPRINGS. The Councils of Arles (443–452), Tours (567), and Toledo (681 and 693) all decried worship of stones in ruined sanctuaries; as late as 1410, British archbishops were still calling for elimination of rituals at the sites.

At the same time, religious credit accrued to those who damaged or destroyed the ancient stones. Superstitious belief in the stones' powers had kept them standing long after their builders had passed away—indeed, it does so today—but during the Middle Ages, priests and their followers attacked many stones. One of the most significant reminders of this period is the immense stone phallus called Longe Pierre or Long Peter in Brittany, which would have stood some three stories tall but now lies broken into several pieces on the ground. That so many stone circles and other vestiges of the megalithic civilization can still be seen in Celtic lands today testifies to the continuing power the stone monuments hold over the spiritual imagination.

Sources: Aalen, F.H.A. *Man and the Landscape in Ireland.* London: Academic Press, 1978; Bord, Janet, and Colin Bord. *The Secret Country: An interpretation of the folklore of ancient sites in the British Isles.* New York: Walker and Co., 1976; Cooney, Gabriel. *Landscapes of Neolithic Ireland.* London: Routledge, 2000; Crawford, E.G.S. *The Eye-Goddess.* Chicago: Delphi Press, 1994; Gimbutas, Marija. *The Language of the Goddess.* London: Thames & Hudson, 1989; Grinsell, Leslie V. *Folklore of Prehistoric Sites in Britain.* London: David & Charles, 1976; O'Sullivan, Muiris. *Megalithic Art in Ireland.* Dublin: Country House, 1993.

Meg Mullach (Maug Moulach, Maggie Moloch)   Scottish folkloric figure. One of the many BROWNIES who aided humans with their ceaseless work, Meg took care of the castle of Tullochgorm, which belonged to the Grant family. Although Meg looked like a small child, she had an impressive head of HAIR, whence she was sometimes called Hairy Meg. (Some versions of her story say that she had hairy hands and that she sometimes reached down chimneys to steal children.) Once she helped a stingy farmer who, realizing that she would do all the work of the farm for free, fired all his farmhands; Meg responded by asking for her wages too. As it was forbidden to offer recompense to a brownie (see LAYING THE FAIRIES), Meg was within her rights when she disappeared upon receiving her wages.

Meiche (Mechi, Merca)   Irish hero. The great war goddess MÓRRÍGAN had one son, Meiche, who had THREE hearts; coiled up within each of his hearts were three SERPENTS that, if allowed to grow to maturity, would break forth from his body and devastate the land. MAC CÉCHT, a warrior of the TUATHA DÉ DANANN, averted the disaster by killing Meiche and throwing the burned remnants of his body into the Barrow River.

Source: Gwynn, Edward. *The Metrical Dindshenchas.* Part II. Vol. IX. Royal Irish Academy, Todd Lecture Series. Dublin: Hodges, Figgis, and Co., Ltd., 1906, p. 63.

Meilge   Irish hero. When Meilge killed a fawn that turned out to be the bewitched maiden AIGE, her brother FAIFNE punished him by uttering a SATIRE so fierce that boils popped out on Meilge's face. Meilge replied in bloody fashion: He had the poet-satirist killed.

Meleagant (Melwas, Meleagraunce, Mellyagraunce)   Arthurian hero. In Arthurian legend, a king or giant named Meleagant kidnapped queen GUINEVERE and held her against her will until the beloved knight LANCELOT came to her rescue (or, in some versions, until a saint named Gildas talked him into freeing her). In order to reach her, Lancelot had to cross a strange bridge that went either underwater by a long route or above the water on a knife-edge. Eager to be at his lover's side, Lancelot took the upper track, wounding himself horribly in the process. In Guinevere's chamber, he joined her in bed, leaving the sheets bloodied. He failed to consider that his friend KAY, also wounded seriously, was asleep in the same room. Although Lancelot crept away before dawn, Meleagant found the blood and charged Kay with sexually assaulting the queen. Too weak to defend himself, Kay was defended by Lancelot, who then freed Guinevere. Meleagant is called the king of Somerset, the SUMMER LAND, which makes it probable that he was originally either a god or a FAIRY king.

Mellts   Welsh god. This obscure Welsh god appears to have been an ancestral divinity.

Melor   (St. Melor)   British and continental Celtic hero. Many SAINTS in Celtic lands are disguised versions of Celtic heroes and gods, for the migration of mythological motifs from earlier times to later figures is a constant in human culture. In Cornwall and Brittany we find stories of St. Melor, a supposed early medieval priest who was murdered and decapitated under the orders of his evil uncle.

As his assailant carried away the severed HEAD, it began to speak. The murderer grew faint with fear as Melor instructed him to strike the ground with his staff. Pure water gushed out, while the staff took root and flowered into a lovely fragrant tree. As a result, healing WELLS in forests were dedicated to St. Melor; there are dozens of such shrines in Brittany as well as a famous one at Linkinhorne in Cornwall. Such tree-shaded wells were HEALING shrines; Melor appears to have stepped in for an earlier healing god or goddess, permitting pagan rituals to continue under Christian protection.

Melusine   (Melusina)   Continental Celtic folkloric figure. Melusine was the daughter of a beautiful water FAIRY named Pressina who, according to a French folktale, chose a human man for her mate. Common to such unions was a vow demanded by the wife—in this case, that the husband should never see her while she was delivering a child. As with other such reckless humans, Pressina's husband grew too excited when he heard she had delivered triplets. Rushing into the birth chamber, he confronted an angry woman who reminded him of his promise, then disappeared with the children. (In some versions of the story, Pressina took the form of a huge SERPENT to give birth.)

The eldest of Pressina's THREE daughters was Melusine; her sisters were Meliot and Palatina. All were reared on a magical ISLAND typical of the Celtic OTHERWORLD. Melusine grew up angry at her father for breaking his promise and therefore denying them the comforts of human life. When she grew old enough to take action, she orchestrated a raid on her father's castle, confining him and all his attendants inside a magical mountain. When Melusine returned home, she did not find her mother happy at this vengeful action; instead, Pressina cursed her to become a snake for part of every Sunday.

Like her mother, Melusine finally found love with a human man, Raymond of Poitou. And like her mother, she put limitations on her husband: in this case, that he never enter her rooms on Sunday. Of course human husbands never keep such a vow, and when Raymond saw his part-snake wife one Sunday, she disappeared in fury at his betrayal and thereafter haunted his family as a kind of BANSHEE.

Melwas   See MELEAGANT.

Men-an-tol   Cornish mythological site. Near the village of Lanyon in Cornwall, a megalithic monument was famous for curing childhood ailments as well as spinal deformities. The huge round boulder with a hole in its center was the site of a ritual in which the afflicted were pulled through the stone, naked, and then rolled on the grass THREE (or three times three) times. The stone can also be used by the hale and healthy for DIVINATION, for if one put two brass PINS on the rock and asked a question, the dancing pins would tell the answer.

See also HEALING STONES.

menhir   Mythological and folkloric site. Often called a STANDING STONE, the menhir is a single, usually enormous, stone erected upright in the ground by the people of the mysterious MEGA-LITHIC CIVILIZATION some 6,000 years ago. Sometimes the stones were "dressed" or worked into a specific shape, but usually they were erected without alteration. There is considerable speculation about how ancient people moved the stones from their original location, sometimes many miles from their eventual homes, and engineered them into place.

Mercury   British and Continental Celtic god. With the arrival of the Roman legions, scores of Celtic gods who were radically localized—found only in one place or among one tribal group—were renamed after Roman gods. Whether the many gods renamed "Mercury" were originally similar, and what the god's original powers were, is difficult to determine. Caesar claimed that Mercury was the god most worshiped among all those of the Celts and that he was the most often depicted in art. Under his Roman name he remained popular among the Celtic peoples of both the Continent and Britain.

Celtic Mercury was shown with a COCK, ram, or GOAT, all symbols of virility and masculine prowess; he was never a warrior like the Celtic MARS, but rather a god of commerce and prosperity. He carried a bag or purse of money, suggesting success at transactions. Although always shown in Roman dress, Mercury often wore a TORC, the twisted neck-piece that indicated prestige and power. Occasionally the Celtic Mercury was imagined as a messenger or herald

of the gods, although this typically Roman vision was rare in comparison to Mercury's importance as a god of traders and commercial prosperity.

At times the winged double-snake caduceus, a classical emblem still used by doctors and pharmacists, was shown as one of Mercury's attributes, suggesting powers of HEALING. The god was often connected with ROSMERTA, a healing water goddess who was never Romanized. The couple was especially worshiped in Braint, a healing shrine in Gaul.

Several gods have been argued as the original of the Romanized Mercury. TEUTATES, the god of the tribe, and ESUS, the woodland god, are both described with the name Mercury by the poet Lucan. Some local names survive including:

- **Mercury Artaios,** "bear" or "ploughed land."
- **Mercury Arvernorix, Avernus.**
- **Mercury Cimiacinus,** a god of roads in Britain.
- **Mercury Cissonius.**
- **Mercury Cultor,** "the farmer."
- **Mercury Dumaitis, Dumias,** "hill" or "mound."
- **Mercury Iovantucarus.**
- **Mercury Moccus,** possibly "PIG," known from one inscription in France.
- **Mercury Visucius.**

Merlin   (Myrddin, Myrdinn, Merddyn, Merddin, Merlinus)   Arthurian hero. Aside from the triangulated lovers LANCELOT, GUINEVERE, and king ARTHUR, the great magician Merlin is the most renowned character in the Arthurian legends. He was the power behind the throne, creating and maintaining the fair realm of CAMELOT. Even before Arthur's citadel was built, Merlin was engaged in adding to Britain's architectural heritage, for it was he who erected STONEHENGE on Salisbury plain, raising the STONE CIRCLE from its original site in Ireland and flying it by MAGIC across the sea to its present site.

Merlin's gifts were recognized early. As a boy he was chosen to become a foundation sacrifice—a HUMAN SACRIFICE offered to stabilize the foundation of a new building and to protect it, through his death, from shifts in the earth that could damage the structure—but he saved himself by going into a visionary trance and uttering an extended PROPHECY about the land's future rulers and challenges.

The vision was centered on a great DRAGON that the boy Merlin saw in the foundation's pit. That dragon led him to envision the greatest king the land would ever know. Arthur would never have been conceived without Merlin's assistance, for he transformed UTHUR PEN-DRAGON into the semblance of count GORLOIS of Cornwall so that Arthur's father could have his way with beautiful but loyal IGRAINE, Gorlois's wife. In one night of passion with the disguised Uther, Igraine conceived the future king; Uther then killed Gorlois and took Igraine as his wife.

When Arthur was old enough to claim his inheritance, Merlin led him to a sword in a huge stone; this unnamed weapon is not to be confused with EXCALIBUR, the magical gift of the mysterious LADY OF THE LAKE that later kept Arthur safe from being wounded in battle. The sword in the stone could only be removed by the rightful king. Though many had tried, none had succeeded in removing it from its rocky prison, but with one tug, Arthur freed it and revealed his destiny, as Merlin knew he would.

Merlin served as Arthur's confidante and adviser during the happy years at Camelot when the ROUND TABLE knights quested for glory. Despite his magic, Merlin either did not see or could not stop the erosion of Camelot's power and prestige, nor Arthur's eventual defeat. Merlin himself never died but lives on somewhere in an OTHERWORLD where he was trapped by his lover, the FAIRY QUEEN or sorceress VIVIANE (sometimes, MORGAN). Some tales say that Viviane feared he might be attracted to other women, others that she wished to ensure his immortality. Using the very enchantments he had taught her, Viviane trapped Merlin in a tower or encased him in a great TREE in the magical forest of BROCÉLIANDE, where he continues to live, immobile and powerless.

Behind this figure of literature and legend is the ghost of an earlier, possibly divine, figure called Myrdinn, after whom the island of Britain was called Clas Myrdinn or "Myrdinn's enclosure." In Welsh sources, Myrdinn was said to have been a warrior who, having gone mad (perhaps the basis for the related figure of MYRDINN WYLLT) from the horrors that he witnessed at the battle of Arfderydd, fled to Scotland, where he meditated until he attained the power of prophecy. Some argue that Myrdinn was the SUN divinity worshiped at Stonehenge; that argument assumes the deity was male rather than female, an unproven assertion. Upon the arrival of Christianity, Myrdinn was said to have taken the treasures of the land and nine BARDS and gone into retirement in an island off Wales.

Source: Geoffrey of Monmouth. *Histories of the Kings of Britain.* London: J. M. Dent and Sons, 1912, pp. 113 ff.

mermaid (Merrow, Morrough, Moruach, Moruadh, Maighdean-mara, Ben-Varrey, Mary Morgan)   Continental and insular folkloric figure. Half-human, half-fish beings are found in the folklore of all Celtic lands, from the west of Ireland across Scotland and England to the coasts of France. These figures most often appeared as female, although male merfolk are occasionally known. They had much in common with other half-human beings such as SWAN MAIDENS and SEAL people but had special powers as well.

A mermaid was a kind of sea FAIRY, an OTH-ERWORLD creature who swam in shallow coastal waters, often with the intention of drawing humans into the brine and to their deaths. In some tales, mermaids did so because they found human men irresistibly attractive; in these tales they are typical FAIRY LOVERS. Their sweet singing lulled people to sleep wherever water could lap over them so they drowned; these figures may be confused with the classical siren, a death-messenger who appears as a bird as well as a singing maiden.

Unlike the more common fairy mistresses, mermaids were not necessarily lovely. Some had GREEN teeth or RED noses or PIG eyes. Their hair might be green and scraggly, made up of seaweed or kelp. Despite this, they seemed to attract enough men that sailors were warned to keep watch for them; if they spotted you before you noticed them, you were invariably captured. Mermaids were said to be fond of brandy; they worked in teams to wreck ships carrying it so that they might forage among the wreckage for unbroken bottles. (The red nose many mermen sport was attributed to excessive indulgence.)

Every mermaid wore a little cap called a *COHULEEN DRUITH*, which permitted her to safely swim below the waves and to live in reefs without danger. Should a human man wish to take a mermaid as his wife, it was important to steal the cap and keep it safely hidden. (Similarly, Swan Maidens' feather cloaks and Seal Women's fur coats had to be kept from their view.) If a mermaid found her cap, she put it on and escaped from land, leaving husband and children behind, without a thought or a second glance. As long as she remained ashore, however, the mermaid was a wonderful wife: industrious, loving, sensuous, making the risk of her loss worth taking and her abandonment devastating.

All the coastal Celtic lands had their own versions of the mermaid. In Cornwall the mermaid cloaks an ancient sea-goddess, pictured holding a mirror, possibly influenced by classical interpretations of the seaborne Aphrodite, Greek goddess of lust and love. The Mermaid of Zennor is Cornwall's most famous manifestation; in a small coastal village in Penwith, a girl emerged from the ocean to lure the best singer from the church's choir, Matthew Trenwalla, down to the depths to share her home and her love. Her image can still be seen in the town's church. In Brittany the mermaid was apt to steal away young men and keep them imprisoned underwater, which invariably resulted in the boys' death from drowning.

In England mermaids were associated with freshwater as well as the ocean; the LAKE MAIDENS did not live in running water but only in pools and other still water. The first syllable in their name, which appears to mean "sea" (from the French, *mer*), in fact comes from the Anglo-Saxon *meer* for "lake" or "inland sea."

Manx mermaid tales emphasized their irresistible seductiveness. They lured potential lovers by holding out coral, pearls, and other sea riches—even jewels stolen from ships they wrecked. If a potential mate came to his senses before leaping to certain death and ran away from the alluring mermaid, she heaved stones at his departing figure. If she struck him, he was doomed: even though safely on dry land, he died shortly thereafter.

In Scotland the Maighdean-mara was a half-fish, half-woman who appeared on offshore rocks late at night or near dawn, combing her splendid long HAIR (see COMB). From a distance she looked entirely human, but upon further acquaintance it was clear she had no legs, only a fish-tail. That tail could, if the mermaid desired, be shaken off, making her appearance entirely human. She could then be very helpful to humans, which was not generally the case with her kind.

The Scottish islands are rich in mermaid folklore. On the Isle of Skye fair-haired people were said to descend from mermaids; members of the Morrow, MacMorrow, MacCodrums, and MacMurray families were their living relatives. In Orkney, off the northern coast of Scotland, a mermaid was recorded to have appeared in the sea in the 1890s, her milk-white body, long arms, and unnaturally tiny head visible from shore. In the Hebrides the mermaid did not sport a magical cap as in other lands; instead she had a magical belt that had to be stolen to tame her. Her descendants were said to have the gift (or curse) of foreseeing who would die at sea. In the Shetlands many people believed themselves descended from mermaids, pointing to a small membrane between fingers and toes (actually a natural, although unusual, physiological mutation) as proof.

In Brittany the mermaid appeared as a siren, luring men to their deaths in treacherous waters. Their leader was the pagan princess DAHUT, who floated above her submerged city of YS and sang beautifully to passing sailors. Should a man venture toward her, however, he drowned in the wild ocean waves. Dahut, whose legend describes her murderous love for men, may have been a mermaid before being depicted as a princess, or the opposite may be true. In some parts of Brittany it was said that all mermaids are daughters of Dahut.

In Ireland the moruadh or moruach ("sea-maid") was known from the earliest literature, for in the BOOK OF INVASIONS mermaids played in the waves as the invading MILESIANS approached the shore. The *Annals of the Four Masters* describes mermaids as GIANTS: 195 feet long, with fingers seven feet long and hair measuring 18 feet. The moruadh was a typically sportive and seductive creature who regularly mated with humans; no members of the Lee family ever drowned, because they were descendants of mermaids.

Sir Walter Scott, in *The Bride of Lammermoor,* related the tradition that drinking from a mermaid's WELL was fatal, in this case to those of the House of Ravenswood. The mermaid's most famous literary appearance was in the somewhat sadistic story of "The Little Mermaid" by Danish author Hans Christian Andersen, who described the pains a mermaid underwent to have her tail cut into legs; this was an invention of the author and never part of folklore, but it became well known as a result of the Disney film of the same name. A contemporary vision of the mermaid appears in the film *Local Hero* by Scottish director William Forsythe, in which an elusive mermaid appears as a goddess of SOVEREIGNTY who protects her land.

Sources: Croker, T. Crofton. *Fairy Legends and Traditions of the South of Ireland.* London: William Tegg, 1862, p. 180; Kennedy, Patrick. *Legendary Fictions of the Irish Celts.* New York: Benjamin Blom, 1969, p. 121; MacGregor, Alasdair Alpin. *The Peat-Fire Flame: Folk-Tales and Traditions of the Highlands & Islands.* Edinburgh: The Moray Press, 1937, pp. 105 ff; McKay, John G. *More West Highland Tales.* Vol. 2. Scottish Anthropological and Folklore Society. Edinburgh: Oliver and Boyd, 1969, pp. 117 ff; Spence, Lewis. *The Minor Traditions of British Mythology.* New York: Benjamin Blom, Inc., 1972, pp. 42, 51; Straffon, Cheryl. *The Earth Goddess: Celtic and Pagan Legacy of the Landscape.* London: Blandford, 1997, p. 95.

merman (Dinny-Mara, Dooinney Marrey, Dunya Mara) Irish and Scottish folkloric figure. Although the half-fish FAIRY creatures of the sea were usually female, there are occasional descriptions of mermen in literature and folklore. Unlike the corresponding female, the merman was rarely attractive, having piggy eyes and a bright RED nose from living on brandy salvaged from wrecked ships. Their breath was also unsavory because they enjoyed dining on raw fish. According to the early British historian Holinshed, a merman was captured alive during the reign of England's King John; dubbed the Wild Man of Oxford, he did not live long in captivity.

Merry Maidens British folkloric site. A number of STONE CIRCLES in Britain bear this name. Typically, local legend says the stones were originally women who, dancing on a Sunday, were turned to stone for their blasphemy. In some cases the stones are called "nine maidens," which may refer not to their number but to "noon"— the ninth hour in the ecclesiastical day, whence 'nones,' the midday service—for the hour at which they were transformed.

At Stanton Drew a wedding dance was once so merry that all of Saturday night passed without anyone's noticing. As Sunday morning drew near, a black-clad stranger appeared and took the fiddle from the chief musician. The music the stranger played was impossible to resist. Even the weary, and even those who could not dance, leapt to their feet. On and on the dancers circled, until at dawn they all turned to stone. The fiddler—who was of course the DEVIL—promised to come back to play for them again, but, devils being devils, he did not, leaving them petrified to this day.

The story of dancers being turned to stone is found in many variations: STONEHENGE is sometimes called the GIANT'S DANCE, suggesting an ancient story in which the stones are transformed dancers; in Devon a man named Ragged Dick was turned to stone with his companions when they danced at an inappropriate time; and in the Shetland Islands trolls were turned to stone at Haltadans ("stop the dancing") together with their musician when the sun rose, a clear survival of Scandinavian mythology.

Although dancing was the usual activity punished by petrification, other actions could bring the same result: Doing WITCHCRAFT brought the stony paralysis on Long Meg and her Daughters in Cumbria, while doing farm chores (shearing sheep, digging turnips) on Sunday caused other people to be turned to stone.

Mesca Ulad See INTOXICATION OF THE ULSTERMEN.

Mesgedhera (Mesgeara) Irish hero. This Irish warrior was better known after death than before, for it was a "brain ball" made from his scooped-out brains mixed with lime that severely injured the great king of ULSTER, CONCOBAR MAC NESSA, when hurled by an opponent. The brain ball lodged in Concobor's head, and although the king survived the wound, it led to his death years later when the ball shook loose.

Mess Buachalla (Mes Buachalla) Irish goddess. When the FAIRY QUEEN or goddess ÉTAIN eloped with her fated lover, the fairy king MIDIR, her human husband EOCHAID Airem set off in hot pursuit of the pair. By the time he caught them at Midir's stronghold of BRÍ LÉITH, Étain had given birth to a girl, a daughter conceived with Eochaid. When Eochaid demanded his wife back, Midir responded with a fairy trick: He sent out 50 identical women, one of whom was Étain while the rest were bewitched to look just like her.

True love sees even through fairy GLAMOURs, and a true lover would have been able to tell Étain from the others, but Eochaid was more interested in having a queen to assure him the throne of TARA than in Étain herself. Thus he was unable to tell his real wife from the 49 enchanted versions of her. He picked a woman and took her back to Tara, where she reigned, looking exactly like the lost queen. She was in fact his own daughter, who eventually went mad with the knowledge of their incest. She raved about the countryside, living in the open, for which she gained the name of Mess Buachalla, "the herdswoman" or "The cow herd's fosterling."

Another version of the story says that she was the daughter of Étain and CORMAC, king of ULSTER, who ordered her killed because he wanted a son as heir. But so sweet was the baby that the warriors ordered to carry out the deed left her instead with the herdsman of the high king, Eterscél, whence she got her name. She grew to a woman of great beauty and wed the high king, but not before mating with a bird god named NEMGLAN, by whom she conceived the king CONAIRE.

Source: Gwynn, Edward. *The Metrical Dindshenchas.* Part II. Vol. IX. Royal Irish Academy, Todd Lecture Series. Dublin: Hodges, Figgis, and Co., Ltd., 1906.

Miach Irish god. Son of the physician god DIAN CÉCHT and brother of the herbalist AIRMID, Miach was himself a brilliant doctor and magician who made skin grow around the silver hand of king NUADA, who had been wounded in the great second battle of MAG TUIRED and had thus lost his throne. Dian Cécht had crafted a cunning hand of silver, one that worked just like a real hand, but it was not sufficient to remove the taboo against a BLEMISHED KING. Only Miach's magical healing restored Nuada as king.

Alas for Miach, his brilliance brought him no glory, but death at the hands of his envious father. Because Dian Cécht had tried and failed to heal Nuada, he could not tolerate his son's success. Miach's HEALING powers did not cease with death, for the most powerful herbs in the world grew up on his grave. Airmid tended them until they were ready to harvest, then classified them according to the good they would bring to humanity. Dian Cécht again stepped in, however, scrambling the categories so that the healing knowledge was lost to humankind.

Michael   See ST. MICHAEL.

Midac   Irish hero. From the land of the Danes once came a warrior, Colga of the Hard Weapons, who was offended that Ireland was the only seagirt island not under his control. His invasion brought him against the heroic warriors called the FIANNA, who, despite being outnumbered, defeated Colga's men. Colga himself fell beneath the weapons of OSCAR, one of the greatest of the Fianna.

Colga had brought his young son, Midac, with him to Ireland. The Fianna's leader, FIONN MAC CUMHAILL, decided that rather than kill the boy as an enemy, he should be brought to ALMU and reared as an Irishman. And so he was, but he could not shake his fury at seeing his father killed, and he quietly plotted revenge.

Fionn's men noticed that the boy was sullen and distant, and at length prevailed upon Fionn to send him away. Giving Midac rich lands in counties Limerick and Clare, Fionn also bestowed upon the young man CATTLE and servants so that he would want for nothing. Fionn sent him away and gave little more thought to the boy.

For 14 years, Midac lived peacefully enough near the bright waters of the Shannon. Then the Fianna came hunting on KNOCKFIERNA, a FAIRY hill near Midac's land. A noble warrior approached them, dressed like a Danish warrior, and demanded that Fionn answer some riddling poems. Fionn, who was as gifted with wit as with

strength, quickly saw through the riddles, but he failed to notice the identity of the young man, whom other members of his band immediately knew to be Midac. His identity revealed, Midac invited the band back to his palace for a banquet.

That palace, surrounded by magical ROWAN trees, was a splendid sight—but it was silent and unoccupied. Still undeterred, Fionn entered the palace and made himself comfortable in the grand banquet hall. Midac entered, stared at them, and departed without a word. It was then that Fionn and his warriors realized that a trap had been set; they had been deceived by a GLAMOUR and were really being held hostage in a crude shack. One after another of the Fianna warriors came to their rescue, with DIARMAIT finally lopping off Midac's head.

Fionn was not free, however, for a CURSE had been placed on him that he could not leave Midac's palace until the blood of THREE foreign kings was sprinkled on its soil. And so Diarmait went back, to do battle with three armies and their kings. He was so strong and valorous that, despite being vastly outnumbered, he was able to decapitate all three kings and drag their HEADS into Midac's palace; as soon as the kings' blood struck the floor, it turned back into a rude shack. The story of entrapment in a bewitched palace is a common one in folklore.

Midas of the Mountains, King   See MIDIR.

Mide (Meath)   Irish geographical division; Irish hero. Ancient Ireland was divided into the four PROVINCES still recognized today: LEINSTER in the east, MUNSTER in the southwest, CONNACHT in the west, and ULSTER in the northeast. In addition, there was a fifth province, Mide or Meath, which was not of this world but was instead a mysterious and elusive center point. This corresponds with an Indo-European vision of the world as divided into four physical districts, with the invisible center as the fifth.

During the reign of the historical HIGH KING Tuathal Teachmhair (130–160 C.E.), a county near the center of the island was named Meath, and it is still called "royal Meath" because the island's political center, the hill of TARA, lay within it. The original Mide, however, was not a geographical concept but a spiritual one. The word *Mide* means "neck" as well as "middle" and so has been interpreted as the point at which the abstract idea of the land's SOVEREIGNTY (symbolically, the HEAD) attaches to the physical land itself (symbolically, the body). That joining was said to have occurred on the hill of UISNEACH in the island's center, and even more precisely at a great cracked boulder on the hill, the STONE OF DIVISIONS, in what is now Co. Westmeath.

According to the *Dindshenchas*, the place-poetry of Ireland, Mide was a person as well as a place. A DRUID and son of the otherwise unknown Brath, he was fostered by the goddess of the land, ÉRIU, and lit the first fire on or near Uisneach. The fire blazed for seven years, fed by gifts from all of Ireland's provinces. In the seventh year, other druids objected aloud to keeping Mide's fire ablaze, so he gathered them together and cut out their tongues, which he buried in the hill. He then sat above their tongues, and his teacher, the woman druid GAINE, named the place Uisneach, "over somewhat."

Sources: Dames, Michael. *Mythic Ireland.* London: Thames and Hudson, 1992; Gwynn, Edward. *The Metrical Dindshenchas.* Part II. Vol. IX. Royal Irish Academy, Todd Lecture Series. Dublin: Hodges, Figgis, and Co., Ltd., 1906, p. 43; Rees, Alwyn, and Brinley Rees. *Celtic Heritage: Ancient Tradition in Ireland and Wales.* London: Thames and Hudson, 1998, pp. 118 ff.

Midir   Irish fairy king or god. In one of the most romantic tales of ancient Ireland, the FAIRY king Midir fell in love with the beautiful ÉTAIN. Unluckily, he was already married to the jealous DRUID FUAMNACH, who cast a spell on her rival. Étain immediately turned into a fly—a beautiful fly, but a fly nonetheless. In this form she flew

about until she accidentally drowned in a glass of wine.

A princess drank the glass of wine and soon found herself pregnant (see PREGNANCY THROUGH DRINKING). Her child was the reborn Étain, who grew up to be just as beautiful as in her earlier incarnation. She had no memory of her earlier life as Midir's beloved, and so she married the king of TARA, EOCHAID Airem. Midir had never forgotten her, however, and set about gaining back his beloved.

He arrived at Tara and challenged the king to a game of *FIDCHELL*, with the prize being a kiss from Étain. As he kissed her, memory flooded back to Étain, and she remembered her earlier life as Midir's beloved. Together, they flew away through the skylight at Tara, joined by a golden chain.

In addition to this romantic tale, Midir also appears in the story of the movement of his people, the TUATHA DÉ DANANN, from the surface of Ireland to a parallel world underground. When the father of the gods, the DAGDA, decided to step down from his leadership of the tribe, his son BODB DERG was selected to replace him. Only Midir—called "the proud"—refused to accept the will of the other gods and launched a war against them. Not only did he not win his goal, but the bloodshed caused the other gods to leave the surface world to hide in their fairy palaces or SÍDHES. Midir lived thereafter in his own sídhe, that of BRÍ LÉITH—Slieve Callory or Ardagh Hill, in western Co. Longford, where he survives in local folklore as Midas, a giant who steals children who walk past his hidden palace.

Source: Gregory, Lady Augusta. *Gods and Fighting Men: The Story of the Tuatha De Danaan and of the Fianna of Ireland.* New York: Oxford University Press, 1970, pp. 88 ff.

Midsummer (Midsummer eve)   Calendar festival. The Celts did not celebrate the SOLSTICES (longest and shortest day of the year) nor the EQUINOXES (days of equal light and darkness in spring and fall) but rather the days in the center of each season (see IMBOLC, BELTANE, LUGHNASA, SAMHAIN). Nonetheless, as the Celts encountered earlier peoples who used the solar pivot-points as CALENDAR feasts, they adopted rituals to mark those days. In addition, the change from the Julian to the Gregorian calendar dislocated some of the old Celtic holidays from their original dates, so that some Lughnasa harvest rituals migrated to become midsummer festivals near the end of June.

The day called Midsummer is not technically the middle of summer at all, but actually the season's beginning on June 21, the day when the SUN is at the closest point to the northern hemisphere that it will be all year and when night is considerably less than day. In some Celtic lands, as in Scotland and Ireland, daylight lasts well into the evening hours on the summer solstice, with as little as five or six hours of darkness; dancing and feasting were common at that time.

In England, girls went out to STONE CIRCLES and whispered the names of their favored young men to the stones, which were said to predict the future on that day. It was also useful to gather the seeds of ferns, to be used in potions of invisibility, and to sow hemp, to be used to see portents, on this day. In Cornwall, girls left their underwear turned inside out and watched, at midnight, for a ghostly form to appear and turn it right, thus finding out the identity of their future husbands. Alternatively, they could pluck a rose, tie it up in a bag, and save it until Christmas, at which time if it were worn to church, the faded rose would irresistibly attract the groom-to-be.

Sources: Briggs, Katharine M. *The Folklore of the Cotswolds.* London: B. T. Batsford Ltd., 1974, p. 14; Hunt, Robert. *Cornish Customs and Superstitions.* Truro: Tor Mark Press, n.d.

midwife Folkloric motif. The midwife who stood at the door of birth—which was, in the past, often the door of death as well—was once a powerful figure. Usually a woman with knowledge of HEALING herbs and medicinal techniques, she was among the Celts also believed to have the power of PROPHECY, a power granted midwives in many other cultures as well, presumably because they saw patterns in the birth that continued throughout the child's life.

Midwives also had a special sort of second sight that permitted them to discover when FAIRIES were stealing human children. A midwife traveling to a late-night birth might encounter such fairies intent on kidnapping; arriving at the home of the laboring mother, she would discover that the child was dead, stolen by those she had encountered. Legend tells of midwives who traveled to the OTHERWORLD to steal back such infants.

Midwives were—with poets and musicians, babies and lovers—the people most likely to be victims of FAIRY KIDNAPPING, for their specialized knowledge was useful to those of the Otherworld. Fairy children were often born weak and in need of intensive care in order to survive. Midwives, unlike others stolen by the fairies, were usually returned to this world unharmed and lived a healthy life thereafter.

Midwinter See NOLLAIG.

Míl (Míl Despaine, Milesius, Míle Easpain) See MILESIANS.

Milesians Irish mythological race. In the Irish mythological history, the *BOOK OF INVASIONS*, we read of the descendants of a hero named Míl Despaine—probably a name invented by the mythological historians from the Latin term "miles Hispaniae" or "soldier of Spain." This mythological ancestor was of the line of the biblical Noah through his son Japheth, whose descendants wandered through SCYTHIA and Egypt before arriving in Spain. One ancestor, Fénius the Ancient, was a consultant on the Tower of Babel and the only person who understood all the cacophony of language spoken there, while his descendant GOIDEL invented the Irish language by mixing them all together. The same Goidel was bitten by a snake in Egypt and was healed by Moses, who prophesied that his descendants would find a place to live without any such noxious SERPENTS.

Leaving Egypt, the ancestors of the Irish returned to Scythia, where they found themselves at odds with those who had stayed behind. The wanderers thus set out again, on boats across the Caspian Sea. MERMAIDS hindered their progress until they hit upon the idea of melting wax and using it to block their ears (a motif apparently adapted from Homer's *Odyssey*). This permitted them to pass unharmed through to the Mediterranean and finally to the shores of Britain. There, climbing a high tower on a fine winter day, Míl's uncle ÍTH saw a misty island to the west and decided to take a group of settlers there.

When Míl heard that Íth had been killed in Ireland by the TUATHA DÉ DANANN, he set sail to exact revenge, but he died on the way. His wife SCOTA reached the shores but was cut down in battle; their sons finished what Míl and Scota had begun, finally winning control of the entire island.

His descendants, the Milesians or Sons of Míl, were the final waves of settlers on Irish shores, displacing the earlier gods and goddesses, children of the mother goddess DANU. Most scholars today believe there is some historical truth, however degraded in transmission, in these Irish legends. In such interpretations, the Milesians were the ancestors of the historical Goidels. The legends of Egyptian and Scythian connections, as well as the Spanish link itself, are generally considered inventions of medieval writers who imagined connections between Scythae and Scoti, Iberians and Hibernians.

milk   Folkloric motif. Celtic people relied on CATTLE for much of their food; for this reason, we find much folklore surrounding milk. A cow typically gives approximately a gallon to a gallon and a half of milk a day for nine months after calving; thus a cow with calf (called a milch cow)

was a valued source of liquid nourishment and of BUTTER and cheese that were made from milk. Milch cows, called in Irish *cumhals*, were so valuable that in ancient Ireland they were the basis of exchange and valuation of other goods and even of people's social rankings (see *ÉRIC*).

Irish myth speaks of the abundant cow, the GLAS GHAIBHLEANN, who did not even need to have a calf to produce milk; she filled to overflowing every vessel brought to her. When an evil person attempted to milk her into a sieve, however, the great cow disappeared from this earth. Attempts to thwart the natural abundance of cows formed part of much folklore. WITCHES were believed to be able to steal milk right out of a cow's udder, without needing a pail, just by passing a needle near the beast (dung-forks, chimney crooks, and other implements were also named as tools for milk theft). The witch could then pass the implement near her own poor cow, which would then give forth the milk of an entire neighborhood. While the witch enjoyed the real milk, the cows she bewitched gave only a thin fluid, which would not form butter or cheese. Milk could be protected by the recitation of MILKING CHARMS.

milking charms   Folkloric ritual. As herding people who relied upon CATTLE for much of their food, those in Celtic lands had many superstitions about protecting their food supply, in particular the MILK that was drunk fresh as well as made into BUTTER and cheese. Various rituals ensured that no one would make off with the milk from a COW: The first drops of milk would be allowed to splatter on the ground; the sign of the cross would be made over the cow's udder; CHARMS and prayers would be spoken.

There were also taboos. No one could step in spilled milk nor cross in front of a cow that had kicked over a milking pail. In Ireland on BELTANE, the feast of summer's beginning on May 1, milking charms were especially necessary, as fairies and witches roved about, trying to steal all the milk out of the cows' udders. Twigs of ROWAN were tied to cows' tails; a Mary Candle was melted and the wax rubbed into cows' hides.

In Scotland milking charms were connected with LUGHNASA, the harvest festival on August 1: Juniper was burned before the barn or stale urine sprinkled on its door; balls of hair were put into the milk pail to keep the milk from being bewitched away. A strong charm involved boiling cow dung into a paste, then adding several straight metal PINS; any witch attempting to steal milk would suffer stabbing pains until she arrived at the farmhouse door with entreaties for mercy. Similarly, putting urine in a bottle and corking it would stop up the kidneys of any thieving witch. Finally, a certain way of keeping the milk flowing was to place the herb pearlwort on the BULL before conception; any resulting heifers would be protected throughout their milking life.

Milucra (Miluchrach)   Irish goddess. The sister of the better-known goddess ÁINE, Milucra became infatuated with the great hero FIONN MAC CUMHAILL—as did Áine, who was known for her lustful ways. Because her sister had sworn she would never sleep with a gray-haired man, Milucra enchanted a lake on SLIEVE GULLION in ULSTER so that it would dye the hair of any swimmer gray. The young virile Fionn, meeting a beautiful maiden on the lake's shores who claimed her golden ring had dropped into the water, volunteered to swim out and retrieve it. He did find the ring, but when he reemerged he was not only gray-haired—therefore unappealing to the sensuous Áine—but also withered with age. The FIANNA captured Milucra and forced her to give their leader a drink that restored his youth, but his hair stayed silver.

Source: Joyce, P. W. *Ancient Celtic Romances.* London: Parkgate Books, 1997, pp. 315 ff.

Minerva (Minerva Medica)   Romanized Celtic goddess. In Rome this goddess of HEALING was absorbed into the powerful Greek warrior goddess Athena, but Minerva was no fighter at all,

except against disease and pain. In Celtic lands the Romans found many similar goddesses whose healing powers were found in the headwaters of RIVERS, in hot SPRINGS, and in other WATER sources. One such goddess can be seen even today carved into the Roman quarries near the River Dee in Chester; she is depicted with OWL and GORGON's head, symbols of the Greek Athena. Julius Caesar said that the Celtic Minerva taught arts and crafts to humanity, but that is not clear from the remaining images.

Sometimes the Celtic goddess was completely renamed, her original name lost to history; in other cases the Celtic name remained. One Minerva was called Vitrix (apparently "victor" or "victorious"), found in many relief carvings of a helmet-crowned female head. Another is associated with BELISAMA, the warrior goddess. The most famous Celtic Minerva was SUL, the goddess of the thermal springs at BATH in Britain.

Sources: Green, Miranda. *The Gods of Roman Britain.* Aylesbury: Shire Publications Ltd., 1983, p. 30; Straffon, Cheryl. *The Earth Goddess: Celtic and Pagan Legacy of the Landscape.* London: Blandford, 1997, pp. 24–29.

Mis (Mish, Miss)   Irish heroine. The towering mountain range of Slieve Mish in Co. Kerry is named for this woman, who was given the mountain as her bride-price, according to the place-lore called the *DINDSHENCHAS.* Daughter of a warrior, she found her father's bloodied body after a battle and, desperate with sorrow, drank his blood, which drove her mad. Mis went into the mountains and lived by killing animals with her bare hands, until a harper named Dubh Rois sang, and she drew near to listen to him. Speaking for the first time since her madness struck, Mis inquired about his musical instrument, which she remembered from her father's house, and then about his sexual instrument, which she did not remember. Tenderly and carefully, he showed both to her.

When Dubh Rois made love to her, Mis lost her wildness and gradually grew to love her rescuer. Her recovery seems to have been complete, for when Dubh Rois was later killed in battle, she did not go mad again but became a BARD to lament his loss. The parallel of this story with the familiar Irish tale of a goddess of SOVEREIGNTY who appears as a HAG until kissed, whereupon she becomes a beautiful girl, has been noted by scholars. The story is also similar, with a gender reversal, to the Sumerian myth of the taming of the wild man Enkidu by the temple woman Siduri.

mistletoe   Symbolic plant. An evergreen parasitic plant that grows on deciduous trees and shrubs, the mistletoe *(Viscum album)* retains some of its ancient symbolic power even today. The British tradition of placing a sprig of mistletoe in the home at the winter holidays, under which kissing rituals take place, is still common in England and America today. The associations of mistletoe with pre-Christian religion are still so strong that it is not used in church decorations, reflecting an ancient belief that it was sacrilegious to bring it into church.

   The Roman author Pliny the Elder said mistletoe was the DRUIDS' most sacred plant, especially when it grew on an OAK—a tree sacred to the Celtic priesthood. He said the plant was harvested in ritual fashion on the sixth day after the new moon. After a ritual banquet, two white BULLS with bound horns were led to the mistletoe-bearing tree and were slaughtered after the plant was cut down with a golden sickle. A mistletoe harvested under such circumstances—called "all-heal"—was believed to be powerful medicine against barrenness and impotence, as well as a remedy for poisons.

Source: Crow, W. B. "The Mistletoe Sacrament." In Matthews, John. *A Celtic Reader: Selections from Celtic Legend, Scholarship and Story.* Wellingborough: Aquarian Press, 1991.

Mithras   Persian deity. Although found in Celtic lands, especially in Britain around the region of Hadrian's Wall, this deity of light was not Celtic but imported by the Roman legions, for there were many legionnaires who were especially devoted to Mithras. His temples, called Mithraea, were the site of the blood ritual called the Tauroboleum, in which a worshiper was drenched in the blood of a newly slaughtered BULL as a kind of baptism. There is no evidence that the rite was used by the Celts, who had their own bull ritual called the BULL-SLEEP.

Moccus   Continental Celtic god. Known from only one inscription that includes his name, which may mean "PIG," this god was identified by the Romans with their deity MERCURY.

Modron   (Madrun)   Welsh goddess. In the Welsh mythological texts called the *MABINOGION*, we find references to this obscure goddess whose name means "mother," making her parallel to the continental Celtic goddesses called DEAE MATRES, "the divine mothers" as well as to MATRONA, "mother." Little myth is attached to her, which has led some to envision her as an early, even pre-Celtic, divinity whose name survived while her narratives and rituals were lost. In Cornwall a SAINT called Madrun or Madron is found, possibly a Christianization of the earlier goddess; rituals at St. Madrun's WELL include dropping PINS into the water to foresee the future health of the petitioner.

Mogetius   Continental Celtic god. An obscure god mentioned in two inscriptions, Mogetius was identified by the Romans with their deity of war, MARS.

Mogons   (Mogounos)   Continental Celtic god. This obscure god may derive his name from a word meaning "to increase," suggesting a divinity of strength and FERTILITY.

Mog Ruith   (Mug Ruith)   Irish hero. Several medieval Irish sources mention this DRUID, whose name has been interpreted to mean "the wheel magician" under the assumption that he used a wheel as a tool for DIVINATION. His legend involves travels to the eastern Mediterranean, where he met Simon Magus, a great magician; there Mog Ruith followed king Herod's command to cut off the head of the early follower of Christ, John the Baptist. For this ancient crime of Mog Ruith's, the Irish have suffered famine and other tragedies.

Some texts give him as the father of the mysterious TLACHTGA, after whom a significant mythological site is named. He is described as MUNSTER's chief druid, who saved their warriors in battle by miraculously drilling a WELL with an arrow or spear. Then he built a fire from the wood of magical ROWAN trees, over which he chanted incantations until he saw clearly enough to prophesy victory. Suited in a bird cloak, he flew into the air and did battle with the opposing druids, while the Munster warriors killed their foes beneath him.

Molling (St. Molling)   Irish legendary figure. A quasi-historical figure who lived in the seventh century C.E., Molling was absorbed into Celtic legends of FIONN MAC CUMHAILL, who is said to have been the saint's foster brother. The magical SMITH, GOBAN SAOR, built Molling's church for him from sacred trees. It was at Molling's church that king SUIBHNE died after living as a madman. Such mythological motifs often were connected with historical figures in order to extend their sacred powers.

Mollyndroat   Manx folkloric figure. On the Isle of Man we find the tale of a GIANT who served an evil DRUID. In a story similar to the familiar European tale of Rumpelstiltskin, Mollyndroat held a woman captive and refused to set her free until she guessed his name. This folkloric figure may be connected with the evil giant MELEAGANT, also known as Mellyagraunce, who in Arthurian legend kidnapped queen GUINEVERE.

Moltinus   Continental Celtic god. His name shares its derivation with contemporary words referring to sheep (English *mutton*, French *mouton*) and has been interpreted to mean "ram." This god is known from only two inscriptions, and unlike many other Celtic gods, he was not identified by the Romans with one of their own divinities.

Mona   See ANGLESEY.

Monday, Tuesday   Folkloric motif. A common tale told of the FAIRIES is that, although they love dancing and singing, they had a limited musical repertoire. They sang, over and over, the words "Monday, Tuesday" (in Irish, *Da Luan, Da Mart*). A hunchback, irritated by their repetitive song, once added "and Wednesday" (*Agus da Cadin*) to their song, causing them great excitement and delight. In gratitude for their new melody, the fairies removed the man's hunch, and he walked away straight as an arrow. Another hunchback in the vicinity, hearing the story, rushed to the same place and waited until the fairies arrived. The moment they started singing he interrupted them with "and Friday" (*Agus da Hena*), and the fairies, incensed at his rudeness, promptly gave him the first man's hump on top of his own.

Mongán (Mongan)   Irish hero. An historical king of the seventh century C.E., Mongán nonetheless is partially mythological. Said to be the son of the sea god MANANNÁN MAC LIR, Mongán ("hairy fellow," a name reputedly given him when he was born with a full head of HAIR) inherited his father's SHAPE-SHIFTING talent as well as his ability to move between this world and the OTHERWORLD.

Mongán was conceived when his divine father disguised himself as a human king, a motif that parallels the story of the conception of king ARTHUR; Mongán is also described as the reincarnation of the Irish hero FIONN MAC CUMHAILL, whose fair wife GRÁINNE ran off with the hero DIARMAIT in a story parallel to that of GUINEVERE and LANCELOT. Thus Mongán, however historical his reign, seems also to reflect an ancient Celtic tale of the goddess of SOVEREIGNTY.

Source: Cross, Tom Peete, and Clark Harris Slover, eds. *Ancient Irish Tales*. New York: Henry Holt and Co., 1936, p. 546.

Mongfhinn (Mongfhin, Mongfhionn) Irish heroine. Her name was used as a charm to keep away evil spirits, but Mongfhinn herself was not especially pleasant. Stepmother or foster mother to NIALL of the Nine Hostages, she tried to poison him but instead killed herself on SAMHAIN night, the feast of winter's beginning on November 1. In some areas of Ireland that holiday was called the Festival of Monghfinn. This obscure figure may have originally been an important goddess, for her name includes the divine syllable *fionn*, "light," and women once prayed to her on Samhain.

monster Folkloric figure. The monsters of one people were often the gods of an earlier people. In many Celtic lands, rather than becoming monstrously large and frightening, the old deities became smaller and rather appealing, like the LEPRECHAUNS and FAIRIES that are found in the folklore of Ireland and Scotland. GIANTS are also found, especially in Britain, behind whose awful visages hide elder gods. Goddesses were often vilified by followers of male-centered monotheism, so that some monstrous female figures, like the CAILLEACH, are derogatory descriptions of powerful early deities. Monstrosity of itself does not always indicate divinity, unless combined with SHAPE-SHIFTING or other magical powers.

moon Cosmological concept. The moon, with its changing phases and its connection with the tides, was a natural object of importance to the Celts as to most other cultures. The Celts originally divided the year according to moons, according to the Roman author Pliny, with the new moon beginning each month as the night began each day. Festivals were celebrated at moonrise; thus we have May Eve, the evening before BELTANE, and Hallowe'en, the evening before SAMHAIN.

Some scholars believe that the moon was especially significant to agriculturalists, because the moon's waxing and waning was believed to influence the growth of plants, just as it does the movement of the tides. An indication of Celtic awareness of the lunar waxing/waning cycle is found in the belief that MISTLETOE and other magical plants should be harvested under a waning moon—the declining light of the luminary indicating that time was ripe for endings. In the Scottish Highlands, similarly, sowing was always done under a waxing moon, with the belief that as the moon swelled, so would the tiny plants within the seeds.

There is also evidence of ancient lunar rituals; the Roman author Strabo tells of night-long dancing among the Celts when the moon was full. Through the 18th century, such dances were held at STONE CIRCLES in the Scottish Highlands. In the 19th century people in the insular Celtic lands still bowed and curtseyed to the new moon, while in Cornwall people merely nodded while reaching into their pockets to touch their money for good luck. In Ireland a full moon brought people to crossroads where they danced beneath its pearly light; the tradition was almost eliminated through priestly opposition but has been recently revived in the area around Ennis, Co. Clare, and other rural regions.

Sources: Carmichael, Alexander. *Carmina Gadelica: Hymns and Incantations*. Hudson, N.Y.: Lindisfarne Press, 1992, p. 578; Hull, Eleanor. *Folklore of the British Isles*. London: Methuen & Co., Ltd., 1928, pp. 61 ff; Leather, Ella Mary. *The Folk-Lore of Herefordshire*. London: Sidewick & Jackson, 1912, pp. 15–16; MacCulloch, J. A. *The Religion of the Ancient Celts*. London: Constable, 1911, pp. 173–179.

Mór (Mor, Mór Mumhan) Irish goddess or heroine. This female figure, whose name means "big" or "great," has been described as the land goddess of the southwestern PROVINCE of MUNSTER; her full name means "the great one of Munster," and the term Mór was often used of territorial goddesses. Like many other ancient goddesses, she shrank into a figure of folktale.

Once, it was said, a woman named Mór arrived with her husband Lear (possibly LIR, an early sea god) at the promontory in Co. Kerry that bears her name. They built a house not far from there, at the foot of Mount Eagle. Lear and Mór lived there comfortably, for the sea brought them anything they wished. (There is an echo in this tale of stories of MERMAIDS who lived off the spoils of ships they had caused to be wrecked at sea.)

One day Mór climbed to the top of the mountain above her and, for the first time, saw how large was the land in which she dwelled. While there on the mountain she was, as they say in the Irish countryside, "taken short," and squatted to relieve herself—a mythological motif found in many stories of creation by goddesses. To this day, the ravines that cut through the mountains of Munster are said to have resulted from Mór's gigantic streams of URINE.

Mór's happiness was destroyed when her sons, the pride of her life, were lured into trying their luck as seamen. As her happiness fled, so did her power, for she withered up in sadness. Her temper grew so bad that her husband left her, sailing north and finally settling far away from his desolate wife.

The vestiges of an ancient goddess can be found in local folklore, for the place where Mór came ashore—Dunmore Head, from Dún Mór, Mór's HILLFORT—was also "Mary Geeran's house," in Irish Ty-Vor-ney Gerane, possibly Tigh Mhorie ni Greine, "the home of Mór, child of the SUN." Dunmore faces the setting sun, said locally to be "Mór on her throne," another suggestion of a sun goddess. Additionally, the story is told that Mór went mad and had to be tamed by the king of the Munster stronghold of Cashel—the same story told of MIS, the goddess

of the Slieve Mish mountains that bisect the peninsula on which Mór was said to live. The two may have originally been the same figure.

A similar GIANT woman of this name is found in the Highlands of Scotland, where she was said to have been the daughter of the otherwise unknown Smûid, who was washed away in a flood while carrying a group of travelers on her back.

Sources: Curtin, Jeremiah. *Hero-Tales of Ireland.* New York: Benjamin Blom, 1894, p. xli; McKay, John G. *More West Highland Tales.* Vol. 2. Scottish Anthropological and Folklore Society. Edinburgh: Oliver and Boyd, 1969, p. 54.

Morann Irish hero. According to several medieval sources, Morann was a wise BREHON or judge, who wore a chain around his neck that, should he begin to speak false words or an unjust sentence, tightened until it strangled him. It was also said that if he placed this chain on the necks of the accused, it worked the same way, strangling them if they lied.

Morda Welsh hero. This minor figure in Welsh mythology was an old man whose job was to tend the fire beneath the goddess CERIDWEN's great CAULDRON. When the blind servant did not see GWION taste the magical brew and so take the WISDOM from the cauldron, Ceridwen was furious and struck him so hard that one EYE fell out.

Mordred (Modred, Modreuant, Medrawd, Medrawt) Arthurian hero. The illegitimate son of king ARTHUR, conceived with Arthur's half sister MORGAUSE through the machinations of the magician MERLIN, Mordred was opposite to his father in all ways. Where Arthur was magnanimous, Mordred was stingy; where Arthur was brave, Mordred was cunning and cowardly, but it was Mordred who finally brought down the great dream of CAMELOT and the ROUND TABLE.

The legends of king Arthur have a basis in Celtic myth, but they were elaborated by many generations of poets and imaginative writers, who used the outline of the tale to paint evocative human portraits. The character of Mordred as Arthur's enemy was established in the 12th century by Geoffrey of Monmouth. Prior to that, as the Welsh hero Medrawd, he was a brave warrior who died in the battle of CAMLAN. After having been absorbed into the Arthurian legend as the great king's son and enemy, Mordred was listed in the Welsh TRIADS as one of the "Three Dishonored Men of the Island of Britain."

Morfessa Irish hero. The magical race called the TUATHA DÉ DANANN came to Ireland from another land with four magnificent capitals, each led by a master of wisdom rather than a king. One of these cities was FALIAS, from which came the great INAUGURATION STONE called the LIA FÁIL. Morfessa, "great wisdom," was the wisdom-master of Falias, who gave the Tuatha Dé the stone when they sailed for Ireland.

Morfran (Morfran fab Tegid) Welsh god or hero. The son of the great goddess CERIDWEN was an ugly child, and to make up for this disadvantage his mother determined that he would become the world's wisest person. She began brewing a collection of herbs that would bring him that WISDOM, setting her servant boy GWION to watch the CAULDRON. But Gwion accidentally drank some of the brew, absorbing with it the wisdom and bringing down upon himself Ceridwen's wrath. Welsh myth says little more of Morfran, save that his ugliness finally proved useful when he escaped the battle of CAMLAN because everyone mistook him for a devil. (See AFAGDDU.)

Morfudd (Morfudd ferch Urien) Welsh heroine. This obscure heroine was the daughter of king URIEN; her mother may have been the goddess MODRON.

Morgan (Morgen, Morgan Le Fay, Morgan la fée, Morgaine, Morgana, Orva, Orna, Oua, Orains, Ornais, Morgain, Moruein, Morganz) Arthurian heroine. King ARTHUR had several half sisters, children of their mother IGRAINE with her first husband, duke GORLOIS of Cornwall. Two are frequently confused because of their similar names and their questionable behavior: the sorceress Morgan and the ambitious queen MORGAUSE, who may have originally been the same figure.

Morgan learned MAGIC while still a child in a convent boarding school; some legends say she furthered her study with the great magician MERLIN. She soon gained great powers of enchantment. When slighted by her lover GUYOMARD, Morgan created the PERILOUS VALLEY where any knight unfaithful to his lady would be trapped by his self-created illusions. She ultimately married a minor king, URIEN, and became the mother of OWEIN, the knight who wed the mysterious LADY OF THE FOUNTAIN in a romantic Arthurian tale.

While her brother ascended to triumph at CAMELOT, Morgan worked to bring disaster on Arthur and his court, stealing and ultimately destroying the magical scabbard of EXCALIBUR, which protected the king in battle. Yet it was to Morgan that Arthur was brought at the end of his earthly life, so that she could take him to the OTHERWORLD, to die or be healed there.

Behind the shadowy woman of legend stands a powerful being whose close connection with the Otherworld is made clear by her alternative name of Morgan Le Fay, Morgan "the FAIRY" or, even more powerfully, "the fate." Early texts describe her as the most beautiful of nine women who lived on a FORTUNATE ISLE where everything was astonishingly fertile; her sisters were Moronoe, Mazoe, Gliten, Glitonea, Gliton, Tyronoe, and Thiten. Like many another FAIRY LOVER, she attempted to seduce men, fixing upon the fine knight LANCELOT as her prey—but without success.

Morgan may be connected with a similarly named goddess of Ireland, the MÓRRÍGAN, a divinity of death and battle. She may have descended from a sea goddess, for the name Morgan survives as a Breton name for sea fairies who kidnap human men, while in Wales LAKE spirits are called Morgans; and the Fata Morgana, a sea mirage of palaces and columns complete with its own watery reflection, was according to medieval legend created by Morgan.

Source: Loomis, Roger Sherman. *Wales and the Arthurian Legend.* Cardiff: University of Wales Press, 1956, pp. 105 ff.

Morgause (Morgawse) Arthurian heroine. Morgause's mother was IGRAINE, the beautiful wife of the duke of Cornwall, GORLOIS. Knowing that only the heroic UTHER PENDRAGON could conceive a king with Igraine, the magician MERLIN enchanted Uther into the likeness of her husband so that the wife would commit adultery without realizing it. Arthur was thus conceived, but Igraine already had several daughters by Gorlois, including MORGAN and Morgause, who became Arthur's implacable enemies.

Yet Morgause also became his lover, unknown to the two of them, through Merlin's meddling. When Arthur realized that he had slept with his half sister, who had conceived the child who would become his murderer, MORDRED, he attempted to have all the children born at that time killed. Morgause protected her child by retreating to far Orkney, where she married the king, LOT. From Morgause, Mordred learned to hate his father/uncle, and with her he plotted the downfall of CAMELOT.

Because of the similarity of their names, their dispositions, and their opposition to Arthur, Morgause and her sister Morgan are frequently confused or conflated; they may have originally been a single figure.

Morholt (Morhold) Irish hero. This Irish GIANT was a warrior who annually came to the land of king MARK of Cornwall, where he claimed a tribute or tax. The strong knight TRISTAN killed him, almost dying from Morholt's poisoned sword. Tristan later fell in love with Morholt's niece, the fair ISEULT.

Moriath (Moriath Morca) Irish heroine. "Sealand" is the meaning of the name of this princess of ancient Ireland, daughter of the king of MUNSTER in the far southwestern corner of the island. Her story began when the high king Cobthach killed his own brother LABHRAIGH Lorc, after which he poisoned AILLIL Áine, the true king. Aillil's son, Labhraigh Moen, was soon banished from the kingdom, but he allied himself with Cobthach's enemy, Moriath's father, Scoriath.

The moment Labhraigh set eyes on Moriath, he fell in love with her. Her father kept his daughter closely guarded, so Labhraigh enlisted the help of his illustrious harper, CRAIPHTINE, who played so sweetly that the entire court fell into blissful sleep, permitting the lovers to pledge their troth to each other. When Labhraigh had to fight Cobthach, his harper came again to the rescue, playing lulling melodies so that the enemy army all went to sleep while Labhraigh's army, prepared with earplugs, stayed wide awake. Upon ascending to the throne of his own region, Labhraigh invited Cobthach to a dinner, trapped him in an IRON house, and burned him to death.

Some versions of this famous story have Moriath as the wooer and her own harper as the miraculous musician, bearing love poems and messages to Labhraigh, who became king with her help.

Source: O' Rahilly, Thomas. *Early Irish History and Mythology.* Dublin: The Dublin Institute for Advanced Studies, 1946, p. 198.

Mórrígan (Morrigan, the Morrigan, Mórrígna, Mórrigu, Mór-Ríoghain) Irish goddess. One of the most important goddesses of ancient Ireland, she was one of the TUATHA DÉ DANANN, the tribe of the goddess DANU; she was also associated with the FAIRY people, for she appears in some texts as a white COW with RED ears, colors that elsewhere indicate an OTHERWORLD origin. The Mórrígan appears in other forms as well: as a gigantic woman who foretells the future of those about to do battle (see WASHER AT THE FORD), as a CROW, as an EEL, as a gray-red WOLF. Such SHAPE-SHIFTING is commonly associated with divinities connected with DRUIDS and BARDS, both of whom were believed to have the power to change their outward appearance at will. The Mórrígan was herself a bard, singing her people to victory at the great second battle of MAG TUIRED; she was also a magician, casting ORACLES and foretelling the future. Most often, however, she took the form of a BIRD to swoop over battlefields, devouring the bodies of the slain.

A war goddess, Mórrígan is associated with the other goddesses of battle: BADB, the scald-crow; NEMAIN, who spreads panic; and MACHA, the speedy horse of battle. Together they are sometimes called the "three Mórrígna," although in other texts Mórrígan herself appears on the list. Thus she is connected with triplicity, which to the Celts meant intensification of power (see THREE), even though the exact trinities vary.

Despite, or perhaps because of, her connection with war, Mórrígan is also depicted as having an immense sexual appetite. In one memorable myth, she had intercourse with the father god, the DAGDA, who came upon her while she was straddling a river and, overwhelmed by her massive charms, fell upon her lustfully. In another tale, she so desired the great hero CÚCHULAINN that she ambushed him, but when he rejected her, she turned upon him in fury and was injured in their fight.

Her relationship to the hero was equally ambiguous in the tales of the ULSTER CYCLE, especially in the precursor tale to the Irish epic, the *TÁIN BÓ CUAILNGE*, called the *Táin bó Regamna*. In that story the Mórrígan lusted after Cúchulainn but also protected him in an almost maternal fashion; she appeared to him in various guises as he single-handedly defended the province of Ulster against the invading warriors of CONNACHT. When he went forth to his death, she attempted, but without success, to stop him.

In the *Táin* the Mórrígan shadows that epic's major figure, queen MEDB, who herself was probably a diminished goddess. The Mórrígan may be an alternative or Otherworld form of Medb, for the cave from which the Mórrígan was said to emerge (see OWEYNAGAT) was Medb's birthplace at Connacht's capital of CRUACHAN. Like Medb she was connected with TARA, where she cooked on a spit that could hold three kinds of food at one time: raw meat, cooked meat, and BUTTER, with the raw cooking perfectly, the cooked remaining unburnt, and the butter not melting away.

She had one son, MEICHE, in whose heart were three great SERPENTS. The hero MAC CÉCHT killed him, because had he lived, the serpents would have split his heart open and devoured all of Ireland. Mac Cécht burned the heart to ashes, then threw the ashes into a RIVER, which boiled to death every living creature within its waters.

The meaning of Mórrígán's name is disputed, with some saying that it means "phantom queen" and others "death queen," while still others derive it from a presumed early Indo-European goddess Rigatona, "great queen." The derivation of her name from the word for "sea," common among early writers, is generally out of fashion. The word *mare* that survives in "nightmare" may be a related word; it refers not to a HORSE but to a phantom or terrifying GHOST.

Yet others have described her as a version of the land goddess known as Flaith or SOVER-EIGNTY, for she was described as a HAG who could transform herself into a young maiden. Additionally, she is identified with a pair of breast-shaped hills called *dá chich na Mórrígna*, "the paps of Mórrígan," near the BRÚ NA BOÍNNE in Co. Meath, which echo the similarly shaped hills devoted to the earth goddess of the province of Munster, DANU.

Sources: Clark, Rosalind. *The Great Queens: Irish Goddesses from the Morrígan to Cathleen Ní Houlihan.* Irish Literary Studies 34. Gerrards Cross: Colin Smythe, 1991; Dexter, Miriam Robbins. *Whence the Goddesses: A Sourcebook.* New York: Pergamon Press, 1990, pp. 88–89; Gregory, Lady Augusta. *Gods and Fighting Men: The Story of the Tuatha De Danaan and of the Fianna of*

Ireland. New York: Oxford University Press, 1970, pp. 85 ff; Herbert, Máire. "Transmutations of an Irish Goddess." In Billington, Sandra, and Miranda Green, eds. *The Concept of the Goddess.* London and New York: Routledge, 1996, pp. 141–151; Hull, Eleanor. *The Cuchullin Saga in Irish Literature.* London: David Nutt, 1898, p. 103; Kinsella, Thomas, trans. *The Táin.* Dublin: The Dolmen Press, 1969.

morris dancing British ritual. In parts of rural Britain, springtime festivals were enlivened by the presence of men dressed in pleated white shirts and white trousers, wearing ribboned caps and bells. A fiddler played while the dancers stepped briskly about, led by a sword-carrying dancer upon whose weapon a CAKE was impaled. This traditional dance had its roots in a springtime ritual of renewal. The phallic symbolism of the sword intensified that of the MAYPOLE, near which the troupe often danced. The festival they celebrated, BELTANE, often ended in licentious behavior appropriate to the burgeoning season.

mother goddess Cosmological concept. As is the case in other cultures, not all goddesses among the Celts have maternal natures; there are goddesses of war and land and power as well as of motherhood. Yet the Celts clearly honored the role of the human mother by deifying the force of maternity in goddesses with simple names such as DEAE MATRES, "the mothers," or MODRON, "mother."

These divinities may harken back to a pre-Celtic period, for there are evidences of mother goddesses from as early as the neolithic period (ca. 4000 B.C.E.) in Gaul, where the Celts did not arrive until ca. 1500 B.C.E. The Celts may have brought their own maternal divinities with them, or they may have adopted the mother goddesses of the indigenous people. Because there are no written documents from pre-Roman Celtic lands, the genesis or evolution of the Celtic mother-goddess figures remains problematic, but it is certain that by the time of the arrival of the Roman legions in 400 B.C.E. the Celts had fully embraced the image of the divine mother.

The mother or group of mothers was the most frequently carved votive image in Romano-Celtic religion, and many of these images are small enough to suggest that they were used to adorn household rather than public altars. Others were substantial enough to be part of public ceremonials; some are believed to have been borne in procession, rather as the image of the Virgin MARY was later carried by the Catholic devout on May 1, the feast of the "Queen of the May," which was originally the Celtic festival of BELTANE.

Such accommodation to the old Celtic cult of the mother was not, however, always the rule, for wholesale destruction of Celtic "idols" was demanded by such fierce opponents of paganism as St. Martin of Tours, who personally destroyed hundreds of images, many of them incontrovertibly feminine visions of the divine.

Source: Berger, Pamela. *The Goddess Obscured: Transformation of the Grain Protectress from Goddess to Saint.* Boston: Beacon Press, 1985, pp. 29 ff.

mound See FAIRY MOUND.

Mound of the Hostages Irish mythological site. On the hill of TARA in central Ireland—sometimes called "royal Tara" because of its associations with mythological and historical HIGH KINGS of the land—there is a small tumulus or artificial mound of earth above a PASSAGE GRAVE built of stone. Called the Mound of the Hostages, the site is associated with the great king NIALL of the Nine Hostages. The term *hostages* seems to imply people held against their will; the word *fosterers* would be better, as the nine young men in question went to Niall's royal seat willingly in order to bind their families to his.

mountain Cosmological symbol. Mountains were sacred to the Celts, but so was everything else in NATURE, which was the residence of the divine. Divine force did not spread itself thinly across the world but tended to condense in specific sacred places. WELLS and RIVER sources were important foci of divine power, as were hills and mountains. Both were typically viewed as feminine powers. A figure connected with high hills in Scotland and Ireland was the HAG named the CAILLEACH, a figure that appears to descend from pre-Celtic times, which has led to suggestions that some mountain worship may precede the Celtic arrivals.

Mountains had additional significance in Ireland as places of royal or political power. Some of this significance may have originated in the simple fact that high hills provide a good view of the surrounding region, therefore assisting defenders in case of assault. The hill of TARA, although not a dominating mountain in its rather rolling countryside, offers such an impressive view over the surrounding lands. Nearby, another small mountain, UISNEACH, became the mystical center of the island; from its summit one can see peaks in virtually all of Ireland.

Mountain Sunday   See LUGHNASA.

mouse   See RAT.

moving stones   Folkloric tradition. Celtic lands are dotted with vestiges of the unknown pre-Celtic people who built STONE CIRCLES and other great undeciphered spiritual monuments. Many traditions and folktales surround such sites, although it is not possible to know the genesis—whether Celtic, pre-Celtic, or Christian—of this lore.

One such tradition holds that the stones were not firmly set in the soil, but were able to move around at will. Usually such movement occurred at midnight, although sometimes at dawn; this did not happen daily but on significant feast days, especially calendar points such as the midsummer SOLSTICE and the Celtic fall feast of

SAMHAIN. The stones got up from their paralyzed position and traveled about the countryside, often going to a nearby LAKE or RIVER to bathe and drink. Sometimes they turned into dancing stones (see MERRY MAIDENS) or just rolled around on the grass. When their brief window of freedom eased shut, the stones once more resumed their usual positions and remained there until their next outing.

Moyturra   See MAG TUIRED.

Mugain (Mughain)   Irish heroine. This sister of the great goddess-queen MEDB became the mother of a hero-king, Aed SLANE, but first Mugain had to learn to be kind to other women. She was co-wife, with MAIRENN, to the king of TARA when she found herself consumed with envy over a beautiful golden headdress that Mairenn always wore. Suspecting Mairenn of hiding something, she bribed a member of the court to pull down the golden headdress and shame her rival. But it was Mugain who was shamed for her behavior, for golden hair instantly appeared on Mairenn's head. Mugain was punished by being forced to give birth to a lamb and a SALMON before she could bear a human child. Some have equated her with MÓR, goddess of MUNSTER.

Source: MacNeill, Máire. *The Festival of Lughnasa, Parts I and II.* Dublin: Comhairle Bhéaloideas Éireann, 1982, p. 326–327.

Mug Nuadat   Irish hero. See EÓGAN.

Muilearach (Muileartach, Muir Larteach, Muilearteach)   Scottish and Irish goddess. A seafaring form of the great goddess figure called the CAILLEACH, this sea HAG was a formidable woman, a bald one-eyed being with a blue-gray face and sharp protruding teeth. She was known throughout the Scottish Highlands as well as in the island of Lewis and Harris and the southern

Hebrides. An ancestral goddess, mother of the king of the mythological land of LOCHLANN, Muilearach lived underwater. She had a HEALING aspect, for the pot of balm she carried could make the sick healthy and the weak strong. Nonetheless she was feared and was killed in a great battle with the hero band called the FIANNA.

Under the name Muireartach, she was an Irish goddess, a one-eyed hag named "eastern sea" who lived beneath the ocean waves with a magical SMITH. She loved merchants who caressed her waves with their boats, but she also loved the treasures they carried and might upend them just to gather them up into her "ill-streaming, bald-red, white-named" presence. The great hero FIONN MAC CUMHAILL killed her after one too many shipwrecks were blamed upon her.

Muime Scottish folkloric figure. Her name means "stepmother" or "foster mother," or "wet nurse." She appears in Scottish folklore as an ambiguous figure, sometimes representing good luck, sometimes bringing the opposite. It was considered an extremely bad OMEN to meet this figure if you were far from home, but nearby she was a helpful sprite. The folkloric figure is believed to hide a memory of Celtic times, when the role of the foster mother was extremely important.

Muircertach mac Erc (Murtach mac Erc, Muirchertach meic Erca, Muircertach mac Erca) Irish hero. A historical king to whom mythological motifs have been attached, Muircertach reigned as HIGH KING of Ireland in the sixth century C.E. His name is puzzling, in that he bears the name of his mother ERC, a princess of Scotland, rather than that of his father Muireadhach, grandson of the famous king of TARA, NIALL. Some scholars have suggested that Erc was originally a goddess rather than a human woman, although that does not fully explain why Muircertach would be named for her.

Muircertach figures in an important tale recorded in the *Annals of Ulster*, in which he wrested the high kingship from the earlier residents of Tara, leaving no survivors. Years later, he met a lovely woman, SIN, who offered herself to him provided he would evict his own wife and children from Tara. He did so, but soon his kingdom was torn apart by fighting. The warriors who attacked Muircertach were sent by Sin. Fearsome warriors they were, too: blue men, men with the heads of goats, and similar MONSTERS.

They were in reality only sticks and stones, enchanted by Sin—whose family Muircertach had killed when he conquered Tara. Muircertach went mad, raging through the rain and snow until he came home and fell into a dream in which he saw demons coming to punish him. Imagining the palace on fire, he leapt into a vat of wine, where he drowned. The fire was another of Sin's illusions, a final revenge for his destruction of her family.

Source: Cross, Tom Peete, and Clark Harris Slover, eds. *Ancient Irish Tales*. New York: Henry Holt and Co., 1936, p. 518.

Muirthemne Irish mythological site. The great plain of Muirthemne was the site of the defeat of one of the mythological races of Ireland, the FIR BOLG, who lost control of the island to the people of the goddess DANU, the TUATHA DÉ DANANN—who in turn lost Ireland to another group of invaders, the MILESIANS.

Mullo Continental Celtic god. The name of this god, associated by the Romans with their war deity MARS, may mean "mule" or "wall," although there is no agreement on which is more likely or what meaning the term would have. Mullo is shown in some images as bearing a RAM-HEADED SNAKE, and he may have been a divinity of HEALING, which that symbol often represents.

Mumu (Muman)   See MUNSTER.

Munanna Irish heroine. In Irish folklore we find the story of this woman who grew weary of living with a boring man. Finding a Viking pirate more to her liking, she set off to sea with him after convincing her lover to kill her husband. Once back home in Norway, however, Munanna's new husband grew worried that she might repeat the behavior. On an outing on a lake, he pushed her overboard to her death. She thereafter haunted him, flying about his boat in the form of a CRANE, a common bird transformation for wronged women.

Munster (Mumu, Muman) Irish mythological site. Ireland was traditionally divided into four parts: LEINSTER, the PROVINCE of wealth in the east; CONNACHT, the province of wisdom in the west; ULSTER, province of war in the north; and Munster in the southwest, province of music and song. A fifth province, MIDE or Meath, symbolized the center; it was not, however, a geographical but a mythological construct.

Munster, which today comprises the counties of Clare, Cork, Kerry, Limerick, Tipperary, and Waterford, is a province of varied landscapes. Its great fertile valleys are among the richest in Ireland. Its MOUNTAINS are the island's highest; each range and many individual mountains are connected with goddesses. Most impressive are the PAPS OF DANU, two identical breast-shaped mountains in central Munster, capped with stone CAIRNS that form nipples.

Although all Ireland was associated with the goddess, Munster was most closely identified with the feminine principle. Many important goddesses derive from the region, including the CAILLEACH, the HAG-like figure who is especially connected with the rocky BEARE peninsula in the south of the province and the similarly rocky Burren in its north; the sea goddess MÓR; and the FAIRY QUEEN ÁINE, whose mountain is visible near the island's most haunted lake, LOUGH GUR. When FINTAN, the magical SALMON of WISDOM, was asked to define the provinces, he said that Munster meant song and celebration, festivals and poetry and the playing of games. Most significantly, Munster symbolizes FERTILITY, for

only with sufficient food can people enjoy the creative arts.

Munster is also the legendary landfall for invaders. Although archaeology shows that most early humans arrived in ULSTER, which is visible on clear days from Scotland and thus attracted early hunters and gatherers, mythology shows wave after wave of invaders arriving on Munster's rocky shores. CESAIR landed at Dún na mBarc on the Dingle peninsula, where the MILESIANS also landed. The currents from Europe that left the medieval Spanish Armada wrecked on the Munster coast may have similarly carried early migrants, so there may be some truth in the legends.

Murias Irish mythological site. One of the four great cities of the magical TUATHA DÉ DANANN, Murias was the place from which the CAULDRON of abundance traveled to Ireland.

Murna (Murna of the White Neck, Murni, Murni Fair-Neck, Muirenn Muncháem, Fuinche, Torba) Mother of the great hero FIONN MAC CUMHAILL, Murna was the descendant of ÉITHNE and thus of the fierce FOMORIAN king BALOR of the Evil Eye. Her father was TADG mac Nuadat, who ruled at ALMU, from which the warrior CUMHALL kidnapped her after his bid for her hand had been refused by her father.

Bringing the matter to CONN of the Hundred Battles, king of TARA, Tadg was told that Cumhall was banished from Ireland for his deed. And so Tadg led the battle in which Cumhall was killed—only nine hours after begetting Fionn upon Murna. She returned home to Almu, to be greeted by a furious father who threatened her life, but Conn intervened and took the woman back to Tara, where she bore her child. When he had grown, Fionn demanded an honor-price (see ÉRIC) from Tadg for the killing of Cumhall, his father. Rather than fight his powerful grandson, Tadg gave him Almu, which became Fionn's seat. Other versions of the story say that Cumhall was killed by the unconquerable warrior

GOLL MAC MORNA, whom Fionn killed in retaliation when he had grown to become Ireland's greatest hero since CÚCHULAINN.

Source: Gwynn, Edward. *The Metrical Dindshenchas.* Part II. Vol. IX. Royal Irish Academy, Todd Lecture Series. Dublin: Hodges, Figgis, and Co., Ltd., 1906–1924, p. 73.

music Art and religious symbol. Music, so much a part of the heritage of Celtic lands today, plays a significant part in many myths. The actual music of the ancient Celts is unknown, for the Celts had no musical notation. Nor do we know the part music played in their daily and ritual lives. Instrumental music is attested by early writers who refer to trumpet-like wind instruments and stringed instruments that resembled lyres, but archaeology finds little support for such references, except occasional depictions on Celtic COINS of the Roman era. The HARP, now an icon of Ireland, was introduced there in medieval times, as was the bagpipe, which migrated to the insular Celtic lands from the Balkans. Both myth and literature refer to singing, still a much-valued art in Ireland and Wales.

In folklore, music plays an important part in FAIRY legends describing the OTHERWORLD melodies that lure mortals into enchanted places from which they find it difficult to escape (see FAIRY MUSIC). Musicians are among the humans most sought-after by fairies, who reward them for playing at fairy celebrations by giving them one of FAIRYLAND's beautiful melodies to take back to earth; the famous "Derry Aire" (sometimes known as "Danny Boy") is the most famous song to come from the fairy world.

Myrddin See MERLIN.

Myrdinn Wyllt Welsh hero. According to the British historian Geoffrey of Monmouth, "Wild Merlin" was a king who, like the Irish king SUIBHNE, went mad and fled to the woods, where he lived in a BIRD costume (or perhaps actually transformed himself into a bird). The name derives from a Welsh legendary figure who became famous as the magician MERLIN.

Mythological Cycle Irish mythological texts. This term is used to describe a series of texts and stories that tell of the ancient divinities of Ireland. The central story describes a contest between mythological races, recorded in the *BOOK OF INVASIONS.* After unimpressive early settlements by the followers of NEMED and PARTHOLÓN, Ireland was occupied by the malevolent FOMORIANS, who twice fought and twice were pushed out by the FIR BOLG. They, in turn, lost their place to the mysterious and powerful TUATHA DÉ DANANN, the people of the goddess DANU, in the first battle of MAG TUIRED. It was at this battle that the heroic king NUADA lost his arm and thus, because a BLEMISHED KING could not reign, lost the rulership of the land.

He was replaced by the half-Fomorian BRES, who although amazingly beautiful was also stingy and mean. After Bres refused to provide sufficient rations for a poet, he was forced from the throne when CAIRBRE spoke a satire so stinging that it raised boils on Bres's face—thus making him too blemished to continue to rule. By this time, the miraculous team of the healing god DIAN CÉCHT and his son MIACH had created a replacement hand for Nuada: Dian Cécht by crafting it from silver, Miach by casting enchantments that caused skin to grow over the artificial limb. Nuada returned to the rulership just in time, for he was needed to lead his people in another battle at the same place as the earlier one.

The second battle of Mag Tuired began on the sacred feast of SAMHAIN and pitted the Tuatha Dé against the again-powerful Fomorians, led by the frightening king BALOR of the Evil Eye, who looked through only one EYE normally but in times of battle allowed warriors to lift the lid on his other eys so that it cast out murderous rays. His own half-breed grandson, the hero LUGH, killed him with a spear, after which the

Tuatha Dé Danann ruled the land until, much later, they were replaced by the MILESIANS, a story that is not considered part of the Mythological Cycle.

mythology Typically scholars use this word to refer to the narrative cycles that underpin a culture's religious rituals and folkways. In some cultures such narratives are codified into writing; divinities then typically become organized into a pantheon, their relationships articulated, and the confusions of identity ironed out.

Because the Celts did not write down their myths but instead recited them, there is no single source or scripture that defines Celtic mythology. In addition, sculptures and inscriptions date from the Roman invasion and were subject to the reinterpretation of Celtic deities according to the Roman pantheon; thus it is sometimes difficult to clearly distinguish what the Celts originally believed. Finally, many literary sources were transcribed by Christian monks, leaving open the possibility that the written myths themselves may be tainted with post-Celtic material.

N

Nabelcus Continental Celtic god. This obscure divinity from the region of Vaucluse in France was associated by the Romans with their warrior god MARS.

na buchtogai See SEA FAIRIES.

name Cosmological concept. The power of naming is commonly connected to spiritual prowess in many cultures, as is evidenced in the Christian myth in which the first humans, Adam and Eve, are granted the power to name all the animals they encounter. Bestowing a name on a child is an important act, one that Roman writers claim was conducted in Celtic Gaul by DRUIDS. Some Irish texts speak of a kind of baptism, with babies dipped in streams or dunked in holy WELLS as their names were given to them. This was not easily supplanted by the Christian rite; in the Hebrides, a long-lasting tradition called for children to be sprinkled with drops of water immediately upon birth, at which time a temporary name was granted the newborn.

In Celtic lands, where the power of the world was held primary, the very sound of a name was so important that to speak it was forbidden at certain times. While at sea, Scottish fishermen would not use the proper names of seabirds that they saw as threatening portents; similarly, names of villages were not mentioned, the places being referred to obliquely instead, apparently to protect those living there from potential harm from FAIRIES or other spirits. Also in Scotland, people did not speak the name of a newborn child until it had been baptized and thus, presumably, protected from FAIRY KIDNAPPING. The tradition of giving nicknames or pet names to people similarly arises from the belief that, if fairy people knew the real name of a loved person, that person would be in danger of being stolen AWAY.

Sources: McKay, John G. *More West Highland Tales.* Vol. 2. Scottish Anthropological and Folklore Society. Edinburgh: Oliver and Boyd, 1969, p. 388; Ross, Anne. *Folklore of the Scottish Highlands.* London: B. T. Batsford, Ltd., 1976, p. 95.

names for fairyland Many names for the OTHERWORLD are found in Irish and Scottish sources, although it is unclear whether these indicated geographically separate locations or are merely variant descriptions of the land's features. The names describe the Otherworld as an abundant flatland, as in MAG MELL ("plain of honey") and MAG MÓR ("great plain"), or as a submerged island, as in TIR FO THUINN ("land under wave"). Perhaps the most common name was TIR NA NOG ("land of youth"), which emphasized the unfading beauty of fairyland's residents.

names for the fairies Folkloric motif. In places where the pre-Christian gods were demoted into FAIRIES, these ancient powers are respected sufficiently that it is still considered dangerous to call them by their real names. Therefore euphemisms are used, some vague, others flattering: Them, the Other Crowd, the Good Folk, the Good Neighbors, even That Lot. In Scotland the common phrase was the Guid Folk, and on the Shetlands the Guid Neighbors, while the people of Wales used the term TYLWYTH TEG, "the Fair Family." On the Isle of Man names for the fairies included Ny Mooinjer Veggey, "the Little Kindred"; Ny Guillyn Beggey, "The Little Boys"; and Yn Sleih Veggey, "the Little People." This verbal habit originated in Celtic beliefs about the power of the word. One famous tale describes how a man was kidnapped by the fairies simply for consistently using the word *fairies* rather than a euphemism when passing their abodes (see FAIRY KIDNAPPING).

names for the Otherworld Folkloric motif. Although, unlike with FAIRIES, there was no taboo against speaking of the OTHERWORLD, we nonetheless find many evocative names that describe the Celtic PARADISE: ILDATHACH, "many-colored land"; MAG MÓR, the "great plain"; MAG MELL, the "plain of honey"; Mag Mon, the "plain of sports"; Mag Réin, "plain of the sea"; TIR FO THUINN, the "land under wave"; TIR NA NOG, the "land of youth"; TIR NA MBAN, the "land of women"; and TIR TAIRNGIRI, the "land of promise." These names sometimes are used of a specific Otherworld realm like the floating ISLAND inhabited by the great FAIRY QUEEN NIAMH of the Golden Hair, but they are more generally interchangeable.

Nanny Button-Cap British folkloric figure. A small sprite known in Yorkshire, Nanny Button-Cap was a good FAIRY who appears in some rhymes and stories; she was apparently a helpful sprite similar to a BROWNIE.

Nar (Náir) Irish goddess. An obscure goddess of this name ("modesty") is known from some texts to have offered a high king of Ireland great riches. She may be a form of the goddess of SOVEREIGNTY more commonly known as Flaith.

Nár Thúathcaech Irish hero. "Shame" is another name for the figure more commonly known as FRIUCH, an argumentative swineherd reincarnated as the great BULL DONN CUAILNGE on whom the great queen MEDB of the western province of CONNACHT set her sights. His name may derive from his role in setting in motion the great carnage related in the TÁIN BÓ CUAILNGE, for it was his whisperings to Medb that encouraged her to marry AILILL mac Máta, who in turn challenged her to prove herself equal to him, whereupon the great CATTLE RAID on ULSTER was launched.

Nás (Naas) Irish goddess or heroine. This obscure Irish goddess, known only as the wife of the great hero LUGH, is familiar in Ireland today because of Naas, a prosperous town near Dublin that still bears her name. The place is said to have been the site of her death or burial. Its ancient importance is suggested by the BUADA or demand that the king at TARA dine on HARES from Naas, for which the town is called Naas na Rí, "Naas of the Kings." Reputedly Lugh instituted the great assembly (see ÓENACH) of Teltown in honor of Nás, although most often that festival was said to have been organized to honor his foster mother, the goddess TAILTIU.

Nasciens (Seraphe) Arthurian hero. Once a pagan ruler named Seraphe, Nasciens ("knows nothing") took a new name when, blinded by his arrogant attempt to look upon the GRAIL, he became a hermit monk who advised the knights who rode out in the quest of the sacred object.

Natosuelta (Nantosuelta) Continental Celtic goddess. Her name has been translated as "meandering river" and "winding brook," either one of which makes it clear that she is a goddess of fresh WATER. Like other Celtic RIVER goddesses, she doubtless ruled the land of her watershed, in this case the River Trent in Britain. The Romanized images of this goddess do not stress her riverine nature. Rather, she is shown holding a pot—which could, arguably, hold river water but could also suggest that Natosuelta was a goddess of the household, for she was occasionally invoked as a protector of the home and HEARTH. Some images show her carrying a house on a sort of pole; on it perched a RAVEN, common symbol of PROPHECY. A shrine to Natosuelta was erected at the Roman settlement of Ad Pontem (today, East Stroker in Nottinghamshire), where she was shown accompanied by an unnamed male deity. On the Continent, she was sometimes associated with the god SUCELLUS, "the striker."

Sources: Green, Miranda. *Symbol and Image in Celtic Religious Art.* London: Routledge, 1989, pp. 24, 26, 42; Straffon, Cheryl. *The Earth Goddess: Celtic and Pagan Legacy of the Landscape.* London: Blandford, 1997, pp. 24, 125.

nature Cosmological concept. The Celtic love of nature has been noted by many writers, from ancient times to the present. However, it is important to note that the Celts, being radically polytheistic (see POLYTHEISM) and seeing divinity as lodged in this world rather than as separate from it, did not think of nature as we commonly do today. Nature was not evil or a source of temptation, as to many Christian believers who describe this world as a failed copy of the original PARADISE. Rather, this world was filled with beauty and splendor, as well as pain.

In one ancient Irish text, princesses EITHNE and FEDELM of CONNACHT asked ST. PATRICK and his followers if their god was "in the heavens or on earth, in the sea, in the rivers, in the mountains, in the valleys." St. Patrick assured the girls that god was, indeed, in all those places, but the saint and the princesses, although in apparent agreement, meant quite different things. Patrick meant that a transcendent god, having created the world, still had power over it; the princesses intended no metaphor but expressed a belief in what is called immanent divinity, god found within nature rather than outside it.

A nature so suffused with divinity seems not to have been the vision of the Irish alone but to have been shared with their Celtic relations around Europe. Supernatural forces were believed to pervade the natural world, which was considered divine. The earth itself was typically feminine, a goddess, as were bodies of WATER, especially RIVERS. For this reason, the Celts worshiped out of doors, in sacred groves called *NEMETONS* rather than in roofed TEMPLES. The forces of nature were not always benign but could be threatening or even maleficent toward humans, who were not seen as separate from nature but as part of it.

Navan Fort   See EMAIN MACHA.

Navel Stone   See STONE OF DIVISIONS.

Nechtan (Elcmar) Irish god or hero. This relatively obscure god appears in the story of the goddess BÓAND, whose river, the Boyne, was said to arise near a small HILLFORT called Síd Nechtain, "the FAIRY MOUND of Nechtan." Sometimes identified with the better-known god NUADA, Nechtan was said to have lived originally in the great stone tumulus called the BRÚ NA BÓINNE with Bóand, his wife. But Nechtan was tricked by Bóand, who wished to sleep with the powerful and well-endowed god, the DAGDA. They eloped together, and to hide the affair the Dagda made the sun stand still in the sky for nine months so that their child could be born before Nechtan realized what had happened. That son, AONGHUS Óg, then tricked Nechtan into giving up possession of the great Brú na Bóinne by claiming that he alone had been left out when fairy palaces were assigned. Thereupon, Nechtan moved to another fairy hill near the river's source.

He lived there, some legends say, in the form of a SALMON, although that figure is more commonly called FIND or FINTAN. The salmon lived on the nuts of WISDOM dropped by magical HAZEL bushes that thrived at the river's source. Anyone who could catch and eat the salmon would be gifted with all its wisdom. Nechtan has been connected with the continental Celtic god NODENS, in whose shrine in Britain sculptures of hooked fish were displayed.

Nechtanebus Irish hero. A supposed Egyptian pharaoh, he was through his daughter SCOTA an ancestor of the Irish people. Scota married Míl, the wandering soldier whose children, the MILESIANS, were Ireland's last settlers, according to the mythological history called the *BOOK OF INVASIONS*. Most scholars believe that work is not factually correct. Despite this doubt, there were indeed several pharaohs by the name of Nechtanebus. The name of the hero or god NECHTAN seems to be derived from this name.

necromancy Cosmological concept. There is some question as to whether the Celts employed what is today called necromancy—speaking with or raising the dead, sometimes with the intention of gathering information that only they possess. Folkloric tales describe WITCHES or FAIRIES as having this ability, but it is unclear whether normal people could attain it. In Irish texts we find a description of a long rite employed by a BARD seeking to gain information through necromancy. Because parts of the greatest Irish epic, *TÁIN BÓ CUAILNGE*, had been lost, the BARD Senchan Torpeist did MAGIC for several days that enabled him to raise the spirit of the great dead hero, FERGUS mac Róich, who had participated in the CATTLE RAID that forms the subject of the poem. The poet managed the difficult feat, memorizing the missing verses and reciting them aloud to an assembly of other poets before dying of the effort.

Source: Evans-Wentz, W. Y. *The Fairy-Faith in Celtic Countries.* Gerrards Cross: Colin Smythe Humanities Press, 1911, pp. 151 ff.

Necthan Scéne Irish heroine. An obscure figure, she appears as the mother of several heroes who lost their lives to the ULSTER superhero CÚCHULAINN.

need-fire Celtic ritual. FIRE was a potent symbol to the Celts, who viewed it as a seed or essence of life. Several times each year, fire festivals were held; these may have begun with the need of agricultural peoples to burn off stubble from fields and brush from cleared forests and later acquired a mythological significance as a solar symbol. In Ireland and on the Isle of Man, such festivals usually included the dousing of house fires throughout the land, to be later relighted from the sacral fires of the festival (see BELTANE).

There would also be times when it was felt necessary to call upon gods and other powers for assistance—when famine threatened, for instance, or when disease ran rampant among herds or humans, or when WITCHCRAFT was suspected (the latter was documented in Scotland into relatively recent times). Then the needed ritual fire would be lit, regardless of the season or date. House fires would be extinguished, and designated celebrants (DRUIDS, in ancient times) made fire with a wooden fire-wheel or with flint. Once the primary fire was burning, each local household would relight its hearth fire from it, thus spreading the intercessory ritual throughout the land.

In some cases, power was believed to come only from certain types of wood, which had to be rubbed together to create a spark for the need-fire. There were often complex rituals connected with the need-fire, such as that the spark had to be captured in hemp, which was then used to light a candle, which in turn lit a torch, and then finally a pile of peat or turf bricks. At times only married men were permitted to swivel the wooden fire-stakes against each other, suggesting a sexual symbolism to the fire-making that was apparently believed constrained by the men's marital status. Water was sometimes made part of the ritual, with a CAULDRON being placed over the blazing fire; when it came to the boil, it would be sprinkled over homes, people, herds, or whatever was in need of protection.

Occasionally need-fires were lit for protection of women in childbirth, and for their children as well, for it was believed that when a newly lit need-fire blazed nearby, FAIRY KIDNAPPING of infants was less likely than if the child were unprotected. The ritual of protection sometimes included carrying a blazing brand from the need-fire around the house or herd in order to purify and protect it.

The tradition of the need-fire lasted long in Celtic lands. It was recorded to have been lit in the year 1767 on the Scottish island of Mull, because a CATTLE disease was spreading rampantly and threatening the stock upon which people depended for food and livelihood. Despite the spread of Christianity and the demonization of ancient rites (the need-fire ritual was called "wicked" by local ministers), the people climbed the hill of Carnmoor with a WHEEL and some spindles made of OAK, a tree sacred to the Celts. All the fires within sight of the hill were doused, and then the fire-wheel was spun in a sunwise direction until sparks flew from it. As this occurred, the witnesses chanted an incantation, whose words are not recorded. According to tradition, the wheel had to make fire before noon, presumably because the sun's energy was waxing or growing stronger until then. For three consecutive days, hours of spinning did not produce sufficient sparks, so people stopped the process until the next day. When the need-fire was finally sparked into life, they took a heifer afflicted with the disease and sacrificed her, burning the diseased part in the blaze. All the hearth fires of the region were then lit from the need-fire, and the rest of the animal was roasted as a sacrificial feast to be shared.

The ritual of the need-fire was practiced by Germanic peoples as well as Celtic, as documented by the great folklorist Jacob Grimm. It is not clear whether the rite began with Germanic tribes and spread to nearby Celts, or the reverse.

Sources: MacCulloch, J. A. *The Religion of the Ancient Celts.* London: Constable, 1911, p. 199; MacGregor, Alasdair Alpin. *The Peat-Fire Flame: Folk-Tales and Traditions of the Highlands & Islands.* Edinburgh: The Moray Press, 1937, p. 21.

Nehalennia   Continental Celtic goddess. One of the most important goddesses of the region we call the Netherlands was Nehalennia, a goddess so popular that many large monuments and carved inscriptions to her have been found in that relatively small geographical area. She was the center of a large, popular, and wealthy cult that involved not only Celts but Roman citizens as well. That she is little known in contemporary texts is probably the result of our ignorance of her mythology. No narratives about Nehalennia survive; we have only the many sculpted images dedicated to her, with their elaborate and quite consistent iconography, to use in interpreting what she meant to her people.

At two major cult sites on the North Sea, archaeologists have found temples filled with large monuments to her. One of these, on the Island of Walcheren near Domberg, emerged from the sea on January 5, 1647, as a storm ravaged the seacoast. When it subsided, a huge temple to Nehalennia, dated to the second or third century C.E., lay uncovered from the seaside dunes. More than two dozen altars and other monuments were part of the complex, which was unfortunately mostly destroyed by fire in 1848. Records show that much pottery and many COINS were found on the site, suggesting commercial activity. It was a rich shrine, made of stone brought from Metz, more than 400 miles away in what is today Germany. Presumably Nehalennia was a special goddess to the sea traders who stopped in this ancient port for provisions, trade, and worship; that they believed she blessed or controlled their activities is clear from the wealth they lavished on her shrine.

Another shrine to Nehalennia was discovered more recently in 1979, when a fisherman working the waters of the Oosterschelde estuary near Colijnsplaat found fragments of altars to Nehalennia. Since then, almost a hundred artifacts have been found in the area, thought to be the temple called Ganuenta, which in late Roman times flooded and sank beneath the waters of the estuary. From these two sites with their wealth of statuary, inscriptions, and other artifacts, it has been determined that Nehalennia—despite our ignorance of her mythology—was a significant, perhaps the most significant, deity to the Celtic residents of the region.

She may have begun as the ancestral goddess of the local Celtic tribe, the Morini, but ultimately she was to become a goddess worshiped by the various travelers through the area, most of them sea merchants and sailing crews who made offerings to her for their continued safety on the often dangerous waters of the North Sea, where her worship seems to have been concentrated. Much of her iconography, not surprisingly, includes nautical imagery: boats, oars, rudders, shells, FISH, dolphins, and sea monsters. She was typically shown as a strong young woman, usually wearing a little cape around her shoulders and a round cap, which have been interpreted as a local costume. Usually she was seated, although sometimes she stood with her foot resting on the prow of a ship or hauling a boat by a rope.

Nehalennia's name has been translated as "leader" and "woman who steers," indicating that her position as goddess of seagoers did not limit her domain but expressed it symbolically. She has been described as a goddess of death, the one who brings her devotees safely home to an OTHERWORLD beyond this one, which was often imagined by the Celts as an ISLAND somewhere off in the western sea. Nehalennia was most often depicted with a DOG, which in other contexts has been interpreted to represent a guardian of the dead. On most statues, these large beasts sit attentively at her feet, ears at the alert, looking more like guard dogs than pets but with a kindly rather than fierce expression on their canine faces.

In addition to her connections with the sea, Nehalennia was also associated with the productiveness of the land. She was depicted surrounded by symbols of abundance: the full CORNUCOPIA, as well as baskets of produce and grain; on the top of many of her altars were sculpted representations of heaped fruits, as though they had been piled upon her altar in offering. So predominant was this imagery that not a single image of Nehalennia has been found that does not include fruits on vegetables: she appears unconcerned with human or animal fecundity, focusing instead on that of the vegetative world.

This combination of nautical and agricultural imagery has been variously interpreted. As a goddess of commerce, Nehalennia naturally would have overseen the ships full of grain that were part of trade in those times; thus she may have been invoked for good harvests that would, in turn, lead to good profits. The imagery may have had a less selfish motivation, however, for Nehalennia may have been envisioned as a goddess of the world's journey through the seasons. The fact that some of her altars show cosmic symbols such as SUN and MOON suggest that Nehalennia's influence was much larger than mere commerce but included all kinds of abundance and prosperity, in this world and the Otherworld.

Sources: Green, Miranda. *Celtic Goddesses: Warriors, Virgins and Mothers.* London: British Museum Press, 1995, p. 179; Green, Miranda. *Symbol and Image in Celtic Religious Art.* London: Routledge, 1989, p. 10.

Nemain (Neman, Neamhan) Irish goddess. One of a trio of war goddesses called the three Mórrígna, Nemain is the least known, the more prominent being BADB ("scald crow") and MÓRRÍGAN ("great queen" or "queen of phantoms"); Nemain's name seems to mean "battle panic" or "frenzy of war." So frenzied did she make warriors that they sometimes mistook their friends for enemies, resulting in tragedies of the kind today called "friendly fire," in which a man is killed by his own comrades. She is described only briefly in various texts as confusing warriors with her weird cries. Like other war goddesses, she was imagined to take the form of a CROW, which like other carrion eaters was often seen hovering over battlefields, waiting for a meal. Because her name may be connected to the Celtic word for an outdoor shrine, NEMETON, she may represent the duty of warriors to protect sacred sites.

Nemed (Neimheadh) Irish god. In the *BOOK OF INVASIONS*, Ireland's mythological history, we read of this man who was an early settler on the island. A direct descendant of the biblical Noah through his son Japheth, Nemed was also descended from the monster god of Britain, MAGOG. Leaving his homeland of SCYTHIA, he arrived three decades after the mysterious people of PARTHOLÓN were wiped out by an unknown plague, but while the malevolent beings called the FOMORIANS still raged through the land. Nemed had set off for Ireland with an armada of ships, but when his seamen saw a tower of GOLD on a shore along the way, they tried to land in order to enrich themselves. The sea was against them, however, and all the boats but that in which Nemed and his wife MACHA were traveling were dashed to bits.

Although Nemed kept on toward Ireland, it took 18 months of sailing before they reached landfall. Nemed's people had to fight three battles to win the right to settle from the fierce Fomorians, but finally that monstrous race was defeated, and Nemed set them to work to build his palace, Rath Chinneich in Armagh. Once that effort was done, Nemed massacred the workers so that they could never build a palace better than his.

It was Nemed who, in honor of his wife Macha (the first of three goddesses or heroines by that name), cleared the first fields in the dense forests of the ancient island. As it happened, Nemed and his descendants, the Nemedians, did not long remain in Ireland. After Nemed's death,

the Fomorians paid back his attack on their people by forcing the Nemedians into servitude. When they tried to escape, their opponents called upon the winds and seas to crush the rebellion, and all but one of the Nemedian ships were overturned into the ocean.

That one carried Macha and Nemed's son, FERGUS Lethderg, who moved to the next island to the east, where with his son Britán (after whom some claim the island was named; other sources cite the goddess BRITANNIA), established himself and became the ancestral father of the British people. Another descendant, Semeon, traveled as far as Greece, where he became the ancestor of the FIR BOLG, who returned to Ireland to fight the Fomorians again. Yet other descendants traveled far to the north where they became the TUATHA DÉ DANANN, returning to win Ireland from both the Fir Bolg and the Fomorians at the two battles of MAG TUIRED.

Related to the Celtic word NEMETON, which means "sacred place" or "grove," the name of this god or hero has been interpreted as meaning "sacred person" or even DRUID. Some historical facts seem to hide in the complex tales of the *Book of Invasions*. The Nemedians were apparently a Celtic people who had resided for some time in Ireland and then moved to Britain, where they remained powerful until the arrival of the Germanic peoples called the Angles and Saxons. Unfortunately, attempts to interpret the *Book of Invasions* in light of actual settlement patterns are invariably conjectural.

Sources: MacAlister, R. A. Stewart. *Lebor Gabála Érenn: The Book of the Taking of Ireland, Part 3.* Dublin: Irish Texts Society, 1941, pp. 115–200; O'Rahilly, Thomas. *Early Irish History and Mythology.* Dublin: The Dublin Institute for Advanced Studies, 1946, p. 76.

Nemedians See NEMED.

Nemetius Continental Celtic god. The grammatical form of the Latinized name has led scholars to presume this figure to have been divine. Nemetius was honored at one site on the west bank of the Rhine. The name is connected to Celtic words for "sacred grove," found also in NEMETON and NEMETONA.

Sources: Cunliffe, Barry. *The Ancient Celts*. Oxford: Oxford University Press, 1997, p. 198; Lonigan, Paul R. *The Druids: Priests of the Ancient Celts*. Contributions to the Study of Religion, No. 45. Westport, Conn.: Greenwood Press, 1996, p. 3.

nemeton   Ritual site. The Celts worshiped not indoors but outside, in groves of TREES and at other sacred sites. There are many evidences that trees played an important part in Celtic religious life, never more so than when rituals were held in forest clearings called *nemetons*, a name related to words in other Indo-European languages (Greek *némos*, "glade," Latin *nemus*, "sacred") and may connect with the ancient Irish root, *nem-*, which meant "heaven" but referred symbolically to anything sacred.

Ancient classical authors made much of the outdoor location of Celtic rituals; Strabo described the OAK groves in which the Galacians met, while Pliny the Elder and Tacitus both spoke of the same among continental Celts. Lucan, in a vivid passage, described groves "untouched by men's hands from ancient times, whose interlacing boughs enclosed a space of darkness and cold shade," wherein "images of gods grim and rude were uncouth blocks formed of felled tree-trunks." He reported a legend that the trees would sometimes appear on FIRE or stricken by earthquake but would in reality be untouched and unharmed. Lucan also offhandedly mentioned that this sacred grove was leveled by Caesar because it was too near some buildings the Romans were erecting.

After Romanization, the word *nemeton* was sometimes used of a stone TEMPLE, when such buildings replaced the sacred groves that gave way to Roman axes. The word became part of the names of many Celtic settlements; thus we have Drunemeton near Ankara, Turkey, where the Celtic Galacians lived; Nematacum and *Nemeton* in Gaul, Nemetobrigia in the Celtic region of Spain called Galacia, Vernemeton in England, and Medionemeton in Scotland.

Nemetona   Continental Celtic and British goddess. The name of this goddess derives from NEMETON, the Celtic word for "sacred grove," for the Celts never worshiped indoors but rather in the open air, especially in groves of TREES that were considered to embody the sacredness of nature. Nemetona's name, which has been translated as "she of the sacred grove" or "the goddess of the shrine" may be related to that of the Germanic tribe, the Nemetes, whose ancestral goddess she may have been; she has also been connected etymologically to the Irish war-goddess NEMAIN, suggesting that part of the role of the warrior was to protect sacred sites. There is some evidence that in parts of Gaul, Nemetona was honored as a god rather than a goddess.

Nemglan   Irish god. This relatively obscure god appears in only one Irish myth, that of the heroine MESS BUACHALLA, to whom he appeared as a BIRD and whom he then seduced. Their son CONAIRE, the king of TARA, was told never to injure a bird because of his descent from that species, which has suggested to some scholars an ancient belief in animal TOTEMS. Nemglan came to Conaire before his INAUGURATION as king, revealing to him the secret requirements for his selection and success.

Nentres   (Nentres of Garlot)   Arthurian hero. This minor figure in the stories of the great king ARTHUR opposed the king at the beginning of his reign but later married ELAINE, Arthur's half sister, and became an ally.

neo-pagan   (neo-Pagan)   Modern religion. This term, which means "new pagan," is used to describe those who attempt to reconstruct ancient religion in ways appropriate to today's world. Some neo-pagans claim that their rites were transmitted in secret for many generations, but there is little proof of such claims; rather, they may refer to family traditions that mix CHRISTIANITY, Celtic religion, and pre-Celtic beliefs, traditions that continue even today in parts of Europe and that are often derided there as SUPERSTITION. Other neo-pagans make no claims of secret information but describe their religion as a reconstruction of ancient beliefs. In both categories one finds groups and individuals involved in the CELTIC REVIVAL.

Nera (Neara mac Niadhain) Irish hero. One of the great literary and mythological texts of Ireland is the *Adventure of Nera*. The tale is set at CRUACHAN, the great palace of the goddess-queen MEDB of CONNACHT, on the magical night of SAMHAIN (November 1), the Celtic feast when the doors to the OTHERWORLD were believed to open. When king AILILL mac Máta asked that someone attend to a hanged corpse, Nera volunteered, only to find the dead man able to speak. The corpse asked for a drink of water, and so Nera hoisted it upon his back to find it a drink, but turning toward Cruachan, saw the palace ablaze. He chased the arsonists to the cave of OWEYNAGAT, where to his wonderment he learned that he had foreseen an attack that would occur the following year on Samhain.

The woman who offered this information became Nera's Otherworld wife, but before settling down with her, Nera returned to Cruachan to warn Medb and Ailill of the attack he had foreseen. The queen and king raided Oweynagat, destroying the army that would have burned their palace. The adventures of Nera were not yet over, for the great war goddess MÓRRÍGAN stole a COW from the herd that Nera's FAIRY wife had given him and took it to the upper world to be bred with the great DONN CUAILNGE, the finest brown BULL in Ireland. When the calf was born, it fell into a fight with the white bull of Connacht, FINNBENNACH, who killed the young bull. When Medb overheard people saying that the fight would have been different had it been the calf's sire fighting, she swore she would someday see such a battle—which indeed came to pass after her raid upon ULSTER, related in the great Irish epic, *TÁIN BÓ CUAILNGE*.

Source: Cross, Tom Peete, and Clark Harris Slover, eds. *Ancient Irish Tales*. New York: Henry Holt and Co., 1936, pp. 248 ff.

Nerbgen Irish heroine. This obscure figure, known as "the vehement," is named in the *BOOK OF INVASIONS* as one of the FIVE wives of the hero PARTHOLÓN, the others being Aife, Elgnad (or DEALGNAID), Cichban, and Cerbnat. She is otherwise unknown.

Nerthus Germanic goddess. There is no doubt that Nerthus is a Germanic goddess, but some aspects of her cult influenced the rituals of Celtic goddesses as well, suggesting that there was a shared source for these rituals or that the geographically close cultures influenced each other. The Roman general and geographer Tacitus describes the worship of Nerthus on a sacred ISLAND to which no human was permitted entry; such islands are found commonly in Celtic lore as an image of the OTHERWORLD. At intervals, however, Nerthus was stricken by a desire to leave her sacred isle to travel among her followers. She was hauled forth on an OX-drawn cart and was greeted with great festivity. All warfare ceased while the goddess was abroad in the land. She was believed, by her passing, to bring FERTILITY to the fields. When her progress was over, Nerthus was conveyed back to her holy island, where those who attended her were put to death, apparently in the belief that no one could be permitted to live who had looked upon the face of the goddess. The image of the goddess drawn upon a CART is found in Celtic contexts as well; HUMAN SACRIFICE, too, may have been practiced by the Celts.

Source: Tacitus. *The Agricola and the Germania.* Trans. H. Mattingly. New York: Penguin Books, 1948, pp. 134–135.

Nessa (Ness, Nes, Assa) Irish goddess. The mother of the great king CONCOBAR MAC NESSA, Nessa was originally called Assa, "gentle one." Her father was EOCHAID, king of ULSTER, who brought up his daughter in dignity and comfort. She was a studious and quiet girl of great personal charisma and beauty who drew the eye of the lustful DRUID CATHBAD. Realizing that she was never without her 12 protective tutors, Cathbad had them all killed one night so that he could gain access to her. Cathbad underestimated the gentle girl: Appalled and infuriated by the violence done her beloved tutors, she gathered a company of warriors and set out to discover who was responsible and to wreak vengeance upon them.

She had never carried arms before, but anger made the girl strong, whence she became known as Nessa, "ungentle." She wandered across Ireland, waging battle wherever she saw wrong done, but she did not find who had killed her tutors. Then, one day as she bathed in a wilderness spring, the culprit found her. Cathbad sprang upon the unarmed, unguarded naked girl and drew his sword on her. "Better to consent to you than be killed without my own weapon," she said. Cathbad forced himself upon her; some legends say that in that moment Concobar was conceived, while others say that Nessa outwitted her rapist by conceiving through magical means. Though she lived with him as a sexual hostage, she did not give birth despite prophecies that she would bear a hero. An OMEN came to her one day: Two WORMS appeared in a pail of water from a holy WELL. Nessa drank them down, thus becoming pregnant (see PREGNANCY THROUGH DRINKING), but through her magical power she assured that the child was born clutching one of the worms, so that no one would mistake the future hero for Cathbad's son.

After Cathbad died, Nessa married again, this time by her own choice. Her husband was FACHTNA, another king of Ulster, but he soon died too, whereupon she was courted by the impressive warrior FERGUS mac Róich, her late husband's half brother, who had assumed the throne. As she had a son already, Nessa worried that Concobar, not being of royal blood, could never become king. So she entreated Fergus to give up his throne at EMAIN MACHA for a year, to allow Concobar to reign in his stead; thereafter all of Concobar's descendants could claim to be of the blood of kings. Nessa was more loyal to her son than to her husband, and after a year Fergus returned to discover that she had conspired to keep him from regaining his throne. Furious, he left Ulster and joined forces with the queen of the neighboring province, MEDB, who soon waged war on Concobar's territory.

Nessa's name has been traced to the language of the PICTS, a people who preceded the Celts in Ireland and Scotland. Some scholars argue that the Picts were matrilineal, tracing a child's family line through the mother's rather than the father's family as in patrilineal descent. The fact that Nessa's father gave his daughter land, in a region where the Picts were strong, seems evidence for this theory. Whether Pictish or not, Nessa's child bore her name, being called Concobar mac Nessa, "son of Nessa," rather than after his father, whether that was Cathbad or a magical worm.

Source: Hull, Eleanor. *The Cuchullin Saga in Irish Literature.* London: David Nutt, 1898, pp. 4–5.

Nét (Néit) Irish god. An obscure Irish divinity known only as the mate of the war goddess NEMAIN and therefore presumed to be a god of war, Nét may be one of the rare Celtic war gods, for Celtic lands were usually under the power of goddesses. Or Nét may be the same figure as NEMED, the husband of MACHA, a goddess with whom Nemain is sometimes confused or conflated. Legends about Nét are contradictory: some name him as a member of the monstrous FOMORIANS, while others say he was one of the magical TUATHA DÉ DANANN. Nét is often connected with the Irish site of GRIANÁN AILEACH, a great stone fortress in the far north of the island whose mythological importance is unarguable although interpretations of its meaning vary.

Neton   Continental Celtic god. This obscure god of the Celtic tribe called the Accetani, identified by the Romans with their war god MARS, may be connected to the Irish warrior divinity NÉT.

Nevydd   See NEVYN.

Nevyn   Welsh folkloric figure. This gorgeous Welsh MERMAID was the beloved of a young man named Ivan Morgan, who lived on the Carnavonshire coast. Like others of her kind, she made a wonderful wife, sensuous and loyal to her human mate. She bore him a son, Nevydd, and a daughter, Eilonwy, and the family lived happily until she grew homesick for the land-under-wave in which she had been reared. While his mother and father were visiting the OTHER-WORLD under the seas, their son Nevydd learned the truth of his heritage and died of shame, whereupon Eilonwy committed suicide out of grief—or at least, she tried, throwing herself into the water. She did not drown, for she was rescued by a handsome merman prince who took her off to live with him in the Otherworld beneath the sea. Nevyn went back to land to claim the body of her son, which she took away with her on a beautiful ship that magically appeared. The legend does not record what happened to the bereaved Ivan. Nyved's name is similar to the Irish FAIRY QUEEN, NIAMH of the Golden Hair; they may originally have been the same figure.

Source: Spence, Lewis. *The Minor Traditions of British Mythology.* New York: Benjamin Blom, Inc., 1972, p. 42.

Newgrange   See BRÚ NA BÓINNE.

Niall   (Niall of the Nine Hostages, Niall Níoganach, Niall Naoi-ghaillach)   Irish hero. One of the greatest of kings of TARA, Niall ruled for more than a quarter century. The meaning of his first name is not known, although it has been translated as "cloud"; no earlier heroes bear it, so the name Niall appears to originate with this heroic figure. The latter part of his name, Níoganach or "of the nine hostages" comes from his agreement to take on as foster sons one boy from each of the five PROVINCES of the land, as well as four from Britain. (Some sources say one was from Britain and one each from Scotland, France, and Wales.) A STONE monument on Tara, still standing today, is said to cover his grave. He is a quasi-historical figure, one of the earliest recorded HIGH KINGS of Ireland and father of the important king Loegaire; Niall is believed to have ruled in the fifth century C.E. His descendants became the Uí Néill (O'Neill) family, one of Ireland's most powerful for more than half a millennium.

Niall was known as a raiding captain who took many captives, following in the footsteps of his father Eochu Muighmheadhon ("lord of slaves") who captured Niall's mother CAIRENN, a British princess, on one of his raids. Eochu already had a wife, MONGFHINN, who naturally favored her own four sons. She persecuted Cairenn and her son until the BARD TORNA foresaw the child's illustrious future and offered assistance to the woman and her baby. It is unclear whether Niall's father was king of Tara or whether Niall was the first of his family to hold that title.

Irish history at that time was thickly encrusted by myth, and so we find stories about Niall that have more legendary than historical accuracy. In one of these, Niall and his four brothers went hunting one day, only to find themselves in a region without game and growing very thirsty. The only water they could find was in a WELL guarded by a HAG so unsavory in appearance that the young men fell back in disgust when she demanded a kiss of them. Only Niall stepped forward to bestow a kiss, and other favors, upon the hag—who, pleased with his performance, revealed herself to be a beautiful young woman in disguise. She told Niall that her name was Flaith or SOVEREIGNTY and bestowed upon him the KINGSHIP of the land.

Sources: Cross, Tom Peete, and Clark Harris Slover, eds. *Ancient Irish Tales.* New York: Henry Holt and Co., 1936, p. 518; O'Rahilly, Thomas. *Early Irish History and Mythology.* Dublin: The Dublin Institute for Advanced Studies, 1946, p. 208.

Niamh (Neeve, Niamh of the Golden Hair, Niave, Niam, Niau)   Irish mythological figure. One of the great FAIRY QUEENS of Ireland, Niamh was so beautiful that no human man could resist her: stately, fair of feature, and crowned with cascading golden locks. Indeed, her very name means "beauty." Daughter of the ocean god MANANNÁN MAC LIR, Niamh lived far out to sea on a magical ISLAND, TIR TAIRNGIRI ("land of promise"), to which she would take her captive and captivated lovers.

The most famous of Niamh's lovers was OISÍN, BARD of the band of heroes called the FIANNA, who left his comrades behind to follow Niamh to her OTHERWORLD. There they lived in a swoon of happiness made even more blissful by the birth of their daughter PLUR NA MBAN ("flower of woman-hood"). Eventually, however, Oisín grew home-sick and begged to go back to Ireland. Niamh had not tired of her lover and was reluctant to let him go into the danger she knew awaited him there, but he persisted, and she relented. She warned Oisín that under no circumstances should his foot touch the ground. Then she put him on a fairy horse and sent him home.

Alas for Oisín, he returned to an Ireland utterly changed, for time passes more slowly in FAIRYLAND than on our earth. The warriors of the Fianna were long deceased, and Ireland had lost its old gods with the coming of CHRISTIAN-ITY. The poet was so shocked that he fell from his horse. All his years came upon him, and he quickly died of advanced old age. One famous poem is based on the conceit that, before dying, Oisín was able to converse with ST. PATRICK, who despite the Fianna poet's great eloquence about ancient pagan ways, was able to convert him and baptize him just before death. In any case, Oisín never saw his beloved Niamh again.

Two less important figures also bear the name of Niamh. One is the mistress of the great ULSTER hero CÚCHULAINN; the other married the son of king CONCOBAR MAC NESSA, whom Cúchulainn served.

Source: Joyce, P. W. *Ancient Celtic Romances.* London: Parkgate Books, 1997, pp. 390 ff.

Nicnevin   Scottish folkloric figure. In some sources, we find this as the name of the figure elsewhere called HABETROT, a beautiful FAIRY QUEEN in a malevolent guise as the leader of the WILD HUNT that steals people from their homes to become entertainments for the fairies.

night   Cosmological concept. Unlike our way of beginning day with dawn, the Celts began it at sundown the night before. Thus Celtic feast days were celebrated on the evening of what we would call the previous day. Hallowe'en is still celebrated at sundown on October 31, the day before the Celtic feast of SAMHAIN, from which it is derived, and BELTANE began with May Eve cel-ebrations on April 30.

Nimue   Arthurian heroine. This Welsh name is sometimes offered as the personal name of the mysterious figure called the LADY OF THE LAKE, the OTHERWORLD sponsor of king ARTHUR who lived on an ISLAND of women somewhere in the fairy mists. The name is also occasionally used of the lover of the magician MERLIN, who otherwise appears as Arthur's half sister MORGAUSE, who in turn has been assumed to be the Lady of the Lake. Even more confusingly, Merlin's lover is called VIVIANE in some texts. Such confusions are com-monplace where mythologies are orally transmit-ted and later written down by imaginative writers.

One common story of Nimue was that she was the daughter of the Roman goddess DIANA, her father having been a human man named Dinas. As the daughter of the woodland divinity, she was naturally raised in the forest, where Merlin first met her. Her first request of him was to teach her to make a tower out of thin air; he did so, not realizing that his life would end when she fashioned just such a prison for him.

Nisien (Nissien, Nisyen) Welsh hero or god. The Welsh god BRÂN THE BLESSED had two half brothers who were opposite in temperament. Gentle Nisien wished only the best for everyone, but his evil brother EFNISIEN did nothing but cause trouble. It was Efnisien who caused the great war that led to Brân's death in Ireland, by a random act of cruelty that caused the king of that land to be set against Wales forever. Nisien tried to intervene, searching for a diplomatic solution and offering apologies for his brother's behavior, but to no avail. Nisien plays a relatively small part in the story, found in the Welsh tales recorded as the *MABINOGION*, and may be simply a positive foil for his evil brother.

Nodens (Nodons) British god. Relatively little is known about this god, whom the invading Romans said was the same as their warrior divinity MARS. A huge temple was devoted to him on the banks of the Severn River at Lydney in Gloucestershire, with a dormitory and several HEALING sites; thus Nodens may have been envisioned as warring against disease. Nodens was also associated with the woodland god SILVANUS, suggesting that healing was believed to occur most effectively in the peace of a natural setting.

Never represented in human form, Nodens may have been pictured as a large DOG—often a healing symbol to the Celts, although also a guardian of the dead—although the canine sculptures found in his sanctuaries may have been intended to represent the god's attendants. His name has not been translated with certainty but may mean "cloud-maker," "wealth-producer,"

or "fisherman." Because of the size and importance of his sanctuary, Nodens is considered one of Britain's most significant Celtic gods; he is sometimes said to be parallel to the similarly named Irish god NUADU and has been linked as well to the Welsh god LLUDD, whose alternative name is Nudd.

Noínden Ulad See DEBILITY OF THE ULSTERMEN.

Nóine (Nóindiu, Noidhiu) Irish folkloric figure. Several curious legends feature this boy who was born after a nine-year gestation. In some, he is said to have been conceived by his mother after a water spirit seduced her when she was frolicking on the seashore; in another, she was made pregnant by the god of poetry, AONGHUS Óg. Upon his birth, Nóine uttered nine mysterious sayings, after which his grandfather died; this motif seems to have come from the more common story of the hero LUGH and his malevolent grandfather, BALOR of the Evil Eye. Some scholars believe that Nóine's tales provided a source for stories about the hero FIONN MAC CUMHAILL.

Noísiu (Naeshe, Naisii, Naoise, Noise, Noaise) Irish hero. One of Ireland's most romantic and tragic legends surrounds this young man, one of the SONS OF UISNEACH and lover of the beautiful heroine DEIRDRE. Doomed by a prophecy to be both immensely beautiful and the cause of war, Deirdre was held hostage by the king of ULSTER, CONCOBAR MAC NESSA, who wished to defy fate and have her for his bride despite the many years that separated them. Although she was brought up without ever seeing a man, Deirdre dreamed of the existence of Noísiu. One day she saw a RAVEN's feather and blood on snow, and she wished aloud to have a man with hair that black, lips that red, skin that white.

Her nurse, the BARD LEBORCHAM, took pity on the girl and introduced her to the man she knew fit that description: Noísiu. Together with his brothers, Ardán and Ainnle, the pair eloped, running from the powerful king Concobar, who pursued them relentlessly. Finally the brothers and Noísiu's beloved Deirdre found peace in the wilderness of Scotland, where they lived a hard but healthy life until Concobar lured them back with promises of forgiveness. Deirdre suspected treachery, but Noísiu yearned for home. As soon as they arrived, Concobar had Noísiu and his brothers killed. Deirdre thwarted his attempt to take her, however, by committing suicide in grief over the loss of her true love, Noísiu.

Noísiu and his brothers were the children of an otherwise obscure man named UISNEACH; some have argued a connection with the important mythological site of Uisneach in Co. Westmeath. Their mother was Elbha, the daughter of the nefarious druid CATHBAD; thus they would have been half brothers to king Concobar himself, according to tales that have Cathbad fathering the king on the gentle scholar Assa, who after his assaults on herself and her household became the warrior NESSA.

Nollaig (In Welsh, Nadolig) Folkloric holiday. Although the Celts did not celebrate the SOLSTICES and EQUINOXES, centering their worship instead on the central days of each season (IMBOLC, February 1, in winter; BELTANE, May 1, in spring; LUGHNASA, August 1, in summer; and SAMHAIN, November 1, in fall), various pressures caused the addition of other seasonal feasts to the Celtic calendar. Earlier cultures had marked the solstices as is evidenced by the orientation of pre-Celtic stone monuments to the sunrise and sunset of those days. With the coming of Christianity, the winter solstice became especially important, for it was the date on which Jesus Christ was said to have been born. This alleged birthday of the savior was, in fact, adopted by the Christian church as a way of adapting the preexisting winter solstice festivals that the new converts were loath to abandon.

Thus Celtic lands developed their own winter solstice rituals, which were called in Scotland "Nollaig," apparently from the Latin *natalis* ("birth") as passed through Welsh. That this festival is not necessarily devoted to the birth of Christ, but is more generically a midwinter feast, can be detected by the fact that it is only sometimes celebrated on Christmas; in some regions it occurs on New Year's Day, while still other regions celebrated the entire week between Christmas and New Year as Nollaig. In Scotland processions of youngsters used to walk from house to house, reciting nonsense rhymes whose words seem to refer to Celtic heroic figures; householders rewarded the singers with food and drink, with the climax of the festivities on HOGMANY or New Year's Day. In Ireland boys hunted WRENS that were then carried around the village to singing and elaborate pageantry. In Irish tradition, if one died during this period, it was a sign of being blessed.

Sources: Campbell, John Grigorson. *Witchcraft and Second Sight in the Highlands and Islands of Scotland.* Detroit: Singing Tree Press, 1970, p. 229; Gardner, Alexander. *Popular Tales of the West Highlands.* Vol III. London: J. F. Campbell, 1892, p. 28; Hyde, Douglas. *Abhráin atá Leaghta ar an Rechtúire: Songs Ascribed to Raftery.* New York: Barnes & Noble Books, n.d., pp. 28, 53.

Noreia Possible continental Celtic goddess. In Roman times this obscure goddess was worshiped in the lands around today's Slovenia, which was settled by both Celts and Illyrians; it is not certain to which ethnic group this goddess belonged.

north (*tuaisceart*) Of the four DIRECTIONS, this one had the most sinister implications for the ancient Irish and, possibly, for other Celtic peoples as well. The SUN was seen to move south on its daily path, as though retreating from the north (a direction geographically defined as the opposite from the Sun's daily position at noon). Because the sunrise direction (*deosil*) was symbolically connected with correctness and the natural order, moving to the left or to the north had the opposite connotations. Words connected with north have, even in modern Irish, negative connections, as with words for "foreboding," "curse" and "anguish," all of which derive from the word for "north." The northern province, ULSTER, is most associated with war in ancient epics.

Source: Dames, Michael. *Mythic Ireland.* London: Thames and Hudson, 1992, p. 46.

Northumbria   Celtic region. In Celtic times, the climatically harsh part of Britain, now known as Northumbria, was called Bernicia; the more fertile southern part was called Deira.

Nothain   Irish heroine. Like other mad women and men of Irish legend (see MIS, SUIBHNE), Nothain was driven mad by war. According to the DINDSHENCHAS, the place-poetry of Ireland, Nothain was a WARRIOR WOMAN who, driven insane by an attack that left her family dead, wandered the countryside, becoming shaggy and wild. Her father, the only one to survive the assault, searched for more than a year before he found her, speechless with grief. After a night spent in his comforting presence, she finally spoke, only to ask if anyone else had survived. Hearing the sad news that the family was all dead, Nothain died of sorrow.

See also MADNESS.

Source: Gwynn, Edward. *The Metrical Dindshenchas.* Royal Irish Academy, Todd Lecture Series. Dublin: Hodges, Figgis, and Co., Ltd., 1906–1924, pp. 29–31.

Nuada (Nuada of the Silver Hand, Nuada of the Silver Arm, Nuadu, Nuadhu, Nuada Argatlám)   Irish god. Leader of the TUATHA DÉ DANANN, the people of the goddess DANU, at the time when they contested with the malevolent FOMORIANS for possession of Ireland, Nuada was a great warrior and fine leader. In the fury of the first battle of MAG TUIRED, his right hand or arm

was sliced off by an opponent. Thus even though victorious, Nuada forfeited his throne, for a BLEMISHED KING could not rule.

The half-Fomorian BRES replaced him but turned out to be so stingy he would not even feed the poet CAIRBRE—an offense against HOSPITALITY that lost Bres his realm, for the BARD cast a SATIRE upon him that raised boils upon his face, thus making Bres too blemished to rule. In the meantime, a silver hand had been crafted for Nuada by the healing god DIAN CÉCHT. Even such a marvelous appurtenance did not satisfy the needs of kingship, for it still constituted a defect. Then MIACH, a brilliant physician and son of Dian Cécht, used his medical and magical skills to cause real skin to grow over the silver arm—thus entitling Nuada to reassume the throne. For his efforts, Miach lost his life, killed by his envious father.

When the Tuatha Dé left the surface of this world to live beneath the earth in their magical swellings or *sídhe*, Nuada became the lord of ALMU, an important early ritual site and magical center of the PROVINCE of LEINSTER. Other sources place his palace at the great tumulus on the River Boyne, the BRÚ NA BÓINNE, claiming that he was the consort goddess of the region, BÓAND. Deceived by her with the god DAGDA, Nuada was further deceived when the son of that affair, AONGHUS Óg, tricked him out of the great palace; NECHTAN, the name sometimes given for Bóand's deceived husband, may be an alternative name for Nuada. Nuada was later euhemerized—made human—in stories that make him an earthly king who fought with the hero FIONN MAC CUMHAILL for control of Leinster. At Almu, Nuada was said to keep one of the great treasures of his race, a sword that could not be escaped once it had been unsheathed.

A minor figure by this name was a human, a DRUID who served the king CATHAÍR MÓR.

Source: O'Conor, Norreys Jephson. *Battles and Enchantments: Retold from Early Gaelic Literature.* Freeport N.Y.: Books for Libraries Press, 1970, p. 7.

Nuala   Irish heroine. This name is often used as a shortened version of FIONNUALA, but it is also given to the FAIRY QUEEN otherwise known as ÚNA, who was the lover of the king of the FAIRIES, FINNBHEARA.

nuckelavee   Scottish folkloric figure. On Orkney, the islands northeast of Scotland, people occasionally reported being set upon by this monstrous centaur, whose one-eyed human head was mounted on a RED-fleshed HORSE's body that had flippers instead of legs. It lived in the sea and from there leapt out to kill humans or CATTLE as its whim took it. The only escape was to dash across fresh water, which this sea-being could not tolerate. The *nuckelavee* was related to the more commonly known WATER HORSE, or possibly to the NYGEL of Shetland.

Source: Douglas, George. *Scottish Fairy and Folk Tales.* West Yorkshire: EP Publishing, 1977, pp. 160 ff.

Nudd (Lludd)   British god. A great temple of the Roman era was dedicated to a god called NODENS, who is believed to be the same as the Welsh god Nudd or LLUDD. Given the location of the temple and the depiction of Nudd as surrounded by tritons, symbols of the sea, he has been interpreted as the god of the RIVER's mouth or estuary and possibly the headlands around it.

In Welsh mythology, the god called Nudd (more commonly, Lludd), was the ruler of Britain and brother of the king of the Continent, LLEFELYS. He built London, but his reign was not entirely happy nor successful. A race of demons attacked the land, then two DRAGONS, then a gigantic magician. With the help of his brother, Nudd was able to conquer all of the plagues.

numbers   Cosmological symbols. As in many other cultures, the Celts saw numbers as mysterious, powerful, even magical. The most important were the numbers THREE and FIVE, but other numbers had significance as well. The Celtic numerical system ended with 10—the number that could be counted on two hands—with larger numbers expressed in terms of multiples (10 times 10) or, more commonly, as a "vast" host or "innumerable" army. In Old Irish we find indications that numbers may have been originally counted in a system of fives, reflected in both mythology and family organization.

Although there is no written evidence of a numerological system whereby each number was given a specific mystical meaning, the repetition of certain numbers suggests such a belief. The iteration of the numbers three and five in various mythological contexts is an especially strong indication that such numerology originally existed and has been lost. Comparison of various myths suggests the following meanings for frequently occurring numbers:

Two—Connected with service or commitment, found in legends of enchanted women chained together in pairs, in pairs of oracular RAVENS that accompany the hero CÚCHULAINN, and in the two loyal hunting DOGS of FIONN MAC CUMHAILL.

Four—Connected with wholeness. Because a hidden fifth was implied (see PROVINCES), four is seen as a diminished version of five.

Seven—Connected with MAGIC, an interpretation that may have been adopted from non-Celtic, possibly Middle Eastern, sources; the most common usage shows typical Celtic multiplication, in the belief that the SEVENTH SON of a seventh son (less frequently, the seventh daughter of a seventh daughter) was especially likely to be magically gifted. In myths about transformation, a span of seven years is common; thus the goddess ÉTAIN was forced to live for seven years as an insect, and the magical LOUGH GUR dries up every seven years to reveal its secrets.

nygel (Noggle, nuggle)   Scottish folkloric figure. On the Shetland Islands, this magical being appeared as a sweet gray pony. But if you mounted it, beware, for it would take you on a fast ride to the sea and dunk you there. Attack by a nygel was far less threatening than that of the invariably fatal WATER HORSE, of which the nygel seems a variant, or of its neighboring MONSTER the *NUCKELAVEE.* The nygel loved millraces—the streams that ran from the old water-powered grain and woolen mills—and grew angry if they were accidentally left running at night; the FAIRY beast forced the wheel to a stop, which wreaked havoc on its machinery.

Nynnyaw (Nynniaw) Welsh hero. This relatively obscure king was a son of the god BELI and, with his brother Peibaw, once waged a war in which all the land was destroyed. The reason for the war: They disagreed on astrological interpretations. Few wars ever were begun for such meager cause, and so the two brothers were turned into animals to teach them a lesson.

Ny Shee Manx folkloric figure. This term, in the language of the Isle of Man, refers to the FAIRY folk called the SÍDHE in Irish.

oak Symbolic plant. Large and impressively long-lived, the oak was one of the most important TREES to the Celts. In part, this was because of the oak's usefulness: It provides abundant acorns, which were in ancient times a favored food of PIGS, whose flesh then became part of the human diet; its long-lasting wood is sought after for building; its bark produces a substance useful for tanning leather. The oak's usefulness extended to the spiritual plane as well; according to Roman author Pliny the Elder, the Celts harvested MISTLETOE from oak trees for ritual use in curing disease and encouraging human FERTILITY.

Oak forests were common in continental Gaul, where we find early evidence of their sanctity: Construction of oak funeral houses by HALLSTATT and LA TÈNE peoples suggests that the tree was connected with the afterlife or OTHERWORLD. The oak may have been associated with a specific god, although which one is not clear, because documents date only to Roman times, when Maximum Tyrius claimed the oak symbolized the father of gods, who lived within the tree; the so-called Jupiter columns (JUPITER being the Roman version of Zeus) found in Gaulish temples have been interpreted as indoor substitutes for great trees dedicated to the god.

Although trees in general were sacred to the Celts, who practiced their rituals in NEMETONS or sacred groves, the Celtic priesthood of DRUIDS held the oak to be the most sacred tree; indeed, the very word *druid* is connected to an ancient word for "oak." The Roman poet Lucan described the druids as using acorns in their prophetic rituals, masticating them until they saw visions; the story is hard to credit, because no hallucinatory substances have been isolated in acorns. Wooden images from the pre-Roman and Roman periods have been found, carved of the strong and lasting wood of the oak.

Belief in the sanctity of the oak survived into the post-Celtic era, when folklore envisioned the oak as a living being that, when cut, cried out or took revenge upon the forester, maiming or killing him as it fell. An oak was believed to make a desperate racket when felled, loud enough to be heard a mile away. FAIRY folk were thought to live in or around oaks; together with the ASH and the THORN, the oak constituted the sacred tree trinity that marked fairy places.

The centrality of the oak in ancient Celtic life can still be detected in names that embody the tree: the Celtic capital of the Galacians in Turkey, Drunemeton ("sacred oak grove"); and the Irish abbey towns of KILDARE ("church of the oak") and of Durrow ("plain of oaks").

Sources: Green, Miranda. *Symbol and Image in Celtic Religious Art.* London: Routledge, 1989,

p. 152; Ross, Anne. *Pagan Celtic Britain: Studies in Iconography and Tradition.* London: Routledge & Kegan Paul, 1967, p. 33.

oakmen　British folkloric figures. Occasionally in the north of England, references are found in oral literature to FAIRY people who lived in great OAKS; an old rhyme holds that "fairy folks/are in old oaks." Especially powerful were oaks that regenerated themselves after being cut; the saplings that came forth in such circumstances were regarded with awe. In the Cotswolds each village had a sacred tree, usually an oak, where fairy beings were believed to hide. The artist Beatrix Potter used the tradition in her book *The Fairy Caravan,* in which oak people wore toadstools for caps.

Source: Briggs, Katharine M. *The Folklore of the Cotswolds.* London: B. T. Batsford Ltd., 1974, p. 121.

oath　Ritual act. Calling upon divine forces to witness the truth of a statement is known in many societies, including those of the Celts, who put great stock in verbal truthfulness—perhaps because they had no written language. Oaths were made by calling upon either gods or elemental powers (SUN, MOON, air), who would punish the speaker for lying; a common form of the oath among the radically polytheistic Celts was, "I swear by the gods my people swear by."

Source: Cowan, Tom. "The Pledge to the Elements." In Patricia Monaghan, ed. *Irish Spirit: Pagan, Celtic, Christian, Global.* Dublin: Wolfhound Press, 2001.

Oberon　(Auberon, Oberycome)　British folkloric figure. Oberon makes a memorable appearance in William Shakespeare's *A Midsummer Night's Dream* as a king of FAIRYLAND whose quarrel with his consort TITANIA prompts him to meddle in the love affair of humans astray in the

forest. Oberon, who also appears in French and British romances, is more a literary than a mythological character. He is associated with the fairy queens Titania and MAB.

Ocean Sweeper　(Aigéan scuabadoir)　Irish mythological object. One of the great treasures of the Irish OTHERWORLD was a boat that moved through the sea under the power of its pilot's thoughts. Brought from the Otherworld by the heroic LUGH, the magic boat became the property of the ocean god MANANNÁN MAC LIR.

Ocelus　Welsh and British god. This obscure god, known from only a few inscriptions, was associated by the Romans with MARS.

Ochall Ochne　Irish mythological figure. A FAIRY king from the western province of CONNACHT, Ochall Ochne played a minor role in the greatest of Irish epics, the TÁIN BÓ CUAILNGE. It was his swineherd, RUCHT, who had an unending argument with another swineherd named FRIUCH; the two were born and reborn in different forms until they became the two great BULLS who killed each other at the epic's end.

Ochren　(Coinchenn, Corrgend)　Irish mythological site. This name is occasionally used of an Otherworldly place beneath the ocean where FAIRY people disported themselves by dancing in labyrinthine patterns.

Octriallach　Irish hero. The monstrous FOMORIANS, one of the early races of mythological Irish settlers, are rarely known as individuals but appear rather as a frightening and murderous mass under the leadership of their king, BALOR of the Evil Eye. An exception is this spy who learned the secrets of the Fomorians' opponents, the TUATHA DÉ DANANN. DIAN CÉCHT, the Tuatha Dé physician, bathed their wounded in the magical WELL of Slaine, which healed all their wounds (it could not, however, reconnect amputated limbs or HEADS). When he discovered this, Octriallach decommissioned the well by filling it with earth, whereupon he was killed by OGMA, the god of eloquence.

Odras Irish heroine. A LAKE in Co. Roscommon, in Ireland's western province of CONNACHT, was named for this brave girl, daughter (or wife) of the hostel-keeper Buchat Buasach. When the MÓRRÍGAN, the great death-queen, stole Odras's cow to mate with her own OTHERWORLD bull, Slemuin the Smooth, Odras was bold—or foolhardy—enough to go after the thief. She traveled to OWEYNAGAT, the cave beneath the great provincial capital CRUACHAN, hoping to redeem her loss. There an enchantment overtook her, and she fell asleep under an OAK tree, just short of penetrating to the Mórrígan's domain. She never awoke, for the Mórrígan turned her into the small lake that bears her name, to keep her from reclaiming her stolen cow.

Source: Gwynn, Edward. *The Metrical Dindshenchas.* Royal Irish Academy, Todd Lecture Series. Dublin: Hodges, Figgis, and Co., Ltd., 1906–1924, p. 22.

Óenach (Aonach) Irish ritual assembly. At regular intervals, the Celtic peoples of Ireland gathered at sacred spots to celebrate seasonal rituals intended to recognize the honor of the natural cycle while restoring the ancient union of the tribe. As the ancient Irish lived in relatively small groups in somewhat isolated spots, such assemblies served many purposes other than the paramount religious ones. HORSES and CATTLE were traded; young people met and courted; laborers were hired; contracts between otherwise distant parties were established. Some of the important Óenachs were those on BELTANE at the sacred hill UISNEACH in the center of Ireland, and on LUGHNASA at the site dedicated to the goddess TAILTIU.

Sources: Aitchison, N. B. *Armagh and the Royal Centres in Early Medieval Ireland: Monuments, Cosmology and the Past.* Rochester, N.Y.: Crithne Press/Boydell & Brewer, 1994; Raftery, Brian. *Pagan Celtic Ireland: The Enigma of the Irish Iron Age.* London: Thames and Hudson, 1994, pp. 81 ff.

Oengus See AONGHUS.

Ogalla Irish mythological site. The Celts revered WATER, both fresh and salt, and many myths are situated at or near water. Streams and WELLS—pure water that springs forth from underground—figure importantly in Irish myth and legend. One such narrative tells of two princesses of CONNACHT, EITHNE and FEDELM, who went to bathe one morning in the holy SPRING of Ogalla, near the great capital city of CRUACHAN. There they encountered men who, dressed in white, looked to them like DRUIDS. They were not; it was ST. PATRICK and his followers.

The girls questioned Patrick about his god. Where, the girls asked, is that god located, whether in the earth or the sky or the sea? Does he have fine daughters, and are his sons beautiful to look upon? Patrick assured the princesses that the Christian god was all they desired (skirting the question of that god's "daughters"). Thus he converted the princesses of Connacht, who then chose to die instantly upon baptism rather than linger in the sinful world. The end of the story is as clearly un-Celtic as the questions the girls posed were pagan.

ogham *(ogam)* Celtic symbolic system. The Celtic people did not practice writing as defined today; they did not use alphabetic letters nor pictorial script to spell out words. Religious, ritual, and historical material was committed to memory by the DRUIDS, who believed that such material was too precious to be written and thus at risk of coming into the possession of those unprepared to understand or appreciate its meaning and value. For this reason we have no written mythology, no prayer books, not even historical works from the Celts themselves. We have instead only writings by people who came into contact with them (often through war) and by later descendants (often Christian monks); thus we must be careful to evaluate written sources on Celtic material to discern political or religious bias.

The fact that the Celts were not literate does not mean they lacked literature or were unintelligent. The lack of interest in—some would say taboo against—writing was based in the importance of speech, which was held to have great power. Even today, eloquent speech is especially valued as a human talent in the ancient Celtic lands.

The Celts did have a symbolic script system called *ogham*, said to have been invented by OGMA, god of eloquence, or by BRIGIT, goddess of poetry. Whether *ogham* developed after contact with and in response to literate cultures is not clear, although many argue that it was inspired by the Latin alphabet. The *ogham* "letters" were lines drawn horizontally and diagonally on wood; there are 20 different combinations of strokes. Epics refer to libraries of wooden wands inscribed with such lines, but wood does not typically endure for centuries; the inscriptions that have been found—fewer than 400—are all carved on stone, most giving only a single name or title. These *ogham* tablets predominantly come from the southwestern Irish province of MUNSTER, where some argue the script was invented in between the third and fourth centuries C.E., but tablets have been found in Wales and Scotland as well. See TREE ALPHABET.

Ogma (Oghma, Ogme)   Irish god. This Irish god is believed parallel or cognate to the continental Celtic god OGMIOS. He was the son of the beneficent father god, the DAGDA, and father of the important goddess ÉTAIN and of the poet CAIRBRE mac Éadaoine. Although he has little legend, Ogma is said to have invented the writ-

ing script called, after him, OGHAM. He was also eloquent of speech and a great poet.

Ogmia   British god. Assumed to be a British version of the continental Celtic god of eloquence OGMIOS and the Irish god OGMA, Ogmia was depicted by Romano-Celtic artists as a curly-haired youth with rays erupting from his head. Nothing is known of his myth or cult.

Ogmios (Ogmioc)   Continental Celtic god. The Greek satirist Lucian of Samosata, in the second century C.E., connected Ogmios with the powerful classical hero HERCULES, although it seems clear that the strength of the Celtic god was rather verbal than physical; Ogmios was depicted as a dark-skinned bald man dragging people around by chains that stretched between his tongue and their ears, symbolizing the power eloquence has over its listeners. For this metaphorical strength he is called Trenfher, "strong man." Ogmios's advanced age suggests that fine speech is a gift of maturity rather than youth. In some contexts, Ogmios, described bringing the dead to the OTHERWORLD, was associated with the Otherworldly divinity DIS PATER.

Ogniad   Irish heroine or goddess. This obscure figure was the daughter of the important FAIRY king MIDIR and mother of the hero SIGMALL, but little is known of her except that she was lawless and self-willed. Whether her own mother was Midir's consort ÉTAIN is unclear from textual evidence.

Source: Gwynn, Edward. *The Metrical Dindshenchas.* Part II. Vol. IX. Royal Irish Academy, Todd Lecture Series. Dublin: Hodges, Figgis, and Co., Ltd., 1906–1924, p. 9.

Ogyrvran (Ogyrven)   Welsh hero. In Welsh folklore and literature, we find mention of this GIANT who owned a CAULDRON from which inspiration arose in the forms of sprites or

FAIRIES. He may be a folkloric memory of a local version of OGMIOS, the Celtic god of eloquence, to whom his name seems related.

Source: Spence, Lewis. *The Minor Traditions of British Mythology.* New York: Benjamin Blom, Inc., 1972, p. 82.

Oirbsen   Irish god. This obscure term was an alternate name or title of the shape-shifting god of the sea, MANNANÁN MAC LIR, who drowned in a lake called Loch Oirbsen (now Lough Corrib).

Oisín (Oshin, Ossian, Oisin)   Irish hero. The poet of the FIANNA, the band of warriors who followed the great hero FIONN MAC CUMHAILL, Oisín was named "little fawn" because of the fur across his eyebrows, left when his mother SADB licked her newborn while still wearing her enchanted DEER shape. He grew into the most eloquent of his peers and, like many other poets, drew the attention of a FAIRY LOVER. In Oisín's case, this mistress the most beautiful fairy of them all, NIAMH of the Golden Hair, who stole him away from his human wife, the blonde beauty Eibhir. Oisín traveled to her land far beyond the western waves, TIR TAIRNGIRI, the land of promise, and lived with her for several happy weeks. Or at least it felt like weeks to Oisín—but because time passes differently in FAIRYLAND than it does here, Oisín was actually away for three centuries, during which time his friends died and Ireland changed almost beyond recognition.

When he finally grew homesick, Oisín prevailed upon Niamh to let him visit earthly reality again. She grudgingly agreed and even provided him a magical horse, warning him that he was under no circumstances to touch the ground. (This common motif in folklore invariably indicates that someone will, in fact, touch the ground.) And so Oisín went home, and he failed to attend to Niamh's warning—although sources differ as to whether Oisín's saddle gave way, or he leaned down to help a beggar, or he was overcome with desire to feel earth beneath his feet again.

In any case, when Oisín touched the ground, his many years instantly came over him. He was no longer the hale and healthy lad who had left Niamh. He grew stooped and gray, then died and turned to dust, all in the wink of an eye. In some versions of the story, Oisín lived long enough to debate the values of Ireland's ancient paganism with ST. PATRICK, and to recognize the value of the Christian way enough to be baptized.

A character named Ossian, invented by the 19th-century Scottish poet James Macpherson, was credited with the creation of a number of poems that Macpherson himself had written, inspired by the oral literature of his native land. When it was revealed that there was, in fact, no ancient Scottish poet named Ossian whose work had been translated, Macpherson was disgraced and the "Ossian forgeries" were dismissed as sentimental. Yet Macpherson's work was influential, especially in Germany where it inspired the emergent Romantic poets.

Sources: Cross, Tom Peete, and Clark Harris Slover, eds. *Ancient Irish Tales.* New York: Henry Holt and Co., 1936, p. 439; Joyce, P. W. *Ancient Celtic Romances.* London: Parkgate Books, 1997, pp. 385 ff; Kennedy, Patrick. *Legendary Fictions of the Irish Celts.* New York: Benjamin Blom, 1969, p. 40.

Olca Ái   Irish hero. The GIANT Olca Ái once so frightened the women of the capital of CONNACHT, Ireland's western province, that they fled across the land and, still terrified, drowned themselves when they reached a large body of water. The LAKE in which they perished bears the name of their leader, ERNE. Some have interpreted the rough-hewn stone sculptures found on White Island in Lough Erne as representing the giant and one of the maidens.

ollam (*ollamh, ollave*)   Irish bardic title. The highest of the seven level of FILI or poet, the ollam was prepared to recite all of the 250 important stories of the land and 100 of the lesser tales.

Ollamh Fódhla (Ollam Fodla, Ollamh Fodhla) Legendary Irish king. This HIGH KING was said to have mounted the throne of TARA in 714 B.C.E. and to have first codified the law of the land. His name seems to mean "poet of FÓDLA," (Fódla being one of the goddesses of the Irish land); as poets were also BREHONS or judges, Ollamh may have held that position before being elevated to the kingship.

Ollipheist Irish mythological being. A large snaky creature, the Ollipheist wriggled through the soil of ancient Ireland, creating a gully down which water flowed to form the River Shannon. See LISCANNOR.

Ollototae Romanized British goddess, or Roman goddess. An inscription to this multiple goddess was found at Chester, although it is unclear whether the divinity was a Celtic goddess translated into Roman form, or a Roman adaptation of the Celtic earth goddess.

Olloudios (Ollouidias, Olludio) Continental Celtic and British god. This relatively obscure Gaulish god may have been a local divinity (GENIUS LOCI) worshiped in a TREE, for his name seems to derive from two words for "great tree" or "giant tree" (ollo-vidio). His special region was the islands off the south of France called the Antibes, where he was honored by the tribe called the Narbonenses. Olloudios was also found in Britain, where in Gloucester he was depicted as having huge ears that stuck out from his head like wings.

Source: Ross, Anne. *Pagan Celtic Britain: Studies in Iconography and Tradition.* London: Routledge & Kegan Paul, 1967, pp. 37, 172.

Olmec (Oílmelc) See IMBOLC.

Olwen Welsh heroine or goddess. The Welsh tale of KULHWCH AND OLWEN centers on this heroine, who may descend from an earlier goddess. There are many indications that she was originally a SUN goddess: her name, which appears to mean "leaving white footprints" or "golden wheel"; her red-gold necklace and many golden rings; her streaming yellow hair; and her power to raise white flowers from every step she took. The hero KULHWCH wished to marry her, but her father YSPADDADEN PENKAWR ("giant hawthorn tree") opposed the match because he believed it would be the death of him (the same motif is found in the apparently parallel Irish story of BALOR of the Evil Eye and his daughter EITHNE, courted by the hero CIAN). Yspaddaden placed 13 obstacles (possibly the 13 lunar months) in Kulhwch's path, but with Olwen's assistance the hero won her hand.

omen Cosmological symbol. To see an omen is not necessarily to see into the future, despite the most common understanding of the word. Omens may be portents hinting at events to come, but they can also point to an event that has already happened in a distant place and so can be a form of far-seeing. Belief in omens has been part of every culture, for there are always those who wish to know more than their senses can tell them. In the case of the Celts, we find omens typically associated with unusual behavior of animals or stars; sometimes it is difficult to discern whether such behavior predicted, or caused, bad luck. In some cases, ritual relief was suggested; for instance, if one caught sight of the new MOON through a window, bowing THREE times to the moon would ward off the bad luck that otherwise followed.

Things out of place or in the wrong season were typically interpreted as omens or portents: A RAT seen at sea was considered among Scots sailors to be a sign that someone aboard would drown. Similarly any peculiar juxtaposition of objects or beings could represent an omen: Those same Scots sailors believed that seeing a rat or mouse in a sieve was a sure signal of danger to anyone at sea that evening, for their boat would spring as many leaks as the sieve had holes.

The Irish specified many omens of death: gaps in a sown field, a hen cackling on the roost, a DOG howling for three nights in a row. Horseshoes were oracular, for if they were found with the closed end pointing away, bad luck was coming, but if pointed toward the finder, good luck was approaching.

Sources: Carmichael, Alexander. *Carmina Gadelica: Hymns and Incantations.* Hudson, N.Y.: Lindisfarne Press, 1992, pp. 176–178; Harland, John, and T. T. Wilkinson. *Lancashire Legends.* London: George Routledge and Sons, 1873, pp. 228 ff; Ross, Anne. *Folklore of the Scottish Highlands.* London: B. T. Batsford, Ltd., 1976, p. 94.

Oona (Ona)   See ÚNA.

Oppida   Archaeological site. This Latin word is used to describe ancient Celtic towns such as that found at LA TÉNE in Switzerland. The large fortified settlements of the sixth–fifth centuries B.C.E. were built in easily defensible positions (on heights or promontories) and were often located near mineral deposits, which provided the settlement's source of wealth.

oracle   Symbolic object or event. Systems of DIVINATION often require the employment of oracles to indicate the future. Flights of birds, unusual weather, untimely blossoming: All these and many other occurrences could predict the outcome of events. Typically oracles were things dislocated in place (a seashell found on a mountain) or time (a tree blossoming in winter). A distinction is sometimes made between OMENS, which predict ill-fortune, and the more neutral or positive oracle. The word is also used to describe a prophet; that usage is more typically classical, as in the Oracle of Dephi in Greece, rather than Celtic.

oracular head   See HEAD.

Orc Triath   Irish mythological beast. The Irish corollary to the Welsh TWRCH TRWYTH was a magical BOAR owned by the goddess BRIGIT.

Orlám   Irish hero. One of the sons of queen MEDB and king AILILL mac Máta of the western province of CONNACHT, Orlám was one of the first to die at the hands of the great hero CÚCHULAINN on the CATTLE RAID known as the *TÁIN BÓ CUAILNGE.* Orlám's charioteer carried his master's head to Medb and Ailill, and for his efforts got brained with a stone thrown by Cúchulainn.

Oscar (Osgar)   Irish and Scottish hero. The son of the poet OISÍN and his human wife Eibhir, he was the grandson of the hero FIONN MAC CUMHAILL. Oscar followed his father by becoming a member of the FIANNA, the band of warriors that fought with Fionn. His name means "deer lover" and refers to his descent from his grandmother, Oisín's mother SADB, who had been enchanted into the form of a deer.

The fiercest of the Fianna warriors, Oscar led the group called "the terrible broom" because it swept clean any battlefield. After the death of his grandfather, Oscar became the head of the mighty band. When they were finally defeated in the battle of Gabhra, Oscar killed the leader of their foes, the high king CAIRBRE, but died of wounds from that battle. His wife, AIDÍN, wept herself to death when his father Oisín bore him away to the OTHERWORLD.

Source: Campbell, J. F. *Popular Tales of the West Highlands.* Vol. III. Edinburgh: Edmonston and Douglas, 1862, pp. 295 ff.

Otherworld   Cosmological concept. This term is used to describe an alternative reality that was the home of spirits and divinities and the beloved dead. This folkloric belief is found in lands where the Celts formerly lived, giving rise to the supposition that it descends from Celtic religion, but there is also the possibility that the Celts adopted the concept from indigenous people whom they conquered. Not a "heaven" like that envisioned by Christian believers as above and separate from this earth, the Celtic Otherworld existed nearby, though just out of reach. Sometimes it rested on an ISLAND in the ocean that floated unfettered through time or space. Such an island might appear only every seven years, or it might move around the ocean and appear in different locations. At other times, the Otherworld was imagined as beneath a hill, often an old fort (see HILLFORT), which opened to reveal an entire vast city. Shadowy and liminal not-here, not-there places such as BOGS, CAVES, and reedy shores were also seen as gates to the Otherworld.

People of this world could visit the Otherworld by accident or design. They could be stolen away, usually by a FAIRY LOVER who wished to take pleasure with a handsome human lover. Musicians were likely to be kidnapped (see FAIRY KIDNAPPING); if they played well for the Otherworldly dances, they might be granted a special tune to play once they returned to earth. Midwives were stolen to help with Otherworldly births; it was important that they not question their kidnappers but do their jobs quietly and hope for a speedy return home. Babies could be stolen, for human infants were more beautiful than those born in the Otherworld; these could be reclaimed through various rituals and tricks (see CHANGELING).

Those of this world did not have to await kidnapping to reach the Otherworld, for at certain times the doors would swing open. Such was the case with the great Celtic holidays of BELTANE (May 1) and SAMHAIN (November 1), which remained magical in folklore long after Christianization of Celtic lands. Liminal times like dawn, and shadowy weather conditions, could also provide moments when the Otherworld could break through to this one, or visitors from this world could gain access there.

In the Otherworld time moved slowly, so that an hour spent there could be a century here. As a result, Otherworldly dwellers did not age and rarely died. There was no illness or pain or bad weather there, but only beautiful sunny days that were passed in dancing and song. Trees of the Otherworld bore fruit and flowers at the same time; the food served there was impossibly tasty but never filling.

Many names are used of the Otherworld: MAG MELL ("plain of honey"), TIR NA NOG ("land of youth"), and HY-BRÂZIL (the island of Bres, after which the South American country of Brazil was named). Some scholars have derived the word AVALON, used of the mysterious and powerful place of Arthurian legend, from the phrase EMAIN ABLACH ("island of apples"), used to describe the Otherworld.

See also NAMES FOR THE OTHERWORLD.

Sources: Evans-Wentz, W. Y. *The Fairy-Faith in Celtic Countries*. Gerrards Cross: Colin Smythe Humanities Press, 1911, pp. 332–338; Löffler, Christa Maria. *The Voyage to the Otherworld Island in Early Irish Literature*. Salzburg Studies in English Literature. Salzburg, Institut Für Anglistik und Amerikanistik, Universität Salzburg, 1983; O'Rahilly, Thomas. *Early Irish History and Mythology*. Dublin: The Dublin Institute for Advanced Studies, 1946, p. 328; Patch, Howard Rollin. *The Other World: According to Descriptions in Medieval Literature*. Cambridge, Mass.: Harvard University Press, 1950, pp. 27 ff.

otter Symbolic animal. Both the Irish and the Scottish Highlanders believed that this sleek, playful water mammal had the powers of the OTHERWORLD. Otters were believed to live in kingdoms like humans, ruled over by an otter king (sometimes called Dorraghow or DOBHARCHÚ) whose skin was worth a fortune. It was hard to catch such a creature, for it was virtually invulnerable; a bit of white fur under its chin showed the only point where it could be killed. Despite the value of the pelt, killing the king otter was costly, for the murderer (whether human or dog) would die soon after, apparently taken out of revenge by the otter-people.

Some felt that the king otter's pelt was worth even that price, for a fragment of the hide would protect an entire household from harm. Soldiers going off to war believed that they would be protected from death at the front if they carried a portion of the skin of a king otter. According to tradition, the only ones who escaped the historic massacre of the followers of Bonnie Prince Charlie at Culloden were those carrying king-otter skin. In Ireland a purse made from the skin of the king otter would be forever filled with coins, making its owner fabulously wealthy.

Sources: MacGregor, Alasdair Alpin. *The Peat-Fire Flame: Folk-Tales and Traditions of the Highlands & Islands.* Edinburgh: The Moray Press, 1937, p. 132; Ó hÓgain, Dáithí. *Irish Superstitions.* London: Gill & Macmillan, 1995, pp. 55–57.

Owein (Owain, Iwein, Yvain, Owein fab Urien) Arthurian hero. In an Arthurian text from Wales (*The Dream of Rhonabwy*), this name is given to a knight of CAMELOT, son of king URIEN and king ARTHUR's sorceress half sister MORGAN. One day, while adventuring abroad, Owein heard of a land that suffered under the scourge of a mysterious Black Knight. He traced the Knight to a forest (see BROCÉLIANDE) and defeated the villain there. There too he found a fountain, guarded by a lovely maiden named LUNED, who helped him win the heart of her mistress, an even lovelier maiden whose only name was the LADY OF THE FOUNTAIN.

Despite pledging to be true to her, Owein was unable to fulfill his vow, leaving her to go adventuring with king Arthur and forgetting to return. The Lady's servant Luned followed him to Camelot, where she shamed him before the other knights for his faithlessness. He fled into the forest, where he finally healed himself sufficiently to become a knight again. Adventuring about the land in knightly fashion, he encountered Luned again, whom he rescued from an imprisoning GIANT. To repay his assistance, Luned arranged a reconciliation between Owein and the Lady of the Fountain.

Oweynagat (Cave of Cruachan, Cave of the Cats) Irish mythological site. In Co. Roscommon, in Ireland's western province of CONNACHT, there is a tiny CAVE of huge mythic importance. Oweynagat is part of the great archaeological complex of CRUACHAN, the ancient capital of the province of Connacht centered on the fort of its goddess-queen MEDB. Still visible and accessible in a small field on the edge of the complex, 700 meters southwest of the great mound where Medb's palace was said to stand, the cave's opening is quite small, some three feet high by four feet wide, formed by a medieval souterrain or underground passage. After that narrow opening, the cave opens up to a huge cathedral-like space.

Oweynagat figures prominently in ancient Irish myth and legend. It was the birthplace of Medb herself. The goddess and fairy queen ÉTAIN, fleeing with her FAIRY lover MIDIR from her human husband, stopped at Oweynagat with her companions, who included her maidservant CROCHAN Crogderg, whose name means "blood-red cup." Midir was said to have wanted to visit a relative who lived in the cave, the otherwise unknown Sinech ("large-breasted one"), for whom he had great affection. At the end of their stay, Crochan was so enamored of the place—which although it seems only a dingy cave, is a great palace in the OTHERWORLD—that she begged to stay. Étain and Midir gave her the cave, and so it was there that Crochan's daughter Medb was born.

Oweynagat also appears in the ADVENTURE tale about one of her servants, a man named NERA who saved Cruachan from an attack by Otherworldly forces with the assistance of a fairy woman whom he met in the cave and married. She warned him that Medb's beautiful palace would be burned to the ground the following SAMHAIN, a warning that brought the forces of Medb and AILILL mac Máta into the cave to eliminate the danger. As with other tales, this one associates the cave with the feast of Samhain.

The cave is also associatcd with the great figure that shadows Medb throughout the epic through which she is most known, the *TÁIN BÓ CUAILNGE* or CATTLE RAID on CUAILNGE—the MÓRRÍGAN, who drove her Otherworldly cattle into the cave each sunset. She may be the one who flew out of the cave, called "the hell-mouth of Ireland" in medieval documents, for apparitions were said to appear there, especially on the magical Celtic festival of Samhain (November 1) when the veils between the worlds were thin and even those without SECOND SIGHT could see beyond this world and into the next.

The Mórrígan was known to have stolen the herds of a girl named ODRAS and to have driven them down into the cave of Oweynagat. Undeterred by Mórrígan's fierce reputation, Odras pursued her, trying to regain the cattle upon which she relied. She got almost to Mórrígan's domain, but the great queen was more powerful than the girl and turned her into a lake.

How the cave got its name is unknown; no CATS appear in its folklore or myth. An oracular cave in Connacht where a cat was consulted by fortune-tellers is recorded in some texts, but its location is not given, so it is unclear whether Oweynagat is intended. Oweynagat is much more commonly associated with CATTLE than with cats; not only does the Mórrígan drive her cattle through the cave, but a woman was said to have traveled underground for many miles, dragged there by a calf to whose tail she clung.

In a text from the 18th century, the cave was described as the "Hell-mouth of Ireland," suggesting that the deities and spirits who had been believed to live within Oweynagat were still imagined as active, if diabolical. The cave is still accessible, although its frighteningly tiny entry makes it one of the least-visited of Ireland's great mythological sites.

Sources: Dames, Michael. *Mythic Ireland.* London: Thames and Hudson, 1992, pp. 237–239; Gwynn, Edward. *The Metrical Dindshenchas.* Royal Irish Academy, Todd Lecture Series. Dublin: Hodges, Figgis, and Co., Ltd., 1906–1924, p. 22.

owl Symbolic animal. The majestic power of the night-hunting owl was recognized by people around the world. To the Celts, the owl symbolized age and its attendant wisdom. The most renowned owl in Celtic literature is the transformed Welsh flower-bride BLODEUWEDD, who was turned into an owl as punishment for betraying her husband and persuading her lover to kill him. We also find an owl (thc Owl of Cwm Cawlwyd) in the Welsh epic of *KULHWCH AND OLWEN*, but the wise bird was unable to provide the hero with the information he needed to find his lover. In Ireland a vestigial owl goddess is found in the figure of Echtach, sister or double of the cannibal goddess Eghchte.

Some have interpreted the great spiraling patterns that appear in eye-like pairs on some pre-Celtic monuments in Ireland, Britain, and France as representing an owl-faced goddess. This controversial viewpoint links those ancient monuments to others in the eastern and central Mediterranean.

ox Symbolic animal. Although this word is not always accurately used, sometimes merely indicating CATTLE, it actually means a castrated BULL, usually of the domestic bovine species. Because removing the testosterone-producing testes from an animal typically produces a more peaceable disposition as well as wcight gain, and because having too many ambitious bulls in a herd could lead to fighting and thus loss of precious animal life, some animals were transformed from bulls into oxen early in life. They then were used for hauling, for their great bulk gave them great strength; they also found their way into the stewpot. Oxen are less important in myth and legend than either COWS or bulls, but occasionally they appear to represent strength and endurance. Similarly, landscape features named for oxen were typically monumental; thus we find, in the west of Ireland, a powerful range of hills called the Ox Mountains.

P

Padfoot English folkloric figure. In Yorkshire, this strange donkey-sized creature appeared as an OMEN of death; it looked like an amorphous shaggy ball with eyes or a woolly white DOG. It could become invisible at will and often roared or rattled to terrify unsuspecting travelers who passed its lair. It was very important never to strike out at Padfoot, for touching it gave the monster power over you.

See also BARGUEST.

Padstow Obby Oss Cornish ritual. In the small Cornish port of Padstow on BELTANE morning (May 1), a HOBBYHORSE ceremony is still held to mark the arrival of spring according to the old Celtic calendar. The celebration has been linked to old Celtic HORSE rituals.

paganism Cosmological concept. All Celtic religion is pagan, for the word defines the polytheistic world as distinguished from the monotheistic. Celtic religion arose before the historical Christ was born and thus before his followers had articulated their message. As Christians made theirs the dominant worldview of Europe, they employed derogatory words to describe anyone who continued to hold to the traditional beliefs of their ancestors. They were "pagans," from the Latin *pagani*, which means "hick" although it is

more formally translated as "a country dweller." Similarly, the word *heathen* was used to describe someone who lived on the heath or moor, poor agricultural land where impoverished people eked out a living and clung to ancestral beliefs. The use of these words betrays the urban background of Christianity's rise and the religious conservatism typical, even today, of the country dweller.

Today the word *pagan* is used in America to describe people, most often urban or suburban, who search for non-Christian spiritual traditions articulating a worldview that seems less dualist, less sexist, or more nature-embracing than they believe Christianity has become. Some scholars argue that the term should not be applied to people who adopt paganism, referring to such seekers as NEO-PAGANS ("new pagans"), to distinguish them from those who practice an unbroken tradition. Such distinctions have given rise to several cults that declare themselves descendants of some religion, often Celtic, that existed in ancient times and was conveyed in secret through the ages. Most such claims are without substance, although there is strong evidence that folklore and place-lore (see *DIND-SHENCHAS*) conveyed ancient beliefs forward to contemporary times.

Palomides Arthurian hero. Not British but a Saracen, an Islamic fighter, Palomides was one of the greatest knights of the ROUND TABLE, who served king ARTHUR in the quest for the sacred GRAIL.

Pamp (Pam) Irish hero. The *BOOK OF INVA-SIONS* gives this as the name of NEMED's father, thus making him an ancestor of the race of Nemedians who were among the early invaders of Ireland. His name is believed to be a late invention, derived from the Latin Pompeius.

Paps of Danu (Paps of Anu, Dá Chich Anann) Irish mythological site. On the road between the scenic Lakes of Killarney and the city of Cork in the southwestern Irish province of MUNSTER, two almost identical rounded hills rise from the Derrynasaggart Mountains. The top of each is crowned with an ancient CAIRN, a rock construction built some 6,000 years ago by unknown people who preceded Celtic settlement in the area. The west Pap has not only a mound surmounted by a cairn but a stone chamber as well. Between the two hills is a stand of ragged rocks called The Teeth.

The Paps are often cloud-hung, but when the mist clears, the cairns create an earth sculpture of nipples atop the rounded breasts of the paired hills. The mountains are called the Paps (breasts) of DANU (sometimes ANU), after a goddess who appears as an ancestral figure but to whom little myth accrues. The monument has been interpreted as indicating that Danu was a goddess of the earth.

Danu is not the only female figure connected with the Paps. The poet CRÉD was said to have built her palace on the side of the hills; a holy WELL on the Paps was dedicated to the strange figure of CROBH DEARG ("red claw"), honored at BELTANE with visits to the well. The only male figures associated with the twin mountains are the BARD CÁEL and the hero FIONN MAC CUMHAILL, both lovers of Créd.

Paradise Cosmological concept. The Celts had no concept that exactly parallels the eastern Mediterranean vision of Paradise as a beautiful, unearthly world that existed before this one, that was lost to us through the human sin, and to which the elect will go after death. Instead, the Celts believed in an OTHERWORLD that could be reached during one's lifetime if one happened to be in the right place at the right time. The Otherworld was not necessarily a desirable destination, for the FAIRIES and minor divinities that occupied it could hold a person against his will and refuse to let him return. Not that the captive would necessarily wish to run, for the Celtic Otherworld was beautiful and satisfying, if somewhat sterile.

Their familiarity with this pleasant Otherworld may have made it easy for the Celts to accept the apparently similar Christian vision of Paradise. Although Christians might be given a visionary glimpse of the world to come, they cannot enter while in their earthly bodies, nor can they readily return from Paradise once they arrive there. As the home of God, Paradise is entirely unshadowed with the ambiguity of the Celtic Otherworld. Thus the differences between Paradise and the Otherworld are profound despite their slight and superficial similarities.

Paris Continental Celtic hero. In the Welsh mythological tale of *KULHWCH AND OLWEN*, a king of this name appears as ruler over the region where the French capital now stands. Most scholars dismiss the assumption that this offers proof of an historical Celtic king named Paris; rather, they say, the city's name probably derives from a local Celtic tribe, the Parisi; the same tribe, or a branch of it, settled in Britain's Yorkshire region. Another legend offers a different idea of how Paris got its name: Because the city was so beautiful, it was named *par-Ys*—"like-YS"—after the lost magical city of Brittany.

Partholón (Partholon, Parthalán, Parthanán) Irish hero. In the mythological history of Ireland, the *BOOK OF INVASIONS*, Partholón was the least significant of the invaders, coming after

CESAIR and before NEMED and his followers. Unlike some of the other races that disguise a history of early settlement, Partholón is believed to have been invented by medieval historians who based his name on Bartholomaeus, a figure from early Christian pseudo-history.

Partholón, it was said, came to Ireland from Greece, where he had killed both his parents and had been blinded in his left eye as punishment. (The theme of the one-eyed leader, which also appears in the stories of BALOR of the Evil Eye and the warrior GOLL MAC MORNA, may be Celtic in origin.) Thirty years after the biblical great flood, Partholón arrived in Ireland with his people, the Partholonians, who settled in after fighting off the monstrous FOMORIANS. Their battle was a strange one: No blood was shed because the fighting took place entirely in the realm of MAGIC.

Life in Ireland was not happy for Partholón, who discovered that his wife DEALGNAID, whom he left alone while he surveyed the land, took advantage of his absence to sleep with their servant Togda; Partholón blamed not his wife but himself, saying that women should never thus be abandoned with their needs for love unsatisfied. Partholón and Dealgnaid had four sons; together they cleared the forests and established farms. After several hundred years a plague struck, and the descendants of Partholón were all killed off, all between one Monday and the next in May. Only TUAN MAC CAIRILL, a SHAPE-SHIFTING BARD, survived. A folkloric remnant of Partholón was an Irish harvest spirit named Parthanán who stole any grain left unthreshed.

Source: MacAlister, R. A. Stewart. *Lebor Gabála Érenn: The Book of the Taking of Ireland, Parts 1–4.* Dublin: Irish Texts Society, 1941, Pt. 2, pp. 253–271; Pt. 3, pp. 2–102.

Partholonians   Irish mythological race. See PARTHOLÓN.

passage graves (Passage tombs)   Mythological sites. Archaeological evidence of an ancient people who preceded the Celts in Ireland, Britain, and Brittany, these stone structures are built of huge boulders, arranged standing upright to form a corridor leading to an inner chamber. The entire structure was usually covered with earth, forming a mound (see FAIRY MOUND), but in many cases this outer covering has worn away, leaving the stone skeleton clearly visible. As was the case with many ancient monuments of the MEGALITHIC CIVILIZATION, these impressive ruins were believed haunted by the Celts, and their superstitious beliefs concerning the tombs make up some of the lasting folklore of the Celtic lands.

patera   Cosmological symbol. The continental Celtic goddess EPONA is frequently shown carrying a flat object upright in her hands. This *patera*, or offering plate, also appears in other contexts: held by a deity, offered up by a human worshiper, filled with fruit or other produce, or entirely empty. Some have interpreted the object not as a plate but as a small frame drum.

Patrick   See ST. PATRICK.

pattern (patron)   Ritual. A series of ritual activities performed on a specific day and usually at a specific site, the pattern (Irish usage) or patron (in Brittany) is apparently Christian but descends from a Celtic, or sometimes pre-Celtic, original. Examples are numerous: visiting holy WELLS at ancient ritual times, climbing MOUNTAINS on Celtic holidays, traveling along a certain road or path while performing specified actions. The pattern often included walking in circles, leaving specified offerings, reciting specific prayers, or drinking well water. In some cases the actions could be effective at any time, while at other locations the pattern had to be done on a certain day and at a certain time. These rituals, which still continue today, are described as Christian by their practitioners, who may be aware of pagan antecedents but who are rarely bothered by them.

pech (peht, pict)   Scottish folkloric figure. In Lowland Scotland, this name used of the OTHERWORLD creatures otherwise known as FAIRIES apparently derives from an ancient historical people called the PICTS. As is common with fairy races, the *pech* was fair-skinned and red-haired (see RED) and might be mistaken for a human except that they were extraordinarily short. Despite their dwarfish height, they were strong and agile; they formed great lines in order to haul stones from quarries to construct their castles. Like many Otherworldly peoples, the *pechs* could not bear sunlight and fled to their residences each dawn.

Peg O'Nell   British folkloric figure. Figures of legend are often earlier deities in degraded form. This seems to be the case with Peg O'Nell, connected with the River Ribble in Lancashire; the Ribble once bore the name of the RIVER goddess BELISAMA, who was worshiped at its source and on its shores. That her worship may have involved HUMAN SACRIFICE is suggested by some scholars who have found in the figure of Peg O'Nell a vestige of that dreadful rite. Peg was said to have been a servant girl who drowned in the Ribble and, to punish those who failed to rescue her, came back every seven years to steal another victim. (In Ireland, we find a similar seven-year cycle of drowning connected with ÁINE, a fairy queen and ancient goddess of the haunted LOUGH GUR.) On Peg's Night, when the Ribble rises to snare a new victim, it was considered appropriate to make propitiatory sacrifices of small birds or animals to the river spirit. A headless stone statue at Waddow Hall on the river's banks is believed to represent Peg or, in alternative theories, the goddess Belisama.

Peg Powler   British folkloric figure. A haunting GREEN-haired spirit of the River Tees between the counties of Durham and Yorkshire, Peg Powler may be a degraded descendant of the ancient Celtic RIVER goddess of the area. She was said to wander about, especially on Sundays, luring young and old folks to a watery death;

those who drowned in the Tees were said to have been eaten by Peg Powler. When foam gathers on the waves of the river, it is called "Peg Powler's suds" and is said to be "Peg doing her laundry," while a white slick means she is milking her cow and is called "Peg Powler's cream."

péist (bruckee)   Irish folkloric figure. A monstrous SERPENT or reptile, the *péist* appears in a number of legends, including many in which it is overcome by ST. PATRICK. Typically the *péist* is associated with WATER, usually fresh rather than oceanic: it lives in a LAKE and can only be successfully killed when submerged. It is also called the OLLIPHEIST.

These beasts are especially common in the area of west Co. Clare called the Burren, where place-names like Poulnapeasta ("water dragon's lair" or "péist-hole") are found. Near Corofin a pool that changed color and was marked with several funnel holes was believed to harbor a brown, hairy, big-eyed MONSTER.

Pelagianism (Pelagius)   Cosmological concept. The fifth-century Christian philosopher Pelagius is believed to have been a Celt, British or Irish (his opponent, St. Jerome, claimed Pelagius was "stuffed with Irish porridge"), who gained many followers in the early church with his "happy heresy." Pelagius believed that all of creation was good and that the human enterprise was to learn to love all that exists. Opposing this vision was that of the North African cleric Augustine, who had been greatly influenced by the dualistic philosophy of the Persian sage Mani in his youth, an influence that he never entirely shed (see DUALITY). St. Augustine's combat with Pelagianism was one of the defining moments for the emerging Christian church. A brilliant and charismatic leader, Augustine argued fiercely against the Pelagian vision, which reflected a typical Celtic view of NATURE.

Pelleas (Pelles)   See FISHER KING.

Pellinore Arthurian hero. Brother of the FISHER KING Pelles, Pellinore was a great knight of the ROUND TABLE and, in some texts, father of the pure PERCIVAL.

Penarddun (Penardun) Welsh heroine. The daughter of the important goddess DÔN and the sea or death god BELI, Penarddun was one of the consorts of king LLYR. She is sometimes called the mother of Llyr's daughter BRANWEN as well as his sons BRÂN THE BLESSED and MANAWYDAN (some sources give another woman, Iweriadd, as mother of the first two). With another man, Eurosswyd, she had two sons of opposite temperament: the gentle NISIEN and the evil EFNISIEN. All of Penarddun's children figure prominently in the mythological Welsh tales collected in the *MABINOGION*; she herself has little legend and appears to be an ancestral figure.

Penn Cruc Welsh god or hero. The Welsh equivalent of the Irish harvest god of similar name, CROM CRUACH, Penn Cruc was worshiped at ancient mounds and STONES.

Percival (Perceval, Parsival, Parsifal, Parzifal) Arthurian hero. The son of the Welsh princess HERZELOYDE and the warrior GAHMURET, Percival was brought up in a cottage without knowledge of his illustrious parentage, and he became a knight noted for his simplicity and purity. The quest for the GRAIL—the cup that Jesus of Nazareth used at his Last Supper, later brought to Celtic lands by the mysterious JOSEPH OF ARIMATHEA—makes up a major part of the Arthurian legends. The story of the Grail quest begins with the knight Percival wandering in a barren land. Its ruler had been wounded (see FISHER KING) and could do nothing other than fish from a boat, although nothing ever came to his line. Dining with the king, Percival suddenly had a vision of a chalice and a bleeding lance. Trying to be polite, he said nothing about the curious experience. The vision ended, and the

castle suddenly disappeared, leaving Percival alone in the woodland, wondering how the Fisher King and his lands could be saved.

The quest for the Grail was thus launched. Percival returned to ARTHUR's court, and the knights of the ROUND TABLE set off, each of them experiencing a different quest that matched the needs of his soul. Percival finally was able to rediscover the Grail Castle and this time asked the necessary questions: Whose is the cup, why does the lance bleed? His questions restored the king to health, and thus the land bloomed again, and Percival succeeded the Fisher King on the throne of the reborn land.

The great Breton writer Chrétien de Troyes first wrote of Percival in 1175 C.E. (*Perceval, ou Le Conte du Graal*); he appears in Thomas Malory's *Morte d'Arthur* as Sir Percival; and he is Parzifal in the Germanic versions of the story that became part of German composer Richard Wagner's operatic cycle.

Source: Loomis, Roger Sherman. *The Grail from Celtic Myth to Christian Symbol*. New York: Columbia University Press, 1963; pp. 196–222.

Peredur Welsh and Arthurian hero. In one of the great romances of Wales, we learn of this callow young man who, enduring many trials and succeeding at many quests, became a noble and admired knight. His character, somewhat altered, became the basis for the Arthurian knightly hero PERCIVAL. Some have found in his name an echo of the GRAIL itself, for *per* means "bowl" in Brythonic Celtic; any connection to the Grail, however, does not appear in most versions of Peredur's tale.

Perilous Bed Arthurian site. Unknown in the physical world, the Perilous Bed magically appeared before knights who quested for the sacred GRAIL. It looked soft and inviting, but anyone who lay down upon it was punctured by invisible knives, until GAWAIN destroyed the threatening object.

Perilous Seat (Siege Perilous) Arthurian site. Like Celtic INAUGURATION STONES, the Perilous Seat recognized true heroism; only the finder of the GRAIL could sit in it without disappearing. In some texts, PERCIVAL sat on the Perilous Seat after his first and failed encounter with the FISHER KING; the stone cracked apart to indicate his unworthiness, but he later repaired it, sitting upon it after successfully finding the Grail and knitting the stone back together.

Perilous Valley Breton mythological site. Within the legendary forest of BROCÉLIANDE in Brittany, there was a haunted valley that had been cursed by MORGAN, half sister of King ARTHUR and lover of the unfaithful GUYOMARD. To assuage her wounded feelings, Morgan enchanted the valley so that any man who had ever betrayed a woman would find himself lost in the Perilous Valley, wandering as though PIXY-LED, unable to find the way out. The green valley would seem, to a faithless knight like Guyomard, to be filled with monsters—all of his own imagining. In the heart of the valley was a lake called the FAIRY's Mirror, from which nightmares rose like mist. No matter how many knights happened into the valley, each would think himself alone. Finally one of the knights of Arthur's own court, the young GAWAIN, found himself snared in Morgan's trap, and LANCELOT went to save him. As Lancelot has never been untrue to his beloved GUINEVERE (his adultery with ELAINE of Corbenic, whereby the hero GALAHAD was conceived, did not count because he was inebriated and believed himself to be making love to Guinevere), he was able to dispel the enchantment and free the captives.

phantom islands Mythic symbol. ISLANDS that appeared and disappeared in cloudy mist were believed to be entrances to the OTHERWORLD where FAIRIES, divinities, and the dead dwelt in endless sunny pleasure. These phantom islands could be seen out in the ocean or on lakes; some appeared regularly, usually on a seven-year cycle, but others appeared once in the mist and were never seen again.

Pict (pl., Picts, Pictii; in Irish, Cruithin, Cruithne; in Welsh, Prydyn, Priteni) There is some evidence that what we know as Celtic religion and mythology includes vestiges of the beliefs of the apparently non-Celtic ancient people called the Picts, or "painted ones," a name that may derive from a tradition of tattooing their bodies. Some argue that the Picts were Celts from such tribes as the Caledonii and the Maecatae, for some Pictish rules had names that seem to have been in the Brythonic (P-Celtic) language. Others claim that the Picts were a distinct ethnic group, speaking a non-Indo-European language. In either case, the Picts may have been matrilineal (see MATRILINY) basing descent on the mother's line rather than the father's, as we find many of the most ancient and presumably Pictish figures named in that way (like the Welsh GWYDION son of DÔN and MOBON son of MODRON), while later heroes and heroines bear patronymics, based on the names of their fathers.

The Picts lived in what is now Scotland, where they left traces in the form of stone carvings of symbolic animals and objects such as BULLS and HORSES, SERPENTS and RAVENS, HAMMERS and COMBS; these carvings may have represented religious beliefs or tribal totems. They were allies with Celtic tribes in fighting the invading Romans; it was against these fierce northern warriors that the great Hadrian's Wall was erected. They continued to be an historical force until the ninth century C.E., when they united with the Scots in a joint kingdom, after which all traces of their language died out.

pig Symbolic animal. The pig is important in Celtic religious symbolism, as might be expected among people for whom it provided a vital meat source, second only to the CATTLE that also figure so significantly in myth and folklore. Early pigs were smaller and fiercer than today's domestic variety; they lived half-wild in the forests, rather than confined to sties, and grew fat on the "mast" or acorns found under OAKS that were themselves sacred to the Celts. In early Celtic culture the pig was a funeral animal; a connection with the warrior class is also suggested by the occasional depiction of a BOAR on a helmet, although this may have been an evocation of the animal's fierceness when cornered.

Mythical and folkloric pigs include, most notably, the ever-regenerating pigs belonging to the DAGDA in the Irish OTHERWORLD; any number of people could slice pork off the creature, which would be found whole and hearty the next day. Also in Ireland, the great boar—a transformed man—that killed the hero DIARMAIT Ua Duibne is found, as is the enchanted sow Caelchéis, who was brought to her doom by a harper's music. In Celtic Gaul there is evidence of a god named MOCCUS ("porker"), whom the Romans assimilated to their Mercury. On the Isle of Man the Arkan Sonney or "lucky piggy" is an Otherworldly creature that, like others of its fairy kind, could be distinguished by its RED ears and white skin; it brought good luck if you could catch it, but few ever did.

Sources: MacKenzie, Donald A. *Scottish Folk-Lore and Folk Life: Studies in Race, Culture and Tradition*. Glasgow: Blackie & Sons, Ltd., 1935, pp. 56–71; MacNeill, Máire. *The Festival of Lughnasa, Parts I and II*. Dublin: Comhairle Bhéaloideas Éireann, 1982, p. 185.

pilgrimage Cosmological concept. The symbolism of the pilgrimage—a journey to a sacred place—is that of the journey of life, tending inevitably to its conclusion in death and the afterlife. The conception, familiar to both Christian and Islamic religions, had little place in Celtic thought. Not that the Celts did not travel to holy sites; there is strong evidence that they did, evidence that continues in the PATTERNS or rituals held at such sites even today. However, travel and pilgrimage are not the same. There was no holy center for Celtic reli-

gion, no place where anyone could come at any time and expect to find an unchanging sanctity. The center was more a cosmological concept (see MIDE) than a geographical one; in addition, sites were connected to specific days and even hours. Thus pilgrimage did not exist in the conventional sense among the Celts; rather, people traveled for various purposes to many sites, usually near home rather than far away.

pin Symbolic object. Small pointed bits of metal or bone—pins and needles—were common offerings at Celtic holy sites, especially those related to water, such as WELLS and RIVER sources. Because pins were used to fasten cloth together, they may have been symbolic prayers for healing or "sewing up" of broken bones and even broken hearts.

In FAIRY lore, tiny pins were secreted in the clothing of those who were victims of FAIRY KIDNAPPING. Upon returning to this world from the OTHERWORLD, the erstwhile captive would remain in a comatose state until the vestiges of fairyland were located and removed.

pishogue (piséog, pistrog) Irish folkloric concept. The term "pishogue" or "pishoguery" is still used in Ireland to dismiss old ways ("it's just a pishogue") and occasionally to describe false tales got up to seem like folklore. Originally the word meant an Otherworldly bewitchment that caused the world to seem quite different than it really is (see GLAMOUR).

pixy (pigsie, piskie) British folkloric figure. One of the most commonly recognized names for the Otherworldly beings of FAIRYLAND, this word was used in the West Country of England and in Cornwall. Like other such beings, pixies typically wore GREEN or RED, had red hair and pointed ears, and were shorter than humans. Often they squinted as though they could not bear the light of day; indeed, they preferred the nighttime. (In Cornwall the piskie was somewhat shorter, older, and more wizened than the British pixy.) Also typical was their mischievous manner; they enjoyed leading people astray (see PIXY-LED) and rousing the animals in the dead of night. They could be friendly and helpful as well, like BROWNIES and other household spirits, offering aid with housekeeping and farmyard chores. As with other such races, it was important to ignore the pixy's contribution to the household economy, because praise or gifts would cause the pixy to be "laid" or driven away (see LAYING THE FAIRIES).

Source: Crossing, William. *Tales of the Dartmoor Pixies: Glimpses of Elfin Haunts and Antics.* Newcastle upon Tyne: Frank Graham, 1890.

pixy-led (pixy leading, pouk-ledden) Folkloric motif. Wherever we find belief in FAIRIES—in other words, in the ancient Celtic lands—we find the tale that they entertained themselves by leading humans astray. They cast a GLAMOUR or PISHOGUE over a scene so that everything seemed strange. A path disappeared, a gate went missing, a road dissolved: they remained real in the physical world, but the pixy-led traveler simply could not find them. Round and round the traveler turned, looking desperately for a familiar landmark, but until the pixy decided to lift the spell, it was to no avail. Being pixy-led was most common at liminal times and places (at dusk, in BOGS, at lakeshores) and on the ancient Celtic feasts, especially SAMHAIN on November 1. That Shakespeare knew of the superstitions about being pixy-led is clear from his description of Puck's doings in *A Midsummer Night's Dream:* "to mislead night-wanderers, laughing at their harm."

Several antidotes to being pixy-led have been recorded: carrying IRON, wearing clothing backward or inside out, wearing hobnailed boots, carrying SALT in the pocket, whistling or singing while walking. Although none offered a guarantee, such actions offered some protection against fairy mischief. See also STRAY SOD.

place-lore Many European place-names are of Celtic origin, especially those ending in variants of *-dunum* ("fort," or "town") such as Lyon and Verdun in France (originally Lugdunum and Virodunum) and those including *nemeton* ("sacred grove") such as Nanterre (Nemetodurum). In addition to names, we find Celtic influence in the stories told of landscape features. As Celtic religion was radically polytheistic, envisioning divinities as related to specific places and the people who live there, place-lore was an important part of religion.

The naming of places oriented speakers and listeners spiritually as well as geographically. In ancient Ireland the remembering of place-names and the stories connected with them was an important duty of the poetic class (see BARD); even today, Irish poetry often includes the naming of specific places, although contemporary work gives less information about the mythological lore connected with them. A specific form of poem told the tales of important places; these place-lore poems are collectively known as the *DINDSHENCHAS.* Some of the stories were invented by medieval poets to fill in gaps in what was known of locations, but in many cases the poems, compiled in the 12th century, provide lore that dates back far into the Celtic past. A century later, another collection expanded the poetic place-lore and added interpretations in prose; together the volumes make up one of the most comprehensive, although difficult to interpret, works on Irish place-names.

Other Irish place-lore was never recorded in writing but remained in local oral tradition. Such material presents specific challenges to the scholar, who must determine whether the tale was an invention, a misinterpretation or misunderstanding, or a true myth. The study of place-lore is less developed in Celtic lands outside Ireland.

Plant Annwn (Plant Annwyn, Plant Rhys Dwfen) Welsh folkloric figures. The "tribe of the OTHERWORLD" and the "tribe of Rhys the Deep" were names for Welsh FAIRY people. The

Plant Annwn lived below the surface of LAKES, where they kept their red-eared CATTLE (the *Gwartheg y Llyn*) and teams of white DOGS (*C'WN ANNWN*). Like other such beings, the Plant Annwn could intermarry with humans, but should the restrictions they put on their mates be broken, they would instantly disappear. The Plant Rhys Dwfen were a subspecies of fairy who were extremely facile at marketing and thus grew very wealthy.

planxty   Folkloric motif. The music of the OTHERWORLD was, according to all who heard it, more beautiful by far than anything in our world. The great Irish harper Turlough O'Carolan, who fell asleep one day on a FAIRY MOUND and awoke a musical genius, coined the word *planxty* to describe the special qualities of fairy music. It was not as regular as our music, nor as rhythmic, but its odd dissonance and erratic rhythm produced a hypnotic and melancholic trance that ordinary music could not. Musicians who heard music in strange lonely places could be certain that what they heard was no earthly melody, but beautiful as the melodies were, they were also difficult to remember. Even if a fiddler played it over and over, by the time he reached home the melody had disappeared from memory.

Following FAIRY MUSIC was a certain way to adventure, but there was no easy way to return to human life once you had heard it. On the Isle of Man, a farmer named Lonagher Lowey went into a hill in search of the melodious sounds; there he found a complete town where a magnificent banquet was underway. Having some presence of mind, Lowey poured off the wine he was offered, rather than drinking it, because eating or drinking anything in the Otherworld makes it impossible to leave. He was one of the rare people who returned unharmed from FAIRYLAND.

Source: Killip, Margaret. *The Folklore of the Isle of Man.* London: B. T. Batsford, Ltd., 1975, pp. 37–38.

pledge to the elements   Continental Celtic ritual. In Gaul the following words were used when speaking an oath: "If I break faith, may the skies fall on me, may the seas drown me, may the earth swallow me up whole." The pledge calls upon the air, sea, and earth to bear witness to the speaker's truth. The words show something of the Celtic sense of ANIMISM, of the world being alive and in this case, watchful.

Source: Cowan, Tom. "The Pledge to the Elements." In Patricia Monaghan, ed. *Irish Spirit: Pagan, Celtic, Christian, Global.* Dublin: Wolfhound Press, 2001.

plowing   Ritual activity. The plowing of a field, necessary in spring to prepare the land for seed, is also an archetypal activity that appears in myth and legend. Often it represents the first arrival of a people in a new land; thus the various races of invaders to Ireland are described as clearing and plowing different regions of the land. Typically gods or heroes do the plowing, although goddesses are sometimes involved when they inspire the work. An alternative name for the harvest god CROM DUBH, Soicin, means "little plow," suggesting a double god of spring and fall; the name of MAC CÉCHT, husband of the land goddess FÓDLA ("unplowed land") means simply "plowman," as does the name Airem, borne by one of the mythological kings of Tara.

Plur na mBan   Irish heroine. This minor heroine, whose name means "flower of womanhood," was the daughter of the fairy queen NIAMH of the Golden Hair and her favored love, the human poet OISÍN.

poet   See BARD.

poetry   Cosmological concept. Today poetry is typically understood as an art form, of little religious consequence. To the Celts, matters were different. Words were powerful; indeed, they had such power that they could alter our physical world. Thus a poet's word in ancient Ireland was feared, for a SATIRE could be so stinging that it could raise welts on a person's face; in the most dire situation, appropriately aimed words (connected with matching rituals) could bring about a person's death.

The Celtic BARD was as much a diviner or seer as a maker of lovely words. It seems clear from ancient sources that DRUIDS and poets were, if not identical, at least nearly so; they were similarly trained and may have been seen as different stages of the same career. Both were adept at SHAPE-SHIFTING: a druid literally so, being able to change into various bodies or to become an invisible fog; the poet through metaphoric words that find likenesses between apparently unlike objects and ideas and thus transform one thing into another.

In addition to being seers, poets were also historians. Invention was not prized above accuracy of knowledge; indeed, invention needed to be rooted in tradition. Thus the poet's training included memorization of long passages as well as extemporaneous composition. Such rote learning may have created a light trance or meditative state in which visions of the OTHER-WORLD were more readily seen; thus the long and arduous training in traditional forms may have opened the door to, rather than sealing it against, invention and illumination.

poet's circuit Irish mythological motif. Once an ancient BARD had been fully trained, he or she often traveled through Ireland, meeting other poets, exchanging tales and poems, and engaging in poetic debate. It was while on a poet's circuit that the fair LIADAN met her fated lover, Cuirithir, she refused to interrupt her travels when he proposed to her.

Poisoned Glen Irish mythological site. When the heroic god LUGH killed the monstrous king of the FOMORIANS, BALOR, the victim's evil EYE split the rocks of a small valley, which remains dangerous to this day. The Poisoned Glen is near Dunlewey, in Co. Donegal.

polytheism Cosmological concept. Scholars of religion separate the monotheistic from the polytheistic worldview, the former seeing divinity as singular, the latter as plural. But the subject is more complex than might appear from that division. Implicit in monotheism is dualism, in that whatever is not "god" becomes "not-god"; thus monotheistic religion is inclined to develop a theology that includes evil. Similarly, monotheism typically has associated the divine with something outside or above this world; thus NATURE becomes less holy in monotheistic religion because it is created by god rather than being god itself. Finally, all monotheisms are based on the concept of a masculine divinity; there is no monotheistic religion that excludes a male god, while all exclude a female image of the divine. All three of today's most powerful monotheistic religions (in order of development: Judaism, Christianity, Islam) arose in a relatively small region in the eastern Mediterranean; they are desert religions with an emphasis on imagery appropriate to that geographical region.

Polytheism, the belief in multiple divinities, is more widespread and has been the predominant religious system for most of the world over most of the world's history. Polytheism is typically far less dualistic than monotheism, although such dualistic cults as the Persian Manichaeism are known. More typically, evil is seen not as a cosmic force at war with god/good but as part of the natural cycle that is less comfortable, more frightening, less understood. Thus death is not the opposite of life, but a natural part of it. This does not mean that polytheistic peoples view death with less fear or that they mourn their lost loved ones less; it does mean that death is not typically defined as unnatural.

The Celts appear to have been polytheistic to the extreme; this is assumed because, although the names of more than 200 Celtic gods and goddesses are recorded, few are known from more than one site. It is possible that the number of divinities may have been somewhat smaller if each god had many titles, as the second person of the Christian trinity is known as "Jesus," "Lord," "Christ," "Savior," "Son of Man," and so forth. Sometimes the same image appears in different locations under different names; it is difficult to know if that indicates regional or tribal manifestations of a similar divine power or the same god under different titles.

Unlike the Greeks and Romans, the Celts had no organized hierarchical pantheon, no list of gods and goddesses arranged in order of power. Rather, there seems to have been a concept that divinity was deeply linked to place and, through place, to people. In Irish, the word TUATH meant a people and the place they lived; each region had a divinity that represented the land, the land's SOVEREIGNTY, and the people connected with that land. This is most forcefully expressed by the goddesses of the Irish land, but similar conceptions seem to be found in other Celtic regions, where numerous divinities personify the powers of SPRINGS, RIVERS, river sources, lakeshores, and other sites.

From this place-based polytheism, some scholars have argued, grew a passionate love of the natural world, which is found expressed in Celtic poetry and in the folkways of Celtic countries. Rituals were linked to the passage of seasons; OMENS were drawn from the flight of birds and from other natural phenomena; stories were told that explained the ways myth and place intersected. Some have argued that there was an implied monism in Celtic culture—that while not seeing a single divinity as monotheism does, the Celts saw a unity in nature that could be expressed as a singular being—but there is no evidence of a hierarchy that places one god above others. Thus the arrival of Christianity in Celtic lands meant the adoption of and adaptation to a new worldview.

Source: Cunliffe, Barry. *The Ancient Celts.* Oxford: Oxford University Press, 1997, pp. 184 ff.

pooka (*púca, phouka;* in Wales, *pwca;* in England, pouke, puck) Irish folkloric character. The spectral figure of the pooka was a familiar part of Irish folklore, although there is great diversity in its description. Often it was said to be a white HORSE, but sometimes it appeared as a BLACK DOG. It also could appear in the form of a GOAT, who lived in the woods and had a tremendous capacity for leaping over fences and other obstacles. It may not derive from Celtic mythology, which knows nothing quite like it, but from that of the Danes, who had a similar figure called Pukí. The pooka became, in Welsh, pwca, who appears as Robin Goodfellow, the half-goat, mischief-making Puck whom Shakespeare evoked in *A Midsummer Night's Dream.* In Britain the puck was a SHAPE-SHIFTER who tended to appear in human form.

Sometimes the pooka was friendly, helping farmers who treated it kindly, as in the story of the boy who made friends with a pooka and soon found that a half-dozen were living in the barn, doing the farm's work. As with any such OTHERWORLD being, however, the pooka refused pay, and when the boy made a little suit for the pooka, it disappeared. In the famous story of the Pooka of Kildare, the being appeared as a donkey, but when given clothing by the farm workers it disappeared.

Often the pooka was a harbinger of doom, indicating bad luck on the way. One tale describes how a pooka, in the form of a goat, leaped onto a man's shoulders; when he went home, he took to his bed and was unable to move for three weeks with intense pain, although there was no visible mark from the attack. The pooka attacked most often after SAMHAIN, the Celtic feast of November 1 when winter began, and was thought by some to be the cause of plants' blighting in that season. In its horse form, it would take its victims on a wild ride, flying through the air in terrifying fashion and leaving the unfortunate rider far from where he started.

The Irish center of pooka appearances is in the southwestern province of MUNSTER, where a castle called Castle Pooka near Doneraile (where the English poet Edmund Spenser wrote *The Faerie Queene*) is said to be haunted by one; a rock called Carrig-a-Phooka, west of the little market town of Macroom, is a common site of visitation; and on the island of Melaam near Kenmare, frightening noises attributed to the pooka are regularly emitted during storms and dark nights. The pooka makes an important appearance in the modern Irish comic novel *At Swim-Two-Birds* by Flann O'Brien (Brian O'Nolan).

Sources: Croker, T. Crofton. *Fairy Legends and Traditions of the South of Ireland.* London: William Tegg, 1862, p. 135; Kennedy, Patrick. *Legendary Fictions of the Irish Celts.* New York: Benjamin Blom, 1969, pp. 124–126.

portals to the Otherworld Cosmological concept. The Celtic OTHERWORLD was not a place apart from this world; there was no heaven high above or hell down far below. Rather, the Otherworld existed in a kind of parallel time and place, near to this world but not accessible. Certain sites and times, however, offered portals to the Otherworld. Then the veil between worlds, always thin, became even thinner; then people could pass from one world into the other. Such places include ancient sites, both Celtic and pre-Celtic. DOLMENS, which are door-like structures of stone built by pre-Celtic people for unknown reasons, were especially likely to be places where one could enter the Otherworld. Similarly STONE CIRCLES, also artifacts of the pre-Celtic period, served as ways to enter there; Celtic HILLFORTS made ideal portals as well. Certain times also made an approach to The Otherworld easier; most significant were the two ancient Celtic holidays, BELTANE on May 1, and its opposite day, SAMHAIN on November 1, when the forces of the Otherworld could easily enter our world, and those from this side could slip over to the Other.

portal tombs See DOLMEN.

portent See OMEN; PROPHECY.

portune British folkloric figure. The wizened and wrinkled portune was a typical BROWNIE-type fairy, delighted to help with farm work provided no payment was offered; it was also necessary to resist the temptation to replace their wrinkled, ragged old coats. They were especially useful in hauling and doing other heavy work. Portunes lived on frog meat, roasted on hot coals. The name may come from a mispronunciation of the Roman god of the sea, Neptune, although the portune has no connection to the ocean. Occasionally, the portune revealed his FAIRY nature by turning mischievous and driving horses into swamps, laughing hysterically at their wild attempts to escape.

power of the word see POETRY.

powrie *(dunter)* Scottish and British folkloric figures. Noisy spirits, they set up a racket in old buildings and towers; when the noise grew impossibly loud, death or ill fortune was approaching the hearer.

pregnancy through drinking, eating Mythic motif. There are a number of Celtic myths in which a goddess or heroine is made pregnant though the mouth, by eating or drinking. Most commonly, the pregnancy results from drinking down a WORM or other insect that has drowned in water or wine. The divine beauty ÉTAIN, cursed by the wife of her lover, became a fly and drowned in a cup of wine, which a princess drank; when she gave birth nine months later, Étain was reborn in a new (but still beautiful) form. The hero CONCOBAR MAC NESSA was born clutching a worm, for his mother, the ravished scholar NESSA, wished to prove that her son's father was a worm she drank rather than the DRUID who held her hostage; his paternal line being in doubt, Concobar bore his mother's name. This motif is found in many other cultures, including the Chinese, where emperors were commonly said to have been born through miraculous conception after their mothers ate or drank something unusual. Some have argued that such myths disguise an ancient matrilineal succession, with property and names being passed through the mother's family.

prophecy Religious ritual. The difference between a prophecy and an OMEN (or portent) is that the first is the result of a ritual embarked upon to find information about the future, while the second is an unsought gift. Omens such as the flight of birds simply existed, like acts of nature, although interpreting their meaning was a skill learned by the Celtic priestly class of DRUIDS. Prophecy, by contrast, could be courted by initiates, and the druids practiced various ritual techniques that produced a trance or altered state that permitted a view into hidden matters. Prophecy permits early vision of the future; in this, it is a specialized form of DIVINATION, which can also include learning about secrets hidden in the past or present. Thus one might use divination to find out who had committed a crime but prophecy to discover whether the culprit would be caught.

The Celts used both prophecy and divination from earliest times. Both Diodoros of Sicily and Strabo describe how HUMAN SACRIFICE (probably the killing of prisoners or criminals) was used to foretell the future; the victim was stabbed with a dagger and, as he died, his death agonies were decoded to reveal events yet to unfold.

In Ireland several complex rituals of prophecy and divination were known, including the *IMBAS FOROSNAI*, or chanting into the fingertips, and the *tarbhfleis* or BULL-SLEEP, in which a druid or poet slept inside the hide of a newly slaughtered bull in order to dream the future (especially the identity of the future king).

protection against fairies Folkloric motif. FAIRIES were not evil; however, they were amoral, not tied to the moral and ethical demands of humanity. Thus to protect oneself

against them was not the same as fending off evil, for they were merely playful troublemakers rather than devilish opponents. They commonly tried to lead travelers astray (see PIXY-LED, STRAY SOD); this was a minor inconvenience and could be quite frightening, but even without protection, the fairy eventually grew bored with the trick and released the ensnared human.

More seriously, the fairies attempted to lure useful or attractive people into the OTHERWORLD, to do their bidding until released. Musicians were sought after to play for the endless fairy dances; midwives were useful for delivering fairy babies; and handsome people of either sex were desirable for sexual dalliance. Because time in FAIRYLAND passed so much more slowly than in our world, a day spent there could be a lifetime here; the returnee might find loved ones dead and the world utterly changed. Even more dreadful, the returnee could find this world so flat and dull compared to the beauties of fairyland that death followed soon after.

Therefore it was traditionally considered wise to carry protection against fairies when going on a trip of any distance; indeed, even a short hike could result in trouble, so filling one's pockets with bread or SALT was always a good idea. The fairies stayed away from anything Christian, so crosses were useful, as was holy water. IRON, too, was dreadful to the fairies, so keeping a knife, scissors, or nail in the pocket was considered well advised, as was mounting a horseshoe over entries to house and barn. Four-leafed clovers or SHAMROCKS exuded an oil that, if rubbed on the eye, could remove any fairy enchantment; other useful plants were St. John's wort, daisies, and red verbena. Most effective of all was ROWAN or mountain ash, whose berries the fairies could not endure.

Actions could also break the fairy spell. The most common was turning one's clothing inside out or wearing it backward, the latter presumably based on the idea that the fairies fail to torment someone who seems to be departing rather than approaching. Praying aloud, or singing, or whistling, were held to be efficacious. As fairies were believed to find running water frightening, leaping over a stream put protection between the traveler and the fairy—provided there was not another fairy standing on the distant shore.

province (cóiced) Irish geographical and cosmological concept. The island of Ireland was divided into four main provinces, each with its own significance: LEINSTER in the east, the region of commerce; MUNSTER in the southwest, land of song and women; CONNACHT in the west, the province of wisdom; and ULSTER in the north, the land of war and strife. These regions were mythological constructs; indeed, there was little sense of the provinces as political units, a situation that remains so today.

In addition to the four main provinces, there was a fifth, one that existed even more in the realm of myth than the others. This was MIDE or Meath, the central province. Its boundaries were even less firm than those of the others, because it represented the concept of the center rather than any specific geographical region. Several hundred years ago, the county of Meath was established, but the fifth province of Ireland remains just as elusive as in prehistory.

See also CÓICED.

Sources: Aitchison, N. B. *Armagh and the Royal Centres in Early Medieval Ireland: Monuments, Cosmology and the Past.* Rochester, N.Y.: Crithne Press/Boydell & Brewer, 1994, p. 114; Dames, Michael. *Mythic Ireland.* London: Thames and Hudson, 1992, pp. 14–16; Rees, Alwyn, and Brinley Rees. *Celtic Heritage: Ancient Tradition in Ireland and Wales.* London: Thames and Hudson, 1998, pp. 118 ff.

Pryderi (Gwri) Welsh hero. In the first book of the collection of Welsh mythology known as the *MABINOGION*, this hero was born of the magical woman (possibly originally a goddess) RHIANNON, who married the human prince PWYLL after a strange courtship. Rhiannon appeared on an impossibly speedy mount and was chased by Pwyll, who never could catch up with her. When he finally simply asked her to pause, she willingly did so. Once married, however, their lives were soon unhappy, for when their son Pryderi was born, he quickly disappeared from his cradle. He had been, unknown to the court, snatched away by an Otherworldly hand, but when the monster tried to add a foal from another part of the land to the night's catch, the foal's owner counterattacked, causing the monster to drop the tiny infant and flee. This left the prince far from home, but happily the noble farmer whose horse had been threatened, TEYRNON Twf Liant, adopted him and reared him in safety and comfort under the name of Gwri.

When he learned the truth of his birth, the young boy set out to claim his inheritance. Finding that his mother had been accused of murdering him and was still being punished for this imaginary crime, he set Rhiannon free by revealing the truth of his absence. Rhiannon welcomed him, but named him Pryderi, "care," for all that she had suffered. The family lived happily until their land was set upon by a strange curse that caused its CATTLE and people to disappear in a magical mist, as described in the third branch of the *Mabinogion.* Pwyll had died, and Rhiannon was remarried to the kingly MANAWYDAN; Pryderi too was married, to the fair maiden CIGFA. Unbeknownst to them all, friends of a rejected suitor for Rhiannon's hand still harbored a desire to avenge the humiliation he had suffered. Thus Pryderi was enchanted, together with his mother, and held until their spouses could determine how to free them.

Prydwen Welsh mythological object. This magical boat, said to have been King ARTHUR's, was described by some Welsh legends as able to navigate both the waters of this world and that of the OTHERWORLD. The name was also used occasionally of Arthur's shield.

puck British folkloric figure. The most famous little FAIRY in English letters is "that merry wanderer of the night," Puck or Robin Goodfellow of William Shakespeare's *A Midsummer Night's Dream.* The puck was well-known to country dwellers as a kind of POOKA, a ghostly haunt that caused mischief wherever it went. A small good-natured creature, the puck lived to make trouble, leading travelers astray whenever possible (see PIXY-LED), pushing furniture about to make people fall flat on the floor, laughing at the annoyances he caused. Like any such being, a puck was friendly enough and could be induced to assist in farm labor, provided no reward or recompense was offered.

Under the name of ROBIN GOODFELLOW, the puck was described in the 17th-century British folklore as a half-human son of OBERON and a country lass who took the fairy lord's fancy. Robin was a normal child until the age of six, when he realized his ability to shape-shift, which he used to become a kind of ROBIN HOOD, causing mischief to the rich but helping the poor. Some of these motifs have been traced to the Celtic myth of the half-human fairy king and sea god MANANNÁN MAC LIR.

Source: Evans-Wentz, W. Y. *The Fairy-Faith in Celtic Countries.* Gerrards Cross: Colin Smythe Humanities Press, 1911, p. 220.

Puck Fair Irish folkloric festival. On a weekend near the ancient Celtic harvest festival of LUGHNASA, a strange ritual is held in the small village of Kilorglin in the southwestern province of Ireland, MUNSTER. A wild GOAT is captured in the mountains near the town, then ceremoniously brought into the square and crowned king. Hoisted above the square, the Puck rules over three days of events: Gathering Day, Fair Day, and Scattering Day. Festivities range from horse shows to outdoor games to music and drink. At the end of the fair, the Puck is taken back to the mountains and released. Locals claim the festival dates back to time immemorial, but some scholars suggest that it is a relatively recent invention, perhaps 300 years old. The fact that the goat is not found as an important symbolic animal in Celtic culture, as well as the use of the word PUCK, which derives from British rather than Irish sources (for Irish, see POOKA), supports the latter argument.

Purr Mooar Manx folkloric figure. On the Isle of Man, this OTHERWORLD specter haunted people in the form of a PIG.

Pwyll (Pwyll Prince of Dyfed, Pwyll Pendefig Dyfed) Welsh hero. One of the primary heroes of the collection of Welsh mythological narratives called the *MABINOGION*, Pwyll appears in the first branch of the series, where he was asked by an Otherworldly king, ARAWN, to exchange places with him. Arawn was being hounded by a murderous enemy and rival, HAFGAN, and hoped that Pwyll would be able to save his country. Pwyll agreed, and taking on the appearance of Arawn, ruled well in the Otherworld. So honorable was Pwyll that he refused to make love with Arawn's queen, though she did not realize another man's soul inhabited the semblance of her husband's form. At the end of the year, Pwyll met the enemy Hafgan in single combat—a classically Celtic motif—and defeated him, thus further bonding him to the grateful king Arawn.

Back in his own world, Pwyll found himself infatuated with a beautiful woman who appeared on a white HORSE that no one could catch. For many nights he chased RHIANNON to no avail, until finally he called out to her to stop. She did, and they were soon happily married, but their happiness was short-lived, for after their son PRYDERI was born, Rhiannon was discovered raving with blood on her face, while the child was nowhere to be found. Believing his wife had killed and eaten their child, Pwyll punished her by making her act as a horse, carrying visitors on her back into their castle. She thus served for many years before their son Pyrderi—who had in fact been kidnapped by a spectral arm and rescued by a distant farmer—returned to free her from her burdens. Pwyll's reign thereafter was without disturbance and abundantly successful.

Source: Gantz, Jeffrey, trans. *The Mabinogion.* New York: Barnes & Noble Books, 1976.

questing beast (Beast Glatisant) Arthurian figure. This monstrous but unexplained hybrid combined the bodies of SERPENT, DEER, and leopard. Although it had only four legs, the sound of 30 hooves was heard whenever it ran. A knight—variously called PELLINORE and PALOMIDES—pursued it endlessly, perhaps because it was really human, a boy transformed to animal shape by the horror of seeing his mother torn apart by wild DOGS.

quintessence Cosmological concept. This word, derived from the Latin word for FIVE and indicating a distilled essence, describes the mystical center or MIDE, a place that is both everywhere and nowhere, a pivot point around which the world turns. Although Mide exists as one of the five PROVINCES of ancient Ireland, it was not limited to one location until the medieval period, before which it was a shifting boundless space. See UISNEACH; TARA.

R

Ragallach (Raghallach) Irish hero. This obscure figure was said to have been king of CONNACHT, the western PROVINCE of Ireland, in the seventh century C.E. There is some historical evidence of his life, although the elaborate tales told about him are partially legend.

Because of his greed for power, Ragallach arranged to have his only possible rival for the throne killed—his nephew, who came to him with guards but was shamed into leaving them behind, permitting the king to kill him with ease. Because of this heinous act, the DRUIDS prophesied that Ragallach would be killed by his own children. To avert this fate, Ragallach announced that all his children should be killed.

His queen, Murieann, hid their daughter (who is never named in the legends) in the woods, where she was found and reared by a poor woman. The daughter grew into a splendid beauty whose reputation reached the king; in keeping with his greedy temperament and not knowing her identity, he demanded that the girl be brought to him. Murieann was so insulted by the king's obvious infatuation that she fled from the court.

Several saintly men fasted in protest against the king's behavior, with the result that he was magically ensnared on the next BELTANE night, the feast of summer's beginning. A magnificent STAG was seen racing through the land.

Ragallach gave pursuit and wounded the animal. The injured stag leapt into a river and swam away, shortly followed by the king, who found the beast's body at last, being divided among hungry peasants. He claimed the meat, but the men fell upon him and killed him in the dispute. Nothing more is said of the daughter whose beauty caused the king's downfall, although it is said the queen Murieann died of jealousy. Nor is it explained how the prophecy was fulfilled, unless the starving peasants were the king's actual or metaphorical children.

Ragnell Arthurian heroine. After an enchantment had been cast upon her, turning her into a LOATHY LADY or CAILLEACH, Ragnell maintained her sweet good humor and helped GAWAIN, a knight of the ROUND TABLE, learn the answer to the riddle of what women really want. Despite her uncomely appearance, the fine knight fell in love with the wise and kind Ragnell. When they married, she told him that she could be a lovely woman during the day and a HAG at night, or the opposite, and asked him which he preferred. When he gave her the power to make the choice herself, she emerged from her enchantment, becoming a beautiful young woman and revealing that women want to make their own decisions. She may be a form of the goddess of SOVEREIGNTY. Ragnell's tale became the basis for the medieval English poet Geoffrey Chaucer's "Wife of Bath's Tale" in the *Canterbury Tales*.

rainbow Cosmological symbol. The bright bridge of colors that decks the sky after a rainstorm has drawn many legends to itself in Celtic lands, as in other cultures. In Celtic areas of Germany the rainbow was believed to leave traces of GOLD wherever it touched the earth; the belief gave rise to the production of a coin with a slightly concave surface called a *regenbogenschüsselchen* (rainbow-coin), which was thought to have healing powers. In Ireland the LEPRECHAUN or fairy shoemaker was similarly said to hide his gold at the end of a rainbow.

ram-headed snake Continental Celtic religious symbol. An unnatural combination of mammal and reptile—and, occasionally, of FISH as well—can be found in some religious art from Gaul, especially after the Roman occupation. The significance of this being, unique to the Celtic lands, is not known and can only be surmised from the way that Celtic artists showed it with deities and as an ornament on religious artifacts. The ram and ram-headed snake are sometimes shown with CERNUNNOS, the god of wild lands, and thus may have been linked with FERTILITY.

rat British folkloric animal. Whether the rat and mouse were originally believed to have magical powers among the Celts is unclear, but some vestige of that belief is found in the British Cotswolds, where they were thought to have prophetic or precognitive powers. When rats or mice suddenly left a house, it was believed to foretell a death the family. In Scotland seeing a rat or mouse in a sieve meant the likely death of someone at sea, as did seeing a rat swimming by when one was in a boat.

Source: Briggs, Katherine M. *The Folklore of the Cotswolds*. London: B. T. Batsford Ltd., 1974, p. 127.

rath See HILLFORT.

Rath Irish hero. In an Irish tale, a sailor named Rath let himself be serenaded by a MERMAID and her friends—who then tore the man to pieces. Mermaids were not believed to be generally murderous beings, but falling asleep to their Otherworldly music was something to avoid, for they were inclined to steal humans AWAY to become their lovers (see FAIRY KIDNAPPING).

Rath Chinneich Irish mythological site. The location of the mythological palace of one of the first settlers of Ireland, NEMED, Rath Chinneich has never been found, although it is believed to have been in Co. Armagh.

Rathcrogan See CRUACHAN.

Rath of the Synods See TARA.

Ratis Continental Celtic goddess. The name of this obscure Gaulish goddess may be connected with the word for a HILLFORT or settlement *(rath)*; she was a protector of such fortresses.

raven Symbolic animal. The distinction between raven and CROW is not always clear to the untrained eye, nor are they clearly distinguished in Celtic myth. The two birds are related members of the genus *Corvus*, with the raven being considerably larger and typically a more northern bird than the crow. They have common eating habits, devouring carrion rather than, as with birds of prey like the EAGLE and the hawk, hunting their food live.

This dietary predilection meant that ravens and crows were often seen flying over battlefields, waiting to feast on the slain. It was easy to link the birds to war goddesses like the Irish MÓRRÍGAN and BADB, who were said to take the form of the birds when encouraging bloodshed.

At the same time, the birds were seen as oracular, a form of the goddess who washed the clothing or armor of those doomed to die (see WASHER AT THE FORD) in the next day's battle. As a symbol of the OTHERWORLD, the raven could indicate rebirth as well as death; thus the birds's meaning is far from simple and can seem self-contradictory.

Ancient tradition was carried through the ages in folklore that claims that ravens are unlucky. If one is seen when ground is being broken for a house or when other new projects are initiated, its appearance foretells a bad end to the project. If they take to hanging around a house, it is considered a sure sign that one of its occupants is near death.

rebirth   See REINCARNATION.

red   Symbolic color. There were two colors most often associated with FAIRYLAND or the OTHERWORLD: GREEN and red, with the latter being the more popular color for TROOPING FAIRIES, while SOLITARY FAIRIES tended to favor green. As a result, the color was considered unlucky, even when on clothing or scarves worn by humans: Women wearing red petticoats were avoided in the west of Ireland until recent times. Even more ominous was red hair or hide, whether on human or animals. Combined with white, red hair was a sure sign of fairy origin. Thus fairy CATTLE were believed to be white with red ears; a dog or cat born with the same coloring was believed to be of fairy blood or a CHANGELING. Red-haired people were, by the same reasoning, believed to have fairy blood.

There are many superstitions about such red-haired people and animals. It was considered very bad luck to meet a red-haired woman first thing in the morning; a traveler might return home rather than risk continuing a journey that started with such an evil portent. A person dressed in red could prove unlucky if he or she passed in the morning or when one was beginning a project. Red-eared animals were believed

to have similar powers to predict (or possibly bring on) difficulties.

Red Branch   Irish warrior group. The warriors of the Red Branch were the protectors of the northern PROVINCE of ULSTER, rather as the later heroic band, the FIANNA, protected the eastern province of LEINSTER. The most famous Red Branch warrior was the peerless CÚCHULAINN, who single-handedly fought off the invading army of queen MEDB of CONNACHT. Some scholars have seen in stories of the Red Branch warriors a foreshadowing of the later ROUND TABLE knights who served king ARTHUR.

Red Branch Cycle   See ULSTER CYCLE.

Redcap   British folkloric figure. His little hat was RED because he washed it regularly in blood from his victims, whom he frightened to death from his haunts in old ruins. His eyes were red, too, perhaps from staring into the darkness, ever on the watch for new prey. Should you encounter, while adventuring around old castles, a wizened old man with wild hair wearing IRON boots and carrying a big iron weapon, the only thing to do was to hold up a Bible, which caused Redcap to emit a horrific scream before disappearing. Occasionally this figure appeared as a kind of useful BROWNIE, eager to help around the house, but generally he was a fearsome spirit to be avoided.

Red Etin   British folkloric figure. This British ogre was ugly to look at (having THREE heads is not typically considered handsome) but not necessarily unfriendly. His interest was CATTLE: his own, which were large herds of OTHERWORLD creatures (often with RED ears, a sign of their FAIRY origin), and others', which he protected for no fee. He may descend from an Otherworldly guardian figure.

In one tale from Scotland, Red Etin appears as a GIANT from Ireland to whose home the son of a widow came, thinking to spy on him from a hiding place. Unfortunately, Red Etin detected the presence of human blood. "Be he from Fife," he bellowed, "or be he from Tweed, his heart this night shall kitchen my bread." He was not so cruel as he sounded, for he gave the young man three chances to avoid becoming dinner, and with the help of magical animals, the boy survived.

Reid, Thome Scottish folkloric figure. This is the name given to a visitor from the OTHER-WORLD who, according to Sir Walter Scott, appeared in 1576 to a Scottish woman named Elizabeth (Bessie) Dunlop of Ayrshire. Bessie was surprised one morning to be greeted by a gray-bearded man dressed all in gray except for a black bonnet (unusual colors for Otherworldly apparitions, who tended rather toward wearing RED or GREEN). He spoke to her, offered her riches if she would give up being Christian, and then disappeared when she refused.

Undiscouraged, he came back again and again. Bessie invariably refused his demand, but she learned that the spectral man's name was Thome Reid and that he had been a soldier killed in battle. Sometimes Thome appeared accompanied by small beings, "good wights," as he called them, who lived with him in FAIRY-LAND. However persuasive he was, Bessie continued to refuse to join him there, accepting only his advice on how to heal her neighbors. She became a renowned herbalist who wanted only food as her fee. For four years Thome continued to visit Bessie, all the while encouraging her to abandon this world for the Other. Her loyalty to this world and its religion was not rewarded, however, for she was ultimately convicted of WITCHCRAFT and burned at the stake.

reincarnation (rebirth) Cosmological concept. There is some dispute as to whether the Celts believed in reincarnation. The term is often used in describing the east Asian religious and philosophical belief that a human being is born again and again in human form, with the activities of one life affecting those of the next (the Hindu concept of karma). When a soul is believed to occupy various forms, both human and animal, the proper term is not reincarnation but TRANSMIGRATION OF SOULS.

Caesar claimed that the DRUIDS believed that, after death, the individual was given a new life, which explained why Celtic warriors were so fearfully brave on the battlefield, since they knew they would find another body when the one they occupied was killed. Caesar was writing about the culture he tried to conquer, so he may not be an entirely credible source. Diodoros of Sicily similarly argued that the Celts believed in reincarnation, but he attempted to show the similarity of the Celtic belief system and that of the Hellenic philosopher Pythagoras, who believed that we would be born again in various forms, not always human. Many Celtic legends describe mythic beings reborn in various forms (see ÉTAIN, TUAN MAC CAIRILL, FINTAN, FRIUCH, TALIESIN), but whether this was believed to happen to the common individual is not clear.

What the Celts believed about the afterlife is debatable. The fact that gods and goddesses as well as heroines and heroines were occasionally reborn may not mean this was the usual fate of mortal beings, but rather might emphasize their uniquely divine qualities—for Celtic deities were not necessarily immortal. The idea of an OTHERWORLD where the newly dead join the shades of the earlier dead, as well as the magical beings and divinities who lived there, does not necessarily imply reincarnation. Such descriptions of Celtic belief may be influenced by the Christian conception of heaven as a place where the dead enjoy the presence of god forever. The question of Celtic belief in reincarnation is thus still an open one.

Source: MacCulloch, J. A. *The Religion of the Ancient Celts.* London: Constable, 1911, pp. 348 ff.

religion See CELTIC RELIGION.

Rhiannon Welsh goddess or heroine. It is probable that, like other major characters in the compilation of Welsh myths called the *MABINO-GION*, the magical horsewoman Rhiannon was originally divine. Her name has been connected with a presumed ancient goddess named riga-tona, "great queen." We find among the continental Celts (and, to some extent, in Britain as well) a HORSE goddess named EPONA, who may be a figure parallel to Rhiannon, since Rhiannon throughout her legend is associated with HORSES. The connection of Rhiannon to horses has led some scholars to link her with the SUN, often depicted by the ancient Celts in equine form.

As she appeared in the Welsh myth, Rhiannon was an OTHERWORLD woman who rode her speedy white horse around an enchanted spot. The king of the region of Dyfed, PWYLL, encountered her there and gave chase, but his mortal horse was no match for hers. Three times they raced, and finally he called out for her to stop, whereupon she did, admitting she had heard of his prowess and had come to seek him. Rhiannon soon became Pwyll's wife and queen—though not until he defeated another contender for her hand, GWAWL.

Life was not long happy for the pair, however, because after Rhiannon gave birth to their son PRYDERI, she was found one BELTANE morning with blood on her face and the child mysteriously gone. Everyone jumped to the conclusion that Rhiannon had gone mad and killed her child, but the blood was actually DOG's blood, for finding the boy missing, the nursemaids had killed a puppy and smeared its blood on Rhiannon's face while she slept.

The nursemaids did not confess their secret, and so Rhiannon was punished. She was given a curiously light sentence: to serve as a mount for all visitors to the castle, bringing them from the gate on her back. She was ultimately released from bondage by the appearance of her son Pryderi, who had been stolen by a spectral figure but later saved and reared by a distant nobleman, TEYRNON Twf Liant.

Rhiannon was widowed later in life, but soon remarried. The problems that plagued her first marriage came back to haunt the kingdom, which abruptly and mysteriously turned barren when her son Pryderi assumed the throne. Rhiannon and her new husband, MANAWYDAN, joined Pryderi and his wife CIGFA in scraping a living from the increasingly empty land. Finally they gave up and found residence in a city far to the east (perhaps London), where they eked out a living as artisans, an occupation at which they were quite talented. In fact, they incurred the wrath of the less-talented local craftsmen, who rose up to drive them away.

Fearing for their safety, the family group returned to the wilderness of Dyfed, but Rhiannon and her son immediately became enchanted and disappeared. Unwilling to abandon his wife even though he had no idea where she was, Manawydan searched for clues until he discovered that the family of Gwawl, the former suitor humiliated when Pwyll won Rhiannon, had come to punish them. After a suitable accord was reached, Rhiannon and Pryderi were freed from enchantment and returned to this world.

Several scholars have connected Rhiannon with the goddess of the land's SOVEREIGNTY, for her presence in Dyfed made the land abundant, while her absence made it barren. She has also been connected with the goddess of war whose name resembles hers (MÓRRÍGAN has some of the same linguistic roots), especially because, like Mórrígan, Rhiannon is associated with BIRDS—in her case, THREE magical birds who fly always around her shoulders, singing so sweetly that the dead awaken and the living fall into a trance.

Sources: Dexter, Miriam Robbins. *Whence the Goddesses: A Sourcebook.* New York: Pergamon Press, 1990, pp. 93–94; Gantz, Jeffrey, trans. *The Mabinogion.* New York: Barnes & Noble Books, 1976; MacCulloch, J. A. *The Religion of the Ancient Celts.* London: Constable, 1911, pp. 98 ff, 110 ff; Ross, Anne. *Pagan Celtic Britain: Studies in Iconography and Tradition.* London: Routledge & Kegan Paul, 1967, p. 225;

Straffon, Cheryl. *The Earth Goddess: Celtic and Pagan Legacy of the Landscape.* London: Blandford, 1997, pp. 38–39.

Rhonabwy Welsh hero. This minor hero is most notable for being skillful at DIVINATION; he dreamed of the great king ARTHUR before he came to power.

Rhun Welsh hero. This human hero figures in a curious story of faithfulness and betrayal. ELPHIN, the bumbling, boisterous king, bragged that his wife was more faithful than Rhun's. To disprove this slight upon his wife, Rhun traveled to Elphin's court and attempted to seduce the queen. When she refused his advances, Rhun drugged her and chopped off her ring finger. He brought this arrogantly to Elphin, not realizing that the queen and her handmaiden had swapped identities; the bread dough under the fingernail, something a queen would never endure, told the story. Rhun continued in his competition with Elphin, next wagering with him as to whose HORSES were faster. Through a trick engineered by the canny BARD, TALIESIN, Elphin won the race and sent Rhun home.

Rhydderch Hael (Rhydderch Largus, Rhydderch the Generous) Arthurian hero. Owner of a CAULDRON of abundance, Rhydderch is an otherwise obscure figure in Arthurian legend.

rí *(ri)* See KINGSHIP.

Riada Irish hero. The son of a king of MUNSTER Riada escaped a famine by taking his people on a long trek to happier climes. He first settled in Co. Antrim, in ULSTER, then boated across the Irish Sea to Scotland; both kingdoms were called Dál Riada after him.

Richis (Riches) Irish heroine. This satirist challenged the great hero CÚCHULAINN after he

had killed her foster son, CRIMTHANN NIA NÁIR. Despite her bravery, she lost her life as Crimthann had done.

Rifath Scot Irish hero. According to the mythological history, the *BOOK OF INVASIONS*, this ancestor of the Irish race was one of the workers on the biblical Tower of Babel. When, to punish human arrogance, God cursed all the workers by causing them to speak in different languages, Rifath Scot began speaking Scots Gaelic. One of this descendants, GOIDEL, created the final version of the language.

Rigani Continental Celtic goddess. This name has been interpreted to mean "great queen." It may be a title of ROSMERTA rather than indicating a separate goddess.

Rigatona (Rigantona) See RHIANNON.

Rigisamus (Rigonemetis) British and continental Celtic god. His name meant "most kingly" or "most regal," and dedications to this otherwise obscure god have been found both in Britain and France. The Romans equated him to their warrior god MARS, as they did a similarly named divinity called Rigonemetis, "king of the sacred grove."

Rigru Roisclethan (Rígru Rosclethan) Irish heroine. This woman of the OTHERWORLD appeared to the king at TARA once, wailing horribly and leading a mooing cow. She warned king CONN of the Hundred Battles, who had attempted to kill her son, and told him that the land would suffer so long as the lustful queen BÉ CHUMA remained in power.

Ríonach (Riona) Irish heroine. The mother of the Christian St. Colman was a member of an important family in the province of CONNACHT. When Ríonach was seen to be pregnant, ambitious would-be kings realized that her heritage would elevate her child to royal status (see MATRILINY) and thus prevent them from gaining the throne. These rivals hunted down the pregnant woman who, in despair, jumped into the Kiltartan River near Gort, Co. Galway, intent upon death.

She did not, drown however, but floated downriver. She landed near Corker, dragged herself from the water, and gave birth beneath a magical ASH tree. Two monks—one blind, one lame—found her there with her infant son. Ríonach begged them to baptize the baby, but there was no water within reach. One monk grabbed some wet RUSHES, whereupon a holy WELL burst forth at that spot. The blind monk washed his eyes, restoring his sight; the lame monk bathed his leg, restoring his ability to walk. Colman grew up to become the patron SAINT of the region. Although a Christian tale, this story has many Celtic motifs.

Ritona Continental Celtic goddess. This obscure divinity was known in Gaul as a goddess of fords; she may have been, like many other Celtic goddesses, connected with RIVERS as well.

river Cosmological concept. Rivers, sacred to the Celts, were almost invariably described as goddesses. Many rivers in Celtic lands still bear the ancient names of the goddesses who were believed to live within them or whose deaths caused the release of their waters. Typically the river goddess was pictured as a maternal presence who provided food to those along her banks; among the continental Celts, the river was often associated with the group of goddesses known collectively as DEAE MATRES, "the mothers." Whether through FISH caught in her waters, grain watered by them, or meat from CATTLE who drank along her shores, the river goddess was the great provider for the Celtic people. Her waters were sometimes associated, as a result, with MILK, and the river goddess herself with a COW.

The source of a river was especially sacred. The Celts believed that where WATER first emerged from the ground, to swell into a river by joining with smaller tributaries, great HEALING power resided. Offerings were often made at these river sources, suggesting that rituals were performed there to promote recovery from illness or injury.

Similarly, SPRINGS were considered sacred, especially hot springs that became healing shrines. There is in fact significant therapeutic benefit to be gained from bathing in hot springs, which can relieve the pains of chronic ailments like arthritis. Several important Celtic sites, like Bath in England, show evidence of having been used in pre-Celtic times; in many cases, the invading Romans continued to employ the springs for their own medicinal purposes.

Some scholars argue that folk beliefs in hauntings or FAIRY activity around holy wells and rivers is a vestige of ancient Celtic religion. The legends of many FAIRY QUEENS connect them to water. This interpretation, although common, is somewhat controversial.

Among the Celtic river divinities (together with the rivers they ruled) are the goddesses ABNOBA (Danube, Avon), ALAUNA (Alaunus, Alun), BELISAMA (Ribble), BERBA (Barrow), BÓAND (Boyne), BRIGANTIA (Braint, Brent), Cluta (Clyde), COVENTINA (Carrawburgh), DANU (Danube), DEE/Deva/Divona (Dee, Dive), ERNE (Erne), FIAL (Feale), GARRAVOGUE (Garravogue), ICAUNA (Yonne), MATRONA (Marne, Madder, Moder, Maronne, Maronna), NATOSUELTA (Trent), SABRINA (Severn), SEQUANA (Seine), SÍNANN (Shannon), and the folkloric figures PEG O'NELL (Ribble) and PEG POWLER (Tees).

Although rivers were typically seen by the Celts as feminine forces, there are occasional breaks in the pattern. Occasionally a god appears as consort of a river goddess. Even less frequently, river gods alone are found; whether the feminine consort has been lost is not known. Gods of rivers (and the rivers to which they were connected) include Danuvius (Danube), NODENS (Severn), and the folkloric figures TAVY and DAVY JONES

(Tavy). More typically, gods ruled healing springs (see BORVO, APOLLO Grannos, LUXOVIUS).

River sources, which are often similar to springs, frequently had a male spirit resident within them. Commonly he took the form of a fish, like the SALMON of WISDOM (sometimes named FINTAN) who lived in the spring at the source of the Boyne or the Shannon in Ireland, gorging on nuts from magical HAZEL trees and growing wise. On the Continent, especially in Brittany, there are legends of EELS and trout who live in sacred springs. Seeing such a being, either leaping from the water or swimming beneath its surface, was extremely lucky.

Sources: MacCulloch, J. A. *The Religion of the Ancient Celts*. London: Constable, 1911, pp. 42, 46, 180 ff; O'Rahilly, Thomas. *Early Irish History and Mythology*. Dublin: The Dublin Institute for Advanced Studies, 1946, p. 3; Ross, Anne. *Folklore of the Scottish Highlands*. London: B. T. Batsford, Ltd., 1976, p. 78.

Roan (roane)   See SILKIE.

Robin Goodfellow   British folkloric figure. In his play *A Midsummer Night's Dream*, Shakespeare conflated the figure of the mischievous FAIRY named PUCK with Robin Goodfellow, son of a fairy king (sometimes, OBERON) and a human mother. According to British folktales, Robin Goodfellow got into such trouble as a child that his mother threatened to whip him, prompting him to run away and become a tailor's apprentice. He continued to make mischief until threatened again, whereupon he ran away once more, this time looking for his father. The reunion was a pleasant one, for Robin's father taught him the art of SHAPE-SHIFTING, after which he settled down and became a hard working, helpful BROWNIE.

Robin Hood   British folkloric figure. The figure known as Robin Hood, who stole from the rich and gave to the poor, may have some historical basis. Robin allegedly lived in medieval times in Sherwood Forest with the fair Maid Marian and his band of merry robbers, including Little John and Friar Tuck. There were, indeed, many highwaymen who lived in the English forests in those days. One of them seems to have caught the popular fancy, although the Robin Hood cult has always been more literate than oral, enjoyed more by the upper than the lower classes, despite Robin's supposed personal bias toward the latter.

The allegedly historical Robin Hood was born Robin Locksley in Brandfield Parish, Hallamshire. When he accidentally wounded his stepfather and feared the violent retribution of the law, Robin fled to Loxley forest, where he met a GIANT hermit named Little John. (A nearby grave was exhumed in 1784 and a thighbone 30 inches long was discovered, so Little John, too, may have some basis in fact. Because bad luck struck the excavator, the bone was reburied and is now lost.)

There have been a number of controversial scholarly attempts to find a mythological basis for the Robin Hood legends. Most propose a connection between the alleged highwayman and the GREEN MAN, a spirit of vegetation and fertility. By this interpretation, Robin Hood was once Robin of the Wood, also known as JACK-IN-THE-GREEN, who ruled as king of the May while Maid Marian was its queen. Such figures were especially associated with the BELTANE festival but were also occasionally attached to the MID-SUMMER festivals of late June. A spot in Loxley forest called Robin Hood's Bower was said in local church records to be a site for Beltane festivities involving a green-clad man; that custom still survives at nearby Castleon, while at ABBOTS BROMLEY men still perform the horn dance around a cross-dressed Maid Marion.

Some legends support the contention that an historical highwayman's deeds became grafted upon an earlier figure whose mythic duties included creation of the landscape. One such tale tells how Robin Hood and Little John challenged each other to a leaping contest. Robin said he could jump all the way over Wormsley Hill, but when he tried he knocked out part of the hill with his heel, which became Butthouse Knapp. When Little John jumped, he too snagged the hill with his heel, with the result that Pyon Hill was formed. Together these hills are still called Robin Hood's Butts. Robin still protects the region, for folklore says that treasure hunters who attempted to dig there found their tools disturbed and GORSE growing every day over what they had dug the day before. Such mischief is typically the work of FAIRIES, so this legend connects Robin and Little John to the OTHERWORLD realm.

Sources: Bord, Janet, and Colin Bord. *The Secret Country: An interpretation of the folklore of ancient sites in the British Isles.* New York: Walker and Co., 1976, p. 76; Briggs, Katherine M. *The Folklore of the Cotswolds.* London: B. T. Batsford, Ltd., 1974, p. 35; Spence, Lewis. *The Minor Traditions of British Mythology.* New York: Benjamin Blom, Inc., 1972, p. 106.

Roc   Irish hero. Part of the mythic background for the romantic tale of DIARMAIT and GRÁINNE regards this man, who had an affair with the goddess Duibhne, wife of the gloomy god DONN. When a child was born of the affair, the outraged and cuckolded husband Donn crushed its skull. Roc knew MAGIC and saved his child by turning it into a great BOAR. If not human, at least the child was alive; it grew to monstrous size, living on the great mountain above Sligo called BEN BULBEN. Duibhne then returned to her husband and had another child, Diarmait, who later lost his life in combat with his beastly half brother.

Roisin Dubh   (Dark Rosaleen)   Irish folkloric figure. This name is given in AISLING poetry to a dark-haired maiden who wanders the roadways alone, hoping to meet a king strong enough to break her bondage. She is a late form of the ancient goddess of SOVEREIGNTY.

Rollright Stones   British mythic location. This great STONE CIRCLE at the border of Oxfordshire and Warwickshire has attracted many legends. One claims the Rollrights as COUNTLESS STONES that deflect any attempt to discover their exact number. A clever baker tried to count the stones by putting a loaf of bread on each one, intending to gather the loaves and count them, but he never seemed to have enough loaves to cover the stones (or loaves may have disappeared as he placed them on the rocks). Some scholars believe these legends arise in an ancient tradition of offering food to the stones.

A significant legend about the Rollright Stones concerns an invading king who heard a prophecy that he would be king of the whole island if he ever saw the town of Long Compton. He set off, but some of his own knights opposed this goal and, when he was camped near the location of the Rollright Stones, began to plot against him. Fearing treachery, the king set off in the night, but before he could mount the rise from which he would see Long Compton, he met a WITCH who turned him into the King Stone— and his whispering knights into stones as well. If the spell ever is broken, the king and his army will conquer England, but for now they remain petrified, while the witch who holds them lives on as an ELDER tree in the vicinity. Some claim to have seen the stones sneak to a stream under cover of darkness, looking for a drink of water to quench their thirst. And every midnight, for a moment, the stones come to life and dance, while the King Stone drinks his fill. Although the stone circles themselves are pre-Celtic, there is evidence of a Celtic HILLFORT in the area as well.

Romano-Celtic   Archaeological term. This phrase is used to describe the divinities and religion of the continental Celts and of Britain, as depicted in art after the Roman conquest of those regions. The Celts did not portray their deities in human form, although there is some early evidence of animal-bodied gods and goddesses; more typically, abstract symbolism was used, which can be difficult to interpret. That the Celts did not suffer from limited artistic skill is clear from the speed with which they picked up the new mode of imagery; within decades of Roman occupation, figurative sculptures in clay and bronze and stone were found in shrines and temples. These show divinities in typically Roman garb (although sometimes with the clearly Celtic TORC or neck-ring) but with Celtic symbols like the DOG, the HAMMER, and the headpiece with ANTLERS. Sometimes the inscriptions use Roman names; thus we have many Celtic MERCURY figures depicting a god who may have ruled commerce. Sometimes the Roman name was used with a Celtic one, as with Sulis Minerva, the healing deity of the hot springs of BATH in England; occasionally only the Celtic name was inscribed on the deity's image, as with NEHALEINNIA, an important goddess of the Netherlands and its sea trade.

In addition to its cultural influence, the Roman occupation had an economic and social impact upon the Celtic inhabitants of the Continent and the island of Britain. By contrast, the Romans never colonized Ireland; thus there are no Romano-Celtic artifacts from that land. Therefore it is not easy to interpret Celtic archaeological finds from the Roman provinces. The same is true of literary texts; as the Celts did not use writing (see OGHAM) to record their history and religion, relying instead on oral transmission, we have no indigenous material with which to compare that written by Romans and other observers.

The cultural scene was further complicated by the importation of non-Roman religious cults—like those of the east Asian goddess Cybele and the Persian god MITHRAS—into Celtic lands by the Roman legions. The Celts were spiritually adaptable (see POLYTHEISM) and may have welcomed some of the new religious visions and opportunities. Taken together, these historical facts mean that the interpretation of Romano-Celtic material presents special problems for scholars, and there is much disagreement and controversy over the meaning of various texts and artifacts.

Rómit Rígóinmit Irish hero. This obscure figure plays a minor role in the story of the *INTOXICATION OF THE ULSTERMEN*, when he appears with the rest of king CONCOBAR MAC NESSA's men at the fort of queen Cú Roi. He is a black man with huge, bulging eyes who serves as Concobar's fool, entertaining the court with his jests and antics.

Ronán Irish hero. The Irish myth of Ronán recalls the more famous Greek story of Phaedra, who fell in love with her stepson, was rejected by him, and vengefully accused him of raping her. Ronán married a much younger woman who fell in love with her stepson, closer in age to her than her husband. When the young man refused her advances, she reported to Ronán that the boy had raped her—for which Ronán put his son to death. When the truth was revealed, Ronán died of grief and his wife committed suicide.

Another Ronán (also called Rodán and Ruadán) was the cause of the desolation of the great central hill of TARA, once the most important political and spiritual capital of the land. When Tara's king, DIARMAIT, condemned him for hiding a relative accused of murder, Ronán cursed the king and Tara itself. From that time forward, Tara was never again as powerful as it had been in Celtic times.

Source: Cross, Tom Peete, and Clark Harris Slover, eds. *Ancient Irish Tales.* New York: Henry Holt and Co., 1936, p. 538.

Rosault Irish legendary monster. This vast being lived in the sea but somehow came ashore in Co. Mayo, where it began vomiting. With each regurgitation, more beings were killed: plants, sea creatures, even humans, until the monster itself expired.

rose Symbolic plant. The fragrant flower of midsummer, the rose was used in DIVINATION and MAGIC. Just as it represents romance today, in Celtic lands it was connected with love and loyalty. In the British Cotswolds the rose was used in making magical spells to attract love or to capture the wandering interest of a lover.

Rosmerta Continental Celtic goddess. Her name, interpreted to mean "The Great Provider," suggests that she was a goddess of abundance to her people in northeastern Gaul. The fact that she was sometimes depicted holding a CORNUCOPIA or horn of plenty supports this theory, as does her association with the god whom the Romans called MERCURY after their divinity of commerce. Rosmerta was often shown without a consort, however, or accompanying an image of the emperor; from this scholars have argued that she was an important goddess whose prestige may have even outweighed that of Mercury, said by the Romans to be the chief god of the Celts.

Occasionally Rosmerta was described as a goddess of a SPRING, which to Celtic people may have represented HEALING. This association might also expand upon her meaning as a force of abundance, for springs at the sources of rivers were connected with the symbolism of the fertile RIVER goddess. Rosmerta's name has been associated with a Celtic word for protection and FERTILITY, and she is sometimes depicted holding the CAULDRON of rebirth. Rosmerta's myth is unknown, as are the specifics of her ritual.

Rothniam See FISHER KING.

Roth Ramach Irish mythological object. This powerful vehicle, called a "flying wheel," was a means of transport for the WITCH or goddess TLACHTGA and her father, the magician MOG RUITH. On the Roth Ramach, they flew easily through the air, even as far away as Italy. The ruins of the magical machine are said to be visible in a stone near Dromline in Co. Tipperary.

Round Table Arthurian legendary object. The great table around which the knights of king ARTHUR at CAMELOT gathered was originally built for Arthur's father, UTHER PENDRAGON, perhaps in the OTHERWORLD. During Arthur's reign, the table symbolized equality between king and knights as well as among the heroic knights themselves, who formed a spiritual brotherhood. When MORDRED, Arthur's illegitimate son by his half sister MORGAUSE, took Camelot from his father, he struck the center of the Round Table and destroyed it—and with it, the hope for harmony and peace that Camelot promised.

rowan (mountain ash, wild-ash, quickbean, quicken tree) Symbolic plant. Not really an ASH tree at all, the delicate-leafed rowan (genus *Sorbus*) was associated with FAIRIES, WITCHES, and the OTHERWORLD across the Celtic lands. Rowan is often found near STONE CIRCLES and other ancient monuments, as well as in graveyards, which may have given rise to the mystical connections of the tree. It was said to offer a foolproof way of detecting witches; the unripe berries, before they turned RED, could be waved over a suspected witch, who would instantly confess. "Rowan, amber, and red thread puts witches to their speed," says a Scottish rhyming proverb.

Pounded and strained, the berry juice was a prophylactic against bewitchment; it is unclear whether the juice was swallowed, used to mark the skin, or simply carried on the threatened person. Crosses made of rowan wood were thought to avert the evil EYE; sticks of rowan wood were useful for driving CATTLE to pasture, because they did double duty in keeping away potentially thieving spirits. Planting rowans around a house or at the property line was held to be good magic against the envy of witches; occasionally the ash was substituted. Rods made of rowan wood were used in casting SPELLS. Like other FAIRY TREES, rowans tended to be long-lived in areas where people believed in fairies, because terrible luck was said to follow cutting one down.

Ruad Irish goddess. In place-lore surrounding the once-magnificent falls (flooded by a hydroelectric project in the mid-20th century), at Assaroe, in Co. Sligo this maiden was said to have given her name to the waterfall (Ess Ruad) when she died there. ABCÁN, the dwarf poet of the magical TUATHA DÉ DANANN, took Ruad from the OTHERWORLD to this world in his bronze, tin-sailed boat, so that she might seduce a human lover, AED Srónmár. The sounds of MERMAIDS singing, or of music pouring from a FAIRY MOUND, caused Ruad to forget herself and leap into the white waters of Assaroe, where she drowned. Assaroe is also said to be named after a male figure, the Ulster king Áed Ruad, whose name combines that of the titular goddess and her human lover.

Source: Gwynn, Edward. *The Metrical Dindshenchas.* Royal Irish Academy, Todd Lecture Series. Dublin: Hodges, Figgis, and Co., Ltd. 1906–1924. Reprinted Dublin Institute for Advanced Studies, School of Celtic Studies, 1991, Part 4, pp. 3–9.

Ruadán (Ruadan) Irish god or hero. In the *BOOK OF INVASIONS*, the mythic history of Ireland, this heroic warrior was described as the son of the goddess BRIGIT and the half-Fomorian king, the beautiful but ungenerous BRES mac Elatha. In the great second battle of MAG TUIRED, Ruadán was injured fatally after being discovered spying on the enemy; his mother came to the battlefield and began to cry out in a way that became the traditional KEENING (from Irish *caoin,* "lamenting") used at Irish funerals.

Ruadh (Rua) Irish hero. One of the figures in Irish legend who was snared by a FAIRY LOVER, Ruadh was sailing one day when his boat was becalmed off the north coast of Ireland. He set off to swim for help but instead found himself beneath the waves, where he was taken up by nine lovely princesses, one of whom bore him a child. He eventually left the women, including the mother of his child, promising to return—then stayed away in

Norway for seven years, never intending to return. When he did come back, the nine fairy maidens intercepted his boat, throwing his son at him so that both died.

Source: Gwynn, Edward. *The Metrical Dindshenchas.* Part II. Vol. IX. Royal Irish Academy, Todd Lecture Series. Dublin: Hodges, Figgis, and Co., Ltd., 1906–1924, pp. 27–35.

Ruad Rofessa (Ruadh Ró-fhesa) Irish god. This name, which means "the red one who has great knowledge," was given to several Irish deities, notably the god of fertility, the DAGDA, although it was also used of the mysterious OTHERWORLD figure of death, DONN. The legends about Ruad Rofessa are confused and confusing; it is unclear whether he was originally a separate ancestral god who became connected with other divinities, or if the name was merely an honorific title.

Rucht Irish hero. Little known in Irish myth under his human name, this man is famous as FINNBENNACH ("white horn"), the greatest BULL of the western PROVINCE of CONNACHT. That bull was originally a swineherd named Rucht, who argued with another swineherd named FRIUCH. Their enmity was so deep-seated that, reborn time after time, they continued to fight: as STAGS, as RAVENS, and finally as WORMS. Not much damage can be done by fighting worms, and besides the two were across the island from each other. They set in motion the next stage of the battle, for one worm encouraged the great queen MEDB to marry AILILL mac Máta, while the other warned DÁIRE to expect an invasion of Ulster by Medb. Then the worms were swallowed by COWS that gave birth to them again as bull-calves.

By the time the bulls had grown up, the stage was set. Medb, offended that her husband owned Finnbennach and thus was her social superior, set off to find a bull of equal value. The only one was Rucht's enemy of so many lifetimes, now reborn as the brown bull DONN CUAILNGE. The battle for the bulls is the subject of the greatest Irish epic, *TÁIN BÓ CUAILNGE*. When they finally were brought together, Rucht and his age-old enemy fell again to fighting. Rucht was killed, his bull body spread in pieces across the land, but Friuch did not live long after his victory, dying of exhaustion and loss of blood upon his return home.

Rudianus Continental Celtic god. An obscure god known only from several inscriptions in France that invoked his aid, he was identified by the Romans with their warrior god MARS.

Rudiobus Continental Celtic god. An obscure Gaulish god, Rudiobus is known only from a single artifact: a HORSE statue, which may have represented either the god in equine form or an offering to him. He has been connected with the Romano-Celtic MARS, who appears under the name of MULLO, possibly "mule."

Rudraige (Rory) Irish hero. A relatively obscure figure in Irish mythology, he was one of the leaders of the FIR BOLG, a race of invaders—the third group to arrive in Ireland—who were put to the sword by the more powerful TUATHA DÉ DANANN.

rune Non-Celtic alphabet. The word *rune* is occasionally mistakenly used for the OGHAM alphabet; it is more appropriately applied to the early alphabet of Scandinavia. Occasionally the word is also applied by folklorists to a rhyming chant or CHARM.

rushes Symbolic plant. In Scottish fairy lore, rushes were said to mark FAIRY hiding places. This is in line with the idea that entries to FAIRY-LAND were found in places that were neither one thing nor another; a spot where rushes grew, being wet but still solid ground, formed such a liminal place.

Ruturugus Irish hero. One of the sons of the Irish invader PARTHOLÓN, he was said by Giraldus Cambrensis to have left his traces on "things still living," although whether that means that his genetic inheritance was still visible or that he was reincarnated in other forms is unclear.

Ryons (Riance) Arthurian hero. The cloak of this king of Wales was trimmed, not with fur, but with the beards of warriors he had killed. When he demanded king ARTHUR's beard, the king of CAMELOT refused and conquered Ryons's land instead.

Sabraan British goddess. This obscure goddess is known from a single Romano-Celtic TEMPLE built on a site in Gloucestershire that is believed to have been inhabited from pre-Celtic times; thus she may have been derived from or connected to a pre-Celtic goddess of the region.

Sabrina British goddess or folkloric figure. A goddess of this name is believed to have been honored as the divinity of the Severn River in Britain; as many Celtic goddesses were seen as embodied in a RIVER and its watershed, this interpretation is supported by evidence from both insular and continental sources. Like many goddesses, Sabrina survived not as a divine but as a folkloric figure, one who appears in the famous "Masque of Comus" by English poet John Milton.

Milton based his Masque, a dramatic entertainment, on the legend of Locrine, king of Loegria (an ancient name for the English Midlands), who was defeated by an invader named Humber. Among Locrine's subjects was a lovely maiden, Estrildis, to whom the conquering Humber took a fancy, despite being already married to the powerful princess Gwendolen of Cornwall. Rather than choose between his marriage vows and his infatuation, Humber hid Estrildis in an underground chamber, where she conceived and bore their child, Sabrina.

When his powerful father-in-law died, Humber thought himself free of any consequence of his infidelity and brought forth Estrildis and Sabrina from their dark confinement. Gwendolen, furious at her husband's betrayal, marshaled her father's troops and marched upon him. When she proved victor, she demanded that the unfortunate woman and her child be drowned in the Severn. This late legend seems to support interpretations of Sabrina as the resident spirit of the river.

Source: Spence, Lewis. *The Minor Traditions of British Mythology.* New York: Benjamin Blom, Inc., 1972, p. 15.

sacral kingship Cosmological concept. This term is used by some writers to represent the idea that KINGSHIP was not only a political role within Celtic society but a sacred one. Although there is evidence to support this contention, the phrase is a controversial one because of its use in other, non-Celtic, contexts.

Kings were often chosen from families of royal blood, but at other times a man from a lesser family might be chosen through DIVINATION by DRUIDS or through feats of arms. Once elevated through the ritual of INAUGURATION, the king was expected to follow a series of rules and to abide by certain taboos (see *BUADA* and

GEIS). Such understandings of Celtic kingship are generally accepted today.

Far more controversial is the theory, generally discounted but fiercely upheld by a minority of scholars, that Celtic kings became human sacrifices in times of need or disaster. There are some mythological hints of such sacrifice (see CONAIRE), but most scholars argue that a king was driven from power rather than killed if crops failed or other misfortunes occurred. Whether this constitutes a sacred kingship as the term is used in other contexts is still debated.

sacred grove   See NEMETON.

sacrifice   Cosmological concept. Sacrifice—the offering up of one thing in order to gain another—was practiced by the Celts, as by virtually all other peoples. Goods of various sorts were offered to gods and goddesses at regular intervals and, most significantly, in times of danger. Typically an object was damaged in some way before being sacrificed; as the Celts usually worshiped outdoors rather than in temples, the object would be deposited in a natural site. Thus a piece of jewelry might be smashed or a TORC twisted out of shape before being thrown into a LAKE or buried in a BOG. An animal might be killed; sometimes the entire animal was burned, so that no part of it was used for human food, but there are also evidences of portions (sometimes the best meat) being sacrificed, while other portions became part of a feast. Sometimes a distinction is made between sacrifice, which requires that something be alive or once alive, and offerings, which were never alive; thus artifacts like coins and jewelry constitute offerings, while plants and animals, to say nothing of humans, are sacrifices. More frequently, the term "sacrifice" describes anything offered to the gods and placed beyond human use.

See also HORSE SACRIFICE; HUMAN SACRIFICE.

Sources: Hull, Eleanor. *Folklore of the British Isles.* London: Methuen & Co., Ltd., 1928, p. 157;

Wait, G. A. *Ritual and Religion in Iron Age Britain.* BAR British Series 149(i) Oxford, 1985, pp. 122 ff.

Sadb   (Saba, Sabia, Sava, Sadhbh, Blaí)   Irish heroine. The beautiful maiden Sadb, daughter of the great magician BODB DERG, was turned into a DEER by one of his magical enemies, Fear Doirche. Her sister DAIREANN became infatuated with the great hero FIONN MAC CUMHAILL and drove him mad when he rejected her, but that punishment did nothing to gain his affection. Instead he regained his sanity and fell in love with a mysterious woman who visited him at night after he had saved a fawn from being killed by his hunting dogs. After many nights of pleasure, the dark DRUID—her father's enemy—found that Sadb had managed to slip out of her deer form and enjoy the hero's affections. He cast a darker spell upon her so that she could never regain her womanly form.

Heartbroken, Sadb fled from her lover, who searched Ireland for nearly a year. Then, near the great flat peak of BEN BULBEN, he found a deer nursing a human infant. Recognizing his lover and their son, Fionn took the boy from her tenderly, naming him OISÍN ("little fawn"). Little more is heard of Sadb, who apparently lived out her years as a deer, but we hear much of her son, who became the greatest poet and one of the finest warriors of Fionn's band, the FIANNA. Some legends say that Sadb was so tender of heart that she died of shame and sorrow after discovering how cruel her lover, Fionn, was in battle.

sain   Irish and Scottish concept. The term, meaning roughly "to make holy," is used of the actions of saints attempting to remove pagan associations from a sacred place. ST. PATRICK of Ireland, for instance, dipped his pastoral staff in many holy WELLS, thus permitting ritual to continue at the sites under Christian protection. Once sained, a place was considered to be protected against evil spirits and FAIRIES, both of which can be seen as vestigial forms of ancient Celtic and pre-Celtic divinities.

Sainnth   Irish hero. In some texts, this is the name of the father of the goddess or heroine MACHA, an otherworldly woman who was forced to race with the king's horses. Little else is known of him.

saints   Folkloric figures. The Catholic Church now requires candidates for sainthood to go through an elaborate three-stage process, being declared "venerable," then "blessed," and finally "saint." That process was not put into place until the 10th century, however, under Pope John XV. Before that, saints were declared by popular acclaim, which provided the opportunity for more than one pagan divinity to creep into the prayer book with "saint" preceding his or her name. Some of the more egregious miscreants (like the Italian god of erections once known as St. Priapus) were struck from the rolls in reforms orchestrated in 1983 by Pope John Paul II, but other saints of doubtful historicity remain, including Ireland's beloved St. BRIGIT, who bears suspicious resemblance to a Celtic goddess of the same name. Neither Brigit nor Patrick are likely to lose their place in the church calendar, given their importance to the Irish church.

In addition to converted divinities, there were other saints, real humans, to whom mythological and magical motifs accrued: in Ireland, Aedh Mac Breic, who flew through the air; St. Ailbe, who was suckled by wolves; St. Bega, who was betrothed to Christ in her infancy but became a nun instead; dragon-slaying St. Finnbar; St. Flannan, who traveled to Rome on a boat made of stone; St. Cury of Brittany, who lived off the same self-regenerating fish for years; and King ARTHUR's Welsh friend St. Gwynllyw. These mythological accretions may have been added through a folkloric process, whereby through continual retelling the stories of local saints and divinities and even FAIRY folk became confused and confounded; or through

the efforts of early monkish writers who created a literary character from a mortal saint, fleshing out historical facts with recognizably powerful mythological motifs.

Source: Kelly, Sean, and Rosemary Rogers. *Saints Preserve Us!* New York: Random House, 1993.

Saitada   British goddess. This obscure goddess of the Tyne valley is believed to have represented grief and suffering.

salmon   Mythic figure. The salmon of Celtic myths is almost invariably a symbol of WISDOM, perhaps because of the FISH's own remarkable life-journey. Hatching from eggs laid in freshwater pools and RIVERS, often deep inland, the fish travel to the ocean, where they live for some years. No one knows what biological mechanism triggers the fish's return to the pool or river of its origin; nor do scientists know how the salmon navigates to a location it has only seen once before. The unerring ability of the fish to find its home, where it spawns (females laying eggs and males providing milt, or sperm) and dies, is one of the wonders of nature. Migrating salmon flood into rivers, intent upon their reproductive task, providing food for animals and humans in the few spring weeks of the spawning season.

The salmon of wisdom appears in several important myths of the insular Celts: In Ireland it appears as FINTAN, the one-eyed ancient who lived many lifetimes; in Wales the salmon of Llyn Llwy is the oldest and wisest of earthly beings. Several Celtic sculptures from Gaul show fish in contexts that suggest that the connection of salmon and wisdom was shared by Celtic people on the continent as well.

The most elaborate myths are found in Ireland, where the salmon of wisdom lived in a pool of water or a WELL surrounded by magical HAZEL trees. Variously called the well of SEGÁIS or CONNLA'S WELL, and described as the source of the Boyne and the Shannon rivers, this pool was a liminal place, neither entirely in this world nor in the OTHERWORLD, but linking the two. The surrounding hazels dropped nuts into the water, filled with all the world's wisdom, which caused bubbles of inspiration called *eó fis*. The fish—which could be either singular or multiple—ate the nuts, thus growing wise.

Some legends claim that the extra nuts washed out into the river and could be snared and eaten directly by a seeker after wisdom. More often, the fish themselves had to be caught and devoured in order for the wisdom to pass into a human being. Only two people ever tasted the salmon of wisdom. The great hero FIONN MAC CUMHAILL did so, when he was a boy serving the druid-seer FINNÉCES. The DRUID hooked the fish and set it to cooking, but it spattered some grease onto the boy's thumb. When Fionn sucked it, he discovered that he had absorbed all the fish's wisdom. (This fish is sometimes named Goll Essa Ruaid, the one-eyed salmon of ASSAROE, after the pool beneath the mythological waterfall where he lived.) Also successful was the goddess SÍNANN, who caught the salmon that lived in the pool beneath the white mountain Cuilcagh in Co. Cavan. When she ate the fish and was flooded with its wisdom, the well rose up and drowned her and the wisdom she had absorbed.

The mythological salmon of wisdom survived into very recent times in Irish folklore. Red-fleshed salmon were seen as fairy creatures from the Otherworld (see RED); holy wells, even those dedicated to Christian observance, were visited in the belief that salmon or trout (even, occasionally, EELS) living there could, if they made their appearance, bring good fortune to the viewer. Attestations of HEALING that occurred when a fish was seen leaping from a holy well continue to occur even today in parts of Ireland.

Sources: Kennedy, Patrick. *Legendary Fictions of the Irish Celts.* New York: Benjamin Blom, 1969, p. 219; Ó hÓgain, Dáithí. *Myth, Legend and Romance: An Encyclopedia of the Irish Folk Tradition.* New York: Prentice-Hall Press, 1991, p. 203.

salt Symbolic material. The Celts based much of their early wealth on salt, for there are extensive salt mines near their great center at HALLSTATT in Austria. Salt was a necessity for ancient inland people, who used the mined mineral to preserve meat through winter, making ham and jerky as well as salted fish. Salt was not only used by the Celts but also traded for valuables from distant places. There is no evidence that salt had any religious importance among the continental Celts, who viewed it entirely as a commodity of trade.

Among the insular Celts, however, salt became connected with the belief that a world of mischievous and sometimes dangerous FAIRIES was near to hand, which required that salt be always carried on one's person. This belief may derive from the fact that salt is a preservative; it might thus preserve one from fairy mischief. Fairies found salt abhorrent and avoided any travelers who carried it; even salt water could do in a pinch. There are tales of people nearly stolen by the fairies but then abruptly let go, who later find a forgotten few grains of salt in the seams of a pocket. Similarly, someone carrying salted meat or fish, even on dangerous days like SAMHAIN on November 1, could pass unmolested by fairy sites.

Fairies also could be kept away by carrying IRON—another of the earliest Celtic trade items—in the form of nails and scissors. It is not clear whether fairies were kept at bay because they loathed the mercantile world of trade, because they were pre-Celtic deities driven away by the salt-and iron-bearing Celts, or for another reason.

Samaliliath (Malaliach) Irish hero. Very few members of the obscure race called the Partholonians are named in Irish myth, but one who is remembered is this hero, who invented brewing and thus brought ALE to Ireland.

Samhain (Sauwin, Samuin, Samain, Sauin, Samonios) Celtic holiday. The Celts are typically described as having four great holidays, one for each of the year's seasons. IMBOLC (February 1) marked the beginning of spring, BELTANE (May 1) of summer, and LUGHNASA (August 1) of the fall harvest season. Most important was Samhain (November 1), the festival of winter's beginning when, folklore says, the people of the OTHERWORLD came to our world to blight vegetation with their breath, so that on the following day nothing remained green and growing.

Samhain was the equivalent of New Year's, for just as the Celtic day began at sundown, so the year was believed to begin with winter. Some scholars, arguing that there is little evidence of these holidays on the Continent and pointing to their appropriateness to Ireland's seasonal changes, contend that the "traditional Celtic" holidays are in fact only Irish. Others believe that because absence of evidence does not constitute proof to the contrary, we can assume that the festivals found among the Celtic Irish were celebrated as well by other Celtic peoples.

Samhain is the Celtic holiday most observed today, for it has become the children's holiday of Hallowe'en, celebrated with decorations, costumes, and pranks. Christianized into All Saints' Day, the feast was carried to the New World and was adopted not only in North America but in lands invaded by the Spanish (some of whom were descendants of Celts from Galicia), where it became Día de los Muertos, the Day of the Dead. Thus Samhain is arguably the most long-lasting and widespread of the Celtic feasts.

Samhain was part of the agricultural calendar in two important ways. Firstly, it marked the day upon which PIGS were killed; the sound of desperate squealing must have added to the fearful quality of the feast, although there would also be seasonal treats like blood pudding to be enjoyed. In addition, COWS were brought down to protected winter pastures on Samhain, after six months in the mountains with their milk-maids. The movement of animals to and from seasonal pastures continued well into modern times in Ireland.

While it is not known how the festival might originally have been celebrated, evidence from Irish mythological texts suggests that consumption of alcoholic beverages was part of the feast. Every story in which drunkenness figures (the *INTOXICATION OF THE ULSTERMEN*, for instance, and the *Adventure of Nera*, as well as descriptions of the feast of kingly INAUGURATION called the Féis Temro) is said to take place at Samhain. As there is archaeological evidence of brewing vats but little evidence of storage vessels of the sort found in wine-making regions like Greece, it is possible that grain from the recent harvest was brewed and the mixture drunk during the Samhain season. Once the ALE was gone, life returned to normal until the next Samhain.

There is some evidence that FIRES were lit on hilltops on this occasion, as on other Celtic feasts. Although the hill of TARA is deeply associated with Samhain in mythology, the Samhain fire was not lit there. The nearby hill of TLACHTGA in Co. Meath has been proposed as the central fire for this festival, as has UISNEACH for the opposite feast of BELTANE. As the harvest's end, Samhain was a feast of both plenty and fear, for although food had been gathered against the dark winter, there was no way to predict what that season might bring. Thus DIVINATION rituals were probably part of the event from ancient times.

If we know little of how the ancient Celts celebrated the feast, we have ample evidence of how Samhain was viewed by later peoples. Innumerable legends and ghost stories are linked to the holiday, when the veil between this world and the Otherworld was lifted so that FAIRIES and the dead could come forth, readily visible to even those without second sight. Fairies were especially prone to stealing humans on Samhain. For this reason, people stayed close to home or, if forced to walk in the darkness, carried IRON or SALT or turned their clothing inside out (see PROTECTION AGAINST FAIRIES). Fairies rode forth on the WILD HUNT, hordes of them pouring out of their FAIRY MOUNDS and riding through the night, kidnapping people they encountered on the road. For this reason, it was considered ill-advised to walk near a fairy mound on Samhain night, even more so than on ordinary nights.

The dead also came forth from graveyards to visit their old haunts; some traditions claim that they were friendly, seeking to enjoy the familiar fruits of human life once more, while others viewed the returning dead as dangerous. Those who viewed the dead as friendly often set out a "dumb supper" of the favorite foods of the departed; their return was anticipated with respect and only a touch of fear, and the next day's empty plates were pointed to as evidence of their visit. Those who viewed the dead as dangerous believed that, like the fairies, they were likely to steal away loved ones and carry them into the Otherworld of death.

On the Isle of Man, Samhain was said to be the time when fairies specialized in stealing human victims (on the opposite feast of Beltane, they were more interested in stealing MILK and other animal products). It was also a night of divination. Women made *Soddag valloo* ("dumb CAKE") on Samhain night; baked directly on the embers of the hearth fire, the cake was eaten in silence by the young women of the household, who then—without turning their back on the fire—retreated to their beds, in the hopes of dreaming of their intended lovers.

Such divination was a common part of Samhain rituals. Girls hid beside a neighbor's house, their mouths full of water, a pinch of salt in each hand, as they listened for the names of eligible young men; the first one spoken would be the husband of the girl who heard his name. Nuts were burned in the hearth and their patterns interpreted for clues about the future. Molten lead was poured into water, the shapes it formed indicating the future occupations of the inquirers. Those born on Samhain were believed to possess this divinatory skill in everyday life; should they be born with a CAUL or other indication of spiritual power, they might be greatly feared and respected.

Some writers assert the existence of a god named Samhain, brother of CIAN, who lost the great COW of abundance, the GLAS GHAIBHLEANN, to the evil Fomorian king BALOR of the Evil Eye, but most find no evidence of such a figure.

Sources: Burne, Charlotte Sophia. *Shropshire Folk-Lore: A Sheaf of Gleanings, Part II.* Yorkshire: EP Publishing, 1974, pp. 378–390; Hull, Eleanor. *Folklore of the British Isles.* London: Methuen & Co., Ltd., 1928, pp. 227–247; Markale, Jean. *The Pagan Mysteries of Halloween: Celebrating the Dark Half of the Year.* Rochester, Vt.: Inner Traditions, 2000; Ó hÓgain, Dáithí. *Myth, Legend and Romance: An Encyclopedia of the Irish Folk Tradition.* New York: Prentice-Hall Press, 1991, p. 105; Paton, C. I. *Manx Calendar Customs.* Publications of the Folk-lore Society, reprinted. Nendeln/Liechtenstein: Kraus Reprint Limited, 1968, p. 76; Sjoestedt, Marie-Louise. *Celtic Gods and Heroes.* Trans. Myles Dillon. Mineola, N.Y.: Dover Publications, Inc., 2000, pp. 47–56; Whitlock, Ralph. *The Folklore of Wiltshire.* London: B. T. Batsford, Ltd., 1976, p. 64; Wilde, Lady. *Ancient Legends, Mystic Charms and Superstitions of Ireland.* London: Chatto and Windus, 1902, p. 78.

Samhair Irish heroine. The daughter of the great hero FIONN MAC CUMHAILL, Samhair married a man who, to please her, built a bed held up by three enormous pillars. Thus the palace of Samhair and her husband Cormac Cas was called Dún-tri-lag (now Duntryleague, Co. Limerick), "the fort of the three pillars."

Sampait (Sempait) Irish heroine. The story of this strong and self-confident woman appears in the DINDSHENCHAS, the place-poetry of ancient Ireland. She was a BARD and a herdswoman who, when tending her flocks one day, was set upon by a nobleman named Crechmael. Believing that he had the right to her body because she aroused him, Crechmael attempted to rape Sampait. She trussed him up like a pig for slaughter and killed him—by strangling him, one story says, while another says that she smashed in his skull in retaliation for his attempted crime.

Source: Gwynn, Edward. *The Metrical Dindshenchas.* Royal Irish Academy, Todd Lecture Series.

Dublin: Hodges, Figgis, and Co., Ltd., 1906–1924, pp. 23–25.

sanctuary Celtic ritual site. The most common forms of Celtic sanctuary are the NEMETON or tree grove and the sacred water-source (SPRING, WELL, or pond). The latter was known as far back as the LA TÈNE period, for dozens of sacrificed weapons and other objects have been retrieved from such ancient shrines. Typically the Celts worshiped in the open air, but three kinds of sacred buildings are known, which archaeologists call the Belgic type, the VIERECKSCHANZEN, and the Celto-Ligurian. The first is a typical temple, a structure built for ritual and SACRIFICE in which rich hoards of jewelry, weapons, and other metal objects have been found. The second is a rectangular building similar to the Belgic temple but lacking any sacrificial goods. Finally, the rare Celto-Ligurian site, resulting from Roman influence, appears much like a classical temple structure.

sanding the steps Cornish ritual. On New Year's Day in Cornwall, it was traditional to pay boys to put sand on the steps of houses and other buildings in hopes of attracting good luck for the ensuing year.

Sarras Arthurian site. This city was the source of the GRAIL and the destination of the knights who quested in search of that sacred object. The name appears to derive from the term "Saracens," used in the medieval period to describe eastern Mediterranean or Islamic warriors. Some texts claim it as the site of GALAHAD's death.

satire Irish ritual. In modern times satire has been defined as a literary work in which wit and irony are used to discredit vice and folly. Among the ancient Irish satire had a similar, but more urgently moral, purpose, and it was specifically poetic in form. The greatest satirical work in post-Celtic Irish literature, Jonathan Swift's bitter "A Modest Proposal," which proclaimed that English landlords should devour "suckling children" because they were already eating the parents alive, had much in common with its ancient forebears. Whereas today satire is sometimes used to expose political injustices but at other times has a merely playful or even a malicious purpose, in Celtic Ireland satire was more carefully targeted speech: It changed society.

The role of the BARD was to balance the power of the king (see KINGSHIP), who was required to offer generous HOSPITALITY to all and to follow his sacred vows—his *BUADA* and *GEIS*—to the goddess of the land's SOVEREIGNTY. Should the king fail, barrenness and famine could result, so it was the poet's duty to create a satire so powerful that its very words would raise boils on the king's face or otherwise cause deformation. Then, because a BLEMISHED KING could not rule, the failed leader would be forced from power. Satires occur in several important Irish myths, notably in the expulsion of BRES mac Elatha from the kingship of TARA after he proved ungenerous, and in the stories of difficulties caused by the bitter poet AITHIRNE.

Because satire was legally considered an assault, it could not be recklessly employed. An honor price or *ÉRIC* was demanded in cases of unjust satire, including the coining of insulting nicknames, the repetition of satires by other poets, and the mocking of a person's physical appearance. There was a legal requirement that the satire be based in truth, for ancient legal tracts refer to what we would today call slander. Because the purpose of satire was not simple cruelty, it was illegal to compose satires about people after death; such compositions required payment of the person's full honor price to their relatives (see *FINE*). Even satires based in truth required the poet to pay restitution—but a praise-poem sufficed and balanced out the damage done by the satire.

Source: Kelly, Fergus. *A Guide to Early Irish Law.* Dublin: School of Celtic Studies, Dublin Institute for Advanced Studies. Early Irish Law Series, Vol. III, 1988, pp. 137–139.

Scantlie Mab British folkloric figure. An assistant to HABETROT, the spinning FAIRY, Scantlie Mab was an unattractive hooked-nose being, admired for her devotion to her OTHER-WORLD mistress.

Scáthach (Skatha, Scáthach nUanaid, Scáthach Bunand, Scathach) Irish heroine. One of the great WARRIOR WOMEN of Irish legend, Scáthach ("shadowy one") lived on the island named for her—what is now the Isle of SKYE, off Scotland. There she made warriors into heroes, for only Scáthach knew the secrets that brought her such students as the great CÚCHULAINN, who vowed he would find her or die trying. The latter was a frighteningly real possibility, for to get to Scáthach's school, candidates had to pass the Bridge of the Cliff, a great chasm that Cúchulann could only cross by performing his great SALMON-leap (whether there was any connection to the salmon of wisdom is unclear).

Scáthach's curriculum was challenging. Students learned strangely named martial arts: apple-feat, thunder-feat, supine-feat, salmon-feat of a chariot-chief; use of blade, spear, staff, and rope; hero's call; use of the magical weapon called the GÁE BULGA. Not only did Scáthach teach her students, she also foretold their futures. In Cúchulainn's case, she refused to do so—because she saw that he would murder his only son, CONNAL, who in some versions of the story was, also Scáthach's grandson.

Some legends say that Cúchulainn attempted to battle with Scáthach for ownership of Skye. After days of exhausting combat they sat down and together ate the HAZEL nuts in which the world's WISDOM was hidden. With the clarity of his inner vision, Cúchulainn realized he would never beat Scáthach, and he returned to Ireland, leaving the island of Skye to the warrior woman. The gift that Scáthach made to the hero upon his departure, the great weapon called the Gáe Balga, has been compared to the sword EXCAL-IBUR, offered to king ARTHUR by his mysterious protector, the LADY OF THE LAKE.

Some writers use the tales of women warriors such a Scáthach, as well as historical figures such as Cartimandua and BOUDICCA and comments by classical authors about Celtic women's prowess in war, to argue that Celtic women fought alongside men. Others refute such evidence, pointing to laws that limit women's activities or offer protection to women in times of war.

Sources: Hull, Eleanor. *The Cuchullin Saga in Irish Literature.* London: David Nutt, 1898, p. 72; Straffon, Cheryl. *The Earth Goddess: Celtic and Pagan Legacy of the Landscape.* London: Blandford, 1997, p. 179.

Scéne (Skena) Irish heroine. An obscure figure in the BOOK OF INVASIONS, she was the wife of the great BARD named AMAIRGIN. She died as their people, the MILESIANS, were attempting to invade Ireland.

Scenmed Irish heroine. A WARRIOR WOMAN, she led her army into battle against the great ULSTER hero CÚCHULAINN after he abducted her niece EMER, but the hero used the battle skills he had learned from another amazonian woman, SCÁTHACH of Scotland, to defeat Scenmed.

Sceolan (Sceolang) Irish mythological beast. The story of this DOG is one in which SHAPE-SHIFTING plays an important role, for Sceolan would have been human except that his mother UIRNE had been bewitched into canine form; she was later restored to humanity, but her twin pups, Sceolan and BRAN, were not. Sceolan's uncle, the hero FIONN MAC CUMHAILL, adopted both dogs into the FIANNA, his band of warriors, where they served well as hunters, fighters, and sentinels.

Scota Irish heroine. A vague figure in Irish legend, she was called a daughter of the pharaoh Cingris in the BOOK OF INVASIONS, which combined ancient Irish lore with biblical legend. Another woman of the same name was also a pharaoh's daughter, but this time he was named NECHTANEBUS; she was wife of the Irish invader Míl, thought to represent a Celtic tribal ancestor (see MILESIANS). Scota may have been a Celtic ancestor goddess, for the people of Ireland were called in ancient times "scoti" or "scots," a name that later came to rest in another Celtic homeland, Scotland.

Scythia Mythic site. Several Irish texts, notably the BOOK OF INVASIONS, claim that the Irish originated in Scythia. Although there was no actual ancient land by that name, there was a migratory group in eastern Europe called the Scythians. Noted for their horsemanship and their impressive gold, they may have in fact interacted with the Celts in their original homeland in central Europe, as the similarity of swirling LA TÈNE art and some Scythian patterns suggests. Poet and propagandist Edmund Spenser used the mythological association of the Irish and Scythians to argue that, being barbarians, the Irish should be exterminated—so that their lands could then be distributed among apparently non-barbaric English settlers like himself.

Source: Spenser, Edmund. *A View of the State of Ireland.* Ed. Andrew Hadfield and Willy Maley. Oxford, England: Blackwell Publishers, 1997, p. 44.

sea fairies (*na buchtogai*) Scottish and Irish folkloric figures. The creatures of the OTHERWORLD, the FAIRIES, did not only live beneath the hills and in the midst of impassible bogs; they also lived on ISLANDS in the sea, especially ones that disappear often behind misty clouds, or even in the ocean's waves. Sea fairies usually disguised themselves as SEALS, just as their freshwater counterparts the SWAN MAIDENS changed into swans. Marriage between water fairies and humans was apparently very common, if folklore that claims seal ancestry for many coastal families is to be believed.

seal (seal people, silkie, selkie, roam roane) Scottish and Irish folkloric figure. A sleek furred mammal that lives in cold seas, the seal is found along Ireland's west and northern coast (occasionally on the east coast, as near Skerries), in many coastal regions of Scotland and, most significantly, on the Scottish islands. On land, seals tend to live in colonies, sometimes quite large ones; in the water, they are strong, graceful swimmers who feed on fish and other sea life.

Many arctic people make seal meat an important part of their diet, but this was never the case in Ireland or Scotland, where eating seals was considered a form of cannibalism. The idea that seals are enchanted people (sometimes, fallen angels) is found in both lands, at times confused with MERMAID legends. This notion may be Celtic in origin or may derive from one of the other strata of culture; the appearance of seal people in Scandinavian folklore suggests an ancient derivation from that region. Some scholars remark upon the claim of seal ancestry by certain coastal families—in Ireland, the Coneelys, Flahertys, MacNamaras, Sullivans, and many families on Achill Island; on the Hebrides, the MacPhees; on the Scottish mainland, the MacCondrums; on the Isle of Skye, all fair-haired people. This may reveal an ancient totemic system; the taboo on members of such families killing seals or eating their meat points in the same direction.

Seals do bear some resemblance to human beings, especially in their wild moaning calls and in the direct gaze from their soft dark eyes. Fishermen sometimes spoke or sang to seals, who were thought to speak back, usually begging that no harm come to them or their young. In Donegal, on the northwest coast of Ireland, it was believed that seals were human beings wearing fur coats. Women of the seal people were thought to make splendid wives, except that their children had webbed toes and fingers. As with SWAN MAIDENS, a man had to steal their animal-cloak and keep it hidden, for if the seal woman ever found her skin, she would disappear instantly into the ocean. Some tales claim that silkies were not born as seals but were human girls drowned at sea and transformed. Women, too, could find seal lovers, by sitting on lonely rocks and weeping into the sea. Such lovers were kind and gentle, but prone to sudden disappearances.

In Orkney, seals still congregate at Sule Skerrie, home of the Great Silkie of a famous ancient ballad, who sang, "I am a man upon the land, I am a Silkie on the sea," in order to seduce a human woman into bearing his half-seal child; the child then returned to the ocean, only to be killed by the woman's husband while in his seal form. More recently, the image of the seal maiden inspired American director John Sayles's movie, *The Secret of Roan Inish*, in which some apparently human children discover that they are the offspring of a silkie.

Sources: Curtin, Jeremiah. *Hero-Tales of Ireland.* New York: Benjamin Blom, 1894, p. 150; Douglas, George. *Scottish Fairy and Folk Tales.* West Yorkshire: EP Publishing, 1977, p. 155; Hull, Eleanor. *Folklore of the British Isles.* London: Methuen & Co., Ltd., 1928, pp. 155–156; MacGregor, Alasdair Alpin. *The Peat-Fire Flame: Folk-Tales and Traditions of the Highlands & Islands.* Edinburgh: The Moray Press, 1937, pp. 95 ff; Spence, Lewis. *The Minor Traditions of British Mythology.* New York: Benjamin Blom, Inc., 1972, p. 53.

seanachie   Irish folkloric figure. The *seanachie* or storyteller was an important figure in rural Ireland up until the late 20th century. A vestigial form of the ancient BARD who memorized the history and myth of the people, the *seanachie* spun yarns that were often based in the same material, though degraded by time and distance.

Seanchán Toirpéist (Senchán, Senchán Torpéist, possibly Senchán mac Uarchride)   Irish hero. This BARD may have lived in the late sixth-early seventh century C.E., but he certainly did not live the life ascribed to him by his biographers. Like some Irish SAINTS of the period, Seanchán

was mythologized—given magical powers such as raising the dead and fighting with magical CATS. He is thought to have been attached to the court of the legendary king GUAIRE of CONNACHT, at whose court he learned that none of Ireland's poets could recite the important epic, the *TÁIN BÓ CUAILNGE*, in its entirety. Determined to remedy this loss, he traveled to the grave of one of the *TÁIN*'s heroes, queen MEDB's lover FERGUS mac Roich; there Seanchán (or his son, Muirghein) invoked the hero from the OTHERWORLD. Fergus materialized and recited the *Táin*, and, Irish poets having been trained in feats of memory, Seanchán memorized it even as the words were spoken. When the ghost of Fergus appeared again at Guaire's Court, Seanchán fell over dead. Variations of the story exist, including one in which Seanchán died of shame at his failure to recite the *Táin* when requested by the king, leaving it to his son to restore his reputation through the magical invocation of Fergus.

Source: Ó hÓgain, Dáithí. *Myth, Legend and Romance: An Encyclopedia of the Irish Folk Tradition.* New York: Prentice-Hall Press, 1991, pp. 384 ff.

Searbhan (Sharvon the Surly, Sharvan, Searban)   Irish hero. In the romantic tale of GRÁINNE and DIARMAIT, this GIANT and magician helped the escaping lovers by letting them hide in his magical ROWAN tree. He warned them not to eat the berries, but Gráinne still craved the magical fruit, and Diarmait killed Searbhan so that they could eat it. The giant's dying screams revealed the couple's location to FIONN MAC CUMHAILL, who was pursuing them.

second sight   Folkloric motif. In the ancient Celtic lands, whether on the Continent or on the islands of Britain and Ireland (and in areas of the New World where people of Celtic heritage settled), we find a common superstition that some people can see things invisible to the physical eye. Folklorists have theorized that this is a degraded remnant of Celtic belief in an OTHER-WORLD that is sometimes visible, sometimes hidden. This was an important part of Celtic religious belief; DRUIDS and other BARDS (who were considered seers as well as verbal artificers) practiced some techniques of DIVINATION that they believed permitted them to see things hidden in past, present, or future.

In the Scottish Highlands, someone who possessed second sight was called a *taibhsear,* while the vision itself was called *taibhs.* Another term, *da-shealladh,* does not translate literally as "second sight" but as "two sights," for it was believed that everyone can see ordinary reality through "one sight," but only gifted people can see the otherwise invisible world. This Otherworld included GHOSTS of the dead who walked casually and without hindrance among the living, invisible to most people but as real as a living body to the second-sighted. People with second sight also could see the FETCH, a duplicate person who appeared before a death, walking the path the funeral would take, and FAIRIES, visible to the ordinarily sighted only at liminal times and places.

Like other unusual traits, second sight was not necessarily believed to be a gift; it was rarely envied, and seers often wished to be rid of it. It was generally hereditary but could make its appearance in anyone who suffered a trauma or spiritual awakening.

Sources: Campbell, John Grigorson. *Witchcraft and Second Sight in the Highlands and Islands of Scotland.* Detroit: Singing Tree Press, 1970, p. 120; MacDougall, James. *Folk Tales and Fairy Lore in Gaelic and English.* Edinburgh: John Grant, 1910, pp. 183–185; Ross, Anne. *Folklore of the Scottish Highlands.* London: B. T. Batsford, Ltd., 1976, pp. 33 ff.

Seelie Court British folkloric motif. The opposite of the UNSEELIE COURT, this group of TROOPING FAIRIES brought only blessings to those they passed as they traveled through the land on the great holidays of BELTANE and SAMHAIN.

Segáis (Segais) Irish mythological site and goddess. In the tale of BÓAND, goddess of the RIVER Boyne, this was the name of the secret WELL of wisdom (sometimes called CONNLA'S WELL, although it is possible the two sites were distinct). Despite prohibitions, Bóand chose to travel to the well, placed by some high in the mountains of Slieve Bloom, while others say it was the source of the Boyne itself, near Edenderry in Co. Kildare.

Like other mystic wells, it had the power to grant WISDOM to anyone who drank from its waters or, alternatively, ate the FISH that swam within it. When Bóand approached, the well rose up suddenly and drowned her, carrying her out to sea. Thereafter, its waters could never return to the tiny space of the well, and the great river watered the land. The same story is told of the goddess of the River Shannon, SÍNANN, thus making this well the source of two of Ireland's most important rivers; both tales are often held up as warnings against women seeking wisdom but can as readily be seen as creation myths.

Segáis is also a name given to Bóand herself. The place-poetry of Ireland, the DINDSHENCHAS, says that she was called by that name in the OTH-ERWORLD, and that the other name for the Boyne is Sruth Segsa, "river of Segáis." If the well were in the possession of Bóand from the start, as this implies, rather than of her husband NECHTAN, the likelihood that her drowning was not punishment but creation is heightened.

Source: Gwynn, Edward. *The Metrical Dindshenchas.* Vol. III. Royal Irish Academy, Todd Lecture Series. Dublin: Hodges, Figgis, and Co., Ltd., 1906–1924, pp. 27–39.

Segomo (Segamonas, Neta Segamonas) Continental Celtic god. This now obscure divinity (possibly "the victor" or "the victorious one") once had a wide following, as is evidenced by inscriptions to him in Britain as well as in Gaul.

Sele (Seelie) British and Scottish folkloric figure. Variations of this name appear all over Britain and Scotland; it has multiple referents, including FAIRY folk and sacred hills, folkloric figures and festivals. Although found in Celtic lands, the word may not be Celtic in origin; it is related to Old Norse *saell*, "happy," and old Teutonic *saeli*, "blessed," as well as to Sil and Silly, Sal and Sally, names used of female figures in folklore and tales. The SEELIE COURT was a British and Scottish name for a troop of good fairies (evil fairies being called the UNSEELIE COURT). Connections have been suggested to the magical MERMAID, the SILKIE, and with the sun goddess SUL.

Semias   Irish hero. The members of the magical TUATHA DÉ DANANN came from four cities, each of which was ruled by a master of WISDOM. Semias was such a master in MURIAS; he owned a great CAULDRON of abundance, which he bestowed upon the beneficent god DAGDA.

Senach   Irish goddess. This obscure divinity is invoked in a magical charm as having control of seven periods of time; she was nursed by FAIRY women but is otherwise unknown.

Senchas Mór   (Senchas Már, Senchus Mor) Irish text. An important collection of laws from approximately the fifth century C.E., when Celtic influence still held sway in Ireland, the *Senchas Mór* offers a view into the world of the BREHONS, judges of the DRUIDS. Although Christian influence was already prominent and may have affected this legal tract, it is nonetheless one of the earliest collections of legal documents known in Ireland. The text includes some mythological references, for example, the derogatory description of AILILL mac Máta, husband of CONNACHT's queen MEDB, as a man of hasty judgment, and the comment that BARDS were the judges in the time of the great ULSTER king CONCOBAR MAC NESSA.

Source: *Senchus Mor.* Dublin: Alexander Thom, 1856.

Senua   British goddess. In 2002 a "new" Celtic goddess was discovered, her broken silver statue part of a hoard of 26 precious objects hidden in the earth at her shrine in Hertfordshire during the late third century, apparently when some disaster threatened, and found by an amateur archaeologist using a metal detector. The Romanized sculpture was much degraded by time, but British Museum X rays of votive plaques, which showed Senua in the garb of MINERVA, revealed the goddess's name. Senua appears to have been a goddess of water, honored at a small SPRING and associated with HEALING. Her emergence from the earth after 1,600 years of burial is a reminder that it is impossible to know what aspects of Celtic religion still remain unavailable to modern eyes.

Sequana   (Sequena) Continental Celtic goddess. The RIVER Seine originally bore this goddess's name. Sequana was especially honored at the Seine's source, Fontes Sequanae ("springs of Sequana") near the French town of Dijon. There, a Roman-era shrine has been found where hundreds of COINS were offered to the bronze image of a crowned woman, her arms aloft: she is mounted in a boat shaped like a DUCK, which holds a berry in its beak. While other Celtic goddesses such as RHIANNON are connected to BIRDS, Sequana is the only one whose emblem is a waterbird; thus she may have combined the HEALING qualities of the river goddess with the bird goddess's OTHERWORLD aspects. Another Gaulish river goddess, NATOSUELTA, is similarly depicted with a bird, but in her case it is the RAVEN, typically a symbol of death.

Sequana's healing powers can be recognized from the many bronze and silver models of legs, eyes, breasts, and other body parts that were deposited in the river source; such offerings usually indicated the organ in need of healing. She may have been a very important goddess, for the Romans did not change her name to a Latin one; all inscriptions use only her original Celtic name. A tribe named the Sequani may have been connected to Sequana, perhaps envisioning her as their divine ancestor.

Source: Green, Miranda. *Symbol and Image in Celtic Religious Art.* London: Routledge, 1989, pp. 40, 157.

serpent (snake) Symbolic animal. Although the snake is not found in all Celtic countries (Ireland being famously free of them), the serpent exists in all Celtic mythologies; it never appears alone but always as the companion of a divinity. On the Continent, the snake was a typical symbol of warrior gods, perhaps because of its connections with wealth and FERTILITY. Often the snake was depicted with HORNS, suggesting a combination of reptile and mammal; the RAM-HEADED SNAKE often appeared with the woodland god CERNUNNOS. The Romans associated gods who accompanied snakes with MERCURY, their divinity of commerce.

The alleged extermination of snakes from Ireland by ST. PATRICK was impossible, as they are not indigenous to that island. Nonetheless we find them in myth, usually as female figures such as the she-monsters CORRA and CAORANACH. Some interpret the dispatching of the serpent goddess as a memory of the dispute between arriving Christians and an older, goddess-honoring paganism; others find a hidden seasonal myth in the stories, with the serpent representing the winter goddess who gives way to her double, the blooming spring. In his role as serpent-destroyer, Patrick may have stepped in for an earlier hero god, for in the DINDSHENCHAS we find the god of healing, DIAN CÉCHT, slaying a serpent who would otherwise have devoured all the CATTLE in Ireland.

Snakes do live in Britain, where the adder was given special mythological consideration as the island's only poisonous native snake. It was said to be a wise creature but very wily. In the Scottish Highlands the adder was associated with the weather-controlling HAG, the CAILLEACH.

Sources: Carmichael, Alexander. *Carmina Gadelica: Hymns and Incantations.* Hudson, N.Y.: Lindisfarne Press, 1992, p. 584; Green, Miranda. *Symbol and Image in Celtic Religious Art.* London: Routledge, 1989, pp. 93, 141; Ross, Anne. *Pagan Celtic Britain: Studies in Iconography and Tradition.* London: Routledge & Kegan Paul, 1967, pp. 151 ff; Wilde, Lady. *Ancient Legends, Mystic Charms and Superstitions of Ireland.* London: Chatto and Windus, 1902, p. 8.

serpent stone (serpent's egg, druid's glass, serpent bead, adder stone, Clach Nathrach, Glaine Nathair) Symbolic object. Of all the methods of DIVINATION and HEALING that the DRUIDS used, the most powerful and the most mysterious employed the serpent stone, a round bit of glass that had magical powers.

The Roman author Pliny claimed that a warrior of the Vocontian Gauls was executed by emperor Claudius because he carried an *ovum anguinum* or serpent's egg when he went to court. The Romans seemed to fear the power of this object, which Pliny said could only be formed in summer, at a certain phase of the MOON. Then, countless serpents would writhe about each other, secreting a ball of liquid from their bodies and hunting it into the air while they hissed vociferously. (Except for the ball of liquid, this is an accurate description of the mating habits of some snakes, such as the garter snake, in which scores, even hundreds, of male snakes surround a single fertile female, all squirming about in an attempt to fertilize her.) The serpents were apparently generating the stone for their own use, for they would set out in mad pursuit of any person who stole the object; only a man on a fast horse could outpace the furious reptiles, and then only if he could speedily cross water, since the snakes would be stopped by a running stream.

Although Pliny claimed he saw one as big as an apple, typically serpent's eggs were closer to the size of a nut. In addition to its apparent efficacy in lawsuits, the stone was used in healing. Those who suffered from bewitchment could be cured by a glass of water, so long as the stone had been dipped in it. Long after the druids had passed into memory, folklore still described such stones as treasured medicine. In the 19th century, serpent stones were said to be found among heather, where a snake had left its spittle after slithering in a circle.

Sources: Campbell, John Grigorson. *Witchcraft and Second Sight in the Highlands and Islands of Scotland*. Detroit: Singing Tree Press, 1970, pp. 84 ff; Cármichael, Alexander. *Carmina Gadelica: Hymns and Incantations*. Hudson, N.Y.: Lindisfarne Press, 1992, pp. 38–80; Curran, Bob. *Complete Guide to Celtic Mythology*. Belfast: Appletree, 2000, p. 27.

Sétanta (Cúchulainn) Irish hero. When he was a boy, the great ULSTER hero CÚCHULAINN was called by this name, but when he grew old enough to fight, he adopted a new name that represented a debt of honor.

Setlocenia British goddess. Only one inscription has been found to "She of the Long Life," apparently a goddess of prosperity and longevity.

seven Daughters of the Sea Irish divinities. These obscure goddesses were invoked in an incantation or *CÉTNAD* used to learn how long someone would live. "I invoke the seven Daughters of the Sea," the invocation says, "who fashion the threads of the sons of long life. May three deaths be taken from me! May three periods of age be granted to me! May seven waves of good fortune be dealt to me! Phantoms shall not harm me on my journey in flashing corslet, without hitch. My fame shall not perish. May old age come to me! Death shall not find me until I am old."

Although otherwise unknown, these figures may be connected to the Seven Sisters whose name is given to several holy WELLS and ancient STONE CIRCLES across Ireland. Seven was a magical number in Ireland, although that sanctity may be the result of Christianization; THREE and FIVE were more commonly sacred to the Celts.

seventh son Folkloric motif. In several areas of Celtic influence, we find a belief that some people are gifted with SECOND SIGHT because of their place in birth order. The seventh son of a seventh son is reputed to be such a gifted—or cursed—individual. In the Cotswolds it was believed that such people could see the double of a person who was about to die (see CO-WALKER). The belief survives in some areas of America where significant immigration from Celtic lands occurred.

Sgeimh Soluis Irish heroine. The great band of warriors called the FIANNA became unpopular after the death of their leader, FIONN MAC CUMHAILL, because they grew greedy and violent. This woman, granddaughter of the great king of TARA, CORMAC MAC AIRT, refused to pay tribute to the Fianna before her marriage. They attacked and, at the battle of GABHAIR, were utterly defeated.

shamanism See CELTIC SHAMANISM.

shamrock Symbolic plant. There is no evidence that the clover or wood sorrel (both of which are called shamrocks) were sacred to the Celts in any way. However, the Celts had a philosophical and cosmological vision of triplicity, with many of their divinities appearing in THREE. Thus when ST. PATRICK, attempting to convert the DRUIDS on BELTANE, held up a shamrock and discoursed on the Christian Trinity, the three-in-one god, he was doing more than finding a homely symbol for a complex religious concept. He was indicating knowledge of the significance of three in the Celtic realm, a knowledge that probably made his mission far easier and more successful than if he had been unaware of that number's meaning. When the shamrock appeared with four leaves instead of the usual three, it was believed to be valuable for making FAIRY OINTMENT.

Source: Carmichael, Alexander. *Carmina Gadelica: Hymns and Incantations*. Hudson, N.Y.: Lindisfarne Press, 1992, pp. 155–156.

Shan Van Vocht   See SPÉIR-BHEAN.

shape-shifting   Cosmological concept. In myth and folklore from Celtic lands, we find frequent mentions of shape-shifting or moving between bodies. In myth this is often associated with the powers of BARDS and DRUIDS, who could transform their appearance without losing their essence. The great poet of the MILESIANS, AMAIRGIN, spoke a long poem upon first setting foot in Ireland that described his various incarnations as "a wave of the sea, a SALMON in a pool," while similar poems are credited to the Irish TUAN MAC CAIRILL and the Welsh TALIESIN. While it is quite possible to read these poems as simple lists of natural phenomenon, then construction argues against that reading, for each line starts with "I am," as though once having taken the shape of another being, the poet thereafter remains partly salmon, hawk, star.

In myth, too, we find tales of people who change from one form to another. Often the cause is enchantment, as when SADB, mother of the heroic poet OISÍN, was turned into a DEER; or when AIGE's beauty provoked so much envy that a spiteful FAIRY transformed her into a doe; or when the evil AÍFE was changed into a CRANE in appropriate punishment for cursing FIONNUALA and her brothers to be SWANS for 900 years. Sometimes the shape-shifter desired the new form: ÉTAIN and MIDIR flew away from TARA in the form of swans, a bird that mates for life just as they had mated for eternity; CIAN turned himself into a PIG to elude the SONS OF TUIREANN; the Welsh CERIDWEN transformed herself many times in order to capture her thieving servant GWION.

Most fairies were believed adept at shape-shifting, although some of the smaller breeds (SPRIGGANS and the like) were trapped within a single body. Monstrous fairy races like the WATER HORSE changed their shape when they wished to bring harm; a handsome young man could change to murderous equine form in the blink of an eye. Some argue that fairies did not really change form but placed a GLAMOUR around themselves, causing viewers to see them differently than they are, but the difference would be irrelevant to witnesses.

In folklore the power to change shapes at will was assigned to WITCHES, who typically assumed the shape of a common animal—most often a HARE—in order to sneak about stealing MILK and BUTTER, driving CATTLE crazy, and otherwise doing evil. If one hit a HARE in the leg and it escaped, it was certain that the next day an old witch would be limping about the village. Thus what may have begun as a magical act showing the druid's control over the physical world diminished, in folklore, to local mischief.

Source: Henderson, George. *Survivals in Belief Among the Celts.* Glasgow: James MacLeose and Sons, 1911, pp. 107 ff.

Shee Finnaha   Irish mythological site. The palace of LIR, one of the kings of the TUATHA DÉ DANANN people, was said to be located near the town of Newtown Hamilton, on the borders of counties Armagh and Monaghan in today's Northern Ireland.

Sheela na Gig   (Sheela-na-gig, Sheila na Gig, Síle na gig, Sheela Ny Gig, Síle na gCíoch) Irish goddess or folkloric figure. Smiling lewdly out from rock carvings, the Sheela na Gig can still be seen: a grinning, often skeletal face, huge buttocks, sunken or absent breasts, bent knees, and a vagina held open. The stones have in most cases been incorporated as gargoyles in Christian churches, usually over the entrance, although some are found in castles, mills, and other buildings.

The figures, commonplace in Irish and British villages, drew the attention of scholars in the 19th century. The prudery of the era, however, often resulted in the figures being misidentified (in one case, as a male fool holding his heart open) or misinterpreted (as dirty jokes). Generally, the figures were believed pagan, an ancient goddess brought into churches as an attempt to co-opt the devotion of her followers.

More recently, scholars place the date of creation of the Sheelas in the Christian Middle Ages—most date to the 12th century—and consider her a Christian icon. But what does she mean? Some interpret her as a warning against lust, but more recently connections have been drawn with folklore that connect this figure with the HAG goddess.

Her name has been variously translated as "hag," as a vulgar word for female genitalia, and as "the holy lady." She has been called a FERTILITY figure, but her grinning face and genital display are complicated by the apparent ancientness of her flesh and the fact that she generally lacks breasts. In a few areas, rock scrapings were taken from the Sheela's vulva and used as a means of promoting fertility and safe childbirth.

Her location over doors is often interpreted as meaning she is apotropaic, intended to ward off evil; folklore that women could drive away evil by revealing their genitals supports this interpretation. Some figures, however, are placed lower in walls; many of these show evidence of having been constantly touched in the genital area, perhaps as a ritual for good luck or HEALING; at Ballyvourney in Co. Kerry, a ritual still remains of touching a Sheela (there said to be the image of the local saint, GOBNAT) with a handkerchief on the saint's feast day, February 11. A few Sheelas have holes in the head, as though horns were once placed there.

Despite the known Sheelas being dated, with little dispute, to the Christian era, pagan antecedents have been found. A small carving at TARA and a grotesque grinning figure from Lough ERNE are among the figures that suggest that the Sheela's posture and exaggerated features may derive from an ancient divinity, probably a goddess. Similarly, the appearance of skeletal hags in Irish myth (see DA DERGA) suggest to some a connection either to the multiform goddess of SOVEREIGNTY or to the pre-Celtic divinity called the CAILLEACH.

Several dozen Sheela figures can still be seen *in situ* in Britain and Ireland, while others have been moved to museums: but there is evidence that hundreds more once existed and were destroyed, either through prudery or a thrifty need to use the stone elsewhere. Whether the Sheela na Gig is a Celtic figure, a remnant of the pre-Celtic past, or an apotropaic sculpture meant to represent a Christian conception of the impurity of the female flesh is still debated. The Sheela na Gig has been used in recent times as an image of women's power by feminist artists in Celtic lands.

Sources: Anderson, Jorgen. *The Witch on the Wall: Medieval Erotic Sculpture in the British Islands.* London: George Allen & Unwin; Marron, Fiona. "Encounters with Remarkable Sheela na Gigs." In Monaghan, Patricia. *Irish Spirit: Pagan, Celtic, Christian, Global.* Dublin: Wolfhound Press, 2001, pp. 297–306; McMahon, Joanne, and Jack Roberts. *The Sheela-na-Gigs of Ireland and Britain: The Divine Hag of the Christian Celts, An Illustrated Guide.* Cork: Mercier Press, 2000.

sheep Irish folkloric animal. Although sheep-rearing has been an important part of the Irish economy for hundreds of years, there is virtually no mythology in which they appear; BULLS and COWS, by contrast, are extremely common in myth. There are some folkloric references to sheep: It was considered unlucky to meet them early in the morning, and it was considered best to knit in the evening, when the sheep were sleeping.

Source: O'Sullivan, Patrick V. *Irish Superstitions and Legends of Animals and Birds.* Cork: Mercier, 1991, p. 80.

Shellycoat Scottish monster. This huge water monster lived in the port of Edinburgh, where it hid under a coat of shells in order to torment the sailors who tried to pass out to sea. When not at work wreaking havoc, Shellycoat left his coat under a rock and became vulnerable to attack, for without it he was powerless.

Source: Spence, Lewis. *The Minor Traditions of British Mythology.* New York: Benjamin Blom, Inc., 1972, p. 18.

shinny Scottish ritual. In Scotland, this ball game, a bit like hurling, used to be played on the day of the winter SOLSTICE.

shoemaker Irish folkloric figure. Shoemakers have a greater stature in Irish folklore than the average craftsman probably because of the famous figure of the FAIRY shoemaker, the LEPRECHAUN. Shoemakers appear as clever men who can cause trouble with their cleverness, as in the tale of the man who learned shoemaking from the fairies; he made shoes for the parish priest, who was unable to say Mass whenever he wore the shoes.

Source: Ó Catháin, Séamus, and Patrick O'Flanagan. *The Living Landscape: Kilgallian, Erris, County Mayo.* Dublin: Comhairle Bhéaloideas Éireann, 1975, p. 130.

Shoney Scottish god. Until the 1600s, a tradition on the Isle of Lewis and Harris honored this otherwise obscure divinity of the sea. Every SAMHAIN the fisher folk of the island would carry out a mug of ALE and pour it into the ocean, calling out to Shoney to accept the mug in return for filling the boats with fish. Some have seen him as the basis for the seamen's folkloric guide, DAVY JONES.

Source: Spence, Lewis. *The Minor Traditions of British Mythology.* New York: Benjamin Blom, Inc., 1972, p. 28.

sídhe (shee, *sidhe*, *síd*, *sí*) Irish folkloric figure. This word has two meanings in Irish folklore. The primary meaning is a FAIRY MOUND, a hill beneath which people of the OTHERWORLD live, out of sight of those with normal vision but visible to those with SECOND SIGHT. By extension, the word is also used to mean the FAIRIES themselves, as a shortened vision of the phrase "people of the sídhe."

Many legends interpret the people of the sídhe as the TUATHA DÉ DANANN, the ancient tribe of the goddess DANU who were driven underground after their defeat by the MILESIANS, Ireland's first human invaders. Each important divinity was provided his or her own sídhe, as MIDIR was given BRÍ LÉITH and ÚNA the mound of KNOCKSHEGOWNA.

Sigmall Irish hero. The grandson of the FAIRY king MIDIR and son of Midir's lawless daughter OGNIAD. Although Midir's consort ÉTAIN may or may not have been Sigmall's grandmother, Étain is said to live now and forever in the OTHERWORLD with Sigmall.

Source: Gwynn, Edward. *The Metrical Dindshenchas.* Part II. Royal Irish Academy, Todd Lecture Series. Dublin: Hodges, Figgis, and Co., Ltd, 1906–1924, p. 9.

Silbury Hill British mythological site. Although built many centuries before the Celts arrived in Britain, the massive artificial mound of Silbury Hill, near the STONE CIRCLE of AVEBURY, is often mistakenly described as Celtic. Covering more than five acres, the pyramidal mound has attracted much folklore, including the story that the DEVIL built it, all in one night, dragging rock and earth to the site in a huge sack. Rumors abounded that a knight named Sil (Seal, Kil, Zel) was buried within it, mounted on horseback and surrounded by all his treasure, hence the name Sil-bury. Excavations turned up no knight, and certainly no treasure. Instead, it was discovered that the entire mound is carefully constructed in layers of organic and inorganic material—peat and rock—making the whole hill a huge SPIRAL. Silbury has been connected with harvest rituals to the earth goddess.

Sources: Dames, Michael. *The Silbury Treasure: The Great Goddess Rediscovered.* London: Thames and Hudson, 1976; Straffon, Cheryl. *The Earth Goddess: Celtic and Pagan Legacy of the Landscape.* London: Blandford, 1997, pp. 14–15; Whitlock, Ralph. *The Folklore of Wiltshire.* London: B. T. Batsford, Ltd., 1976, p. 23.

Silkie Scottish folkloric figure. Taking her name from the silk clothing she wore, this Scottish house-goddess sneaked into homes to clean whatever was left in disorder; too-careful housekeeping was as bad as slovenliness, for if she found nothing to clean, Silkie messed up the rooms instead. Some have connected her with the harvest goddess SELE and with the FAIRY folk called Silly WITCHES, while others consider her a form of the BROWNIE. The name silkie (or selkie) is also used for the apparently human SEAL race.

Source: Briggs, Katherine M. *An Encyclopedia of Fairies: Hobgoblins, Brownies, Bogies, and Other Supernatural Creatures.* New York: Pantheon Books, 1976, pp. 364–365.

Sillina British goddess. Although her existence has not been proven, scholars believe there was a goddess of this name who gave her name to the Isles of Scilly, where an impressive Roman-era shrine was found.

Silvanus Roman god. This Roman name was sometimes applied to indigenous Celtic woodland gods, most of whose names have been lost as a result of the INTERPRETATIO ROMANA.

Sin Irish heroine. This Irish FAIRY woman is probably a remnant of an early goddess, for she was said to have created wine from water and swine from leaves to feed the battalions of warriors she had created with her spells. She appears in a tale of the king MUIRCERTACH MAC ERC, whom she seduced and drove mad to punish him for killing her family when she was a child.

Sínann (Shannon, Sinann, Sionann, Sionnainn, Sinand, Sineng) Irish goddess. The granddaughter of LIR—apparently the hypothesized ancient sea god who was father of the ocean ruler MANANNÁN MAC LIR, rather than the human king who was father of the heroic FIONNUALA—Sínann was goddess of Ireland's most important river, the Shannon, which waters one-fifth of the island. Like other Celtic RIVER goddesses, she was seen as ruling both the river's waters and the land it irrigated.

Her legend is very similar to that of another important Irish river goddess, BÓAND. Warned that she should not approach a WELL—variously named the well of SEGÁIS and CONNLA'S WELL—wherein wisdom was hidden, Sínann ignored the prohibition. In some sources she, like FIONN MAC CUMHAILL, caught the SALMON of WISDOM who swam there and, upon eating its flesh, became the wisest being on earth; in others, she merely arrived at the well in search of wisdom. In either case, the result was the same: the well broke forth from its bounds in a great flood, drowning Sínann as it carried her to sea. Thereafter the river could never return to the limiting confines of the well and instead watered the land. Although often interpreted as a cautionary tale, warning women against seeking wisdom, Sínann's story can also be seen as a creation myth, in which she sacrifices herself to establish the land's FERTILITY.

A minor story told of Sínann claims that the hero Fionn mac Cumhaill was set upon by several fierce warriors at Ballyleague, near the northern end of the great LOUGH REE. Almost overcome by the number of opponents, Fionn was rescued by Sínann, who arrived with a magical stone that, when Fionn threw it, killed all his enemies at once. Fearful of the power of Sínann's stone, Fionn threw it into the river, where it remains hidden in a low ford. Should a woman named Be Thuinne ever find it, it would indicate the world's end is near.

Source: Gwynn, Edward. *The Metrical Dindshenchas.* Vol III. Royal Irish Academy, Todd Lecture Series. Dublin: Hodges, Figgis, and Co., Ltd, 1906–1924, Reprinted Dublin Institute for Advanced Studies, School of Celtic Studies, 1991, Vol. III, pp. 287–291.

siren See MERMAID.

Sirona (Dirona, possibly Tsirona)   Continental Celtic goddess. Many inscriptions in France and other continental Celtic lands invoke this HEALING goddess, whose name has been translated as "star." Although Sirona was often connected with the Celtic APOLLO, she also stood alone. She was frequently depicted with SERPENTS and EGGS, suggesting a connection both to rebirth and to FERTILITY.

Source: Green, Miranda. *Symbol and Image in Celtic Religious Art.* London: Routledge, 1989, p. 43.

Sithchenn (Sithchean)   Irish hero. This DRUID and SMITH was asked to prophesy for NIALL of the Nine Hostages and his four brothers. Sithchenn did as asked, but in a strange way: He set fire to his own forge, and then observed what items the young men grabbed as they fled the burning building. Niall rescued the anvil, the smith's most important tool, leading Sithchenn to predict that the boy would grow up to become leader of all Ireland from the great royal seat of TARA.

skriker *(trash)*   British folkloric figure. When death approached, this portentous figure appeared like a BANSHEE, predicting the event to come. Sometimes the skriker wandered the forests of Yorkshire and Lancashire, screaming; or like other FAIRIES he engaged in SHAPE-SHIFTING, transforming himself into a terrifying DOG.

Skye   Scottish mythological site. The Isle of Skye off Scotland's west coast, largest of the Inner Hebrides, was named for the woman warrior SCÁTHACH.

Slane (Sláine, Áed, Slaine)   Irish hero and mythological site. Although Slane himself is a minor figure in Irish mythology—being a leader of the FIR BOLG, who were defeated by the magical TUATHA DÉ DANANN—the place of his burial is famous. It was on Slane hill, overlooking the great bend in the River Boyne near the impressive ancient mounds called BRÚ NA BÓINNE, that

ST. PATRICK lit a fire one BELTANE. On nearby TARA, the DRUIDS were gathered to light the first fire of that festival night, and seeing the upstart blaze on a spiritually insignificant hill, went right over to hear the word of the Lord and the sermon of the SHAMROCK from the man who would bring Ireland into Christendom. Another Slane was a doctor of the Partholonians, one of the mythological races that invaded early Ireland.

Slemuin   See ODRAS.

Slieve Gullion (Sliab Cuilinn, Sliab Cuillinn)   Irish mythological site. In Co. Armagh, a strange geological formation, a circular valley formed by ancient volcanic action, is centered around the legendary mountain of Slieve Gullion. The peak was named after, the FAIRY king CUILENN, whose home it was said to be. More prominent in the region's mythology is the CAILLEACH, the great HAG goddess who formed the landscape and controlled the weather. She was said to live in the CAIRN that tops the mountain, which was built by the people of the pre-Celtic MEGALITHIC CIVILIZATION and was called by local people Cailleach Birrn's house. From that point, she once threw a huge rock across the valley; she was a GIANT, so the boulder seemed like a pebble to her. It landed miles away, in the Dorsey Ramparts, where it was honored until recent times. The great hero FIONN MAC CUMHAILL was said to be buried in the cairn, although the story of how his body got there is not recorded.

Slievenamon (Slievenaman, Sliab na mBan, Mountain of the Women; Sliabh na Bhan Fionn, the Hill of Fair Women)   Irish mythological site. In the southeast of Ireland, this CAIRN-capped hill was named for the contest held by Irish women who wished to bed down with the heroic but aging FIONN MAC CUMHAILL. The winner of the contest, GRÁINNE, may have been fleet of foot, but she was also fickle of heart, for at her wedding feast she noticed the handsome hero DIARMAIT and, putting a spell upon her husband-to-be and the wedding party (or possibly drugging them), eloped with the young man.

sluagh Scottish folkloric figures. The "Host of the Unforgiven Dead" were not FAIRIES, for they rode forth only at night. They were the GHOSTS or souls of those who had died without being forgiven for earthly transgressions; they were trapped in this world and could not move on to the OTHERWORLD. They could never travel in daylight, being forced to reside always in gloomy night, and they waged endless war upon each other, leaving stripes of their blood behind each morning.

Smertrius (Smertrios, Smertrio) Continental Celtic god. The name of this relatively obscure god includes a syllable, *smer-*, also found in the name of the goddess ROSMERTA and apparently meaning "protection." One sculpture believed to be of Smertrius shows him as a strong, bearded man with a snake's tail.

Smirgat (Smirnat) Irish heroine. One of the wives of FIONN MAC CUMHAILL, she was a prophet who revealed to the hero that if he ever drank out of a horn, he would die. Fionn took the warning seriously and always used a goblet.

smith Irish and continental Celtic mythological figure. From the beginnings of Celtic culture, metalcraft was one of the Celts' main sources of wealth. Smiths, those who smelted metal (especially IRON and GOLD) from ore and formed it into useful and ornamental objects, were greatly revered. In myth, the smith (see GOIBNIU and GOVANNON) became associated with MAGIC and alchemy; in Irish folklore, he was connected with the magical COW of abundance, the GLAS GHAIBHLEANN.

snail bead Symbolic object. Like the SERPENT STONE, the strange Scottish TALISMAN called the snail bead was said to have been formed naturally, in this case by snails gathered into a great mass and secreting a mysterious fluid. Such stones were rare and difficult to obtain, but they were worth the trouble for their HEALING power: dipping the bead into a glass of water would create a healing potion. Anyone wearing the bead on his person would be protected from all bad luck.

Source: Campbell, John Grigorson. *Witchcraft and Second Sight in the Highlands and Islands of Scotland.* Detroit: Signing Tree Press, 1970, p. 88.

snatching by the sídhe See FAIRY KIDNAPPING.

solar divinities See SUN.

solitary fairies Folkloric figures. In Irish and Scottish folklore FAIRIES appeared either as TROOPING FAIRIES, who spent their time with others of their kind, dancing and making merry, or solitary fairies, who preferred their own company to that of others and were typically ill-natured. The most famous solitary fairy was the LEPRECHAUN, the miserly fairy shoemaker who hid his wealth away; the wary *CLURICAUNE* was another solitary fairy.

Source: Briggs, Katernine M. *An Encyclopedia of Fairies: Hobgoblins, Brownies, Bogies, and Other Supernatural Creatures.* New York: Pantheon Books, 1976, pp. 375–376.

solstice Calendar feast. The word means "sun sitting still," and the sun does, indeed, appear to stand still on the several days surrounding the summer and winter solstices on June 21 and December 21, the year's longest day and longest night, respectively. The changes in length of daylight and night slow and become almost imperceptible, before beginning again as the solstice period concludes. Although the solstices were not marked by the Celts, they must have known how to calculate them, as their own annual feasts were based upon this knowledge. See CALENDAR.

Sons of Tuireann Irish heroes. A long and complex ancient story (*Oidheadh Chlainne Tuireann* or *The Tragedy of the Sons of Tuireann*) tells of the brothers BRIAN, IUCHAIR, and IUCHARBA, children of the important goddess DANU (or DONAND) and the otherwise obscure TUIREANN, son of the god of poetry OGMA and the craft goddess ÉTAN. The three set off to ambush their father's enemy, CIAN, known from other tales as the clever man who seduced the fair captive EITHNE despite her father BALOR's attempt to keep her hidden from all men.

Cian, realizing he was about to encounter the heavily armed sons of his enemy, transformed himself into a PIG (see SHAPE-SHIFTING), but not fast enough, for the brothers changed into DOGS and hounded him nearly to death, permitting him to turn back into human form before they finished him off. Just as the Sons of Tuireann had taken up their father's cause, so did Cian's son LUGH, who demanded a heavy honor-price (see *ÉRIC*) for his father. Brian and his brothers performed seven impossibly difficult deeds, but the eighth was beyond their strength, and so Iuchair and Iucharba died, and Brian soon after. The tragedy of their deaths led the ancient Irish to name this tale among the THREE SORROWS OF IRELAND, the others being the stories of the SONS OF UISNEACH and the CHILDREN OF LIR.

Sources: Cross, Tom Peete, and Clark Harris Slover, eds. *Ancient Irish Tales*. New York: Henry Holt and Co., 1936, p. 49; Joyce, P. W. *Ancient Celtic Romances*. London: Parkgate Books, 1997, pp. 37 ff.

Sons of Uisneach (Usnech, Usna) Irish heroes. It is not known whether the paternal name of these Irish heroes is connected to the great Irish mountain UISNEACH, for little is said of their father in the sad tale, which is remembered as one of the THREE SORROWS OF IRELAND, the others being the stories of the SONS OF TUIREANN and the CHILDREN OF LIR.

The tale begins with a prophecy by the chief DRUID of ULSTER, CATHBAD, who declared at a feast that the child born that day would be the world's most beautiful woman, but that she would bring sorrow to the province. Some of the court wished to have the child killed immediately, but king CONCOBAR MAC NESSA was intrigued. He determined to have DEIRDRE brought up to be his companion and bedmate, and so she was raised under the tutelage of LEBORCHAM (sometimes described as a woman poet, sometimes as a male forester).

Nonetheless Deirdre's heart was open to love. One day she saw a RAVEN drinking blood from snow, and she wished aloud for a man whose hair was that black, whose lips were that red, whose skin was that white. Wise Leborcham knew that only one man was that beautiful: NOÍSIU, oldest of Uisneach's sons. She arranged for the pair to meet in secret, thus sealing their fate. Knowing that the king would be severely displeased with losing his future consort, the couple fled, first across Ireland and then to Scotland, accompanied by Noísiu's brothers Ardán and Aínnle. In Scotland they lived happily on wild food in the forest, under the protection of the region's king.

Concobar could not forget the fated beauty, and so he arranged for a treacherous invitation. Promising that all would be forgiven, he invited the three brothers and Deirdre back to Ulster. Despite forebodings, Deirdre agreed to go, in part because the honorable FERGUS mac Róich was the messenger. As soon as he arrived in Ireland, the Sons of Uisneach were killed, whereupon Deirdre herself died—either by suicide, throwing herself from a chariot, or simply from a broken heart. Thus the tragic heroine is known as Deirdre of the Sorrows.

Source: Cross, Tom Peete, and Clark Harris Slover, eds. *Ancient Irish Tales*. New York: Henry Holt and Co., 1936, p. 239.

Souconna Continental Celtic goddess. This otherwise obscure RIVER goddess may have ruled the Saône, a river in eastern France, which bore her name in ancient times; however, there may have been two goddesses of the same name, for an inscription found at some remove from the river also mentioned Souconna.

south   Cosmological concept. In the spiritual geography of Ireland, NORTH represented the DIRECTION opposed to the solar cycle, because from the northern hemisphere the SUN moves always toward the south from dawn to noon. Thus south is *deosil* in Irish, a word that also means to move in a way congruent with the natural order. The southwestern PROVINCE of MUNSTER takes on some of the mythological significances of its direction, representing poetry and song; it is also considered the province most connected with women and the feminine.

Sovereignty (Sovranty, Lady of Sovereignty, Flaith)   The goddess of the land was envisioned in Celtic Ireland as bride of the king, wedded to him at his INAUGURATION. The figure of Sovereignty is varied: It can be the unnamed loathy HAG who offers NIALL a drink at her sweetwater well, then demands a kiss in recompense; it can be ÉRIU, titular goddess of the island; it can be fierce and willful MEDB, who weds one king after another.

If the figures vary, the concept they embody remains stable: that the king's duty is to maintain the land's FERTILITY through righteous behavior. This meant that he had to offer HOSPITALITY to all who came, to rule wisely, and to honor the sacred vows and taboos (see BUADA and GEIS) that came with his office. Should he fail to do so, his reign would be forfeit—if not his life, as was the case for CONAIRE, who, despite years of successful rulership, broke his sacred vows and died a horrible death as a result. The hag who came to him at DA DERGA's hostel to proclaim his death may be a punitive form of the goddess of Sovereignty.

See also KINGSHIP.

Sources: Green, Miranda. *Symbol and Image in Celtic Religious Art.* London: Routledge, 1989, p. 10; O'Brien, Marie Cruise. "The Female Principle in Gaelic Poetry." In S. F. Gallagher,

ed. *Woman in Irish Legend, Life and Literature.* Irish Literary Studies 14. Gerrards Cross, Bucks: Colin Smythe, 1983, pp. 26–37.

sow   See PIG.

spéir-bhean (spear-ban, sky woman)   Irish heroine. A late (16th–18th century) version of the goddess of SOVEREIGNTY through whose right a king could rule in Ireland, the *spéir-bhean* was depicted by BARDS of the time as a beautiful young woman, possibly from the OTHERWORLD, who wandered the roads searching for the land's true leader. Her name was sometimes given as CATHLEEN NI HOULIHAN, sometimes is ROISIN DUBH or Dark Rosaleen. Sometimes she appeared as the Shan Van Vocht (Sean-bhean Bhocht), the "poor old woman," who recalls the HAG who turned young again when kissed by the rightful ruler. The most famous version of the *spéir-bhean* is found in William Butler Yeats's play *Cathleen ni Houlihan* written for the revolutionary leader Maude Gonne.

Source: Clark, Rosalind. *The Great Queens: Irish Goddesses from the Morrígan to Cathleen Ní Houlihan.* Irish Literary Studies 34. Gerrards Cross: Colin Smythe, 1991.

spells   Ritual action. The use of verbal MAGIC has a long history in Celtic lands, for BARDS were believed to have the power to transform the physical world by the sheer power of their speech. In folklore this belief was translated into the idea that rhyming spells can bring HEALING (when the words are used to bless) or pain (when cursing is intended). Sometimes brief ceremonies accompanied the repetition of the rhyme—dipping stones in water, rubbing parts of the body—but these were less important than the rhyme or recitation itself.

See CURSE.

Source: Campbell, John Grigorson. *Witchcraft and Second Sight in the Highlands and Islands of Scotland.* Detroit: Singing Tree Press, 1970, p. 57.

spiral Mythological motif. Celtic art is renowned for its interlacing spirals, which especially deck the metalwork (shields, jewelry, and tools) found in their lands throughout the duration of the culture. The motif continued to appear as late as the Christian Middle Ages, when such masterworks as the Book of Kells, with its ornate spiraling ornamentation, were created. Though the spiral is associated today with the Celts, it is possible that they adapted it from the imagery left them by the people of the MEGALITHIC CIVILIZATION, who carved great spirals across their stone monuments. Many pre-Celtic spiral designs, like the triple spiral of Ireland's Newgrange (see BRÚ NA BÓINNE), are complex artworks that suggest a spiritual importance. Whether and how the spiral was transmitted from pre-Celtic to Celtic people has not yet been studied.

Source: Meehan, Aidan. *Celtic Design: Spiral Patterns.* London: Thames and Hudson, 1996.

spontaneous speech See *DÍCHETAL DO CHENNAIB*

spriggans Cornish folkloric figures. These ghosts of the ancient race of GIANTS were transformed into FAIRIES, who served as bodyguards to other fairies. They were mischievous, though not usually dangerous, preferring to scare off those who might intrude upon fairy gatherings rather than, for instance, murdering them. Like many fairies, they were inveterate thieves, slinking about the countryside stealing BUTTER and other valuables.

spring Mythic site. WELLS and springs can be difficult to distinguish, for they both serve similar purposes in myth and legend as well as being similar freshwater sources. Both were viewed as having HEALING powers, even at a distance, so that water brought from a holy well or sacred spring could help someone unable to travel there. Especially potent were thermal springs or "hot springs," where early people could relax in naturally warm (indeed, sometimes scaldingly hot) waters; even into Roman times the great thermal spring at BATH was visited by throngs seeking cures for physical and emotional pain. Many scholars have proposed that pre-Celtic peoples also used these sites, so rituals there may have derived from a mixture of religions. Earlier peoples may have seen the sites as openings to the womb of the earth mother, but the Celtic heritage seems clear in the connection, found throughout the Celtic world, of water with abundance, fecundity, and health.

spring equinox Calendar feast. The Celts did not mark the two EQUINOXES, when daylight and darkness are of equal length, nor the SOLSTICES in winter and summer, as most other peoples of the world do; rather, they marked the points in between, in their great festivals of SAMHAIN (winter), IMBOLC (spring), BELTANE (summer), and LUGHNASA (autumn). Yet there are vestigial celebrations in Celtic lands that suggest that earlier dwellers had marked time in the more conventional way; orientations of STONE CIRCLES and such megalithic monuments as the BRÚ NA BÓINNE in Ireland show that equinoxes and solstices were important to those earlier dwellers.

Sreng Irish hero. Less renowned than NUADA, his opponent in single combat in the first battle of MAG TUIRED, Sreng was a warrior of the FIR BOLG who, sent to meet the invading TUATHA DÉ DANANN, realized that his people would be unlikely to beat their magically armed foe. His own people refused to listen to his counsel, so Sreng fought with the Tuatha Dé king Nuada, cutting off his arm and causing him to lose his KINGSHIP.

stag Mythic animal. The horned male of the DEER held a significant place in the iconography of the god CERNUNNOS, who wears antlers in many sculptures and reliefs.

standing stone Mythic site. Hundreds of pillar-like stones still stand throughout all the ancient Celtic lands, sometimes in groups (see STONE CIRCLES) and sometimes alone. Erected by pre-Celtic people of the MEGALITHIC CIVILIZATION some 6,000 years ago, such monuments are evidence of an early civilization with great engineering skills and an apparently deep religious sense. See also DOLMEN.

Starn Irish hero. Two obscure figures carry this name. One was a brother of the invader PARTHOLÓN; the other, son of NEMED, was father of the poet TUAN MAC CAIRILL. Neither plays much role in myth.

St. George British saint and folkloric hero. The cross on the British flag today is an emblem of this saint, said to have been a soldier from the Holy Land who suffered martyrdom by the Romans. What such a figure has to do with England has baffled many; some believe that, like ST. MICHAEL and ST. PATRICK, St. George took the place of an earlier mythological hero who protected the land by slaying DRAGONS.

Many scholars argue that St. George stands to England as St. Patrick to Ireland: as the symbol of Christian dominance over ancient pagan ways. Patrick killed the goddess-demons CORRA and CAORANACH, while George slew the dragon that haunted the wilder places of Britain, where the old ways remained strong the longest. As with St. Michael, George's churches often stand in ancient holy spots. The image of George killing the dragon may have been an icon of the victory of Christianity over Celtic paganism.

St. Michael Scottish and British saint and folkloric hero. In Christian cosmology, Michael was one of the archangels of heaven who, tempted by the bright angel Lucifer to oppose the divine will, refused and remained at God's side in a great angelic battle. His appearances in Christian legend are numerous, for he witnessed the burning bush with Moses and spoke with Abraham. This angel-saint plays a significant role in British and Scottish folklore, perhaps standing in (as ST. PATRICK may in Ireland) for an earlier mythological hero figure. He was a specialist at removing threatening DRAGONS from the land, an honor he shared with ST. GEORGE; the dragons have been variously interpreted as indicating residual pagan influences beaten down by Christianity, or earlier mythic beings who were bested by a Celtic god or hero. Many sites or churches dedicated to St. Michael were built on ancient sacred sites, notably the tower atop the TOR in GLASTONBURY, further supporting the theory that his legends are influenced by Celtic or even pre-Celtic material.

St. Michael's feast day on September 29, called Michaelmas, is close enough to the autumnal EQUINOX that harvest festivals have collected around that day; in the Scottish islands a special harvest-bread called *struan* or *struan Michael* was until recently served as part of the ritual festivities. In Ireland "Michael's portion" was an offering at harvest time.

stoat Irish mythological animal. This small red-brown Irish land mammal, which looks rather like a weasel, was viewed anthropomorphically and thought to have human characteristics such as living in families and holding rituals for their dead. They were dangerous, for their saliva could poison a full-grown man; they were also mischievous and prone to thieving. It was not good luck to encounter a stoat when setting out on a journey, even a short one, but one could turn the luck to good by greeting the stoat as a neighbor.

Source: Ó hÓgain, Dáithí. *Irish Superstitions.* London: Gill & Macmillan, 1995, pp. 32 ff.

stolen bride See FAIRY KIDNAPPING.

stone Mythic motif. The mysterious pre-Celtic people of Ireland, Britain, and Brittany were astonishing stonemasons, building structures that lasted almost 6,000 years; they also carved their art onto the stones, leaving an unreadable but provocative record of their beliefs. The Celts, who moved into these lands thousands of years later, saw no similar depth of symbolism in stone. They did, however, adapt the impressive sites—see BRÚ NA BÓINNE and STONEHENGE—to their own rituals, including the important one of kingly INAUGURATION. At Tara the impressive boulder called the LIA FÁIL was said to roar or shriek when the true king sat upon it; at Ireland's center the STONE OF DIVISIONS was said to map the four provinces of the island.

Adapting earlier stone structures to ritual use was made easier by the fact that the Celts saw the world in a pantheistic way, believing that NATURE was animated by divinity and was therefore sacred. Stones, like TREES and running WATER, therefore were significant evidences of divine power.

stone circles Mythic site. Hundreds of stone circles, ranging from tiny to enormous, dot the islands and peninsulas of the traditional Celtic lands. Built by the people of the MEGALITHIC CIVILIZATION thousands of years before the Celts emerged into the historical records, the stone circles were often kept as sacred spaces, being left relatively undisturbed while fields and towns were built around them. (In the case of AVEBURY, the town was built within the stone circle, one of the largest in Britain.) Although there were periods in historical times when the stones were moved or destroyed, in general folklore (often mislabeled "superstition") preserved them, for the archaeological sites were believed to be the habitations of the FAIRY race.

Source: Harbison, Peter. *Pre-Christian Ireland: From the First Settlers to the Early Celts.* Thames and Hudson, 1988, p. 94.

Stonehenge British mythological site. On the Salisbury Plain rises one of the ancient world's most famous monuments, Stonehenge. For hundreds of years, the great STONE CIRCLE was wrongly associated with the Celts, who lived in the area thousands of years after the erection of the stones in ca. 4000 B.C.E. The builders lived so far before historical time that we have no information about who they were, what language they spoke, or what they believed, but the similarity of Stonehenge to other such monuments (notably Carnac in Brittany and BRÚ NA BÓINNE in Ireland) has led scholars to speak of the MEGALITHIC ("big stone") CIVILIZATION, named for their monumental constructions. Like other great megalithic monuments, Stonehenge was built with reference to the stars. It is carefully aligned to permit a particular illuminating moment on the morning of the summer SOLSTICE; both Carnac and Newgrange at the Brú na Bóinne were aligned to the moment of sunrise on the winter solstice. Whoever the builders were, whatever their beliefs, they possessed impressively accurate information about the solar system.

Although its original myth and meaning are lost, Stonehenge in historical times attracted many legends. The third-century B.C.E. writer Apollonius claimed that it was a temple to APOLLO and called the worshipers there Hyperboreans ("beyond the wind god Boreus"). Later stories claimed that the great magician MERLIN built Stonehenge in a single day, bringing the stones by magical levitation from Ireland; they were called the GIANTS' DANCE because they had earlier been carried off through enchantment from Africa by Irish giants. Another story credits the DEVIL with building the stone structure, all in one night, chuckling at the surprise of the local population when they awoke to find the massive building where, the evening before, there had been only a flat plain. A monk, overhearing the Devil's bragging, interrupted him, whereupon the Devil threw one of the huge stones at him—which nicked his heel before falling to the ground, thereafter to be known as the Heel Stone. These legends hide a bit of truth. Although it is unlikely that teleportation was the means of transit, it is true that the stones come from a distance, some having been carried—perhaps rolled on logs—from as much as 26 miles away.

Despite scholarly agreement on the lack of connection between Celts and Stonehenge, the local antiquarian and man of letters John Aubrey argued, in the 17th century, that the site was a DRUID temple. In recent years the Order of British Druids (established in 1781) has claimed the right to celebrate their rituals within the stone circle. Robed in white in the pale dawn, the group may indeed be reenacting the presence of Celtic peoples within the circle at that time, but with no documentary evidence of Celtic use of the site, such a reconstruction can only be considered imaginative theater.

Sources: Spence, Lewis. *The Minor Traditions of British Mythology.* New York: Benjamin Blom, Inc., 1972, p. 84; Straffon, Cheryl. *The Earth Goddess: Celtic and Pagan Legacy of the Landscape.* London: Blandford, 1997, p. 99; Whitlock, Ralph. *The Folklore of Wiltshire.* London: B. T. Batsford, Ltd., 1976, p. 76.

Stone of Divisions (Aill na Mireann, Ail na Múenn, Catstone, Navel Stone) Irish mythological site. Upon the flanks of the sweeping hill UISNEACH, mythic center of Ireland, a huge boulder lies, left there by the retreating glaciers some 10,000 years ago. It rests about halfway down the hill, a half-mile away from the summit, from which almost all of Ireland can be seen on a clear day.

Locally called the Catstone, although there is no legend or myth to explain the name, the great glacial erratic is more formally known as the Stone of Divisions, because its shattered face is believed to include a map of the four provinces of Ireland. With a good imagination one might, indeed, see MUNSTER, CONNACHT, ULSTER, and LEINSTER mapped in the cracks of the rock. Local legend has it that the stone marks the grave of the goddess ÉRIU, for whom Ireland is named. The stone is also sometimes called the Navel Stone of Ireland. The phrase would seem to indicate that

it marked the point where the land was once connected to an immense mother, but little legend exists to further describe this phrase.

In the BOOK OF INVASIONS, the arriving MILESIANS encountered three goddesses in turn, each standing on a mountain; each obliged them to promise that the land would be named after her (see BANBA, FÓDLA). Upon arriving at Uisneach, their poet AMAIRGIN decided that the land should bear Ériu's name, as it does to this day.

Source: Dames, Michael. *Mythic Ireland.* London: Thames and Hudson, 1992, pp. 196–199.

St. Patrick (Patrick, Patricius, Pádraig, Pátraic, Cothraige) Irish saint and folkloric hero. It is interesting that no contemporary author from the fifth century C.E. mentions this name, for that is when the great St. Patrick was said to have been converting Ireland; Gildas and Bede, two important historians of the era, make no reference to a man named Patrick, which has caused some commentators to doubt that he ever existed. Although that is a minority opinion, most writers agree that folkloric and mythological motifs gathered around an historic figure, so that anything written about Patrick must be viewed with great caution in terms of its historicity.

According to the various *Lives* written in early Christian times and the two autobiographies reputed to have been written by the saint himself, Patrick was born in Britain to a family of well-off Romanized Celts. Even such a genteel upbringing was insufficient protection against sea pirates, who kidnapped the lad and sold him into slavery in Ireland (traditionally, in ULSTER). For six years, until he was 22, Patrick was a farm worker, apparently learning the language of his captors. Then he escaped and made his way to the Continent.

There, he experienced a vision in which he was instructed to return to Ireland in order to convert the inhabitants to Christianity. Legend does not record what kind of training he received for this mission, but it tells much about his arrival in Ireland. Proselytizing among his former captors, Patrick used his knowledge of Irish religion in order to explain the mysteries of Christianity. The best known of his evocative explanations is his use of the SHAMROCK, probably the common clover, to show how the Christian divinity can have three persons (father, son, holy spirit) while being still one god; in this, Patrick employed the familiar Celtic motif of triplicity in an innovative fashion (see THREE).

The shamrock speech was said to have occurred on "Easter," although the pre-Patrician Irish Celts would not have celebrated that Christian feast. Rather, they were celebrating the springtime festival of BELTANE, which involved lighting fires on hilltops across the land. As the people waited expectantly for the fire to blaze from the top of TARA hill, home of the high king, they were surprised instead to see a light from an inconsequential little hill nearby. The druids rushed to SLANE to see who dared such a sacrilege and found Patrick there over his offending fire.

Most of Tara's court was, according to legend, easily converted, but some of the DRUIDS did not wish to give up their power to the new hierarchy of priests and monks. Thus there are a number of legends in which Patrick was said to engage in combat with the druids—legends that are filled with un-Christian imagery suggestive of the Celtic worldview. In one such story, Patrick was challenged to a magical combat by a druid, who enchanted a garment that Patrick was to wear. Patrick did the same, and the druid died horribly after putting on his garment, while Patrick's associate escaped unharmed (the great saint did not, apparently, risk putting on the enchanted garment himself). Some druids continued to threaten Patrick, but he passed through their midst without their seeing him. He could read in the dark by the light of his own glowing fingers; rain never touched him no matter how severe the storm. Such magical events are clearly legendary rather than historical. The insertion of a druidical prophecy claiming that Patrick would come to convert the land seems a

later interpolation designed to support the claims of the new religion.

In several legends Patrick directly confronts the pagan world that his religion replaced. In one such story, he encountered the princess of CONNACHT one morning at the holy spring of OGALLA, where they had come to bathe. The girls, EITHNE and FEDELM, mistook Patrick and his monks for druids and began to discuss religion with them. Learning that Patrick served a new god, the girls asked questions that give insight into the religious expectations of the Celts at the time, asking, for instance, where his god lived, whether in the earth or the sky or the sea? Satisfied by Patrick's answers, the girls accepted baptism and then died instantly, to assure themselves of remaining unstained by sin. In a similar tale, Patrick encountered OISÍN and Caoilte, members of the heroic FIANNA who had been stolen away and carried to the OTHERWORLD. (Variants of the tale say Patrick met only one, usually the poet Oisín.) He debated with them which religion held more promise, showing Christianity to be the more hopeful worldview, and thus converted the pagan sages. Such literary texts are useful in gaining insight into what values and ideals Celtic Ireland held, as well as those brought from abroad by the proselyting Christians.

Also legendary were Patrick's combats with various Otherworld powers. He split the HAG GARRAVOGUE into four parts with his staff; he battled the water monster called CAORANACH, sending her to a watery death (or perhaps not, depending on the legend consulted); he fought with the demon CORRA atop the mountain now called CROAGH PATRICK in his honor; he smashed the idols of CROM CRUACH. And, in the most familiar legend, he drove the snakes out of Ireland (see SERPENT). That last is entirely fabricated, as there were no snakes in Ireland at the time of his coming; this has been typically interpreted as indicating the driving forth of pagan Celtic divinities from the land.

Many sites in Ireland that are now devoted to reverence of St. Patrick were originally pagan sites that were SAINED or converted with the coming of Christianity. The most prominent of these is Croagh Patrick (locally known as "the Reek," from a word meaning "mountain"), the pyramidal mountain where Patrick is reputed to have fought with the demon Corra before flinging her into the sea at the mountain's base. Ruins have been found on Croagh Patrick's summit suggesting that religious observance there stretches back into the neolithic period, some 6,000 years ago. Today it is the best-known Patrician site in Ireland. On Reek Sunday in late July (see LUGHNASA), thousands of pilgrims climb the steep path to the summit, some of them barefoot, some on hands and knees.

St. Patrick's feast day of March 17 is celebrated as a holiday in many countries where Irish influence has been strong. It was not traditionally a day of national importance in Ireland itself until recent times, being more typically an ethnic celebration of descendants of the Irish diaspora.

Sources: MacNeill, Máire. *The Festival of Lughnasa, Parts I and II.* Dublin: Comhairle Bhéaloideas Éireann, 1982; Ó hÓgain, Dáithí. *The Hero in Irish Folk History.* Dublin: Gill & Macmillan, 1985, pp. 5 ff.

stray sod (lone sod, *fod seachran*) Irish folkloric motif. While the idea of being lured off your intended path by FAIRIES usually entails the fairy placing a GLAMOUR spell upon a site, in Ireland the fairy people had a simpler, more portable expedient. They put a stray sod—a little piece of enchanted grass—on the path and then watched as people became PIXY-LED or helplessly confused as to their location. It was possible to hide a stray sod in plain sight, even in the middle of a road. When a passerby's foot struck the sod, all the surroundings became unfamiliar. Trapped this way, a traveler could wander for hours, growing ever weaker and more exhausted, until the mischief-making fairy put everything right again.

stream Irish and Scottish mythological site. All flowing WATER was sacred to the Celts; most

RIVERS were named for goddesses, who were imagined as generously watering the land. In a diminished way, streams and brooks had the same HEALING quality. Most significant was the crossing or joining of THREE streams; as anything occurring in threes was significant to the Celts, such sites were considered magically potent. In Scotland, as the sun rose, if you filled cupped hands with water from the point of meeting, you could have good luck and good health, as long as you spoke the following invocation: "I will wash my face, in the nine rays of the sun, as Mary washed her Son, in the rich fermented milk."

Source: Ross, Anne. *Folklore of the Scottish Highlands.* London: B. T. Batsford, Ltd., 1976, p. 53.

Strid British folkloric site. Near Bolton Abbey in West Yorkshire is a narrow pass in the River Wharfe called the Strid. There, on BELTANE morning, a woman was said to appear, riding a white HORSE; she was thought locally to be the goddess of the watershed, VERBEIA. Those who crossed the river afterward were warned to be careful, for the goddess's appearance often prophesied death from drowning.

Source: Clarke, David, with Andy Roberts. *Twilight of the Celtic Gods: An Exploration of Britain's Hidden Pagan Traditions.* London: Blandford, 1996, pp. 96 ff.

stroke (Elf-stroke, fairy stroke) The full or partial paralysis that we now know to be caused by an interruption of blood to the brain or a clot therein was believed, in the past, to be punishment for offending the FAIRIES, who would "stroke" the offender in punishment. Those who lapsed into coma were believed to have been taken AWAY and CHANGELINGS put in their place. Cutting down FAIRY TREES, plowing through FAIRY MOUNDS or otherwise interfering with fairy business could bring on stroke. Many sites of legendary importance were protected for generations by this belief.

struan   See CAKE.

Sualtaim mac Roich. (Sualtam mac Roy, Subaltach, Sualtach)   Irish hero. Foster father of the great ULSTER hero CÚCHULAINN, Sualtaim was given the princess DECHTIRE in marriage after she became pregnant by drinking water in which a magical WORM was swimming. Sualtaim plays little part in myth, except to warn the court of EMAIN MACHA about the advance of queen MEDB's armies in the *TÁIN BÓ CUAILNGE*. Unfortunately he turned so quickly on his horse, the Grey of MACHA, that his own shield lopped off his HEAD—which continued to call out warnings until the men of Ulster awakened from Macha's curse and protected their land.

Súantrade   Irish hero. The music of this legendary harper was so sad that people died of broken hearts just hearing it.

submerged city   Mythic theme. The image of a city under the water of a lake or the sea is common to Celtic lands: Ireland's INCHIQUIN lake and LOUGH GUR both were said to have cities on their rocky bottoms; in Wales we find tales of the Lowland Hundred in Cardigan Bay; in Brittany the magical city of YS rested in the sea off Pointe la Raz. Some of these were FAIRY cities, for which the OTHERWORLD is sometimes called Land Under Wave; some were originally surface cities that sank, either because of the decision of their residents to withdraw from this world, or because they were cursed by an evil power. As there are in fact sunken settlements in the areas covered by the Irish and North Seas and the Atlantic Ocean as the glaciers retreated, there may be some historical memory embedded in these apparently fanciful tales.

Sucellus (Sucellos)   Continental Celtic god. The name of this important Celtic god seems to mean "the striker," and in his arms he carried the symbol associated with his name, a great HAM-MER or MALLET like the one that a similar god, the DAGDA, carried in Ireland. Found across Gaul, sometimes in connection with the goddess NATOSUELTA, he was not renamed by the invading Romans for one of their gods, although he was sometimes associated with their woodland god Silvanus. Sculptors showed him as a mature bearded man with a fine head of curly hair, gazing benevolently at the viewer. He wore native, not classical, clothing—a tunic and a cloak. Sometimes Sucellus wore a crown of leaves or was joined by a hunting dog.

His hammer has been variously interpreted. It was so important to his identification that sometimes the hammer alone, with no human form, stood for the god. It was not usually connected with lightning, as with other hammer gods such as the Greek Zeus and the Scandinavian Odin. Rather, the hammer has been interpreted to mean the power of vegetation, driving itself up through the earth; thus Sucellos is described as a FERTILITY god or a god of the wildwood. Perhaps because his hammer could reawaken life, he was also seen as a god of healing.

Source: Green, Miranda. *Symbol and Image in Celtic Religious Art.* London: Routledge, 1989, pp. 46, 75.

Suibhne (Sweeney, Mad Sweeney, Suibne, Suibne mac Colmain, Suibhne geilt)   Irish hero. When Suibhne, a king of a small region of ULSTER, went to war to support the king of the province, he did so with a cloud hanging over him, for he had recently mistreated a monk, St. Rónán, who cursed him. The saint traveled to the battlefield to attempt to make peace, but Suibhne again insulted him, this time also killing one of Rónán's clerics, and the saint cursed him again.

When the battle started, it was fierce and horrible. Whether because of Rónán's curse or because of the horror of war, Suibhne went mad and abandoned his post on the battlefield.

Thinking himself a bird, he climbed a YEW tree. Each time he was found by his supporters, he fled again, always finding another tree in which to make his home. Finally he arrived at a monastery, thought to have been at Rosharkin in Co. Antrim or Gleann na nGealth (the Glen of the Lunatics) in Co. Kerry, where a relative disguised himself as an old woman—the only one Suibhne trusted—and finally brought the king back to his throne. Then the old woman came to him and reminded him how high he used to jump when he was mad. Suibhne tried it again and lost his wits again. He lived for a time with another madman, Alladhán (also called Fear Caille), who tried to leap into a waterfall and drowned; after that, Suibhne partly recovered his sanity. When he reached his old palace, he would not go in for fear of capture and went away lamenting his life. He wandered across Ireland until he reached a monastery in Co. Carlow, where he spoke with the resident saint, MOLLING, and was in the process of dictating his adventures to a scribe when, in a jealous fury, the husband of the monastery's cook stabbed him with a spear.

Suibhne is not listed on any of the rosters of historical kings, so it is believed that he was an Irish version of the figure known in Welsh mythology as MYRDINN WYLLT, "wild Merlin." The magician, well known in the story of King ARTHUR, went mad as a result of the massacre he witnessed in the battle of Arfderydd. Like Suibhne, he hid out in the woods, living off wild foods and making prophecies.

During his mad days, Suibhne spoke in sensuous poetry, and thus he is an attractive figure for poets; both the American poet T. S. Eliot and the Irish Nobel laureate Seamus Heaney have used him as a poetic persona, while the mid-20th-century Irish poet Austin Clarke wrote a long poem entitled *The Frenzy of Suibhne*.

Source: Ó hÓgain, Dáithí. *Myth, Legend and Romance: An Encyclopedia of the Irish Folk Tradition.* New York: Prentice-Hall Press, 1991, pp. 394–395.

Suideachan Irish mythological site. On the slopes of the MUNSTER mountain Knockadoon can be seen AÍNE's "birth chair," a rock outcropping that was said to be an entry to the OTHERWORLD. There this goddess or FAIRY QUEEN sat, arranging her long golden hair with a golden COMB. As recently as a century ago, sightings of Áine on her chair were not uncommon, although those who witnessed her appearance were likely to drown thereafter or to go to insane from the vision of her unearthly beauty. The chair was sometimes said to be the possession of an otherwise mysterious figure called the FAIRY HOUSEKEEPER, suggesting an identity between the two magical feminine figures of haunted LOUGH GUR.

Sul (Sulis, Sulis Minerva) British goddess. At the small city of BATH in central southwestern England, hot springs bubble forth at the rate of a million gallons a day. They were called by the Romans AQUAE SULIS, "the waters of Sul," and the site was a significant center for commerce and HEALING, a combination of Lourdes and the Mayo Clinic where people came to pray and bathe in the steaming waters, hoping to be cured of their ills. For many centuries after the legions left Britain, the baths were buried under silted-up deposits, but in the 17th century they were rediscovered by antiquarians. Today the great columns of the main bath are open to the sky; from their level, one can look up to see the medieval cathedral, its base several stories above the once-buried Roman baths.

The Romans associated the goddess of the thermal springs with their healing divinity, MINERVA or Minerva Medica ("medical Minerva"), so that she is sometimes called Sulis Minerva; in a bronze sculpture found in the temple precinct, Sul is shown as a warrior maiden. More important, scores of inscriptions—many written on lead and deposited in Sul's waters—reveal how active the shrine was in ancient times. More than 6,000 coins have been retrieved from the spring, most of Roman date. As goddesses of WATER are known in other Celtic lands, it is assumed that Sul is the local form of that divine category.

Sul's name suggests that she was a SUN goddess, for it is connected to words that mean both "sun" and "eye." Despite this pointed connection, some scholars continue to look for a male sun divinity in the area, even suggesting that all inscriptions to Sul contain a misspelling of the word for "pig." As a sun goddess, Sul would be connected with such figures as BRIGIT, who in Ireland was associated with holy WELLS (in that case, rarely thermal) that were said to have healing properties. Like Brigit, too, Sul was said to have been served by a college of priestesses who tended an eternal flame. Occasionally Sul appears in the plural (see SULEVIAE); the same name is occasionally given to Brigit.

Sources: Green, Miranda. "The Celtic/Goddess as Healer." In Billington, Sandra, and Miranda Green, eds. *The Concept of the Goddess.* Routledge: London and New York, 1996, pp. 28 ff; Straffon, Cheryl. *The Earth Goddess: Celtic and Pagan Legacy of the Landscape.* London: Blandford, 1997, pp. 94 ff.

Suleviae Continental Celtic goddess. Several dozen inscriptions have been found to this multiple goddess, whose name seems to mean "the many Suls," thus connecting her with the British healing goddess SUL. Caesar associated this team of divinities with the Roman goddess MINERVA, who ruled HEALING.

Summer Land (Summer Country) British folkloric site. This name is often used to describe the OTHERWORLD, where the weather is always fair, flowers bloom endlessly, and fruit hangs ripe off the trees. It is also used in some texts to describe the land of MELEAGANT, the ogre who held queen GUINEVERE hostage until the fine knight LANCELOT rescued her.

sun Cosmological concept. In the 19th century, scholars sometimes spoke of mythology as a form of poetry, a collection of primitive narratives about the forces of NATURE. Primary among these forces was the sun, whose presence at the center of our solar system and impact on earthly life made it a likely candidate for divinity in many cultures. So insistent were scholars of that early period in finding solar connections to various gods that a backlash began. Today, "solar mythology" is disdained, and as result antiquated attitudes about mythology have remained unexamined for more than a century.

Primary among these attitudes is the presupposition that the sun is invariably a masculine symbol. In fact, dozens of cultures from Japan to South America, from the arctic to Arabia, have seen the sun as feminine. Yet examination of solar mythology generally halted while the assumption was still made that that the Celts saw the sun as a male figure—as a god. Many candidates are proposed as the "Celtic sun god," including LUGH and LANCELOT, yet there is no definitive statement in any Celtic-language text that shows a god being honored as the sun.

There is, however, significant evidence that the Celts saw the sun as a goddess. Indeed, the name of one goddess, SUL, means "sun." In the Irish language the word for "sun" has been feminine in gender since the first recorded usage; this word, *grian*, is occasionally used for a minor goddess figure who may be connected with or the same as the more prominent heroine GRÁINNE. A few scholars are hesitantly examining this question, but the general prohibition against solar mythology means that it has not been substantively explained.

Sources: Green, Miranda. *Celtic Goddesses: Warriors, Virgins and Mothers.* London: British Museum Press, 1995, pp. 114–115; Green, Miranda. *Symbol and Image in Celtic Religious Art.* London: Routledge, 1989, p. 37; Hull, Eleanor. *Folklore of the British Isles.* London: Methuen & Co., Ltd., 1928, pp. 67 ff; Monaghan, Patricia. *O Mother Sun: A New View of the Cosmic Feminine.* Freedom, Calif.: The Crossing Press, 1994, pp. 61–86.

superstition Cosmological concept. When one religion is replaced by another, one, either through conversion or conquest, the earlier religion rarely disappears entirely. Rather, its beliefs and rituals remain, although the context and meaning was forgotten. Thus in the ancient Celtic lands today, we find a general revulsion at eating horse-meat, considered a useful food in some areas of the world; this may derive from the old reverence for the HORSE among the Celts. Similarly, beliefs in the BANSHEE and other FAIRY beings, viewed as superstition today, represent an earlier belief system in vestigial form.

Source: Henderson, George. *Survivals in Belief Among the Celts.* Glasgow: James MacLeose and Sons, 1911.

Sutugius Continental Celtic god. A few inscriptions from France attest to the existence of this god, believed by contemporary scholars to have pre-Celtic roots and equated by the Romans with their warrior god MARS.

swallow Folkloric animal. In Ireland the swallow was considered a helpful bird; to kill one brought bad luck.

swan Folkloric animal. The swan was often, like the SEAL, seen as a transformed human; occasionally the swan was believed to be a bewitched nun. It was considered lucky to see seven swans flying, because seven years of good luck would follow; seeing a multiple of seven brought that many more years of good luck. Hurting or killing a swan, conversely, brought bad luck to oneself and one's entire community. See SWAN MAIDEN.

swan maiden Irish, Scottish, continental Celtic folkloric figure. The story of a young woman who is half-bird appears throughout the ancient Celtic lands. Sometimes the girl was said to be under an enchantment, which might or might not be broken; other times, no reason was given for the maiden's double nature. In the dark of night, such maidens took off their swan plumage and left it beside the lakes in which they swam, naked and beautiful. Should a man find the feather cloak of such a woman, he could make her his wife by stealing it, whereupon (like a SEAL woman) she became a happy and hardworking helpmeet. Should the swan maiden ever find her feathers, she instantly converted herself to bird form and flew away, leaving her children behind without so much as a backward glance.

That this fairy tale has mythological roots is generally unquestioned. The BIRD is associated with religious imagery across Europe; it is found among the Celts as far back as the HALLSTATT period. Many bird divinities had solar associations (see SUN), while waterbirds were connected to thermal SPRINGS that were believed to hold the night-sun's energy. One of the largest and most graceful of waterbirds, the swan was sometimes depicted as part of a team pulling a chariot or cart, each swan connected to the others by a small chain. That motif appears in Irish mythology in the story of CÁER and AONGHUS ÓG, who, after falling in love, flew away together linked by a golden chain.

When a swan-woman married, she often demanded that her husband follow specific rules; the FAIRY QUEEN or goddess ÁINE, for instance, demanded that her husband, the Earl of Desmond, express no surprise at anything their children did. Should the rules be broken, the swan-wife and her children would instantly depart, as Áine and her son GERÓID IARLA did, turning into waterbirds which still can be seen on the magical LOUGH GUR. A few scholars have proposed that these legends recall a period when women made specific demands in the negotiation of a marriage contract.

Sources: Ross, Anne. *Pagan Celtic Britain: Studies in Iconography and Tradition.* London: Routledge and Kegan Paul, 1967, p. 234; Ross, Anne. *Folklore of the Scottish Highlands.* London: B. T. Batsford, Ltd., 1976, p. 54; Stuart-Glennie, John S. "Incidents of Swan-Maiden Marriage." In Dorson, Richard M., ed. *Peasant Customs and Savage Myths: Selections from the British*

Folklorists. Vol II. Chicago: University of Chicago Press, 1968, p. 523 ff.

swarth   Scottish folkloric figure. A magical double of a person, the swarth was dangerous to meet on the road, because seeing the image of yourself was an almost certain prophecy of death's approach. If, however, you were brave enough to speak with the swarth, you could gain magical knowledge and SECOND SIGHT.

Sweeney   See SUIBHNE.

sympathetic magic   Cosmological concept. In many cultures and mystical traditions throughout the world, it was believed that objects of a specific shape or form affected other similar objects; thus a girl combing her hair at home in the evening could attract the attention of a dangerous MERMAID, who also used a COMB at that hour and liked to drown sailors. Another form of sympathetic magic was the supposition that parts always remain connected to the whole; thus discarded HAIR and nails had a subtle power over the person from whom they originally came. (See also EXTERNAL SOUL.)

taboo See *GEIS*.

Tadg (Tighe, Tadc) Irish hero. This name is common in Irish history and mythology. The most prominent bearer was Tadg mac Nuadat, grandfather of the hero FIONN MAC CUMHAILL; Tadg has been interpreted as a form of the god NUADA, although his name implies that he was Nuada's son. A more obscure Tadg was foster father of the great king of TARA, CORMAC MAC AIRT. When Cormac was a boy, he killed some BADGERS and brought them home for dinner. His foster father, revolted by their bloody appearance, refused to eat them. It was well that he did, for they were his SHAPE-SHIFTING cousins. Another Tadg was the son of the canny hero CIABHÁN who traveled to the OTHERWORLD to meet the beautiful FAIRY QUEEN CLÍDNA.

taghairm Scottish ritual. A peculiar magical ritual is known from Scottish texts, which describe how conjurers roasted live CATS over coals until a giant cat named Big-Ears appeared; he may be a folkloric descendant of the ancient king of the cats, known in Ireland as Irusan. The rite of taghairm was known down through the 17th century, but it was strongly discouraged by the clergy, who proclaimed that anyone who performed it was instantly condemned to hell.

Tailtiu (Taillte, Tailtu) Irish goddess. The mythological history of Ireland parallels what archaeologists believe is its historical reality: waves of invaders landing, sometimes doing battle with their predecessors, sometimes intermarrying with them, sometimes both. The goddess Tailtiu stands at the boundary of two of these groups, the FIR BOLG and the TUATHA DÉ DANANN. She may have been a member of the Fir Bolg, although she is also said to have been a Spanish princess; in either case, she has been described by modern scholars as a goddess diminished into human form.

Tailtiu was married to EOCHAID mac Eirc, the last Fir Bolg king, an ideal ruler during whose reign only truth was spoken in the land, which bore abundant crops under fair skies. Eochaid was killed at the first battle of MAG TUIRED, when the Fir Bolg battled the magical invaders, the Tuatha Dé Danann. Thereupon Tailtiu married EOCHAID Garbh, who despite the similarity of name to her first husband, was a member of the victorious Tuatha Dé.

Tailtiu traveled to the center of the island, where even today the land is the richest in Ireland, and began to clear fields for planting, but the effort of felling the dense Irish forest killed her. As she died, she asked that her funeral go on forever, with HORSE racing and games and festivities. And so her foster son, the god LUGH, established the August festival that, strangely, bears his name (LUGHNASA) rather than hers.

On Lughnasa each year at TELTOWN, on the River Blackwater in Co. Meath, a great ÓENACH or assembly of the tribes was held, devoted to trading, match making, and celebration as well as to ritual athletic contests appropriate to the season. Horse-racing may have been part of the festivities, for there are legends that teams swam across the nearby river as dawn broke. The Great Games at Teltown, also called the Tailtin Games in Tailtiu's honor, took place through medieval times; a smaller-scale festival was held at the same site through the 19th century.

The Óenach Tailten was the most important of the ancient Irish festivals, because it was held closest to the seat of political power, the hill of TARA, whose kings sponsored the event. Other Lughnasa festivals (see CARMAN, TLACHTGA) were dedicated to goddesses who died; as earth goddesses, they may have represented the dying vegetation that fed humanity.

Source: Gwynn, Edward. *The Metrical Dindshenchas.* Royal Irish Academy, Todd Lecture Series. Dublin: Hodges, Figgis, and Co., Ltd., 1906–1924, pp. 147–163.

Táin See CATTLE RAID.

Táin bó Cuailnge (Cattle Raid of Cooley) Irish epic. The greatest extant piece of Irish mythological literature tells of a great CATTLE RAID upon a region now known as the Cooley peninsula; hence the piece is sometimes anglicized as the *Cattle Raid of Cooley*. Part of the ULSTER CYCLE of myths, the story was recorded in the Middle Ages by Christian monks at the important central monastery of Conmacnoise, but its material dates to earlier times. Presumably the tale had been conveyed orally, as was the tradition among Celtic BARDS, for centuries before being transcribed.

Besides the tale itself, there are a number of *remscéla* or fore-tales that described the reasons for the cattle raid. These include some of the most famous stories in Irish literature: how the maiden NESSA was raped by the DRUID CATHBAD and gave birth to a king who bore her name, CONCOBAR MAC NESSA, and how she then conspired to put her son on the throne of ULSTER by stealing it from FERGUS mac Róich; how the goddess or FAIRY woman MACHA came to earth to live with the human farmer CRUNNIUC, who wagered that she was faster than the king's horses and thus brought about her death, screaming the curse that caused the DEBILITY OF THE ULSTERMEN whenever they were attacked; how the lustful king Concobar hid away the resplendent maiden DEIRDRE, who nonetheless escaped captivity with her beloved NOÍSIU and his brothers, the SONS OF UISNEACH, who were later traitorously killed by the king; how the great hero CÚCHULAINN was begotten, grew to manhood, wooed the fair EMER, and unwittingly killed his only son; and how two angry pigkeepers were reincarnated time after time, always arguing with each other, until they found themselves in the bodies of two powerful bulls, the great white FINNBENNACH and the brown DONN CUAILNGE.

All these stories set the stage for the *Táin* itself. MEDB, queen of the western province of CONNACHT, was lying abed one morning with her husband AILILL, comparing their net worth. Medb contended that she owned as much as or more than Ailill, while Ailill believed she did not. And so they called for their wealth to be counted, and indeed, Ailill was proven to be right: He had one bull more in his herds than Medb did. To make matters worse, the great White Bull had been born in Medb's herds but had migrated to Ailill's. Since under BREHON law Medb's status as a wife was contingent upon her comparative wealth, she set about bringing her possessions up to par with her husband's.

Discovering that the equal of the White Bull was in the province of Ulster, on the Cuailnge peninsula, Medb sent word to the lord of that region, DÁIRE mac Fiachna, promising a fortune in gold and her own willing thighs as well, in return for the loan of the bull for a year. She hoped that a powerful bull-calf would be sired on one of her own cows by the great brown

DONN. Dáire was perfectly willing to make the loan, but when his men heard Medb's warriors bragging that they would take the bull whether his owner agreed or not, a furious Dáire withdrew his consent. So, just as her men had said, Medb set out to steal what she could not rent.

Medb had an advantage in her raid. Because of the curse of Macha, the warriors of Ulster suffered a debility whenever they were attacked, falling down in an agony that resembled labor pains. This went on for four days and five nights—plenty of time for Medb's army to be into Dáire's fields and off with the bull. And so she assembled a great army at her capital city of CRUACHAN and prepared her raid on Ulster.

While all of Ireland's great warriors assembled to do her bidding, Medb encountered a woman bard or DRUID named FEDELM. She was a magnificent figure mounted on a chariot, dressed in gold and red embroidery, staring with unseeing eyes at the chaos around her. When Medb asked whether she had the IMBAS FOROSNAI, the ability to see the future, Fedelm said she had. So Medb asked her to predict the outcome of her quest. "I see crimson, I see red," Fedelm warned. Medb decided to ignore this clear warning, however, so as not to be deterred from her plan. The seeress, she announced, had seen only the wrath and rage of warriors. And so the die was cast.

The armies set out from Cruachan right after SAMHAIN. As cattle-raiding was typically a summer activity, they were marching off-season, at a time they would not be expected. Ailill himself went along to support Medb's raid, as did her lover Fergus mac Róich, who was still angry at Concobar for cheating him out of the throne of Ulster and for manipulating him into causing the deaths of the sons of Uisneach. They foresaw a pleasant march through an unmanned land, with only victory ahead as they walked past the suffering Ulstermen.

They did not foresee that Cúchulainn would oppose them. The great hero was not an Ulsterman, so he did not suffer from the provincial debility; indeed, he was ready to fight against any invader. On a tree, Cúchulainn posted a warning, written in OGHAM letters, challenging any single warrior to combat.

And so they came, one after another, to fight against Cúchulainn. One after another they died: the handsome FRÁECH, Medb's sons MAINE and ORLÁM, even Cúchulainn's boyhood friend FERDIAD. The great winged goddess MÓRRÍGAN came to help Medb, but even she could not stop the slaughter. Yet while Cúchulainn was fending off warriors, Medb sneaked past and stole the brown Donn. As she was escaping across the land with her prize, the men of Ulster recovered from their curse and leapt into action. Although they won the battle, they lost the bull, which Medb brought back to Connacht with her retreating army. There the two reincarnated swineherds, the white bull Finnbennach and the great brown Donn Cuailnge, did as they had always done. They fell to fighting, with the brown fatally wounding the white and then, himself, dying of the exertion.

This was the ending of the story of the *Táin*, although there was a late tale added: of how the epic was partially lost, then restored by the son of Ireland's chief bard, SEANCHÁN TOIRPÉIST, who called up the ghost of the great warrior Fergus at his grave. As Fergus had been a party to the raid, he was an excellent source for the missing material. The poet who performed the invocation, frightened by the apparition of Fergus's ghost in the king's court where he was reciting the lost tale, fell over dead upon its conclusion.

Sources: Hull, Eleanor. *The Cuchullin Saga in Irish Literature.* London: David Nutt, 1898, pp. 111 ff.; Kinsella, Thomas, trans. *The Tain.* Dublin: The Dolmen Press, 1969.

Taise   Irish heroine. This minor figure of legend became one of the wives of the hero FIONN MAC CUMHAILL in order to free her father, ABARTA, from imprisonment by the FIANNA.

Taliesin (Taliesin Pen Beirdd, Telgesinus) Welsh hero. Like other great Celtic BARDS, the poet Taliesin, whose work has been dated to the sixth century C.E., was said to be the reincarnation of an earlier mythic figure. Originally he was the boy GWION, servant to the great goddess CERIDWEN. Because Ceridwen's son AFAGDDU was born ugly, his mother decided to give him the gift of inspiration and POETRY to make up for it. And so she brewed, in her magical CAULDRON, a potent mixture of herbs that needed to be stirred constantly as they cooked for a year and a day. Whenever she was busy about other things, Ceridwen assigned Gwion the duty of stirring. It happened that he was at the pot when the mixture bubbled over, burning Gwion's finger. Stung by the pain, the boy popped his finger into his mouth, thereby absorbing all of the magical power Ceridwen had intended for her son.

The first gift his new vision endowed was an image of how furious Ceridwen would be when she found out what he had done. So Gwion ran away. Ceridwen, when she found her potion destroyed, ran after him. With the new power of SHAPE-SHIFTING that he had gained from the brew, Gwion transformed himself into a HARE, but Ceridwen became a greyhound in hot pursuit. Every time he changed, she changed as well: FISH and OTTER, BIRD and HAWK, with Ceridwen always a hair's breadth away from capturing the errant servant boy. Then, when Gwion turned himself into a grain of wheat, Ceridwen became a hen and ate him up.

In Celtic myths eating often leads to pregnancy, and so it was with Ceridwen, who gave birth to Gwion and set him adrift on the sea. A nobleman, ELPHIN, found the baby floating near shore and took him home, raising him tenderly as his own child, calling him Taliesin, "radiant brow." Taliesin grew to be the most eloquent poet in the land, one who could see through the veil to the OTHERWORLD. Like the Irish poets AMAIRGIN and TUAN MAC CAIRILL, Taliesin spoke of many incarnations, both human and animal. He is said to be buried in a stone grave in Dyfed, called Bedd Taliesin; anyone who sleeps there wakes up either a poet or insane. The work that comes down to us as Taliesin's may have been indeed composed by a poet of that name, but the famous name may have attracted to itself poems from the oral literature; the line between fact and myth is easily blurred in Taliesin's case.

Sources: Bord, Janet, and Colin Bord. *The Secret Country: An interpretation of the folklore of ancient sites in the British Isles.* New York: Walker and Co., 1976, p. 59; Jackson, Kenneth, et al. *Celt and Saxon: Studies in the Early British Border.* Cambridge: University Press, 1963, p. 29; Nash, D. W., "Taliesin in Song and Story." In Matthews, John. *A Celtic Reader: Selections from Celtic Legend, Scholarship and Story.* Wellingborough: Aquarian Press, 1991, pp. 179 ff; Matthews, John. *Taliesin: Shamanism and the Bardic Mysteries in Britain and Ireland.* London: Aquarian/Thorsons, 1991.

talisman Symbolic object. The distinction between a talisman and an AMULET is not invariably maintained, as the words are sometimes used as synonyms. While both words indicate magical objects, a talisman draws good luck or the blessing of gods to the owner, while an amulet wards off evil spirits and bad luck.

Tamara Cornish and British folkloric figure. The nymph of the RIVER Tamar, which forms the boundary between Cornwall and Devon, was originally a maiden who wandered the land freely, despite the annoyance this brought to her parents, two earth-dwelling GNOMES. Two GIANTS, Torridge and TAVY, fought over her, and the argument caused all three of the lovers to dissolve into the rivers that bear their names. Although the legend itself was first transcribed in the 17th century, it is likely that it elaborates on an earlier tale, for the ancient geographer Ptolemy named the Tamar as a major river of the region. While the story of Tamara is similar to that of other Celtic river goddesses like BÓAND and SÍNANN, this story is unusual in having male divine figures dissolving to form rivers.

Tam Lin (Tamlane, Tam-a-Lin)   British folk-loric hero. One of the most famous FAIRIES of the British border country was Tam Lin, a lascivious young man who haunted Caterhaugh Wood and lured maidens away from their families in order to ruin them. He had once been human, but the queen of FAIRYLAND tricked him into passing over its borders, thus trapping him forever. A young girl named Janet fell deeply in love with Tam Lin and tried to bring him back to this world. Following Tam Lin's instructions, Janet went out on SAMHAIN night to watch the WILD HUNT pass on the road. When a milk-white steed appeared, she knew Tam Lin would be riding it, so she grasped him as he rode by and, just as he had predicted, found herself holding an eel, a bear, a lion, even a spike of fire. In spite of these tricks, she did not let go and so finally freed him from his enchantment.

tangie   Scottish folkloric figure. This strange being occasionally appeared around water, both fresh and salt, on the Orkney islands. Sometimes he looked like a human being, at other times like a fierce WATER HORSE. The *tangie's* name seems to derive from the local word for seaweed, *tang*.

tanist (tanáiste)   Celtic social role. According to many ancient and medieval authors, Celtic leaders had an elected assistant called a tanist. The English poet Edmund Spenser, who spent most of his life in Ireland, noted that even in the 17th century the Irish still elected their kings and, at the same time, a tanist who assumed the leadership role upon the king's death. Just as the king was not necessarily the eldest of a royal family, so the tanist was chosen for his talent and strength rather than for family prestige or position. Some theorists believe that the tanist was a religious as well as a political role, possibly deriving from the Celtic belief in the power of TWINS.

Tara (Temair, Temuir)   Irish mythological site. Perhaps the most famous ancient site in Ireland,

Tara is a small hill in Co. Meath that has been renowned at least since Celtic times—perhaps even before, as there are stone monuments on the hilltop from the pre-Celtic period. Ireland's mythic history, the *BOOK OF INVASIONS*, tells how the early invaders, the FIR BOLG, erected the first structures on the hill, although the Stone Heap of the One Man, their supposed work, is not known at Tara today. The place-poetry of Ireland, the *DINDSHENCHAS*, says that the name of the hill under the Fir Bolg had been Druim Cáin; the earlier people of NEMED had called it Druim Léith, after LIATH who had cleared its slopes so that there would be enough sun for crops to grow; even before that it had been called Forduim, a hill on which magical HAZEL trees grew.

It was at Tara that the Fir Bolg king received news of the arrival of yet another wave of invaders—this time the magical TUATHA DÉ DANANN—and at Tara that he mustered his hosts for the first battle of MAG TUIRED. In that monumental event, the Fir Bolg were defeated and forced to cede Tara to the newcomers. The Tuatha Dé changed the name of the hill to Cathair Crofhind and installed four treasures that they had carried from the mysterious cities of their origin, including the LIA FÁIL or Stone of Destiny, a great pillar ("a stone penis" according to some texts) that screamed when a true king touched it. Whether the stone that stands on Tara today is the same stone is unknown; some sources contend that the Scottish Stone of Scone (see INAUGURATION STONES) that rested for centuries in Westminster Abbey and upon which the English royals were crowned, is the real Lia Fáil.

There were also two great flagstones called Blocc and Bluigne, which fit tightly together except when a true king arrived, when they would open up so that he might pass between them. These stones, if they ever existed outside myth, are no longer to be seen on the hill. There was also a great Banquet Hall, the vestiges of which can be seen as earthen embankments on the hill. Legend has it that the Hall had nine separate areas for the various levels of society that would meet there, but no such divisions are visible today.

Despite their victory over the Fir Bolg, the Tuatha Dé Danann were not the wisest rulers. Soon they were at war again, this time against the combined forces of the Fir Bolg and the monstrous FOMORIANS. Under the leadership of LUGH, the Tuatha Dé once again won over their foes at the second battle of Mag Tuired, from which they returned to Tara rejoicing.

They were not to remain forever as Tara's rulers, for a new and even stronger race arrived in Ireland several hundred years later. Against the MILESIANS, even the Tuatha Dé could not prevail. They were forced to accept banishment to the OTHERWORLD while the Milesians settled upon the green and fertile surface of Ireland. A doorway to that Otherworld was thought to exist on Tara, for it was described in a medieval poem as "the secret place on the road of life," but its location is lost, or secret.

It was to Tara that the Milesian leader ÉREMÓN carried the body of his beloved wife, TÉA, who had asked that she be buried on the most beautiful hill in Ireland. This motif is found on other sacred mountains as well: TLACHTGA, for example, is said to have been buried beneath the mountain that bears her name, and the island's eponymous goddess ÉRIU rests on the slopes of the sacred central mountain, UISNEACH. Nothing is known of Téa except her dying wish.

Téa is not the only divine figure connected with Tara, for its goddess of SOVEREIGNTY was variously said to be ÉTAIN and MEDB. Étain was said to have been the reincarnated lover of the FAIRY king MIDIR, who in her human form married king EOCHAID of Tara, from whom Midir won her by gambling. Medb, although more typically associated with the great capital of the province of CONNACHT called CRUACHAN, is also said to have married nine kings of Tara, one after the other; a HILLFORT on the site bears her name. Finally, the heroine or sun goddess GRÁINNE is associated in myth with Tara, for she was to have been married at the palace there before she eloped with one of her husband's retainers.

Another mythic being, the COW goddess of abundance, is also found on Tara's heights, for

there is an earthworks called the Mound of the Cow (now lost) and two WELLS, one dedicated to the White Cow, the other to her calf. Some texts provide the name Glas Teamhrach for the mound, apparently referring to the magical cow GLAS GHAIBHLEANN, which gave milk endlessly to anyone who needed it.

The great ÓENACH or assembly of Tara was held on SAMHAIN, the day when the veils between this world and the Otherworld were lifted; it was not held at Tara itself but at the nearby hill of Tlachtga (now called the Hill of Ward), from which the seasonal fires blazed. It is recorded that Samhain was the time of the *feis Temrach*, the INAUGURATION feast when Tara's king ritually married the goddess of the land. Some evidence suggests that the assembly was held every THREE years rather than annually. The association of Tara with the beginning of winter makes it parallel to its twin mountain, Uisneach, where the opposite feast of BELTANE was celebrated with great double fires.

Among the many ancient structures and earthworks on the hills is the so-called Rath of the Synods, a pre-Celtic site from the MEGALITHIC CIVILIZATION that later became important to the Christian Irish, who believed incorrectly that it had been the site of bishops' councils in the early days of the Church. The site is now partially destroyed because in the 19th century a group of British believers tore through the earth in search of the biblical Ark of the Covenant, which they thought had been buried within it by the daughters of the last king of Israel. Although they never found the Ark, they destroyed much of this ancient structure in their attempt.

Visitors to Tara today enter the site through the yard of a church once dedicated to ST. PATRICK but now converted to an educational center. Almost directly ahead the ruined Rath of the Synods is visible. To the right, the long earthworks called the Banqueting Hall stretch in two parallel lines; the name is probably incorrect, but it is not known for what reason the structure was designed. Down the hill beyond the Banqueting Hall is a small rath named for GRÁINNE, errant wife of the hero FIONN MAC CUMHAILL, who may have originally been a goddess of Sovereignty. The larger rath, dedicated to Medb, is separated from the main monuments by distance, lying almost two kilometers away; the rath was once part of the ancestral estate of the Anglo-Irish author Lord Dunsany, commonly regarded as the inventor of the literary genre of fantasy fiction.

A cut on the north side of Rath Medb's bank, presumably the entrance, is aligned with the oldest site at Tara, the Mound of the Hostages. A pre-Celtic PASSAGE GRAVE, long covered by rubble, was excavated in the 1950s so that the chamber is now visible. Remains buried beneath the mound have been dated to some 3,500 years ago, suggesting that the tales of Tara's antiquity as a sacred site convey some truth. The name of the mound suggests that it was used as a prison, but it refers rather to the famous king of Tara, NIALL of the Nine Hostages. He took on nine foster sons from various parts of the land; their relationship to the king of Tara is questionably translated with the word "hostage."

Near the Mound of the Hostages, two smaller mounds rise from the green hilltop. One is the Forradh, also called the King's Seat or Place of Judgment; in the *Dindshenchas*, this monument is called the Mound of Téa and is said to be her grave. Atop this mound stands the upright Lia Fáil, approximately one-half of it visible above the ground. Nearby rises a mound nearly identical in size to the Forradh; called Cormac's House, it is as yet unexcavated and is associated in myth with the great king CORMAC MAC AIRT.

Other monuments at the site include Rath Lóegaire, dedicated to Tara's king at the time of St. Patrick's arrival; the Sloping Trenches, site of a mythical massacre of more than 3,000 maidens who are thought to have belonged to a college of priestesses; several holy wells; and minor structures and earthworks. Together, these monuments make Tara as important a site today, although for different reasons, as it was in its storied past.

Sources: Gwynn, Edward. *The Metrical Dindshenchas.* Part I. Royal Irish Academy, Todd Lecture Series.

Dublin: Hodges, Figgis, and Co., Ltd., 1906–1924; Ó Ríordáin, Seán. *Tara: The Monuments on the Hill.* Dundalk: Dundalgan Press, 1992; Raftery, Brian. *Pagan Celtic Ireland: The Enigma of the Irish Iron Age.* London: Thames and Hudson, 1994, pp. 65 ff; Rees, Alwyn, and Brinley Rees: *Celtic Heritage: Ancient Tradition in Ireland and Wales.* London: Thames and Hudson, 1998, pp. 146 ff.

Taran   Welsh god. This obscure god is mentioned once in the compilation of Welsh mythology, the *MABINOGION*; he is assumed to be similar to the continental Celtic thunder god, TARANIS.

Taranis (Taranos, Taranoos, Taranucnos) Continental Celtic god. This god was associated both with lightning strikes and with the fire that often follows. His name derives from a Celtic word for "thunder" and is thought refer to the god depicted with a HAMMER, although that god is also identified as SUCELLUS. The Romans, who believed Taranis to be the chief Celtic divinity, typically associated him with their own chief god JUPITER, although there is no evidence that Taranis stood at the head of a pantheon. The Roman poet Lucan claimed that Taranis, the "master of war," was honored with HUMAN SACRIFICES that required the victims be burned alive.

tarans   Scottish folkloric figure. Spirits of unbaptized infants were called by this name in Scotland. They were encountered in wild places, weeping over their inability to reach heaven. The belief appears to combine Celtic and Christian views of the afterlife, mixing up the OTHERWORLD with the Christian Limbo where unsoiled but unsanctified souls spend eternity.

Tarbhfheis   See BULL-SLEEP.

tarroo-ushtey   Manx folkloric figure. The WATER BULL of the Isle of Man was not as dangerous as such creatures normally are. Whereas in other lands, such water monsters devoured people and CATTLE outright, the *tarroo-ushtey* merely blighted the crops. As with other FAIRY creatures, this one could be warded off with a wand of ROWAN.

Tarvostrigaranus (Tarvos Trigaranus) Continental Celtic god. This obscure god is known from two stone sculptures at Paris and Trier, where he was depicted as a BULL with THREE CRANES or other waterbirds perched upon him. He may be similar to or identical with the god ESUS.

tatter-foal (shag-foal) British folkloric figure. A kind of BOGEY or bogle, the tatter-foal was a shape-shifter (see SHAPE-SHIFTING) who appeared in many forms, including that of a monkey, but most commonly a shaggy baby HORSE.

tattoo Celtic ritual. Although the word itself comes from the South Pacific, there is some evidence that the Celts decorated their bodies with permanent markings. The tribal name of the Scoti has been translated (perhaps fancifully) as "the scarred ones," while the name of the PICTS may mean "the pictured ones" or the "engraved ones." Roman writers describe Celtic warriors as painted with the blue dye-plant woad, while COINS from the imperial era show faces with what seem to be tattoos. Whether the apparent tattoos were marks of status, totemic markers, or religious symbols is unknown.

Tavy Cornish folkloric figure. The river spirit Tavy warred with another GIANT, Torridge, over the hand of the beautiful maiden TAMARA. He won her, but only after all three dissolved into rivers, for only the Tavy joins the Tamar, while the Torridge flows elsewhere. The name Tavy has also been suggested as the origin of the sea spirit DAVY JONES.

Téa (Tea) Irish goddess or heroine. This obscure figure gave her name to the great royal site of TARA in the center of Ireland. Little else is known of her, except that its first earthen walls were built at her request and that she died at Tara, giving her power to the hill.

Tech Duinn (House of Donn) Irish mythological site. A small rocky island off the BEARE peninsula in west Co. Cork was believed to be the home of DONN, a shadowy early god who ruled the OTHERWORLD of death. Unlike later visions of the Otherworld as a magnificently beautiful land, Tech Duinn was a frightening place of darkness and dread. Its relationship to the more typical Otherworld is unclear.

Tegau Eurfron Welsh heroine. One of the THREE SPLENDID WOMEN of CAMELOT, Tegau Eurfron rescued her husband from a venomous snake. She herself was bitten and lost one breast as a result. It was replaced with a breast made of gold, which matched her golden hair.

Tegid Welsh mythological site. What is now called Lake Bala in northern Wales—the largest LAKE in that land—appears in mythology as Llyn Tegid, home of the great goddess CERIDWEN. It was there that she brewed her magical potion in a CAULDRON, which she left the young boy GWION to watch while she did other chores.

When he accidentally swallowed some of the brew, thereby gaining both WISDOM and poetic talent, Gwion fled the scene. The omniscient Ceridwen knew what had happened and pursued him. Despite his newfound SHAPE-SHIFTING ability, Gwion was at last eaten by the goddess, who gave birth to him again as the great BARD, TALIESIN. The lake's mystical character remained in local folklore, for it was believed that Lake Bala's depth could never be measured; anyone who tried would be greeted by a booming voice demanding that the measurement cease. DRAGONS were reputed to live in the lake's bottomless lower regions.

Tegid Voel (Tegid Foel, Tegyd Foël) Welsh god. This obscure god or GIANT was the consort of the great HAG goddess, CERIDWEN; little else is known of him, although the LAKE where the pair made their home (now Lake Bala) bore his name.

teinm laeda (tienm laído) Irish ritual. The ancient Irish form of DIVINATION called *teinm laeda* seems to have been what is today called psychometry—finding information from objects by touching or holding them. A verse or incantation may have first been recited, and the DRUID employing this technique may have touched the object in question with a wand of HAZEL or other magical TREE.

Legend suggests that direct transmission of information was also possible: Holding a bone, the BARD Moén mac Etnae was able to discover not only that it was the skull of a DOG, but also the name of the deceased pet. Sometimes this form of divination is associated with chewing the thumb, as the hero FIONN MAC CUMHAILL did in order to prophesy. The *teinm laeda* was prohibited by ST. PATRICK, as was the better-known trance method called *IMBAS FOROSNAI*, apparently because both required a SACRIFICE or prayer to a pagan god or goddess.

Telgesinus Welsh hero. In one Welsh text, this name is given for the great BARD, TALIESIN, who instructed the magician MERLIN in the secret ways of the universe.

Telo Continental Celtic goddess. This name, found on inscriptions to the HEALING spirit of the SPRING at Toulon in the French region of the Dordogne, is believed to name a goddess, although Telo may have been a god.

Teltown Irish mythological site. On a farm in Co. Meath, near the River Blackwater, a large, long HILLFORT rises from a pasture. Nondescript as it may be today, it was in ancient times one of the most renowned sites in the land, for it was

there that the king of royal TARA presided over the annual games in honor of the goddess TAILTIU, who gave her name to the hillfort and, even today, to the townland that surrounds it. The games were part of the harvest assembly called the Óenach Tailten, held on the Celtic feast of LUGHNASA, the feast was named for Tailtiu's foster son, the god LUGH, who established the games and the assembly in her honor when Tailtiu died of exhaustion after clearing Ireland's central pasturelands.

Teltown was not only a site of games and trading; it was also the location for the so-called Teltown marriages, trial marriages contracted at a mound across the road from the main center of activity. At this spot, long known as the Crockans, stood a wooden door pierced by a hole through which young couples held hands while plighting their troth. If the match did not prove successful within a year and a day, the pair could return to the Crockans and undo the union.

Games at Teltown continued through medieval times, and the assembly, was held until the 19th century. Such continuity may have an even longer history, for one of the earthworks at Teltown, the so-called Rath Dubh ("black rath") may be built above a PASSAGE GRAVE; the site may have been selected because it was already sacred to the pre-Celtic people.

Source: Raftery, Brian. *Pagan Celtic Ireland: The Enigma of the Irish Iron Age*. London: Thames and Hudson, 1994, p. 82.

Temair (Temuir) See TARA.

temple Ritual structure. The Celts did not erect buildings for worship as did their conquerors, the Romans. They preferred to gather outdoors in *NEMETONS* or sacred woods, where SACRIFICES and offerings were made; on hilltops like UISNEACH and TARA, where great FIRES were lit on festival days; and at holy WELLS where such ceremonies as INAUGURATION might be performed.

There is, however, some archaeological evidence of buildings that are variously called temples or castles, which may have been used for assemblies that included religious ritual. At the first century B.C.E. British site called MAIDEN CASTLE in Dorset, evidence of a circular building has been found; since the circle had cosmological significance to the Celts, this round building is interpreted as having a religious purpose. Similarly, the remains of circular buildings have been found in Ireland at EMAIN MACHA and DÚN Ailinne. At Emain Macha there are indications of a central post which may have represented the central TREE in a grove. Despite such occasional finds, there is no clear evidence that Celtic people were generally in the habit of protecting themselves from the powers of nature as they worshiped.

Tephi Irish heroine. This obscure figure appears in the place-poetry called the *DINDSHENCHAS* as one of the early builders of the ramparts at the royal hill of TARA. She was an Egyptian pharaoh's daughter, a fierce warrior who was carried away by Camson, an otherwise unknown champion. At Tara, Tephi used her staff and her brooch to trace the outlines of the great earthen walls that were called, after her, the Rampart of Tephi. She died in Ireland and was buried elsewhere, possibly in Spain. The story may be a reflection of the building of the capital of ULSTER by MACHA, who similarly traced out its raths with the pin of her brooch; alternatively, the story of Tephi may have inspired that of Macha.

Tethba Irish goddess or heroine. This little-known goddess was said to have given her secret name to the lands she most loved, now parts of Co. Westmeath in the Irish midlands. Such stories are typically told of the goddess of the land's SOVEREIGNTY, the consort of the king.

Tethra Irish hero. This obscure divinity is called the FAIRY king of the OTHERWORLD. Nothing is known of him except that he was a member of the magical race called the TUATHA DÉ DANANN, who were banished from the surface world by the conquering MILESIANS after losing the second battle of MAG TUIRED.

Teutates (Toutatis, Totatis, Teutate) Continental Celtic god. This god's name appears to mean "ruler of the people," from the Celtic word for "tribe," which suggests an ancestral god. Dedications to Teutates are most commonly found in Gaul, occasionally in Britain, never in Ireland; he is sometimes connected to, or considered an alternative form of, the god COCIDIUS, while the Romans believed he was similar to their warrior god MARS and to their god of commerce, MERCURY. The Roman author Lucan said that Teutates was honored by HUMAN SACRIFICE, with the victims offered to him being drowned on SAMHAIN, the feast of winter's start on November 1.

Teyrnon Welsh hero. In the story of RHIANNON and her son PRYDERI, this is the name of Pryderi's foster father, who unwittingly saved the boy from being devoured by a monster. Seeing a huge claw descend from the heavens on BELTANE night, aiming at a newborn foal, he rushed to its defense. Slashing at the claw, Teyrnon caused it to drop its burden: the stolen child, which Teyrnon and his wife brought up as their own.

Them (They, Them Folk, Themselves) See NAMES FOR THE FAIRIES.

thinness Cosmological concept. The Celts believed that reality was not all the same everywhere. While common reality was opaque and solid, there were also "thin places" where the OTHERWORLD was near. These included FAIRY TREES that grew alone in the center of a rocky field; BOGS where people could be lost and drowned; and ISLANDS that appear remote or close according to atmospheric conditions. There were also "thin times" in the year, turning points at which Otherworld forces could penetrate to our world, or dwellers here could happen into that world. Although each day had a thin time at twilight, there were two days every year when time grew so thin that the two worlds collided: the two Celtic feasts of BELTANE on May 1 and SAMHAIN on November 1. The idea of thinness in time and place may be connected to the belief in SHAPE-SHIFTING, the ability to transform one's body into that of an animal, a plant, or even a fog.

Thirteen Treasures of Britain British folkloric motif. Just as Ireland had four great treasures brought from the OTHERWORLD and signifying the SOVEREIGNTY of the land, so British lore names 13 objects of Otherworldly origin that reside in this world to betoken the rightful ruler. The great king ARTHUR brought them back from the Otherworld kingdom of ANNWN. The treasures are: the sword of RHYD-DERECH, which would burst into flame when born by a rightful king; the bottomless hamper of Gwyddno; the mead-dispensing horn of BRÂN THE BLESSED; an impressively speedy chariot; a HORSE-attracting halter; a knife that replenished the food it carved; a CAULDRON that would not boil food for cowards; a whetstone that sharpened only the weapons of the brave; a coat that only fit the noblest warriors; a crock and a dish that served whatever the hungry desired; a self-playing chessboard; and the mantle of invisibility.

thistle   Symbolic plant. This prickly plant with a soft purple blossom symbolizes Scotland; it was believed to show the location of buried treasure and of forgotten graveyards.

Thiten   See MORGAN.

Thomas the Rhymer (Thomas Rymour, Thomas of Ercildoune, True Thomas)   British hero. The most renowned visitor to FAIRYLAND was the historical 13th-century poet, Thomas Learmont, of Ercildoune on the Scottish-English border. He attracted the attentions of a lustful FAIRY LOVER, who stole him away (see FAIRY KID-NAPPING) and held him a happy captive for seven years. When it appeared he might be taken away by the DEVIL to pay off an old debt of his mistress's, however, the fairy queen relinquished Thomas to the human world. She gave him an ambiguous gift: prophecy, without the ability to lie, which caused Thomas no end of trouble when he returned to earth. Some versions of his story say that, at the end of his life, he returned to fairyland, where he is seen by other visitors, attentively at the side of his happy mistress.

thorn   Symbolic plant. One of the most powerful and magical plants known in Celtic lands is the thorn tree (variably species *Prunus* and *Crageaeus*). The blackthorn *(Prunus)* blooms each spring near the BELTANE festival on May 1; beside its sweet white flowers are sharp, pin-like thorns that can easily puncture flesh. The thorns limit the usefulness of this tree, except as a CATTLE hedge, but its magical use is significant, for the tree protected humans against the FAIRY people. It was hedged about with precautions to keep it from losing that power; it was especially important not to cut the trees on May 11 or November 11, for the trees would take vengeance against the woodsman. The related whitethorn was similarly a protective plant, but its wood had to be kept out of doors, for fairies had extrasensory awareness of its presence indoors and would haunt the house where it was kept.

Hawthorns too bloom in spring, when their pink blossoms are among the season's most extravagant. Bathing in the dew from hawthorn blossoms on Beltane assured the seeker of perpetual beauty. The tree was angry if cut, and sometimes frightening animals emerged from an injured hawthorn, chasing or injuring the woodcutter. Those who cut down thorns were especially prone to FAIRY STROKE, the paralysis that struck when a fairy touched one's flesh, however gently. When the thorn appeared in a group of THREE with an ASH and an OAK tree, that was taken as a certain sign of fairy activity in the area.

Sources: Briggs, Katherine M. *The Folklore of the Cotswolds.* London: B. T. Batsford Ltd., 1974, p. 120; Spence, Lewis. *The Minor Traditions of British Mythology.* New York: Benjamin Blom, Inc., 1972, p. 108.

three Cosmological concept. The Celts, both continental and insular, saw three as a significant and powerful number; only FIVE appears more often in mythological or ritual contexts. The number itself was considered sacred, and anything that appeared in three parts (see SHAMROCK) represented this religious value. In Wales a series of short poems called the TRIADS encodes much mythological material; in Ireland we find stories showing kings and heroes suffering the THREEFOLD DEATH.

Many Celtic divinities appear in triplicate, as do the DEAE MATRES or MOTHER GODDESSES of Gaul and the supernatural triple-horned BULL of Britain. Triplicity seems, in many cases, a way of intensifying the power of a figure. Although goddesses are most often tripled (see MÓRRÍGAN, MACHA, BRIGIT), gods are occasionally elevated into a trinity; the continental god LUGOS appears to be a tripled form of the god LUGH, and three-headed figures have been found, although they are not clearly male or female. In addition to emphasizing a figure's importance, the number three has been described as indicating a complete cycle: past, present, and future; mother, father, and child.

The sanctity of the number three may have represented, or been represented by, a threefold division of social functions: the sacred, the warlike, and the fertile. Each person in society had a place according to the function he or she performed; thus BARDS and DRUIDS may have been granted more power than warriors and kings; goddesses of SOVEREIGNTY would presumably have symbolized the third function, as well as farmers and others who created the abundance that society enjoyed. Support for such an argument is found in tales such as that of CESAIR, who arrived in Ireland with only three men to serve her 50 women—a story that incorporates the other most significant number, five, in expanded form.

Sources: Cunliffe, Barry. *The Ancient Celts.* Oxford: Oxford University Press, 1997, p. 187; Green, Miranda. *Symbol and Image in Celtic Religious Art.* London: Routledge, 1989, p. 169; Powell, T. G. E. *The Celts.* London: Thames and Hudson, 1980, pp. 154 ff.

threefold death Celtic ritual. Although the question of whether the Celts practiced HUMAN SACRIFICE is not settled, there are evidences in Irish myth of a kind of sacrificial death with three parts—often stabbing, burning, and drowning. (Another version of the threefold death probably involved strangling, cutting, and drowning.) At times, the various forms of execution were parceled out among the gods; thus among the continental Celts, those sacrificed to the thunder god TARANIS were burnt, those offered to the ancestral god TEUTATES were drowned, while those who went to the TREE god ESUS were hanged.

In Ireland several texts refer to the threefold death: MUIRCERTACH MAC ERC was wounded, then as he tried to escape his burning house, he fell and drowned in a vat of wine; the failed king CONAIRE similarly was wounded, stricken with an unquenchable thirst, then burned alive. A body found in Britain's Lindow BOG (see LINDOW MAN) showed that the victim, who had a noose around his neck, had his throat slashed before being drowned in the bogwater. If, as some argue, the Celts believed in REINCARNATION, the ritual offering of a human life to attain a community good, such as relief from plague or famine, might have been seen as a noble way to die.

Three Sorrows of Ireland Irish mythological tales. The three stories known by this name are among the most poignant in Irish mythology. They include the tale of DEIRDRE of the Sorrows and her lover NOÍSIU, as well as his brothers, the SONS OF UISNEACH; the slaughtered SONS OF

TUIREANN; and the heroic girl FIONNUALA and her brothers, the CHILDREN OF LIR.

Three Splendid Women Welsh heroines. Three women of king ARTHUR's court were known in the Welsh TRIADS as the Three Splendid Women. They were the faithful and challenging ENID, the model wife; the helpful TEGAU EURFRON; and the obscure but beautiful DYFR.

Tiddy Mun British folkloric figure. Those who made their living from the now-drained fens of England had a complex folklore that is now regrettably mostly lost. Among the spirits they believed lived in the watery fens was Tiddy Mun (apparently, "tidy man"), a gentle white-haired soul who protected those who cared for the land. When the fen waters rose in stormy weather, the fen people would pray for his intervention: "Tiddy Mun! Tiddy Mun! you without a name, walking lame, harm none, Tiddy Mun, harm none, harm none." With the draining of the fens to expand agricultural land, Tiddy Mun's special habitat was lost, and he has not been recently seen.

Tigernmas (Tiernmas) Irish hero. A quasi-historical king of TARA, Tigernmas was a devotee of the cruel god CROM CRUACH; he also brought GOLD-smelting to Ireland, thus establishing one of its most important ancient industries.

time Cosmological concept. The concept of time is not standard throughout the world; each culture's calendar reveals its values and philosophy. To the Celts, each day began at sundown of what we would consider the previous day, and just as NIGHT preceded day, so winter preceded spring, with the beginning of the year marked at the feast of SAMHAIN on November 1. The year appears to have been divided, not into four seasons, but into the two seasons of summer and winter; each of those seasons, however, was further divided into two, a beginning and an end-

ing. A similar division has been found in some ancient sources that suggests that each month was divided into two equal parts.

The year's 12 lunar months alternated between 29 and 30 days. To reconcile this 354-day calendar with that of the sun, a 13th month was added every 2½ years; at the end of two such cycles—that is, every five years—the 13th month was an occasion of celebration and sacrifice. Six such five-year units, or 30 years, composed something that Pliny calls an "age," which may have meant a generation. Time was linked to history, which was important to the Celts, who invested effort in memorizing long genealogies, but there was also the OTHERWORLD, where time and space were radically different from those in our world and where the gods and FAIRIES lived.

Source: Brunaux, Jean Louis. *The Celtic Gauls: Gods, Rites and Sanctuaries.* London: Seaby, 1988, pp. 45–48.

Tine Ghealáin (Jack-o-Lantern, Jack of the Lantern) Irish folkloric figure. What is called in other lands the will-o'-the-wisp, a light seen over bogs at night, was said in Ireland to be a lantern carried by a dead gambler doomed to wander forever because, although his soul was too stained to enter heaven, he had won his way out of hell by beating the DEVIL at cards. His name was applied to the hollowed-out turnips (in the New World, pumpkins) used at SAMHAIN, when the veils between the worlds were thin.

Tintagal Cornish mythological site. A Norman castle on a steep headland overlooking the Irish Sea, Tintagal is often described as the site of king ARTHUR's conception by his father, UTHER PENDRAGON, upon his mother IGRAINE, although there are other contenders to places that contact for the same identification. The castle dates to the 12th century, but there is evidence of occupation at the site some seven centuries earlier; even earlier, the territory was known in the ancient world for its exports of tin.

Near the castle itself is what appears to be an INAUGURATION STONE: a small depression in the rock called King Arthur's Footprint.

Tir fo Thuinn (Tir-fa-Tonn, Land Under Wave) Irish mythological site. One of the many names given to the OTHERWORLD or FAIRYLAND, Land Under Wave refers to the tradition that LAKES and the ocean hide the route between this world and the other. Stories of cities beneath lakes or on the ocean bed, and of MERMAIDS and MERMEN who live there, are common in all coastal Celtic lands.

Tir na mBan (Tir na Ban) Irish mythological site. The Land of Women, one of many names given to the Irish OTHERWORLD, seems to have applied specifically to mysterious floating ISLANDS where FAIRY QUEENS like NIAMH of the Golden Hair reign. Such islands were famous, or notorious, for the FAIRY KIDNAPPINGS that were launched from their shores.

Tir na nOg (Tir Na n-og) Irish mythological site The Land of Youth was one of the many names given to the OTHERWORLD, often confused or conflated with FAIRYLAND, because the ancient gods called the TUATHA DÉ DANANN were banished from this world and turned into FAIRIES. The name derives from the fact that no one ever grows old in the Otherworld; instead its inhabitants lead a charmed life, dancing and loving, eating from the endlessly fruiting trees and never having to face death. Local legend around the enchanted LOUGH GUR claims that the entrance to Tir na nOg is beneath the LAKE's waters.

Tir Tairngiri Irish mythic location. The Land of Promise was the domain of the beautiful NIAMH, a FAIRY QUEEN who chose her lovers from the human sphere and employed FAIRY KIDNAPPING as a means of courtship. As daughter of the ocean god MANANNÁN MAC LIR, Niamh lived on a magical ISLAND that, like other areas in FAIRYLAND, was ideal in all ways: perfect weather, endlessly fruiting trees, beautiful people.

Titania British folkloric figure. In Shakespeare's *Midsummer Night's Dream*, this name is given to the FAIRY QUEEN. While the name itself is not Celtic, deriving from a title of the Roman goddess DIANA, the conception of FAIRYLAND as ruled by such a regent is typical of British folklore.

Tlachtga Irish mythological site and goddess or heroine. Less known than the nearby hill of TARA, Tlachtga nonetheless has deep mythological significance as the site of the great ÓENACH or assembly of SAMHAIN, the festival of winter's arrival on November 1. Now known as the Hill of Ward and located near Athboy in Co. Meath, Tlachtga is the site of impressive earthworks from the Celtic period. Its significance lasted into historical times, for in 1168, the high king Rory O'Connor called together an island-wide assembly there.

Tlachtga rises near the western edge of Ireland's central plain, called BREGA in early texts, now covering most of Co. Meath. Like other significant mountains in the midlands, Tlachtga is not tall or striking, but its summit offers a vista of almost half of Ireland. The mythic hills of Tara, SLANE, and LOUGHCREW are visible on a clear day. A large series of earthworks forming a circular HILLFORT were likely topped with wooden palisades to form a protective wall. Four large banks fan out from the circle, forming a shape similar to the Rath of the Synods on Tara. Nearby are several WELLS, one of which has the unusual name of DRUID's Well; it may be the source of the water known from an ancient poem as one of the appropriate offerings to the king at Tara.

Although not much attention has been paid to Tlachtga by scholars and archaeologists, it held considerable significance in ancient times. Its curious name includes the word for "earth" in modern Irish, *tlacht*, from which some have proposed a lost goddess of that name; the second syllable appears to mean "ray" or "spear" (see GÁE BULGA). Some ancient texts claim that the hill got its name from a WITCH, daughter of the magician MOG RUITH. In a confusing tale, she is said to have traveled to Italy to study with the great magician Simon Magus, from whom she learned to make a flying wheel or ROTH RAMACH, with which she was able to sail back to Ireland. Somehow, the THREE sons of Simon Magus tracked her there and raped her on the hill that bears her name. There too she died, in labor with the three sons of the three brothers, and there she is buried. Like the parallel figure of TAILTIU, Tlachtga was honored with a festival organized in her memory by the god LUGH.

Sources: Gilroy, John. *Tlachtga: Celtic Fire Festival.* Glanmire, Co. Cork: Pikefield Publications, 2000; Gwynn, Edward. *The Metrical Dindshenchas.* Royal Irish Academy, Todd Lecture Series. Dublin: Hodges, Figgis, and Co., Ltd., 1906–1924, Reprinted Dublin Institute for Advanced Studies, School of Celtic Studies, 1991, pp. 187–191; Raftery, Brian. *Pagan Celtic Ireland: The Enigma of the Irish Iron Age.* London: Thames and Hudson, 1994, p. 82.

tober   See WELL.

tochmarc   See WOOING.

togail   See DESTRUCTION.

Toice Bhrean   Irish folkloric figure. In some legends from near the enchanted LOUGH GUR, this is the name given to the FAIRY HOUSEKEEPER who sits at the LAKE's bottom, knitting endlessly. The name means "slattern" or "lazybones" and refers to the story that the lake was formed (like LOUGH NEAGH) when the assigned guardian left the lid off a sacred well, which overflowed to form the lake. For her lack of attention, Toice

Bhrean was condemned to spend eternity at the lake's bottom, beneath a magical tree that grew there. Only once every seven years did she see daylight, when the lake's waters evaporated for a few moments.

toili   Welsh folkloric figure. Sometimes at night, a funeral seemed to pass through a village. All the villagers were visible, passing slowly and mournfully behind a casket, headed toward the cemetery, but all those villagers were really tucked safe in their homes, for the spectral procession was the *toili* or ghostly funeral. Those with SECOND SIGHT could sometimes see them passing in the daytime as well. The appearance of the *toili* was invariably a premonition that someone's death was imminent. It was important to turn aside if one saw the *toili* pass, for anyone swept up in its parade would die.

Tommy Rawhead   (Rawhead-and-Bloody-Bones, Old Bloody Bones) British folkloric figure. Informants in the last century differed as to where this frightening BOGIE lived, some contending that he was a water demon who haunted BOGS and other somber places, while others believed he lived under stairs and in unused cupboards. The creature was ugly beyond words, seated on top of a pile of bones with blood dripping out of his mouth.

Tom Thumb   British folkloric figure. Although the tale of a man the size of a man's thumb only dates to medieval times, the motif of tiny people is consistent with Celtic FAIRY lore. Tom's adventures took him to the court of king ARTHUR at CAMELOT, where he arrived in the belly of a SALMON which was intended for the king's supper.

toot mounds   British mythological site. Many round hills that can be found in the English countryside go by the common name of "toot mounds," presumably related to an Indo-

European real word meaning "to stick out" which evolved into such words as "tit" and "teat." Because of their breast shape, some of the hills were topped by pre-Celtic people with CAIRNS to form nipples, reinforcing the idea that the earth was seen as a womanly, probably maternal, body. The most famous such hills are in Ireland and are known as the PAPS OF DANU.

Tor British mythological site. Near the small town of GLASTONBURY in southwestern England, a strange pyramidal hill rises. Called the Tor, it was renowned as an entrance to the OTHER-WORLD and as the home of the king of FAIRY-LAND, called in Welsh GWYNN AP NUDD. The Celtic saint Collen met the FAIRIES and their king on the hilltop, where he saw a beautiful palace filled with dancing figures. When asked how he liked it, Collen threw holy water at the palace, whereupon everything disappeared.

The Tor is connected with many Arthurian legends, for some contend that Glastonbury was none other than AVALON itself, the Isle of Apples where the great LADY OF THE LAKE conducted ARTHUR. On the hilltop stands a tower dedicated to ST. MICHAEL, who although a Christian figure may have been absorbed into an earlier god or hero; upon the tower is carved BRIGIT milking a COW, an image that is also found in other Glastonbury sites. The tower stands near an Iron Age settlement, showing that there has been continuous habitation in the area for more than 2,000 years.

Beneath the hill are two WELLS. One, the famous Chalice Well or Blood Spring, has waters stained with iron so that they appear RED as blood. The other, the White Spring, has no such coloring. The presence of TWIN wells with waters of different colors would doubtless have drawn the attention of ancient people to this powerful site.

A figure of this name appears in Arthurian legend as a common-born man who desired to become a knight of the ROUND TABLE and who, after succeeding in that goal, was revealed to be the illegitimate son of king PELLINORE.

Torba See MURNA.

torc (torque) Celtic religious object. Throughout the ancient Celtic lands, archaeologists have found SPIRALS of coiled metal, often of GOLD and often elaborately decorated. These torcs can be massive or slender, and their use is made clear from sculptures and bas-reliefs. They were worn about the neck, with the opening facing to the rear. However beautiful the workmanship, the torcs do not seem to have been simply ornamental, for they are found around the necks of gods and goddesses, as though indicating a divine stature. Worn by humans, they may have had a similar meaning—of religious dedication—or may have been indications of high social rank. The bodies of BOG PEOPLE are often found wearing torcs, suggesting that they may have been HUMAN SACRIFICES rather than criminal executions.

Torc Triath Irish mythological figure. The king of BOARS, this figure is parallel to the Welsh TWRCH TRWYTH; some texts say it was one of the magical possessions of the goddess BRIGIT.

Torna Irish hero. A minor character in the story of the great king of TARA, NIALL of the Nine Hostages, Torna was a BARD who prophesied a great future for the baby Niall and offered assistance to his mother CAIRENN.

totem Cosmological concept. This word is used by scholars to refer to an animal (occasionally, plant) believed to have been the ANCESTOR or ancestral mother of a tribe. Because of this ancient connection, the members of that tribe were forbidden to kill or eat the flesh of their onetime relative. Vestiges of such a belief system are suggested by certain folk beliefs, such as the supposed descent by some coastal Irish families from SEAL women, and by mythological tales such as that of the king CONAIRE, who was forbidden to kill birds because his mother was descended from them.

Toutiorix Continental Celtic god. Known only from a single inscription, this god seems to have been an ancestral god or personification of the tribe, similar to TEUTATES. The Romans identified Toutiorix with their healing god of the sun, APOLLO.

transmigration of souls (metempsychosis) Cosmological concept. Scholars do not agree on whether the ancient Celts believed in REINCARNATION, although there are some texts from Roman times that appear to refer to such a belief. Among those who do accept the idea, most agree that humans were not necessarily reborn as humans but rather experienced what is called transmigration of souls, moving into the bodies of various animals, birds, and even insects. Irish mythology is filled with references to such events, as when the fair ÉTAIN was changed into a fly and impregnated her own mother so that she could be reborn as a human; the warring swineherds FRIUCH and RUCHT, who were reborn as RAVENS and STAGS and BULLS; and the great BARD TUAN MAC CAIRILL, who lived as an EAGLE and a SALMON.

trash (guytrash)   British folkloric figure. A form of the SKRIKER, this evil being appeared just before death as a shaggy DOG (*trash*) or a COW (*guytrash*).

tree Cosmological concept. Trees were not, to the Celts, merely large woody plants. They were also religious symbols of the highest order. The tree occupies many levels of reality, with its roots hidden in the dark underground and its branches reaching for the sky. For this reason, the tree represented wisdom: In both Irish and Welsh, the words for tree (*fid* and *gwydd*) and wisdom or wise one (*fios* and *gywddon*) are related.

This sense of the sanctity of trees is recorded by the earliest writers, for Tacitus describes the dark groves of ANGLESEY, where the DRUID orders made their last failed stand against the invading Romans, while other classical writers claimed that the Celtic NEMETONS or sacred groves were horrific places where the trees were stained with the blood of HUMAN SACRIFICE. Whether this is true or represents anti-Celtic propaganda, several sixth century B.C.E. sites in Germany (at Goloring and Goldberg) seem to indicate that shrines were built around a huge central post, believed to represent a sacred tree. The same building style was found in Ireland, at the great capital of ULSTER called EMAIN MACHA. In addition, in some regions of Roman Gaul have been found the tree-shaped JUPITER columns, carved of stone but perhaps originally made of wood.

Many tribal names on the Continent suggest that people saw themselves as descended from trees: Eburones from YEWS, Lemovices from ELMS. Individual names, too, referred to trees, as with Guidgen ("son of wood") and Guerngen ("son of alder"). In Irish mythology we find figures bearing tree names, like Mac Cuilen ("son of holly") and Mac Ibar ("son of yew"). All these names suggest that the tree's upright form was seen as parallel to that of humans, so much so that trees could establish human families.

Individual trees were honored into historical times in Ireland. There, legend says that FIVE great trees were especially magical: the Tree of Ross, a yew that grew from a seed of a tree in the biblical PARADISE, bore fruit without ceasing; the Tree of Mugna, an OAK, produced 900 bushels of acorns every year, as well as the same amount of APPLES and nuts; the Tree of Tortu, an ASH, was so huge that when it fell, it reached across the island; the Tree of Dathi, named for a poet that it killed as it fell; and the many-branched tree of UISNEACH, which grew on the sacred mountain in the center of the island. The trees were planted by an otherwise unknown mythological figure named Trefuilngig Tre-eochair, who carried a branch from the land of the setting sun. As he passed over Ireland, berries fell from the branch, from which the five great trees all grew.

Medieval Irish law, called the BREHON laws after the druidical judges who originally articulated them, treated trees like people by dividing them into classes. There were seven noble trees, for which fines or ÉRICS had to be paid if they were cut down or injured; these were the oak, HOLLY, HAZEL, apple, BIRCH, ALDER, and WILLOW. Other trees had lesser value in the legal system. These were the peasant trees (elm, hawthorn, aspen, quicken), the shrubs (blackthorn, ELDER, spindle, test-tree, honeysuckle, bird-cherry, and white hazel), and the herbs (GORSE, HEATHER, broom, bog-myrtle, and rushes).

The most sacred tree was undoubtedly the oak, which was honored by the druids, who also believed in the magical potency of the MISTLE-TOE that grows parasitically on that species. That the Celts hung on to their sense of the sacredness of trees long into Christian times can be detected through the many and continued warnings by Christian clerics and rulers against tree worship. In the seventh century, the archbishop of Canterbury pronounced that "no one shall go to trees, or wells, or stones, or enclosures, or anywhere else except to God's church, and there make vows or release himself from them." Were people not using trees, along with holy WELLS and ancient stones, as sites of prayer and petition, there would have been no reason to inveigh against the practice. Three hundred years later, King Edgar felt compelled to "enjoin that every priest to zealously promote Christianity and totally extinguish every heathenism; and forbid well-worshiping and necromancies, and divinations, and worship with various trees and stones." In Ireland, COINS are still offered to sacred trees (see BILE) at holy wells; the practice is discouraged—because metal pounded into the bark has killed more than one sacred tree—but survives nonetheless.

Sources: Clarke, David. *Ghosts and Legends of the Peak District*. Norwich: Jarrold Publishing, n.d., p. 16; Green, Miranda. *Symbol and Image in Celtic Religious Art*. London: Routledge, 1989, p. 151; Hull, Eleanor. *Folklore of the British Isles*. London: Methuen & Co., Ltd., 1928, pp. 118–135.

tree alphabet (Beth-Luis-Nuin) Cosmological concept. The Celts arranged the most familiar and valuable TREES of their lands into a series that had mystical meaning and could be used for DIVINATION. These formed the OGHAM alphabet, each letter of which was named for a tree. The *ogham* letters were drawn using a system of horizontal and diagonal lines; the letters and sounds these symbols stood for are represented below, along with the tree that each letter was linked with. The sound of each letter is the same as the initial sound of the tree's Irish name.

B	Birch (beith)
L	Rowan (luis)
F	Alder (fearn)
S	Willow (saille)
N	Ash (nuin)
H	Hawthorn (huathe)
D	Oak (duir)
T	Holly (tinne)
C	Hazel (coll)
Q	Apple (quert)
M	Vine (muinn)
G	Ivy (gort)
NG	Broom/fern (ngetal)
STR	Blackthorn (straif)
R	Elder (ruis)
A	Fir/pine (ailm)
O	Gorse (onn)
U	Heather (ur)
E	Aspen (edhadh)
I	Yew (ido)
EA	Aspen (ebhadh)
OI	Spindle (oir)
UI	Honeysuckle (uileand)
IO	Gooseberry (iphin)
AE	Beech (phagos)

This alphabet has been the source of some controversy, with some scholars dismissing its importance, while others stress it. It was not used as our alphabet is, as a means of transcribing literary works and other compositions for later reading, but rather as a divinatory tool and as a means of memorizing.

Tree of Tortu (Irish mythic object, Ash of Tortu, Tree of Dath-î)   One of the five great TREES of Ireland, it was an ASH, one of the most sacred trees to the Celts. The tree of Tortu was so huge that when it was felled it stretched across Ireland.

tree soul   Scottish folkloric symbol. Just as a human soul could lodge in a rock or an animal, the EXTERNAL SOUL could also reside in a tree. This belief may derive from the widespread Celtic belief in the sanctity of TREES.

Tregeagle (John Tregeagle, Jan Tregeagle) Cornish folkloric figure. Once in Cornwall, legend says, lived an evil man who pledged his soul to the DEVIL after killing his wife. He outwitted his fate, however, because he was so selfish that he would not leave earth after his death but remained to interfere with neighbors who wished to use his land. Finally a local clergyman, intent on saving even lost souls, gave him the task of emptying a pool with a seashell, which he did until he wearied. At the moment he stopped to rest, the devil appeared and dragged him away, "roaring like Tregeagle," as the Cornish saying goes.

Source: Spence, Lewis. *The Minor Traditions of British Mythology*. New York: Benjamin Blom, Inc., 1972, p. 96.

Trenfher   See OGMIOS.

Trewa   Cornish folkloric site. At this region near the town of Zennor, WITCHES were said to meet for their MIDSUMMER festival, lighting fires on Burn Downs and dancing around, casting spells and otherwise concocting magic and mischief. The festival was centered on a strange rock formation called Witches' Rock, which local superstition holds is certain protection against bad luck, if one touches it nine times at the stroke of midnight.

triad   Welsh and Irish literary form. Because of the mystic importance of the number THREE and to facilitate memorization by providing a standard formula, poets and other BARDS composed many short poems that listed three examples of qualities, people, and places. Triads list the THREE SPLENDID WOMEN of king ARTHUR's court, the THREE SORROWS OF IRELAND, and many other groups. Scholars examine the triads for the mythological material they encode.

Source: Bromwich, Rachel. *Trioedd Ynys Prydein: The Welsh Triads*. Cardiff: University of Wales Press, 1961.

Triduana   British goddess. In a story similar to one told of Ireland's BRIGIT, this minor British goddess is said to have pulled her eyes out of her head to avoid an unwanted suitor. As Brigit was a triple goddess, and Triduana's name includes the syllable for "three," it is possible this was a local title of the goddess.

triplicity   See THREE.

Tristan   Cornish hero. The story of Tristan and his fated love, ISEULT, is one of the great romances of the Celtic world. He was a young warrior, strong and vigorous; he was talented in the arts, being a fine musician and storyteller. And he was handsome as well, easy on the eyes of the many maidens who swooned after him, but Tristan was fated to love and be loved by the wife of his king.

When that king—Tristan's uncle, MARK of Cornwall (sometimes, Cornouille in Brittany)—discovered a hair of the most glorious gold, he determined to marry the woman to whom it belonged. That woman was Iseult, and Tristan traveled to Ireland to escort her to her wedding. On the way, Iseult's handmaid BRANGIEN gave the two a potion to relieve their thirst. It was no ordinary drink, however, but a magic brew from Iseult's mother, who to assure her daughter's happiness had concocted a potion for her wedding night. As she was meant to do with her king, Iseult fell in love with the handsome knight Tristan.

The couple tried to be true to their vows to king Mark, and the wedding went forward but eventually Tristan and Iseult consummated their love. Despite their happiness, Iseult finally returned to her husband. Heartbroken, Tristan married a woman with the same name, but he could not bring himself to sleep with her, and when he heard the false news that his beloved Iseult was dead, he died himself.

The story, long viewed as only a romantic tale, has its basis in the myth of the goddess of SOVEREIGNTY who chooses as her mate the strongest and most virile lover. The same story appears in variations throughout the Celtic lands: in the story of king ARTHUR, his queen GUINEVERE, and her knight LANCELOT in Britain; and in the Irish myth of the aging hero FIONN MAC CUMHAILL, the glorious GRÁINNE, and the handsome DIARMAIT.

trooping fairies Folkloric motif. FAIRIES came in two varieties: SOLITARY FAIRIES like the LEPRECHAUN kept their own company and avoided others of their kind, and the more common trooping fairies who lived together in great palaces where they danced and sang the day away. (Some writers add a third category of fairy being: the domestic fairy like the BROWNIE who, although living without other fairy kin, was nonetheless sociable to humans.) Generally these fairies caused little trouble to humans who left them alone, although sometimes they rode forth on the WILD HUNT to steal babies and brides AWAY to FAIRYLAND.

trow Scottish folkloric figure. On the Shetland and Orkney Islands, these figures represent the most common kind of FAIRY. Like the Scandinavian trolls, from whom their name probably derives, the trows did not like sunlight and so were nocturnal creatures. Unlike trolls, trows were not typically turned to stone by sun-

light but were merely paralyzed, to return to life at nightfall.

Trows were found in two varieties. The sea trow lived beneath the waves, like a MERMAID or SEAL, while the land trows could be GIANTS or human-sized gray-coated fairies. If you met one on the road, he walked backward rather than toward you. Seeing one was unlucky, but overhearing them talking to each other brought good luck.

Sources: Keightley, Thomas. *The Fairy Mythology.* London: H. G. Bohn, 1870, p. 105; MacGregor, Alasdair Alpin. *The Peat-Fire Flame: Folk-Tales and Traditions of the Highlands & Islands.* Edinburgh: The Moray Press, 1937, p. 104; Spence, Lewis. *The Minor Traditions of British Mythology.* New York: Benjamin Blom, Inc., 1972, p. 52.

Tryamour Arthurian heroine. In the poetry of Marie de France, this FAIRY LOVER traded wealth for sex with the knight LAUNFAL but, like any such woman, made one demand: that he never boast about her. He was unable to fulfill his promise, as is common in such cases, but Tryamour was less punitive than others of her race and permitted Launfal to join her in the OTHERWORLD.

Trystan (Drystan, Drystan fab Tallwch) Welsh hero. In a Welsh-language version of the familiar tale of TRISTAN and ISEULT, the hero and heroine are named Trystan and ESYLLT, and she is the wife of king March ap Meirchion. The couple eloped to a forest, where they were besieged by March's three armies. The battle was bloody and brutal, and when it appeared that Trystan might win, king ARTHUR was called in to negotiate a truce. That wise king told them to share the woman's favors, with one having her in the summer, the other in the winter. March chose first: he wanted winter, when nights were longest, but Trystan tricked him, claiming that because yew trees are green year-round, he would keep Esyllt forever. Trystan may have derived from the lore of the PICTS, a mysterious northern British people whose cultural background is unknown.

Tuag   Irish heroine. At the age of 15, this lovely girl caught the eye of the god of the sea, MANANNÁN MAC LIR, although she had been reared on the royal hill of TARA by the high king CONAIRE himself. To ensure that she was kept safe, Conaire decreed that no man should approach Tuag's home. Many nobles and kings came to court to seek her hand, but Manannán was determined to wed her, so he sent his BARD, the dwarf FER Í, as his emissary. Fer Í disguised himself a woman and crept into her chambers, where he sang a lullaby so potent that she fell into a dreamless sleep. Continuing to sing to the girl, Fer Í hoisted her onto his shoulders and carried her away. Later, exhausted from carrying her strong body on his small shoulders, he set her down while he rested. Unfortunately, he chose his resting place poorly, for the waters of the Bann River rose and carried Tuag away, drowning her.

Similar stories are told of many river goddesses, such as BÓAND and SÍNANN, so Tuag may be the goddess of the Bann River. Its estuary, Tuag Inber, bears her name. Three great waves were said to dash against Ireland's coasts: the wave of the FAIRY QUEEN CLÍDNA, the Wave of Rudraige, and the wave that strikes the shores at Tuag Inber.

Source: Gwynn, Edward. *The Metrical Dindshenchas.* Royal Irish Academy, Todd Lecture Series. Dublin: Hodges, Figgis, and Co., Ltd., 1906–1924. Reprinted Dublin Institute for Advanced Studies, School of Celtic Studies, 1991, pp. 61–63.

Tuairisgeal   (t-Urraisgeal)   Scottish folkloric figure. When the king of Ireland was out riding in Scotland one day, he met this strange man who lured him into gambling. Tuairisgeal seemed an easy mark: First he lost his wife, then his horse. The third time, Tuairisgeal won, earning the right to ask anything of the king. He wanted only one thing: the answer to an unlikely question. How had his father died? The king did not know, so he set off to find out. Riding Tuairisgeal's horse and helped by Tuairisgeal's wife, the Irish king finally found himself in the court of Greece, where he learned that Tuairisgeal's father had been a monster who had turned children into WOLVES. The king of Greece lost several children to the monster, and at last when his daughter was threatened by a monstrous claw, she was protected by angry wolves—her transformed brothers and sisters. One bit off the monster's hand, after which the king of Greece tracked the creature to his home and killed it. The wolfish children were immediately restored to their human forms, and the king of Ireland had to bring bad news back to the mysterious gambling stranger.

Source: McKay, John G. *More West Highland Tales.* Vol. 2. Scottish Anthropological and Folklore Society. Edinburgh: Oliver and Boyd, 1969, p. 3.

Tuan mac Cairill   (Tuan Mac Carell)   Irish hero. The brother of the early Irish invader PARTHOLÓN, Tuan survived the plague that killed off his people and lived on in a series of forms, including a STAG, a BOAR and an EAGLE. After many such REINCARNATIONS, Tuan became a SALMON that was eaten by a woman who became pregnant (see PREGNANCY THROUGH DRINKING, EATING). Reborn as a human, Tuan remembered all his lives, which made him a great and eloquent BARD. A similar story in Wales told of the boy GWION who, eaten by the goddess CERIDWEN while SHAPE-SHIFTING, was reborn as the bard TALIESIN.

It was Tuan who narrated the mythological history of Ireland called the *BOOK OF INVASIONS.* He did so as an expert witness, having lived through almost all of Irish history. Some texts claim that Tuan was the same as the salmon of WISDOM, otherwise known as FINTAN.

tuath   Irish concept. This word, often translated as "tribe," had a more complex meaning in ancient Irish than merely a group of people, for it also referred to the land upon which that group lived. Each tuath chose its own king. Ireland had approximately 150 tuaths, hence the large number of kings in Irish mythology and history. Some scholars assert that the usual number of members of a tuath was approximately 3,000, leading to a proposed total population for the island of nearly a half-million people. A similar word appeared in continental Celtic languages, where it became the basis for the name of an apparent tribal god, TEUTATES.

One ancient legal text says that not only does each tuath need a king, but other offices must be filled as well: BARD, churchman, and scholar. Kings were paid taxes (usually in food) by the tuath and could call upon the able-bodied men to assist in protecting the land and its people. Most people stayed within the physical territory of their tuath virtually all their lives, seeing their friends and relations (and their enemies as well) at regular festivals and assemblies called ÓENACH. While most legal rights were confined to the territory of the tuath, the bard or poet had the right to travel beyond the tuath's boundaries and to be treated according to the expected standard.

Source: Kelly, Fergus. *A Guide to Early Irish Law.* Dublin: School of Celtic Studies, Dublin Institute for Advanced Studies. Early Irish Law Series, Vol. III, 1988, pp. 3–4.

Tuatha Dé Danann (Tuatha Dé, De Danaan, de Danaan, Fir Dea)   Irish mythological race. According to the mythological history of Ireland, the *BOOK OF INVASIONS*, the penultimate invaders were a magical race, distant descendants of the earlier children of NEMED. They fought against the monstrous FOMORIANS and the tough FIR BOLG, defeating both to earn the right to rule the land. They kept control of Ireland for nearly 3,000 years, until the final migratory wave struck the island shores. The MILESIANS fought bitterly against the Tuatha Dé, who refused to give way. Finally a treaty was pro-

posed, whereby the land would be divided. The Milesians took the surface world, while the Tuatha Dé took the rest: the misty ISLANDS out to sea, the bottoms of LAKES, and the FAIRY MOUNDS. And so they departed, yet never left, Ireland. They became the FAIRY people, immortal presences that still interacted with their human neighbors, especially at times when the veils between the worlds lifted, like the magical festivals of BELTANE on May 1 and SAMHAIN on November 1.

The Tuatha Dé Danann get their name from DANU, the goddess from whom they were descended; for this reason they are also called Fir Dea, "men of the goddess." They include many of the greatest divinities of Ireland: BRIGIT, goddess of healing, smithcraft and poetry; ÉRIU, after whom the island is named; BÓAND, the white cow goddess of rivers; the three war goddess, BADB, MACHA, and the MÓRRÍGAN; the good god DAGDA; MANANNÁN MAC LIR, god of the sea; the envious physician DIAN CÉCHT; the many-gifted LUGH; and many others. When they were driven from the surface world, they each established a SÍDHE or palace, some of which were especially famous, such as KNOCKSHEGOWNA, where ÚNA lived, and BRÍ LÉITH, home of the loyal MIDIR. There they lived immortal, pleasant lives surrounded by beauty and song, only venturing to this world to engage in FAIRY KIDNAPPING and similarly amoral activities.

Source: MacAlister, R. A. Stewart. *Lebor Gabála Érenn: The Book of the Taking of Ireland, Parts 1–4.* Dublin: Irish Texts Society, 1941, pp. 91–314.

tuathal   See DIRECTIONS.

Tuireann (Turrean)   Irish hero. Like a parallel figure, UISNEACH, Tuireann receives little attention in Irish mythology, although the story of his three sons' deaths is one of the THREE SORROWS OF IRELAND. The young warriors set out after CIAN, a hero with whom their father was at war. When he realized he was surrounded, Cian turned into a BOAR and attacked, but the SHAPE-SHIFTING warriors turned into DOGS and brought him down. They permitted Cian to resume his human shape just before he died. For this murder, the SONS OF TUIREANN had to perform a series of exhausting tasks, from which they died. Their father, who was the consort of the great goddess DANU (sometimes called DONAND in this tale), himself died of sorrow at hearing the news.

Tuiren   See UIRNE.

tulman   Scottish folkloric site. This word is used in Scotland to describe the palace inside a FAIRY MOUND.

turning the jacket   Irish folkloric symbol. Like carrying IRON or SALT, turning one's clothing backward or inside out is supposed to be a sure protection against FAIRIES, who otherwise might kidnap a traveler AWAY.

Turoe Stone   Irish mythological site. In a field outside the small town of Loughrea near Galway City, a human-sized boulder stands upright, its top swirling with ornate bas-reliefs. It originally stood near a rath called Feerwore but was moved in historical times to the current site. The ornamented stone appears to be in the LA TÈNE style, suggesting that it is Celtic in origin. What purpose it was intended to serve is unknown, but four other pillar stones are known in other parts of Ireland: at Castle Strange in Co. Roscommon, Killycluggin in Co. Cavan, Mullaghmas in Co. Kildare, and Derrykeighan in Co. Antrim. Such stones may have been symbolic central points, like the STONE OF DIVISIONS on the hill of UISNEACH, which is said to be Ireland's exact center. A replica of the Turoe Stone can be seen in the National Museum in Dublin.

Source: Harbison, Peter. *Pre-Christian Ireland: From the First Settlers to the Early Celts.* London: Thames and Hudson, 1988, p. 158.

Tweedie   Scottish folkloric figure. This minor water spirit was the child of a water demon who lived in the Tweed River.

twins   Cosmological concept. Although THREE was the most significant number to the Celts, there is also evidence that they saw symbolic value in the number two. Celtic mythology frequently pictured goddesses who gave birth to twins. Typically one twin was light and the other dark or, as in the case of the Welsh NISIEN and EFNISIEN, one good and the other evil. The Romans associated such twin gods with their own Dioscures, Castor and Pollux.

Twrch Trwyth (Twrch Trwyd)   Welsh monster. In the tale of *KULHWCH AND OLWEN*, the human hero Kulhwch sought the hand of the fair Olwen, but her father YSPADDADEN PENKAWR refused to permit the wedding until the groom had performed 40 impossible tasks. The most difficult was the capture of a COMB, razor, and scissors from the horrifying Twrch Trwyth, who appeared to be a monstrous BOAR but was in reality a bewitched king trapped in animal form for his misdeeds. With the help of MABON, freed from bewitchment to help with the quest, the great boar was found and captured. Given that Kulhwch's name means "pig-run," the connection between hunter and prey appears close.

tylwyth teg (fair family)   Welsh folkloric figure. This name is often used as a NAME FOR THE FAIRIES in Wales; there as in other Celtic lands, it was believed impolite or unlucky to refer the FAIRIES by their real names. The king of this fair family was GWYNN AP NUDD. Small, childlike beings, the *tylwyth teg* wore homespun clothes of blue, unlike most fairies who wore GREEN or RED. Petroleum was their BUTTER and toadstools, their bread.

Tyronoe   See MORGAN.

Uaithne (Uathe) Irish folkloric figure. The harper who served the beneficent god, the DAGDA, Uaithne eloped with the Dagda's consort BÓAND, with her he had three children, including the musician SÚANTRADE, who inherited his father's great talent. The name is also given to the Dagda's magical HARP, which would only sing when its owner demanded it.

Uathach (Uathach of the Glen) Scottish mythological figure. The daughter of SCÁTHACH, the WARRIOR WOMAN of the Isle of Skye, Uathach met the budding hero CÚCHULAINN at the border of her mother's lands (the "glen" in her title) and challenged him. Despite putting forth enormous effort, neither could win against the other. Realizing that she had met her equal and finding that enormously attractive, Uathach then set about helping Cúchulainn with his studies in the martial arts. Although they shared a bed as well as lessons, Cúchulainn finally left Skye to return to his home in Ulster, abandoning Uathach to return to his intended wife EMER, to whom he had pledged fidelity. A variant of the tale says the hero wounded Uathach and then, when another lover arrived to help her, killed him, although whether he acted out of jealousy or defensiveness is unclear; in another tale, Uathach gave Cúchulainn his greatest weapon, the mysterious magical GÁE BULGA, as a reward for his sexual performance.

Uath mac Imoman Irish mythological figure. In the Irish story of the *Feast of BRICCRIU*, the warrior Uath mac Imoman challenged all of Ireland's heroes to a test of their courage: He would let them cut off his head, if they would do the same afterward. Two of ULSTER's finest warriors refused, but the great CÚCHULAINN agreed, despite knowing that Uath had FAIRY blood and thus was able to regrow his head. Cúchulainn's courage was rewarded, and he went uninjured, for the blade of Uath's sword refused to kill him. For this peculiar feat, Cúchulainn was hailed as the land's greatest warrior, an honor that troublemaking Briccriu used to stir up the rest of the warriors against him.

Ucuetis Continental Celtic god. This obscure god, consort of the goddess BERGUISA, was depicted carrying a HAMMER, which may indicate that he was a parallel to the Irish god of fertility, the mallet-wielding DAGDA, or a local form of the hammer-bearing god SUCELLUS.

Uffington See WHITE HORSE OF UFFINGTON.

Uicce Irish hero. This obscure leader of the MILESIANS was, according to the *BOOK OF INVASIONS*, an important early Irish warrior of whom little is now known.

Uigreann (Uirgriu)   Irish hero. Although this obscure hero plays only a small role in Irish mythology, that role is significant, for he was killed by the great hero FIONN MAC CUMHAILL. Fionn, in turn, was killed by Uigreann's five sons, who all cast their spears at once.

Uirne (Tuiren, Tuirn, Tuirreann)   Irish mythological figure. The mother of the favorite hunting dogs of the heroic FIONN MAC CUMHAILL was his sister or aunt, Uirne, who was transformed into a DOG by a jealous rival for the affections of her husband ULLEN. Uirne was pregnant when the enchantment struck her, and so her children were born as TWIN puppies, BRAN and SCEOLAN, who grew up to become Fionn's companions. While their mother was released from the spell, her twins remained forever trapped in canine form.

Uisneach (Usnech, Usna, Uisnech, Usliu, Usnach, Usnoth)   Irish mythological site. In the geographical center of Ireland, a low hill rises among the rolling lands near the village of Ballymore, between Athlone and Mullingar in Co. Westmeath. Although from its base Uisneach is a nondescript hill, the view from its summit is extraordinary, for almost the entire island can be seen from that single vantage point. Ireland's bowl shape, with mountains along the seashore rim and a great interior plain, is clearly visible from the top of the mountain that was, in ancient times, recognized as the island's magical center (see MIDE).

In Celtic cosmology, the center is not so much a physical as a metaphoric or spiritual location, and thus Uisneach shares with the hill of TARA the title of Ireland's center. In a manner typical of the Celtic view of DUALITY, Uisneach and Tara make up a pair of TWINS that may, in ancient times, have represented two different kinds of power. Tara's associations are predominantly with the political and kingly history of the land, while Uisneach—now little known compared to Tara, whose fame remains widespread— was the center of spiritual power, the domain of the DRUIDS rather than the kings. The connec- tion between two hills was recognized by ancient geographers such as Giraldus Cambrensis, who called them "alike as two kidneys."

Despite their apparent equality, however, it is Uisneach rather than Tara that is more significant in mythology. For it was on Uisneach that the last wave of invaders, the MILESIANS, met the greatest goddess of the land, ÉRIU. They had previously met her two sisters, FÓDLA and BANBA, each standing upon her own mountain. In each case, the Milesians had promised to name the land after the goddess, provided she let their armies pass unopposed. Fódla and Banba each in turn stood aside, permitting the Milesians to pass to the center of the island, where they met the superlative Ériu. In awe of her power and opulence, the Milesians cast their earlier promises aside so that the island could bear her name, as it still does today.

When Ériu was killed, local legend says that she was buried beneath the STONE OF DIVISIONS, a great, naturally placed boulder on the side of Uisneach that is said to mark the exact point where the four PROVINCES come together. The Stone, sometimes called "the naval of Ireland," is described as showing, on its broken surface, the map of Ireland. More commonly, it was not a goddess killed on the hill but the god LUGH, who was set upon by three gods, MAC CUILL, MAC CÉCHT, and MAC GRÉINE, the last being Ériu's husband. The myths are somewhat fragmented and self-contradictory, but the connection of the hill with the magical center of the island and with its tutelary goddess are invariable.

Apparently the first dwellers on the hill were the FOMORIANS, ancient monsters who warred with the magical TUATHA DÉ DANANN. The Fomorians required that the Tuatha Dé pay tax on all their kneading-troughs, querns, and baking stones, as well as for every male of the tribe. Anyone who refused to pay the taxes had his nose cut off. After the Tuatha Dé conquered the monstrous Fomorians, Uisneach became the home of the strange DRUID MIDE, whose name means "middle"; thus the magician doubles the metaphorical meaning of the hill itself.

Mide lit a huge fire on the hill, fed with tributes from all the other druids of Ireland. When they objected to paying this tax, Mide had them all killed and their tongues cut out; he had the tongues buried in the hill, sitting above them (the source of the hill's name, "over somewhat," although it may also refer to the hill's prospect; the name is also translated as "proudly," for Mide sat proudly over the druids' tongues). Another legend credits the igniting of the Uisneach fire to the druid or fire goddess DEL-BÁETH, from whose blaze FIVE great points of light streamed forth. Some scholars have interpreted the mutilation motif as indicating cultural change and the social oppression that often attends on it.

Fires were important in the mythology of Uisneach. They were also important ritually, for it was on that hill that the first BELTANE fire of each year was lit. Reconstructions of an island-wide ceremony suggest that the hill of Tara responded to the twin fires on Uisneach's summit with its own fires, whereupon the other hilltops of Ireland were similarly set ablaze. Yet early documents also suggest that Tara remained dark, its role in the ceremonies being taken up by other nearby hills such as KNOCKAULIN and TLACHTGA.

Into historical times, Beltane fires were lit on Uisneach, and CATTLE driven between them as a ritual prayer for protection against disease and bad magic. Uisneach was also the site of a great ÓENACH or assembly, presumably held at Beltane. Until recent years, the assemblies continued in nonreligious form as cattle fairs, for the fertile region around Uisneach is one of the most renowned for its herds.

The connection of Uisneach hill to the mythological figure of the same name is unclear. Little narrative exists about the warrior Uisneach, whose wife Ebhla was the daughter of CATHBAD, the evil DRUID who figures prominently in the ULSTER CYCLE, and his wife Maga, an otherwise obscure daughter of the god of poetry, AONGHUS ÓG. The SONS OF UISNEACH figure in a story known as one of the THREE SORROWS OF IRELAND (see DEIRDRE).

Sources: Dames, Michael. *Mythic Ireland.* London: Thames and Hudson, 1992; Gwynn, Edward. *The Metrical Dindshenchas.* Part II. Vol. IX. Royal Irish Academy, Todd Lecture Series. Dublin: Hodges, Figgis, and Co., Ltd., 1906; Joyce, P. W. *Ancient Celtic Romances.* London: Parkgate Books, 1997, p. 36; O'Rahilly, Thomas. *Early Irish History and Mythology.* Dublin: The Dublin Institute for Advanced Studies, 1946, p. 171.

Ulfius   Arthurian hero. One of the knights who served UTHER PENDRAGON, Ulfius assisted his master's plot to SHAPE-SHIFT into the form of duke GORLOIS of Cornwall, so that he might take his pleasure with the virtuous IGRAINE without the lady knowing of the deceit. Ulfius's loyalty continued when he became chamberlain to king ARTHUR, the child conceived as a result of the deception.

Uliad   (Uliadh, Ultonian) Irish mythological figures. This term, now out of fashion, was used to refer to the people of the land of ULSTER, one of Ireland's four great PROVINCES.

Ullen   (Ullan, Illann, Iollann) Irish hero. The husband of UIRNE, sister (or aunt) of the hero FIONN MAC CUMHAILL, Ullen was indirectly responsible for her bewitchment. A woman DRUID became enamored of Ullen and, gaining no attention from him, turned his wife Uirne into a DOG out of spite. This won the druid what she desired, because Ullen slept with her to win back his wife's human form.

Ulster   Irish mythological site. One of the PROVINCES of ancient Ireland, Ulster is not synonymous with the political unit now called by this name, for the old provincial boundaries included three counties (Monaghan, Cavan, and Donegal) that are part of the Republic of Ireland, as well as the six counties that make of Northern Ireland (Armagh, Antrim, Down,

Derry, Fermanagh, and Tyrone) and are part of the United Kingdom. In myth, Ulster was associated with war, as the stories of the ULSTER CYCLE make clear. FINTAN, the SALMON of WISDOM, when asked to describe the attributes of the various provinces, connected Ulster with battle, strife, pride, and conflict. The capital of the ancient province of Ulster was EMAIN MACHA; after the fall of Emain Macha, GRIANÁN AILEACH became the capital.

Ulster Cycle (Red Branch Cycle) Irish mythological texts. The series of tales about the PROVINCE of ULSTER that make up the Ulster Cycle are among the most renowned in Irish literature. The Cycle begins with MACHA, a goddess or FAIRY QUEEN who was betrayed by her human husband. He wagered that she could outrun king CONCOBAR MAC NESSA's best horses, and so she did, despite being ready to give birth to TWINS. As she died bearing her children, Macha leveled a curse that all the men of the province would fall down in intense pain whenever invasion threatened (see DEBILITY OF THE ULSTERMEN).

This left the province vulnerable to attack, which it suffered when queen MEDB of CONNACHT marched upon the land, intent upon seizing the great bull DONN CUAILNGE, in order to settle a dispute with her consort AILILL mac Máta. The greatest of Ulster's heroes, CÚCHULAINN, held off Medb's encroaching armies, for he was not born of Ulster blood and was therefore exempt from Macha's curse. Other stories in the Ulster Cycle include the tragic tale of DEIRDRE and the SONS OF UISNEACH, the story of NESSA the raped maiden, and of DECHTIRE the miraculous mother.

Úna (Oona, Oonagh, Nuala) Irish heroine. The beautiful FAIRY QUEEN of MUNSTER, the southwestern province of Ireland, Úna lived in the great mound of KNOCKSHEGOWNA (Cnoc Sídhe Úna) in Co. Tipperary. Despite her association with Munster, Úna took as her lover the powerful fairy king FINNBHEARA of the western

province of CONNACHT. Although he constantly cheated on her with non-fairy women, she did not hold it against the human race, to whom she was beneficent. One of the most famous stories of Úna tells how, annoyed by a drunken piper, she turned herself into a calf and, with the piper clinging to her back, made a massive leap to the shores of the Shannon River. When the piper appeared undismayed by his calf-assisted flight, Úna forgave him his bad piping and returned him to the place from which she had stolen him.

Uncumber (Liberata, Livrade, Wilgefortis, Saint Uncumber) British folkloric figure. It is possible that the SAINT of this name disguises an ancient goddess of the region around Burton, in Sussex, where Uncumber is still honored. She has strange duties for a Christian saint, for Uncumber was charged with freeing wives from the encumbrance of their husbands. Once called Wilgefortis, Uncumber was a pagan princess of southern France who, threatened by her father with an unwanted marriage, prayed to be made unattractive to men and woke up with a beard.

Undry (Uinde) Irish symbolic object. This name is sometimes given to the great CAULDRON of the beneficent god DAGDA, which fed everyone who needed food and refused no hungry person.

Unseelie Court British folkloric motif. The FAIRIES who screamed through the earth on their WILD HUNT are known by this name, which means "unseemly" or "unholy." While some fairies, like BROWNIES, were helpful to human beings, the TROOPING FAIRIES of the Unseelie Court were dangerous. Anyone who saw them was a potential victim for FAIRY KIDNAPPING. Good fairies who danced and sang but did not kidnap mortals formed the SEELIE COURT.

Urban (Urban of the Black Thorn) Arthurian hero. This guardian figure stood at a RIVER ford, protecting his land from invasion. Magical birds helped him: One, killed by PERCIVAL, was revealed to be an enchanted woman. He plays little part in Arthurian legend.

Urien British mythological figure and Arthurian hero. In the works of the early mythographer and historian Nennius, we learn of four ancient warriors, one of them named Urien. With the others—Dhydderch, Gua-Ilaug and Morcant—Urien attacked the ruler Theodric, who held out against him for three days on the island of Lindisfarne before succumbing to their mightier force.

In Arthurian legend, Urien was the king of Gore and husband of king ARTHUR's half sister, the sorceress MORGAN; their son was the heroic knight OWEIN. In some texts, Urien is mated with the otherwise obscure MODRON, whom he met at a RIVER ford, where they had intercourse, a motif that occurs as well in tales of the Irish goddess MÓRRÍGAN. Urien's name was adopted by poet William Blake for one of his earth spirits, although there is no evidence from earlier texts that he was a god or FAIRY.

urine (urination) Mythological motif. In Irish and Scottish mythologies, female creator figures carve out gullies and ravines down the sides of mountains by letting out enormous gushes of urine. MEDB stopped the CATTLE RAID on ULSTER to urinate, thus carving out a gulch that can still be seen today. More commonly, the HAG goddess called the CAILLEACH, along with her regional forms such as MÓR, is credited with this landscape-creating behavior.

Urnfield Period of Celtic culture. The earliest period of Celtic culture is called the Urnfield, named for the practice of cremating the dead and then burying the ashes in huge ceramic urns. Whether this period (ca. 13th–8th century B.C.E.) should be called Celtic is arguable, as it is not known for certain what language those buried in Urnfield cemeteries spoke, and therefore whether they were Celtic or not.

uruisg (*urisk*, water-man) British folkloric figure. A stupid and slovenly kind of FAIRY who haunted lonely waterfalls, the *uruisg* was not especially threatening to humans, except for pretty girls who could be terrified by his leering and lurching. Sometimes the *uruisg* appeared like a BROWNIE, willing to help with farm chores provided no recompense was offered, but more typically he hid from human contact.

Uscias Irish hero. The mysterious cities from which the TUATHA DÉ DANANN, Ireland's magical race, originated were each governed by a master of WISDOM. Uscias was the master of the city of FINDIAS, from which the unerring sword of king NUADA reached Ireland.

Usnach (Usnoth)   See UISNEACH.

Uther Pendragon (Uthr Bendragon) Arthurian hero. The father of the great king ARTHUR, Uther Pendragon ("dragon-head") desired the faithful IGRAINE, wife of GORLOIS the duke of Cornwall, and with the assistance of the great magician MERLIN he had his way with her. While Gorlois was away fighting some of Arthur's men, a man looking exactly like him arrived at his home and went immediately to bed with his wife. Gorlois was indeed far away, and the apparent duke was Uther, under a GLAMOUR to appear as Igraine's husband. Once Arthur's mother had conceived him, his father played little additional role in his legend.

Source: Geoffrey of Monmouth. *Histories of the Kings of Britain*. London: J. M. Dent and Sons, 1912, pp. 147 ff.

Varia (Vaum)   Irish heroine. An Irish folktale tells of this nagging woman who was married to an unusually lazy man named DONAGHA. When he was gifted by the FAIRY people with two wishes, he wasted one by asking that the load of wood he was carrying would grow feet so that it could walk by itself. When Varia cursed her husband for his foolishness, he wished that she was far, far away from him. Instantly he got his wish. She was lifted high in the air, touching down at at Teach na Vauria in Co. Kerry, while he was transported to Donaghadee, at the other end of the island in Co. Down.

Vates   Continental Celtic social role. This Latin word may have entered the language of Rome from an original source in a Celtic language. The word, which means "prophet," refers to a social caste of diviners who, like DRUIDS and BARDS, served the religious needs of the people.

Venus   Continental and British goddess. Throughout the Celtic lands occupied by the Roman legions, diminutive figures of clay have been found that represent an ample-breasted woman wearing a hooded cloak, or naked and clad only in the cloak of her long hair. Because the figures often emphasize the public triangle, they are interpreted as FERTILITY figures and are called by the name of the Roman goddess of infatuation, Venus. The name or names that the Celts used for this goddess has been lost.

The name of Venus is also given to a famous statue in Brittany that represents a clearly non-local goddess, Isis of Egypt; but the current shape has been carved over an earlier one, creating an awkward though womanly form. Whether the Venus of Quimpilly represents a remnant of an earlier local goddess cult or an imported divinity is unknown.

Verbeia (Verbia)   British goddess. One of the many RIVER goddesses of Celtic lands, Verbeia was the resident spirit of the River Warfe, known from inscriptions at a Roman fort in Yorkshire. The name, which may mean "winding river" or "she of the cattle," may not be original, but a Latinized form of a Celtic name. Local legend has it that the river goddess appeared on BELTANE morning, on May 1, in the form of a white HORSE; anyone seeing the apparition should be wary of drowning in the river's spring flood. Such threatening tales have been interpreted as indicating a folk memory of HUMAN SACRIFICE (see PEG POWLER). Horses are not typical familiars of the Celtic river goddess, who is more likely to appear as a COW, so the connection of the animal with Verbeia may indicate a confusion with the mare goddess EPONA.

A sculpture found at Ilkley in Yorkshire shows the goddess holding two long snakes in her hands, possibly representing the watery waves of her river. Some scholars have seen evidence of a solar cult in Verbeia's iconography, which includes SPIRALS and WHEELS.

Viereckschanzen (sing., Viereckschanze) Continental Celtic site. Across the Celtic regions of Europe, archaeologists have found these ritual enclosures, surrounded by a square or rectangular ditch. Some show evidence of timber buildings, presumably shrines or TEMPLES, within them; burials too have been found on these sites, as well as the remains of what appear to have been animal offerings. Often there are indications of a WELL in the enclosure.

Vindonnus (Vindonus) Continental Celtic god. The Romans equated this HEALING god with their own APOLLO; he was worshiped in what is today called Burgundy and may have had special power over EYE diseases.

Vinotonus British god. This obscure god may have been connected with wine-making or grape-growing, for his name seems to include the syllable for "wine," *vin-*. A shrine dedicated to Vinotonus, found on the Yorkshire moors, points to his powers as a god of wild NATURE, as does his identification by the Roman legionnaires with their wildwood god SILVANUS. The two associations may be linked by the tendency toward wild behavior of wine-drinkers, or the connection with wine may be a false etymology.

Vintius Continental Celtic god. This obscure god was equated by the Romans with their TWIN god Pollux, an unusual identification that unfortunately does not much illuminate the god's meaning. His name seems to suggest a connection with wind, as does the fact that Vintius was honored by Celtic sailors.

vision See AISLING.

Visucia Continental Celtic goddess. This obscure goddess is known from several inscriptions in southwestern France; sometimes she is seen with a consort, Viscucius, whose name is the male form of her own. It is unclear what her character or powers were.

Vitiris (Vitris, Venus, Hvitiris) British god. Many inscriptions to this popular god have been found in northern England, in contexts that suggest that he had nonnative as well as Celtic followers. However, nothing is known of what he represented, although he is sometimes depicted with a PIG or a SERPENT.

Viviane (Vivienne, Nimue) Arthurian heroine. The FAIRY LOVER of the great magician MERLIN, Viviane may be the same figure who appears in some legends under the name NIMUE, who may in turn be the mysterious LADY OF THE LAKE, protector of king ARTHUR. Viviane is usually credited with Merlin's magical demise. Various reasons are given for her actions toward him: that she was angry when he refused to share his magical knowledge with her, that she was jealous of his wandering affections, or that she wished to save him from the pain of growing old. In any case, she encased the magician in a tree, where he still lives today. Or perhaps she just bewitched him so that he believed he was encased. The location of Merlin's prison-tree is usually given as the legendary forest of BROCÉLIANDE in Brittany.

Vosegus Continental Celtic god. Although like many other divinities of his region, Vosegus is known only from Roman-era inscriptions and sculptures, he is believed to have been the wildwood god of the Vosges mountains in eastern France, which bear his name to this day.

votive deposits Celtic ritual. It was common practice among the Celts to make offerings at holy places. COINS, PINS, and other jewelry, swords and other weapons, clay sculptures of divinities or human forms—any could be offered to the divinity resident in a place, in hopes of gaining some boon or averting some danger. RIVER sources, WELLS, LAKES, and thermal SPRINGS were especially favored locations for making such offerings.

vough (*fuath*, *brollachan*) Scottish folkloric figure. This terrifying female BOGIE or KELPIE was the most fearful apparition encountered in the Scottish Highlands. She could be captured but not held; one apparently successful hunter found, when his companions gathered around to admire his catch, just a smear of jellyfish into which the monster had dissolved. Her name means "hatred" or "aversion," which is how she was generally greeted.

Although usually female, the *vough* occasionally appeared as male. Both had webbed feet and noseless faces; they usually wore GREEN, the FAIRY color. They disliked daylight but enjoyed intercourse, sexual as well as conversational, with humans; thus some families, like the Munroes, claimed to have *vough* blood in their veins (see also SEAL; SWAN MAIDEN). The word *brollachan* appears to describe the *vough* in its immature or larval stage.

Sources: Campbell, John Grigorson. *Witchcraft and Second Sight in the Highlands and Islands of Scotland.* Detroit: Singing Tree Press, 1970, p. 188; McKay, John G. *More West Highland Tales.* Vol. 2. Scottish Anthropological and Folklore Society. Edinburgh: Oliver and Boyd, 1969, p. 14; Spence, Lewis. *The Minor Traditions of British Mythology.* New York: Benjamin Blom, Inc., 1972, p. 23.

vow   See *GEIS.*

voyage (Imram; pl., Imrama)   Irish literary text. One of several categories of literary text from which we derive our knowledge of Irish mythology (see also AISLING, DESTRUCTION, WOOING), the voyage tales describe how a hero travels to the OTHERWORLD and what he encounters there. Some voyage tales have aspects of the aisling (dream-poem); a few have elements of SATIRE. Some famous examples of this genre include the *Voyage of BRAN*, in which a human is lured by a FAIRY LOVER to leave his home; and the *Voyage of MAELDUIN*, in which the hero encounters several frightening Otherworld women while at sea. A similar but distinct form, the ADVENTURE, also describes trips to the Otherworld but pays less attention to the actual journey, focussing instead on the destination.

W

waff   British folkloric figure. In Yorkshire this name was applied to what is called elsewhere a CO-WALKER, a spirit double that appeared just before someone's death. Unlike what occurred in other traditions, however, death could be averted if one spoke sharply to the waff, which became frightened and departed, leaving the speaker a few more years of life.

wake   Irish ritual. After a religious funeral, Irish people today typically gather to share food and drink, stories and music. The tradition is a long-standing one, with possible roots in the pagan past, when the deceased were believed to have gone over to an OTHERWORLD from which they could occasionally return, especially on SAMHAIN night when the veils between the worlds were thinnest. Similarly, the wake may have its roots in a belief that the beloved dead are most vulnerable to FAIRY KIDNAPPING when newly deceased; the wake then served to protect against fairy influences. In contrast, the worldwide fear that the dead may drag the living into the Otherworld with them may have given rise to wake amusements as a means of protecting the living.

Until recent times, the non-Christian aspects of the wake were significant, so much so that priests attempted to discourage traditional games that may have descended from old rituals.

Gathering to "wake the dead" occurred before, rather than after, the funeral service. The body was laid out, face uncovered, often in the parlor or best room; thus the deceased was able to "attend" the wake. Loud KEENING—wailing or sobbing, usually by women—announced that the wake had begun. Although members of the family might keen, unrelated women of the community assisted, expressing grief through loud cries.

During the wake, it was traditional that someone always sit with the body, so that the deceased was never alone while there were people in the house. Visitors arrived over the next 12 to 24 hours, paying respects to the corpse and then finding their way to food and drink. Anyone was welcome, no matter how distantly they knew the family or the deceased; no one was turned away.

Despite the somberness of the occasion, visitors made quite merry, for it was considered ill fortune for a wake to be without laughter. Much of the merriment was verbal, for jokes and stories, puns and rhymes were part of the occasion. Jokes could become quite insulting, with ridicule and mockery formalized in games like "Making the Stack" (a gossip game) and "I Have a Question" (a self-revealing game). Then there were indoor athletic contests, including "lifting the corpse" (not in fact that of the deceased, but any corpulent visitor willing to stiffen his body), wrestling and arm wrestling, and piggyback riding (called "driving the pigs across the bridge")—all likely to cause some commotion in the narrow confines of an Irish cottage.

Some of the games hint at a belief in personal rebirth, as when mourners pretended to be dead and were awakened by their fellows. Others focused on the cyclical rebirth of life implied in sexuality, for kissing and courting games like Frumso Framso, in which ardent kisses were exchanged among virtually all at the wake, were common.

Source: Ó Súilleabháin, Seán. *Irish Wake Amusements*. Cork: Mercier Press, 1967.

Warna Cornish heroine or goddess. The patron saint of shipwrecked mariners, honored on the Isles of Scilly off Cornwall (see SILLINA), may have originally been the goddess of that region or its waters. History records a local habit of leaving offerings at Warna's sacred WELL in an effort to attract the wealth of wrecked ships to the islands; this rather predatory prayer seems at odds with Warna's alleged protective function.

Source: Straffon, Cheryl. *The Earth Goddess: Celtic and Pagan Legacy of the Landscape*. London: Blandford, 1997, p. 83.

warrior women (bangaisgedaig) Mythic motif. Throughout the ancient Celtic lands, we find goddesses whose speciality was war: British ANDRASTE, Irish BADB, Gaulish CATHUBODUA. We also find goddesses and heroines who were warriors: the Irish MEDB of CONNACHT led her armies into battle against the province to the north, ULSTER; the great SCÁTHACH of the Isle of Skye trained heroes like CÚCHULAINN; Scáthách's daughter (or double) AÍFE not only trained with heroes but bore children to them. Beyond such mythological material, we find historical evidence of women who led their tribes into battle, as did the British queens BOUDICCA and Cartimandua, and of women who fought alongside their men to protect their lands and families.

Nonetheless there is general scholarly agreement that Celtic women were not typically warriors.

Source: Clark, Rosalind. *The Great Queens: Irish Goddesses from the Morrígan to Cathleen Ní Houlihan*. Irish Literary Studies 34. Gerrards Cross: Colin Smythe, 1991.

washer at the ford (*bean nigh, bean nighe,* washer-wife, washing fairy) Irish and Scottish folkloric figure. A form of the BANSHEE or death prophet, this spectral woman appeared before a death, washing the clothes of the doomed in a river, stream, or small pool. A passerby heard a noise that sounded like water rippling; it was the sound of her slapping at the laundry in the cold water. She appeared as a small GREEN-garbed woman with RED webbed feet.

Occasionally the washer was said to be the ghost of a woman who, dying in childbirth, left laundry unfinished, but most agree that she was a member of the FAIRY race. Like others of her kind, the washer was generally prescient, able to see other things in the future besides imminent death; thus if you could catch a glimpse of her before she saw you, you could demand a prophecy, which was always accurate. Such fortune-telling was risky, however, because the washer could injure those caught spying on her, inflicting broken bones by waving her washing.

The washer appeared most often before battles, when she had a great pile of laundry to do; the more brutal the battle, the greater her workload. As a result, she was sometimes associated with the war goddess BADB or with the phantom queen MÓRRÍGAN.

Sources: McKay, John G. *More West Highland Tales.* Vol. 2. Scottish Anthropological and Folklore Society. Edinburgh: Oliver and Boyd, 1969, p. 32; Spence, Lewis. *The Minor Traditions of British Mythology.* New York: Benjamin Blom, Inc., 1972, p. 22.

wasteland Mythological motif. Their myths suggest that the Celts believed that if a king were wounded in body or spirit, his land would cease to bear fruit and his people would starve. Many myths revolve around the question of the BLEM-ISHED KING, but it is unclear how such beliefs affected the lives of actual rulers. The most significant literary use of the motif appears in works inspired by the GRAIL legend, in which the FISHER KING was wounded in his genitals (or more discreetly, his thigh) and the land became barren. Exhausted and in pain, the king was unable to rule but only fished in the increasingly sterile LAKES. In Irish legend a BARD was to create a SATIRE fierce enough to drive the failed king from the throne, but in Arthurian romance knights instead sought the sacred Grail to release the land from its endless winter.

water Cosmological concept. The Celts saw fresh water as sacred, whether it ran in RIVERS and SPRINGS or was still in LAKES and WELLS. This appreciation for a vital part of the ecosystem is appropriate to a people to whom NATURE was a source and residence of divinity. Water often appears as a dividing line between this world and the OTHERWORLD; thus FAIRIES live in cities at the bottom of lakes or on islands in the middle of rivers. Water from holy wells, usually devoted to a SAINT or diminished deity, was held to be a HEALING medicine.

water bull (tarbh uisge) Scottish folkloric figure. Like the more common WATER HORSE, this creature from the realm of the FAIRY was unfriendly to humans; it often stood guard at the entranceway to FAIRY MOUNDS or palaces.

water horse (aughisky, agh-iski, eachuisge, each uisge) Scottish and Irish folkloric figure. This horrible being rose from beneath the waves of LAKES or from the ocean, looking like the strongest and most powerful horse ever seen. If you mounted it—unable to resist the temptation to ride as fast as the wind—you would soon regret your decision. The water horse galloped away, so fast that the rider suffocated from lack of breath;

or the animal plunged back into the water, drowning the victim. Even worse were the water horses that grazed quietly by a riverside with no bridge; an unwary traveler who thought to keep clothing dry by riding the horse to the other side found that, once halfway across the river, the water horse dove down and tried to drown the rider.

For those who wanted to risk such a death, it was important to point the water horse's head inland, for if he ever saw water, the rider's fate would be sealed. The creatures, which came out most often in November, were wily enough to take on forms other than equine; sometimes they appeared as helpless maidens or handsome youths, but if you offered them a hand, they turned instantly into a ravening beast who tried to eat you alive. (For this reason it was deemed wise to check the smile of apparent humans you meet at watery places; any sign of green vegetable matter stuck between the teeth was a signal that the water horse had been grazing and shape-shifted when you appeared.) Humans were not their only diet; they also ate CATTLE, so it was dangerous to leave a herd unattended on a lakeshore. Sometimes they inexplicably left the organs of their victims in the grass, to be found by grieving relatives and frustrated herdsmen.

It was almost impossible to kill a water horse, although if you could snare it and hold it over a fire—difficult to do, given the monster's size—it melted into a puddle of slime. Some legends say that all lakes were the residue of ancient water horses, melted away at their death.

See also CABYLL-USHTEY.

water-leaper (llamhigyn y dwr) Welsh folkloric figure. Like the WATER BULL or the WATER HORSE, this monster (a kind of giant toad) hid in the water until a man or beast walked by, whereupon it leaped out, grabbed its prey, and dragged it underwater to eat it.

waulking songs Folkloric motif. The songs that were sung by groups of women as they "waulked" or shrank woolen fabrics to make them waterproof were filled with mythological and folkloric references. Because of the conservative force of such oral transmittal, the material in the songs is often ancient. With the invention of mechanical looms and machines to process woolens, the tradition of women's singing has been in serious decline, although some contemporary artists like Scotland's Capercaille have recorded and made available some of the age-old, heavily rhythmic, songs.

Wayland (Wieland) British folkloric or mythological hero. Like the Irish GOBAN SAOR, Wayland is a folkloric remnant of a mythological character. The SMITH was, to the Celts, a magical being with powers that exceeded those of normal humans; the Germans had similar beliefs, so it is difficult to know whether the smith whose name appears in British legend and folkloric sites derives from one or both cultures. The lameness attributed to Wayland was a likely import from the Mediterranean, where the smith god Vulcan was depicted as crippled. Wayland's handicap was imposed upon him by a legendary king, Nithland (Nidud) of the Niars, who cut his hamstrings, the better to trap him at the forge. Wayland got revenge by killing the king's son and raping his daughter. Among Wayland's many gifts was the forging of supremely effective weapons, such as EXCALIBUR, the sword borne by king ARTHUR.

weasel   See STOAT.

well (tober, tubber)   Mythological site. Hundreds of so-called holy wells are still in active use in Ireland, Scotland, and Wales; in Ireland approximately 3,000 have been recorded. Although usually dedicated to a SAINT, there is clear evidence that they were originally pagan sites, perhaps pre-Celtic but certainly honored in Celtic times. Because fresh WATER was not only a necessity for health and life but also a symbol of the magical OTHERWORLD, wells—

where cool, clean water sprang up from near bedrock, more like a small stream than a deep pit—were especially revered. They were the sites for INAUGURATION of regional kings, who would drink the water as a pledge of fidelity to the SOVEREIGNTY goddess. They were also used, as they still are today, for HEALING rituals. Often the water was believed especially potent on specific days, including the Celtic holidays (IMBOLC, BELTANE, LUGHNASA, SAMHAIN). Later, holy wells were honored as Christian sites, often given saints' names that echoed, like BRIGIT, a Celtic divinity. Rituals at holy wells continue to this day in parts of Ireland and other Celtic lands, usually involving a solemn procession around the water, decoration of nearby trees with ribbons called *CLOOTIES*, and placement of stones, COINS, or other offerings in or near the well's water.

Wells were believed to have the power to move if offended by ill-considered behavior; taboos were especially strong against placing any kind of litter or garbage in the well. Tales abound of wells departing from one region in the middle of the night, accompanied by FAIRY LIGHTS; the next day the well would be found in its new home in a competing district. Such stories doubtless had the advantage of helping to keep a region's water supply free of pollution.

Wells appear in many myths, usually guarded by a woman, who might be young and beautiful (see LADY OF THE FOUNTAIN) or haggard with age (see CAILLEACH). Some narratives warn that women should not approach certain wells, especially those wherein the SALMON of wisdom swam. Goddesses such as BÓAND and SÍNANN ignored the advice and traveled to the well of SEGAIS or CONNLAs well, only to be drowned when the well rose up and chased them across the land, forming rivers that bear the goddess's names (the Boyne and the Shannon respectively). While usually cited as a warning against women's ambition for learning, the connection of wells with women guardians suggests that the myths may have been altered or that they are in fact creation narratives, for by tempting the well out of its bounds, Bóand and Sínann create the fertile watersheds of Ireland.

Sources: Bord, Janet, and Colin Bord. *Sacred Waters: Holy Wells and Water Lore in Britain and Ireland.* London: Granada, 1985; Brenneman, Walter, and Mary Brenneman. *Crossing the Circle at the Holy Wells of Ireland.* Charlottesville: University of Virginia Press, 1995; Burne, Charlotte Sophia. *Shropshire Folk-Lore: A Sheaf of Gleanings, Part II.* Yorkshore: EP Publishing, 1974, pp. 412–434; Gribben, Arthur. *Holy Wells and Sacred Water Sources in Britain and Ireland: An Annotated Bibliography.* New York: Garland Publishing, 1992; Hull, Eleanor. *Folklore of the British Isles.* London: Methuen & Co., Ltd., 1928, pp. 106–117; Rackard, Anna. *Fish Stone Water: Holy Wells of Ireland.* Cork: Atrium, 2001; Westropp, T. J. *Folklore of Clare: A Folklore Survey of County Clare and County Clare Folk-Tales and Myths.* Ennis, Co. Clare: Clasp Press, 2000, pp. 49–53.

well dressing   Folkloric ritual. In some areas of rural England, notably in Derbyshire and the Peakland district, a springtime tradition is still practiced wherein flowers, seeds, and other natural objects are embedded in clay to form pictures, which are then displayed at holy WELLS. The tradition, which doubtless harks back to rituals of veneration addressed to the wells, continues as a source of civic and community pride. Some of the patterned flower creations are quite elaborate and artistic.

west   Cosmological concept. To the Irish, the direction of sunset was also the direction of the OTHERWORLD. FAIRY beings like NIAMH of the Golden Hair came from the west to lure humans to their lovely but sterile world. ISLANDS off the west coast, such as Inisbofin (the island of the magical white COW), were magical because of their location. Unlike some other cultures, the Irish did not necessarily see west as a symbol of death, except insofar as FAIRY KIDNAPPING took humans AWAY to another world.

Among Ireland's PROVINCES of Ireland, the westernmost is CONNACHT, one of the most culturally traditional regions; thus in Ireland's spiritual geography, west represents WISDOM and tradition.

See BUILDING TO THE WEST.

wheel   Symbolic object. As a HORSE-rearing people who traveled in CHARIOTS, the Celts learned how to made wheels early in their cultural history. Later the wheel became an image of divinities, especially those associated with the SUN, which was imagined wheeling through the sky; rituals in honor of the sun often took the form of rolling wheels (sometimes set ablaze) down a hill. As a chariot wheel, the sun became connected with war, and it was often depicted with warrior gods.

white   Cosmological concept. Words translated as "white" are often found in names and titles of Celtic divinities. The word might be better translated as "shining" or "radiant," for it refers to a quality of light rather than the absence of color. Many deities and heroic figures bear names that suggest they were seen as emanating brilliant light: BÓAND (or BÓ FIND), the Irish COW goddess, whose brightness may be the light reflecting off her RIVER, the Boyne; FINTAN the SALMON, who swam in the sacred WELL and whose flesh carried all the world's WISDOM; and the brilliant hero FIONN MAC CUMHAILL.

White Horse of Uffington   British mythological site. Near Oxford, at a high point of the Berkshire downs, a huge earth sculpture can be seen up to 20 miles away: the flowing, swirling lines of the White Horse of Uffington, created by digging shallowly in the ground. Because the earth is chalky at that spot, removing the grassy turf from the surface created a startling white line in the green grass.

While there are several such British sculptures of great antiquity (see CERNE ABBAS GIANT), only one depicts the image of a HORSE; other chalk-outlined white horses exist, but they are much later in date and unconnected to Britain's prehistory and Celtic era. Almost 400 feet long, the White Horse looks down on a valley called the Vale of the White Horse, where ceremonial horse-racing may have occurred; a nearby small mound called DRAGON Hill shows signs of wear on its top, as though spectators stood there watching events in the valley below. Folklore claims that the hill is flat because ST. GEORGE buried a dragon there; such legends often indicate an important pre-Christian site that needed to be SAINED or sanctified in terms appropriate to the new religion. On the hilltop above the White Horse can be seen the remains of an ancient HILLFORT called Uffington Castle, its steep earthen sides high enough so that, within it, a visitor can see nothing but the sky above.

While it is not certain who carved the White Horse into the hillside, most scholars today believe it was of Celtic origin, perhaps built by the Dubunni who lived in the area. The flowing style recalls horse patterns found on Celtic COINS of the Roman era; one such coin shows a horse almost identical to the one carved into the hillside. Even presuming a Celtic origin, however, archaeologists are not settled on whether the figure represents a divinity and if so, which. Among the Celts, the horse was the emblem of the goddess EPONA; there is no known horse god, nor is the White Horse anatomically a stallion. As the White Horse appears to be running from east to west, it may symbolize the SUN traveling across the sky from dawn to sunset.

While the White Horse itself is an impressive earth sculpture it is even more impressive that it remains at all, for grass would soon obliterate the design were it not continually pulled out. Today the National Trust cares for the monument, but in the past it was "scoured" or cleared of encroaching grasses every seven years, when a huge local festival was held. For as much as 2,000 years, the people around Uffington kept the horse clearly outlined on its height, long after the reason for its creation and its meaning were lost.

Sources: Marples, Morris. *White Horses and Other Hill Figures.* Gloucester: Alan Sutton, 1981, pp. 28–66; Newman, Paul. *Gods and Graven Images: The Chalk Hill-Figures of Britain.* London: Robert Hale, 1987, pp. 19–41.

White Lady   Folkloric figure. In both Britain and Ireland, this term is used of FAIRIES and of the GHOSTS of human women. There is no parallel masculine term.

Wicca   Modern religion. Although some self-identified Wiccans believe they practice an ancient religion, most contemporary scholars trace the development of the rituals and philosophy to mid-20th-century England. Celtic holidays are celebrated (as are the solar holidays of EQUINOXES and SOLSTICES), but contemporary Wicca is not a Celtic religion.

See also WITCHCRAFT.

wicker man   Celtic ritual. According to Julius Caesar, the Celts occasionally fashioned a huge human form from wicker, the bent branches of WILLOW trees. Within this wicker prison, they confined animals and humans and then set fire to the vast structure. As Caesar had been fighting a military campaign against the Celts for years, it is not clear that this report is anything other than wartime propaganda. However, it inspired a CELTIC REVIVAL movie, "The Wicker Man," in 1973.

widdershins   See DIRECTIONS.

Wild Hunt   (Wild Host, Fairy Rade)   Folkloric motif. The idea that the FAIRIES regularly leave their OTHERWORLD residences and ride wildly about the surface world, snatching people from their homes and carrying them AWAY, was found throughout the ancient Celtic lands. In Wales the leader of the Wild Hunt was GWYNN AP NUDD, king of the dead, who rode with the red-eared hounds called the CWYN ANNWN; he rode on storm clouds to collect the souls of the newly dead, to take them to the afterlife. In Scotland King ARTHUR was said to ride on storm winds with the Wild Hunt, and the unforgiven human souls of the SLUAGH made their own wild night rides. At times, only dogs (see GABRIEL HOUNDS) forayed across the sky, baying like hounds of hell. Gazing on the riders was dangerous, but those who put a sprig of protective ROWAN over their doors could watch the procession in safety. Some scholars believe that this folkloric motif grows from Germanic or Scandinavian roots.

willow Folkloric plant. The water-loving willow (genus *Salix*) comes in many forms, from the majestic weeping willow to the scrubby pussy willow that marks the spring. The folk reputation of the plant as a healer has been scientifically verified, because a chemical in its bark is the equivalent of aspirin (whose name, salicylic acid, includes the Latin name for willow).

Winefride (Winifred) See GWENFREWI.

winter solstice See NOLLAIG.

wisdom Cosmological concept. To the Celts, wisdom was not an intellectual construct; wisdom did not arise from reasoned thought but arrived as a gift from the OTHERWORLD of gods, FAIRIES, and the dead. In Irish mythology the god ECNE (Wisdom) was the son of three gods of craftsmanship and knowledge, which suggests that wisdom was thought to arise through the body. Wisdom is also depicted as connected with the watery element, for it could be gained by eating the flesh of a magical SALMON that swam in a secret WELL (see CONNLAS; WELL SEGAIS); it was something earned through effort rather than bestowed like grace, yet the effort was more Otherworldly than mundane. Finally, wisdom was associated with the arts and especially with

POETRY, for DRUIDS and BARDS were often called by names that expressed their wisdom.

witch Folkloric motif. Folktales and legends are filled with stories of people—usually old women, although occasionally men—who have magical powers to enchant and bewitch. At times the powers attributed to these witches resemble those of the CAILLEACH and other weather divinities, for they could raise storms with their CURSES. Witches traveled easily: They could fly across the land, and if they needed to cross the ocean, any vessel would serve, including sieves and eggshells. They were shape-shifters (see SHAPE-SHIFTING) who assumed animal form to work mischief in the area, often stealing the neighbors' BUTTER rather than making their own, taking MILK from the udders of the cows, and bringing fish up onto shore so they could pick them up. They preferred to disguise themselves as HARES or CATS but could also be RAVENS or mice, gulls or sheep.

Sources: Campbell, John Grigorson. *Witchcraft and Second Sight in the Highlands and Islands of Scotland.* Detroit: Singing Tree Press, 1970; Harland, John, and T. T. Wilkinson. *Lancashire Legends.* London: George Routledge and Sons, 1873; p. 248.

witchcraft Cosmological concept. In a famous and controversial book in the mid-20th century, Margaret Murray proposed that the European pagan religion continued to be practiced after Christianization, and that reports gathered by priests of the Catholic Inquisition proved that groups still met in ancient rituals ("sabbats") despite the apparent conversion of the people. Further, she argued that some pockets of rural Europe had kept such traditions alive into the present. Many popular books continue to claim that witchcraft is an ancient religion, practiced continually and without alteration; more serious practitioners recognize that the rituals of contemporary witchcraft (see WICCA) arose in the mid-20th century in England and represent an attempted reconstruction of European paganism. In addition to this contemporary usage, there is a long-standing belief in Celtic lands that WITCHES can cause distress and mischief, but such witches were seen as magically gifted individuals who did not need a coven to work their spells.

Witta Contemporary religion. An invented NEO-PAGAN religion that purports to be an ancient form of Irish paganism, Witta has no basis in any Celtic history or tradition; even the name is an invention.

wodwose (*woodwose*, wild men) British and Scottish folkloric figure. In the forests, it was long believed, lived great hairy wild men, shy beings who avoided human contact but did no harm to anyone. Some traditional British dances and mummers' parades include cavorting imitations of the *wodwose*. The image of the wild man is also found in mythology; in Ireland mad king SUIBHNE lived in a tree, while in legends of king ARTHUR the great magician MERLIN similarly went insane and hid in the forest (see MYRRINN WYLLT).

wolf Symbolic animal. Although now extinct in the ancient Celtic lands, the wolf once hunted through their forests. The wolf shares symbolic meaning with its relative, the tame canine DOG, as a creature that could see into the OTHER-WORLD. In some ancient texts we find references to wolves as SHAPE-SHIFTING people. The Irish *Leabhar Breathnach* tells of people who, descended from wolves, could still change into that form to prey upon their neighbors' cattle, while Giraldis Cambrensis describes a family who turned into wolves every seventh year because of a curse, retaining human language and having prophetic powers. On the Continent the god DIS PATER was sometimes clad in wolf-skin; Julius Caesar reported that the Gauls believed themselves descended from wolves.

wooing (*tochmarc*) Irish mythological text. Among the various categories of Irish narratives are those that tell of the courtship of a woman or goddess. Although all Irish literary texts were written down by Christianized monks, the female characters in such texts are often more vigorous and self-willed than the category title might imply. ÉTAIN, for instance, willingly goes along with an invitation to commit adultery; BECFHOLA grew bored with king DIARMAIT of TARA and took a FAIRY LOVER.

worm Folkloric figure. Looking rather like a SERPENT but entirely fantastic, the worm is a DRAGON figure that derives from Scandinavian mythology, which arrived in Celtic lands with the invading Vikings. That connection may explain why worms are typically found in seaside areas, where Vikings might have landed.

The famous Lambton Worm was an eft, the immature adult form of a newt, which grew to enormous size after being thrown into a WELL by a man sacrilegiously fishing on Sunday. It was hard to conquer because its breath poisoned the air and, every time it was cut in two, it joined itself together and attacked again. In the same way, the Dragon of Loschy Hill would never have been destroyed if a DOG had not carried away the hacked-off parts and buried them, so they could not reassemble themselves. The most famous worm today is surely the Loch Ness Monster, which might also be classified as a SERPENT from the alleged reptilian shape of its head.

Aside from the monstrous worm, there is the mythological creature that makes women pregnant through the mouth (see PREGNANCY THROUGH DRINKING, EATING). This worm is tiny and apparently can breathe underwater, for most miraculous conceptions take place when a woman drinks a glass of water in which the worm is swimming. Many heroes are born from such worm insemination; CÚCHULAINN, to make sure that his parentage was clear and that he was not the child of incest, emerged from the womb clutching a worm in each hand.

wren Symbolic animal. Many species of BIRDS attract legends, but only the stately SWAN has more symbolic significance than the wren, a tiny, nondescript brown bird especially associated with the winter season. In ancient times the bird was considered a prophet, although its cries were notoriously hard to interpret; the glossarist Cormac refers to the wren as "the DRUID bird."

Killing a wren brought bad luck, even death; such ill fortune could extend itself to the herds, which were thought to give bloody milk after a wren's murder. In Brittany, even to touch a wren or its nest would bring acne; worse, lightning could strike the home of such an invader, or the hand that touched the wren's babies would wither and drop off.

One day each year, however, the taboo had to be broken: On a date near the winter SOLSTICE, the year's longest night, boys killed a wren and brought it from house to house, begging for alms "to bury the wren." On the Isle of Man it was servants who hunted the wren, suggesting that the power to blight was not entirely removed, and families might wish to protect themselves by demanding that the hired help put themselves at risk. After capturing the wren, the hunting party fixed it to a long pole and walked around the village, chanting, "We hunted the wren for Robin the Bobbin, hunted the wren for Jack of the Corn; we hunted the wren for Robbin the Bobbin, we hunted the wren for everyone." The wren was then buried, with great ceremony, in the village churchyard, after which Christmas festivities began. Feathers from the buried wren were believed to protect the owner against death at sea.

Source: Frazer, James George. *The Golden Bough.* Vol. II: *Spirits of the Corn and of the Wild.* New York: St Martin's Press, 1913, pp. 317–318.

wulver Scottish folkloric creature. Half-human, half-WOLF, the *wulver* lived like a WOD-WOSE and generally left people alone, although at times he could be helpful to those in need, leaving wild food on their doorsteps.

Y–Z

Yallery Brown British folkloric figure. This evil FAIRY was named for its yellow-brown hair, which made an odd frame around its withered and aged face. Yallery Brown worked mischief even to those who tried to help or befriend him; he was a fairy to be avoided. As he lived in the British Fens, which have long since been drained, he may be no longer a danger to anyone.

Yann-An-Ord (John of the Dunes) Breton folkloric figure. Along the shorelines of Brittany, this unpleasant creature wandered, calling like a seabird; he was a form of the male siren called the YANNIG. He looked like a little old man in a raincoat, rowing in a boat just off shore. He especially created a din at sundown.

yannig Breton folkloric figure. A dangerous FAIRY of Brittany, the *yannig* ate the unwary who did not hide when he called three times.

yarkins British folkloric figure. A member of the Tiddy Folk (see TIDDY MUN), the yarkins lived in the Fens, the great Lincolnshire wetlands that were drained in the 18th century to expand agricultural land. The people of the Fens had a complex and elaborate folklore featuring many fantastic FAIRY creatures; like the Fens themselves, these tales are now virtually lost. Little is now known about the yarkins, except that they demanded offerings to keep the earth fertile.

Ychen Bannog Welsh folkloric figures. These calves of the DUN COW were long-horned and strong; they were also friendly to humans and lured the monstrous AFANC out of its protective LAKE so that it could be killed.

yew Symbolic object. The yew (species *Taxus*) is a sturdy evergreen that can grow to an impressive girth and age. Perhaps for this reason, yews were associated with the OTHERWORLD, with death, and with immortality; they are commonly found in graveyards throughout Britain and Ireland. In mythology a yew betokens transformation, as when the Welsh hero LLEU LLAW GYFFES turns into an EAGLE at his death and perches in a yew tree. Modern science is just learning of healing chemicals found within yew trees, such as taxol, used in fighting breast cancer; as with many ancient beliefs, the Celtic connection between yews and immortality may encode some scientific knowledge.

Yew of Ross Symbolic object. In Irish tradition there were several TREES of great legend, one of which was the Yew of Ross, which the DIND-

SHENCHAS tells us was as broad as it was tall; it bore apples, acorns, and nuts, all at the same time.

y fuwch frech (y fuwch laethwen lefrith) See DUN COW.

Ygerna See IGRAINE.

y mamau (bendith y mamau) Welsh folkloric figures. "The Mothers" was a name given in some Welsh tales to the OTHERWORLD figures otherwise known as FAIRIES. The meaning and significance of the term is unknown; it is unclear whether the fairy folk were believed to be ancestral figures, as the name suggests. *Bendith y mamau*, "the Mothers' blessing," means good luck brought by the fairies.

Ynys Gutrin (Ynys Wydrin) Welsh mythic site. A legendary place that cannot be seen with physical vision, "glass ISLAND" was a women's domain, inhabited only by nine beautiful maidens.

Ynys Wair Welsh mythic site. What is now known as Lundy Island, in the ocean waters off Bristol, was once known as Ynys Wair, the island of Gwair or GWYDION, the magician-BARD who figures so prominently in the mythological tales collected as the *MABINOGION*.

Youdic Breton mythological site. Legend claims that the mouth of hell can be found in the region of Brittany's known as Finistère ("earth's end"), in the BOG of Yeun. Because the Celts did not see the OTHERWORLD as infernal, this legend may be of Christian origin.

Yr Hen Wräch Welsh folkloric figure. The great HAG who lived in the BOG near Aberystwyth sneaked into town on cold misty evenings and breathed on the people there, after which they came down with fevers, chills, and coughing. She appears to have been a protective spirit of the bogs, for she has been inactive since people started burning coal and gas rather than peat. At seven feet tall, with yellow skin and black teeth, she was a frightening figure.

Ys (Is, Ker-Ys, City of Ys) Breton mythological site. One of the great tales of Brittany is that of the pagan princess DAHUT, who spurned the new religion of Christianity despite her father's GRADLON's devoutness. Instead, she gathered the *KORRIGANS*, the FAIRIES who lived in the sea, and had them build her this great crystalline city off the Breton peninsula, in an area so low that it had to be walled to keep the water out (the name means "low town"). It was located in the Baie de Trépassés, "Dead Men's Bay," a treacherous part of the Atlantic that is rich not only in fish but in the wealth of wrecked ships.

Its great seawalls protected Ys from the storms that ravaged the coast. At certain times, the sea-gates were opened, so that the city's wastes could be carried away through an elaborate sluice system. Dahut kept the key to the seawalls on a silver chain around her neck.

The people of Ys grew wealthy and contented. Dahut was content as well, living a life that was both sensual and rapacious, killing men after she had her way with them. As a result, the great city of Ys was doomed; the seawalls broke (or perhaps Gradlon or one of Dahut's lovers opened them) and Ys sank beneath the waves. Some legends claim that you can still see it under the waves at Douarnenez on certain days when the sea is calm and the sunlight just right.

Source: Guyot, Charles. *The Legend of the City of Ys.* Trans. and illus. Deirdre Cavanagh. Amherst: University of Massachusetts Press, 1979.

Ysgithyrwyn Welsh mythological figure. In the story of KULHWCH AND OLWEN, one of the tasks set for the hero was snaring a tusk from this OTHERWORLD boar.

Yspaddaden Penkawr (Yspaddaden Pencawr, Ysbaddaden Bencawar) Welsh mythological figure. The "great GIANT" or "chief giant" of Welsh mythology appears in the romance of *KUL-HWCH AND OLWEN*, in which the titular hero, condemned to marry no other woman than Olwen, asked the assistance of his cousin, king ARTHUR. With Arthur's knights, Kuhlwch located Olwen's home after a year's search. There he discovered that Yspaddaden Penkawr, who needed four men to lift his eyelids, had no intention of letting his daughter marry—because a prophecy had said that he would die on the day of her wedding. He attacked the company, but they defended themselves well, and finally Yspaddaden offered Olwen to Kuhlwch, provided he satisfy 13 difficult challenges and 26 minor ones. Ultimately the hero did so, and as prophesied, Yspaddaden was killed on Olwen's wedding day. Many motifs in the story recall that of BALOR in Ireland.

Yvain See OWEIN.

Yvonne and Yvon Breton heroine and hero. A folktale from Brittany, presumably of Celtic origin, tells of a young woman who attracted the eye of the SUN with her beauty, diligence, and patience. He carried her off to his home in the sky one day, and a year later the family had heard nothing more of her. With his five brothers, Yvon started walking toward the western horizon, hoping to find the land of the sun. After many adventures, the brothers were discouraged—all but Yvon, who continued through trials and tribulations until he found his sister, happily at home in the sun's house. When he returned home, Yvon discovered that ages had passed and that all memory of his family had disappeared from the land.

Source: Luzel, F. M. *Celtic Folk-Tales from Amorica*. Trans. Derek Bryce. Dyfed, Wales: Llanerch Enterprises, 1985, pp. 7–18.

Zeus See JUPITER.

BIBLIOGRAPHY

Aalen, F. H. A. *Man and the Landscape in Ireland.* London: Academic Press, 1978.

Aitchison, N. B. *Armagh and the Royal Centres in Early Medieval Ireland: Monuments, Cosmology and the Past.* Rochester, N.Y.: Crithne Press/Boydell & Brewer, 1994.

Allason-Jones, Lindsay. "Coventina's Well." In Billington, Sandra, and Miranda Green, eds. *The Concept of the Goddess.* London and New York: Routledge, 1996, pp. 107–119.

Almqvist, Bo, Séamus Ó Catháin, and Páidaig ó Héalaí. *The Heroic Process: Form, Function and Fantasy in Folk Epic.* Dublin: The Glendale Press, 1987.

Anderson, Jørgen. *The Witch on the Wall: Medieval Erotic Sculpture in the British Islands.* London: George Allen & Unwin, 1977.

Ashe, Geoffrey. *Mythology of the British Isles.* London: Methuen, 1990.

Barrett, W. H. *Tales from the Fens.* London: Routledge & Kegan Paul, 1963.

Basford, Kathleen. *The Green Man.* Ipswitch: D. S. Brew, Ltd., 1978.

Baugh, Albert C., ed. *A Literary History of England.* New York: Appleton-Century-Crofts, 1967.

Bedier, Joseph. *The Romance of Tristan and Iseult.* Trans. Hilaire Belloc. New York: Vintage Books, 1965.

Berger, Pamela. *The Goddess Obscured: Transformation of the Grain Protectress from Goddess to Saint.* Boston: Beacon Press, 1985.

Billingsley, John. *Stony Gaze: Investigating Celtic and Other Stone Heads.* Berkshire, England: Capall Bann Publishing, 1998.

Bitel, Lisa M. *Land of Women: Tales of Sex and Gender from Early Ireland.* Ithaca: Cornell University Press, 1996.

Bord, Janet, and Colin Bord. *Sacred Waters: Holy Wells and Water Lore in Britain and Ireland.* London: Granada, 1985.

———. *The Secret Country: An interpretation of the folklore of ancient sites in the British Isles.* New York: Walker and Co., 1976.

Bourke, Angela. *The Burning of Bridget Cleary.* London: Pimlico, 1999.

Bradley, Ian. *Celtic Christianity: Making Myths and Chasing Dreams.* New York: St. Martin's Press, 1999.

Brenneman, Walter, and Mary Brenneman. *Crossing the Circle at the Holy Wells of Ireland.* Charlottesville: University of Virginia Press, 1995.

Breton Folktales. London: G. Bell & Sons, 1971.

Briggs, Katherine M. *An Encyclopedia of Fairies: Hobgoblins, Brownies, Bogies, and Other Supernatural Creatures.* New York: Pantheon Books, 1976.

———. *The Fairies in Tradition and Literature.* London: Routledge & Kegan Paul, 1967.

———. *The Folklore of the Cotswolds.* London: B. T. Batsford Ltd., 1974.

———. *The Personnel of Fairyland.* Cambridge: Robert Bentley, 1954.

Briggs, Katherine M., and Ruth L. Tongue. *Folktales of Britain.* London: Routledge & Kegan Paul, 1965.

Bromwich, Rachel. *Trioedd Ynys Prydein: The Welsh Triads.* Cardiff: University of Wales Press, 1961.

Brunaux, Jean Louis. *The Celtic Gauls: Gods, Rites and Sanctuaries.* London: Seaby, 1988.

Buchan, Peter. *Ancient Scottish Tales.* Darby, Pa.: Norwood Editions, 1973. Originally published Peterhead, 1908.

Burne, Charlotte Sophia. *Shropshire Folk-Lore: A Sheaf of Gleanings, Part II.* Yorkshire: EP Publishing, 1974.

Buttimer, Neil, Colin Rynne, and Helen Guerin, eds. *The Heritage of Ireland.* Cork: The Collins Press, 2000.

Byrne, Patrick. *Irish Ghost Stories.* Cork: Mercier Press, 1965.

Callan, Barbara. "In Search of the Crios Bhride." In Patricia Monaghan, ed. *Irish Spirit: Pagan, Celtic, Christian, Global.* Dublin: Wolfhound Press, 2001.

Campbell, J. F. *Popular Tales of the West Highlands.* Vol. III. Edinburgh: Edmonston and Douglas, 1862.

Campbell, John Grigorson. *Witchcraft and Second Sight in the Highlands and Islands of Scotland.* Detroit: Singing Tree Press, 1970.

Carbery, Mary. *The Farm by Lough Gur: The Story of Mary Fogarty.* London: Longmans, Green and Co., 1937.

Carmichael, Alexander. *Carmina Gadelica: Hymns and Incantations.* Hudson, N.Y.: Lindisfarne Press, 1992.

Carr-Gomm, Philip. *The Druid Renaissance.* London: Thorsons, 1996.

Cashman, Seamus, and Seán Gaffney. *Proverbs and Sayings of Ireland.* Dublin: Wolfhound Press, 1974.

Chadwick, Nora. *The Celts.* New York: Penguin Books, 1971.

Clark, Rosalind. *The Great Queens: Irish Goddesses from the Morrígan to Cathleen Ní Houlihan.* Irish Literary Studies 34. Gerrards Cross: Colin Smythe, 1991.

Clarke, David. *Ghosts and Legends of the Peak District.* Norwich: Jarrold Publishing, n.d.

Clarke, David, with Andy Roberts. *Twilight of the Celtic Gods: An Exploration of Britain's Hidden Pagan Traditions.* London: Blandford, 1996.

Coghlan, Peg. *Irish Saints.* Cork: Mercier Press, 1998.

Column, Padraic, ed. *A Treasury of Irish Folklore.* New York: Wings Books, 1967.

Condren, Mary. *The Serpent and the Goddess: Women, Religion and Power in Ancient Ireland.* San Francisco: Harper & Row, 1989.

Cooney, Gabriel. *Landscapes of Neolithic Ireland.* London: Routledge, 2000.

Cosgrove, Art, ed. *Marriage in Ireland.* Dublin: College Press, 1985.

Courtney, M. A. *Cornish Feasts and Folklore.* Penzance: Beare and Son, 1890.

Cowan, Tom. *Fire in the Head: Shamanism and the Celtic Spirit.* San Francisco: HarperSanFrancisco, 1993.

———. "The Pledge to the Elements." In Patricia Monaghan, ed. *Irish Spirit: Pagan, Celtic, Christian, Global.* Dublin: Wolfhound Press, 2001.

Coxhead, J. R. W. *Devon Traditions and Fairy-Tales.* Exmouth: The Raleigh Press, 1959.

Crawford, E. G. S. *The Eye-Goddess.* Chicago: Delphi Press, 1994.

Crawford, H. S. *Irish Carved Ornament.* Cork: Mercier Press, 1980.

Croker, T. Crofton. *Fairy Legends and Traditions of the South of Ireland.* London: William Tegg, 1862.

Cross, Tom Peete, and Clark Harris Slover, eds. *Ancient Irish Tales.* New York: Henry Holt and Co., 1936.

Crossing, William. *Tales of the Dartmoor Pixies: Glimpses of Elfin Haunts and Antics.* Newcastle upon Tyne: Frank Graham, 1890.

Cunliffe, Barry. *The Ancient Celts.* Oxford: University Press, 1997.

Curran, Bob. *Complete Guide to Celtic Mythology.* Belfast: Appletree, 2000.

Curtin, Jeremiah. *Hero-Tales of Ireland.* New York: Benjamin Blom, 1894.

———. *Tales of the Fairies and of the Ghost World Collected from Oral Tradition in South-West Munster.* New York: Lemma Publishing Corp., 1970. Originally published, London: David Nutt, 1895.

Dames, Michael. *Mythic Ireland.* London: Thames and Hudson, 1992.

———. *The Silbury Treasure: The Great Goddess Rediscovered.* London: Thames and Hudson, 1976.

Danaher, Kevin. *Folktales from the Irish Countryside.* Cork: Mercier Press, 1967.

———. *In Ireland Long Ago.* Cork: Mercier Press, 1964.

———. "Irish Folk Tradition and the Celtic Calendar." In Robert O'Driscoll, ed. *The Celtic Consciousness.* New York: George Braziller, 1981, pp. 217–242.

———. *The Year in Ireland.* Cork: Mercier Press, 1922.

Davidson, Hilda Ellis. "The Legend of Lady Godiva." In *Patterns of Folklore.* Totowa, N.J.: Rowman & Littlefield, 1978.

Davidson, L. S., and J. O. Ward. *The Sorcery Trial of Alice Kyteler.* Binghamton, N.Y.: Medieval and Renaissance Texts & Studies, 1993.

Day, Brian. *Chronicle of Celtic Folk Customs.* London: Hamlyn, 2000.

Deane, Seamus, ed. *The Field Day Anthology of Irish Writing.* Vol. 1. Derry: Field Day Publications, 1991.

Delaney, Mary Murray. *Of Irish Ways.* New York: Harper & Row, 1973.

Delargy, J. H. *The Gaelic Story-Teller, with some Notes on Gaelic Folk-tales.* London: Proceedings of the British Academy, 1945.

Dexter, Miriam Robbins. "Queen Medb, Female Autonomy in Ancient Ireland, and Irish Matrilineal Traditions." In Jones-Bley, Karlene, Angela Della Volpe, Miriam Robbins Dexter, and Martin E. Huld, eds. *Proceedings of the Ninth Annual*

UCLA Indo-European Conference. Washington, D.C.: Institute for the Study of Man, 1998, pp. 95–122.

———. "Reflections on the Goddess Donu." *The Mankind Quarterly,* Vol. XXXI, Nos. 1 & 2, Fall/Winter, 1990, pp. 45–58.

———. *Whence the Goddesses: A Sourcebook.* New York: Pergamon Press, 1990.

Dillon, Myles. *The Cycles of the Kings.* Dublin: Four Courts Press, 1994.

———. *Early Irish Literature.* Dublin: Four Courts Press, 1994.

———. *There was a King in Ireland: Five Tales from Oral Tradition.* Texas Folklore Society. Austin: University of Texas Press, 1971.

Dillon, Myles, ed. *Irish Sagas.* Cork: The Mercier Press, 1968.

Dillon, Myles, and Nora Chadwick. *The Celtic Realms.* London: Weidenfeld and Nicolson, 1967.

Dorson, Richard M., ed. *Peasant Customs and Savage Myths: Selections from the British Folklorists.* Vol II. Chicago: University of Chicago Press, 1968.

Douglas, George. *Scottish Fairy and Folk Tales.* West Yorkshire: EP Publishing, 1977.

Ellis, P. Berresford. *The Cornish Language and its Literature.* London: Routledge & Kegan Paul, 1974.

Ellis, Peter Berresford. *Celtic Women: Women in Celtic Society and Literature.* Grand Rapids, Mich.: William B. Eerdmans Publishing, 1995.

Eogan, George. *Knowth and the Passage-Tombs of Ireland.* London: Thames and Hudson, 1986.

Evans, J. Gwenogbryn, ed. *The Book of Taliesin.* Reprint, Llandebrog, North Wales: Old Welsh Texts, 1940.

Evans-Wentz, W. Y. *The Fairy-Faith in Celtic Countries.* Gerrards Cross: Colin Smythe Humanities Press, 1911.

Folk-Lore and Legends: Scotland. London: White and Allen, 1889.

Frazer, James George. *The Golden Bough.* Vol. II: *Spirits of the Corn and of the Wild.* New York: St Martin's Press, 1913.

Gantz, Jeffrey, ed. and transl. *Early Irish Myths and Sagas.* New York: Penguin Books, 1984.

Gantz, Jeffrey, trans. *The Mabinogion.* New York: Barnes & Noble Books, 1976.

Gardner Alexander. *Popular Tales of the West Highlands.* Vol III. London: J. F. Campbell, 1892.

Geoffrey of Monmouth. *Histories of the Kings of Britain.* London: J. M. Dent and Sons, 1912.

Gilroy, John. *Tlachtga: Celtic Fire Festival.* Glanmire, Co. Cork: Pikefield Publications, 2000.

Gimbutas, Marija. *The Language of the Goddess.* London: Thames & Hudson, 1989.

Graves, Robert. *The White Goddess: A Historical Grammar of Poetic Myth.* New York: Farrar, Straus and Giroux, 1948.

Green, Miranda. "The Celtic/Goddess as Healer." In Billington, Sandra, and Miranda Green, eds. *The Concept of the Goddess.* London and New York: Routledge, 1996, pp. 28 ff.

———. *Celtic Goddesses: Warriors, Virgins and Mothers.* London: British Museum Press, 1995.

———. *Celtic Myths.* Austin: University of Texas Press, 1993.

———. *The Gods of the Celts.* Gloucester: Alan Sutton, 1986.

———. *The Gods of Roman Britain.* Aylesbury: Shire Publications Ltd., 1983.

———. *Symbol and Image in Celtic Religious Art.* London: Routledge, 1989.

Gregory, Lady Augusta. *Cuchulain of Muirthemne: The Story of the Men of the Red Branch of Ulster.* In *A Treasury of Irish Myth, Legend and Folklore.* New York: Gramercy Books, 1986.

———. *Gods and Fighting Men: The Story of the Tuatha De Danaan and of the Fianna of Ireland.* New York: Oxford University Press, 1970.

———. *Visions and Beliefs in the West of Ireland.* Gerrards Cross: Colin Smythe, 1970.

Gribben, Arthur. *Holy Wells and Sacred Water Sources in Britain and Ireland: An Annotated Bibliography.* New York: Garland Publishing, 1992.

Grinsell, Leslie V. *Folklore of Prehistoric Sites in Britain.* London: David & Charles, 1976.

Guyot, Charles. *The Legend of the City of Ys.* Trans. and illus. Deirdre Cavanagh. Amherst: University of Massachusetts Press, 1979.

Gwynn, Edward. *The Metrical Dindshenchas.* Royal Irish Academy, Todd Lecture Series. Dublin: Hodges, Figgis, and Co., Ltd., 1906–1924. Reprinted Dublin Institute for Advanced Studies, School of Celtic Studies, 1991.

Harbison, Peter. *Pre-Christian Ireland: From the First Settlers to the Early Celts.* London: Thames and Hudson, 1988.

Harland, John, and T. T. Wilkinson. *Lancashire Legends.* London: George Routledge and Sons, 1873.

Healy, Elizabeth. *In Search of Ireland's Holy Wells.* Dublin: Wolfhound Press, 2001.

Healy, Elizabeth, with Christopher Moriarty, Cerard O'Flaherty. *The Book of the Liffey: From Source to the Sea*. Dublin: Wolfhound Press, 1988.

Henderson, George. *Survivals in Belief Among the Celts*. Glasgow: James MacLeose and Sons, 1911.

Henry, Sean. *Tales from the West of Ireland*. Cork: Mercier Press, 1980.

Herbert, Máire. "Transmutations of an Irish Goddess." In Billington, Sandra, and Miranda Green, eds. *The Concept of the Goddess*. London and New York: Routledge, 1996, pp. 141–151.

Herity, Michael. *Rathcrogan and Carnfree: Celtic Royal Sites in Roscommon*. Dublin: Na Clocha Breaca, n.d.

Herm, Gerhard. *The Celts: The People Who Came out of the Darkness*. New York: St. Martin's Press, 1975.

Hubert, Henri. *The Rise of the Celts*. New York: Dorset Press, n.d.

Hull, Eleanor. *The Cuchullin Saga in Irish Literature*. London: David Nutt, 1898.

———. *Folklore of the British Isles*. London: Methuen & Co., Ltd., 1928.

Hunt, Robert. *Cornish Customs and Superstitions*. Truro: Tor Mark Press, n.d.

———. *Cornish Folk-Lore*. Truro: Tor Mark Press, n.d.

Hyde, Douglas. *Abhráin atá Leaghta ar an Rechtúire: Songs Ascribed to Reftery*. New York: Barnes & Noble Books, n.d.

———. *Beside the Fire: A Collection of Irish Gaelic Folk Stories*. London: David Nutt, 1890.

Jackson, Kenneth Hurlstone. *The International Popular Tale and Early Welsh Tradition*. Cardiff: University of Wales Press, 1961.

Jackson, Kenneth, et al. *Celt and Saxon: Studies in the Early British Border*. Cambridge: Cambridge University Press, 1963.

Jestice, Phyllis G. *Encyclopedia of Irish Spirituality*. Santa Barbara, Calif.: ABC-CLIO, 2000.

Jones, Noragh. *Power of Raven, Wisdom of Serpent: Celtic Women's Spirituality*. Edinburgh, Floris Books, 1994.

Jones, T. Gwynn. *Welsh Folklore and Folk-Custom*. London: Methuen & Co., Ltd., 1930.

Joyce, P. W. *Ancient Celtic Romances*. London: Parkgate Books, 1997.

Kavanagh, Peter. *Irish Mythology: A Dictionary*. Newbridge, Co. Kildare: The Goldsmith Press, Ltd., 1988.

Keightley, Thomas. *The Fairy Mythology*. London: H. G. Bohn, 1870.

Kelly, Eamonn. *Sheela-na-Gigs: Origins and Functions*. Dublin: Country House, 1996.

Kelly, Fergus. *A Guide to Early Irish Law*. Dublin: School of Celtic Studies, Dublin Institute for Advanced Studies. Early Irish Law Series, Vol. III, 1988.

Kelly, Sean, and Rosemary Rogers. *Saints Preserve Us!* New York: Random House, 1993.

Kennedy, Patrick. *Legendary Fictions of the Irish Celts*. New York: Benjamin Blom, 1969.

Kiernan, Thomas J. *The White Hound on the Mountain and Other Irish Folk Tales*. New York: Devin-Adair, 1962.

Killip, Margaret. *The Folklore of the Isle of Man*. London: B. T. Batsford, Ltd., 1975.

Kinsella, Thomas, trans. *The Tain*. Dublin: The Dolmen Press, 1969.

Kirk, Thomas. *The Secret Commonwealth of Elves, Fauns, & Fairies*. London: David Nutt, 1893.

Koch, John T, ed., with John Carey. *The Celtic Heroic Age: Literary Sources for Ancient Celtic Europe and Early Ireland and Wales*. Andover, Mass.: Celtic Studies Publications, 2000.

Lamb, Cynthia. "Following the Black Dog." In Patricia Monaghan, ed. *Irish Spirit: Pagan, Celtic, Christian, Global*. Dublin: Wolfhound Press, 2001, pp. 43 ff.

Leather, Ella Mary. *The Folk-Lore of Herefordshire*. London: Sidewick & Jackson, 1912.

Lenihan, Edmund. "The Fairies Vs. the Money Economy." In Patricia Monaghan, ed. *Irish Spirit: Pagan, Celtic, Christian, Global*. Dublin: Wolfhound Press, 2001, pp. 122 ff.

———. *In Search of Biddy Early*. Cork: Mercier Press, 1987.

———. *The Savage Pigs of Tulla*. Cork: Mercier Press, 2000.

Lincoln, Siobhan. *Ardmore: Memory and Story*. Co. Waterford: Ardmore Pottery Shop, 2000.

Litton, Helen. *The Celts: An Illustrated History*. Dublin: Wolfhound Press, 1997.

Löffler, Christa Maria. *The Voyage to the Otherworld Island in Early Irish Literature*. Salzburg Studies in English Literature. Salzburg, Institut Für Anglistic und Amerikanistik, Universität Salzburg, 1983.

Logan, Patrick. *The Holy Wells of Ireland*. Gerrards Cross: Colin Smythe, 1980.

———. *The Old Gods: The Facts About Irish Fairies*. Belfast: Appletree Press, 1981.

Long, George. *The Folklore Calendar*. London: Senate, 1930.

Lonigan, Paul R. *The Druids: Priests of the Ancient Celts.* Contributions to the Study of Religion, No. 45. Westport, Conn.: Greenwood Press, 1996.

Lonigan, Paul, "Shamanism in the Old Irish Tradition." *Eire-Ireland*, Fall 1985.

Loomis, Roger Sherman. *The Grail from Celtic Myth to Christian Symbol.* New York: Columbia University Press, 1963.

———. *Wales and the Arthurian Legend.* Cardiff: University of Wales Press, 1956.

Luzel, F. M. *Celtic Folk-Tales from Amorica.* Trans. Derek Bryce. Dyfed, Wales: Llanerch Enterprises, 1985.

Lysaght, Patricia. "Aspects of the Earth-Goddess in the Traditions of the Banshee in Ireland." In Billington, Sandra, and Miranda Green, eds. *The Concept of the Goddess.* London and New York: Routledge, 1996, pp. 152–165.

MacAlister, R. A. Steward. *Lebor Gabála Érenn: The Book of the Taking of Ireland, Parts 1–4.* Dublin: Irish Texts Society, 1941.

———. *Lebor Gabála Érenn: The Book of the Taking of Ireland, Part 5.* Dublin: Irish Texts Society, 1956.

MacCulloch, J. A. *The Religion of the Ancient Celts.* London: Constable, 1911.

———. *Celtic Mythology.* Chicago: Academy Publishers, 1996.

MacDougall, James. *Folk Tales and Fairy Lore in Gaelic and English.* Edinburgh: John Grant, 1910.

———. *Waifs and Strays of Celtic Tradition: Argyllshire Series, No. III; Folk and Hero Tales.* London: David Nutt, 1891.

MacGregor, Alasdair Alpin. *The Peat-Fire Flame: Folk-Tales and Traditions of the Highlands & Islands.* Edinburgh: The Moray Press, 1937.

MacKenzie, Donald A. *Scottish Folk-Lore and Folk Life: Studies in Race, Culture and Tradition.* Glasgow: Blackie & Sons, Ltd., 1935.

MacKillop, James. *Fionn mac Cumhaill: Celtic Myth in English Literature.* Syracuse, N.Y.: Syracuse University Press, 1986.

MacManus, Dermot. *The Middle Kingdom: The Faerie World of Ireland.* Gerrards Cross: Colin Smythe, 1959.

MacNeill, Máire. *The Festival of Lughnasa, Parts I and II.* Dublin: Comhairle Bhéaloideas Éireann, 1982.

Mahon, Bríd. *Irish Folklore.* Cork: Mercier Press, 2000.

———. *Land of Milk and Honey: The Story of Traditional Irish Food and Drink.* Cork: Mercier Press, 1991.

Malone, Caroline. *English Heritage Book of Avebury.* London: B. T. Batsford, Ltd./English Heritage, 1989.

Markale, Jean. *Courtly Love: The Path of Sexual Initiation.* Rochester, Vt.: Inner Traditions, 2000.

———. *The Epics of Celtic Ireland.* Rochester, Vt.: Inner Traditions, 2000.

———. *The Pagan Mysteries of Halloween: Celebrating the Dark Half of the Year.* Rochester, Vt.: Inner Traditions, 2000.

———. *Women of the Celts.* Rochester, Vt.: Inner Traditions, 1986.

Marples, Morris. *White Horses and Other Hill Figures.* Gloucester: Alan Sutton, 1981.

Marron, Fiona. "Encounters with Remarkable Sheela na Gigs." In Monaghan, Patricia. Irish Spirit: Pagan, Celtic, Christian, Global. Dublin, Wolfhound Press, 2001

Matthews, Caitlín. *The Elements of the Celtic Tradition.* Rockport, Mass.: Element, 1989.

Matthews, John. *A Celtic Reader: Selections from Celtic Legend, Scholarship and Story.* Wellingborough: Aquarian Press, 1991.

———. *Taliesin: Shamanism and the Bardic Mysteries in Britain and Ireland.* London: Aquarian/Thorsons, 1991.

Matthews, John, and Caitlín Matthews. *British and Irish Mythology.* London: Diamond Books, 1995.

———. *Encyclopedia of Celtic Wisdom: A Celtic Shaman Sourcebook.* Rockport, Mass.: Element, 1994.

Márkus, Gilbert. *Adomnán's Law of the Innocents.* Glasgow, Scotland: Blackfriars Books, n.d.

McCarthy, Bairbre. *Irish Leprechaun Stories.* Cork: Mercier Press, 1998.

McCrickard, Janet. *Eclipse of the Sun.* Glastonbury: Gothic Image, 1994.

McDowell, Patricia. "Soldiers' Heart." In Patricia Monaghan, ed. *Irish Spirit: Pagan, Celtic, Christian Global.* Dublin: Wolfhound Press, 2001, p. 22.

McGarry, Mary. *Great Fairy Tales of Ireland.* New York: Avenel Books, 1973.

McKay, John G. *More West Highland Tales.* Vol. 2. Scottish Anthropological and Folklore Society. Edinburgh: Oliver and Body, 1969.

McMahon, Joanne, and Jack Roberts. *The Sheela-na-Gigs of Ireland and Britain: The Diving Hag of the Christian Celts, An Illustrated Guide.* Cork: Mercier Press, 2000.

McNeill, F. Marian. *The Silver Bough: Scottish Folk-Lore and Folk-Belief.* Edinburgh: Canongate Classics, 1989.

Meaden, George Terrence. *The Goddess of the Stones: The Language of the Megaliths.* London: Souvenir Press, 1991.

Meehan, Aidan. *Celtic Design: Spiral Patterns.* London: Thames and Hudson, 1996.

Merriman, Brian. *The Midnight Court.* Trans. Frank O'Connor. Dublin: The O'Brien Press, 1989.

Meyer, Kuno. *Aislinge meic Conglinne: The Vision of MacConglinne.* London: David Nutt, 1892.

———. *The Voyage of Bran Son of Febal to the Land of the Living.* London: David Nutt, 1895.

Moane, Geraldine. "A Womb Not a Tomb: Goddess Symbols and Ancient Ireland." *Canadian Women's Studies: Les cahiers de la femme.* Vol. 17, 1997, pp. 7–10.

Monaghan, Patricia. *O Mother Sun: A New View of the Cosmic Feminine.* Freedom, Calif.: The Crossing Press, 1994.

Neeson, Eoin. *Celtic Myths and Legends.* Cork: Mercier Press, 1998.

Newman, Paul. *Gods and Graven Images: The Chalk Hill-Figures of Britain.* London: Robert Hale, 1987.

Nicolaisen, W. F. H. "Concepts of Time and Space in Irish Folktales." In Patrick K. Ford, ed. *Celtic Folklore and Christianity: Studies in Memory of William W. Heist.* Center for the Study of Comparative Folklore & Mythology, University of California, Los Angeles. Santa Barbara: McNally and Loftin, 1983, pp. 150–158.

NightMare, M. Macha. "Bridy in Cyberspace." In Patricia Monaghan, ed. *Irish Spirit: Pagan, Celtic, Christian, Global.* Dublin: Wolfhound Press, 2001, pp. 292 ff.

Nutt, Alfred. *Cuchulainn, The Irish Achilles.* London: David Nutt, 1900.

O'Brien, Marie Cruise. "The Female Principle in Gaelic Poetry." In S. F. Gallagher, ed. *Woman in Irish Legend, Life and Literature.* Irish Literary Studies 14. Gerrards Cross, Bucks: Colin Smythe, 1983, pp. 26–37.

Ó Catháin, Séamus, and Patrick O'Flanagan. *The Living Landscape: Kilgallian, Erris, County Mayo.* Dublin: Comhairle Bhéaloideas Éireann, 1975.

O'Conor, Norreys Jephson. *Battles and Enchantments: Retold from Early Gaelic Literature.* Freeport N.Y.: Books for Libraries Press, 1970.

Ó Danachair, Caoimhin. *A Bibliography of Irish Ethnology and Folk Tradition.* Cork: The Mercier Press, 1978.

O'Driscoll, Robert, ed. *The Celtic Consciousness.* New York: George Braziller, 1981.

O'Faoláin, Seán, ed. *The Silver Branch: A Collection of the Best Old Irish Lyrics.* New York: The Viking Press, 1937.

O Farrell, Padraic. *Irish Proverbs and Sayings.* Cork: Mercier Press, 1980.

———. *Superstitions of Irish Country People.* Cork: Mercier Press, 1978.

O hEochaidh, Séan. *Fairy Legends of Donegal.* Trans. Máire MacNeill. Dublin: Comhairle Bhéaloideas Éireann, 1977.

Ó hÓgáin, Dáithí. *Fionn mac Cumhaill: Images of the Gaelic Hero.* Dublin: Gill & Macmillan, 1988.

———. *The Hero in Irish Folk History.* Dublin: Gill & Macmillan, 1985.

———. *Irish Superstitions.* London: Gill & Macmillan, 1995.

———. *Myth, Legend and Romance: An Encyclopedia of the Irish Folk Tradition.* New York: Prentice-Hall Press, 1991.

———. *The Sacred Isle: Belief and Religion in Pre-Christian Ireland.* Cork: The Collins Press, 1999.

O'Kelly, M. J. & C. O'Kelly. *Illustrated Guide to Lough Gur.* Blackrock, Co. Cork: O'Kelly, 1997.

O'Rahilly, Thomas. *Early Irish History and Mythology.* Dublin: The Dublin Institute for Advanced Studies, 1946.

Ó Ríordáin, Séan. *Tara: The Monuments on the Hill.* Dundalk: Dundalgan Press, 1992.

Ó Súilleabháin, Séan. *Irish Wake Amusements.* Cork: Mercier Press, 1967.

O'Sullivan, Muiris. *Megalithic Art in Ireland.* Dublin: Country House, 1993.

O'Sullivan, Patrick V. *Irish Superstitions and Legends of Animals and Birds.* Cork: Mercier, 1991.

Palmer, Roy. *Britain's Living Folklore.* Newton Abbot, London: David & Charles, 1991.

Parry-Jones, D. *Welsh Legends and Fairy Lore.* London: B. T. Batsford, Ltd., 1953.

Patch, Howard Rollin. *The Other World: According to Descriptions in Medieval Literature.* Cambridge, Mass.: Harvard University Press, 1950.

Paton, C. I. *Manx Calendar Customs.* Publications of the Folk-lore Society, reprinted. Nendeln/Liechtenstein: Kraus Reprint Limited, 1968.

Piggot, Stuart. *The Druids.* London: Thames and Hudson, 1968.

Powell, T. G. E. *The Celts.* London: Thames and Hudson, 1980.

Power, Patrick. *Sex and Marriage in Ancient Ireland.* Cork: Mercier Press, 1976.

Rackard, Anna. *Fish Stone Water: Holy Wells of Ireland.* Cork: Atrium, 2001.

Radner, Joan Newlon. "The Significance of the Threefold Death in Celtic Tradition." In Patrick K. Ford, ed. *Celtic Folklore and Christianity: Studies in Memory of William W. Heist.* Center for the Study of Comparative Folklore & Mythology, University of California, Los Angeles. Santa Barbara: McNally and Loftin, 1983, pp. 180–200.

Raftery, Brian. *Pagan Celtic Ireland: The Enigma of the Irish Iron Age.* London: Thames and Hudson, 1994.

Rees, Alwyn, and Brinley Rees. *Celtic Heritage: Ancient Tradition in Ireland and Wales.* London: Thames and Hudson, 1998.

Rhys, John. *Celtic Folklore: Welsh and Manx.* Oxford: Clarendon Press, 1941.

———. *The Welsh People.* London: T. Fisher Unwin, 1906.

Rolleston, T. W. *Myths and Legends of the Celtic Race.* Boston: David D. Nickerson & Company, 1923.

Ross, Anne, "The Divine Hag of the Pagan Celts." In Venetia Newall, ed. *The Witch Figures.* London: Routledge & Kegan Paul, 1973, pp. 139–164.

———. *Folklore of the Scottish Highlands.* London: B. T. Batsford, Ltd., 1976.

———. "Lindow Man and the Celtic Tradition." In Stead, I. M., J. B. Bourke, and Don Brothwell. *The Lindow Man: The Body in the Bog.* Ithaca, N.Y.: Cornell University Press, 1986, pp. 162–169.

———. *Pagan Celtic Britain: Studies in Iconography and Tradition.* London: Routledge & Kegan Paul, 1967.

Ross, Anne, and Michael Cyprien. *A Traveller's Guide to Celtic Britain.* Harrisburg, Pa.: Historical Times, 1985.

Rowland, Jenny. *Early Welsh Saga Poetry.* Cambridge: D. S. Brewer, 1990.

Ryan, Meda. *Biddy Early: Wise Woman of Clare.* Cork: Mercier Press, 1980.

Senchus Mor. Dublin: Alexander Thom, 1856.

Sheehan, Jeremiah, ed. *Beneath the Shadow of Uisneach: Ballymore and Boher, County Westmeath.* Ballymore, Co. Westmeath: Ballymore-Boher History Project, 1996.

Sjoestedt, Marie-Louise. *Celtic Gods and Heroes.* Trans. Myles Dillon. Mineola, N.Y.: Dover Publications, Inc., 2000.

Slavin, Michael. *The Book of Tara.* Dublin: Wolfhound Press, 1996.

Smythe, Daragh. *A Guide to Irish Mythology.* Dublin: Irish Academic Press, 1996.

Spence, Lewis. *The Minor Traditions of British Mythology.* New York: Benjamin Blom, Inc., 1972.

Spenser, Edmund. *A View of the State of Ireland.* From the first printed edition, ed. Andrew Hadfield and Willy Maley. Oxford, England: Blackwell Publishers, 1997.

Squire, Charles. *Mythology of the Celtic People.* London: Bracken Books, 1996.

Straffon, Cheryl. *The Earth Goddess: Celtic and Pagan Legacy of the Landscape.* London: Blandford, 1997.

Tacitus. *The Agricola and the Germania.* Trans. H. Mattingly. New York: Penguin Books, 1948.

Thomas, N. L. *Irish Symbols of 3500 BC.* Cork: Mercier Press, 1988.

Trevelyan, Marie. *Folklore and Folk-Stories of Wales.* London: Elliot Stock, 1909.

Turner, R. C. "Boggarts, Bogles and Sir Gawain and the Green Knight: Lindow Man and the Oral Tradition." In Stead, I. M., J. B. Bourke, and Don Brothwell. *The Lindow Man: The Body in the Bog.* Ithaca, N.Y.: Cornell University Press, 1986, pp. 170–176.

Wait, G. A. *Ritual and Religion in Iron Age Britain.* Oxford: BAR British Series 149(i), 1985.

Wakeman, William F. *Handbook of Irish Antiquities.* Dublin: Hodges, Figgis and Co., 1891. Republished London: Bracken Books, 1995.

Walsh, Maeve. *A Guide to Irish Mythology.* Cork: Mercier Press, 2000.

Weston, Jessie. *The Legend of Sir Lancelot du Lac.* London: David Nutt, 1901.

Westropp, T. J. *Archaeology of the Burren: Prehistoric Forts and Dolmens in North Clare.* Ennis, Co. Clare: Clasp Press, 1999.

———. *Folklore of Clare: A Folklore Survey of County Clare and County Clare Folk-Tales and Myths.* Ennis, Co. Clare: Clasp Press, 2000.

White, Carolyn. *A History of Irish Fairies.* Cork: Mercier Press, 1976.

Whitlock, Ralph. *The Folklore of Wiltshire.* London: B. T. Batsford, Ltd., 1976.

Wilde, Lady. *Ancient Legends, Mystic Charms and Superstitions of Ireland.* London: Chatto and Windus, 1902.

Woodward, Ann. *English Heritage Book of Shrines and Sacrifice.* London: B. T. Batsford Ltd., 1992.

Yeats, W. B. *Fairy and Folk Tales of the Irish Peasantry.* In *A Treasury of Irish Myth, Legend and Folklore.* New York: Gramercy Books, 1986.

INDEX

B